Children in Films

Children in Films

(Volumes 1 to 8)

Andrew Musgrave

Lightship Guides & Publications

ISBN-13: 978-1481862257
ISBN-10: 1481862251

Published as separate volumes in 2012

First Published as a combined volume in 2013

Lightship Guides and Publications

By the same author

Fun Runs and Guns
(Trips and Trails through Yemen and Saudi Arabia)

Samak Fishing in Yemen

This book comprises the eight volume series, *Children in Films*, each volume of which is published separately.

1. Gender Roles and Themes
2. Families, Step-kids & Orphans
3. Tomboys, Adventurers & Talented Kids
4. Childhood Friendships: Peers, Pets & Grown-ups
5. Make-Believe, Horror and the Supernatural
6. Puberty & First Love
7. Childhood Trauma: Illness, Death, Divorce & War
8. Physical & Sexual Abuse

A Note about References

Sources of quotations taken from film dialogue or from DVD 'extras'
are listed in the Appendix of Films at the end of this book.
All other sources are noted as references in the endnotes.

"The children now love luxury; they have bad manners, contempt for authority; they show disrespect for elders and love chatter in place of exercise. Children are now tyrants, not the servants of their households. They no longer rise when elders enter the room. They contradict their parents, chatter before company, gobble up dainties at the table, cross their legs, and tyrannize their teachers."

(Not taken from an ill-informed comment about the vagaries of modern youth, but attributed to Socrates *(400 BC)*.

VOLUMES 1 TO 8

1. Gender Roles and Themes..19

2. Families, Step-kids & Orphans...71

3. Tomboys, Adventurers & Talented Kids..........................143

4. Childhood Friendships..191

5. Make-Believe, Horror & the Supernatural.....................261

6. Puberty & First Love..317

7. Childhood Trauma...377

8. Physical & Sexual Abuse...455

9. Curtain Call...523

Tables, References and Appendix.................................529

Index...559

CONTENTS OF ALL VOLUMES

1. Gender Roles and Themes..**19**

Contents for Volume One...**21**

Introduction...**23**

Gender Agenda...**25**
The Girl as a Unique Species..*25*
The Boy as Urchin or Angel, Mouse or Man...*28*
Gender Imbalance..*30*

Roles & Reactions..**32**
Emotional and Psychological Impact on the Child Actor..................................*33*
Coping with fame..*35*
Child Labour Laws and Stunt Doubles...*39*
Exploitation of the Child Actor...*42*
Age appropriate roles...*45*

Talents **48**
Natural Talent...*48*
Casting – lucky breaks and who you know...*51*
Stage School Training / Pushy Parents...*53*
Astonishing performances and Oscar nominees..*56*
Oscar and Bafta Winners and Nominees...*58*

Themes **60**
Adult themes and hard-hitting moral messages..*60*
'Coming-of-Age'...*64*
Multiculturalism...*65*

Endnotes for Volume One **68**

2. Families, Step-kids & Orphans...**71**

Contents for Volume Two..**73**

There's No Place Like Home..**75**
The Statistics: How the Media has Deceived Us..*76*

The Importance of the Family..**78**
Happy Families *79*
Mother's Role..*80*

Sibling Rivalry..*81*

Papering over the Cracks **85**
Strains & Betrayals in Family Relationships.......................................*85*
The Need for Compromise..*85*
Favouritism, Feeling Unwanted and Runaways....................................*86*
When the Bough Breaks...*90*
Traumas creating Fractious Families...*91*
Neglect of the Family: The example of Enid...*92*
Rebelliousness..*94*
The Rejected Child...*96*

Family Reunions...**99**
Searching for Family..*101*
Thwarted Searches...*106*
The Child as Matchmaker...*107*

Broken Homes...**109**
The Single Mother / Missing Father-Figure..*111*
Single Fathers...*114*
The Unwanted Orphan / Institutionalised Kids...................................*118*
The Fostered Child..*121*
Motives for adopting...*123*
Trying to remember Mother/Father...*130*

Home Alone: Kids in Charge...**132**
The Blue Lagoon..*132*
Vulnerable Girls Forced to Seek Help...*133*
Kids Abandoned to Struggle Alone..*135*
Boys Home Alone...*137*
The Ultimate Struggle: Survival of the Fittest.....................................*138*

Endnotes for Volume Two...**140**

3. Tomboys, Adventurers & Talented Kids.........................**143**

Contents for Volume Three...**145**

Introduction...**147**

Crossing Gender Boundaries..**148**
Billy Elliot: boy breaking the mould...*150*
The Tomboy...*151*
Tomboy (2011): The Film..*156*
Hollywood's Tomboy Legends: Hayley Mills & Mary Badham............*158*

The Talented Child...**160**
Musical talent...*160*

Creative Talents..*163*
Striving against the Odds...*164*

Sports Starlets..**168**
The Great Pretender: girls masquerading as boys...............................*169*
Climbing...*170*
Soccer...*171*
Water sports..*173*
Dance..*175*
Getting the Parents' Support...*177*

The Adventurers / Just Good Fun..**179**
The Adventure Journey as a Rite-of-Passage.......................................*179*
The Amazons: Girl Adventurers...*184*
Just Good Fun..*187*

Endnotes for Volume Three..**189**

4. Childhood Friendships..**191**

Contents for Volume Four...**193**

Making Friends..**195**
The Rule of Gender...*195*
Best Friends Forever...*196*
Breaking into the Clique: On the periphery of friendship groups.......*200*
Group Dynamics: The Rejected Child...*202*
Childhood Sweethearts: Overcoming the Gender Barricade..............*204*
Sharing the same frying pan: friends thrust together..........................*206*

Inter-Racial Bonding..**210**
American Segregation...*210*
South African Apartheid..*213*
Australian Aboriginal Culture..*214*
Cross culture bonding..*217*

Children bonding with Adults...**221**
The Retarded Adult Companion..*224*
Travelling Companions...*226*
The Drifter and Loner as replacement father-figure and object of first crush....*231*

The Child's Best Friend: Animals and Children....................................**237**
Animal Welfare over Child Welfare...*239*
The Pet as Provider of Unconditional Love...*240*
The pet as a lesson in life and death...*242*
The Call of the Wild...*246*
The Child as Rescuer of the Helpless..*249*
The Horse Lover..*252*

Let us down to the sea again: Dolphins and Whales, Seals and Sea-Lions.....................255
The Pet as a Punishment.....................256

Endnotes for Volume Four.....................**258**

5. Make-Believe, Horror & the Supernatural.....................**261**

Contents for Volume Five.....................**263**

Introduction.....................**265**
Gender, Colour and Make-Believe.....................265
Girls With Mysterious Powers.....................266

Make-Believe.....................**270**
Alice in Wonderland.....................271
Folk Tales.....................273
Little Otik (Otesánek).....................275
Santa Claus.....................276
Fairy Tales.....................278
Magic.....................282
The Harry Potter Series.....................284
Witches and Witchcraft.....................286

Horror.....................**289**
Ghosts.....................293
Vampires.....................298
Werewolves.....................300
The Child-Killer: Children who Kill.....................301

The Supernatural.....................**307**
Religion.....................307
Devil Possession.....................312

Endnotes for Volume Five.....................**315**

6. Puberty & First Love.....................**317**

Contents for Volume Six.....................**319**

Coming of Age.....................**320**
Puberty.....................321
Masturbation.....................323
Steps towards the Adult World.....................325
Body Parts.....................326
How babies are perceived to be conceived.....................329

Children in Love.....................**333**
Just Good Friends.....................334
A Word of Advice: Rehearsing that First Kiss.....................337

The First Kiss..339
Unconventional Kisses: the bizarre and audacious......................................343
Snogging..345
Enduring Affairs..347
Spurned Love...349

Unorthodox affairs...**352**
Affairs with Older Men...352
The Penalty for Being Precocious...355
Lesbian Affairs..357
Gay Boys and the Effeminate..360
Hermaphrodite Children..362

Child Nudity on Screen...**365**
What is indecent, and are we, as viewers, breaking the law?........................367

Endnotes for Volume Six..**375**

7. Childhood Trauma..**377**

Contents for Volume Seven..**379**

Childhood Trauma: Introduction..**381**

Separation and Divorce: Its Impact On The Child....................................**382**
The Comedic Approach to Divorce...384
The Serious Approach to Divorce..386

Illness and Disability..**389**
Coping with a Disability...390
Contracting a Disability...396
Contracting a Disability: The Brooke Ellison Story......................................398
Contracting a Disability: Lorenzo's Oil..400
When the Child becomes Ill...402

Underage Pregnancy...**404**
Observing Pregnancy in Others...404
Coping with Pregnancy..405
Pregnancy: the boy's responsibility...407

Death...**409**
Platitudes...410
Terminal Illness...412
Psychological Effects of the Death of a Parent on the Child........................414
Misunderstanding in the Child's Mind about death.......................................419
Muteness as a reaction to the Death of a Parent...421
Death of a Friend...421
Guilt feelings that arise as a loved one dies..424

Life After Grief: Coming to terms with and Rationalising the death of a Parent............426
Taking on the burdens of responsibility when adult carers can't cope..........................428
The Afterlife...429
When death is of no concern...431

The Impact Of War...433

Vulnerable Refugees 434
Ethnic Cleansing..437
Resistance Fighters..440
Witnesses to the Atrocities of War..441
Evacuees..444
Keeping Home Fires Burning..445

Moving To A New Home...447

Fear of not being able to make new friends...448
Regrets of the past...449
Beneficial Moves...452

Endnotes for Volume Seven..453

8. Physical & Sexual Abuse...455

Contents for Volume Eight...457

Child Abuse: Introduction...459

Physical Abuse...462

Making a Stand against Abuse...462
Neglect...463
Bodily Harm..466
Violently Abusive Parents...468
Racial Abuse / Prejudice...470
Kidnapping and Abduction..473
Slavery / Child Bondage..478

Bullying...483

Name-Calling...483
The Bully and Victim...484
Cyber-bullying...485
Bullying: Passive Resistance..486
Standing up to the Bully...489
Ill-Treatment by Adults...490

Sexual Abuse..495

Paedophilia..495
Little Girls Loved: Salacious Relationships with Children..498
Boys and Older Women..502
Paedophilia: Seeking Justice and Revenge..503

Empathy with the Perverted..*506*
Adults Targeting Children / Grooming..................................*508*
Molestation..*514*
Child Prostitution..*515*
Therapy for Abused Victims..*518*

Endnotes for Volume Eight..**521**

9. Curtain Call..**523**

Curtain Call..**525**

Tables, References and Appendix....................................**529**

Table (i): Films Depicting Broken Homes v Families with Both Parents
....**530**

Living with Mother only (or mum + stepdad)........................*530*
Living with Father only (or father + stepmum)......................*531*
Living with other Relatives..*531*
Fostered, Living in Orphanage, or having No Guardians.........*532*
Living with both Birth Parents...*532*

Table (ii): Films in Which Children are Required to Kiss..........**534**

References & Further Reading..**537**

Appendix: List of Films..**538**

Index..**559**

Volume One

Gender Roles and Themes

"I've made films with children before.
I know working with children can be very difficult,
but very pleasing when it is finished."
(Françoise Truffaut on the filming of *Pocket Money*.)

"Each one of these children is amazing
– a little pocket of stardust."
(says Pam Ferris playing the headteacher in *Nativity!*)

CONTENTS FOR VOLUME ONE

1. Gender Roles and Themes..**19**

Contents for Volume One...**21**

Introduction..**23**

Gender Agenda..**25**
The Girl as a Unique Species...*25*
The Boy as Urchin or Angel, Mouse or Man..................................*28*
Gender Imbalance..*30*

Roles & Reactions...**32**
Emotional and Psychological Impact on the Child Actor....................*33*
Coping with fame..*35*
Child Labour Laws and Stunt Doubles...*39*
Exploitation of the Child Actor...*42*
Age appropriate roles...*45*

Talents **48**
Natural Talent...*48*
Casting – lucky breaks and who you know.....................................*51*
Stage School Training / Pushy Parents..*53*
Astonishing performances and Oscar nominees..............................*56*
Oscar and Bafta Winners and Nominees.......................................*58*

Themes **60**
Adult themes and hard-hitting moral messages...............................*60*
'Coming-of-Age'..*64*
Multiculturalism..*65*

Endnotes for Volume One **68**

INTRODUCTION

As someone who enjoys watching docile films which do not involve violence, guns, swearing or gratuitous sex I had assumed I would be happy watching child-centred films, or films in which children have an acting role. I was shocked therefore when researching this book to discover that some of the most violent, shocking, and frightening films are films that involve children.

From *Hard Candy*, in which a groomed fourteen-year-old turns the tables on her thirty-year-old paedophile predator, as we watch in gruesome horror as she systematically castrates him; to *The Omen* in which the satanic Damien is possessed by the antichrist; to girls with special powers such as *Firestarter*, where Drew Barrymore can cause spontaneous combustion to the men pursuing her; or Harry Novak's *The Child* (1977), in which eleven-year-old Rosalie is in league with a monster who haunts and mutilates its victims.

There are scary movies in which children are both victims and perpetrators in ghost stories – *The Dark* (2005), *The Children* (2008), *The Turn of the Screw* – or 'undead' children tearing raw flesh from a living pig in *Zombies*. In others, children shriek with demonic possession as in *The Exorcist* and *Audrey Rose*. In *Orphan* (2009), a nine-year-old takes terminal revenge on the children and adults who have opposed her, as does the infant Michael Myers from the *Halloween* series, found still clutching the deadly dagger. In *The Reaping*, a little girl is the catalyst for the whole flourish of seven plagues, one sweet innocent scared girl causing rivers of blood, boils, swarms of locusts, flies and maggots, and thunderbolts from the sky!

No doubt it is because little children are so vulnerable that they evoke empathy when we witness them being abused. Likewise, they provoke startling shock when we see them as the abusers, a tool so perversely exploited in horror films. Director, Jaume Collet-Serra had no qualms about this for he says in the introduction to his horror movie, *Orphan* (2009), "When writing scripts for horror films, children are always a taboo that you want to tap into."

The director seeks to shock in other ways, too. Tirades of swear words emit from the lips of children, from Georgia Groome in *London to Brighton*, and from Evan Rachel Wood in *Thirteen* (2003), and an endless dribble of revulsion from Leo Fitzpatrick in *kids* (1995), while in *Hope and Glory* regurgitation of swear words becomes part of initiation into the gang for Sebastian Rice Edwards.[1] Others, like us to be astounded at their audacity, expecting us to titter as a seven-year-old uses words like *hard-on* (Jennifer Beck in *Tightrope*), or a ten-year-old uses *penis* and *vagina* as everyday vocabulary (Abigail Breslin in *Definitely, Maybe*), while in *Billy Elliot* Nicola Blackwell is scripted to have an embarrassing conversation with Jamie Bell about 'having sex' while we are expected to pretend to be amused and impressed by their guile. "If you like, I'll show you my fanny." Even Steven Spielberg in his child-friendly blockbuster *ET* had no qualms about Henry Thomas uttering "Penis Breath!" In other films, we are horrified at the unforgiving exploitation of children as in *I am Slave*, *Stolen* (2011), or *Lilya 4-ever* – all cases of children trafficked into a horrendous world of abuse.

However there are also charming films involving the delightful and cute: Emma Bolger in *Heidi*, Georgina Terry as *Pollyanna* – surely every parent's dream of an ideal daughter – or Mark Lester from *Oliver!* whom many a mother would wish to pamper. Others we find endearing – Margaret O'Brien's Tooti in *Meet me in St Louis*, Macaulay Culkin in *Home Alone* (1990), Brandon de Wilde from *Shane*. Even the biblical rants of Natalie Wood in *Driftwood* are appealing. Others are real tearjerkers: Keisha Castle-Hughes in *Whale Rider*, Justin Henry in *Kramer v Kramer*, Alicia Morton in *Annie* (1999).

I had originally tried to restrict this book to films depicting children using the Nabokovian criteria of the child as being between eight and fourteen, but I have strayed beyond the goalposts in both directions. For Nabokov, the ages delimited a fantasy for the sexual stage in a child's development, but for Sula Wolff, writing in *Children Under Stress*, this is the age when a child emerges from an egocentric view of the world to take a more realistic and cooperational cognisance of its own interactions, and is able to identify his/her existence in relationships with others. Between these ages the child is more socially, democratically, cooperatively and rationally aware.[2]

This is also the age of cuteness, when the audience, including me (and probably you too) are coaxed by the innocence and comeliness of the child, and the ingrained desire that lies within us to nurture them, as we become blinkered to our more objective perceptions. John Candy was aware of this in *Uncle Buck*. Seven-year-old Gaby Hoffman is staring at him doughy-eyed and irresistible, knowing her alluring looks can wheedle any request as she wraps him round her little finger. "Don't look at me like that," he begs. "It's not fair!"

GENDER AGENDA

While our children are taunting our sensibilities as horrors and hoydens, they are double-crossing our expectations of them in their gender roles, too. Society has implanted certain traits to characterise little girls as opposed to little boys, and we have been induced over generations to see them in that light: the brash boy adventurer, donned in his superman confidence, whose scrapes and entanglements must be borne manfully without retreating to mother's apron strings; the girl-child bearing fairy wings, binding the limping limb of a stray dog, and returning to father's welcoming hug for approval.

This is *sugar and spice* verses *puppy dogs' tails* conceptualisation. But the movie industry is subtly manipulating our vision of such gender differences. Children have had no say in this matter, of course. They are just stage-managed puppets. All children appearing on our TV screens or in our Odeons and Multiplexes are there at the beck-and-whim of the production teams that have deployed them, teams whose goal is to excite by the stretching of incredulity and the crossing of sacrosanct boundaries. When we see children challenging our expectations of them, they are simply following the stage directions given them by the directors and scriptwriters who, in collusion together, are changing our perception of the gender status of the child.

This is partly the purpose of this book: to report how children are playing their part in maintaining or infringing our cultural perceptions of their roles that girls will be girls, and boys will be boys.

The Girl as a Unique Species

"I'm not a dwarf, I'm a girl!" says Lucy Pevensie to Mr Tumnus in *The Lion, the Witch and the Wardrobe*, as if she were a new species needing defining. Billy's granddad in *Hope and Glory* would agree: "They are a different species, you know, Bill. Love them, but don't try to understand them."

As a male and daughterless I am intrigued by the enigma of the girl-child, they have an indefinable mystery to them. "We are women," explains seventeen-year-old Jane Withers in *The North Star*, "Different things go on in our heads." Although some have ordinariness in common with both sexes of children, others have male tendencies giving them the label 'tomboy', as Tatum O'Neal exemplifies in *Bad News Bears* or Hayley Mills in *Tiger Bay*.

But girls also have that indefinable uniqueness. Every female reader will understand their secretive world, the special best friend and confidant (as in *Beaches*, and which becomes a repressive twin relationship in *Me without You*), the shattering anguish and isolation when best friends fall out (*Thirteen* (2003), *32A* and *Water Lilies*), the make-believe world they play in of dolls, and mothers and fathers (*Tideland* and *Cría Cuervos*), the desire to nurture, the nurse in them (*Eyes of an Angel*), their love of animals (*Lassie* (2005)), especially horses (*Dreamer*), their vulnerability (*Water* (2005) – no boys are forced into being child brides at the age of eight to marry dirty old women, this is only a dilemma for the young girl). Whether these stereotypical traits are true, is this why in the majority of films in which little girls feature, they are so frequently portrayed as vulnerable, from a broken home, or fatherless, or as an orphan?

Men, who can never put themselves in the shoes of a little girl, can only try to empathise with them for their vulnerability but without patronising them for any weaknesses. Gordon John Sinclair certainly found them confusing in *Gregory's Girl*. Having turned up for a date with the girl of his dreams, he is stood up, only to be taken out by a string of substitutes standing in for his Dorothy. "It's not a joke," he is told. "It's just the way girls work. They help each other." Or as a young Elizabeth Taylor tries to explain to the two boys who just shot her dog in *The Courage of Lassie*, "You wouldn't understand, you're only boys." And how can you explain to a distraught jilted boy the baffling quip made by Julia Roberts to her stepdaughter, twelve-year-old Anna, in *Stepmom*, "The point of 'going out' with someone is so that they can be dumped!"

Alex McKenna knew how to take advantage of her gender in the Australian movie, *Joey* (1997). "That's right, I am a girl! Which means I'll get all the love and attention I'll ever want," says the thirteen-year-old. But being an ambassador's daughter comes with its drawbacks, for referring to visiting diplomats she adds, "All they ever do is slobber all over my hand and tell me how cute I am."

It is this cuteness factor that inspired Maurice Chevalier to warble about his *Gigi*, "Thank Heavens for little girls!" while Miss Hannigan sarcastically croaks in *Annie* (1982),

> *"Some women are dripping with diamonds,*
> *Some women are dripping with pearls,*
> *But lucky me!*
> *What I'm dripping with is little girls!"*

But this cute factor can be a dangerous tool exploited by the movie business and perpetuated by us the loyal audience. As James Kincaid points out in his book *Erotic Innocence* "Why do we yearn to see twelve-year-olds, and avert our eyes from kids of fifteen?... We want cute, and adolescents are not cute."[3]

The mystery of girlhood is further deepened as Charlotte Gainsbourg says to her brother in *The Cement Garden*, "Secretly you'd love to know what it is like to be a girl." Girls have a different kind of strength, and their confidence can be channelled in different directions. Artists may picture them as statues of beauty, others see fairy-like qualities in them, dirty old men may see them as objects of desire, and the predator may see them remotely as playthings, or more tangibly as objects to abuse.

Lucile Hadzihalilovic recognised these ambiguities in the preamble to her film *Innocence* (2004). She realised the audience reaction to her film would vary between men and women. "Naturally, I think it is easier for women to identify with the young girls (in her film). They'll understand more quickly and directly. Their own lives will be evoked. For men, however, viewing the young girls (in her film) may be problematic," she admits. This contrast in the reactions of different genders is apparent in *Hounddog*, too. According to director, Deborah Kampmeier, "There was a polarised response between men and women to Lewellen's sexuality. So many men felt the young teen was being provocative with her sexuality, whereas the women said 'no, no' she's just being natural – alive in her body."[4] (Lewellen is being played by a spirited precocious Dakota Fanning who has to depict a disturbing rape scene – an exceptional ask for any actor, let alone a fourteen-year-old minor.)

Girls are considered more vocal than boys, (and according to Eileen Quinn in *Annie* (1982) "easier to get used to,") using language skills to resolve problems by diplomacy. "I've been here three times," says Detective Miglioriti to Jodie Foster who is trying to cover up for an absentee father in *The Little Girl who lives down the Lane*, "And each time I've noticed how good you are with words. The way you speak: you're very careful. You're too goddam careful!" I guess the male/female differences in communication are rudely exaggerated in *Magic Island*. "That be the problem with men. They never speak when they should, and they speak when they have nothing of importance to say," complains Jessie-Ann Friend. More characteristically, boys use guttural growls of grunts as Duckworth generates: "P'Tang, Yang, Kipperbang, uhh."

A difference between the genders can be noticed as punishments are meted out, too. Richard, in *Return to the Blue Lagoon*, receives a spank on two occasions, while his playmate, Lily (Courtney Phillips), who was equally to blame, goes unblemished. I do not even think the spankings were scripted. I believe the actress, Lisa Pelikan, just slapped him instinctively, because that is what you do to boys. There are exceptions: Brooke Shields receives a thrashing in *Pretty Baby*, as does Patty McCormack in *The Bad Seed*, and the palms of Perdita Weeks are made raw in *The Rag Nymph*, as are Dakota Fanning's in *Hounddog*. Hailee Steinfeld is given one hell of a thrashing in *True Grit* (2010), not because she had done anything wrong, but because she was stubbornly determined. She had been previously warned, "Your headstrong ways will lead you into a tight corner some day." Her abuser was a man, US Ranger Le Boeuf, feeling threatened emotionally by this upstart of a girl, and the only way he could find to impose his dominance is to bend her over his knee and bring a switch to her backside.

How deeply ingrained are these gender stereotypes for, as a male, I found these punishments meted out to a girl distressing and untypical, more so than to a boy. However, Capt Von Trapp's smacking of Brigitta's bum (for reading a book) in *The Sound of Music* was more comic than severe. Isn't this a bent trait of some males: the desire to tap the girl's bum? The action wasn't helped by Brigitta's pleasurable smile. "Tooti, remind me to spank you after supper," (says Leon Ames to Margaret O'Brien in *Meet me in St Louis*).

Here is another gender stereotype that I am aware some readers may cringe from and disagree with. You hold back from switching a girl because they are more likely to burst into tears. Are not many romance movies based on the idea that the leading man falls for the tearful woman feigning a hard-luck story? (Rex Harrison falling for Gene Tierney in *The Ghost and Mrs Muir*. "The one thing I can't stand is a woman crying," he says, then instantly falls in love with her.) The pitiful crying waif wins over the man who can't bear to see her distress. It is this ability to cry at a whim that sets girl actors apart.

Personally, I acknowledge it influences my rating of how talented a child actor is according to how sincerely (or falsely) they can burst into tears and get me and the audience blubbering with them (along with portraying other emotions, too), and a study by Nancy Signorelli concurs that 44% of female characters cry or whine on camera, compared to only 24% of men.[5]

Niki Caro commenting on her film *Whale Rider* says, "It's amazing working with children. They are so straight forward." Adults have developed techniques to mask their hurts and feelings whereas "Here is a child who is so emotionally available," referring to her lead actress, eleven-year-old Keisha Castle-Hughes. The adult Jodie Foster used a similar phrase to describe eleven-year-old Abigail Breslin's role in *Nim's Island*. She is "so emotionally accessible." No doubt, both references were related to the need for the child to burst into tears. We don't expect boys to cry. There is some degree of discomfort in watching Wil Wheaton cry on the shoulder of best friend River Phoenix in *Stand by Me*; he certainly restrains his tears until his other buddies are out of sight, as does Piggy (Daniel Pipoly) in *Lord of the Flies* (1990). But witness a girl in distress and the whole film is a winning tearjerker. We will mention shortly how Keisha Castle-Hughes won an Oscar (deservedly so) on the back of her performance in which her crying reduces a whole cinema into blubbering sympathisers.

"That's why all children should be girls," says Annie the maid in *It's a Wonderful Life*.

The Boy as Urchin or Angel, Mouse or Man

The movie industry has helped perpetuate the myth of the boy adventurer, from *Greystoke* abandoned to the jungle, to Mowgli adopted by wolves, and the infant *Superman* ejected as an orphan from his planet Krypton. Whether he is *Harry Potter* sparring with Voldemort, Sabu trailing the infidels beyond the Khyber Pass in *The Drum* (1938), Short Round accompanying *Indiana Jones*, or Alex Rider in *Stormbreaker*, all remain fitting disciples following the stride of our legendary heroes. It is what we expect of boys. And what we perceive to be the romantic aspiration of the schoolboy dreamer.

Most children do not have the jungle as their playground: Sam Huntington as Mimi-Siku in *Jungle 2 Jungle*, and Charley Boorman in *The Emerald Forest* are exceptions. For others, their adventures are accomplished in their own concrete wildernesses of colliery pit heaps for Billy Casper (David Bradley) in *Kes* (1969), and urban towpaths for William Eadie in *Ratcatcher*, railway tracks for the four intrepid adventurers in *Stand By Me*, or the bomb craters and dereliction of wartorn London for Billy (Sebastian Rice Edwards) in *Hope and Glory*. But it is this willingness to explore with a modicum of bravado that is expected of the boy-child. Albeit, Ryan's Slater's trek across Chinese mountains in *Amazing Panda Adventure* was only achieved with the help of a girl, Yi Ding, and *Harry Potter* could not succeed without the inspiration of Hermione, while Ethan Hawke's aerial flight in a make-shift space capsule in *Explorers* was made partly to impress the girl of his dreams. "If she can do it, I can do it too!" asserts Ryan, afraid of being omitted from the panda rescue. "Oh Jack, you are the bravest boy I've ever met," says Jessie-Ann Friend to the thirteen-year-old in *Magic Island*, but only because the girl has accompanied him stride for stride alongside the alleged hero. The boy is projected as the explorer but he has no permit to monopolise the trail.

He is thrust into a competitive environment in which he has to assert himself to the fore; and as he matures, to demonstrate his macho nature at attracting admiring female on-lookers and thus preserving the survival of the fittest syndrome. His is a world of rough and tumble mock fights as the foursome demonstrate in *Stand by Me*, of the bloody hog chase in *Lord of the Flies*, and of throwing stones in *Killer of Sheep*. "Real men don't mess about dreaming," says Abigail Cruttenden to Duckworth in *P'Tang, Yang, Kipperbang*. Michael Thompson states in *Best Friends, Worst Enemies*, "When boys run into conflict, they often push and shove to resolution. When girls disagree, they'll usually try to compromise."[6]

The boy must resort to manly roles, for that is what is expected of him. Christopher Atkins builds the house, and designs the spears to fish the creeks in *The Blue Lagoon* (while Brooke Shields is able to scoop the fish with her hands); it is Peter who is given the sword by Aslan in *The Lion, the Witch and the Wardrobe* (while Lucy has power to heal with the phial of medicine); and Gary Warren receives the steam engine in *The Railway Children*, for he wants to be an engineer (though his sisters watch aghast while it is derailed). Boys: the explorers, the inventors, the mechanics. "Danny, finish your rocket, instead," says Mark Lester's prudish mother in *Melody*, after she finds the eleven-year-old sketching nudes. Somehow, this boy has misread the script!

But as well as macho man, the movie industry likes to exploit the child that has not made the grade. Through the director's viewfinder, the bullied boy transcending torment makes for great entertainment. Regrettably, none of this enhances our morality or the boy's self-esteem, for his adversaries are usually overcome by supernatural means and not by the child's own intuition. "Please don't make me go to school today," pleads Cayden Boyd in *The Adventures of Sharkboy and Lavagirl*. "They'll make fun of me." This boy can only cope with his daily torment by inventing a fantasy world in which he becomes the superhero. In *Let the Right One In*, it takes another superhuman (the vampire girl, Eli) to put a dramatic stop to the bullies who have taunted Oskar, struck him with switches and dumped his clothes in the school urinals. While in *Munchie*, Jaime McEnnan has to call upon a scary-looking gnome to perform his miracles for him.

So, though the movie industry has perpetuated the myth of the boy adventurer, his indestructibility has been humanised by River Phoenix providing a comforting shoulder for Wil Wheaton's tears, and by Macaulay Culkin quaking in his bedroom in *Home Alone* (1990). "Only a wimp would be hiding under the bed," he admonishes himself.

The daring director explores these more effeminate traits from a serious standpoint: the mummy's boy, the son despised by father for his sissy stance; the *Billy Elliot* who exchanges boxing for ballet (Jamie Bell); Tom (Ned Birkin) in *The Cement Garden* who willingly dons a blouse, dress and blond wig to avert a spell of school bullying; Buddy (Eric Lloyd), who only knows how to bake and sew and clean because he has been adopted by a trio of spinsters in *A Christmas Memory*.

To the boy, the female of the species is incomprehensible. The boy has to despise the girl. "Girls, they're snotty nosed gits, they are," says Ornshaw (Jack Wild) in *Melody*, while Josh Hutcherson in *Little Manhattan* acknowledges that since first grade, "the iron curtain came down, girls on one side, boys on the other," with no interaction in between, afraid to catch a dreaded cootie that comes from even accidentally touching a girl. Michael Thompson noted this same dilemma, suggesting that for primary aged children, "One of the most powerful and consistent rules about gender is to spend most of one's time and energy in single-sex groups," and the punishment for violation of these rules is "teasing, rejection, gossip."[7] You just need to see the huddle of boys spectating around the periphery of a dance hall in *Run the Wild Fields* to bear this out. Even as a youth, Jude Law discovered the reality of this when told by his sports-mad buddies to choose between them or his girlfriend, Clare Danes, in *I Love You, I Love You Not*. (The boy chose his teammates!)

The whole of *Little Rascals* highlights these differences. The gang of infant boys have their own clubhouse where they meet as *The Woman-Hater Club*, and woe betide any girl that tries to approach. Girls are definitely an alien species. To the girls, boys mean "bogeys and bugs", "fighting and farting", "and they don't listen". To the boys, all the girls want to do is talk. Alas, Alfalfa (Bug Hall) has fallen for Darla (Brittany Ashton Holmes) and needing a place to woo her, smuggles her into the clubhouse while the gang are off elsewhere. Whoa. This poor boy has to be rescued from this love affair.

When it comes to the opposite sex, the boys have to spend part of their adolescence in no-man's land and dream. While girls of their age are dating older youths, the desolate urchin has to resort to other means to satisfy his lust. This becomes a standing joke for girls, and exploited for its frivolity by filmmakers – once a taboo subject, male masturbation is approached with less reserve (though still widely avoided in reference to the preteen girl). Oh the embarrassments, the secrets, the telltale signs! John Albasiny in *P'Tang, Yang, Kipperbang* wearing a glove in bed to avoid the temptation of idle hands, to placate God, in the hope his prayer will come true: just one kiss from Abigail Cruttenden. Christopher Atkins, sitting alone on the rocks beside his *Blue Lagoon*, taunted by Brooke Shields, "I know what you're doing!" Andrew Robertson posing in front of his mirror in *The Cement Garden* warned by his mother, "Every time you, you know, do it, it takes two pints of blood to replace it!" "You're going to go blind," shouts Renato's (Guiseppe Sulfaro) father in *Malèna* as he hears the bed violently creak in the room above. Only in *Babel* are we expected to watch without tittering as two child shepherd boys take a secretive break from watching their flocks. "I have to go urgently," says embarrassed Charlie after his first kiss with Marcie Brady in *The Brady Bunch*. "Something's come up!"

"That's how it is with men," gossip the old Anatolian hags in *Times & Winds*. "Sweet as little boys, they become like their fathers when they are fathers themselves!" And the apology granted by Elle Fanning in *The Nutcracker* (2010)? "Sorry about my brother. Boys are like that!"

Gender Imbalance

As in so many other occupations, there is a history of prominence for men in the movie industry, an imbalance that sees the male dominating principal roles. Stacy Smith, in a study with University of Southern California, revealed that just 30% of actors are women, and just 27% of actors with a speaking part are female, and that certain distributors (Fox, Paramount, & Universal) had an even higher imbalance with just 25% women,[8] (implying, of course, that 75% of actors are male). Obviously, women are leading characters in a multitude of films, and most viewers will have their favourites who are glittering stars: Julia Roberts, Jodie Foster, Helena Bonham Carter, Kate Winslett, Jean Simmons. Yet, men run the movie industry. 83% of directors, writers and producers are men, just 17% being women.[9]

I can confirm these findings. At the end of this book is an appendix listing the films I consulted in preparation for this series, *Children in Films*. Of the five hundred films listed, only 14% are directed by a woman (86% of directors are men). When considering script and storywriters of the screenplay, the balance is redressed only fractionally: 26% of women are involved creatively as writers. And even when women *are* involved, it seems their company employers first direct them towards writing or directing repeats and sequels, such as the *Doctor Dolittle* update (1998), the repeat of *Freaky Friday* (1994), *The Parent Trap* (1998), *Pollyanna* (2002), *The Railway Children* (2000), *Turn of the Screw* (2009), *The Secret Garden* (1993), *Lord of the Flies* (1990), and *My Girl 2*. It's as if the production company felt these could only be entrusted in a female hands where a template already existed.

When women actors reach a pinnacle, it is more likely to be in glamorous roles in which the attractive, agile, slim female is the requisite. Where are the modern day Margaret Rutherfords or Hattie Jacques?

According to Stacy Smith, "Females are more likely than males to be young, thin, and shown in tight or revealing attire. This prototype illuminates the hypersexualisation of females in film, reinforcing a culture of lookism within the industry." The actress is more likely to be the love interest for the lead male, and to be designated domestic roles of housewife or caregiver. As the woman ages and loses her attractive qualities, she is then likely to be discarded in the industry's dustbin. Stacy Smith's study notes that only 24% of actresses are over the age of forty, compared with 39% of male actors. The young girl is more highly prized than the young boy: 18% of female actors are under twenty-one compared with just 12% of males. These females are emphatically exploited for their looks. "They are more likely to be sexualised with revealing clothing, partial nudity, thinness, and attractiveness."

In Volume Six (*Puberty & First Love*), we highlight how this demand has been passed down to teenage and preteen girls who, in a surprisingly large proportion of movies, are required to strip off for shower/bath scenes. Stacy Smith's study also noted that in films directed, produced, or written by women there was a lower percentage of female characters "in sexually alluring attire" and less partial nudity (i.e. showing cleavage, midriff, upper thigh). Nancy Signorelli notes that 42% of female film actors are likely to be seen in sleepwear/lingerie compared with just 11% of men; and 58% of women receive compliments about their looks on film compared with 24% of male film characters.[10]

Children watching movies, or taking part in them are likely to be subconsciously indoctrinated as they see other girls and women portrayed in an exploited or suggestive role. 69% of girls and 40% of boys say they have "wanted to look, dress, or fix their hair like a character on television." And a small proportion have dieted or exercised to mimic that appearance.[11] "Stereotypical depictions of women as sexy or domesticated may facilitate the development and maintenance of attitudes, beliefs and aspirations that are limiting."[12] This is borne out in a study by Vernae Graham et al, 58% of children interviewed thought the female characters seen on television were 'better-looking' than females they know in real life, and 61% thought the actresses were thinner – traits the child may feel obliged to emulate. Characteristics that the children in her survey most associated with the female actress were "worrying about appearance or weight, crying or whining." The male actor is more likely to be portrayed as "playing sports, and wanting to be kissed or have sex." According to Matt James, Kaiser Family Foundation, "The media is a powerful tool that can either reinforce negative stereotypes or present strong role models for young girls and boys today."[13] From the evidence of these studies it appears as if the negative stereotypes are more likely to be reinforced.

Nancy Signorelli notes that in movies, 31% of women compared to 7% of men are seen preening or grooming, and 19% of women are seen doing gender-stereotyped chores compared to just 1% of men. Further, 44% of female film characters can be seen crying or whining compared to 24% males, while male characters are more likely to be using physical force, working hard, and taking risks.[14] According to Geena Davis, "Kids need to see entertainment where females are valued as much as males."[15]

Roles & Reactions

For some it begins in the school hall, doubling as a stage for the Nativity play. For others, a local drama club keeps them off the streets. For many, they have parental footsteps to follow and try to emulate, while others are plucked anonymously from the mundane into a strange world of fantasy and falsity. All arrive with dreams and ambitions into an industry that offers the child bright lights and glamour, but discards them at a whim. Each acting apprentice arrives with pre-conceived ideas about the role they are to play in the theatrical sphere, but inevitably they are wrong, duped by the exploitative expectations of the public and the media.

I wonder how many children making their debut as a preteen child, dreaming the whole world is at their feet, are aware that if they wish to progress into a career in movies as adults (with no guarantee of stardom) they will be required to portray intimacy on stage, kiss in front of the camera (and in front of millions of hidden viewers), bare all, take part in simulated sex scenes, and be mobbed by the 'adoring' paparazzi to the point of breakdown, and will have their very personal dilemmas – their drug-taking, their extra-marital affairs, their indiscretions and petty shop-lifting, their therapies and hours in rehab – scrutinized in every gossip magazine around the globe, and have millions of sad men and boys drooling over them in their closets. For in many films, even in this liberated era, this is still the main role of the lead lady – to be a pretty female, a sex goddess, in a movie business filled with groping men – while the male actor is expected to be the handsome hulk pinned scandalously to the bedchambers of adoring acned adolescents (and spinsters).

Further, they will be self-employed with an irregular income, probably having to oddjob at Tescos in between contracts, and if they want a pension, they will have to resort to performing parts of elderly characters. For it is only the small percentage of the most highly successful that acquire any wealth from the career.

These are the roles expected of our young actors, and even if the theme they are depicting does not warp their mentality, the audiences' critique of them certainly will. Veteran actor Simon Callow would concur with me. Innocent dressing up games with his grandma while a kid led him twenty years later "on a television production set naked in bed with another person, while a dozen people stand behind the camera recording every breath and flick of an eyelash."[16]

1940s actress Deanna Durbin must have had a premonition of what to expect. At the screen test she was attending with her pushy mother, the young adolescent broke down saying, "I don't want to be an actress. You are all torturing me!"[17] But she was living in an age when American parents thrust their children to the stage to collect the accolades, and in particular, the wage packets and royalties that they themselves missed in their own careers. Deanna was an innocent bonny-looking songster, yet she was typecast into a Lolita-ish personality fabricated by the media. She was only a fresh-faced girl of just thirteen, impotent at shaking off her unwanted label. American darling in her teenage years, she made a rapid exit from showbiz once she came of age and had any personal choice in the matter.

The fact that all the cinematic nymphets of the 1940s – Deanna Durbin, Shirley Temple, Judy Garland, Elizabeth Taylor, plus Carol Lynley, Hayley Mills and Sue Lyon of the 1960s – tried to escape from the media-imposed labels by marrying while still teenagers, often to men much older than themselves, shows how traumatic it is being a teenage darling, a nymphet esteemed by a nation.[18] 'Our Shirley', 'our Judy', 'our Liz' – their names are phrased as if a nation owns them, and has a right to react, admire, manipulate, and criticize them as if they were their own personal lapdogs. I realise I too am guilty of it in this book. I take a pride in 'our actors', and have used the term within these pages to express a fondness for our legends, past or future.

Alas, all 'our' teenage brides ended up divorced within two years, only for the media to again rant (unjustly) at the fickleness of famed youth.

Emotional and Psychological Impact on the Child Actor

I am curious to know how the child perceives the role he/she is playing. Most children can naturally portray child-like attributes of love, tears, obedience, playing and scrapping. Unlike young actors from pre-war eras and the fifties and sixties, the child of today is mollycoddled and should not be so adept at playing fear, or being abused, despite this being an important demand of modern scriptwriters for whom adult themes are becoming ever more explicit. Yet today there is such a plethora of visual media for a child to copy from, they are able to play such parts with conviction. Evidently, nine-year-old Isabelle Fuhrman prepared for her dark murderous role in *Orphan* (2009) by watching adult-rated movies such as *The Silence of the Lambs* and *Dangerous Liaisons*.[19]

Some children playing parts in adult films are not even able to watch the playback of the movie they have starred in due to the age-restrictions for viewers. I hope the little girl playing with her dolls outside the doorway was denied the opportunity to watch her performance at a screening of *kids* (1995), a movie full of explicit sexuality, violence and drug taking. Sue Lyon was not legally permitted to see her own acting in adult-rated *Lolita*, while underaged Nastassia Kinski intended to watch her own performance in *To the Devil a Daughter* but promised, "I'll probably cover my eyes."[20] Eight-year-old actress Heather O'Rourke claimed to have watched *Poltergeist* (1982) 'over and over again' before her own untimely death at the age of twelve, while Scarlett Johansson bragged about watching *The Silence of the Lambs* when she was just eight.[21] What was the psychological impact on six-year-old Laura Vaquero in the Spanish film, *Alas de Mariposa*, who as an infant had to smother her baby brother with a pillow in a desperate attempt to deflect her parents' rejection of her? Adult movies have an age-restriction placed on them for a purpose: to prevent premature psychological scarring of a child viewer. This places a dichotomy on the part of young actors and their guardians. It seems parental neglect is making a mockery of the Board of Classification's attempt to protect the innocence of our youth.

Alison Graham (in a *Radio Times* editorial) focuses on the needless violence children are required to portray. Referring to an episode of the TV drama *Waking the Dead,* she reflects on the unnecessary depiction of nine-year-olds torturing each other in which Danny Emes stubs lighted cigarettes on another kid while the victim screams in terror. Other scenes depict a child stabbing a tormentor in the eyes, and in another, a child is chained with a bag over his head.

Alison Graham (justifiably in my view) describes this as "vile and unflinching make-believe sadism carried out by infants on other infants… This is the dramatised torture of small children by other small children… It has no part in entertainment – ever. You can try to justify it dramatically, but you will fail because it is indefensible."[22] It is at times like these that thoughts of the James Bulger murder focus into view, with the potential horror of copycat crime.

If this had such an emotional impact on a professional drama critic, just think what psychological damage this must have imposed on the child actors themselves. No doubt, much of the horror was fabricated in the editor's cutting room and the children may not even have been aware of the actual violent acts they were depicting. But any child actor must be sorely tempted to watch the production they have 'starred' in, even if it is adult-rated. This is where the psychological scarring can begin.

Infant Rafiella Brookes has a similar gruesome task to perform in *The Children* (2008), stabbing her mother in the eye with a pencil. Yet the director, Tom Shankland, seems to justify this as innocuous, that kids live in a gory world of make-believe, that it is only adults who worry about the impact of such actions. In the words of one of the crew members, Jane Karen, "For kids, who are quite gory in their play anyway, it's not such a big leap for them; but with adults, we get very sensitive about how we are going to explain this." Fellow actor, Jeremy Sheffield, explains how they prepared the child cast by "playing games and wink murder with the kids to make it clear it is just a game." This included spending time in the prosthetics department, stabbing fake eyeballs and watching blood come spurting out! [23]

I was particularly impressed by the stance taken by the adolescent Natalie Portman, who in the words of Barry Norman, "had shown unusual promise as a twelve-year-old nymphet in her first film, *Leon*, where her appearance attracted steamy appreciation." When offered the title role in *Lolita* (1997) she turned it down because "she thought it unhealthy to portray young girls as sex objects." [24] This sensible young girl has matured into an Oscar winning adult for her role in *Black Swan*. Perhaps the versatility of roles she has pursued has allowed her greater freedom to develop her acting talent than say, Brooke Shields, who was trapped into being typecast, after appearing in *Pretty Baby*, for sensationalist child exploitation roles.

Maybe, Natalie Portman had seen the warning signs from Sue Lyon who played title role in the first *Lolita* (1962) film. The fifteen-year-old Miss Lyon recognised "*Lolita* exposed me to temptations no girl of that age should undergo:" overnight fame, money, endless parties, and handsome (older) actors. "I defy any pretty girl who is rocketed to world stardom at fifteen in a sex-nymphet role to stay on a level path thereafter." [25]

While Sue Lyon and 1960s self-proclaimed Lolita, Tuesday Weld, were weighed down with the struggle of shaking off their promiscuous reputation, Hayley Mills could not shake off her reputation as sweet innocent everyone's favourite Disneyfied child actor. She even wished she *had* accepted the role of *Lolita* when offered the part by Stanley Kubrick. She felt this would have allowed her to grow up. "I seemed forever doomed to be a little girl. Whatever I did I knew nobody wanted me to change."[26]

Other child actors are unable to socialise with their peers, because of their performance schedules, growing up in an environment filled with adults, and tutored by adult teachers in between takes. Prodigies like Dakota Fanning, despite starring alongside a string of famous faces – Tom Cruise, Robert de Niro, Queen Latifah, Denzel Washington – seem often to be the only child in the cast. This must surely stunt her social capacity and warp her stance on life. No wonder all the actors who work alongside her praise her for being so grown up and thinking like an adult. At least, in *Hounddog* she had other playmates to hobnob with. Her contemporary, Daniel Radcliffe, said of her, "She was freakish as a child. She couldn't play a kid. I was watching a nine-year-old girl thinking, Jesus Christ, you're forty. No problem with me, Emma (Watson) and Rupert (Grint) over that. We were kids." [27] This, of course, was not Dakota's fault. She was an admirable child actor given difficult emotional parts to play.

In the case of Heather Ripley, who plays Jemima in *Chitty Chitty Bang Bang*, she had no friends to play with for the fourteen months of filming. Having to move south from her hometown of Dundee to be able to perform at the Pinewood Studios in London, she was deprived of her family and friends. For a child of eight, this seems inexcusable. She tells how in desperation she wrote a message on the window of her London flat to try to gain the attention of the little girl who lived across the road from her – "Will you be my friend?" [28] What she had missed most was her father. When she was finally able to return home from filming over a year later, she found that father had divorced and her family had fallen apart. Not the fairy tale ending the film had projected. Yet she had other traumas to contend with too. When cast for her role as Jemima she was told she was perfect, except for the Scottish accent. "We'll get that out of her," she was assured, but the infant girl feared that meant having an operation. When you hear the final clipped Oxford English of the little girl in the movie, you can tell her Scottish roots have been ripped from her.

Writing in *Radio Times,* Mark Lawson casts a similar shadow concerning the privations of our aspiring actors. Speaking of Emma Watson, Daniel Radcliffe, and Rupert Grint, the idolised stars of the *Harry Potter* series, "What would it be like to know that millions of people on every continent possess almost twenty-four hours of home movies of your adolescent development?" [29]

Later, we mention how Emma Watson and her co-stars required a bodyguard, and this is becoming the norm in this unpredictable world. Yet this is not a new phenomenon. Sandy Descher, a child star of the 1960s received a number of kidnapping threats, and the FBI was involved when a woman stalker fantasized about her as her long lost daughter. [30] Jodie Foster, the twelve-year-old pimped for sex in *Taxi Driver*, required bodyguards after she became idolised and pestered by John Hinckley, the man who subsequently attempted to assassinate President Reagan.

Coping with fame

Not realising how prophetic her words would be when she wrote them, Joanna Rowling, says of *Harry Potter*, "This boy will be famous. There won't be a child in the world who won't know his name." How true this turned out, for today every child knows the names of the stars playing their characters: Daniel Radcliffe, Rupert Grint, Emma Watson – three multi-millionaire child stars.

Many young actors have had no experience of acting at all prior to being in a blockbuster movie. The transition from being a little anonymous schoolkid to being a massive international sensation can take just months. What an incredible emotional pressure that must exert on the child – and the tremendous responsibilities laid upon those who nurture and protect them. For example, the aforementioned trio of wizards thrust into international recognition in the *Harry Potter* series. At least they must have had an inkling of what was in store for them, for the novels by J K Rowling had generated a reading revolution in primary classrooms nationwide. Yet, these were just three out of thousands who queued around the block for their auditions for a part in the blockbuster series. Fortunately, these are three kids, now international superstars, who have not been fazed by the journey. For Rupert Grint, he finds the adulation positive and not something to hide away from.

By contrast, a year before Keisha Castle-Hughes was nominated for an Oscar for best actress, the eleven-year-old was sitting in her New Zealand primary school with no acting ambitions. By chance, the director of *Whale Rider* entered her classroom searching for a girl who would fit the role of a Maori girl, and Keisha was unaware she had been spotted from among her classmates. In the words of Niki Caro, "She was extraordinary. She took it all in her stride!" And her Oscar nomination was a rare achievement for a child.

Similarly plucked from obscurity and now wallowing in glory is Matthew Lewis who, as an avid reader of the Harry Potter novels begged his mother, "If ever they make a film of it, will you take me to see it?" Beyond his dreams, he finds himself actually playing Neville Longbottom in the billion-dollar series.[31]

New found fame can have an impact on the actor. This may be detrimental or positively enhancing. Patty McCormack was considered freakish by her schoolmates. Having shocked the public by playing the part of a serial child murderer in *The Bad Seed*, her fellow students had difficulty coming to terms with her fame while she was acting on Broadway. I assume she implies she was bullied and picked on and pointed out as being 'different'. But Patty says her reception was much more positive when she went to California where other Hollywood school kids were more used to celebrity children. Brooke Shields claims she was 'cold-shouldered' on enrolling at Princeton University. "I was shattered. Everyone thought I was just a movie star playing at being a student. They all thought it cool to ignore me, and I was broken-hearted."[32] Heather Ripley, playing Jemima in *Chitty Chitty Bang Bang*, spent the next thirty years of her life trying to forget the film, because as an eight-year-old she found the experience so dismal.

Ramona Marquez, who featured in *Enid* (2009), but who rose to celebrity status as an infant through her improvised humour in the TV comedy series *Outnumbered,* says concerning being recognised in the streets, "I really like it cos people that never talked to me before come up and talk to me now." But this is a nine-year-old girl still trying to rationalise her fame for she counters by saying "I don't like it when people point me out in the street and flash mobile phones in front of me to take my picture," or when "they just look at you whispering. That's quite annoying."[33]

It was this incessant stalking by the paparazzi that annoyed adolescent Scarlett Johansson, too. "I don't think there's any kind of preparation for sudden celebrity. Like, you're buying a slice of pizza and somebody's outside photographing you, which is weird; that's not normal! It's very uncomfortable!"[34] This promising starlet was advised by Drew Barrymore, "Whatever you do, don't go into acting for the fame. Because if you do, you're going to end up unhappy."[35]

Emma Watson, girl star of the *Harry Potter* series, is also aware of the double-edged sword of the fame game. "I know it sounds strange, but I really don't feel famous. It's quite surreal." This despite *Vanity Fair* naming her as Hollywood's highest paid female with earnings over £20 million. She has to be accompanied by bodyguards but tries to keep a low profile when she goes out. "Occasionally people stop me (in the street) but I'd rather deal with that than not go out at all. That'd be really tragic." She tells how when she was a younger actress she and her co-stars would try to hide from their bodyguards and guardians.[36] As to her co-star, Daniel Radcliffe, he does admit avoiding the underground, being worried about potential problems in confined spaces.[37]

Emma Watson's pot of gold pales into insignificance when compared to the phenomenal earnings of America's idolised childhood sweetheart, Shirley Temple, who on her tenth birthday had become the seventh highest paid American, was "the most photographed human being in the world," and received over five-hundred fan-mail letters every single day.[38]

Although it is outside the movie sphere, the experiences of Hollie Steel epitomises the emotional impact that fame and performance make on a fragile girl of nine. Taking part in *Britain's Got Talent 2009* the little songbird from Rochdale soared through the audition rounds with her angelic renditions. But when the realism of the semi finals hit her, with thirteen million TV viewers either willing her through or waiting for her to trip up, the little girl stutters through her performance and bursts into tears. The real life drama is worsened as the production team tell her that there is no time available to allow her to sing again, but her continued tears provoke Simon Cowell to take pity. He allows her to perform again and the British public vote her through to the finals. The irony of all this is that the next day the fate of this one little girl reached headline news in many of the national newspapers and radio broadcasts, and a debate raged among journalists and well-meaning members of the public as to the rights and wrongs of putting our children into the media spotlight, with the term 'child exploitation' being bandied around.

Hollie's problems did not end there. Following her rise to recognition, like many vulnerable children in her age group, she was targeted by paedophiles, receiving several inappropriate messages on her facebook page, and several kids much older than her wanted to 'befriend' the preteen girl. Now she can only view the internet in the presence of her parents or schoolteachers.

In the case of child singing wonder, Lena Zavaroni, the pressure of being in the public spotlight led her to anorexia, and an early death from pneumonia. She thought she looked too plump. One newspaper headline described her fate as 'the little girl who paid the price for fame.'[39]

On UK TV, BBC3 broadcast an interesting documentary about how a fourteen-year-old girl copes with the pressures of sudden fame. Although the girl was not a film star, she gained an equal amount of exposure on Internet face-book. It is helpful to focus on this here, for it illustrates the challenges facing immature children who achieve unexpected stardom. Fortunately, in this particular case we are dealing with a confident, eloquent, and sensibly chaperoned teenager, Rebecca Flint, a resident from the Isle of Man.

The documentary was called *Beckii: Schoolgirl Superstar at 14.* For weeks, Rebecca would dance Japanese danjo in front of the webcam in the "privacy" of her own bedroom, without her parents' knowledge. She gave herself a new identity, Beckii Cruel, and within a few months, she had received thirteen million hits on-line from the Japanese public.

When a Japanese video producer contacted her, obviously her parents then became involved. Her father, being a policeman, sensibly ensured she was steered along strict lines. In eight months, she made six journeys to Japan where she had become a celebrity. Rebecca was successful because her face and figure fitted the oriental image of a manga icon – large eyes, moon faced, pointy chin, and regardless of whether she could sing or dance well, she paraded in short dresses and Japanese costumes. "She is a total cootie," the reporter was told following a photo shoot for a lads' mag. She is like "a dolly, pure, innocent, with an angelic look."[40]

For Rebecca, she is loving it. "Wonderful! I like doing TV," she cheers, striding down the studio corridor having just been watched by twenty-five million people on live TV. In the streets of Tokyo, she is mobbed by fans that want her autograph and to be photographed with her. Her only complaint is her cheeks hurt from too much smiling!

For her father, he realises this may "just be fuelling dirty old men," but he counters by saying that any clothing catalogue can also turn on dirty old men. Though there is a Lolita aspect to it, in Japan that is normal and "part of the wider picture." So the documentary tells us.

For mother, after intercepting an alarming e-mail from an admirer whose comment about Beckii was "nice up-skirt", mother now checks her daughter's routines to ensure nothing is too overt, such as panty-peeps, or bra-straps showing.

Rebecca is disappointed that the bulk of her fans are middle-aged men, though she assumes not every one of these will be bad or seedy. Yet, she does also get a reasonable proportion of young female viewers, she claims with a hint of optimism.

Her admiring fans often send her exotic gifts right across the world. The documentary shows her receiving and opening an expensive electric bass guitar. This is from an infatuated man who regularly makes a twelve-hour trip across Japan to admire her at concerts. (The parents now describe this former stranger as a friend of the family!) Rebecca acknowledges she "feels uncomfortable about him spending so much money (on her). It's very sweet of him, but he needs a reality check." Fortunately, this sensible fourteen-year-old has her feet very firmly on the ground.

The parents are willing for her to sacrifice her GCSEs, or rather postpone them, realising they have "only a short window" of success, and they are happy to maximise this while the girl is earning in excess of £50,000.

Uncle Max saw a similar potential for the Von Trapp children in *The Sound of Music*. As the family have to make a secretive hurried escape over the mountains to Switzerland, he reflects, "I shall miss all of them. I shall miss all the money I could make from them!"

However, Rebecca Flint has one advantage over other child stars, such as Ramona Marquez mentioned above. She is famous only in a country on the other side of the world, so she is not constantly haunted by a parade of parasitic admirers back on the Isle of Man, where she lives. Even her own schoolteacher had been unaware of her talent and Japanese fame! Some of her peers at school occasionally taunt her by singing her dance routines behind her back, but surely isn't this form of teasing normal for any child growing up, celebrity or not? Tom Felton mentioned similar taunting from school peers following his Harry Potter role as Malfoy, but he accepts this as part and parcel of being a celebrity.[41] Other children confronting the negative side of fame include *Britain's Got Talent* winner fourteen-year-old George Sampson who was "viciously punched in the street while waiting for a bus," and who was jeered in Warrington clubs for daring to move out of the home town where he was brought up.[42]

Rebecca has (so far) avoided the unpleasant side of fame – for she is anonymous in her own country. An actor can only achieve fame by being recognised. Most people can name or recognise a child actor, being able to put a name to a character they see on the screen. It surprises me, therefore, when some directors give no credit to the child actors in their films. Why is it that Elizabeth Taylor, before she became famous, did not appear in the credits for the 1944 version of *Jane Eyre*? Or the brilliant children's movie *Nanny McPhee* – not a single child actor was credited. We all know Colin Firth, Celia Imries, Imelda Staunton, Emma Thompson – all are familiar faces and take top billing. But the children: none of this film would have been possible without them, yet none of them appeared in the cast list as the credits rolled, no glory for them in seeing their names in print. Maybe there was a sociological reason they were denied credit. Maybe psychologists felt such exposure would be detrimental to them. If I were a child, I would feel conned – like being denied a trophy I had justly won.

Daniel Radcliffe confirmed this when being interviewed by Will Lawrence for *Radio Times*: "I remember I cried when my name came up in the titles at the end of the film. I felt very proud, and liked seeing my face on posters."[43] Alas, now he is older he says he does not even notice them. As Professor Snape snidely remarks to Daniel Radcliffe, "Clearly, fame isn't everything, is it Mr. Potter?" (*Harry Potter and the Philosopher's Stone*), and as Gildaroy Lockhart tells him, "Fame is a fickle friend, Harry." (*Harry Potter and the Chamber of Secrets*)

Child Labour Laws and Stunt Doubles

Judy Garland, who had been acting since the age of two and a half, said of poor Margaret O'Brien while sharing the limelight with the rising star in *Meet me in St Louis*, "That little girl is not having any life. I've been there and I know what I'm talking about." She was referring to the pressure placed on young children who have to act and rehearse at all hours. Margaret O'Brien however when interviewed about this as an adult denied it having been a trouble. By then, in 1944, child labour laws had been introduced in America, which were not in place during Garland's childhood. O'Brien also had access to a teacher, and except for the Halloween scene was never expected to work after dark.

This concern about children missing out on their normal childhood was commented on by Patty McCormack reflecting on the 50th anniversary of her appearing as a child actress in *Bad Seed*. She had been a child of eight and a half working in Broadway Theatres when the stage play *Bad Seed* was made – and this was not her first theatrical role either. "My working as a child was so normal for me that I didn't think about not having a life." Henry Jones, who plays handyman LeRoy, was additionally concerned the girl was not getting any schooling. Patty relied on other cast members for her companionship. She says of Nancy Kelly who played her mother in the production, "She was like a second mum to me. She had no children of her own at that time, so she enjoyed our relationship."

Missing out on a childhood was a trait of children caught up in the early days of cinema. Mary Pickford, the diminutive darling of American cinemagoers for the first quarter of the twentieth century was supporting her single mother, brother and sister before she was even a teenager. Her childlike looks and flowing locks ensured her action in child roles in *Rebecca of Sunnybrook Farm*, *Little Annie Rooney*, *Pollyanna*, and *Poor Little Rich Girl* well into her thirties. She could confidently claim, "I intend to stay young indefinitely,"[44] and she needed to if her family were to keep their head above poverty.

Joe Wright, the director of *Atonement*, mentions that the hours Saoirse Ronan was allowed to work after dark were carefully monitored when filming the nighttime scene of searching the expansive grounds of the mansion gardens. Likewise, under French laws no filming was permitted after dark, so the lighting for the nighttime woodland scenes in *Innocence* (2004) had to be specially adjusted to make it seem dark, even though it was daytime. Director, Jay Russell, was made aware of the reasons for these recommendations when filming the nighttime scene in a cemetery in Jackson, USA, for *My Dog Skip*. They were filming with the children among the gravestones when real-life shooting began between violent youths who used the graveyard as their own private nighttime haunt. Film crew, actors, and children had to hide behind tombstones and crawl out to safety.

Commenting on the restrictions for the nine-year-old actress Ramona Marquez, rehearsing for *Outnumbered*, Tim Dowling[45] mentions that nine-year-olds can work a maximum of three hours a day in forty-five minute chunks, which does not allow for much continuity when filming. All filming must be completed before 4:30 pm, so if a scene extends beyond those hours then the director has to play as stand-in for the little girl's part "with eyes drawn on and stuck to his chest" while filming continues, so the other actors know in which direction to look. Inconveniently, the sequence is then cut and pasted in the editing room. JJ Abrams, filming *Super 8*, tells how his main core of child actors were only used for facial scenes. To avoid overworking his young cast, all the scenes in which the children's backs were to the camera were performed by substitute actors.

Blair Treu, director of *Little Secrets*, says he had access to his child actors for 5½ hours a day. He further explains how his lead actress Evan Rachel Wood would perform an intense scene, then go off to an algebra class, and return to take up where she left off.

The biggest shock comes when an actor changes from being a child into a youth. Alexia Skinitis writing in the *Radio Times* tells how Dakota Blue Richards, once she had turned sixteen was appearing in Channel Four's *Skins*. Dakota says, "This was my first job after turning sixteen so I was no longer covered by child protection laws or given a tutor on set, which meant I had to work twelve to fourteen hour days and then try to do my homework when I got home.[46] She describes this as her worst job (having previously starred in *The Golden Compass* and *Dustbin Baby* while aged eleven to thirteen).

The director of *Blame it on Fidel*, Julie Gavras, acknowledged how tiredness quickly set in among the child actors and how easy it was for them to lose concentration. In particular, the little boy (Benjamin Feuillet) found it difficult. When he auditioned for the part, he thought the filming would take one day, not several months. What's more, he found it frustrating having to repeat action again and again. He complained that his director "tells him off for making too many mistakes." Maybe the director's problems were compounded by her own attitude. "I don't see children as children. To me they are mini adults," says Julie Gavras. What is more, "all the actors are a bit scared when children are around." Perhaps it is the unpredictability of the child that makes them difficult to work with. More likely, it is the unaccommodating incompetence of the crew that makes the child uncomfortable in the first place.

Benjamin's problems pale into insignificance compared to those of eight-year-old Heather Ripley. Filming for *Chitty Chitty Bang Bang* was scheduled for four months but ended up taking fourteen months. Reflecting on her role thirty years later, Heather recalls the "endless boredom of sitting around waiting for shooting to begin, or for it to stop raining. After six months of filming the novelty had completely worn off and I was sick to the back teeth with it."[47]

In *Toto le Héros*, the children would play board games in between sets and would run around getting in the way. But for this film, the crew were patient with them, and the children, reflecting back as adults, remembered how they were well looked after.

Kevin Corcoran, who acted alongside Hayley Mills in *Pollyanna*, was so insatiably curious about wildlife it distracted him, wandering off between takes, to the annoyance of the director.[48]

Boredom certainly was not a problem in *Cheaper by the Dozen 2*, a film in which two families, one with twelve children, the other with eight, get to mingle and compete together. Already rapport had grown up between the kids from the first film. Now with twenty child actors on site, each of whom had a double and stunt stand-ins, a veritable village grew up ("visible from Mars," according to director Adam Shankman) and being based at a lakeside camp, every day the children would be water trampolining, swimming, fishing, riding on motorboats and water-skiing, playing crazy golf and having karaoke nights. They had of the time of their lives. Comic actor Steve Martin agrees, "It was very hard controlling all the children." For glamour actress Carmen Electra, she found it "overwhelming at times what with all the animals and kids!"

Some films require more practical safety precautions, such as the special breathing units made available under the practice water pools for the underwater sequences in which Abigail Breslin took part in *Nim's Island*. Abigail also tells how, as well as working on set (based in Queensland, Australia) she had three hours of schooling each day, with access to a tutor.

I wonder if they thought safety precautions were necessary in 1965 when the whole Von Trapp family tumble out of their rowing boat capsizing it into the cold Austrian Lake (in *The Sound of Music*). Evidently, Kim Karath as five-year-old Gretl swallowed so much water she was sick and threw up on Heather Menzies.[49]

For some sequences it is easier to just use an adult stage double to replace the child for the trickier scenes, or for the more emotional, traumatic or explicit scenes. These doubles are so brilliantly and seamlessly edited in that it is hard to see when a replacement is being used. Reese Witherspoon as Dani in *The Man on the Moon* used a double for the naked diving scene. One of the camera team stood in for Brooke Shields in *The Blue Lagoon* for the intimate scenes and for some of the naked underwater shots.

Some directors choose to use a stunt double even when the element of risk is only slight. If an accident did occur, as well as being hurtful to the child it can also put back the filming sequence by days, even months, if for example, an accident results in a limb being put in plaster. Jodie Foster refers to this in the filming of *Nim's Island*. She could easily have pretended to fall off the jogging machine herself, but the director decided it was not worth risking an interruption to the shoot if a delaying accident had occurred to the lead lady. So, stunt doubles are not just used because something may be dangerous. They are used to avoid undesirable delays.

We mention in Volume 4 (*Childhood Friendships*) how we seldom see girls actually riding their ponies in movies, despite ponies being considered a young girl's best friend. No doubt, a child falling off would cause severe delays, let alone fractured limbs.

Were safety issues even considered for the film *Killer of Sheep*? Children play and scrap in the dirt, and throw real stones at each other. And it hurts. You can see the children wince painfully as stones hit their bodies, as they leap across rooftops, and as dust gets in their eyes from the dirt fight.

In *London to Brighton*, twelve-year-old Georgia Groome was allowed to smoke fags to make her part look authentic, but herbal cigarettes were substituted for tobacco.

Director Danny Boyle was aware of many potential dangers for his child actors in *Slumdog Millionaire*, yet went ahead with the action regardless, using the crossing-of-fingers and hoping-for-the-best technique, while his child stars race beside moving trains, clinging on for dear life, and hanging suspended upside-down on the side of a speeding locomotive. Though the children are suspended by wires, he still vocalises his worries, "What if the kid stumbles?" He realises it is very tough, but he felt he could take no further precautions. This is, however, a director who admirably considers the well being of his Indian cast. In a country that has few laws restricting child labour, Danny Boyle decided to film all the night scenes during daylight hours, and the children were put into schools where they could learn English.

Exploitation of the Child Actor

In his book *Erotic Innocence*, James Kincaid describes a conference he attended in California about the abuse of child actors. This was led by former child stars, now adults, reflecting on the abuse they suffered as children in the film industry. Quoting from a speech made by Barry Gordon (President of the Screen Actors Guild), "If your child is in show business and has been there since the age of three, get it out of your head that he is normal." Bobby Potter (a stunt double) states that kids are mistreated on sets, labour laws are twisted. What seems like a glamorous career "masks what sometimes edges towards drudgery, exploitation, or even child slavery."

1940s child actress Peggy Ann Garner agrees, "While adult performers could voluntarily place themselves on the movie capital's slave block, Hollywood's children were given no such option. Too young to vend the product which they soon discovered was themselves, they constituted a commodity in which only grown-ups dealt... Spoiled darlings in the eyes of an envious public, we were actually child labourers working to support our families... In the end it became clear, no matter how much we loved our parents or wanted to believe they loved us, our real value to them seemed measured only in terms of performance and earning power."[50]

These are American kids we are referring to, not some Third World street kid. Eddie Hodges tells how his acting childhood was a series of lessons in deceit, given a sense of being special and talented but dumped as his cute years passed him by. "We sacrifice our mental health for the Hollywood dream." Gene Reynolds further argues this slavery view. "The child actor is a slave surrounded by a confusing array of masters: parents, coaches, directors, agents, managers, all controlling the child as if the child is not there." To evade child labour laws some directors would cross the inter-state border to film, in a state where there were fewer restrictions on child acting.

This is partly our fault, as viewers, as voyeurs. As Kincaid argues, "Why do we yearn to see twelve-year-olds, and avert our eyes from kids of fifteen? We want cute, and adolescents are not cute. It's children we seem to long for, and we relentlessly throw them away when we're finished with them...It really is a swim and then sink reality, given that all but a tiny number of child performers are given the book once and for all at puberty."[51] Despite Kincaid's pessimistic opinion, several youths do buck the trend as Jamie Bell (*Billy Elliot*), Daniel Radcliffe (*Harry Potter*), George Sampson (*StreetDance*), Elijah Wood (*Paradise* (1991)), and Jared Rushton (*Honey, I Shrunk the Kids* and *Big* (1988)) all demonstrate.

Andrew Collins reaffirms this, writing in *Radio Times* about the successful British actor Freddie Highmore (star of *Spiderwick Chronicles*, *Golden Compass* and others). "What made him adorable and unique aged twelve might mature into something altogether less marketable."[52] Cary Guffey, four-year-old star of *Close Encounters* must have been aware of this when he retired from acting aged thirteen. "I don't want the greatest thing I do in life to be something I did when I was four."[53] Likewise, *Coronation Street* child star, Emma Woodward, quit acting aged eleven because her parents "wanted her to lead a normal life as she prepares to start secondary school."[54] The movie industry does recognise this state of affairs. This is the message behind *Life with Mikey*. Washed-up former child star Mikey (Michael J Fox) realises he is no longer cute and the public do not want him. So, he redirects his talents into running an agency, promoting the younger Christina Vidal, instead.

Daniel Radcliffe, interviewed by Emma Brockes, mentions this ambiguity. "I've been asked a thousand times if I'll end up like Macaulay Culkin, but I've never been asked if I'll end up like Jodie Foster or Tobey Maguire or Elijah Wood or Christian Bale," (all of whom have made it through the adolescent lottery of rejection). He quotes from William Goldman's memoir, *Adventures in the Screen Trade*, 'All stars are temporary, only actors last.'[55] The movie *Dickie Roberts, Former Child Star* bears this out. Dickie (David Spade), now an adult, harks back to his childhood days when he was popular TV entertainer. Now he is considered a has-been, and is longing for the comeback that never materialises. Even lodging with a family can't reawaken dormant youthfulness – customs and cultures move on, the children he lodges with treat him as an old fogey, and call him '*stranger danger*'.

Tony Dow purports a further psychological abuse of the child actor. "The child is made an object of voyeurism, a creature in this really strange fishbowl, where everybody is looking at you." Such children learn one thing only – how to be objects of attention and desire, adept at pleasing people and being cute. And staring into this fishbowl, we can observe their "changeless bodies and eternal cuteness…Children are being posed before us on movie and TV screen in answer to deep and terrible cultural needs that have everything to do with our desires and nothing to do with the welfare of the children."[56]

Marianne Sinclair suggests that actors enter this fishbowl voluntarily, expecting to be gawped at and revelling in it. "Isn't becoming a movie actress all about trying to 'sell' one's looks and sex-appeal on screen?" She further intimates that in the early days of cinema, young girls (those younger than the age of consent and even preteens) would try to use their premature Lolita-ish sex appeal as bribes to secure acting roles, and that famous names such as Charlie Chaplin, Roman Polanski, and Errol Flynn all succumbed to (or more probably took advantage of) this manipulation.[57]

In the case of Brooke Shields and Jodie Foster, the child Lolitas of the 1970s, their exploitation was that of sexploitation. A US judge deemed the nude photos taken of Brooke Shields at the age of ten were 'so lascivious' they would 'result in serious injury to Miss Shields.' The young Brooke was touted as the world's sexiest eleven-year-old. "I don't try to look sexy, really I don't," despairs the girl when she is twelve. The media, the glossy magazines, and we the viewers and readership have some questions to answer. Jodie Foster, placed in a role of child prostitute in *Taxi Driver* researched her character by actually visiting New York's red-light district. She was only twelve! Marianne Sinclair describes these two sexploitated children, Brooke Shields and Jodie Foster, as "two pretty babies lost in an ugly world of big money and porn-hungry audiences, always on the look-out for new, even sicker kicks."[58]

These are the experiences of American actors, from the 'land of the free'. As director of *Little Secrets*, Blair Treu says, "In Hollywood, kids are forced to grow up fast." I cannot think how other nationalities treat their child actors. I did, however, watch a TV documentary on the Chinese State Circus in which children appeared to be abused liked chunks of meat. Preteen gymnasts had their limbs forcibly and cruelly doubled back behind them in an attempt to extend their flexibility. Several of the children ran away from the cruel regime only to be tearfully brought back, forced to apologise and be grateful for their chance in life. This was all too degrading. Alas, what was so pitiful, was a friend of mine said how she went to watch a performance of the Chinese State Circus describing how fantastically talented and agile these youngsters were, but quite unaware of the deep distress and exploitation caused to reach that level of skill.

On a more trivial level, yet showing how children are not consulted and are not in charge of their own bodies, just being there to do what they are told, twelve-year-old Jodie Foster complained of having her hair bleached against her wishes and her eyebrows plucked in *Bugsy Malone* and Scott Baio was not happy about having his hair cut short.[59]

Australian child actress, Everlyn Sampi, actually ran away during the filming of *Rabbit Proof Fence*. This girl had aborigine blood and was playing the part of an aboriginal girl, Molly. It was part of her nature not to be tied down. 'Everlyn did not adapt readily to the demands of film making, trying to run away and driving Noyce (the director) to despair. "We tried desperately to recast," he says, "but we just could not find anyone who was nearly as charismatic and talented as her... The more she rejected us the more convinced I was that she was another version of the real Molly, her disdain for authority, her scepticism that she had to do what the white man had told her because it was good for her... She *is* Molly."'[60]

Marie Antoinette's oft quoted 'Let them eat cake' could be an apt maxim to use for child actors. I certainly don't decry Rebecca Flint earning £50,000 from her internet Japanese django routine,[61] as long as she is not exploited and the kitty goes into *her* trust fund.

James Kincaid, writing in *Erotic Innocence*, makes mention of the monetary exploitation of child actors by their parents. You would expect child stars like Shirley Temple or Macaulay Culkin to have "piled up big bucks to provide themselves with a future", but like most child actors on reaching maturity they discover their financial pot has already been spent by greedy parents. This is partly because American law granted to the parent "the custody, services and earnings of the unmarried minor and partly because kids are easy to blackmail."

In particular, Kincaid mentions Lauren Chapin, a child star famous for her role in *Father knows Best*. Parents are automatically entitled to 75% of a child's earnings. But when she reached sixteen and wanted her 25% she had to resort to the courts, who decreed the parents should hand over 10% of that figure. In other words, the courts granted her just 2½ per cent of her earnings!

Sybil Jason found her earnings had been siphoned off by an uncle, mirroring the experience of other child stars when they reach twenty-one: they find the cupboard bare.[62] Aged just fourteen when Jena Malone discovered her mother was going on a spending spree using the child's earnings, she sued her mother (and won) "for emancipation under California's *Jackie Coogan Law*, charging that her mother had mismanaged her earnings, drained her college savings, and failed to pay taxes."[63]

The *Jackie Coogan Law* was set up in the year 2000 to ensure all the earnings of minors are deposited in trust funds. Any withdrawal by parents is now deemed to be theft under US Law. The law was named after the boy who assisted Charlie Chaplin, yet who discovered when he came of age that the earnings from his hard earned labour had already been spent by his parents.[64]

The adult Natalie Wood, perversely exploited as a child by her over-ambitious mother, once she became a mother herself declared that no child of hers would be thrust into the movie business. She planned to give her children the childhood she was denied as a childstar. "My baby's going to have a childhood," she announces in *The Mystery of Natalie Wood*. "My children are going to have normal lives."

Age appropriate roles

"Don't they grow up fast!" We come across the phrase referring to Anna Paquin in *Fly Away Home*, and to Hayley Mills in *In Search of the Castaways*. Even Madeleine (Allison Forster) in *Gregory's Girl* catches the eye of Gregory's window-cleaning friend: "They grow up fast don't they. Ten years old and the body of a woman."

Some 'child' actors are obviously in their twenties. The challenge for the director is to find older actors who can pass for a younger age. Obvious examples of this are Jenny Agutter and Sally Thomsett who played the girls in *The Railway Children* but were more than five years older than their character. In particular, Sally Thomsett, aged twenty at the time but playing a ten-year-old girl, was told to carefully keep her true age a secret so as not to deprive the film of its magic for the younger age group. In between takes, Sally Thomsett had to be discreet about having a sneaky fag lest the press be hovering, and this adult (masquerading as a child) was certainly banned from visiting the pub, lest the 1970s equivalent of the paparazzi became aware. Hayley Mills complained of similar restrictions. She had a reputation as a sweet innocent wholesome Disney girl, so woe betide if she dared be seen having a fag or a drink, even as a young adult.[65]

This age differential was also true for Judy Garland in *The Wizard of Oz*, the use of ponytails and loose clinging garments giving a more childlike look. Julie Harris was twenty-five when she played twelve-year-old Frankie in *The Member of the Wedding*! Surely, this extreme of age differential is an insult to the acting ability of our children. Were there really no talented young girls in the early 1950s when this film was made who could have filled this role? Or was the director frightened, as the saying goes, of working with animals and children? Perhaps Noel Coward's proverbial Mrs Worthington would not permit her daughter to take the stage. Maybe I could understand this casting if controversial themes were being depicted but this was not the case in any of the afore-mentioned films.

Such an age-differential may be justified in the 1919 film *Broken Blossoms* in which a twenty-six-year-old Lilian Gish was playing her fifteen-year-old character (aged twelve in the book by Thomas Burke) – a brutalised waif befriended by an older Chinese man in seedy London. Scott Jacoby was twenty when he played the schoolboy magician alongside Jodie Foster in *The Little Girl who lives down the Lane*. This is a lad who had to sit in the bath to have his back scrubbed by thirteen-year-old Jodie Foster and then jump naked into bed with her. Perhaps, in this instance, the young girl was inappropriately cast. Mark Webber was also twenty when acting as a fifteen-year-old schoolboy in *Snow Day*, but since he was required for a kissing scene, maybe the older age was more appropriate. The same can be said for the gangly eighteen-year-old, Gordon John Sinclair, in *Gregory's Girl*, pretending to be in class 4D. But Mary Pickford was thirty-two as she played the twelve-year-old imp in the 1925 silent movie *Little Annie Roonie*! Ginger Rogers was also thirty-one as she masqueraded as a twelve-year-old in *The Major and the Minor*, awakening sexual passions at a military camp, though in this case, her ruse was used to avoid paying full fare on public transport, rather than hood-winking the audience.

Dana Hill was seventeen when she played the groomed preteen Jennifer Philips in *Fallen Angel*. Actor Richard Masur had coaxed her into joining his paedophile ring, so I guess an older actress was more appropriate for this role. Dana Hill had looked particularly young for her age. At the age of ten she had been one of America's leading child athletes, ranked third nationwide for the half mile race. Yet she contracted diabetes that stunted her growth making her aptly suited for child-like characters but which also led to her premature death in her early twenties.

To cast a seven-year-old in the role of Helen Keller would not have achieved the phenomenal impact made by sixteen-year-old Patty Duke in her astonishing performance as the deaf and dumb mute in *The Miracle Worker*. It would have been inappropriate to cast an actual fourteen-year-old in *Benny's Video*, a boy fascinated by the electrocution of a pig using a stun gun – the boy replaying the sequence on his video over and over again to satisfy his fatalistic curiosity. (Seventeen-year-old Arno Frisch plays the part of the fourteen-year-old.)

In the case of boys, it is not so easy to substitute a husky-voiced, stubble-chinned youth as a preteen. This must be a casting nightmare: having to perform a re-take with a post-pubescent youth who was an angelic lad when filming began a few months back. Julie Walters tells of such an outcome during the filming of a *Harry Potter* movie. Rupert Grint's voice broke during filming the invisibility cloak scenes over the period of a few months, creating a continuity problem,[66] as did Scot Baio's in *Bugsy Malone*.[67]

Likewise, it must be difficult casting infants when they grow so quickly during the course of a year, and the ten-year-old lass who achieves a growth spurt in both dimensions. Some girls who may be pre-pubescent at the start of filming have to tape and hide their newly budding breasts if the filming doesn't stick to deadlines. Patty McCormack reminiscing about her role in *The Bad Seed* mentions having to be 'strapped up' for subsequent roles when she was twelve. Ang Lee, director of *Sense and Sensibility* referring to Emilie François playing eleven-year-old Margaret Dashwood, states, "She grew like bamboo shoots" during the course of the production.

Probably an adult may feel proud to be able to pass as a child. But it must be more disconcerting for small (in stature) children to have to play the part of infants. Most five- or six-year-old infants are actually played by nine- or ten-year-olds, such as Mara Wilson in *Matilda* and Susan Gordon in *The Five Pennies*. However, this age differential would not have been disconcerting for ten-year-old Mary Badham playing the part of six-year-old Scout in *To Kill a Mockingbird*, for her performance led to a credited Oscar nomination (beaten only by another child actor, Patty Duke). With all these parts, I assume the director preferred the confidence of the older girl, to the indiscipline and inexperience of an infant. An infant may be a scene-stealer, but can also be a scene-destroyer.

Some producers actually earmark child actors in their early childhood and are willing to wait a few years for them to reach the necessary maturity for the part, as with Dakota Fanning in *The Secret Life of Bees*. This surely is a risky business if the children don't mature in the expected way, or their attitude changes, or that fleeting flirtation with a drama club does not mature into dramatic ambition, and school exams or the new boyfriend takes precedence over rehearsal and filming.

My deciding to restrict this series to actors aged between ages eight and fourteen is only a loose guideline, and anyway, the age of the actor often has to be deduced from when the film is released rather than the age the child performed the part – this could be a difference of at least one year and maybe two. In other words, a child who was thirteen when the film was released might only have been eleven when the filming took place, or when he/she was shown the script. Consider this a dilemma for a child asked to play with dolls as Lindsey Lohan in *Life-Size*, while a child at the same age might be asked to play a child prostitute, as did Georgia Groome in *London to Brighton*.

That actors of such contrasting age differences are procured for the roles of children, particularly of girls, is explained by Marianne Sinclair who considers the whole history of the movie business as a way of subtly projecting the image of a seductive Lolita. The Lolita of the cinema takes on two distinct guises: "the girl-child pretending to be a vamp through grown-up attitudes and reactions" or "the young woman turning herself back into the little girl through childish clothing and posturing."[68] For examples of the first category, Humbert is swiftly pencilling into his poem of newcomers to the class register names such as Brooke Shields, Pamlyn Ferdin, Patricia Gozzi, Dominique Swaine. For the second category scribble into Humbert's secret diary Lilian and Dorothy Gish, Leslie Caron, Mary Pickford, and Colleen Moore, and lock it securely from the gaze of 'that Hayes woman'.

TALENTS

Natural Talent

In the majority of cases, the young actors parading for our pleasure seem quite natural and accomplished in their performances. You only need to watch a school play to see the difference. Where children have had just half a dozen rehearsals getting them ready while mucking about with their mates to act in front of their parents, teachers and peers – for one night only – it is only fair to expect wooden, droll and garbled performances on the school stage or in the village hall. But for professionally made films where the children have been coached by the finest tutors and have been on set or on location for weeks and months, and maybe have spent time in drama school before that, then more polished performances are expected. The film *Nativity!* amusingly bears this out as a class of untalented reluctants are coaxed into a glittering successful troop.

In the main, the child is only as good as the director allows him/her to be, and a sequence of takes can iron out weaknesses, as can the editor's cuts. In fact, if the child appears to be natural without any exceptional outbursts or overacting, and if the speech is audible then the director has done his/her job. It is only when you see a weak performance – and these are few and far between – that you realise how effective the vast majority of films are, and just how naturally talented are the children that perform in them. Daniel Radcliffe (of *Harry Potter* fame) quotes his dad: "If you can do the thing that people don't expect you to do, and do it better than they expect you to do it, you'll have a career!" [69]

Karen Lury, in her book *The Child in Film* reiterates how children are successful when they are natural and have not been stage trained. As well as the over-coaching of Margaret O'Brien that we refer to shortly, she considers the example of Anna Paquin who received criticism from Jeremy Irons following her Oscar award as best supporting actress at the age of eleven in *The Piano*. 'She didn't have to act, she just had to be natural,' complains Irons, as accomplished adult actresses such as Emma Thompson and Holly Hunter were passed over for a juvenile upstart. It is because children are childlike that they attain instant success and appeal. It is their "littleness, cuteness, prettiness, and precocity. When the child actor ages, the apparent inherent qualities which made them a star will no longer be manifest." Further, Ms Lury contends that the performance, the tears on cue, just happens, and the most effective performances can be captured from child actors who are akin to puppets who do as they are told without individual guile, intention or agency. [70]

According to Jeremy Irons, Anna Paquin symbolizes a misunderstanding on the part of audiences and critics alike: her naturalness being misinterpreted as Oscar-winning brilliance. In the same vein, Ana Torrent (*Spirit of the Beehive*, *Cría Cuervos*) receives similar plaudits for her natural ability to convey bewildered lost innocence, seldom seen in one so young. In fact, critics rave at this remarkable attribute in this little girl. And yet, will there be a Spanish insurrection if I toss into the bullring that maybe, just maybe, Ana herself was simply a sad bewildered lost juvenile, whose emotions had been drained from her; a fearful sprite that I and a multitude of sympathisers would wish to cradle from the evils that haunt her? Karen Lury remarks on this girl, too, by quoting Marsha Kinder: "Ana Torrent, the child actress… with a brooding sensitivity that captures every nuance of emotion… her luminous dark eyes confront us with a bold knowing gaze, conveying a precocious intelligence, passion and intensity… Yet her pale oval face and slender birdlike frame create a fragility that also marks her as a victim – a delicate instrument for the registering of pain."[71]

Currently, the buzz name among child actors is nine-year-old Quvenzhané Wallis being touted for an Oscar nomination for her phenomenal characterisation of Hushpuppy in *Beasts of the Southern Wild*, and admired by American film critic Roger Ebert as a "force of nature, uniquely and particularly herself."[71a]

It is rare that acting is poor. The most notable exception in my opinion was *Lost in New York* in which two little girls had to talk together in a graveyard, sit reading a book, and climb up some rocks to enter a cave. But whenever the cameraman focused on them, smirks appeared on their faces as they tried to stifle their giggles, but the editor made no attempt to cut these frames, considering his production to be an 'Art' film. However, the adults seemed even weaker in their performances in this film. Similarly, in the well-lauded Japanese production of *Nobody Knows*, the eldest girl actor Suki, played by Hanae Kan, tries desperately to hold back a grin as the camera focuses on her face for the first few occasions, leaving me to ponder whether all directors actually rehearse with the child in front of the camera. Hushpuppy (Quvenzhané Wallis) however could have the camera focused between her eyeballs and still the little girl could outstare and outfrown even the best of cameramen.

At least we knew what the children were saying in *Lost in New York* and *Nobody Knows*, for these were French and Japanese films respectively and the words were subtitled. Unfortunately, where a child has a regional accent, whether this be Glaswegian as in *The Ratcatcher*, Liverpudlian Scouse in *Under the Mud*, Texan or Gulf American as in *The Reaping*, Irish (*The Magdalene Sisters*), broad Yorkshire (*Lassie* (2005) and *Kes* (1969)) or urban street talk (*Knights of the South Bronx*), understanding some of the dialogue can be tough-going especially where the child is required to walk and talk simultaneously. Abigail Breslin's directors (Mark Levin & Jennifer Flackett) were guilty of allowing this in *Nim's Island*. Nim's speech was garbled, and words incoherent as she tried to smile, walk and talk. So is the highly praised Dakota Fanning whose casualness and nasal tones often result in words being muffled, especially as she plays Cassie in *Push*. Dakota has arguably been the best child actress of recent years, but her producers needed to work on her diction. Maybe it is sound recordists who are to blame, for the clarity of her enunciation in the animated *Coraline* is crystaline clear.

Eleven-year-old Keisha Castle-Hughes deservedly won an Oscar for her role as a Maori girl in *Whale Rider* but you have to strain your ears to catch her words as she narrates the introduction and postscript to the film. We miss the key points to the story line as her nasal New Zealand accent is muffled, something that could easily have been rectified by a re-take. Maybe Niki Caro, the director, didn't predict her film would be such a phenomenal success. For the course of the rest of the film, the young girl's diction is perfect and her performance superb. It is not only children who can be inaudible. Armin Mueller-Stahl, the adult actor in *The Dust Factory* speaks with a quiet European accent; much of it is inaudible, strange considering he was such an experienced adult actor, and whose accent is comprehendable in *Jakob the Liar*. Likewise, the whispering of adult Zelda Rubinstein playing Tangina is equally incoherent in *Poltergeist* (1982). Contrast this with Patty McCormack who, having had elocution coaching as a child, is crystal clear in her *Bad Seed* performance as Rhoda, as is Georgia Groome in *Angus, Thongs and Perfect Snogging*. Sometimes, you see, success can be achieved with a little effort.

In *Death Defying Acts*, although Saoirse Ronan's performance as Benji was fine on the whole and usually her diction of a Scottish accent was clear, we are left wondering at the critical time what the actual important words were. This is like someone telling a joke in a pub. You listen to the clear dramatic telling of the story. But the joker guffaws at his own joke just as he tells the punchline, which comes out garbled, and so the listener has no idea what the actual joke was. I am afraid the same could be said of *Death Defying Acts*. At least in *The Brady Bunch Movie*, Olivia Hack's lisp was effectively exploited to humorous effect. The obnoxious next-door neighbour could never decipher what the twelve-year-old was saying. After listening to an incoherent sentence for the third time, the riled man could only surrender in ignorant assent to what she was asking.

A film I found particularly baffling was *The Annunciation*, which could fit into the 'so bad it was brilliant' category. The words were not a problem, for they were subtitled from Hungarian, though the language was poetically archaic and surely beyond the comprehension of the cast of child actors. The whole film seemed to be a day's outing to the countryside for a drama group of preteen children, and the youngsters expected to perform strange allegorical drama sequences and mimes while keeping a straight face. And yet it was fascinating and mesmerising.

Occasionally child actors may be required to burst into tears and this can seem false. But hey, how do you get them to cry believable tears without saying 'imagine your dog has just died, or your mum is in hospital with an incurable disease?' These are actual cruel methods used by some parents to induce a winning performance from their child. Judy Garland was threatened with abandonment to coax startling performances from her. The mother of Natalie Wood shredded a live butterfly before the infant's eyes to ensure she screamed on cue.

Earlier, we mentioned how tearfulness is a quality one associates with vulnerable little girls. The lost waif who resorts to tears to engender pity is endearing. We have just mentioned Keisha Castle-Hughes performance in *Whale Rider*. Her tearful singing of a Maori speech is incredible. Her character, Pai, had written a prize-winning speech that she is to recite at a school concert, and she has to do so in front of her grandfather – her honoured guest. But because of a tiff, her grandfather does not show up. There is just an empty seat in the front row of the assembly hall as Keisha tearfully begins her speech and song. The tears well in her eyes, floods begin, and she brilliantly blubbers her way through the song. As the director comments, "Keisha singing her speech, literally breaks your heart." As a girl, "she's so little, and totally inexperienced, and yet she's absolutely a match for any of the adult actors."

Likewise, Perla Haley-Jardine's traumatic howling for her mother in *Genova* is deeply moving. She is inconsolable as Colin Firth desperately tries to comfort her, stricken as she is with guilt for causing the death of her own mother. Another effective outpouring of grief is matched by ten-year-old Mae Whitman who explodes into tearful desperation in *Hope Floats* as her father finally announces to the wife he is separated from, "I want a divorce." The girl hurriedly packs her bags and races after her father as he drives away, hoping he will take her with him. Danuel Pipoly, playing Piggy in *Lord of the Flies* (1990), grates the deepest reaches of your soul as he despairs at the helplessness of his predicament. As Dominique Swaine had an attention-grabbing argument with the predatory Humbert Humbert in *Lolita*, so too in *Beaches* (1988), Mayim Bialik's tantrum after her song-and-dance audition was brilliant, and Evan Rachel Wood's screaming panic was bloodcurdling in *Down will come Baby* as her friend drowns in the lake. You can feel your whole body being pricked as the same actress launches into a defiant tirade against her mum in *Thirteen* (2003).

As if to confirm how naturally the young girl can slot into her role, Terry Gilliam tells of ten-year-old Jodelle Ferland playing Jeliza Rose in *Tideland*, "I didn't direct Jodelle. I watched with amazement. She would choose to do things, which surprised me. She plays a little girl *like* a little girl, and not how a sixty-four-year-old director thinks a little girl should be." Jodelle immerses herself into her role-play of childish make-believe almost like a person with a split personality.

Charles Laughton described Billy Chapin, his lead boy in *The Night of the Hunter*, as an 'acting technician' for his "innate ability to understand the construction of a scene, its impact and its performance," while Bobby Driscoll was described by director Lloyd Bacon as "The greatest child find since Jackie Cooper played *Skippy*."[72] Dakota Fanning attracted similar plaudits from many of the superstars she acted beside (see *Astonishing Performances*).

Casting – lucky breaks and who you know

In the French movie *Innocence* (2004), no girls with acting experience were cast because the director, Lucile Hadzihalilovic, thought they might not be natural enough for she wanted to depict the innocent naivety of pre-adolescent girls. A similar stance was taken by her fellow compatriot, the French director Mia Hansen-Løve, in *Father of My Children*. She on purpose chose children with no acting experience so they would be entirely natural. In fact, when the parents of one of the girls practised a scene at home with their daughter, the director had to undo the efforts of the parents in order to recover the natural spontaneity of the child – "to get back the freedom she had lost." Likewise, Vincente Minnelli tells of how he had to 'un-train' Margaret O'Brien to regain the naturalness she had shown in *A Journey for Margaret* for his production of *Meet me in St Louis*. After the success of her first film, the little girl had been coached in Shakespearean methodology, which Minnelli had to undo to reawaken her natural talent. This we see at her sparkling best in *The Secret Garden* (1949). Emma Thompson, the award-winning scriptwriter for *Sense and Sensibility*, tells how they rejected their favoured candidate for the part of eleven-year-old Margaret Dashwood at the auditions because they overheard the parents trying to coach the child resulting in a loss of spontaneity. The aspirant candidate was evidently passed over, replaced by acting novice Emilie François, a delightful find who lit each scene with her vivacity.

For the uncomfortable to watch New York-based movie, *kids* (1995), director Larry Clarke chose streetwise kids who were familiar with ghetto-style culture of dope, drink, and brawls to produce a hard-thumping tale of immorality and the dangers of unprotected sex. In this case, however, his cast were youths, Leo Fitzpatrick, Chloé Sevigny, and Justin Pierce (who committed suicide just a few years later), though there is some ambiguity concerning the ages of the two girl victims, Sarah Henderson and Yakira Peguero, who were supposedly thirteen years of age and who had to endure prolonged intercourse scenes.

This idea of casting children with no acting experience, bringing them straight off the street, seems to be a common occurrence. We found it with *Innocence* (2004), *Father of My Children*, and in *Whale Rider*, and Danny Boyle used kids straight from the Mumbai slums for *Slumdog Millionaire*. It even occurred in the mid-twentieth century despite the competition from pushy parents who coached their infant child from an early age. The parents of Gigi Perreau (*Has anyone seen my Gal*) took her along "for the ride" to the MGM studios in Hollywood where their son was being auditioned for a film role. Gigi herself was too young to express an acting ambition. But director Mervyn LeRoy spotted the two-year-old and offered her the part in *Madame Curie*. The same good fortune befell Heather O'Rourke who, as a five-year-old, was spotted by Steven Spielberg having a meal with her mother while awaiting her older sister perform in *Pennies from Heaven*.[73]

Similarly finding herself in the right place at the right time was Jodie Foster accompanying her older brother, Buddy, for a *Coppertone Suncream* commercial. "I could not leave her in the car, so she had to come with us," says her mother, Brandy Foster.[74] Her subsequent history is… well, history. After a career as a successful child actor, Jodie is now a leading adult star and film director.

Another accidental casting was seven-year-old Donna Corcoran (*Million Dollar Mermaid*). Clarence Brown had already auditioned over six hundred young girls for his film *Angels in the Outfield*. He was desperate. He noticed Donna, the daughter of one of the maintenance men, wandering aimlessly around the courtyard and was immediately impressed, signing her up for the part, with father's permission of course. "I've never seen a beginning juvenile with more promise," said Clarence Brown. A similar accidental meeting occurred as the legendary Al Johnson found young Davey Lee wandering aimlessly.[75]

Other actors have struck it lucky by chance meetings with influential people in the movie world. David Holt (*Beau Geste* and *Tom Sawyer*) had the good fortune to move next door to actor Charles Hickman, while Dickie Moore lived next door to film producer Joseph Schenck. Ann Carter's (*Curse of the Cat People*) Anglo-Irish parents moved from New York to California to find they were living next door to an employee of the film studios. Consequently as a five-year-old, Ann was introduced to the film director, Herbert Brennon, who personally coached her in acting techniques. According to Marc Best (*Those Endearing Young Charms*), she met with success because she resembled one of the leading actresses of the 1930s/40s, Veronica Lake.

As a four-year-old living in Santa Rosa in California, Natalie Wood (*Driftwood, Miracle on 34th Street*) and the other villagers appeared as extras in *Happy Land*. Natalie made such an impression on the director he sent for her for his next movie *Tomorrow is Forever* – her bilingual skills, Russian and German, being effectively utilised. In the biographical movie, *The Mystery of Natalie Wood*, we witness the infant Natalie (real name, Natassia Gurdin and played brilliantly by Grace Fulton) being sent by her overly pushy mother to sit on the director's lap to be sure she gets noticed!

Cora Sue Collins was rushed to an audition by her parents who had only heard at the last moment of an acting opportunity for their daughter. But in their haste they hadn't noticed how dirty her face and hands were. While they were scolding their child for being so dirty the casting director was attracted to the moppet for being far more in character than the other perfect immaculate brats who had turned up for a role in *They just had to get Married*.

For others, however, finding their dream role is a round of dispiriting auditions, in competition with hundreds of other hopefuls, and in the case of the *Harry Potter* cast, against thousands of others queuing optimistically around the block outside London theatres. Nina Kervel was one of four hundred girls auditioned for the part in the French movie *Blame it on Fidel*. The director, Julie Gavras, wanted to make a rational, considered choice and took six months to do so. Even so, she had a stand-in available – just to keep Nina on her toes. Jay Russell considered over a thousand boys until he found his lead for *My Dog Skip*, and Hailee Steinfeld was one of fifteen thousand girls who applied for the part of Mattie in *True Grit* (2010). According to Alan Parker, it took a year to find and audition the young cast for *Bugsy Malone*, and the director had to see ten thousand kids.[76] Mara Wilson (child actress with roles in *Mrs Doubtfire*, *Matilda* and

Miracle on 34th Street) describes this tedious round of auditions as 'brutal and dehumanising'.[76a] As an adult, she withdrew from acting, turning her attention instead to playwriting.

British TV channel, *More 4*, broadcast a TV documentary, *Babes in Hollywood*, about the pilot season tutoring courses in California, where hundreds of aspiring young actors and actresses pay thousands of dollars in their quest for stardom. Establishing themselves with agents and photographic portfolios, they may spend $5000 per month for several months trying to arrange that evasive lucky break. But the kids (and their parents) are being exploited, like cattle in a market, being sold false leads and taken to dispiriting auditions. "When you have money, all the termites come along and start eating it up," explains one commentator. The odds on any child actually becoming a movie star are no better than winning the lottery, and most of the children just have to pack their bags and head for home at the end of the season. Contrast this with Katie Jarvis, with no acting aspirations, plucked from the streets of London by director Andrea Arnold, who was witnessing the girl arguing with her boyfriend at a railway station, and chose her as the lead in *Fish Tank*.

Others, according to Joan Collins[77], gain their first steps to stardom via what she calls 'the casting couch'. She, as a vulnerable teenager in the early 1950s, was enrolled by this method. Some claim that DW Griffiths, Charlie Chaplin, and Roman Polanski all secured their aspirant under-aged nymphets by this means: the Gish sisters, Lilita McMurray, and Nastassia Kinski; and that, yes, it still goes on today, suggests Ms Collins. The price of fame *can* be bought, but not for cash!

Yet, some studios inadvertently let potential stars slip through their grasp, for instance, ten-year-old Elizabeth Taylor, making her debut screen performance in *There's One Born Every Minute*. "The kid has nothing," declared the casting director as the future megastar was released from contract – an action he spent a lifetime regretting.[78]

Stage School Training / Pushy Parents

In the early to mid twentieth century, many desperate parents pushed their child to a professional career from an early age. Perhaps the parents were themselves on stage; others wanted to pursue the ambition by living out their dream through their child. Virginia Weidler was the daughter of an opera star, which helped her be selected as a five-year-old for a role in *Autumn Crocus*. Like Natalie Wood, she too was multilingual: in English, German and French.[79] According to Marianne Sinclair, most parents pushing their infant children into the movies "showed no mercy. They took little creatures scarcely old enough to stand or speak, and like buck sergeants, drilled them to shuffle through a dance step or mumble a song. They robbed them of every phase of childhood to keep the waves in the hair, the pleats in the dress, the pink polish on the nails."[80]

The Mystery of Natalie Wood convincingly shows the traumatic childhood endured by the young Natasha Gurdin whose mother ruthlessly catapulted her into an acting career. Mother's methods were certainly effective, for Natasha (renamed Natalie Wood) became one of the most successful actresses of the 1960s, until her early demise in that mysterious drowning at the age of forty-three. But we see a girl devoid of her childhood, not allowed to mix with other children, compelled into genuine emotional acting by the cruel words of her unsympathetic mother – a mother who wouldn't even allow her daughter to see a doctor after her wrist broke. Natalie lived with the deformity for the rest of her life, hiding it behind a bracelet. And boyfriends were certainly taboo. As she becomes a rational yet repressed teenager she yells at her mother, "My children are going to have normal lives."

In early twentieth century America, a popular form of entertainment were the vaudeville acts: bands of itinerant actors and actresses travelling the country, often with musical and dancing talents, who would tread the circuits looking for acting work. Husband and wives would travel as teams, and it was productive to utilise their progeny to act alongside them in the pantomime-style shows.

Edith Fellows was born into such a family of entertainers; her parents were stage performers, her grandmother a popular singer. So Edith was performing as soon as she could walk, travelling with her parents' theatre group, getting opportunity to dance, play several musical instruments and sing on the radio from an early age. It was only natural she would sidle into acting from the age of eight with a little help from her well-connected grandmother. Other infant stars – Mickey Rooney, Mitzi Green, Sybil Jason, Sharyn Moffett, Sherry Jackson – followed their parents onto the stage, sometimes working alongside them. Like Edith Fellows many of these infant stars will have missed much of their childhood by being part of an itinerant stage troop in which the child is expected to work by acting, dancing or singing.

Many of the cutest young girls were enticed into acting following a modelling career. To some it may seem perverted seeing parents push their children in front of a photographer to become a child model at the infant age of three, four or five. This became the springboard for their acting careers. Margaret O'Brien (*Meet me in St Louis*, *Jane Eyre*), whose mother herself was formerly a stage dancer, got her first film role (*A Journey for Margaret*) because the director had seen her cute modelling photo in a magazine. Ironically, Margaret (whose real name was Gladys) had no singing or dancing experience, yet she achieved fame for her brilliant song-and-dance routine in *Meet me in St Louis*.[81]

Peggy Ann Garner also entered the world of acting via a modelling career – as an infant! So, she was used to bright lights and cameras from an early age. She also had dance lessons and her tutor recommended her for stage school, which resulted in a theatre role. Her parents, so in awed of her success, took the gamble of moving to Hollywood where she obtained several minor roles, but it wasn't until she was ten that Peggy Ann received star roles in *Pied Piper* and *Jane Eyre*.

Patty McCormack was also modelling at the age of four. But aged seven she had a TV role, which led to acting on Broadway before her incredible success with *The Bad Seed*. At least, none of them had Brooke Shield's overly pushy mother who at the age of just ten had her posing naked in a modelling studio, which directed her subsequent path of controversial nude roles in *Pretty Baby*, *The Blue Lagoon*, *Just You and Me Kid*, and *Endless Love*, all while she was a juvenile.

Young girls don't volunteer for these roles, they are gently coaxed into them by mothers with an unconventional sense of morality. Jodie Foster, aged twelve, offered the part of a hooker in *Taxi Driver* initially dismissed the role as something more suitable for a twenty-one-year-old. "At first I didn't want to do it," she said, her older brother advised against it, and the California welfare authorities insisted she cooperate with a child psychologist; but pushy mother ensured her little girl took the role: "You can't miss the opportunity of acting alongside Robert de Niro," said her mother.[82]

Brooke Shields' on-camera activity pales into insignificance alongside that of Eva Ionesco who, at the age of twelve indulged in naked simulated sex in the banned film *Adolescent Malice*.

She, and her co-star Lara Wendel, remained naked for much of the screening and their 'willingness' to perform in sex scenes caused national controversy in Italy, Germany, and the Netherlands. That these children were targeted as performers relates to how their parents projected them as promiscuous and vulnerable to manipulation. Ms Sinclair suggests that behind every Lolita is a pushy mother, a B-rate actress who never made it in show business and wants to "claw her way to the top" through her daughter.[83] That Eva Ionesco sued her mother while still a teenager reveals how she was coerced into sexual roles as a child. Not only were the children in *Adolescent Malice* misled by their parents, the producers of this film, in attempting to highlight the sexual proclivity of our pubescent youth, actually re-created and perpetuated the abuse by doing so.

Other parents already working in the movie business themselves or in film production naturally steer their children towards acting roles, for to follow in father's footsteps is often the goal of many children, particularly if their parents are successful and renowned. Lisa Minnelli must surely be the most celebrated, the daughter of Judy Garland and director Vincente Minnelli. Hayley Mills had parts playing alongside her famous father John Mills and mother Mary Bell. Both Dakota Fanning and younger sister Elle have followed in their father's footsteps, as also did Tatum O'Neal who at first starred alongside Ryan O'Neal before stealing the plaudits from him. Even director François Truffaut, needing a preteen for a kissing scene in his film, *Pocket Money*, called upon his daughter, Eva Truffaut, for this role. Director Charles Bennett used his six-year-old daughter, Angela, in his arthouse film about a black ghetto, *Killer of Sheep*. Among the boys who follow their parents' path into the movie business we find Brandon de Wilde (*Shane*), Jackie Jenkins (*National Velvet*), Dean Stockwell (*Kim*); and who did director Andrew Birkin find to play a young lad who dresses in girl's clothing? His own son, Ned Birkin, had to be coaxed into the role.

Drama is high on the curriculum in modern day schools. Many of our young actors have been attracted into theatre groups as a result of dedicated teachers. Yorkshire actress, Georgie Henley, was tempted into the Ilkley Upstagers Theatre Group, and this led to a sequence of parts as Lucy in the *Chronicles of Narnia*. Georgia Groome's participation in a TV workshop in Nottingham led to her role in *London to Brighton* (a part her mother disapproved of, showing that not all parents are pushy). Yet, as we saw with *Innocence* (2004) and *Father of My Children*, currently there is a trend among directors to reject the drama school student who may have had natural childlike reactions trained out of them.

This may not be such an alarming concept when considering the rights of the child. Myriads of irate parents would be opposed to this, especially those who have skimped by sacrificing their earnings to pay thousands of pounds to have their aspiring child coached and tutored in top schools, e.g. London's *Italia Conti Academy*. Some children have been channelled into these ambitions since the age of seven or eight, and have spent their entire school life following the hope of a dream. But these are the naïve dreams of glamour-craving parents and glitter-loving kids. How can career choices be made by a child so young? By all means, coach and nurture the child, but if by the age of fifteen the child discovers life has other things to offer, then he/she should be permitted to steer a new course without any feelings of regret or betrayal, and irrespective of any loss of financial investment made. Any other reaction is nothing less than child abuse inflicted by blinkered self-promoting parents, pretending it is for their child that they have made these sacrifices. My pontificating is also applicable to aspirant sports enthusiasts and musicians who don't reach the grade of parental expectations.

Astonishing performances and Oscar nominees

Once in a while you witness a piece of astonishing acting that makes you sit up with a start. Among the girls: Linda Blair as the possessed Regan in *The Exorcist*, Ellen Page with her hard punching dialogue in *Hard Candy*, the sultry obnoxiousness of Charlotte Gainsbourg in *An Impudent Girl*, the tomboyish playfulness of Mary Badham in *To Kill a Mockingbird*, Margaret O'Brien's rants at bedridden Colin in *The Secret Garden* (1949), and Dominique Swaine's fit of temper as she argues with Humbert in their squalid tenement in *Lolita*. Who can remain dry-eyed after Jenny Agutter's joyful race into her father's arms in *The Railway Children*, "Daddy, my daddy!"

From among the boys, step forward Haley Joel Osment (*The Sixth Sense*), Jamie Bell (*Billy Elliot*), Freddie Highmore (as Charlie Bucket, and in *The Spiderwick Chronicles*), the playful exuberance of Christian Bale in *Empire of the Sun*, and Brandon de Wilde nominated for an Oscar in 1953 as best supporting actor in *Shane*.

An example of a child being entirely natural can be found in *Alice in the Cities* in which eight-year-old Yella Rottländer, who had been searching Wuppertal for her granny's house, sits silently in a café in Germany pawing at her ice cream, to the background strains of the jukebox playing 'On the Road Again'. Intermittently and with perfect natural timing she breaks the lull in the conversation, ultimately dropping the bombshell of a comment to see how her escort reacts, "My Gran doesn't really live in Wuppertal." There is also a similar piece of brilliant timing of 'dropping the bomb-shell' when Natalie Portman says to the hotel receptionist in *Leon*, "He's not really my father – (long dramatic pause) – he's my lover!"

For a little girl of just seven can the superb performance of Margaret O'Brien in *Meet me in St Louis* be bettered? Her cheeky dance routine, her display of joy, fear, and tears, her clarity of diction, all provided her with a credited Oscar. What's more, the director Vincente Minnelli was worried she was having so much fun on the nighttime filming of the Halloween scenes, how could she act frightened when having to approach the house of a scary man and his dog? But of course, she accomplished it with ease, her frightened eyes near popping from their sockets, her confident but quivering voice chuckling inside her with the fun of it all.

Most of our modern child actresses are wondrously accomplished and several are exceptional having been treading the boards since they were toddlers, and are now leading lights in the adult spheres – Scarlett Johansson, Jodie Foster, Natalie Portman, Lindsay Lohan, Kirsten Dunst. The boys, however, have less prominence – Mickey Rooney, Ethan Hawke, Christian Bale making it through the adolescent chasm of rejection.

Others will shortly be following their example. Dakota Fanning is one child actress that producers have ear-marked at an early age and have been willing to wait several years till she had reached the required maturity for the role she had been reserved to play. As well as being selected for *The Secret Life of Bees*, Dakota was the obvious choice for the part of Fern Arable in *Charlotte's Web*, in the words of Barry Norman, "the young, precociously confident Dakota Fanning."[84] She was then lined up for major parts in the more violent blockbusters of *Man on Fire* and *Push*. Even Terry Gilliam was recommended to try to get Dakota for his film *Tideland*, though in the end he chose the more naturally innocent and child-like Jodelle Ferland instead. As soon as he had decided to make *The War of the Worlds*, Steven Spielberg immediately thought of Dakota Fanning to be the lead alongside Tom Cruise. Spielberg says of Dakota, "She is the best juvenile actor working today. She thinks with an adult's heart. She's intuitive about human nature." Tom

Cruise says of her, "Dakota is enormously talented…. innately talented…. and very bright. Fun to be with too." She was only ten going on eleven!

The producer of *Charlotte's Web* claimed there to be no one other than the remarkably talented Dakota considered for the part of Fern Arable. "There was never anyone we wanted more than Dakota. Not even close… Dakota combines great wisdom with youthful glee." The plaudits for this youngster seem to be endless. Speaking about her performance in *Dreamer*, Kris Kristofferson compares her to "Bette Davis reincarnate." Kurt Russell likens her to Goldie and Meryl Streep. Further, he says of her, "It's hard to call Dakota a little girl – she's a unique special person, a terrific actress. I'm blown away by her." Dakota was eleven at the time! As a ten-year-old in *Hide and Seek* (2005) she was likened to a child of thirty, such was the maturity with which she performed! "I've never seen an adolescent girl portrayed so well," says Ed Lachman (director of photography) referring to her role in *Hounddog* (2008).

All these compliments of her *are* justified. She *is* a remarkable actress. But as I mentioned earlier, like Keisha Castle-Hughes and Abigail Breslin, her diction can be poor, and you have to strain to understand her words. In *Dreamer*, she repeats the same quotation about horses on three different occasions, but I could still never grasp the garbled last line. Maybe it's my English ear that is not tuned to southern American drawl, yet as exemplified by Patty McCormack, good diction can be worked at, and the adults in these films did not pose a problem with their accents.

Writing in the *Radio Times* about Tatum O'Neal's performance in *Bad News Bears*, Jason Caro says of this eleven-year-old, "she has more screen presence than dad Ryan O'Neal ever had." [85] Of Eliza Dushku acting as ten-year-old Alice in *That Night*, John Ferguson writes, "The young Dushku is a revelation." [86]

Sandrine Blancke is another actress that the director has nothing but respect for. Speaking of the eleven-year-old's performance in *Toto le Héros*, director Jaco Van Dormael says of her, "Sandrine had an extraordinary understanding of emotions. She grasped the meaning of a scene and what her character was going through. Sandrine followed up this film with a further deeply emotional performance in the French film, *A Shadow of Doubt*.

J G Ballard, autobiographical author of *Empire of the Sun* describes the acting of young Christian Bale as "the best by a child in the history of cinema." [87] Sinyard explains how the boy appeared in every scene undergoing a complete transformation of character, "from immaculate English schoolboy to the begrimed deranged survivor." [88]

Carroll Ballard, director of *Fly Away Home*, says of his thirteen-year-old child star Anna Paquin, "Anna is usually ahead of everybody in knowing emotionally what is expected of her." This girl had already received an Oscar for her part in *The Piano*. Likewise, writing in *The Radio Times Guide to Films*, David Parkinson says of the lead actress in the Disney movie *The Journey of Natty Gann*, "Meredith Salenger was so good in the role of the fourteen-year-old in search of her lumberjack father that it beggars belief that she did not go on to be a star." [89] If brilliant child actors disappear into the ether, what is the destiny for Dakota, or will she just disappear from the public's adulation like Shirley Temple?

Oscar and Bafta Winners and Nominees

The diversity of roles that a child is called upon to portray is awe-inspiring. The incredibly talented among them have been distinguished by receiving credited Oscars or the British equivalent, Baftas. But spotty teenaged boys don't get nominated. Nor do black children. Pretty blond teenage girls do, and so do cute-looking preteens, both girls *and* boys. But overweight, fat, or bespectacled youngsters don't get a look-in. The cute factor is uppermost and we have already iterated Kincaid's words *we want cute.*

Jamie Bell aged fourteen was an exception, receiving a Bafta in 2000 as *Billy Elliot,* and Salvatore Cascio in 1990 as best supporting actor in *Cinema Paradiso.* We have already mentioned the best actress nomination for Keisha Castle-Hughes for her lead role in *Whale Rider* in 2003. Similarly, Mary Badham attracted an Oscar nomination for best supporting actress in *To Kill a Mockingbird.* As a ten-year-old in 1962, she was the youngest girl to be nominated for an academy award. In the same year, Patty Duke claimed an Oscar for her role as Helen Keller in *The Miracle Worker.* In 1945, seven-year-old Margaret O'Brien received a special Oscarette for her endearing performance as Tooti in *Meet me in St Louis.*

Saoirse Ronan is becoming a recognised star. Having been understudy to Catherine Zeta-Jones in *Death Defying Acts* it didn't take her long to be among the 2007 Oscar nominees in *Atonement* and she has since appeared in *The Lovely Bones.* Abigail Breslin set her career off to a flying start by being nominated in 2006 for best supporting actress for her role as little girl in *Little Miss Sunshine* when she was only ten years old, and she has continued to shine in *Nim's Island* and *My Sister's Keeper.* Another ten-year-old nominee for best supporting actress was Patty McCormack for *The Bad Seed* in 1956, and Tatum O'Neal received an Oscar in 1973 as Addie in *Paper Moon,* and as we have mentioned, Anna Paquin in *The Piano.* Most recently fourteen-year-old Hailee Steinfeld has received both Oscar and Bafta nominations for her role in *True Grit* (2010).

Other actresses trod the boards in their childhood building up experience to claim an Oscar in their adult career. Reese Witherspoon, starring as an adolescent with a crush on boy next door in *Man on the Moon,* in later life gained an Oscar in 2005 in *Walk the Line.* Ellen Page as a teenager confronting a predatory paedophile in *Hard Candy* was nominated for an Academy Award for playing *Juno* in 2007. Natalie Portman, having starred as a young teen being trained for a vendetta by a gunman in *Leon* won a Golden Globe and gained an Oscar nomination in 2004 for best supporting actress for *Closer,* and then captured everyone's hearts in her Oscar winning role in 2011 in *Black Swan.* Scarlett Johansson has become one of the leading ladies in modern cinema winning an Oscar in 2003 for *Lost in Translation* and a nomination for *Girl with a Pearl Earring.* Yet, she started off convincingly as a child actress in *Manny & Lo, My Brother the Pig,* and *The Horse Whisperer.* By contrast, in what I thought was an unconvincing movie – *Phenomena* – Jennifer Connelly was not to be deterred for she received an Oscar for her supporting role in *A Beautiful Mind.*

Who will we be applauding in the future? An adult Dakota Fanning, Freddie Highmore or Abigail Breslin? Perhaps Jodelle Ferland, in my opinion the best and also under-rated young actress of our time. But my money is on Dakota's younger sibling Elle Fanning. Already lauded in *Babel, The Curious Case of Benjamin Button, Pheobe in Wonderland* and *The Nutcracker,* director JJ Abrams says of her in *Super 8:* "this twelve-year-old girl just has this super real unbelievable skill –

she's an incredibly talented actress." The maturity of this girl caused her to be cast as a sixteen-year-old in *Ginger and Rosa* (2012) when she herself was just thirteen.

But surpassing all these, in my opinion, is the emotional performance of Jena Malone in *Bastard out of Carolina*. So chillingly knowledgeable was her reaction during the molestation scene, and the way she yielded to being picked up by her head and hurled around like flotsam in the arms of her ruthless abuser, this pained innocent depicted the suffering of a generation of abused females, and doggedly rose above it. She made me feel really, really sorry I am a member of that cruel gender called male. What is worse, this powerfully truthful film, classified *R* in the USA, has been ignored in the UK and gets no listing in any British film guide.

THEMES

There is a wide range of themes that children are asked to portray in the movies. Other volumes in this series tackle topics as diverse as family relationships, crossing gender boundaries, making friends with children and adults of different race and colour, the child's world of fantasy and horror, first tentative steps into puberty and first love, facing the trauma of divorce, illness or death, and finally coping with bullying, physical and sexual abuse. For some of these themes, the child can act with knowledgeable confidence when they lie within their limited life experience and are not controversial.

But in several of the categories, the child is asked to step outside their comfort zone to explore an experience totally new to them. This may be a first kiss, the death of a loved one, physical violence, imagining ghosts or psychic phenomena. It is in these circumstances that the director needs to tread gingerly, wrapping the child in proverbial cotton wool, chaperoning them through controversy, and being patient to address their misunderstandings.

Does a director have purpose or a message to convey beyond just entertainment? *Hidden in America* scripts an appeal for the *End Hunger Network*. *Peck on the Cheek* specifically set out to highlight the civil war in Sri Lanka, while *Lilya 4ever*, *I am Slave*, and *Stolen* (2011) all have specific messages regarding child trafficking. *Mom at Sixteen* tackles the repercussions for a school-aged teenager having a child. Many bracket their movies in the overused label *rites-of-passage*, while others doff their hat to controversies related to racism and cultural identity, but neglect to be multiculturally inclusive.

Adult themes and hard-hitting moral messages

Although there are some films that are thoroughly enjoyable, tempting us to watch them again and again – *The Wizard of Oz*, *The Railway Children*, *The Sound of Music* – others deal with traumatic themes giving a thoroughly hard-hitting message but leaving a bitter taste in the mouth. These films are equally well produced and convincingly portrayed by the child actor, but they are films you watch once only, for any more than that is too traumatic. I'm thinking of *Liar, Liar* dealing with the heart rending decisions an abused child has to make to expose her abusive father; *Hard Candy* where a child groomed on the Internet is taken home by her predator; *The Woodsman* in which a paedophile released from prison has to make choices concerning a little girl he meets in the park. Other films we watch only once, squinting between the chinks in our fingers, just to say we have watched them, and never again unless we are addicted to nightmares – *The Omen*, *The Exorcist*, *Let the Right One In*, *The Amityville Horror*, *Audition*, *Benny's Video*.

Films can be classified according to a theme, with edifying messages concealed in the screenplay, as if there is something ethically moral to be gleaned from a film. Examples are inter-racial relationships, or films that tackle the subject of bullying, teenage pregnancy, underage sex, or bereavement such as the loss of a parent.

The dilemma here for the filmmaker is that he/she is out to entertain. As soon as the director implants a discreet message about moralistic behaviour there is the danger of alienating the audience. For example, in a drama handling underage sex and teenage pregnancy, if there is an overt message warning of indulging in certain types of relationships the target audience may be deterred from watching. You can't offer someone an apple while telling them don't take a bite. The balance a director has to make when dealing with sensitive themes is how to entertain, and even titillate, while still trying to get the message across.

Manny & Lo is one such example of a film in which a sixteen-year-old runaway becomes pregnant but is unwilling to visit a clinic for treatment. Instead, the girl and her younger sister (a preteen Scarlett Johansson) take a maternity nurse hostage for the duration of the birth. The film is entertaining and questionably describes itself as a comedy, but in so doing, trivialises a serious issue and seems unwilling to explore the real emotional quandary of either child. A similar comment can be made about *Juno* in which Ellen Page puts her new-born up for adoption.

Regrettably, the reverse is true about *Liar, Liar*, a moralistic tale portraying the dilemma of an eleven-year-old girl who has been sexually molested by her father. This film so honestly and fully depicts the trauma and the consequences of a child who dares to say 'no' by reporting the abuse. The distressing courtroom battle she has to face in order to be believed could possibly be too much for a young viewer going through the same hell, but in desperate need of guidance.

Some films specifically set out to show the emotional impact on the child, of events and how the young actor interprets them. In *Blame it on Fidel*, "We are watching a little girl watching the world around her and what is forced on her." The Parisienne nine-year-old Anna has to comply as her once bourgeois family radicalise into socialists, foregoing their previous affluent life-style. "Everyone knows it's the children who suffer first."

The Argentinean film, *XXY*, makes us aware of the emotional quandary that a hermaphrodite child has to face, the impact of her bisexuality on her parents, and her relationships. The director tries to balance the effect on the parties involved, but not without us being voyeurs and unwitting viewers of a freak show, but a freak show that has to be aired if it is to get its message across.

In other films a child may feel he is being deprived, either of a loved one if there is a death or divorce, of his friends if the family are moving home, or of love and security if he is growing up in an abusive environment. It requires a talented child to understand how to navigate the emotional stepping-stones across the quagmire of domestic tribulation. The performance by Justin Henry was remarkable as he portrayed the bewildered infant in the tug-of-love *Kramer v Kramer*, which in Sinyard's words is "the film that makes the biggest emotional meal of this theme."[90]

There are many films that blatantly tackle controversial issues in a true and sensitive fashion without being overly sensational. And yet, I notice that film critics do not rate them highly. In particular, I am referring to *My Sister's Keeper*, *The Brooke Ellison Story*, *The Woodsman*, *Fallen Angel*, and *Liar, Liar*, all of which I found gripping to watch and thorough in their handling of sensitive issues. Maybe it is the frank honest approach they make; perhaps it is the sugary sweet optimism the films depict; whatever it is, I believe the criticisms are unfair. A case in point is *Mom at Sixteen*, a powerful film that opens the debate among its teenage audience regarding the disadvantages of casual sex and unexpected pregnancies. According to the *Radio Times Guide to Films*, "The movie clearly means well but the moralising is decidedly off-putting,"[91] and yet a glance at the reviews on the internet by non-professional viewers indicate its appeal as hard-hitting entertainment providing a helpful consideration of pertinent issues. In my opinion, the media *should* be taking a moralistic educational stance, and films like these should be applauded and not be underrated.

How does a director approach working with a child in a film dealing with adult themes? Nicole Kassell, director of *The Woodsman*, says you have to be completely up-front with the child and her parents, with no hidden agendas. Hannah Pilkes was playing an eleven-year-old who befriends a sex offender while bird watching in the park. *XXY* partly addresses this problem by casting an older actress, Inés Efron, to masquerade as the teenager. As for Patty McCormack, musing fifty years after playing the role of a nine-year-old child serial killer in *The Bad Seed*, she claims perhaps it's not such a big deal, "Kids have wonderful imaginations. They can pretend better than older people." In fact, Eddie Murphy speaking about *Dr Dolittle* states, "The greatest thing about being a kid is you can pretend." As I mentioned earlier, it must have been unsettling and baffling for Laura Vaquero to smother her younger brother in *Alas de Mariposa*, and I wonder how that impacted on her psychologically in later years.

Danny Boyle, director of *Slumdog Millionaire*, marvels at the way his child actors cope with the difficult themes they are depicting, in particular, he says of thirteen-year-old Tanvi Ganesh Lonkar, "She has an acceptance beyond her years." When her childhood sweetheart, Jamal, is kicked out of the apartment by his older brother, Salim, she is aware she is going to be raped by the older boy, and knowingly assents to prevent a fraternal spat. The director tells us how he "carefully explained to the parents" the role their daughter was required to depict and that the rape would be implied and not acted out.

Georgia Groome has to take on the role of a preteen prostitute, though not in the salacious way that Brooke Shields did in *Pretty Baby* or Jodie Foster in *Taxi Driver*. Georgia plays the character of eleven-year-old Joanne in *London to Brighton* as a runaway picked up off the streets by a gang serving a millionaire who 'liked his girls young'. She is thrown into a frightening whirlpool of violence and confronted with issues of paedophilia, smoking, drug and alcohol abuse. This was an uncomfortable film to watch and the child actress herself admitted she "found it very scary playing against Derek, for he was so like his real character" – a hard-hitting, no-nonsense control-freak, taking out his own insecurity onto others. "He made me cry without needing to put any thought into it at all," says the girl in the post-screening interviews. Even her own mother wasn't happy initially when she read the script. Even so, mother passed the buck by giving her still immature daughter the decision whether to proceed with the part or not. Georgia was asked, "Has the role changed you in any way?"

"It's made me grow up quite a lot," replies Georgia. "Everyone thought I wouldn't understand what was going on. Mum was so surprised how naturally the swear words came out of my mouth. It has made me more aware (of what can happen to vulnerable little girls) but not really changed me very much as a person." But, of course, she can only see from the inside looking out. Others who know the girl well may be more objective. Georgia Groome was playing the gritty role of a vulnerable child. Her use of gutter language was realistic and expected in such a role.

Sue Lyon had made a similar comment shortly after her role in *Lolita* (1962) that "Being Lolita hasn't changed my life in any way. Why should it? I'm just the same." But reflecting on this ten years later, she realised what a confused stage her post-Lolita years were, and "my destruction as a person dates from that movie." Linda Blair went through precisely the same denial phase following her Oscar nominated role in *The Exorcist*. "Both she and her mother hotly insisted that becoming a celebrity had not changed little Linda one bit," but a few years later, having moved in with an older boyfriend at the age of fifteen, having been threatened by mad gunmen who decried her role as a 'Devil-possessed nymphomaniac' and having gone on the run from the FBI for peddling drugs, she acknowledged, "I grew up fast," and that growing up in Hollywood "burnt people out."[92]

To add to this arrogant assumption that the child believes she knows it all, Jodie Foster, allaying fears that playing a child hooker in *Taxi Driver* would corrupt her, countered, "There was nothing to worry about on that score, as I'd known about it for ages." Likewise, we are told that eleven-year-old Brooke Shields, playing a child prostitute in *Pretty Baby* was kept distant from the adult sex scenes that were not filmed in sequence, "so she doesn't follow the story." But Brooke says the contrary: "Sure, I knew what was going on with the sex scenes and everything in New Orleans. I pretend I don't know. It works better for me to be dumb."[93]

It is when we as an audience abuse the innocent ignorance of the child for cheap laughs, maybe then we need to shift our focus. Why was seven-year-old Jennifer Beck required to ask of Clint Eastwood in *Tightrope*, "What's a hard-on?" The only purpose of this dialogue is to allow us to chuckle at the ignorance of the child. Then when ten-year-old Abigail Breslin in *Definitely, Maybe* shows how knowledgeable she is about sex education by coming out with the line, "Just when did you put your penis in mum's vagina?" we too are expected to titter at the brazen remark. Both are instances of child exploitation, the film director using the child for a cheap laugh, and we the audience are by association equally guilty. In *Little Rascals*, an infant boy (Jordan Warkol) is required to tell us about a new girl from across the street who came over to play, and as a way of deterring her, "I whipped out my lizard", and we are meant to guffaw at his audacity; while in *Oranges are not the Only Fruit*, Emily Ashton complains to the ice-cream vendor, "They're fornicating next door!" 'Out of the mouths of babes and sucklings...' In Volume Six (*Puberty & First Love*), I consider further whether children are being exploited in their portrayal of sexual themes, and whether we are implicated as voyeurs.

This concept of chaperoning a child through the upsetting portrayal of child abuse had added difficulties in *Lilya 4-ever*. Swedish director Lukas Moodysson had to film in Estonia with a cast of Russian speakers. This instantly presented a language barrier and he had no way of being assured his actors were improvising with a suitable dialogue. Oksana Akinshina had to play the part of sixteen-year-old Lilya, a girl who was raped and trafficked for sex. Although in the post-film interview the director was asked what precautions he took to protect the actress from the distressing nature of the script, all he could reply was, "It was important to protect Oksana and not exploit her," but having no Russian and no suitable translator he was not able to communicate adequately with the girl. For most of the sex scenes, Oksana was omitted and an adult female photographer was substituted to take Oksana's place. When even the cameraman found this too upsetting the director himself had to do the filming which he acknowledged was an emotionally difficult experience, for he had to lie directly underneath the actor who was simulating the rape. This vividly drove home to him (and hopefully to us the audience) the horrific nature of systemised child abuse.

Jodie Foster can verify this. Playing the part of a girl gang-raped in *The Accused*, she claims, "It was one of the most cruel, devastating, overwhelming experiences I've ever gone through."[94] These are scenes we do not expect the child actor to know how to portray – and yet Dakota Fanning has to demonstrate just that in the rape scene in *Hounddog*: the fourteen-year-old contorts her face in pain, stabs her hand on a nail to try to evade the painful hurt and intrusion of being raped. Thirteen-year-old Chloë Grace Moretz had to portray the same torture in *Let Me In*. She was playing the part of Abby (Eli in John Ajvide Lindqvist's novel) raped by a vampire when she was twelve. This was all too horrendous and was omitted from the final cut, and only appears in the deleted scenes on the DVD. According to director, Matt Reeves, Chloë's mother found watching her daughter portray this scene so upsetting she had to leave the set. Even more distressing is watching the performance of Jena Malone in *Bastard out of Carolina*. The violent sexual assault this preteen has to endure, the realism of the abuse barely censored, is sickening and soul destroying.

'Coming-of-Age'

Two vogue phrases – or should that be *vague* phrases, because it covers such a diversity of scenarios – used in the media for this age group is *coming-of-age* and *rites-of-passage*. The terms refer to the transition stage between childhood and adulthood as the child confronts for the first time various adult themes and learns to come to terms with the life changing forces that are occurring around them and within them. This might involve exposure to drug culture, as Jeliza Rose helps her junkie father inject himself with heroine in *Tideland*. It may refer to the distress resulting from the death of a parent or a childhood friend as Vada experiences grief in *My Girl* (1991) as her friend Thomas J dies of a bee sting allergy, or the child's first confrontation with a corpse, the target for the expedition from Castle Rock for the four lads in *Stand by Me*. In this film, Wil Weaton gets another rude awakening: "Chopper was my first lesson in the difference between myth and reality." Chopper was the legendary guard dog at a junkyard, but whose existence was made vividly real as the boy makes a desperate escape from its jaws.

Coming-of-age could involve taking on the early role of motherhood by helping to look after the youngsters as was the responsibility for Yildiz in *Times & Winds* until she stumbles on a cobble dropping the baby on the road. For Christie (Sarah Bolger) in *In America* (2003), her maturing responsibility has sanely kept her parents together following the death of their young son. "Don't little girl me! I have been carrying this family on my back for over a year," says the ten-year-old.

The adventure is well used by filmmakers as an initiation into the real world: the child transported from its comfort zone into an edifying or terrifying eye-opening quest.

The rite-of-passage for fourteen-year-old Mattie Ross (Hailee Steinfeld) in *True Grit* (2010) was to raise an expedition to bring her papa's murderer to justice, in which she embarks (in her own words) on a "glorified 'coon hunt" in which she witnesses killings, hangings and she herself revengefully shoots Tom Chaney.

The aimless wandering of Jenny Agutter and her younger brother (Lucien John), in *Walkabout*, was at once an attempt to evade the horror of their father's violent suicide bid while maintaining proper prim conduct in the desolate outback. But the lesson they learnt was that life is as equally harsh as the burnt-out shell of the vehicle they have abandoned. Life is raw. The gruesome juxtaposition of the cruel hunter-gathering sequence with the nubile naked water nymph swimming carefree in the billabong, the festering innards alongside bare flesh, glimpses of tantalising breasts merging with the death throws of clubbed animals, show the boundary between life, love and death is delicately fragile.

For Nina Kervel in *Blame it on Fidel* coming-of-age meant being fobbed off over issues of politics, abortion, and sex, all of which were impinging on her character's life; while for Christian Bale in *The Empire of the Sun* it meant surviving by himself following the accidental separation from his parents during the Japanese occupation of Shanghai in 1941. As a boy alone, devoid of the protection of his parents, he is confronted face to face by his former housemaid, a lady he formerly exploited while a petulant spoilt brat. Now free of her subserviency, the woman slaps him on the face as retribution for all the times he had taken her for granted. As Sinyard puts it: "That slap signals a brutal division between the old world of comfort and complaining, and the new world of scavenging and survival."[95]

But for the majority of movies *coming-of-age* or *rites-of-passage* refers to the build up to and the experiencing of that first mind-blowing kiss, when that glass barrier separating the yearnings of puppy love is shattered, as Duckworth struggled to do in *P'Tang, Yang, Kipperbang*, or that caused Josh Hutcherson so much dilemma in *Little Manhattan*, or Sandra Wilcox so much joy in *My American Cousin*. "No hanky-panky, understand?" the boxing lads are warned in *Billy Elliot*, as the girls' ballet class have to share their gym facilities. Other films then explore, usually in a light-hearted trivial way, the puzzling changes brought on by puberty, a brother noticing his naked budding sister emerging from the bath in *Toto le Héros*, the purchase of the first bra as in *32A*, the ghastly horrors of the first period for Anna Chlumsky in *My Girl* (1991) and for Brooke Shields in *The Blue Lagoon*. Beyond this is the total immersion into the teenage culture of drugs and sex as shown in *kids* (1995), and ultimately the trauma (or ecstasy) of premature pregnancy as in *Manny & Lo*, *Mom at Sixteen*, and *Juno*.

Multiculturalism

In this age of multiculturalism, I am alarmed there is a disproportionate lack of actors from black or ethnic minorities on the screen. Perhaps part of the reason for this is because several movies were made at a time when American and British culture was white-dominated. Also, many films made today are based on novels written before our Westernised population was so diverse, and the character featured in the book may be a white child. If a Caucasian girl was visualised by Charles Dodson as he wrote *Alice in Wonderland* then I suppose it would be inappropriate to cast a black or oriental girl in that role, especially as devotees cry foul when any deviation in made from the classics. Likewise, the characters in *Matilda* or *Charlie and the Chocolate Factory*, *Bridge to Terabithia* or *Charlotte's Web* were based on white-skinned children.

Of course, there are films depicting black and Asian kids. Nate Parker provides controversial black company in *The Secret Life of Bees*, Keke Palmer plays a girl from a poor Los Angeles neighbourhood in *Akeelah and the Bee*, Aleisha Allen and Philip Daniel Bolden play the demanding youngsters in *Are We There Yet*, Raven-Simoné in *Doctor Dolittle*, Jurnee Smollett as the voodoo loving daughter in *Eve's Bayou*, Sabu the young Indian prince in *The Drum*, while Everlyn Sampi plays a mixed-race Australian Aborigine in *Rabbit Proof Fence*. All the above movies are concerned with ethnic issues and so it would be appropriate for a non-white actor to play the part.

Karen Lury acknowledges this in her book *The Child in Film*. "While there have been successful black child performers in popular music and television the peculiar history of American filmmaking in the 20th century demonstrates a lack, an almost complete absence, of the little black girl as major character or as star... The little black girl, it seems, has been lost and nobody is looking for her." Further, she says of casting Dakota Fanning in *Man on Fire*, "White blonde and translucently fair-skinned and fragile-looking, recreates an all too familiar scenario in which the little girl must always be white because... she must inherit the legacy that is sustained by all those other little white girls loved and lost, stolen and avenged."[96]

This concept of the white Arian child is taken still further in *Race to Witch Mountain* in which pure blond AnnaSophia Robb and Alexander Ludwig play chase with the US military. The irony here is that these children are not representing earthlings at all. They are interplanetary aliens, sent to Earth on a mission to avert an intergalactic war. Has the movie industry duped even extra-terrestrials into believing the ideal human form is pretty, slim and blond?

It is encouraging therefore to find a black girl, in *Station Agent*, in which eleven-year-old Raven Goodwin plays Cleo. The film is set in a wooded rural middle class community in upstate New Jersey, so it is pleasing that a non-white girl was cast for this role, for they could easily have chosen someone white, or even a boy. The story is about an adult dwarf (Finbar McBride) who had recently moved into the community. Everyone finds him so odd (because of his size) and he is taunted by the usual bullying jokes. But it turns out that Finn, the dwarf, is the only normal person in the village. All the others have their own problems that make them larger than life as well as larger in stature.

Now, seen in this perspective, the casting of Raven Goodwin was not so innocuous, for she also was chosen as an odd contrast, an overweight black girl who stands out from the norm by means of her colour and her size. At least this girl, who is possibly taunted at school herself, sees nothing odd about the dwarf man (she even asks him what class he is in at school!). But when she invites the man to her school to give a talk on trains, is she inviting the man as a knowledgeable friend or as a freak? Certainly, the class of children are more interested in his size issues than in his lecture on trains.

Angela Burnett is a dutiful six-year-old black daughter who croons to her dolls in the recently rediscovered black arthouse movie, *Killer of Sheep*. *Lovely and Amazing* features a black girl (Raven Goodwin) living in a white family: the girl is adopted. In *Precious*, Gabourey Sidibe plays the bullied fifteen-year-old girl of the title, illiterate, overweight, and pregnant; a black girl who through self-assertiveness transcends the humiliation received from her classmates and mother.

Following the success of her childhood movies of *Akeelah and the Bee*, *Knights of the South Bronx*, and *Cleaner* (2007), Keke Palmer progressed to being the lead performer in the comedy sitcom series *True Jackson VP*, as a high school student holding down a top job in a fashion company. But she is no longer a girl-child. This does not provide us with an example of a black girl encroaching on the traditional preserve of the cute white middle class lass.

For this we have to look to Steven Spielberg to buck the trend in his sequel to *Jurassic Park: The Lost World*. In this, he casts Vanessa Lee Chester as the black adopted daughter of Dr. Malcolm who unwittingly smuggles herself into dangerous encounters with the cretaceous beasts – the usual preserve of the delicate white Arian child who has to be protected from the ravenous monsters. Yet, instead of playing scared like her predecessor (Ariana Richards), Vanessa Lee remains laid-back and unfazed by the ominous dinosaurs, as if she is perpetuating the perceived stereotype of Afro Caribbean culture. Never does she allow a scream to emit from her lips, or a nervous widening of the eyes, and the only condescension she would make to fear is to hold the hand of her tall white-skinned father.

Although Rebecca Hall gives a fine performance as Sophy in the TV drama *The Camomile Lawn*, Mary Wesley actually describes her in the book as having oriental features, the product of a traveller's fling in the Far East. So I was surprised a mixed-race oriental girl was not cast for the role.

James Kincaid recognised the predominance of white kids in the American acting spheres. He mentions that 99% of child actors are white, and 75% are blond. "When children *really* become valuable commodities, these kids are mostly white upper-middle class kids."[97] Nancy Signorelli's study indicates 85% of film characters are white, with 6% as African-American.[98]

What the film industry needs is 'multicultural interchangability'. Will a time come when audiences are ready to accept a black Alice in Wonderland, an Afro-Caribbean Superman, or an oriental Cathy in Wuthering Heights, or will literary critics remain uncompromisingly rigid in their perspectives? Even middle-eastern Jesus is more typically played by a white man and not an olive-skinned Arab; and who was chosen to play Mary in *The Nativity Story* (2006)? New Zealander Keisha Castle-Hughes, imbibed with Maori blood. At least the adult Eddie Murphy was able to buck this trend in his role as *Dr. Dolittle*, Diana Ross plays Dorothy in the 1978 version of *The Wizard of Oz* (*The Wiz*) and Sheffield-based Solomon Glove takes the role of a black young Heathcliff in the latest version of *Wuthering Heights* (2011) more in keeping with the swarthy dark character Emily Brontë described in her novel, though his counterpart, thirteen-year-old Cathy (Shannon Beer) remains pale-skinned.

However, in moralising about a serious issue we are flippantly informed, "Racial prejudice is only a pigment of the imagination."[99]

ENDNOTES FOR VOLUME ONE

1. The actual phrase this ten-year-old was required to say was 'bugger off sod bloody fuck'
2. Sula Wolff, Children Under Stress p17-34
3. Erotic Innocence: The Culture of Child Molesting by James Kincaid
4. Deborah Kampmeier, director of Hounddog being interviewed for The Making of Hounddog.
5. Nancy Signorelli, University of Delaware Reflections of Girls in the Media, 1997 (Internet)
6. M Thompson et al Best Friends, Worst Enemies, p165
7. M Thompson et al Best Friends, Worst Enemies, p163
8. Stacy L Smith Gender Oppression in Cinematic Content Annenberg School of Communication & Journalism, University of Southern California, 2007. Internet p4
9. Stacy Smith, ibid p6
10. Nancy Signorelli, University of Delaware Reflections of Girls in the Media, 1997 (Internet)
11. Lake, Sosin & Snell Associates for Children Now and the Kaiser Family Foundation
12. Stacy L Smith Gender Oppression in Cinematic Content Annenberg School of Communication & Journalism, University of Southern California, 2007. Internet
13. Vernae Graham et al, Kaiser Family Foundation, California (Internet)
14. Nancy Signorelli, University of Delaware Reflections of Girls in the Media, 1997 (Internet)
15. Geena Davis, Institute on Gender in Media Research (Internet)
16. From an article by Charlie Gray, Radio Times 14th April 2012, p9.
17. Marianne Sinclair Hollywood Lolita p76
18. Marianne Sinclair Hollywood Lolita p76
19. Andrew Collins, Radio Times 10th March 2012.
20. Marianne Sinclair Hollywood Lolita p133
21. Chris Roberts Scarlett Johansson: Portrait of a Rising Star p22
22. Alison Graham Radio Times 2-8 April 2011 p59
23. Quoted from the extras on the DVD disc, The Children.
24. Barry Norman Radio Times Supplement 23 April 2011, p8
25. Marianne Sinclair Hollywood Lolita p115
26. Marianne Sinclair Hollywood Lolita p120
27. Daniel Radcliffe being interviewed by Emma Brockes in Radio Times, 11 Feb 2012, p12.
28. Chitty Chitty Bang Bang: After they were famous, shown on ITV1, December 2011. Heather Ripley's co-child actor, eight- year-old Adrian Hall did not have the same friendship deprivation for, living close to the Pinewood Studios, he was able to return home to family and friends every day after filming.
29. Radio Times 20 November 2010, p10
30. Wikipedia: Sandy Descher 6 Sept 2010
31. Radio Times, 16 July 2011
32. Marianne Sinclair Hollywood Lolita p157
33. Tim Dowling, Radio Times 3/4/10 p13
34. Chris Roberts Scarlett Johansson: Portrait of a Rising Star p12
35. Chris Roberts Scarlett Johansson: Portrait of a Rising Star p25
36. Will Lawrence writing in Radio Times 20 Nov 2010, p15
37. paraphrased from Radio Times, 16 July 2011
38. Marianne Sinclair Hollywood Lolita p49
39. Lena Zavaroni won the TV talent show Opportunity Knocks aged 10 in 1974. The Talent Show Story ITV1, 28 Jan 2012.

40. Cootie: An ambiguous American term of endearment, partly in reference to being cute; an alternative meaning is to do with body and head lice, and maybe unpleasant genital warts. In Little Manhattan infant schoolchildren are playing. A girl touches one of the boys on the shoulder, and the boy recoils – "she touched you, you've got a cootie!" Thompson in Best Friends Worst Enemies uses the term as a form of affection as a chapter title.

41. Harry Potter: Behind the magic ITV2

42. Mail Online, 17 April 2010

43. Will Lawrence Radio Times 20 Nov 2010 p12

44. Marianne Sinclair Hollywood Lolita p40

45. Tim Dowling Radio Times 3/4/10

46. Alexia Skinitis Radio Times 12 Feb 2011

47. Chitty Chitty Bang Bang: After they were famous, shown on ITV1, December 2011.

48. Marc Best Those Endearing Young Charms, p50

49. Sound of Music internet

50. Marianne Sinclair Hollywood Lolita p43

51. James Kincaid Erotic Innocence

52. Andrew Collins Radio Times 13 Nov 2010 p44

53. Andrew Collins Radio Times 13 Nov 2010 p45

54. The People 8 August 2004, p9

55. Daniel Radcliffe being interviewed by Emma Brockes in Radio Times, 11 Feb 2012, p10.

56. James Kincaid Erotic Innocence pp299-306

57. Marianne Sinclair Hollywood Lolita p7-11

58. Marianne Sinclair Hollywood Lolita p148-154

59. Bugsy Malone: After they were famous, ITV 2003.

60. Brian Pendreigh from the IO Film website Film Inside Out

61. See previous section, Coping with Fame.

62. James Kincaid Erotic Innocence p 302,303

63. Soylent Communications 2012, NNDB: Tracking the world. Article: Jena Malone. Internet

64. Coogan Law Screen Actors Guild.mht, 2012.

65. Marianne Sinclair Hollywood Lolita p120

66. ITV2: Harry Potter and the Deathly Hallows: Part 2 – behind the Magic

67. Bugsy Malone: After they were famous, ITV 2003.

68. Marianne Sinclair Hollywood Lolita p11

69. Radio Times 16 July 2011, p14

70. Karen Lury, The Child in Film, p145ff

71. Marsha Kinder, *The Children of Franco in the New Spanish Cinema* in Quarterly Review Film Studies Spring 1983, p59-60. Quoted from Karen Lury ibid p108

71a. Quoted by Caroline Frost in Huff Post Entertainment, 9 Nov 2012

72. Marc Best Those Endearing Young Charms p30, & p80

73. From Wikipedia 'Heather O'Rourke' listing source as: Spielberg, Steven; Royal, Susan (2000). "Steven Spielberg in His Adventures on Earth". In Friedman, Lester D.; Notbohm, Brent (Google Book Search). Steven Spielberg: Interviews. Jackson, Mississippi: University Press of Mississippi. p. 88. ISBN 9781578061136

74. Marianne Sinclair Hollywood Lolita p145

75. Marc Best: Those endearing young charms

Radio Four: Saturday Live, 19 Nov 2011. Director Alan Parker is being interviewed by Rev Richard Coles.

76a. Yahoo! Movies UK 19th April 2012.

77. Joan Collins was being interviewed on Radio Five Live, 13th Sept 2011

78. Radio Times Guide to films 2010, p 1152

79. Marc Best: Those endearing young charms

80. Marianne Sinclair Hollywood Lolita p49
81. Gladys changed her name to Margaret O'Brien on the back of her acting debut in A Journey for Margaret.
82. Marianne Sinclair Hollywood Lolita p150
83. Marianne Sinclair Hollywood Lolita p11
84. Barry Norman Radio Times 18/09/2010
85. Radio Times Guide to Films 2010 p79.
86. Radio Times Guide to Films 2010 p1149.
87. Neil Sinyard Children in the Movies quoting The Guardian, 17 Mar 1988, p11
88. Neil Sinyard Children in the Movies p53
89. though Meredith Salenger did not disappear from acting, having a modicum of roles when she reached adulthood.
90. Neil Sinyard Children in the Movies p98
91. David Parkinson Radio Times Guide to Films 2010 p774
92. Marianne Sinclair Hollywood Lolita p115-116, 127-128
93. Marianne Sinclair Hollywood Lolita p150,154
94. Marianne Sinclair Hollywood Lolita p155
95. Neil Sinyard Children in the Movies p53
96. Karen Lury The Child in Film p104
97. James Kincaid Erotic Innocence p 305,306
98. Nancy Signorelli, University of Delaware Reflections of Girls in the Media, 1997 (Internet)
99. Book of British Lists by Hunter Davis, p84

Volume Two

Families, Step-kids & Orphans

"You see, he understood the children.
He had the knack of entering their world
and becoming part of them."

(Cathy Brenner's mother reminiscing about her dead husband
in Hitchcock's, *The Birds*.)

CONTENTS FOR VOLUME TWO

2. Families, Step-kids & Orphans..**71**

Contents for Volume Two...**73**

There's No Place Like Home...**75**
The Statistics: How the Media has Deceived Us..*76*

The Importance of the Family...**78**
Happy Families *79*
Mother's Role...*80*
Sibling Rivalry...*81*

Papering over the Cracks **85**
Strains & Betrayals in Family Relationships..*85*
The Need for Compromise..*85*
Favouritism, Feeling Unwanted and Runaways...*86*
When the Bough Breaks..*90*
Traumas creating Fractious Families...*91*
Neglect of the Family: The example of Enid...*92*
Rebelliousness..*94*
The Rejected Child...*96*

Family Reunions...**99**
Searching for Family..*101*
Thwarted Searches...*106*
The Child as Matchmaker...*107*

Broken Homes...**109**
The Single Mother / Missing Father-Figure..*111*
Single Fathers...*114*
The Unwanted Orphan / Institutionalised Kids..*118*
The Fostered Child..*121*
Motives for adopting...*123*
Trying to remember Mother/Father...*130*

Home Alone: Kids in Charge...**132**
The Blue Lagoon..*132*
Vulnerable Girls Forced to Seek Help...*133*
Kids Abandoned to Struggle Alone..*135*
Boys Home Alone...*137*
The Ultimate Struggle: Survival of the Fittest...*138*

Endnotes for Volume Two...140

THERE'S NO PLACE LIKE HOME

"Home is the nicest word there is!" declares little Laura Wilder in the *Little House on the Prairie* having just moved into her new abode, while in *The Wizard of Oz* the whole tearful audience concurs with Dorothy that the best place to be is back home, among the family, where there is comfort and security, a sentiment that could be echoed in household after household across the world: "There is no place like home." Many films would like to give the impression that the home is the ideal, the paradise that all little children should aspire to be in, the reassurance and comfort of mother and supportive father, in a happy family unit.

Prairie girl, Laura Wilder, had it lucky. She already had a home, a happy nuclear family, with mum, dad, and two sisters. But for Kansas Dorothy that was just an ideal. Dorothy was, after all, an orphan. She was coming home from Oz to Auntie Em, and her uncle, and to the farmhands. No mother, father, or brothers and sisters for her.

Klaus Baudelaire is talking to his sister, Violet, in *Lemony Snicket's A Series of Unfortunate Events*, "Home is where our parents put us to bed at night, where they teach us how to ride a bike, or get all choked up on our first day at school." But *their* parents had just died in a fire. They have come to the realisation that without parents, in particular, without mother, they will never know home again. "Do you think anything will feel like home again?" Violet responds.

This is just the state of affairs that film directors like to exploit. For every film depicting a little child living happily with his/her mummy and daddy, there are three others where the child is from a broken home, fatherless, motherless, or orphaned, and in the care of stepparents, guardians, or in a household where a single parent is desperately trying to raise the child.

Yet the true ratio should be a reversal of those statistics. In the UK, one-third of children live in a broken home (though the new vogue term seems to be *blended family* [1]). Two-thirds of children still live with their birth mother *and* father, yet by my reckoning based on a sample of 500 films reviewed for this series of books, directors and scriptwriters would have us believe that three-quarters are from broken homes, and not one third. I describe this in more detail below in the section, *The Statistics*. [See also Table (i) for a listing of films depicting one-parent households or broken homes contrasted with the traditional family unit.]

In this volume, we focus on the importance of the family as an ideal. The child is searching for perfection (though seldom finding it) within a nuclear unit of mum, dad, and siblings. In such circumstances, the family is the provider of nurture, and the film is there to show us (assuming films have a purpose beyond entertainment) that when the child strays from the path out of the embrace of protective parents, then all the dangers of the big bad wolf materialise.

Barry Norman, writing in *The Radio Times* about why the *Wizard of Oz* has such a unique status is "the incomparable way it touches on and deals with every child's deepest fear – that of being whisked away from the comfort and security of home to a strange and frightening place…. Despite Oz being a glittering, colourful wonderland, home is still where safety lies." [2] Tom Hanks playing an overgrown thirteen-year-old stepping outside the comforting warmth of the family unit in *Big* (1988) also found it a scary adventure. Though the 'lad' gained a glimpse of life beyond childhood, like Dorothy he needed the safety reins of familiarity and of being mothered: "I miss my family. I want to go home!" he mopes.

In other films, a parent is missing and the scriptwriter casts the child as a tool to try to mend a broken relationship, to find the missing partner or parent, the missing link to perfect domestic bliss. Examples of these are *No Reservations*, *The Parent Trap*, *Miracle on 34th Street*, *Home Sweet Homicide*.

Others, such as *A Father's Choice*, *Hidden Places*, *Kramer v Kramer* play on our emotions by showing us the realities of a broken home, the tensions and crises that can arise when a single parent struggles to raise the child.

Then there is a devious set of films that unnecessarily depict a child from a broken home, trying to make us, the audience, more sympathetic to the characters, thus warping the statistical evidence that children mostly live with both birth parents. *Explorers* is guilty of this, as is *Russkies* and *The Little Unicorn*.

Finally, there are some films which feature children who have to cope without parents at all. I don't mean orphans in an orphanage, or adopted children, nor even *Oliver Twist* who at least had Fagan as housekeeper, nor free-spirited *Eloise at the Plaza* who had a nursemaid to nanny her. Rather I mean, kids in charge of themselves, learning to run their lives independently and adult-free as William Golding wrote about in *Lord of the Flies*. For example, *Nobody Knows*, *The Cement Garden*, *The Blue Lagoon*.

The Statistics: How the Media has Deceived Us

What initially goaded me into writing this book, was watching film after film that seemed to exaggerate the myth that the broken home is the normal status of modern households. True, the problem is worsening, but the media is painting a fabricated picture of the true nature of the family. When one reads headlines such as '*Most Teenagers live in Broken Homes*',[3] or listen to radio talk-shows berating one-parent families for the ills of modern society, and even politicians bandying phrases such as '*Broken Britain*',[4] it is only logical to conclude that family structure has collapsed, and that we are raising a generation of children in households without the child's birth parents.

The movie industry perpetuates this myth. Table (i) lists the films I have reviewed for this series of books. Out of 500 films reviewed, 71% of children are depicted in the movies as coming from one-parent families, broken homes, or living with a step-parent. Only 29% are shown living with both their natural birth parents. Yet in the real world, a reverse of these statistics is the reality. In the UK, 62% of children live with both their birth parents.[5] In the US, the proportion is similar: 61% of under-eighteens live with both biological parents.[6] In Sweden, the ratio is even more promising: 72% of children under 18 live with both birth parents.[7]

We have to conclude the movie industry is being sensationalist as it tries to convince us otherwise. It is far more appealing to depict a child that is vulnerable, a child yearning for its lost mum or dad, and its desperate struggle to adjust to a world that has deprived it of love. This is what attracts an audience, and what makes money. The wholesome, happy, well-nurtured child, despite being the norm, does not keep the wheels of the movie industry clanking along.

It is disturbing to learn how this is distributed between ethnic groups. While in 2010, 75% of white children lived with two married parents, only 61% of Hispanic children did so, and alarmingly just 35% of Black children lived with two married parents.[8] [9]

Although the situation is misrepresented in the media, it becomes further upsetting to discover, as Mary Park tells us, that 40% of children will experience the divorce of their parents before they reach adulthood.[10]

THE IMPORTANCE OF THE FAMILY

The movie industry is riddled with torrid love affairs, men and women fulfilling the urge to marry and inevitably start a family. The magic of these affairs is kept alive (for a short while) with the arrival of kids. But then the focus changes. The acknowledged benchmark appears to be seven years of marital bliss. Up until then, relationships may remain rosy, but after that, as over-familiarity and routine set in, fractures develop in the marriage. The nurture of the children then becomes the overriding factor, as the parents have to make new compromises and sacrifices.

Demi Moore in *Now and Then* describes it thus: "This whole baby thing baffles me," she says. "You have it, you raise it, you inevitably screw it up, they resent you, you feel guilty for them resenting you. Then *it* has a baby, which only perpetuates the vicious cycle."

Inevitably it is the child who suffers and this becomes the tool for filmmakers to wield so perversely, reprimanding parents for being too self-centred, or unwilling to compromise.

The lives of a perfect family living in unity do not make for interesting viewing, so filmmakers seldom focus on this. And when they do, it is in the form of a spoof, such as *The Brady Bunch* or *The Addams Family*. Tribulations in a broken marriage are far more entertaining.

Some families do come close to the ideal: the Darlings in *Peter Pan* ("There never was a happier, simpler family"); the aforementioned Wilders in the *Little House on the Prairie*; the Buckets in *Charlie and the Chocolate Factory* ("I wouldn't give up my family for anything, not for all the chocolate in the world"). Even the Bakers in *Cheaper by the Dozen 1 & 2*, despite appearing to be chaotic and dysfunctional, are in fact a cohesive cooperative democracy. *In America* (2003) is a wonderful advert for the selfless struggle for family unity, as Christie (Sarah Bolger) chants in her nightly prayer, "Mum, dad, Christie and Ariel, altogether in one happy family." *The Railway Children* and *Little Women* also provide examples of an ideal unified family, assumedly once the fathers have returned (though we are never shown the families gelling once the father *has* returned).

Several films present a cohesive family structure as the basis for further adventures: *Charlotte's Web*, *Little Miss Sunshine*, *Honey, I Shrunk the Kids*. Here, mum's intentions are positive. "We've just got to get this family back together," she says to crazy inventor dad, Rick Moranis, as his miniaturised brood are rummaging through the jungle that is their backyard. In my viewpoint, this is how family life should be projected if we are to keep the perspective proportionate.

When fractures do appear, it is usually the father who is blamed for putting his career first, as in *Meet me in St Louis*, *One Fine Day*, or *Angus Thongs and Perfect Snogging*, though in *Enid* it is the selfishly blinkered mother (prolific author Enid Blyton) who is to blame. *Field of Dreams* should fit into this category had it not been for the baffling support given by the wife in an already impoverished household in which a father sacrifices everything on a psychically inspired whim (he uses all the housekeeping money to build a sports-field, simply because he thought he saw the ghost of a former ballpark star).

In other families, rifts develop due to the illness of a child, as in *The Horse Whisperer*, *Mandy* (1952), *My Sister's Keeper*, and *Lorenzo's Oil*. It is films like these that really help us appreciate the anguish of families tearing apart.

Happy Families

So, what of films that depict the warmth of the family in a positive light? "It's not much, but it's home," says Ron Weasley showing Harry Potter around his home in *The Chamber of Secrets*. But for Harry, it seems like heaven, with a mum, a dad, and a bunch of happily interacting kids.

Meet me in St Louis stresses the wholesomeness and security of the family unit living in turn of the century middle America. Though based around life-styles in the 1900s, it was filmed in 1944 when the family unit was disrupted by the Second World War, when fathers were away on the battle front, when there was a national yearning for families to be reunited. The film depicts a happy nuclear family during the course of a year, the two older daughters searching for the appropriate boy to wed, while the two younger preteen girls get up to playful tricks. The family exudes cosy warmth until father drops a bombshell by announcing that after Christmas, because he has been offered a new job in New York, the whole family will pack up and join him on the big venture.

Alas, the news only creates opposition as all the family members, one by one, see their cherished dreams shatter. For the youngest, Tooti, played by the exceptional seven-year-old Margaret O'Brien, it is the thought of losing the secure comfort of familiarity, regardless of whether the move would be an advantageous adventure for the whole family. Father comes to realise that family unity and stability are far more precious than an ambitious career move. "We can be happy anywhere as long as we're together… Home is here right in our backyard."

Little Women conveys a similar affability. Based on the classic novel by Louisa May Alcott, the story is about four teenage girls brought up in a small rural community in Massachusetts, the warmth of growing up in a close-knit family, the interaction of living without the distractions of modern-day technology. They play together in the snow, they confide, squabble, sing carols together around the piano, and prepare outfits for dances and balls. The film is a happy blend of family harmony tested by their recent loss of status and affluence. With father away, and with the gradual deteriorating illness of the second eldest sister, Beth, the story delves into the sacrifices they make for each other – Jo selling her hair to make money for the family, giving away their butter on Christmas Day (their one and only luxury) – and of the happy reunions when dad finally returns. "At last we are again family, like we always should have been."

In the same vein, Bob Cratchet's impoverished family in *Scrooge* are only too happy for any mercies, and who gladly give away their presents, if only their family are all together around the Christmas hearth.[11]

Sometimes you have to dig deep to discover the heart. When the Oprah Winfrey TV crew turn up at the Baker's household to interview Kate Baker about her newly published book in *Cheaper by the Dozen 1*, they witness the bedlam in the family of twelve independently-minded kids. The producer talks down his mobile, "You don't want to come here. It's the furthest thing from a happy family." This family exudes chaos, and there are disasters at every turn as the two adults try to pursue their separate careers; for comic actor Steve Martin it is football coaching, for Bonnie Hunt it is being an author.

Yet, it is a democratic family showing loyalty, cooperation, and concern. As Hilary Duff says to Alyson Stoner, "There are times when I want to kill you, but I'd kill *for* you all the time." It is just that family unity becomes punctured from time to time. Like, when father goes for a top coaching job with the Chicago Stallions, he is too often absent from home. "At least we get to see him on TV," complain the kids sarcastically. "Once we were a family. Now we're a supporters' club." Dad sees why the family is falling apart and gets chance to put things right again. "If I screw up raising my kids nothing I do will matter much."

The sequel, *Cheaper by the Dozen 2*, conveys a similar aspiration. Father misuses his family to try to outdo his nemesis, former college rival, Jimmy Murtaugh. But when the kids don't want to play ball he starts to realise, "Parenting is not a popularity contest. The tighter you hang on, the more they're going to pull away."

Other family films portray the happy contented family to be the ideal state. *Peter Pan*, the parentless child from Neverland, stares longingly into the nursery window of the Darling's abode at three contented children living with mummy, daddy, and Nanny the dog. In *Charlie and the Chocolate Factory*, Willie Wonka offers little Charlie Bucket the whole factory and chocolate for the rest of his life, on one condition: if only he comes and lives with him, Willie Wonka. But Charlie declines. For, although Charlie Bucket shares just a one-roomed house, he shares it contentedly with his parents and grandparents as well.

These films provide heart-warming messages of the contented family group gelling together for a happy ending: the Darlings, after Wendy and John have returned from Neverland; the Smiths, after Tooti and Agnes shame their parents into staying in St Louis; Cary Grant, having just recovered from a run on the bank, reunited with his wife, his son, and with his daughter in his arms, for the conclusion to *It's a Wonderful Life*, just in time for Christmas.

Alas, there are only so many times you can convey the family as a happy idyll. Modern critics demand gritty reality. Few families are in continued perfect harmony. Regrettably, directors have all rushed to the opposite side of the boat and the vessel is toppling, the family misrepresented by fallacies and fractures. Perhaps it takes a war or a national tragedy or even Scrooge-induced impoverishment to restore the family to its pedestal.

Mother's Role

While in former days, father was depicted as the breadwinner, and stay-at-home mum was in charge of domestic arrangements and thus more highly rated in the affections of the child, even today in an era when both parents go out to work mother is still considered the heart of the household. Obviously, there are some films that buck the trend, in which the domesticated father struggles with the household chores – *Kramer v Kramer*, *Corrina, Corrina*, *Fly Away Home*. In fact, as we shall see, the single father has gained disproportionate focus in the movies. But various mantras seem to make the mother irreplaceable:

"It takes a woman's heart or a child's presence to make a home," says Mr. Pendleton to *Pollyanna*. And, we are told in *Silent Hill*, "Mother is God in the eyes of a child."

"Mother," says Liesl, rolling the word over her tongue and considering the possibilities. "That sounds so nice. I like calling you mother," as the newly wedded Maria returns from her honeymoon in *The Sound of Music*.

For Laura Ingalls (Melissa Gilbert) in *The Little House on the Prairie* "Her smile is the last thing I see at night, and the first thing I want to see in the morning."

Yet, the mother is not always idolised in the teenager's eyes. "Why can't I get her to love me?" despairs Mrs Frank in *The Diary of Anne Frank*. The reassurance she is offered is not very convincing: "All girls shut out their mothers at this age. They give all their love to their fathers." In *The Mommy Market*, Anna Chlumsky and her two brothers are dissatisfied with their mother (Sissy Spacek) and try to trade her in at a magical market. But they discover no one is ever perfect. The substitute mothers never live up to their expectation of a real mum. "She's your ma, and she knows best," says Uncle Remus to Bobby Driscoll in *Song of the South*, and then goes on to show how short-sighted and unimaginative the mother proves to be.

In *Shattered Family*, the foster mother of eleven-year-old Gregory Kingsley (Tom Guiry) tells the court, "A good mother is someone who loves her kids, but also puts that love into action." Alas, in this case, the birth mother did not make the grade and custody is awarded to the more caring foster parents.

Sibling Rivalry

In general, scriptwriters make their young actors out to be a genial bunch. Siblings are more likely to be portrayed as cooperating rather than squabbling. *Cider with Rosie*, *The Railway Children*, *Swallows and Amazons* all depict families in happy unity. Even when eleven-year-old Margaret Dashwood (Emilie François) complains in *Sense and Sensibility*, "We never talk about things," theirs is only a friendly spat between sisters worried over future suitors.

In *Are We There Yet*, *Snow Day*, and *Whistle down the Wind*, siblings put up a united front to ward off oppressors: an unwanted interloper making inroads towards mum; a snowplough man who insists on thwarting dreams of a day off school; and hiding the kittens from uncaring adults intent on drowning them.

Domestic squabbles between brother and sister are less likely to be shown than cooperation. In *Honey, I Shrunk the Kids*, Amy O'Neill feels duty bound to protect her younger brother (Robert Oliveri) as they explore their Lilliputian backyard. In *Walkabout*, Jenny Agutter guides her younger brother (Lucien John) through the outback, escaping the horror of their father's suicide and murderous attempt.

This is the role of the older girl perpetuated on screen for our edification. She is protector and nursemaid to her younger brother, willing to absorb the taunts and intimidations of her charges, remaining loyal to the tender calling of her gender; Kristy Swanson caring for her younger twin siblings in *Flowers in the Attic*, Violet (Emily Browning) cradling the infant Sunny throughout *Lemony Snicket's A Series of Unfortunate Events*, just as Tara (Eliza Bennett) does in *Nanny McPhee*.

"I don't care if Annabel is not like me. I love her anyway," declares Asher Metchik about her older sister (Gaby Hoffman) in *Freaky Friday* (1995). Wendy even takes on the acknowledged role of mother in *Peter Pan*. "Be sure to take your medicine," she tells the Lost Boys. Jenny Agutter's mothering of her young charge takes the form of pestering nannying (in *Walkabout*): "Put your shirt on... don't scuff your shoes... don't go off too far... don't do that!" For Sandrine Blancke in *Toto le Héros* and Charlotte Gainsbourg in *The Cement Garden*, traits that are more incestuous are hinted at in the brotherly-sisterly interactions.

By contrast, in families where there is an older brother and a younger sister, the younger girl is more likely to be abandoned by the older brother, who has the more important calling of adventures to commit to, without the hindrance of annoying younger brats.

The older brother is not portrayed as compassionate like his female counterpart. Robbie (Justin Chatwin) and Dwayne (Paul Dano) reprimanded for not caring for their younger sisters (Dakota Fanning and Abigail Breslin) in *War of the Worlds* and *Little Miss Sunshine*. Leaf Phoenix has a marooned Russian sailor to protect instead of caring for his younger sister (real-life sibling, Summer Phoenix), in *Russkies*, while in *Man Without a Face* ten-year-old Gaby Hoffman gets left behind because her older brother Chuck (Nick Stahl) has to join his mates in their dare to see the elusive disfigured man. Seven-year-old Girtie (Drew Barrymore) has to resort to blackmail to be part of the gang caring for *ET*, else she will tell mummy, but Elliott (Henry Thomas) exerts his authority by threatening to rip up Girtie's rag dolls if she splits. Michael (Peter Jones) only agrees to care for his younger Emmeline (Susan Stranks) in *The Blue Lagoon* (1949) after exerting his superiority: "You'll have to do what I say, then." Omri Katz only takes younger moppet Thora Birch trick-or-treating under protest in *Hocus Pocus*.

In *The Lion, the Witch and the Wardrobe* Edmund (Skandar Keynes) yearns for self-respect, power, and to shirk his responsibility of care to younger Lucy. In a bickering household, Edmund's making fun of Lucy's alleged excursions into Narnia, Peter's attack on his brother for being beastly; both incidents trigger the resentment which leads Edmund into betraying his siblings to the Queen of Narnia, in the hope that he himself will become king and his brother will be made subservient.

In those families where there is a sibling with a disability, a 'normal' child becomes resentful because mother's time is devoted to the other child, establishing a rivalry for parental attention. In *Phoebe in Wonderland*, the younger sister asks, "Can I have another sister? I'm fed up with Phoebe (a child with Tourette's Syndrome)."

"Why?" asks the astonished mother. "What does she get that you don't get?"

To which the younger girl replies, "You!"

In *My Sister's Keeper*, teenager Kate (Sofia Vassilieva) apologises on her death bed to her older brother (Evan Ellingson), "I'm sorry, Jesse. I'm sorry I took all the attention when you were the one who needed it most." The family had never realised Jesse had dyslexia because all their attention had been devoted to Kate's leukaemia.

Rarely in the movies does the older boy take uncomplaining responsibility for his younger sister. Exceptions are Gordon John Sinclair's nurture of Madelaine (Allison Forster) for ice cream sundaes and goodnight kisses: "So who's going to be *Gregory's Girl*, then?" and Billy Chapin taking under his wing his infant sister Pearl (Jane Bruce) still clutching that valuable rag doll in which the family's inheritance has been secreted, in *Night of the Hunter*. Instead of praising this dutiful concern on the part of this latter boy, Neil Sinyard denounces the fraternal relationship for "its element of boy chauvinism," – the resourceful and favoured son, "entrusted with a burden that was too much for a child" – compared with the "dim-witted", and in Robert Mitchum's words, "poor, silly, disgusting little wretch" that was his little sister, Pearl.[12]

If any tension is depicted in sibling relationships it is more likely that the girl is portrayed as the victim, whether this be of name-calling, bullying, or aggression. "My embarrassing parents just don't get it," says Scarlett Johansson playing Kathy in *My Brother the Pig*. She is constantly the butt of practical jokes initiated by her obnoxious younger brother, George. The parents seem blinkered to the taunts and physical abuses she receives. "I hate him," she cries, when one morning she wakes up with the pet mouse tied to her big toe. "Honey, he just wants your attention," says dad unconvincingly. Sibling rivalry could be viewed as a positive attribute, when it promotes a productive outcome. Guilt-ridden Kathy drags her snorting brother to Mexico to seek a cure for him.

But tensions do occur. Sometimes this can have a romantic trigger: two sisters chasing the same fellow in *Man in the Moon* and *Little Women*; while in *Slumdog Millionaire*, older brother Salim exerts his superiority as he chucks Jamal out of the house to rape Jamal's childhood sweetheart, Latika (played as a thirteen-year-old by Tanvi Ganesh Lonkar).

Even where there is a more physical rivalry, again it is the girl who is often the victim, and the boy is depicted as the aggressor. For adopted *Jane Eyre*, it was her guardian's spoilt son who cruelly shifts the blame onto the little girl for any misdemeanour. "There is no sight so sad as a wicked child," says Mrs Reed, locking Jane all alone in a scary room. "You should be grateful you are not in the workhouse with all the other orphans."

When siblings of the same gender are together, they can plot against a common enemy: a sibling of the opposite sex. For seven-year-old Gaby Hoffman confiding in her older sister (Jean Louisa Kelly) about her brother (Macaulay Culkin) in *Uncle Buck*, "I don't know why we need boys at all – they are so loud!" Her sister explains, "We need boys so they can grow up, get married and turn into shadows," referring to how her father seems to be absent for much of the time. To the 15-year-old, her younger brother is just an embarrassment: "I've got better things to do than baby-sit you, you little stain!"

For the three children in *Uncle Buck* their interaction is a comedy, a daily sparring match typical of most families. In *Home Alone* (1990), it is the eight-year-old Kevin (Macaulay Culkin) who becomes the victim. "I wouldn't let you sleep in my room if you were growing on my ass," he is told by an older brother, Buzz. "You're a complete idiot. Everyone has to do everything for you." Sent to bed early, Kevin wishes his family would all disappear. When he wakes up next morning he finds he is truly home alone. It is then that regrets flood his conscience. He looks fondly at the family photograph wishing his family would come back again. When the family do eventually return, Buzz makes his fraternal love clear in a way only a brother could do: "Hey Kev! It's pretty cool you didn't burn the place down," and Kevin proudly smiles everything back to normal.

The three orphaned girls, adopted by palaeontologist, Richard Griffiths, in *Balletshoes* seem to gel successfully, thrown as they are into a life of relative poverty after their benefactor disappears. The three Fossil girls, Pauline (played by Emma Watson), Petrova (Yasmin Paige) and Posy (Lucy Boynton) make a pact together so that, with each other's help, they can individually make a mark on the history of the world. But it is the older girl, Pauline, who achieves success first by taking the lead role in performances on the London stage. With her success comes arrogance and bossiness resulting in resentment by the other girls. "This is all about you," Petrova complains. "Do you think you are the only one that wants your heart's desire?" Despite the complaints, Pauline is generous, diverting her stage earnings to promote the successes of her two younger sisters.

Margot, in *The Diary of Anne Frank*, in the same spirit uncomplainingly makes sacrifices for the more strong-willed younger teen, Anne. "Why can't you be more like your sister?" Anne's mother rebukes her.

Michelle Trachtenberg tries to deflect her responsibilities as an older sibling in *A Father's Choice*. She plays thirteen-year-old Kelly, older sister to ten-year-old Chris (Yvonne Zima). They have both been through a terrible ordeal of witnessing the death of their mother (shot by a burglar), and had to move back with their estranged father. Kelly had been expected to care for her sister, but she objects, "I don't want to take care of her. I don't want to be her mother. I'm supposed to be a kid."

Carol Stone, playing Macy, younger sister to a schoolgirl mum in *Mom at Sixteen*, has played second fiddle to her older sibling all her life. Now mum's disapproval of her older sister's pregnancy has at last allowed her an unexpected reversal of fortune. "I've waited all my life for this," says Macy. "Since you were little, you were good at everything. Now you're the scrub, and I'm the good kid!"

The current of animosity underpinning the two sisters in *A Company of Wolves* leads to dreams of terminal freedom from a more favoured sibling. Older sister is sent upstairs to fetch her younger sister, Rosaleen, who has locked herself in her bedroom claiming to have a stomach-ache. She keeps repeating a four-letter word as she ascends the stairs and bangs on the little girl's door. "Pest! Pest! Pest! Pest! I expect you've been using my lipstick again," the older girl accuses. But Rosaleen (Sarah Patterson) is dead to the world – soundly asleep in a deep nightmare. Rolling feverishly in her bed, and dolled up in lipstick and rouge, the little girl is dreaming of her older sister being frantically chased through the forest, at first by her gruesome looking dolls, then her teddy bear which has a glint of evil-intent in its eye, and finally by a company of wolves, which capture the sister and devour her. We just see the hint of a pleasurable smirk appearing on the sleeping girl's lips as grandma mourns her: "Your only sister! All alone in the woods and nobody to save her."

The friendship between brother and sister seems solid enough in *The Turn of the Screw* until the governess, Miss Given, starts hallucinating about a possible collusion with the dead Peter Quint. She sees the children frolicking in the grounds of Bly, but to her, the innocent game of roly-poly becomes a vision of sexual intercourse between Quint and the former governess, Emily. She sees Miles ("a little progeny of goodness") thrashing Flora ("she's an angel") as Quint molesting Emily, so she attacks the boy to protect the girl. To little Josef Lindsay and Eva Sayer playing the children, how can a simple childish game be so misinterpreted in the eyes of an adult? As Fester (Christopher Lloyd) says in *Addams Family Values*, "It's just sibling rivalry!"

Yet despite the natural rivalry between siblings, it is rarely their fault when cracks appear in the safe haven that is meant to be home. They have a part to play, but when rifts arise in the domestic household, the familiar mantra 'blame the parents' comes true.

PAPERING OVER THE CRACKS

Strains & Betrayals in Family Relationships

The movies are riddled with stories of family fracas: the hurt child in a family that is falling apart. These are the stories of misfortune that the public demand: gossip, and better still, salacious gossip about indiscretions. Maybe we use them to justify our own inadequacies. The result is that this is now the expected norm. The family today appears broken. Perhaps it has always been so, but in the past adults have been adept at papering over the cracks, giving the illusion that all was well. Perhaps also today our parental resolve is not as enduring, and we allow the slightest of fault lines to fissure into a destructive avalanche of disharmony in family life. Add a measure of parental self-indulgence, friction, and thoughtlessness, and the edifice crumbles.

In films, however, some problems are easily remedied. All it needs is a sprinkle of magic dust. The trouble with George Banks esquire was, like so many other fathers self-absorbed in the workplace, he was blinkered to the needs of his family. "Sometimes a person you love, through no fault of his own, can't see beyond the end of his nose." His children, Jane and Michael, become increasingly difficult and a string of nannies keep arriving and then leaving. "Perhaps if you helped us make a kite..." suggest the children who only want love from their parents. Fortunately, as the wind changes, *Mary Poppins* descends on this scene to help reshape the mould for this family.

But in the real world, Mary Poppins nor her counterpart *Nanny McPhee* exist. Parents have to face their crises using their own intuition. This is how the child sees it, too, as they discover that a sprinkle of fairy dust is not a panacea for domestic strife. Too often, the child feels shame that he or she may be the catalyst for mummy and daddy's nightly arguments.

The Need for Compromise

Compromise is necessary for a family to be successful. One parent needs to sacrifice his/her ambitions to keep the marriage secure. "All you think about is yourself," complains Daniel Tay to his work-obsessed father in *Elf* (2003). "You have two jobs," Eddie Murphy is reprimanded in *Imagine That*, "and one of those jobs is being a father."

Robin (Evan Rachel Wood) encounters the same degree of neglect from her workaholic parents in *Down will come Baby*. Usually it is the father who is criticised, but in this film the mother is forced to refocus. And yet, it is the child who feels the weight of the dilemma as she tries introspectively to discuss her parent's insecurity first with her friend and then with her overly interested neighbour.

Robin lives in Phoenix with mum and dad, but mum has been offered a job in Denver and wants the family to relocate there. Father is just getting his own business off the ground in Phoenix. "What about my career?" he objects. Daughter Robin does not want to move either. "If it wasn't for me they wouldn't have all these problems," reflects twelve-year-old Robin in an attitude common among teenagers who think they may be the cause of family strife. Her father (Marcus) phones up his wife on her business trip, "What we need is for you to come back home and be part of the family."

In the end, Marcus agrees to relocate to Denver, but only (as we discover later) to save the marriage. In the meantime, Robin is abducted. The parents have to forget their differences and work together to locate her. Mother realises she had only selfish motives for the move to Denver and was not thinking of the family. She concludes, "I need a home, and as long as I'm with my family I have that."

When real emotion and tragedy threaten to rip families apart, it is sad to confront a situation in which the children are being obnoxious just for the hell of it. Compromise is required to maintain family unity, but try telling that to the kids. *Our First Christmas* features a widow with one kid and a widower with two kids. The two adults get together, marry, and there is one big happy family. Now the dilemma: every Christmas one family always goes skiing, while the other family always stays at home for a family pageant. Doh!! Though the solution is obvious, the children (Grace Fulton, Maxim Knight and Cassi Thomson) make a pax and pretend they don't see it.

Two families also combine in *Yours, Mine & Ours*. A widower with eight kids and a widow with ten get married. When one rigid regime tries to merge with a happy-go-lucky household, daggers are inevitably drawn and the kids conspire to break up the marriage. Susan Sarandon agrees, while dying of cancer in *Stepmom*, "There comes a time in each family when you've got to be there for each other."

Sometimes, it is just a misunderstanding that makes a child think its family is fracturing. In *Angus, Thongs and Perfect Snogging*, Georgia Groome's father, played by Alan Davies, has earned a job promotion and has to leave Eastbourne for a trip to New Zealand. "We can't go," complains Georgia, "I've got a life. I'll be bored to death by sheep and hobbits." This is a girl who complains of living in Eastbourne: "God's waiting room, where people come to die!"

While father is away in the antipodes, her mum employs a hunky builder in the home, who then takes the woman to salsa classes in the evening. In Georgia's eyes, they are spending too much time with each other, and Georgia assumes the worst: her parents will inevitably be getting a divorce. The girl seeks out the offices of dad's employer, and pleads with the secretary who has asked her why she wants to see the boss. "I was going to ask him if my dad could come back. We don't want him to leave us and stay in New Zealand." Her pleading works. Father is offered promotion in the Eastbourne office, and it transpires the hunky handyman that so tempted her mother, is gay and is no threat to family unity after all!

Eddie Murphy in *Dr Dolittle* realised the problem of his fractious family lay with him when he admitted to his daughters (Raven-Simoné and Kyla Pratt), "Sometimes daddies are the ones who need to change."

Favouritism, Feeling Unwanted and Runaways

"There are no perfect families," Gaby Hoffman observes in *Now and Then*. Those that seem to be, like *The Brady Bunch*, are spoofs. There are always trials and jealousies, preferences, and points of friction. For Josh Hutcherson in *Bridge to Terabithia* and Jurnee Smollett in *Eve's Bayou*, both kids feel unloved thinking their parents prefer their sisters instead. In *Times & Winds*, Özkan Özen knows it to be true, for his parents verbally remind him about the favoured younger brother; whereas Eliza Dushku in *That Night* compares herself with next door neighbour, Sheryl, as evidence that she is unwanted. Whether parental neglect is due to pressure of work, or by disinterest, these examples gleaned from films help reinforce the statistic that the average parent spends just seventeen minutes a day with their kids.[13]

For some of the children, this apparent parental neglect leads to revengeful thoughts of rejecting their own parents, or at least teaching them a lesson. For Özkan Özen in *Times & Winds* there is opportunity to push his neglectful father over a crag; for Brandon de Wilde in *Shane*, it is the thought of the gunslinger being able to whip his father in a fight; while for Jurnee Smollett in *Eve's Bayou*, revenge becomes a reality as a voodoo curse gets out of hand. In *The Secret Garden* (1993), Kate Maberly saw no need to cry when her negligent parents were killed in an earthquake.[14]

Other children draw attention to their neglect by running away, as do Tegan Moss in *The Angel of Pennsylvania Avenue*, Christine Taylor in *The Brady Bunch Movie*, Forrest Landis in *Cheaper by the Dozen 1* and as Zachery Ty Bryan in *Magic Island* and Aidan Pendleton in *Andre* almost do, by packing their bags (though neither ever reaches the front door with it).

Neglect can result in potentially severe traumatisation of the child, and we detail such cases in the final volume of this series of books, *Physical & Sexual Abuse*. Here, we contemplate those films that depict a milder emotional reaction from the child.

Josh Hutcherson, playing Jess Aarons in *Bridge to Terabithia*, lives in a stable but struggling family consisting of mum, dad and four sisters. But he feels unloved in the relationship. During the day there are fracas with his sisters, he finds looking after his younger sister onerous, and his father insists on him doing chores around the family farm. At night, he is aware that while his sisters are tucked up and given a goodnight kiss, he just gets a distant goodnight wave. No doubt, parents commonly expect their adolescent boys to shun physical contact with them, and maybe they were offering him the breathing space most teenage boys crave, but for Jess, he obviously had a heart-felt yearning for attention. It doesn't help when his father tells him to "Get your head out of the clouds."

Alice Bloom also wished for a better relationship with her father in *That Night*. Her father seems to ignore her questions. At the meal table, the man just wants to talk business with his wife. Ten-year-old Alice (Eliza Dushku) goes daily to meet her father at the railway station as he arrives home from work. She opens her arms wide, hopefully, ready for a hug, but all she ever gets is a pat on the head, as if she were a dog. It is not until Alice takes the drastic action of running away does dad finally give her the hug she deserves when she returns. It's the same for Jess in *Bridge to Terabithia*. He only gains the attention of his parents (or is it pity?) after his best friend Leslie (AnnaSophia Robb) drowns in the creek.

Times & Winds is a Turkish film focusing on the strains and stresses of three families living in a rural Anatolian community. In a stunning maquis landscape overlooking the distant Aegean Sea, time ebbs slowly through the daily routines, the call to prayer, the changing seasons and diurnal weather patterns. The villagers mend their roofs, rebuild walls, tend their flocks, make bread, slaughter a sheep, assist with the birth of a calf.

In one family lives Omer. He hates his father because father dotes on the younger son instead of him. Both parents join in the ridiculing of Omer. "Your brother's already surpassed you (at

Maths). You keep wandering in the mountains." A poignant scene is the taking of the family photo with mum, dad and favourite son huddled together in the centre of the camera frame, but with Omer sitting at a distance, to one side.

When Omer's father develops influenza, bad enough to worry the village doctor, Omer hopes this might kill his father. So he sneaks into his father's bedroom at night, opening the window wide in the hope it might acerbate his condition. He also empties the powder from the drug capsules that the doctor has given to father for his cold. When that fails, Omer tries to think of other ways to finish him off – a snake, a scorpion, a knife. One day he has the opportunity to push dad off the edge of a crag and is sorely tempted.

This relationship is mirrored in *Honey, I Shrunk the Kids* by the father's disappointment with his eldest son, Russell. Thomas Brown is frequently derided by his father for not wanting to come fishing, or practise weightlifting. The younger son (Jared Rushton) is the apple in his father's eye. "Only twelve and already thinking about construction. Why can't Russell be like that?"

The girl in *Eve's Bayou* feels her father is ignoring her, too. Father is a doctor in southern states America, head of a happy household, and ten-year-old Eve (Jurnee Smollett) loves him being around. But she is concerned that father prefers her older sister and is not giving her the time she craves. He also stays out on his medical rounds too long, particularly at those houses where certain pretty lady patients live. She is worried the family may become broken if mother finds out he is canoodling with other women. However, when mother does eventually understand her husband is being unfaithful, little Eve does not dutifully seek a way to bring the family back together. Instead, she resorts to voodoo to take revenge on her father.

Children who feel neglected need some method of gaining the attention of their parents. For some, it is the extreme measure of running away. I say extreme measure, for a large proportion of children harbour thoughts at some time in their lives of temporarily running away from home. In the US one in seven children actually do so. The incredible number of runaways on UK and US streets shows how strongly children feel this neglect, combined with a premature and misguided desire for independence.

The Children's Society estimates 100,000 children run away each year in the UK, fleeing family conflict, neglect or abuse.[15] This is a problem that is getting worse. BBC News on-line quote a figure for 2001 as being 77,000, eighteen thousand of whom were under eleven, and one in fourteen were under eight years of age.[16] In the USA, figures of one million child runaways are quoted. According to *About.com*, 'For all children, adolescence is a stressful time of dramatic physical changes, peer pressure and an emerging identity. Those with parental support are usually able to successfully navigate this period, but without it, emotions can overwhelm a child to the point that he or she believes that leaving will bring relief.'[17]

Teenaged Aidan Pendleton felt betrayed in *Andre*, her father spending too much time caring for a seal pup and her younger sister. She felt left out. When father finds her smoking in the barn with her new boyfriend, the inevitable fallout is triggered. She storms to her room and starts packing clothes into a suitcase. Mother follows after her to placate her daughter and without the girl realising, helps by adding more clothes to the suitcase until the girl bursts into tears on mum's shoulder.

For Tegan Moss playing Bernice in *The Angel of Pennsylvania Avenue* her being neglected in favour of her younger siblings is seriously affecting her mental stability. In an effective emotional scene she complains to her father, "Mum pays more attention to Lilly and Jack than she does to me." This is mainly because Megan is the oldest sibling, expected to look after herself. This is

1930s depression Detroit and father is having to leave home to seek work, so the twelve-year-old girl feels she will be further neglected. Mother is blinkered to her own neglect of her daughter. It is not until Bernice runs away that mother realises, "Bernice is something special, but I wish I'd told her so."

Middle child, Jan, is driven to similar desperate measures in *The Brady Bunch Movie*. She has developed paranoid schizophrenia, believing her older sister Marsha is given more attention. She dreams of cutting off her older sister's perfect hair while she sleeps. Jan then runs away, and is picked up by a woman truck driver who explains she too suffered from *middle child neglect*. Her parents and siblings are overjoyed as she returns safely, but this doesn't solve her personal problems.

That these three examples are girls, helps reinforce the statistics that over the age of fourteen, girls are twice as likely to run away from home. Among younger aged children, it is boys who are more likely to be runaways.[18]

Usually, the child that runs away from home finds just that required shift of focus in its own mentality, so that as the prodigal returns to a household where nothing has actually changed, he/she finds there are square holes to take square pegs, as they are lovingly welcomed back. Neil Sinyard comments further on this, citing *ET* and *The Goonies*. "Elliott in *ET* returns with tearful satisfaction to a family, none of whose problems have really been resolved. At the end of *The Goonies*, the children ride to the rescue of their parents' suburban homes, seemingly forgetting that it has been their dissatisfaction with ineffectual parents and their frustration with boring suburbia that had precipitated their desire for excitement in the first place." [19]

Some children may harbour evil revengeful thoughts about their neglectful parents, but other factors miraculously intervene to alter circumstances. For Mary Lennox it was the unexpected death of her parents. For Joey it was the arrival of the gunslinging hero, Shane. While for others, supernatural intervention seems to smooth over a domestic problem.

The inability on the part of a father to endow the child's expectations is taken up by Neil Sinyard who characterises *Shane* as materialising "a need for a heroism that his decent mundane father cannot provide." No matter how faithful, the father does not live up to the expectation of the little boy, Joey.[20]

"My parents didn't want me," says an indignant Mary Lennox in the film of Frances Hodgson Burnett's classic *The Secret Garden* (1993). The superb Kate Maberly plays the resentful child being brought up in early twentieth century India. (In the 1949 version, Margaret O'Brien is equally brilliant with her argumentative patter.) "My mother cared only about going to parties, and father was busy with his military duties." The parents were too busy hobnobbing with the Raja. "Mother didn't even have time to tell me stories." Little Mary was brought up by an Indian maid who did everything for her. Mary was so used to being spoilt and waited upon she didn't even know how to dress herself. "I was angry but I never cried. I didn't know how to cry," says the young girl. This unloved and lonely upbringing made her a sour, friendless girl. Fortunately, when the need was thrust upon her, in time, others were able to penetrate her bickering obnoxiousness.

Chloë Grace Moretz felt neglected in the comedy *Big Momma's House 2*. At first, "Daddy can't waste his time taking kids to school." Nor does he find time to watch his daughter's dance competition – that is, until Big Momma steps in as a cross-dressing supernanny to put him and the family straight. Maybe that's what all relationships require: a supernanny such as *Big Momma*,

Nanny McPhee or *Mary Poppins*, or Lindsey Lohan's Barbie Doll, Eve, in *Life-Size* which magically comes to life, or failing that, just a sprinkle of fairy dust.

When the Bough Breaks

When fractures appear in parental relationships the only thing keeping the family together is the nurturing of the children. In the previous section we considered how children felt neglected, and the impact that made on their belief in the durability of the family structure. These are battles the child faces daily, and though he/she may feel there is no escape they have only limited power to redress the situation. But when it is the parent who feels unwanted, double-crossed, or who bids for a lifestyle change, this can cause the family to rift, rendering the child powerless, as an impotent bystander. Though this happens in one in three households, the children feel isolated, shame that it is happening to them, and try to hide this as a secret (as in *Now and Then* and *Little Secrets*), assuming the problem is unique to them. In Volume Seven (*Childhood Trauma*), we consider in more detail films in which families endure the trauma of divorce, in particular its impact on the child. Here, we focus on those relationships straining to snap, and the messages this sends out to children.

The family break-up might result from a lack of communication – either from a bored over-reliance on each other, as in *Little Manhattan* or *Kramer v Kramer*, or fear of talking to a violent partner, as in *Prince of Tides*, or an increasing build up of resentment as in *Now and Then*. The child feels the weight of guilt, assuming he/she is the catalyst for the break-up and, as in *Me without You*, leads to feelings of inadequacy. There are no instant solutions, as we discover in *Under the Mud*. Happy endings seldom arise, and antagonisms can endure a lifetime.

In *Little Manhattan*, ten-year-old Gabe's parents are separating. "It doesn't make for the greatest living environment," narrates Josh Hutcherson. All the food in the fridge have individual labels on them, and there is embarrassment all round as father has to open the door when mum's new boyfriend arrives. The parents try to press home to the boy, "It's not anybody's fault. It's just that your father and I are a lot more different than we thought."

Gabe has some love problems of his own. "How come love has to end?" he asks his father. Dad explains what happened in his marriage, how stupid little things were left unsaid. "They all piled up, until we barely said anything at all."

The same strains appear in *Under the Mud*. "Our problems will not be solved with a night out," says mother as they raise their five kids in Liverpool. When an old flame appears trying to split them up father realises why he loves his wife, and the ties that bind the marriage together, though seemingly trivial, make a strong tether. The husband realises, "I'd be lost without Sally. I'd miss the million tunes she hums as she does the dishes. I love the way her nose crinkles when she laughs, and the way she always manages to burn the frigging lasagne."

"Mum, is dad not going to live here anymore?" asks Anna Popplewell in *Me without You*. "Daddy likes to come and go," replies mum resentfully, "he's a free spirit, which means we just are not good enough for him, apparently."

"My parents had been fighting for as long as I can remember," ponders Gaby Hoffman in *Now and Then*. And she adds sarcastically, "That offered comfort and consistency." Alas, on one day she overhears her dad say to her mum, "This just isn't working," and the next moment she sees through her bedroom window dad throwing his suitcase into the car and driving off. "I thought he would be back," she reminisces. "A wishful notion I held onto for many years." Now, this is a tale of four girls bonding so, as Gaby says, "The last thing I wanted was to be different from my friends," so she does not confide in her best friends, not until much later anyway.

But one day, out of the blue, Thora Birch asks her, "Do you like your parents?" Gaby thinks a moment how to reply. "I don't really know my parents. As far as I know they are assholes. You see, there are no perfect families." And at last Gaby has the opportunity to confide about her parents' forthcoming divorce.

Another film in which children feel betrayed by their parents is *The Prince of Tides*. As a child, Tom Winger grew up in an abusive household. He, his siblings, and his mother were rigidly fearful of their father in whom they could not confide. One day, Tom's twin sister and mother were raped by three strangers. The older brother saw what was happening and shot the perpetrators. But to avoid incurring the wrath of their father they decided to bury the men, hiding the evidence from their father before he arrived home. Tom bottled up this trauma through his life. Now an adult, Tom is consulting a psychiatrist. Despite his fear of his father, "When I was a child," he tells the psychiatrist, "I thought my father was a god. Now I see him as a man with all his faults." Yet as a man now raising his own family, Tom realises, "I learned that I needed to love my mother and my father despite their flawed outrageous humanity." He sees the importance of family and allows his own children to travel with their unpredictable granddad on his shrimping boat. "In families, there are no crimes beyond forgiveness."

Traumas creating Fractious Families

Later, we discover how the death of Beth in *Little Women* brought a family close again. A similar tragedy occurs in My *Sister's Keeper,* which tests the strength of the bonds that bind the family members together.

My Sister's Keeper is powerful in the way it depicts a family going through crisis – that of a teenage girl trying to survive but gradually succumbing to leukaemia. Kate's parents were faced with an awful dilemma. In her infancy, their daughter had been diagnosed with leukaemia for which there was no cure – unless they genetically engineered another baby who could provide healthy parts for the dying Kate. The parents grasped at this one lifeline little realising the impact it would have on the welfare and happiness of the newborn child. Various painful operations, blood and bone marrow donations from the new child, Anna, helped keep Kate alive though never provided a cure. In the film, issues come to a head when donor child Anna reaches eleven years of age. Father reflects on his once happy family: "Big house, great kids, beautiful wife, but beneath the exterior there are cracks, resentments, alliances that threaten the foundation of our lives."

In order to escape from being a continual donor for the rest of her life, the eleven-year-old Anna, played by Abigail Breslin, takes legal proceedings against her parents. "I want to sue my parents for the rights to my own body." At the same time, Kate knows she is going to die but sees the damage her illness is doing to the rest of the family, the sacrifices they have to make for her, the squabbles and tensions that result. "I don't mind my disease killing me, but it's killing my family too."

So, the bonds that had so securely bound the family are slowly unravelled. A court case ensues. On one side is strong-willed but caring mother desperately trying to help Kate cling to life. On the other side are her children (with the eventual sympathy of father once he has removed his blinkers and the true impact of his decisions has dawned on him). The children are wanting their rights restored: in Anna's case, the rights to her own body; in Kate's case, the right to die.

As a final showdown, when Kate desires a trip to the beach to escape the claustrophobia of the hospice wards, father insists his antagonistic wife join them or else she will have a divorce case to contend with as well.

Mandy is a further example of a family dissolving into disunity when they are forced to confront the treatment of their deaf daughter. The opposing opinions of the parents lead to separation, and divorce proceedings are only averted when the husband rationalises his blinkered attitude. In *Lorenzo's Oil*, the marriage was kept from failing only by the dogged devotion of one of the partners, as the mother sacrifices everything – her health, her friendships, her religion, and her spouse – if only she can provide twenty-four hour comfort to her dying son. Likewise, the marriage in *The Brooke Ellison Story* may well have terminated had the mother not been forewarned that that is the inevitable outcome for parents of a paraplegic child.

Neglect of the Family: The example of *Enid*

An unexpected and eye-opening revelation about the impact of family breakdown comes in the BBC drama *Enid* (2009) about that most popular children's author, Enid Blyton. Enid had written an incredible 750 books, selling half a billion copies worldwide, all about jolly children climbing trees, going exploring, outings to the sea, picnics with raspberry jelly and ginger beer in which the wholesome family was uppermost. She pompously tells a reporter, "Children take from my books a feeling of security, a sense of being, anchored with a sure knowledge of what is right and what is wrong…. I am the guardian of our children's morals."

In this play, *Enid* (2009), we get to see the irony of this remark. Helena Bonham Carter brilliantly plays a ruthlessly determined Enid Blyton bringing up her children either side of the Second World War. Enid never seemed to love her own children; she ignored them, exploited them, and as soon as she could, packed them off to boarding school because she could not tolerate the demands of motherhood. That she was even a mother at all is rather ironic because at first she was unable to conceive. It required a series of hormonal injections before she was even able to give birth to her two daughters, Gillian and Imogen. After one week of having given birth she finds that the baby's crying disturbs her work, so she hires Dorothy as a nursemaid. "I do find them rather trying when they are tiny," says Enid, washing her hands of them for the rest of their lives.

As well as shutting the children out of her life she also shuts out Hugh Pollock, her husband, driving him to drink. This also is an irony, for her husband was her publisher who had first realised her potential – when other publishers had rejected Enid, Hugh Pollock, played by Matthew MacFayden, had encouraged her, published her work, and then married her. However,

Papering over the Cracks

as box-load after box-load of fan mail arrives, this and her writing takes precedence over her husband, her children, and her marriage. Ultimately, Hugh and Enid divorce and she cruelly denies him his attempts to access his own children. "Since I left this house I've hardly drunk a drop (of alcohol)," he tells her. "Why do you think that might be?"

As for her own children, they are daily shunted upstairs to the nursery to be supervised by housemaids. On one occasion she says the sound of her own daughter gaily playing in the garden "is quite intolerable" so the girl is sent in. Enid arranges tea parties for child members of her fan club, but her own children are sent up to the nursery, or they only catch glimpses of the party from the staircase.

It is so distressing watching Sinead Michael act as daughter Gillian, and Ramona Marquez play Imogen as, one afternoon, Gillian and Imogen are sitting in the nursery listening to a live broadcast on the radio from the BBC studios where their mother is being interviewed. When asked by the interviewer what is the secret of your success, Enid replies, "It's quite simple really. I am able to enter the child's world. Children need mothers. Mothers are the heart of any household. I try to spend as much time as I can with my two girls." At this point, the two girls listening to the radio look at each other incredulously, knowing it to be completely untrue. Shortly after this, the older girl, Gillian, is whisked off to boarding school, out of sight and out of mind. Imogen is left on her own to mope, totally bored.

Ramona Marquez plays her part effectively as a pitifully morose little girl (she had recently become darling of the British viewing public for her improvised role in the comedy series *Outnumbered*). One evening Mummy tells her, as a special treat, she will come up and read her a bedtime story. But we watch the lonely Imogen patiently sitting in bed with the book ready, but intuitively knowing Mummy will never come. After a while, in resigned despair, Imogen places the unread book on the bedside table switching off the bedside lamp, feeling barely better off than an orphan.

Enid then hooks up with another man, Kenneth Waters, played by Denis Lawson, and they get engaged. One morning Enid breezes into Imogen's bedroom. "I've got some wonderful news," says Mummy. But Imogen has already braced herself ready to be deflated as she is told that 'Uncle' Kenneth will be her new father. "Trust me," says Enid, just like a character from one of her adventure books, "New beginnings are always marvellous."

"But I just want my *old* daddy," whines Imogen.

Soon after, Imogen is sent off to boarding school to join her sister. Imogen throws back at her mother any last glimmer of tenderness: as they are leaving to catch a train, Imogen locks the car door to deny her mother the smug satisfaction of seeing her off from the station.

What hit hard was the wry satisfied smile on Enid's face as she read one of the fan mail letters from a little boy. "I wish you were my mother…we'd have so much fun!"

Why I felt so angry watching this programme was because the author, who I had admired and had grown up reading her books, was such a heartless mother herself, or at least that was how she was portrayed in this drama.

Much of her attitude to family was a reflection of her own upbringing. The film started by showing us Enid as a child of twelve, played by Alexandra Brain. We see twelve-year-old Enid having fun, going exploring with her own father. She didn't get on well with her own mother whom she despised, though she did love her father. So her world was shattered when after hearing an argument in the house the night before, her mother enters her bedroom in the morning saying, "Wake up. I've got something to tell you. Your father left." A despairing young Enid runs out of bed, racing into father's closet, only to find the coat hangers dangling limply in a bare empty wardrobe with every last trace of her father removed. She curls up like a foetus in the cupboard desolately reminiscing. A lifetime later she confides, "For years I thought it was my fault my father left. I thought I must have done something terribly wrong." This is a common worry among children who feel partly responsible for the broken home.

You would have thought she would have transferred the love she was denied as a child to her own children. Instead, the heartlessness of parenthood was perpetuated by her own inconsiderateness and selfishness, as she meted out the wrongs she felt as a child onto her own family. A family may be a utopian ideal, but when it is fractured it can become a miserable hell.

Rebelliousness

Rebelliousness is really an issue for older teenagers but the seed germinates as the younger teen strives for independence and its own identity. Fourteen-year-old Peggy Ann Garner shockingly stays out after 9pm and dares to wear off-the-shoulder outfits in *Junior Miss*. Oh, the daring! Oh, the rebelliousness! Oh, the scandal! But this was in 1945. This is the distant nightmare of many parents as they start to raise a family, and creates an unspannable chasm once the fearful age is reached. We see this as sultry Charlotte Gainsbourg yearns for the same freedom her older brother enjoys in *An Impudent Girl*, or Jean Louisa Kelly in *Uncle Buck* and Emma Robert in *Wild Child* who believe they are at an age when they can please themselves.

The child starts to become rebellious as rational independent thought evolves in the child's development, in tandem with puberty, and as the maturing child makes comparisons with the parents of his/her friends, who may be perceived as being "more understanding or less 'square'", and as he/she establishes an independent identity.[21] "I don't know what to do," says Judy's (Natalie Wood) father in *Rebel without a Cause*. "She'll outgrow it dear. It's just the age… It's just the age when nothing fits," reassures his wife.

Most films want to portray little children as charming and cute. When they are portrayed as obnoxious young teenagers it is often the older child actress who is called upon to perform. At sixteen, Evan Rachel Wood, playing Tracy, does this brilliantly in the teenage rebel movie *Thirteen* (2003). While happy in her sedate friendship clique, she is jealous of the other more popular girls who seem to receive attention and adoration from the unattainable lads, while she herself is ridiculed for her fashion sense. Chief among the girl idols is Evie, played by Nikki Reed, who as a thirteen-year-old schoolgirl also co-wrote the script.

Observing how Evie and her friends shoplift after school, Tracy is at first revolted; but when a woman inattentively sits next to her on a street bench more intent on her mobile phone, Tracy seizes the opportunity to steal her handbag, which turns out to be a treasure trove containing hundreds of dollars. Tracy takes this to Evie, and immediately they are best friends, shopping extravagantly in the top fashion malls. Tracy's downward spiral has begun, copying her idol's expensive habits, getting her tongue and navel pierced (despite being under aged), smoking cigarettes and dope, attending nightclubs, drinking booze.

Using a sob story of being abused at home, Evie moves in with Tracy, sharing her room. Here, confrontations with Tracy's mother (Holly Hunter) are defused by Evie by fabricating compliments to mum (as Patty McCormick does in *The Bad Seed*), and involving her in the latest fashion trends. She also offers Tracy's mother a sensual kiss on the lips, which both confuses the adult and endears her. Soon, Tracy too is snogging, not only with the hunky boys but also with Evie, so that 'lesbo kiss' becomes part of their vocabulary.

"This is not how I raised you," sighs a despairing mother as she witnesses Tracy's deterioration.

On-going through the film, is Tracy's alarming self-harm – opening the bathroom cabinet to find a razor with which to slit her arms (though she never attacks her wrists). No doubt, this initially had something to do with the breakup of her parents. Why she should continue this while befriending the most popular girl in school is not made clear. It is certainly not an act of bravado, for she keeps the scarring secretly hidden beneath her rolled down blouse sleeve. Maybe, like Natalie Wood in *Rebel without a Cause* she is finding, "Life is crushing in on me."

All the while there are distressing rows with mother, who reaches her wits end. Finally, mother goes berserk, trashing the kitchen, and ripping up the lino. She calls on her estranged husband to help. "She's starting to scare me," says mum on the phone to her ex-husband. But when father arrives, his wimpish conversational approach breaks no barriers.

In the end, mother decides Evie has to move out, but not before Evie's own mother pays a visit placing all the blame firmly on Tracy! "You're a really bad influence, Tracy. You cheat, you lie, you steal."

Tracy ultimately discovers the penalty for her association with Evie. She is left out of Evie's clique, her former friends don't want to take her back, and her abandonment of schoolwork means she will have to repeat seventh grade. The lesson directed at all teenagers is seldom heeded: if only she had known, eh!

Otto Frank proffered sensible advice to his frustrated teenage daughter who couldn't make sense of the world in *The Diary of Anne Frank*. "There's so little that we parents can do to help our children, honey. We can only try to set a good example; point the way. The rest, you must do yourself."

Sula Wolff notices that "adolescent rebellion is often exaggerated in children with excessive dependency needs, stemming from feelings of insecurity," and these extremes result as parents who themselves feel inadequate or threatened as parents "try to insist on continued conformity to their own standards."[22]

James Dean, as the classic *Rebel without a Cause* is one such youth, "hurt, lonely, and looking for kicks, and no one understands him,"[23] who complains that both parents contradict each other – the nagging wife and the inadequate husband. Like other 'rebellion' films, the child/youth alienation leads to dabbling in violence, drugs, promiscuous sex, even extremist religious or moral campaigns.

Some films angle in from a humorous stance: *Wild Child*, *Uncle Buck*. Others are in your face exploitative: *kids*, *Melissa P.* "You know those kind of brawls those drunken parties turn into. It's no place for kids," says Jim's father in *Rebel without a Cause* when he comes to collect him from the police station, while in *My American Cousin*, John Wildman is told "It's alright having a good time, but what about decency and responsibility." For Charlotte Coleman experimenting in lesbian sex in *Oranges are not the Only Fruit*, it was kicking against the rigidity of a strict religious upbringing.

The teenage years must be the most trying for parents fearful of the daily battles with their obnoxious progeny. John Conger hints at avoidance strategies by inferring that the successful parents are those who are "democratic, authoritative loving parents (especially those with relatively traditional values), who allow their children gradually increasing age-appropriate opportunities to 'test their wings'." Children of parents who are "overly-permissive or authoritarian and hostile" are likely to nurture rebellious adolescents who will, for example, develop serious drug problems.[24] The trouble for Jim (James Dean) in *Rebel without a Cause* is his parents' love is "smothering and artificial."[25] "You're tearing me apart!… You say one thing, he says another, and everybody changes back again," referring to the fickle hypocrisy of his mother and father.

Teenage actors don't just portray rebelliousness in the movies. Their own lives may be a one-act play, kicking against the exploitation of their over-indulgent parents. In Volume One (*Gender Roles and Themes*), we highlighted this as a problem. The ambitious parent thrusting her daughter into the limelight, whose childhood is one endless parade of beauty pageants, modelling, and auditions. That Brooke Shields, Eva Ionesco, and Tuesday Weld all split from their mothers in their teenage years hints at the reaction to the straitjackets their parents had imposed on them.

The Rejected Child

This must be the saddest situation in any family: when the child itself is raised unwanted and despised. This may be encountered where the child is adopted, as we shall see later in this volume, but when it is the natural birth parents who reject the child, this must be devastatingly heartless.

Here, it is the divisive issue of gender that raises its ugly head: the unwanted girl. Common in medieval or Asiatic cultures, where the female child is an encumbrance, a financial drain on family resources, to be married off at the earliest possibility, as in *Water*, or just sold off as in *Memoirs of a Geisha*. It is disheartening to discover its actuality in westernised households in the present day. Seldom is it the male child who is rejected.

"Koro, acknowledge your granddaughter," appeals his wife. The old man wishes the girl had never been born. Regrettably, the words are said in earshot of the eleven-year-old girl who had been devoted to her grandfather. The film is *Whale Rider*. The old man Koro is tribal chief of a Maori community who is frustrated by the emigration of his son from New Zealand to Germany, who had abandoned his child to be raised by the grandparents. So, the young girl had been brought up by grandparents who had wanted a boy to perpetuate the tribal traditions. "Take the girl," Koro says to his son on one of his rare visits back to New Zealand. "She's no use to me."

This devastating rejection of the granddaughter had its predecessor in the classic novel, *Heidi*, of which the 2005 version is the latest in a string of cinematic screenings. When Heidi returns from her forced sojourn in Frankfurt to Grandfather's isolated mountain hermitage, Max Von Sydow makes it clear that the nine-year-old girl is not welcome. Grandfather sends her away. But the orphaned girl has nowhere else to go having just made the trek of several hours from the valley bottom. Heidi resorts to sleeping in the barn along with the goats. Yet, at her young age she has rationalised her grandfather's rejection of her. "He was really hurt when I left… He only told me to leave because he was upset… I should never have gone with my aunt… I did try to run away, lots of times."

Like *Whale Rider*, the Spanish film *Alas de Mariposa* further develops this theme of the influential grandfather rejecting the newborn child because it is a girl, and not the desired boy – the heir that could prolong the male family line. But in this film the repercussions are tragically fatal. This movie opens with Grandfather impatiently waiting outside the maternity ward, futilely hoping for news of the birth of his first grandson. All his adult progeny, so far, have only provided unwanted granddaughters. So, when the nurse cheerfully comes into the waiting room to inform him he has a new granddaughter, he angrily turns the other way and leaves the hospital.

"I couldn't give you a son," the mother confesses to her husband, miserably.

But to the father, the child's gender is irrelevant, for this is his firstborn – a baby girl, Ami. "If we have a daughter, that's God's will. It's all right." Father is unconcerned. (Likewise, the father is unconcerned in *Bastard out of Carolina*. "Your mum's worried that if it's a girl I won't love it!" declares Bone's stepdad as they wait outside the maternity ward, before proceeding to sexually abuse his stepdaughter (Jena Malone).)

Unfortunately, the grandfather in *Alas de Mariposa* has moulded the wife's ambitions. "But a son! A father needs a man at his side," she tells her husband. With a girl, "Once she is married – who will remember your name?"

Still the father is unbowed. "A name is not important. What is important is to carry it with dignity."

Unfortunately, the wife Carmen carries the stigma with her as baby Ami grows into a six-year-old girl. The mother is rarely tender with the girl. If ever Ami is invited to kiss her mother, it is always 'a hairy kiss'; the girl's lips can never touch mother's face, but may only kiss her through a curtain of hair.

Neither does the grandfather show any love for the little girl, despite sharing the same house. At least in *Whale Rider*, Grandfather Koro was willing to dutifully raise the child, and the girl loved him back. But for Ami's grandfather, the infant is just an inconvenience. No wonder then, when Ami draws a family portrait, mum points out to her that granddad is missing from the picture.

Ami is always quiet, never laughs, and feels rejected. For a six-year-old she seems self-assured at answering questions with a precise, honest, but brief reply, as if she has learnt to avoid becoming committed to an intrusive conversation. In time, Ami learns to feign sleep in order to avoid a goodnight kiss.

When Carmen becomes pregnant again, the mother won't let her daughter feel her stomach lest in some fateful way that may affect the gender of the child forming in her womb. "So what if it's a boy, or a girl?" protests the father again. "It's still ours."

Ironically, it was the grandfather who had wanted the baby boy, but he dies just before the baby boy is born. When the new baby arrives, Ami is left in the waiting room, unwanted, forgotten, sadly sitting by herself. She is never invited in to enjoy her new baby brother. We see shots of mum, dad, and baby bonding, but Ami is never in them. Like the despised boy in *Times & Winds*, and like Enid Blyton's daughters, she is kept at arm's length.

Now the mother becomes over-protective of her new child. Ami is left out of the relationship. Whenever it is time to breast-feed the new baby, Ami is banished from the room. The mother becomes needlessly neurotic about her child, and has nightmares in which she sees Ami dropping the baby from the balcony. On one occasion, mother comes home worried, she sees the empty cot, and she can see Ami standing alone on the balcony. Putting two and two together, she angrily and brutally beats up the little girl, crying, "Where's my baby? Where's my baby?" only for father to appear from another room with the baby in his arms, unharmed.

On one occasion, Ami falls off a high stool badly injuring herself, and smashing open her skull, needing urgent attention. But the baby is crying, and the baby takes precedence. So Ami gets no love or attention from her mother at all. She curls up on her bed like a foetus and cries herself to sleep.

2. Families, Step-kids & Orphans

So it is made clear to the little girl, that now there is a new baby in the household, Ami is to be further distanced and rejected. No wonder she starts to hate both her mother and her baby brother. So when she is left alone with the TV still on – a film in which a man murders his wife by smothering her with a pillow – Ami naturally is tempted to follow the murderous example, taking a pillow to the baby's cot.

Of course, the death of the baby doesn't solve anything for Ami. Although it was seen as an accident, Ami grows up as an unwanted rejected child. "I have no children," claims the mother on one occasion, overlooking her daughter Ami.

Later in the film, Ami is now an older teenager. She comes home to a cold, unkempt, and unfriendly house. She has just been raped. Desperate for help, she cries to her momma, but she receives no comfort from that direction, and again curls up on her bed as a foetus, just as she did as a child.

FAMILY REUNIONS

"A hundred miles is not a long distance, except when it lies between the ones that you love," says Charles Ingalls in *The Little House on the Prairies*.

Two of our best-loved films (*Little Women* and *The Railway Children*) focus on the strength and resourcefulness of family members while they painfully wait for the return of a loved one.

Two film versions of *The Railway Children* have been made. The most popular tear-jerking version was in 1970, famous for a youthful Jenny Agutter playing the enterprising Bobby, and capturing one of the most dearly remembered piece of action in movie history as she spots her long-lost father on the railway platform, bursting into that famous tearful embrace. In 2000, Jemima Rooper took the role in the thirtieth anniversary re-make of the original film, with an equally moving copycat embrace of her returning father.

The filming begins in London with a happy family, the Waterburys: mother, father, and three children. Birthday boy has been unwrapping his presents and the girls help him play with his new toys. There is a knock on the door and father is carted off by two 'gentlemen' who have arrested him for alleged treason for which he is wrongfully convicted and sentenced to five years servitude. Mother has to be stoical about this and tries to hide the reality of the situation from the children. (Compare this with *The Night of the Hunter*, in which mother gets no opportunity to hide the facts from her two children, for John and Opal actually witness their father's arrest which leads ultimately to death-row.) The Waterburys have to sell their possessions in London to live frugally in the countryside, "simply and in reduced circumstances." "We have to play at being poor for a bit," says mother. A steam train takes them off to a cold dark rural residence – Three Chimneys – located in the 1970 film around Oxenhope and Haworth in Yorkshire, while in the 2000 remake around Sheffield Park in Sussex.

The three children are inventive in their adventures centred on the railway line that passes close to their house. But with the passage of time, the memory of father grows dim so that mother becomes concerned and asks Roberta (Bobby) why she doesn't ask about father anymore. Bobby responds by saying, "How long can you remember someone you really love, even if you can't see them or hear their voice?" Thus, the anguish of separation is intensified.

With the help of the influential railway controller, Bobby has been working behind her mother's back. Strings are pulled. A reprieved father is released from jail, and what follows is one of the most intensely moving reunions in movie history. The vision of father gradually takes shape on the railway platform as the mists of steam slowly clear, and Bobby races into the arms and embrace of her long-lost father, echoing those words which will remain famous through the decades for generations to come: "Daddy, my daddy!"

Frances Griffiths (Elizabeth Earl) gives an equally heart-wrenching sob of delight as she greets her father returning home from the First World War, missing in action presumed dead, in *Fairy Tale* (1997). She and her cousin Elsie (Florence Hoath) have just been blessed by the arrival of fairies in their bedroom, which materialise before their eyes. This should be the most exciting moment in an imaginative girl's childhood, but Frances has a premonition of something far more dear to her heart, as she hears a car door slam. She races down the stairs, opens the front door and disbelievingly races into the arms of the man standing there. "It's my daddy! It's my daddy!" Who needs fairies when you have guardian angels to care for you?

It is not just daughters who wait eagerly for a parent's return. Although *Empire of the Sun* does not have the same dramatic action of the girl racing into the arms of long-lost father, the reunion with the boy's parents is equally as powerful. The Japanese occupation of Shanghai is over; the expatriate children are all gathered in a warehouse, long since separated from their parents. A lorry load of adults arrive searching for their missing offspring. In the clamour, Jamie (Christian Bale) does not even recognise his parents at first, so traumatised has he been from the survival struggle. He has become a "calculating, almost feral creature."[26] He has that distant look that so epitomised the war-struck heroes from *The Deer Hunter*. Nor do his parents recognise him at first, either. Long gone is his immaculate school blazer and the well-kempt British demeanour. Now his face is ruddy, smeared with concentration camp grime, and he sports the stubborn scowl of someone who has been through hell and out the other side. Both child and mother have to double check, till it slowly dawns on Jamie who she is, before gripping his mother in an inseparable embrace, closing his eyes on the horrors he has seen, while the welled-up audience wring out their hankies. In admiration, director Steven Spielberg says of his lead lad, "I felt he was yearning for an escape even deeper than his mother's arms."[27]

The return of father from behind enemy lines is barely less subdued in *Five Children and It*. Freddie Highmore had used his last wish from the Psammead for the safe return of his father during World War Two. Like Colin in *The Secret Garden*, the lad is counting to twenty for a game of hide and seek with his sisters. On the count of twenty he opens his eyes, and there is dad standing before him. Soon the whole family are in a group hug, wish granted, miracle achieved.

In *The Parent Trap* we have eleven-year-old Annie James living in a posh part of London with her divorced mother, wondering why she doesn't have a dad, and wondering why the family photo has been ripped down the middle with father missing. In the vineyards of northern California we have eleven-year-old Hallie Parker living in a rambling ranch with divorced father wondering why she doesn't have a mother, and why the family photo has been ripped up with mother missing. This is a wonderful heart-warming film about a pair of identical twins separated at birth, but both by coincidence sent to the same summer camp in the American backwoods. The girls, both brilliantly played by Lindsay Lohan, or by Hayley Mills in an earlier version, see the mirror images of themselves and are surprised to discover they share the same birthday.

They put two and two together, including the two halves of the torn photograph and realise each is their long lost twin. "If your mum is my mum, and my dad is your dad, and we were both born on October 11th...."

They plot to switch identities and return home to the wrong family so they can meet their estranged parent for the first time in their life, with the intention of duping the parents to get back together again. As Hallie meets her unwitting mum for the first time, "I can't believe it's you... I've missed you so much...it's as if you've been away forever."

The film is a wonderful comedy with several tear-inducing moments, convincingly and seamlessly acted by Lindsay Lohan (1998) and Hayley Mills (1961) about the joys of a family re-uniting. Surely, it can soften the hearts of any parent in a strained relationship.

Why did the parents split up eleven years ago? Mother stormed out in a huff, boarded a 747, and as she says to her former partner, "you never came after me." When father sees this scenario repeating itself at the end of the film, he does chase her. "I made the mistake of not coming after you once before." While we dry our tears, they live as a happy re-united family (at least to the closing credits).

Usually family reunions are joyful affairs, but not always. Eleven-year-old Opal's father is absent in *Run the Wild Fields*, missing in action somewhere in the middle of the Pacific Ocean during World War Two. He has been away for so long Opal has really given up hope. Opal (Alexa Vega) stumbles across a drifter, Tom Walker. He has been badly mauled by some guard dogs. Between her and her mother, they help the injured man to their home where he can recuperate from his wounds. The man stays to help around their American farm. Though he is despised by the community who assume he is a war deserter, Opal and her mother put their faith in the man and gradually a bond grows between them. While other members of the community grieve as they receive telegrams about lost loved ones in the war, Opal intercepts a letter saying father has been found and will be returning home. For Opal this is bad news for it means her new friend Tom will have to move on, so like Jenny in *Driftwood* she hides the critical letter from her mother. When the truth is discovered Opal tearfully tells Tom, "I didn't want daddy to come home. Not now. I wanted you to be my daddy." But as Opal sleeps, Tom packs his bag and silently retreats from the house passing the real returning father on the lane.

In the Irish film *32A*, Ruth has been waiting a lifetime for a reunion with her father. Living in a one-parent household, she has been unaware of her father living in England, until out of the blue he tries to get in touch. She does not even know what her father looks like, but without letting her objecting mother know, she arranges a rendezvous with him under the town hall clock. She is too nervous to go by herself so she asks her friends to accompany her. However, the father also is nervous. Although he waits nearby watching the assembled posse of girls, he fails to make himself known to them. The girls get fed up waiting, so eventually drift away looking for a taxi to take them home. Father, however, re-finds his courage and drives in his own taxi to find them (he is a taxi driver himself). Father picks up the girls in his taxi and anonymously takes them to their home. "How did you know where we lived?" chirps one of the girls. "Hey Ruth, he's your dad!"

And so, Ruth gets to meet her father for the first time in her life. But this is not the emotional union we saw in *The Railway Children*. They do not even shake hands, let alone embrace. But father and daughter do share phone numbers and promise to keep in touch.

Searching for Family

This is the mission of the movie industry: the delicate child (inevitably the girl-child) is lost and needs to be brought back to the homestead. For Meredith Salenger in *The Journey of Natty Gann* this involves travelling independently across a continent, for Amudha and for Dakota Fanning there is the terror of a war-zone in *A Peck on the Cheek* and *The War of the Worlds*, while for Yella Rottländer in *Alice in the Cities* it incorporates a wild goose chase around Germany. While the journey is usually made to achieve a happy reconciliation, for Vincent Rottiers in *Les Diables* the motive is retribution. Others, like Eileen Quinn in *Annie* (1982), just hang around hoping the parents will come for her: "I have been dreaming of my folks for as long as I can remember and I have just got to find them."

Where the journey is a solitary one this shows the indomitable spirit of the resolute child, as Natty Gann, April in *Dustbin Baby*, and Dorothy in Oz exemplify. While adventures for boys are expeditions, the girl's journey is more purposeful: a reunification with lost family members. Boys do seek out lost parents, as *Les Diables*, *War of the Worlds*, and *In Search of the Castaways* prove, but only when accompanying a younger or more vulnerable female sibling. Notwithstanding that Natty is a tomboy, April is streetwise, and *Castaway*'s Mary Grant has the confidence of an intrepid explorer; the message is the same however it is couched: the world is bad and full of dangers, whether that be the motorist who tries to molest Natty Gann, the suicide bomber who befriends Amudha in *Peck on the Cheek*, the wicked witch who attacks Dorothy or the evil wheelers who chase her in *Return to Oz*.

Inevitably, the solitary girl has to put her faith in a stranger as a travelling companion and hope to high heaven they are trustworthy: for *Alice in the Cities* this is the German compatriot Philip, for Natty Gann it is John Cusack; both single adult males, equally lonely, and fortunately not predatory (despite Alice sharing the bathroom with a naked man, and Natty's farewell kiss with Cusack). For Dorothy Gale, her companions are more fanciful: the Tinman, Scarecrow, Pumpkinhead and Tik Tok.[28]

Fourteen-year-old Natty (Meredith Salenger) sets out to find her father in *The Journey of Natty Gann*. The year is 1935. Chicago is gripped by the American Depression, making work hard to find. Natty Gann's widower father, Sol, is offered work far away at a logging camp in Washington State, and he has to leave that very day. He only has time to leave a message with his landlady to inform his daughter Natty and to send her out west to follow him. Natty makes her way to the rail-track where she joins several other men trying to jump train to search for work out west. She is told she is wasting her time. "You know, once your folks are gone, you may think they are coming back, but they figure out pretty quick they are better off where they are," (a statement that becomes a reality in the Japanese drama *Nobody Knows* as we describe in the next section, *Kids in Charge*). Yet, Natty is not dispirited. Her travels get her mixed up with a variety of vagrants all desperate for food and finance gained by any ill-gotten means. "You gotta wise up if you're going to make it, kid." She gets caught by the authorities, shut up in an orphanage, escapes, is involved in a train crash, molested by a man while hitch-hiking, but rescues a maltreated dog which becomes her faithful companion and guard.

A similarly frenzied search for family members takes place in *The War of the Worlds*. In this film, father and daughter, with reluctant son, are frantically trying to relocate their family and are willing to face terrifying dangers to accomplish their goal. This is an exciting film in which Dakota Fanning and her father, played by Tom Cruise, escape the annihilating forces of the invading Martians as described in H G Wells classic novel. Ten-year-old Dakota plays Rachel who, along with her older brother Robbie (Justin Chatwin), has been dropped off at their divorced father's home in New York while mother goes off to Boston for the weekend to visit the grandmother. "Take care of our kids," says mum's boyfriend as they depart. "You've got nothing to worry about!" says Tom Cruise rather prematurely. The Martians inconveniently choose this weekend to attack the Earth causing widespread devastation and death, immobilising all vehicles, clocks and other mechanical and electrical devices.

Others share equally eventful episodes. Amudha in *A Peck on the Cheek (Kannathil Mutthamittal)*, searching for her birth mother in Sri Lankan jungles, gets caught up in gunfire, bombings and warfare. For Mary Grant (Hayley Mills) in *In Search of the Castaways*, her search involves crossing the Andes Mountains, gliding down a glacier during an avalanche, camping out in an Ombu tree to evade Pampas floods, being captured by Maoris, diverting a volcanic eruption, and finally defeating a gang of gun-running pirates, all accompanied by the optimistic crooning of Maurice Chevalier, before finally locating her father.

The trail seldom goes cold, because the belief of the searcher is unbreakable. Only April's search in *Dustbin Baby* is fruitless. Author Jacqueline Wilson at least has her finger on the reality pulse. Mary Grant, however, is forever optimistic. "Captain Grant is our father, and he is not dead," protests Hayley Mills. John Wayne is relentless in his quest to find his niece (Natalie Wood) in *The Searchers*. Arthur Lestrange spends a lifetime searching the coral seas of the Pacific for his marooned son and niece in *The Blue Lagoon*. Some crazed parents even persist in their neurotic search after their child's death. Elliot Hoover (Anthony Hopkins) searching for his daughter *Audrey Rose* for eleven years in the realm of psychics in the hope she has been reincarnated; Donald Sutherland and Julie Christie chasing after the spectre of their infant daughter through the dim passageways and canals of Venice in *Don't Look Now*; Bill Pullman enduring the hauntings and humiliations of the three mischievous ghosts if it will only lead to a reunification with his dead wife in *Casper*. "Yesss! There's a girl in my bed," chirrups the lonely boy-ghost Casper as he sees the adolescent daughter (Christina Ricci) lying there.

In the case of Natty Gann, her father had given up hope of being reunited with his daughter. Having been handed her lost purse by the police, which was found where the train crashed, he fears the worst. So he volunteers for the most dangerous job on the logging camp, neglecting his own safety – a topper, removing the crown of a tree before it is felled.

But the girl is not easily daunted. Natty arrives in Seattle. From there, she is directed into the mountains to find dad's logging camp. Of course, there are always obstacles to her progress, but hey, this is a Disney film so she always overcomes them. At last, she reaches within one mile of dad's camp when there is an almighty explosion; the camp has to be rapidly evacuated along with the wounded. A despairing Natty looks aghast as she stands in the middle of the dirt track as the vehicle carrying her father careers past her down the hill and out of sight. But just as Jane Eyre hears the despairing anguished cry of Mr Rochester carried over the miles of moorland, so too Natty's dad has heard her distressed yell. The truck pulls up further round the bend. Dad gets off and walks back up the hill into the line of sight of his unbelieving daughter. Natty Gann and father race to each other, embrace, and the credits roll.

In Search of the Castaways is a film in which two children sail the oceans in search of their shipwrecked father. In the end, they rescue Captain Grant and the family are reunited: "Mary, Robert…. Oh my dear children, how I've prayed for this day…. so that's my little girl." Wilfred Hyde White and Maurice Chevalier blubber into their handkerchiefs. "By George, they do grow up!"

As for Tom Cruise in *War of the Worlds* who risked his own life and went to hell and back to save his kids, all he gets is an indistinct 'thank-you' whispered by the ex-wife.

A Peck on the Cheek (Kannathil Mutthamittal) tackles seriously the reunion between a child and the mother she never knew she had, the child travelling from safety into a war zone to satisfy her curiosity. This is a Sri Lankan film unashamedly trying to influence and rectify the ethnic instability among the Tamil community. Little Amudha grows up living in India in a happy loving family with both a caring mother and a doting father.

On her ninth birthday, against the advice of their older, wiser relatives, Amudha's parents decide she is now old enough to be told she is actually adopted, the daughter of a Sri Lankan refugee. Overnight, this changes the character of the little girl. Having been a happy carefree child all her life, now suddenly she feels unloved and rejected, and feels antagonism towards her from her siblings. She stops trusting her adopted mother. She becomes unhappy, and on two occasions, she runs away in order to try to discover the identity of her true mother.

Her parents decide the only way to cheer her up and resolve things is to fly out with her to Sri Lanka so that Amudha can meet face to face with her birth mother. However, Sri Lanka is in the grips of a civil war, and her birth mother is one of the mercenaries. Little Amudha does get to meet her natural mother briefly. She tearfully greets her, but with suspicion. But after a minute she is back in the arms of her adopted parents, her curiosity having been assuaged. I guess we have to assume she is again endeared to her adopted parents, if not to her siblings. This is a powerful film, despite its Bollywood-style musicality.

Alice in the Cities is a German film. A lone traveller, Philip, is stranded at New York airport unable to get a flight for Amsterdam until tomorrow. At the checkout desk, he meets a woman with her nine-year-old daughter, Alice, played by Yella Rottländer. They discover they are booked on the same flight tomorrow, so since neither have a place to stay they share accommodation for the night. The next day, the man agrees to accompany the girl to the airport while mother has to go on an errand somewhere. But at the time of the flight mother does not show up. She has left a message asking the man to go on ahead to Amsterdam where the mother will catch up with them. So the man has no alternative but to accompany Alice to Europe.

Of course, on arriving at Amsterdam airport no one turns up to claim the girl. Philip acquires a car and drives Alice across Germany to where she thinks grandmother lives. But the girl cannot remember the address, and thus begins a long adventure zigzagging across Germany searching cities for the possible house that fits the description in Alice's memory.

As a last resort, they go to the police station to report the situation. Unbeknown to them, the authorities have already been searching for the girl, having been reported missing. In the police station waiting-room the girl gets lonely so leaves and re-finds her companion, just like Tatum O'Neal does at the end of *Paper Moon*, and they drive off together again. So now, the police-search for the girl intensifies. The man is now seen as an abductor. They are caught on a car ferry. The man tries ineffectually to explain the predicament. Alice is put on a train to re-cross Germany no doubt to be reunited with a frantic family.

However there is no real conviction of concern on the part of the family. We do not even see the child being reunited. Instead, the child is depicted as a piece of inconvenient luggage that does not even have an adequate luggage label. The film, made in 1970's Germany, is reflecting the demise of the family and making a moral statement about the inadequacy of a single parent with an unwanted child. As for Philip, her escort, "What else can a man do when he gets stuck with a kid and can't get rid of her?" poses Wim Wenders the director. He becomes in a strange way a father to the young girl, a surrogate. In real life the girl actress, Yella, had grown up without a father herself, so in the film she was experiencing for the first time in her life what it was like to have a substitute father-figure.

Worse than a piece of luggage, in *Les Diables* the boy Joseph feels he has been dumped like a piece of garbage. *Les Diables* is about two orphaned children who, having been institutionalised, are desperate to find their family home and the mother who abandoned them at birth. This is a grim and hard-hitting French tale tinged with moments of tenderness and pathos. Vincent Rottiers stars as twelve-year-old Joseph – a tough for his age, street-wise, close-cropped lad who was taken into care soon after he was born. His mother abandoned him on the streets of Marseilles along with his older sister, Chloë.

Chloë is autistic. She has no mental capacity of her own so she is totally dependent on her younger brother. Adèle Haenel, who was later to star in *Water Lilies,* convincingly plays the mentally traumatised girl. She carries a bag of coloured glass chips with her everywhere, which she uses to make a collage of a villa. Chloë is mute, so Joseph assumes the collage to be what she recalls of her childhood home. So, for the umpteenth time in their lives, they are running away, searching for the building in Chloë's mind that hopefully will lead them to their parents. However, I am not sure they wish to be re-united with their parents. More likely, they are wanting revenge.

"You want to find your parents?" asks the supervisor of the children's home.

Joseph spits his reply: "They dumped us like garbage."

"Do you think when you find your house your sister will be normal again?" And Joseph realises the impossibility of his unrealistic dream.

While staying at the orphanage, mother is tracked down, and a meeting is arranged. (Dad is already dead.) When mum arrives she tries to approach Joseph, but he is unable to provide a hug. Joseph, head bowed and cowering, reluctantly holds out his hand, thinking that shaking hands may be more appropriate, but mum turns away and cries. During the course of this contact, mum explains that she left Joseph with Chloë who just happened to be there in the street. "Chloë is not your sister." This is a little confusing, and certainly, Joseph cannot accept this. Chloë being mentally deficient is oblivious to the proceedings.

Joseph cannot face up to this truth so he grabs Chloë by the hand, snatches mum's handbag and the couple run away again. Mother's handbag contains her address so that is where they head. But they are disappointed by what they find – it is certainly not the house in Chloë's picture. It slowly dawns on him that maybe what mum says is true, that Chloë is not his sister. As they continue their travels, they spot a house identical to the collage that Chloë keeps making. He realises this must be Chloë's original home so he decides to take revenge on Chloë's parents. He breaks into the house, spreads petrol around, and sets the house on fire. But as they step back to admire the flames he notices all the other houses in the street are identical to the one he just set alight.

An equally disturbing story featuring children going on a journey is the Italian film *Stolen Children.* But in this film, the children are being removed from their abusive mother to be taken across country to an orphanage in the south of Italy. For the past two years, eleven-year-old Rosetta had been rented out by her mother, for prostitution. The police have rescued the girl and her brother, Luciano. They are being accompanied by a young police officer as they travel by train across Italy. As in *Alice in the Cities,* there is no excitement on the part of the children as they travel closer to their destination. The opposite seems to be true. The relationship with the escort is strengthened and a bond of love ties the children to him. Also, as in *Alice in the Cities* the ending is inconclusive in *Stolen Children.* We never see the children warmly cosseted in their new abode. The policeman advises the children, "You need to love each other. No one else will help you."

Similar words of advice are offered in *Hidden Places* when grandmother tells Becky and her brother: "You need to be angels for each other, to give each other strength and consolation." And in *Lemony Snicket's A Series of Unfortunate Events,* the orphans Violet and Klaus are told, "Take care of each other with kindness, bravery and selflessness…. As long as you have each other you have your family and your home."

Thwarted Searches

April Johnson is an orphan desperately struggling to discover her birth parents, in Jacqueline Wilson's brilliantly moving tale of a child continually being rejected and shunted from one foster parent to the next. This story is *Dustbin Baby* which, although not actually a film, was a full-length drama made for British TV.

In the course of one day, her fourteenth birthday, April reflects on her life so far in a succession of foster and children's homes, thinking about the abuse she received by her first foster parents when she was an infant, how she was bullied in another children's home, and how she became rebellious one day at school when the history lesson was about family trees. The thoughtless teacher had asked the students to write about their parents, grandparents and so forth. April, abandoned as a baby, was found in a dustbin by a café owner. She had no parents, no family tree to cherish or research so she stubbornly refused. However, the insensitive teacher had a change of heart, apologised, and ended up adopting April when she retired. "April," she is told, "You don't have to leave here ever. This is your home." Instead of just having a black plastic bin liner to cart her few meagre possessions in, at last she has her own room, her own chest of drawers, and a wardrobe.

However, despite now having a stable home she is still curious to know who her real birth parents are. She bunks off school and goes in search of the café where she was found as a baby. There she finds a message waiting for her, painted on to the side of one of the refuse bins: "Baby – telephone this number." April phones the number expecting to hear her real mother's voice for the first time in her life. It is a man's voice that answers. "Are you my dad?" April tentatively asks. But the number is the home of the pizza man who found April fourteen years ago. They meet and he is able to explain how he first found her crying her heart out in the trash bin, and how lovely and cute she looked as a baby. However, it is at this point she realises "I guess I will never know my real mum. I could sit next to her on a bus, or brush past her in a shop and neither of us would ever know."

"Are you my dad?" seems to be a recurring theme in child-focused films. We have met the phrase in *Dustbin Baby* and later it is reiterated in *Mischief Night*. In *Paper Moon*, as Addie is being ferried by Moses to her aunt's house, she also asks him if he is her father. Seems a natural question since the man turned up out of the blue to attend her mother's funeral, the only fellow to do so. "I wish I could tell you I was your pa but it just ain't like that." (These parts were being played by Tatum and Ryan O'Neal, who were in real life daughter and father).

The Ice Palace again re-iterates the desire to find out about a lost father. Unn is a desperately lonely Norwegian girl who has trouble making friends at school. "Why don't you play with the rest of us?" asks Siss, her only friend. "I told you never to ask me that," insists eleven-year-old Unn, who seems to be wracked with guilt by a trouble we can only guess at. She has recently lost her mother and now lives a solitary, bored life with her aunt. The secretive undressing game she plays with her only friend is disturbing. She locks the door in case her aunt intrudes. Unn is keen to confide in her friend: "My mum wasn't married … did you know who my father was?" she asks her friend as if maybe Siss had heard some rumour that had so far evaded Unn. Whatever this deep trauma was, Unn wanders off the next day on the way to school into the deep frozen

106

Norwegian wilderness where she gets lost in the magical maze of ice tunnels, until she collapses from exhaustion and dies slowly of the cold.

The Child as Matchmaker

This is more likely to be the girl's role in films with happy endings. The family, deprived of one parent, is only too keen to procure a replacement. Most typically, the daughter of a widowed mum yearns for a new father, or the son of a widower wants to find a new mother. Boys, however, are more suspicious of the new stepparent, as we discover later in the section on *interlopers*. There are some one-parented families, usually those comprising a multitude of children, who are only too happy to find a new mother, as in *Nanny McPhee*, or *The Sound of Music*. The housemaid or the convent nun, anyone will do, as long as it is not the obnoxious suitor that Colin Firth or Christopher Plummer are currently courting, replacing them with someone they know and love. Ten-year-old Gaby Hoffman even chats up a stranger on the ferry in *Man Without a Face* on the look out for a new dad. "I'm only trying to help mum," she claims.

Chitty Chitty Bang Bang is, in essence, just a magical conveyance for providing two headstrong but lonely individuals (Caractacus Potts and Truly Scrumptious) with an instant family comprising two lovable kids: Jeremy and Jemima. The kids were overly keen to adopt Sally Ann Howes as their new mother, this despite her being a nosy parker, and constantly reprimanding them for truanting from school. "Do I need anyone to help me raise my children?" Dick Van Dyke objects sarcastically. And yet eight-year-old Heather Ripley rounds off father's magical story with a fairy tale ending proposed as a question, "and daddy and Truly were married and they all lived happily ever after?"

There are many happy-clappy films in which the daughter, living with single mum, dreams of having a father as well. This was the dream of Natalie Wood and also Mara Wilson, both of whom played seven-year-old Susan Walker in the two versions of *Miracle on 34th Street* (in 1947 and 1994). If only mum would marry the nice man Fred Galley who lives next door. Into their lives stumbles Kris Kringle, the real Santa Claus, who is living in an old people's home in New York. But little Susan is a sceptic, brought up by her mother to only believe in the real tangible world with no make-believe. So, the only way Susan will believe in Santa is if he magically provides a father, a wonderful house with a garden and a swing. Can you guess how this film turns out? I'm getting my wish list sent to Santa right now. "Faith is believing things when commonsense tells you not to."

Santa seems to have quite a responsibility as far as matrimony is concerned. Hallie (Thora Birch) makes a similar request to Santa Claus in *All I want for Christmas*: that their separated mum and dad will re-marry. "You can't ask Santa Claus for that," derides her brother (Ethan Randall).

"Why not?"

"Because he's a fat, jolly guy, not a marriage counsellor."

Nevertheless, undaunted, nine-year-old Thora Birch seeks out Santa at Macy's and settles on to Leslie Nielson's lap. "That's a pretty tall order!" declares Santa, as the girl whispers her wish list.

2. Families, Step-kids & Orphans

But as Christmas Eve arrives, through sabotage and deviousness on the part of the kids, the match is re-made, and the audience get to realise dreams can come true in films, if not in real life.

This 'let's get a fella for my mum' is pursued in *Bad News Bears*, too. Amanda Whurlizer played by Tatum O'Neil lives with single mother. "Why don't you marry my mum?" she says to her mum's ex-partner Mr Buttermaker, played by Walter Matthau in the 1976 version. Sammi Kane Kraft asks the same question of Billy Bob Thornton in 2005. Neither matchmaker is successful.

The string of girls matchmaking a partner for their single parent include Natalie Wood who is instrumental in bringing a couple together in *Driftwood*, as does Abigail Breslin in *No Reservations*. Both girls help smooth over initial tensions between each couple until that important question is popped. In *Curly Sue*, Alisan Porter pairs up her fellow drifter James Belushi with the lawyer who has taken pity on the destitute twosome.

In *Home Sweet Homicide*, siblings Peggy Ann Garner, Dean Stockwell, and Connie Marshall try to set up their widowed mother with Randolph Scott, while more recently, Jadin Gould and Abigail Mavity try to get a date for their widowed dad in *A Kiss at Midnight*. The younger sister, Cassie, who had no recollection of her dead mother, was happy with the status quo. But the older sister, Jennifer, was at the age of having "issues she needs to discuss with a female." The girls find a perfect match and secretly manipulate a date for their dad. Everything is perfect, until both adults discover each are the head of their own rival dating agencies. Then the perfect match breaks, and young Cassie cries in despair, "I thought she was going to be our new mum."

Though it is rare for a boy to have the role of matchmaker, this does happen in *Paradise* (1991). A married couple (Melanie Griffith and Don Johnson) virtually live apart ever since the death of their three-year-old son. Then the son (Elijah Wood) of a friend arrives on vacation. The boy acts as a soundboard to bounce off their thoughts and recollections, and unwittingly brings the couple close again as the adult-child bond grows and the couple see what they have been missing.

Five-year-old, Max (Justin Cooper), performs a similar role in *Liar Liar* (1997). Jim Carrey makes a warm-hearted but unreliable dad, always too busy, or too forgetful, to play with his son. It takes a magic wish over a birthday cake to reform the character of lawyer dad, just in time before mum boards a plane with a new lover.

The dispenser of magic in *Blue Butterfly* seems to be the elusive *Blue Morpho* persistently pursued by terminally ill paraplegic Marc Donato. "Why are you so obsessed with finding me a partner?" his mum asks him. If the butterfly can provide a miracle cure for his cancerous tumour, it can't be such a hard task to link up mum with the entomologist who is leading their expedition.

Alas, with most of these films, the magic ingredient is, well, magic. All these films ever do is play with our emotions, suggesting that dreams may come true, when in reality, they are dashed against the rocks of disharmony, rift and violence.

BROKEN HOMES

For film directors, an easy way to evoke sympathy from the viewer is to feature a child from a broken home, the desolate orphan desperately wanting to locate its father or mother. A child is vulnerable, a girl child even more so, seemingly. Screenwriters and authors hope to be off to a winning start if they can feature a vulnerable child who demands sympathy from us.

There are some films that are genuinely about orphans or depicting children from broken homes, reflecting life in a realistic fashion, and the whole film quite rightly addresses the hardships and loneliness of the children coming to terms with their situation. *Dustbin Baby*, *Peck on the Cheek*, *Kramer v Kramer*, and *Heidi* are just a few examples. But there are a whole host of films that inform us about the broken home almost as an aside. In such films, the fact that the child is from a broken home adds nothing to the story line. The child could have as easily been scripted from a two-parent family, but the director is out to compel us to watch the film more sympathetically because the child is from a broken home. It is used as a flippant aside in *Explorers* as Ethan Hawke asks his friend, "What are your folks like?" and River Phoenix has his chance to tell us of the missing adult. At least it is explained more fully in *Now and Then* as Gaby Hoffman wails, "I really miss my dad."

In *Russkies*, Leaf Phoenix mopes to his younger sister (Summer Phoenix), "Dad's downstairs. They're signing the divorce papers." This is a fun adventure about a trio of American kids capturing a Russian spy – but inevitably we have the unnecessary injection of family spat to twist the reality of domestic harmony.

Earlier in this book, I stated that in real life, 62% of children live with both their birth parents in the UK or US. Yet what is depicted in the movies are families broken, with children brought up by stepparents in blended households, or by single mothers and fathers. According to the movies only 29% live with their birth parents: a veritable twisting of the facts. See Table (i) for corroboration of these statistics.

What goaded me into researching this anomaly was an obscure South African film, *The Little Unicorn*. I am sorry to pick this out as an example, but for me it was the final straw in a stack of movies about parentless kids. *The Little Unicorn* unashamedly depicts eleven-year-old Polly (Brittney Bomann) as an orphan cared for jointly by both her kindly granddad and her uncaring thoughtless Aunt Lucy, then packed off to a girls' boarding school, despite Polly being happy with her friends at the state primary school.

This is an example of a film where the scriptwriter blatantly wanted the girl to be an orphan, to evoke sympathy from the audience. Polly could easily have been living with mum and dad when they decide it is time for her to go to boarding school, but no, she has to be an orphan to give greater impact to her dilemma. We could throw the same accusation at *The Wizard of Oz*, except in the case of Oz, the scriptwriter is only adhering to the storyline of Frank Baum's classic story. Would we be equally fond of this movie had Dorothy been whisked away from mum and dad?

A similar assertion can be made about *Jumanji*. Kirsten Dunst plays Judy, moving into a new house with her brother and her aunty – the parents having died in a car crash in Canada. However, in this case the scriptwriters didn't make them orphans to evoke pity. Instead, they derive humour from it, as Judy tries to fool the estate agent who is showing them around a property that her parents were uncaring. "We barely knew our parents," she fibs. "They were always away – skiing in St Moritz, or gambling in Monte Carlo, exploring darkest Africa. We don't even know if they loved us." But later on, she tries a different sob story with someone else, but her dupe fails. Even so, this distraction of being recently orphaned adds nothing to the adventure story.

I realise that in today's society there are a lot of broken homes, and many children are no longer living with their natural birth parents, and that following the two world wars there were a lot of children with parents who had died. But this is disproportionately reflected in movies. The vast majority of films with child actors feature a boy or girl from a parentless family.

Obviously there are films in which the child grows up with its natural birth mother and father – *Charlotte's Web*, *The Five Pennies*, *Great Balls of Fire*, *My American Cousin*, *Snow Day*, *The Virgin Spring* to name some at random, but comparisons can be drawn by referring to Table (i). In a sample of 500 films which feature child actors, all of which I have referred to in this series of books, 71% do not live with both birth parents, leaving only 29% of the films depicting a child being raised by both birth parents. From this sample of 500 films, 112 (26%) depict the child raised by the mother alone (or with a stepdad), 79 (18%) raised by the single-father (or with a stepmum), 39 (9%) live with other relatives (uncles/aunts, etc), while 77 (18%) are fostered, living in orphanages, or running wild with no parental supervision. There is also a small number of films featured in this series in which the family structure is ambiguous and these are listed at the end of Table (i).

The majority of films play on our emotions by having the child from a broken home, whether this is because one parent has died, or the parents are divorced, or the child is an orphan. We have already pointed an accusatory finger at the best-loved children's film of all time. Dorothy in *The Wizard of Oz* does not live with her parents. At the start of the film, Dorothy, played by the legendary Judy Garland, is restless and runs away from the homeliness of Aunt Em's farmstead mainly to prevent her little dog, Toto, from being put down. [28a] But as every soaked handkerchief that has accompanied the viewer watching this film can bear witness, "There is no place like home." As she is whisked away to Oz, her only concern is to be reunited with her family.

Aunt Em was only trying to dutifully do her best for her niece. Considerable self-sacrifice is required to raise someone else's child. This may be offered grumpily as the aunt helps raise the children in *Whistle down the Wind* or *Tiger Bay* (both standing in to raise Hayley Mills). Later in this volume, we confront those situations where the stepparents are reluctant providers. Usually the substitute parent is well motivated, but the adopted child just does not recognise the love and sacrifice.

"I'm not your son," complains Jason James Richter to the kindly foster parents with whom this obnoxious brat has been place in *Free Willy*. The boy had joined his gang members to raid restaurants for food, and a van delivering an enormous iced birthday cake. Arrested for breaking and entering the North-West Adventure Park, the lad is put to work clearing off the graffiti he has spray-painted onto the whale's viewing tank. Although this is just a side issue, the movie shows how difficult it is, and how much patience is needed to look after a bewildered thirteen-year-old whose only love he wants is from the mother who abandoned him six years back. "My mum's coming back for me," he says storming off. But she never does.

"Sharon's adopted – but I'm still her mother," protests Mrs DaSilva in *Silent Hill*, optimistically. Although orphans can integrate into the fold of a family, a part of the child's soul lies elsewhere. In *Silent Hill*, Jodelle Ferland delves into the horror world of her ancestors, causing horror and despair to the guardian mother as she explores a ghostly underworld in search of her parallel past. *Dustbin Baby* portrays April's heart-breaking search for her roots on her fourteenth birthday.

In the fun comedy *Grounded*, all of the six children are from divorced families. The six unaccompanied children are at the airport on Christmas Eve because they are being shunted from one divorced partner to the other. They cause havoc as they use the airport terminal as an adventure playground. When asked how the children managed to lead the airport staff on a merry dance Spencer (Dyllan Christopher) says, "Divorced kids are just more resourceful, that's all."

Whatever the past history, the child has to make the best nest he/she can from the materials he has been left. Although Aunt Em's pad is not glittery like Oz, for Dorothy it is the only home she has. "We're your only family now," nine-year-old Chiyo (Suzuka Ohgo) is told after her parents have sold her to the *Okiya* in *Memoirs of a Geisha*. "This is your home now!" is echoed in the Indian film *Water* (2005) as eight-year-old Chuyia is locked into the *ashram*, a home for widows, while in *Innocence* (2004) as Iris (Zoe Anclair) asks, "When do I get to go home?" she is told, "This is your home." This phrase recurs in *Zombies: Wicked Little Things*. A widowed mother has just moved into an abandoned house with her two daughters. The place is dilapidated, filthy, nothing works, and the door is smeared with blood. "I want to go home," cries Scout Taylor-Compton. "This is your home," mother has to tell her.

The Single Mother / Missing Father-Figure

There are 13.7 million single-parent families in the USA raising 22 million children. [28b] In the UK there are approx 2 million one-parent families (comprising 3 million children), which represents 25% of households. 90% of these are raised by the single mum. [29] This raises ambiguities for children as they question the absence of a father-figure. Questions like "When is daddy coming home?" or "Who is my dad?" are commonly used by scriptwriters seeking empathy from the viewer.

"He's not coming home, is he?" observes the infant Laurie Lee in *Cider with Rosie*. His older sisters had assured the boy, "Father will be home soon. Yes, he'll be home soon." But the father finds the distractions of the city have a greater hold over him than his family. Toto (Salvatore Cascio) arrives at the same conclusion in *Cinema Paradiso*. "If the war is over, why doesn't dad come back?" he asks his mum. But the question is rhetorical. "I know why," declares the boy. "He's dead."

Likewise, Ben (Asher Metchik) in *Freaky Friday* (1995) asks, "When is dad coming back?"

"They've been divorced for two years, you nerd," responds his obnoxious sister (Gaby Hoffman[30]). "Won't you ever get it out of your thick skull he's not coming back?" This is the natural response of a distraught girl who feels she has to hide her real emotions, being reluctant to admit she is missing dad too.

A similar concern about 'where is father' is raised in the Swedish film *My Life as a Dog*. Twelve-year-old Ingemar (Anton Glanzelius) tells his girlfriend/playmate he has to go away to his uncle's while mum recuperates from a hospital operation. "Where's your dad?" asks the girl (Melinda Kinnaman).

"He's loading bananas at the Equator," he tells her.

"Dad's have obligations, too," she retorts. "He should be here to look after you."

"Yes, but who would load the bananas if he wasn't there?" says Ingemar obviously justifying his argument by repeating an excuse his father had probably used with him.

For Kimberley (Holly Kenny) in *Mischief Night*, growing up in the multicultural community of Leeds in Yorkshire, she had never even known her father. "Who's mi dad?" she probes. "I can't be a Paki if I'm white." Mum is a beautiful blond, and eleven-year-old Kimberley is similarly pretty with sharp blue eyes and long blond hair. "I ain't told her the truth about her dad. Maybe I should have," muses mother. Because mum has transient relationships with Asian men, Kimberley starts to consider the possibility that her birth father may be a Pakistani man. Amusingly, this Arian-looking white girl believingly pronounces, "I'm a Paki, aren't I?" Hidden among mum's things she finds her birth certificate. It says "Father unknown." Understandably, she is told, "We're your family. That's all that matters." In *The Missing* (2003), when Evan Rachel Wood enquires about her father, mother admits she does not even know who the father is: "I didn't get chance to see his face." Assumedly, she had been raped in her frontier homestead in New Mexico.

This leads us to consider what the role of the sexualised male in a partnership is perceived to be. For twelve-year-old Violet (played by Brooke Shields) in *Pretty Baby*, brought up in a brothel, the fatherless daughter of one of the prostitutes, the only value in men-folk is to pay her mother for services rendered. As Italian police cop Antonio says to young Luciano in *Stolen Children*, when enquiring about the boy's absent father, "Some father! He makes babies then disappears." Abigail Breslin makes a similar observation in her role in *My Sister's Keeper*: "Most babies are coincidences… a result of drunken evenings and a lack of birth control. The only people who have trouble making babies are those who actually plan for them." The police cop in *Case 39* makes a comment about both the neglectful parents of Jodelle Ferland. "People have kids, then they decide they don't want to be parents anymore. Then the kids grow up thinking it's their fault."

So what are the detriments for a child living in a fatherless family? Psychologists claim fatherless families give rise to various social and psychological issues ranging from bullying, lack of a role model, to psychological disorders. Further, children from single-parent families are at greater risk of poverty, more likely to have poorer health, and many people hold the unproven view that children of sole parents present a 'major cause of societal ills'[31] due to their involvement in crime and drug taking. Certainly, it is raised as an issue in *Free Willy* with Jason James Richter forced into care following a delinquent phase.

"If your mother can't control you, the court will," Heather Ann Foster is told in *Urban Ghost Story* perpetuating the belief that children from broken homes are more likely to be in trouble with the law. But a mother bringing up a single kid can be hampered in a far more terrifying way. Linda Blair who plays Regan MacNeil in *The Exorcist* is the only daughter of a single mum. As Regan develops abnormal psychiatric behaviour, the doctor blames it on separation from her father, which has in medical jargon induced a nervous reaction of hyper-kinetic activity (but of course, we who have witnessed the exorcism of her devil know otherwise). The psychotic behaviour of Anna Madders (Charlotte Burke) in *Paperhouse* was attributed to the absentee father. In *Nobody Knows*, the absentee father was the one blamed for the lack of schooling for the youngsters: "Your father was the selfish one, disappearing like that." This is a favourite tool of the psychotherapist: to blame childhood traumas back to an adverse relationship with the father (or lack of one).

Yet *Nobody Knows* also painted the virtues of needing a father in a household – the absentee role model. Kyoko is told, "Besides when you don't have a daddy they bully you at school." This is just the crutch needed for bullied twelve-year-old Marcus (Nicholas Hoult) in *About a Boy*. The boy seeks out predatory single male, Hugh Grant, both for consolation after the suicide bid by his own mother, and as a place to escape to – somewhere to chill out by watching tele, just to evade his tearful mum. Mum on her own is not good enough: "It's a bit hard for you to love me when you're dead!" spits the boy. The advantages of surrogate fatherhood are displayed as Grant, like a scapegoat, provides the backing support for the lad's karaoke rendition at the school concert.

Knowing this support of a father-figure to be so crucial to a child, Jack McElhone's mother in *Dear Frankie* maintains the pretence that the man has not abandoned his child but is taking a daily interest in his well-being. In reality, father has long since disappeared while mother stalwartly strives to raise her child alone. Yet the mother guiltily feels the need to pretend to her son that all is well – that father has not given up on his little boy. Mother has fabricated a story that daddy has simply gone away to sea. She has even invented the name of the boat: the *Accra*. Then she goes down to the library where she fabricates a detailed letter to her boy, Frankie, describing the presumed journey the father is taking, while the boy writes back to the non-existent father. So enthusiastic does the boy become, he puts pins into the map on his bedroom wall to show where the boat has docked.

Unbeknown to mother, there is a real ship called the *Accra*, and it is docking tomorrow in Glasgow's port of Greenock where the family live. Frankie is excited that at long last the nine-year-old can meet his pa again, the first time since he was three. Gran tells mum, "Tell Frankie the truth. He must know what his daddy was." But mother ignores this piece of commonsense. Mother now digs an even deeper hole for herself: she pays a man – a stranger – to masquerade as Frankie's long-lost father. So effective is the man's charade that man and boy quickly bond. Frankie proudly announces in the Chippy, "This is my dad!"

The boat leaves two days later. Boy and man make their tearful goodbyes. The film does not have the expected happy ending. Mum and stranger don't fall in love, despite the obvious signs. Not long after, Frankie's real dad dies so mum is able to break the news with some relief. But Frankie has already worked it out. He has two dads.

Meanwhile, in the absence of father, the single mother has to carry on alone, dispensing love and lunch boxes as the children are waved off to school, and steeling herself for the evening battles, squabbles and tantrums as they return. "It's not easy being a mother," complains Cher to Winona Ryder in *Mermaids*. "It's not like you came along with a set of instructions." The daughter desperately wants to confide in her mother about the emotional changes taking place in her teenage years, but she can't vocalise her problems. "Why don't you talk to your daughter?" asks Bob Hoskins after the girl has run away. Cher replies, "I'm her mother. She's the last person I expect to talk to! She's a teenager. I'm surprised she even talks at all!"

In real life, the father is most usually absent due to divorce/separation (for example, *Enid*, *Thirteen*, *War of the Worlds* (2005)). In *Melody* the father is in prison.

But the picture painted in films suggests a high ratio of absentee fathers resulting from the death of the father (as in *Akeelah and the Bee*, *Flightplan*, *Jack Frost*). Part of this may be the influence of war films, or films made in the post war era. Maybe it is sentimentalising the domestic situation, or maybe it is acknowledging reserve about depicting the shame of divorce.

113

In *Doctor Zhivago*, most of the children seem to be fatherless. From Omar Sharif's own son, Tarek, playing the part of Yuri at eight years old, attending his parents' funeral, to Lara's daughter, Lucy Westmore, who had never met her father, the feared military leader Strelnikov. Even the youthful orphan played by Rita Tushingham was unaware her father was the revered poet, Yuri Zhivago.

The single mother struggles on alone, and the movie business helps us admire her for that. In *Hidden Places*, single mum, Eliza, struggles to maintain the orange plantation at the time of the American Depression, her kids foregoing school until the harvest is picked. But help is at hand from the hunky drifter, Gabriel Harper. In *Hideous Kinky*, Kate Winslet plays a mother of two girls who has fled to Morocco to be separated from her husband. They expect support money to arrive from the father, but it rarely comes, so the family have to subsist by going native. It is inevitable, when mum teams up with Moroccan Bilal, that Bea (nine-year-old Bella Riza) whispers in his ear, "Bilal, are you my daddy now?" The 1959 movie *Imitation of Life* also features single mother (Lana Turner) anxious as her daughter goes missing on the beach, only to be rescued by a free-lance photographer who is only too willing to become stepdad.

The movie industry is full of single mothers struggling through the trial of child rearing until along comes a genial father-figure to help with the chores. Table (i) lists the examples reviewed for this series of books. Even the notorious film *Lolita* has the child, Dolores Hayes, coming from a one-parent family in which the predatory Humbert sidles his way into the relationship. He refers to Lolita's mum as "that Hayes woman" who presents the only barrier to his fulfilling his evil ambitions with the nymphet.

Single Fathers

If the image of the broken home is inflated in the movies, the depiction of the single-father is the most exaggerated of all. While children living with just their dad are found in 2½% of households in the real world,[32] in the movies the proportion is 18%.[33] Here, the movie's mission appears to be boasting how socially up-to-date it has become by tackling such a topical concept. But surely, we do not need one in every five films focusing on this when the reality should be one in every forty!

Usually the film depicts a man struggling to cope with the trials of raising kids single-handedly, often reprimanded for not giving enough time for his children as he juggles paternalistic chores with a day-job. "Dad, just forget it," rebukes his son (Peter Billingsley) in *Russkies*. "I thought I could talk to you man to man." "Mum would have had time," yells Vincent Kartheiser in *Alaska* (1996).

Invariably loitering in the background is a woman ready to jump in to save the day. Rarely is the man shown succeeding confidently with fatherhood. (Of course, by comparison, the single mother is never praised nor reprimanded for not having time to raise kids as well as maintain a day-job. *The Telegraph* on-line quotes single-dad, Sunil Vyas, who has a more balanced perspective: "Loads of single mums get through this stuff and no one applauds them, but when a man does it we're seen as incredible." He cites how he was admired by other parents for braiding his daughter's hair!)[34]

We cover more fully in Volume Seven the trauma of separation and divorce, and how children come to terms with an absentee parent. Here, we confine our deliberations to its aftermath, of the daily interactions between child and single dad.

The man who has parenthood thrust upon him reacts differently to a single mum. According to Cary Cooper, Professor of Psychology at Lancaster University, "Men cope with stressful situations by pushing on and getting the job done, but they avoid the emotional aspect of things. They won't ask for support, they internalise feelings and cut themselves off from the rest of the world." This is borne out by Beau Bridges' role in *Hidden in America*[35] of a single parent raising two children in poverty in Seattle in USA. That this is a *man* bringing up his kids seems to make the crisis more pertinent: a single mother raising an equivalent brood just would not have the same impact.

Beau Bridges stars as a father to two children. Mother has recently died of cancer. Because of poverty, they have had to scale down their family home and move into a dismal apartment in Seattle, where father struggles to keep a succession of jobs. But his pride prevents him from seeking charitable aid. Each day father comes home and there is little food for the children to eat. Some days he has to resort to raiding skips at the back of food outlets to get throwaway and out-of-date leftovers. Willa, the ten-year-old played by Jena Mallone, is often poorly, while her eleven-year-old brother (Shelton Dane), plays truant from school. Only a piece of altruism from the father of Willa's friend who happens to be a doctor provides any relief from their impoverishment.

In *A Father's Choice* two sisters are coming to terms with the death of their mother, yet resenting their father. The girls witness their mum being shot by burglars. Social services take them into care. "The girls need a secure and stable home as soon as possible," so the estranged father agrees to take custody of them, the older of the two, Kelly, being played by Michelle Trachtenberg, the younger Chrissie, by Yvonne Zima.

As in *Fly Away Home*, father is like a stranger to them. The girls are used to the cultured life of town, with fine clothes and easy living, but dad lives on a ranch in the country, which means dungarees, mud, and roughing-it. It takes a while for the new lifestyle to grow on them and for a love and trust to build between the threesome. The children show no joy when the estranged father arrives, just a certain inevitability. There are no hugs from the man, just an embarrassed, "I can't believe how much you have grown." Almost overnight, the man has to make rapid changes in his lifestyle from being a carefree rodeo rider to a responsible dad. "I'll have to start being their father again. How the hell do I do that?" Soon the man has a pile of laundry to cope with, as well as being locked out of the bathroom and foregoing his bedroom for the couch, and he, too, has to learn how to braid the young girl's hair.

Kelly taunts him for neglecting them when they were younger. "You just let us go," she complains.

"I did the best I could," replies father defensively.

"It was not good enough," she scoffs. "I hate you!" Chrissie joins in the tirade: "I want to go home." (Billy Elliot gives a similar tirade to his widower father after being banned from ballet classes: "I hate you. You're a bastard!")

Despite what the children think of him he claims, "I'll always be your father."

Then Kelly provides the stinging blow, "You don't know anything about being a father."

But the patience of time, the help of counselling sessions, and the birth of a foal help bond the family back together again, and the movie finishes with Michelle Trachtenberg screaming with delight as at last the three of them play and scuffle on the paddock.

There is a similar imposed reunion in *Fly Away Home*. Anna Paquin as Amy, living in New Zealand with her divorced mother is involved in a car crash. Mum is killed. Father (Jeff Daniels) takes custody of the child, but father lives in Canada. So the grieving girl not only has to come to terms with the death of her mother, she has to live with a virtual stranger, and in a foreign country. No wonder she resents the situation and the quirkiness of her father's weird Heath Robinson contraptions. In her case, a flock of hatchling geese give her purpose to life, and help to make the bond with her father.

Not all single-father movies are so emotionally challenging. When bachelor top sports star Joe Kingman is phoned by his receptionist at his luxury apartment in Boston that there is "a cute young lady waiting for him in the lobby," he replies, "Send her up, Larry," expecting a blind date from one of his many admirers. But what he finds outside is a diminutive eight-year-old, Peyton (Madison Pettis). "Hi! We've never met before," says the girl. "You were married to my mum. I'm your daughter." Welcome to Walt Disney's *Game Plan*.

The problem for the dumbstruck man is, he never knew he had a daughter, having split from his wife eight years ago. But when the girl shows him documentary evidence, her birth certificate becomes a warrant to turn his exclusive flat, filled with every gadget the bachelor pad would ever need, into a playroom. His special athlete's diet is wrong for a kid, he is turfed off his bed, his precious trophies get covered in glitter, his TV programmes get switched. A tutu is put on Spike the bulldog. He even has to downsize his top of the range sports car because there is no back seat for the girl to sit in. This is the last man in the world to be cut out as a father. As Peyton's ballet teacher tells the hunk, "I can see you're the kind of parent who thinks his life is more important than anyone else's."

As with all these relationships (that involve preteen girls), as Peyton is temporarily taken away from him, the reluctant Joe Kingman realises that she was the best thing that ever happened to him. "She's not a distraction. She's my daughter!" And the little girl replies. "I love you daddy. I want to come home."

An ambiguity arises when we consider the impact of the single-father on gender issues. In the case of girls, as she approaches puberty, the relationship with father tends to strengthen. Films featuring daughters wanting a new stepmother are rare, and we explore this further in the section on *Interlopers*. I would have thought that all those baffling emotional as well as biological changes in the pubertal female teen requires a female confederate to confide in, and yet in the movies the girl is lumbered with single dad as a source of intimate and embarrassing advice.

Tatum O'Neal cherished her relationship with her real-life father. "My relationship with my dad is extremely precious. Nobody in the world has a relationship like me and my dad."[36] But relationships with father in a single-parent household rarely run smoothly. Some commentators refer to a strained jealousy between the O'Neal father and daughter, the father being envious of the upstart child's Oscar nomination.

"God! I hate him," says Alex McKenna, playing Linda Ross in the Australian movie, *Joey* (1997).

"Who?"

"My father," says the thirteen-year-old girl.

The father, the American Ambassador, is mulling over in his head why his daughter has gone missing. He is trying to recollect his last conversation with the girl. "How many times did I say to her, 'I don't care?'" And he realises why his daughter is resentful of him, for throughout her life father had always stalled the girl's requests without explanation and using the remark "I don't care." Like Dan Aykroyd in *My Girl*, the father has always been too busy to listen to his child. When the girl eventually turns up, he apologies to her. "I'm so, so sorry," says her dad. The girl who had taken off on a spending spree across Sydney replies, "Yes, you will be when you get your credit card bill!"

Lindsay Lohan has a similar dialogue with her single-father in *Life-Size*. When, yet again, through pressure of work he had failed to turn up for her sports fixture, he apologises. "I should have been there, sorry." But his twelve-year-old daughter rebuffs him, "You wore out sorry a long time ago." When he confides to his work colleagues about his inadequacies as a father, they try to reassure him: "Don't be so hard on yourself, I'm sure she knows you love her."

There are many, many other films featuring children living with just a father (see Table (i)), challenging us to empathise with the motherless child, the father struggling on against the odds. "I've been nice to her. I've been tough on her. Nothing has worked," complains Jeff Daniels about his fourteen-year-old daughter (Anna Paquin) in *Fly Away Home*. "I'm no better a father now than I was when she was three."

Unlike the girl living with single mother wanting to discover their father, there seems not the same urgency for a child living with a single father to obtain a replacement mother, as if a strong relationship with a father is the goal for an adolescent girl. There are of course exceptions: the Von Trap family break this rule as Julie Andrews singsongs her way onto the scene in *The Sound of Music* and ultimately weds the struggling master of the house. Two daughters (Jadin Gould and Abigail Mavity) conspire to engineer a meeting between their dad and his rival dating agent in *A Kiss at Midnight*. And in *Driftwood*, Natalie Wood is only too keen for her guardian Walter Brennen to wed kind understanding Ruth Warrick. So it seems, in films depicting single-fathers, there is always a woman waiting in the wings, ready to come to the rescue of the seemingly impotent father.

The role of the woman in the wings is seemingly to bring order into the chaos. She may simply be a housekeeper (for Gregory Peck in *To Kill a Mockingbird*, or Woopi Goldberg bonding with Tina Majorino in *Corrina, Corrina*. "Where you would be if you didn't have me, I don't know!" exclaims Hayley Mills' housekeeping aunt in *Whistle down the Wind*). In other movies, the woman may represent a love interest, a girlfriend for a lonely man. Invariably she is despised by the child, yet frequently ends up becoming the child's friend or confidant: Jamie Lee Curtis as Dan Aykroyd's assistant in *My Girl*, Catherine Keener providing emotional support for Colin Firth's distressed daughter (Perla Haney-Jardine) in *Genova*, Famke Janssen as consultant to Robert de Niro in *Hide and Seek* (2005) to try to diagnose the childhood trauma of Dakota Fanning. All these women are at first dispassionately shunned by the adolescent loner, yet embraced when their usefulness to the child becomes apparent.

Charlotte Gainsbourg in *An Impudent Girl* is from a motherless family, too. Her widower father is often at a loss what to do with her. "I need three cups of coffee before I can talk to you!" Leone is a housekeeper who assists with daily chores and acts as a stand-in mother for the girl during daytime hours, but the pair are constantly bickering, and there is no love in their relationship. In fact, the woman says of the thirteen-year-old, "It'll be hard to find a girl more rotten than you." But the girl depends on the feminine support, and the dress for the evening piano recital is supplied.

Children recognise the sourness of loneliness as widowhood is thrust upon the father. "Fathers always turn bad once their wives die. They don't care anymore." This was the belief of the children in *Nanny McPhee*. "Father doesn't care for us anymore. Does he read to Chrissy like he used to? Does he play cricket with us like he used to? We hardly see him." The same accusations apply to the Banks' in *Mary Poppins*. If only they would come to the park to fly the kite with us, wishes Michael.

Yet, an abusive relationship with the children can develop as the widower grapples with his parental responsibilities. Bette Midler described her relationship with her single dad in *Beaches* (1988) as "Stifling." It is what caused Georgia Groome to flee her abusive father in *London to Brighton*. Dakota Fanning receives physical abuse at the hands of her father in both *A Secret Life of Bees* and *Hounddog*. "I'm going to kill my daddy one day," she despairs.

When disability wreaks its cruel havoc, then the separated father finds he just cannot face his kids. Riddled with terminal paralysis, Jean-Dominique (Mathieu Amalric) in his memoir *The Diving Bell and the Butterfly* tells his estranged wife don't bring the kids when she comes to visit him. Yet the man reflects, "Even a fraction of a dad is still a dad," as his three kids do finally gather round to kiss the paralysed man whose only physical ability is to blink yes and no. "Fathers' Day," he despairs. "The day when my son wipes the dribble from my lips."

Up until now, we have painted a despondent relationship between single fathers and daughters. Despite motherless girls seeming to be disinterested in acquiring a stepmother, the man-girl relationship seems to be strained. At least this is not the case in *A Little Princess*, in which Sara Crewe (Liesel Matthews) is happily ensconced in Simla, India, with her military father, Capt. Crewe. But even here, all is not well, for the war in Europe beckons, and the girl has to be packed off to a girls' school in New York. For Saoirse Ronan in *The Lovely Bones*, a father's love can reach beyond the grave, as he refuses to give up his demonic search for the paedophile who killed his daughter. "My murderer didn't understand how much a father could love his child." The single father struggling on alone deserves the honour of his kids and the respect of his community. "Stand up, your father's passing," little Scout and Jem Finch are told in *To Kill a Mockingbird*, after their single father, Atticus, had just defended a black man on a rape charge, a brave thing to do in a prejudiced white community.

The Unwanted Orphan / Institutionalised Kids

Charles Dickens opened the eyes of the world to the plight of orphaned children, particularly those trapped in the drudgery of the nineteenth century workhouse. In *Oliver Twist*, Barney Clark cowers dutifully with the rows of other unfortunates, unpicking the fibres from old rope. For him, childhood is one long existence of maltreatment and malnourishment, as his body is pummelled at the end of broom handles and brutal fists, and as his empty food bowl is appealingly raised to the heartless Mr Bumble. Even dog scraps are deemed too nourishing for him. It is not just the *character* of Oliver that is maltreated. Both actors, Mark Lester in *Oliver!* and

Barney Clark, are constantly mal-handled, lifted by the scruff of their necks, thrown across rooms, and shoved through windows and into cellars as if they themselves are just pieces of flotsam. Life with crooked Fagan was positively enhancing compared with the drudgery of fostered enslavement.

Only barely any better were the conditions at the Lowood orphanage that *Jane Eyre* ended up in. Following the death of her parents, an aunt (Mrs Reed) had assumed the responsibility of caring for the girl. But this old dragon ill-treats the girl and unjustly blames her for any misdemeanour. Yet, claims Mrs Reed, she has saved the girl from the workhouse.

When the proprietor of Lowood Institution visits, Jane jumps at the opportunity to escape the harsh Mrs Reed. Little does she realise what she has committed herself to, for the 'school for unfortunate orphaned girls' is cold, damp, poorly equipped, and there is a policy of starving the children on a minimal diet to keep them godly. The girl had to endure a childhood of bullying by the adults, and yet through endurance her life and luck are gradually turned around.

These are all life-affirming dramas. A childhood of drudgery is endured, but the waif always comes out on top. The movie wouldn't be entertainment otherwise. Jane Eyre marries abrasive Mr Rochester. Oliver is saved by an altruistic benefactor. The three 'musketeers' in *Slumdog Millionaire* end with their pockets full. *Annie* ends up fostered by billionaire Mr Warbucks. Even nine-year-old Chiyo, sold by her impoverished parents to the *Okiya*, in *Memoirs of a Geisha*, has some degree of respectability by the end of the film. We get to witness the traumas, the child exploitation, the lack of love, but there is always light at the end of the tunnel.

The three girls thrust into servitude in *The Magdalene Sisters* did however emerge bitter, traumatised and disturbed into their adult life. "What in God's name have we done to deserve this?" weeps Bernadette. "All the mortal sins in the world would not justify this place." What we don't see are the films about institutionalised kids – the Helen Burns of this world (left to die of consumption on the cold damp beds of Lowood Institution) – who enter destitute, and leave in a coffin.

The obscure French film, *Innocence* (2004), does however involve coffins for inmates. The situation at the orphan school is mysterious and secretive. Set in a chateau in the midst of remote Gallic woodland, with five satellite houses, the whole estate is surrounded by a high wall, with further forest beyond. The only access to the estate is by means of a long underground tunnel with a secret entrance. Every year, a new intake of seven-year-old orphans arrive, each mysteriously brought naked in a coffin, and every year the oldest eleven-year-old girls leave. The girls play together, swim, eat, and sleep with the minimal of adult supervision. It is an idyllic setting through all the seasons of the year, with the delights of the forest, the lake, the wildlife. But as in a menacing fairy tale some of the children are restless and feel trapped, and their bid for freedom ends in tragedy.

When little Iris arrives, disillusioned, and desperate to learn about her family and her brother, she talks to her older roommate. "I want to go home."

Bianca tells her, "This is your home."

"Won't someone fetch me?"

"No."

Although in general, life at the orphanage seems simple and happy we occasionally get glimpses of the seedier side of the institution. How is this place funded? All the girls are raised to be pretty, athletic, slender, healthy, wearing regulation white blouses and skimpy wrap-around gym skirts. Once a year, the headmistress auditions for the best ballet dancer who gets the chance to escape to the wider world. As well as their dancing being assessed, their stance, their curvature, and their teeth are inspected as if they were on an auction dais. Where were they going to be sent, one wonders?

In the end, we discover where the secretive older eleven-year-old girls go every night. They go to an auditorium, where the ogling public pay to watch their butterfly dance, as they gyrate and swirl sensually in their body clinging costumes and lithely roving legs. "The show pays the school fees," the girls are finally told. "Who else would pay for you?"

When the oldest girls finally reach twelve, they are quietly led out of the campus into the control of a different set of housekeepers for the next phase of their metamorphism.

In *Sundays & Cybele*, a father wants to be rid of his daughter completely by leaving her with a group of nuns at a French orphanage. In fact her grandmother had cared for Cybele, but now she wants to be relieved of her duties. Cybele (played by Patricia Gozzi) had only ever seen her father on three occasions, and this was one of those occasions – father is taking her to the orphanage. He is using a similar patter to that used by Dr. Stephen in *Driftwood*, trying to palm her off. "I don't want to go to the orphanage," protests Cybele, resisting as she is pulled out of the railway station.

"It's going to be nice," father dupes her. "You're going to have little friends, and then everyone will be kind to you, and on Sundays I'll come to see you". But he never does.

At the railway station, they ask directions from a stranger, Pierre, a war-scarred air pilot still haunted by his memory of killing an innocent girl while fighting in Indo-China. He has amnesia and is thought of by many in the community as a simpleton. Pierre follows the man and girl as they stumble along the dark streets to the austere orphanage gates and overhears as the little girl is handed over to the nuns. The nuns refuse to call the girl by such a heathen name (Cybele was an ancient Greek mystic). So they call her Françoise. "What's going to happen to me? My grandmother doesn't want me anymore. My mother has already abandoned me. My father – he has deserted me." And now the poor girl has even lost her own name.

On the Sunday, when father has failed to turn up and Françoise is hopefully waiting to be collected, Pierre passes the orphanage gates, calls to the nuns pretending to be Françoise's father, and the eleven-year-old girl is only too pleased to have someone come for her. In no time, this unloved girl has found a friend, their intimacy grows, and both look forward to their weekly excursions together every Sunday. Françoise pretends her real dad is dead. "Thank you God," she prays on her knees, "that my dad is dead because you have given me Pierre who is very much nicer." But their games and playfulness grow more intimate and they start to attract the stares and gossip of the locals and passers-by, and this friendship can't be allowed to continue unchecked.

Françoise in *Sundays & Cybele* was an orphan who had found in Pierre a potential father-figure, someone she could love and who would love her in return. But I think we know deep down really how this relationship would have panned out had the police not been called.

With all these despondent and seedy depictions of life for the institutionalised orphan, it becomes pleasurable to indulge in the delights of the heart-warming musical, *Annie*. Miss Hannigan is the drunken housekeeper in charge of New York's Hudson Street Home for Girls, which she runs with a rod of iron (when she is sober), but the moppets know how to exploit her when she is tipsy.

In *Annie* (1982), Eileen Quinn plays the orange mop-top, while Alicia Morton takes up the reins in the 1999 version (*Annie* (1999)). She and her fellow inmates are put through endless chores of mopping and polishing, folding sheets, and being woken at all hours by the temperamental Miss Hannigan. "No one ever cares for you or me when you're in an orphanage," they warble. But the girl gets her lucky break when billionaire Mr. Warbucks sends his secretary to fetch an orphan (to improve his image). Annie is put in the lap of luxury beyond her wildest dreams.

"Why any kid would want to be an orphan is beyond me!" declares Miss Hannigan.

The Fostered Child

Some altruistic carers genuinely wish to nurture the best from their new charges. Such were the plans of Esther's parents in *Orphan* (2009); or Jean Valjean's fostering of Cosette, the 'daughter of a whore', rescued by the successful factory boss in *Les Misérables*; kindly Mrs Wincovsky taking in Millie (Perdita Weeks), as the girl's mother is arrested for soliciting in *The Rag Nymph*; Miss Bean (Juliet Stevenson), the teacher who gives her student, April, a home in *Dustbin Baby*. But when the new guardian is a relative – an uncle, aunt, or (god forbid) a stepparent – then there is always an underlying reticence, assuming responsibility only because 'it is expected of them'.

The movie industry loves to exploit these scenarios, for these are the stuff of ageless fairy tales and folklore. Jane Eyre brought up by irritable Mrs Reed, falsely accused and virtually kept locked in her spooked bedroom. Gillie (Hayley Mills) whose guardian aunt moans, "All my life spent in scrimping and scraping to get a few pennies to bring you up decent, and this is how you repay me!" exasperated by the constant lying and petty thieving of the eleven-year-old, in *Tiger Bay*. Miles and Flora haunting the hollow halls of Bly because their uncle has washed his hands of them in *Turn of the Screw*. Mary Lennox sent to England to stay with an equally uncaring and negative uncle, Lord Craven of Misselthwaite Manor, in a secluded idyll surrounded by the bleak moorland of Yorkshire.

This is the tale of *The Secret Garden*. Ten-year-old Kate Maberly in 1993 and twelve-year-old Margaret O'Brien in 1949, both effectively play the crabby little girl robbed of her uncaring parents during an earthquake in India. "If only I could have known that in a few moments I was going to lose them forever." Sophy (Rebecca Hall) unwanted by her aunt and interfered with by uncle in *The Camomile Lawn*. Even *Harry Potter* dumped on the doorstep of 4 Privet Drive had to endure a boyhood of bullying from the demented Dursleys. *Heidi* unwanted by the aunt who was raising her, and rejected (at first) by grumpy intolerant grandfather. Only Abigail Breslin in *No Reservations* seemed to attract any love from her adoptive aunt.

Just when you expect to evoke pity for the orphaned child, novelist Eleanor Porter turns the situation upside down in *Pollyanna*. She doesn't allow us to pity the parentless eleven-year-old, "Father's gone to Heaven to be with mother," for Pollyanna is infused with the gift of seeing the world – including every mishap and disaster – through rose-tinted glasses. She has no living relatives other than the prim and distant Aunt Polly who lives cloistered in her grand country house having fallen out with locals. Now the grumpy woman has reluctantly agreed to accept

Pollyanna as her ward "because it's my duty." Yet, she recoils from the hugs and vivacity of her little niece.

Despite this, the irrepressible Pollyanna thinks, "I'm so lucky she wants to look after me." Pollyanna lives the 'glad game', finding something to be thankful for in every circumstance, and in the course of time spreads her infectious optimism into the whole community. And the girl is not dispirited by her aunt's negativity. "Aunt Polly is like an old nut. You just need to find a way to crack open the shell and the goodness is inside."

Other than Gillie in *Tiger Bay*, our examples of fostered children have ended up in the lap of luxury (but with the lack of love) in the vaulted halls of rich uncles and aunts. What of the benevolent stranger who takes in the waifs and strays? This was the lot of seven-year-old Jenny Hollingsworth (played by Natalie Wood) in *Driftwood*. The girl is both parentless and homeless. She had been living with her great grandfather as the only remaining inhabitants of Bullfrog Springs, an abandoned ghost town in the Nevada wilderness. All the miners had long since gone so all that remains are the vicar and his great granddaughter. "If ever I die," the old man had told the child, "you are to make your way to Panbucket and report to the sheriff." So now, she is wandering through the scrub of windblown driftwood to 'sillivization'.

A kindly doctor finds her sleeping rough, brings her home, bathes her, puts her to bed, and next day takes the ragamuffin to the store for some fresh new garments. "It's amazing what fine clothes can do!" he admires. Following a quarrel with the mayor's son, Jenny runs back to see her temporary guardian, Doctor Steve. "The Mayor's son said I was an orphan and I'm going to live in an orphanage. That isn't so is it, Doctor Stephen?"

"I'm afraid it is, but you won't mind. The orphanage is a nice place."

"No it's not. It's a horrible place."

"You probably won't have to stay there very long anyway because someone will come along and adopt you and take you home with them to live."

"Then why can't you adopt me?" says Jenny excitedly rising to meet his face. "Adopt me now, Doctor Steve."

He explains he can't. "I'm going away from here too, as soon as I get a letter I'm expecting." So it is in Jenny's interest to make sure that letter doesn't arrive. When the postman comes, she intercepts it, hiding the important letter so that Dr. Steve can't go away.

Dr Steve was lucky. He ended up adopting his delightful charge. But for the foster parents of Esther in *Orphan* (2009), the outcome was brutal. Isabelle Fuhrman plays nine-year-old Esther, a pretty, pony-tailed, articulate, polite, and artistically talented Russian immigrant. Her goal is to be ultimately rid of the devoted foster mother, so she can have her foster dad to herself. "I like it when it's just the two of us," she tells him. "You don't know how long I've waited for a dad like you."

By means of a sequence of planned accidents, various family members are hospitalised so that Esther can finally be alone with her new daddy. The nine-year-old girl cuddles up on the sofa with father, wearing one of mum's sexy dresses. "I love you daddy, I really love you." But father, despite being dazed with drink, is able to see through the seduction and spurns her. This is a horror movie; so expect plenty of knifings, with mother struggling to the bitter end to ultimately drown her adopted daughter once she has discovered the truth.

Of course, these strays are all girls. In the movies, boys are not careless enough to lose their parents to need any fostering. As always, it is the lonely, vulnerable girl who needs a home.

The fostered boy is a rarity in the movie world. Jesse (Jason James Richter) only stays with his guardians under protest in *Free Willy*, and had he not discovered his interest in cetaceans he would have headed for the streets long before. Mr Oakley (John Thaw) only accepts his evacuee boy (Nick Robinson) in *Goodnight Mr Tom* because there is nowhere else to send the lad. Heathcliffe, acquired as a 'playmate' for little Cathy in *Wuthering Heights* was mistreated with the horsewhips with which the youth had to stable. Orphaned Waldo (Luke Gallant) likewise was not allowed to encroach the homestead of his playmates where he was treated little better than a slave in *The Story of an African Farm* because he was black.

Only in *Under the Mud* do we find a Liverpudlian youth interacting with the family that has adopted him, or Bobby Driscoll tolerated by the gran that gives him a home in *So Dear to my Heart*, but the pet black lamb stays outside. He is told, "It's hard enough making ends meet. We can't afford to keep things that don't earn their keep."

Motives for adopting

What motives do parent/guardians have in adopting a child? For *Jane Eyre*, Mr Reed had promised his dying sister he would raise the child as one of the family. But both were now dead. So, for Mrs Reed (Jane Eyre's aunt), she had been lumbered with an unwanted child taken in by her husband, to raise alongside her own children. Jane Eyre was subsequently despised and bullied, and left barely better off than being in the workhouse.

The infant Harry Potter receives the same treatment at the hands of his muggle uncle and aunt, the Dursleys. Left as a baby on their door-step ("they are the only family he has"), Petunia and Vernon Dursley had no option but to raise the wizard orphan alongside their spoilt bullying son Dudley. "They are the worst sort of muggle imaginable," protests Professor McGonagall.

For *Pollyanna*, a disgruntled Aunt Polly adopted the girl solely as a family duty – there was no love involved. In all three cases the child was unwanted, an encumbrance. Others may have an ulterior motive: "I'll raise these orphans as if they were actually wanted," rants the furtive Uncle Olaf, knowing full well he is just about to get his wicked hands on the Baudelaire children's inheritance, in *Lemony Snicket's A Series of Unfortunate Events*.

So why was Jess adopted in *Oranges are not the Only Fruit*? "She's my joy!" says her mum. This new mother is a fundamentalist Pentecostal Christian, and she needs a child through whom she can demonstrate to others her religious fervour.

Someone observes to seven-year-old Jess, "Your mum must love you very much."

"Yes, she does," replies the girl, who doesn't know any better. "That's why she got me," as if she was an item on a shop shelf.

The drama goes on to show how unloving the mother is to the little girl – how Christian principles must come first. While others around her show the girl a little tenderness and hold her hand, mother (played by Geraldine McEwan in an award winning role) never does.

One day Jess' real mother turns up at the door wanting to see her little girl. "She's not your daughter," the impostor is firmly told. "She's mine! You were unfit to have a child. God gave her to me." And with that, she slams the door in the woman's face.

Jess asks, "Was that my real mother at the door?"

"I'm your real mother. She was just the carrying case that bore you."

At least Eddie Fortuna had his heart in the right place in *A Horse for Danny*. Uncle Eddie was an impoverished horse trainer when eleven-year-old Danielle's father died in a car crash. "Would you prefer to go live with your grandparents?" Danny replies, "I'd rather be boiled in oil than go live with my grandma." The uncle adopts the girl (played by Leelee Sobieski) but there are times when he thinks better of it: "I should not have brought you to a race circuit like this. You should be in a nice neighbourhood, with a nice school and play with children your own age."

Danny wants him to clarify: "You wish I wasn't here, Eddie, is that it?"

But no, uncle tenderly coaxes her to sit on his knee. "You're the best thing in my life," he tells her. "I wouldn't trade you for a million dollars." And they rub noses together.

Others, take on the role of foster parents for altruistic reasons, as in *Shattered Family* in which father of eight, Richard Crenna, adopts an eleven-year-old who had been passed between a variety of foster homes because the parents were neglectful and preferred the bottle. But Richard Crenna, who himself had a difficult childhood, realises "it could have been me," and this summarises his motive. He is responding to his wife's admonition: "There are a lot of lonely kids out there in the world, but we can't just bring them all home."

This film is historically pertinent for it is based on a true story of the eleven-year-old Gregory Kingsley who set a precedent by suing his parents for divorce. This sounds pretty drastic and heartless, particularly when you read how the US press twist the headlines. But here is an unhappy child, unwanted by his alcoholic parents, who had farmed him out to a succession of foster homes where he was bullied. Now, for the first time in his life, Gregory (Tom Guiry) has found a loving home environment, with new parents willing to adopt him. But the welfare agency and the birth parents try to thwart the process, believing that at all costs reunification with the birth parents is the best outcome.

The only way for the child to be adopted is by making legal history by taking his parents to court. Like Anna Fitzgerald in *My Sister's Keeper*, the lawyer argues that, "Children are not property. They are human beings that demand all the rights of the constitution." After hearing the evidence, the judge sides with the new foster parents, decreeing that "parental rights are earned through sacrifice, love and responsibility."

By contrast, two recently orphaned girls had to live with their "awful" aunt on a farmstead in the South African Karoo in *The Story of an African Farm*. The date is 1870 and it seemed the normal practice in those days for a relative to bring up orphaned children in the family. Usually there was some sort of financial inducement. In this case, ownership of the ranch once the girls have grown up. The girls, Lyndall and Em (played by Kasha Kropinski and Anneke Weidemann), hate their selfish auntie and cannot wait to leave. Like Mrs Reed in *Jane Eyre*, the stepmom has an over-inflated impression of her generosity. "Out!" she tells the girls after a plate is accidentally broken. "You ungrateful children! After all the love I've given you!"

This was precisely Uncle Vernon's attitude in *Harry Potter and the Chamber of Secrets*. He, like so many other guardians, felt permitted to mistreat their charges because they believe they are doing the child a favour just by having them in the house. "I wish you had been a little more grateful," he says to Harry Potter. "We've raised you since you were a baby. Given you food off our table. Even given you Dudley's second bedroom."

Harry apologises, "I'll be in my bedroom, making no noise and pretending I don't exist."

Sophy, in *The Camomile Lawn*, is the ten-year-old darling of her grown-up nephews and nieces in a pre-war cliff-top Cornish villa, "so small, so sweet, so quiet, so young, compared to the ebullient others, sweet innocence of youth," expresses Mary Wesley in the narrative to her book.[37] Yet, she was the 'little accident' of Uncle Richard's half sister who had since died. Now Uncle

Richard (played by Paul Eddington) is married to Aunt Helena (played by Felicity Kendal).[38] Neither of them was fond of the girl but had adopted her as their duty. Sophy confides to older niece Calypso how Uncle Richard used to put his hand up her skirt, but suggests it didn't trouble her; she just found it 'boring'. In wartime Britain when so many children were left parentless, and many others were re-housed to strangers as evacuees, this regrettably was part and parcel of many a little girl's 'coming-of-age'.

The orphan who can find a guardian who needs and loves the child is far preferable to them being adopted unwanted by an uncaring relative. Nine-year-old Aimee found such a guardian in Senora Emily Delahunty in *My House in Umbria*. A terrorist bomb had exploded on an Italian train killing Aimee's parents and badly injuring other travellers in the same railway carriage.

Emily Delahunty was one such passenger, who after their release from the hospital suggested the other victims come to her Italian villa to convalesce. Thus, Aimee was thrown together with a lonely old spinster (played by Maggie Smith), an elderly gentleman (played by comedian and character actor Ronnie Barker), and a political activist. They bond together feasting on the lush affluence of this idyllic retreat. Aimee is the centre of attention and Senora Emily realises she fills the void in her life restoring to her a purpose and meaning in life. "There has to be love in a person's life. No one can get by in life without giving or receiving it."

Eventually Aimee's American uncle is traced, and he comes to collect the girl. He has plans for enrolling her in an American boarding school. As soon as the girl is taken away, an aura of listlessness pervades the villa, as if its heart has been wrenched out. "Aimee gave us life, and spirit, and new hope for the future." There is a happy ending. The uncle realises how sad the girl has become now she has left the house in Umbria, reconsiders, and returns to the villa where Senora Emily is only too happy to adopt the child.

Just as a little child revived the spirit of a broken adult in *My House in Umbria* so too the grumpy reclusive grandfather is rejuvenated by the arrival of *Heidi* to his remote alpine shack in Switzerland. Heidi, as an orphan, had been raised for a time by an aunt.[39] But now that the aunt had been offered a job in Frankfurt, looking after the young child would be too onerous so she is being dragged up the mountain slopes to make the grandfather take his share of the paternal duties. The cantankerous old man at first refuses to take the girl, but when he realises the girl has nowhere else to go, he accepts her, and both their lives are changed as each depend on the other for love and company. Yet, how they gossip in the village down below! How awful for little Heidi to be left alone with *that* man!

In time, the man cannot visualise an existence without Heidi, but that day comes when the aunt returns and tricks Heidi into accompanying her to Frankfurt to be a play-mate for the crippled girl, Clara. After Heidi leaves, the old man is devastated. Heidi was like *Pollyanna*, a delightful girl who spread warmth and hope in everyone she came in contact with.

Other girls who seemed to slip happily into their new environment include Zoe, played by Abigail Breslin in *No Reservations*. She had been travelling with her mother to visit an aunt (Catherine Zeta Jones) when there is a car accident in which mum is killed and the child orphaned. So, single auntie adopts her. The film does not focus on the trauma of the accident, nor on the trials of being an orphan, but the girl helps smooth the difficult relationships that auntie has at work (she is a top chef), and brings her together with a new male chef (Aaron Eckhart).

In *The Turn of the Screw* (2009) and *The Innocents* (1961), we have two orphaned children, Flora (9) and Miles (10), living in grandeur but placed in vulnerable circumstances. These are two film versions of the same book by Henry James. Both their parents died during the Second World War. Their uncle has taken over reluctant guardianship of the two wards. They live in a grand mansion with servants and house-parents to care for them and they attend private boarding schools. But the uncle has washed his hands of them and rarely visits them – preferring to pay others to do that for him. So there is no love in their upbringing. The uncle appoints a governess, Miss Giddens,[40] to care for the children during their vacations. But this clever story is ambiguous. It is a ghost story but we are never quite sure whether there are ghosts manipulating the two children or whether the new governess is psychologically paranoid in believing the building to be haunted and the children to be possessed.

We are left to draw our own conclusions whether the governess succeeded in preventing two dead lovers from continuing their torrid love affair through the possessed bodies of the two children, or whether it was Miss Giddens' psychosis that caused the manslaughter of young Miles. Either way, one of the orphans dies in the care of its guardian.[41]

In *Jane Eyre*, we have another absentee guardian. Like the uncle in *The Turn of the Screw* washed his hands of the children turning them over to a governess, so too did Mr Rochester who had dutifully become the guardian of French girl Adele, and Jane Eyre was to be her governess. Now, Mr Rochester is a hero figure in English literature whereas the uncle of Miles and Flora is not, despite both abandoning responsibility for their charges to others; this is because of the actions of the governesses. Miss Giddens ends up killing one of her charges, whereas Jane Eyre nurtures her ward and has the sense to marry her master, Mr Rochester. And so Mr Rochester is adulated in literature circles, even though he callously abandoned the care of his ward (Adele) to others.

Joining the list of uncles who are dismissive of their responsibility to adopt, we have Great Uncle Matthew (Gum), played by Richard Griffiths in the made-for-TV drama of the Noel Streatfeild classic, *Balletshoes*. "You are this child's last surviving relative," the bachelor palaeontologist is told. But, the man complains, the child will be miserable staying in this lonely cold house stuffed full of fossils, like a museum. However, the little girl Sylvia (played by Skye Bennett) chirps up, "My parents are dead. I'd be miserable anywhere."

Reluctantly, the man takes in the child, and she grows up to be in charge of his household while he goes gallivanting off on worldwide fossil-collecting expeditions. Yet he cannot be too averse to adopting, for on three occasions when he returns he brings back a package from a remote part of the world: a baby in his holdall. The three babies grow up to be the heroines of the story, Pauline, Petrova and Posy Fossil (Emma Watson, Yasmin Paige, and Lucy Boynton).

Yet the man is the world's worst foster father. He is rarely at home, and disappears for over a decade while the girls are growing up. On his return, when Pauline is fifteen, he cries aghast. "Who are these women in my house? I left you three babies!" Like the uncle of Miles and Flora, Great Uncle Matthew believes he can callously throw his money at his charges and smugly let others do the caring, shirking the duty of love.

As Mrs. Ardvisson says to Ingemar in *My Life as a Dog*, "It's not easy being left over."

The Interloper – Resentment for the Substitute Parent

The child is naturally devastated when one of its parents leaves, whether that be through separation, divorce, or death. In Volume Seven (*Childhood Trauma*) we pursue this trauma more thoroughly. What adds to this disaster is mum's new boyfriend or dad's new girlfriend – the interloper – sidling his or her way into the family home. The child is almost programmed into opposing this intrusion, and will do whatever it can to prevent the new relationship from bonding. Throughout history, the image of stepparent has mushroomed into the child's greatest ogre.

The interloper is opposed by the child on two fronts: rejection of the concept of a stepparent with all the social stigma that attracts, reinforced by centuries of fairy tales in which the stepparent, in particular the stepmother is widely reviled (this despite the child welcoming the fairy godmother!). On the second front, the child believes acceptance of the new stepparent is sure to result in the final severance of contact with the absentee birth parent. The child realises there will now be no way that the distanced father (or mother) will ever return, and that their memory will inevitably be erased.

This is true of Thora Birch who runs away when mum's new man friend announces their engagement in *Paradise* (1991). She had never met her birth father. A new stepdad would render that an impossibility, in her eyes. In a desperate last ditch attempt to locate her birth father she goes to the skating rink where she thinks he is employed. But the man she believes may be dad just doesn't want to know.

"I just want my old dad back," whimpers Ramona Marquez when her mother breezes into her room to tell her she is to have a new father, in *Enid*. Ten-year-old Mae Whitman faces the same disappointment in *Hope Floats*. She is astute enough to realise where mum's new relationship with the local handyman will lead – estrangement from her daddy. 'Helpfully', the girl carries the man's toolkit out of the house to his car in the hope he can be out of their lives forever. In *An Unfinished Life*, it is a cop who is trying to edge his way into a family relationship. When mum arrives back at the ranch in the policeman's car, the eleven-year-old (Becca Gardner) complains, "I don't want him to stay here," knowing where the romance will inevitably lead.

"I really miss my dad," says Samantha (Gaby Hoffman) in *Now and Then*. It is bad enough her parents are going through a divorce proceeding, but when mother introduces her new boyfriend, "Samantha, I want you to meet a friend of mine," she on purpose makes the man uncomfortable. After spluttering wine down his shirt, he is found a discarded old shirt of dad's to wear, with dad's name still embroidered on it. For Gaby, this is the final straw, and she storms out from the interloper, slamming the door behind her.

If the new arrangements are successful, then the stepdad works to ingratiate himself on the child, bribing the girl with presents, taking the boy to the ballpark. In the case of *Liar, Liar*, Cary Elwes just does not have the vivacious energy of Max' real dad (Jim Carrey) and his attempt at 'the claw' becomes an embarrassing flop. Only on rare occasions is the stepdad accepted (in the movies): the persistence of Ice Cube succeeds in *Are We There Yet*, and the cop in *An Unfinished Life* eventually becomes a useful ally, Bob Hoskins becomes a father-figure to Winona Rider in *Mermaids*, while in *Angus, Thongs and Perfect Snogging* the impostor turns out to be gay and not a threat to the harmony of Georgia Groome's family after all. In *Lolita*, a vipers' nest of problems are released as Humbert wheedles his way into the affections of Dolores Hayes and her mother.

More likely, the child is being set up for a life of friction and misery if the intruder is not ousted. The daughters in *Enid* are packed off to boarding school, to be out of the way. In *The Amityville Horror* (2005), mummy's boy Billy Lutz (Jesse James) becomes the butt of the stepdad's masculine assertiveness, as he quakes in fear while the brute crashes the felling axe to the log the boy is holding. Mum ineffectually reassures him, "No one will ever replace your dad."

In *Munchie*, the boy Cage (Jaime McEnnan) is able to call on magical help to be rid of the unwanted boyfriend. The intruder seems to know the potential problems but approaches it in too brash a way: "I know you feel I'm taking your mother away from you," he tells the boy. "Come on, you've got to face the facts: we going to get married." When Cage sees mum and her new

2. Families, Step-kids & Orphans

boyfriend kissing it seems like the end of the world, but enter on stage his magic genie, a gnome named Munchie who has the power to put things right. But instead of mending the relationship between the two males, Munchie scares the man away, so Cage gets to be with just his mum again (irrespective of mum's feelings on the matter).

In *Pan's Labyrinth*, arrival of the new stepdad leads to a fatal confrontation between interloper and child. "When we meet the General I want you to call him father," says mother to her twelve-year-old daughter Ofelia (Ivana Baquero) as they head for the outpost of the military camp in the Spanish hills. Mum tries to cushion the inconvenience: "It's just a word, Ofelia, just a word." But the girl resents this new strict imposition into her life. "Why did you have to get married?" the girl asks her mother. Ofelia is so aloof from her new stepfather, she makes it plain to everyone who will listen to her: "He is not my father. My father was a tailor. He died in the war." Quite possibly, he was murdered by the general himself.

Only rarely is the new stepdad preferred over the birth father, an exception being in *2012* in which John Cusack is shunned by his kids, Morgan Lily and Liam James, because the new stepdad is more fun. Even when Cusack arrives to take his kids camping they find it miserably tedious. Fortunately for Cusack, the end of the world comes to his rescue as they make a frantic implausible bid to reach the arks that become their conveyances of salvation.

New stepmums don't fare any better. You would have thought that every child yearns for a mother. But in the movies, the memory of mum must never be substituted. The legend of the evil stepmother is extant and worms its way subliminally into the conscience of every child. This is a quandary imposed on single-parented children, who fear they will be neglected and abused by the new stepparent, a belief reinforced by every folk story told in the nursery. It was the fear of the children in *Nanny McPhee*. "All father cares about now is getting a nice new wife. Whoever he marries will be vile and treat us like slaves," complains twelve-year-old Thomas Sangster. They show Evangeline, their maid, a massive book of fairy tales. "There is not one stepmother in here who is not even half-way decent. Anyway, whoever likes other people's children?"

The adolescent girl, in particular, becomes hostile when another woman intrudes on her relationship with dad, whether that be Lewellen (Dakota Fanning) giving short-shrift to Robin Wright Penn in *Hounddog*, or Casey (Lindsay Lohan) exasperated by the arrival of Eve in *Life-Size*. "You stay away from him, got that!" she warns the woman after Casey catches her mesmerised father about to start kissing the impostor. Veda's (Anna Chlumsky) reaction to Jamie Lee Curtis in *My Girl* (1991) is to vindictively crash the bumper car into the woman, when dad and girlfriend announce their engagement at the funfair.

Dakota Fanning shows a similar resentment in *Hide and Seek* (2005). Her mother having committed suicide, the girl becomes negative towards any female who may be honing their way onto the widower, Robert de Niro. Dakota's character, Emily, misinterprets the action of one neighbour, a single mother who brings her own daughter to play with the lonely girl. Emily finds it more important to cling to mother's memory than have the opportunity to make new friends. She gouges out the face of the visiting girl's doll to show how unwelcome both are.

Amy (Anna Paquin) shares a similar resentment in *Fly Away Home*. Mother has died in a car crash, and now the thirteen-year-old has to move from New Zealand into her father's home in Canada. The man is almost a stranger to her, because the parents separated when she was three. He lives in a house filled with strange artistic contraptions. But she has just about got used to his quirks when another woman, Susan, walks through the front door. "Do you live here, too?" asks Anna Paquin, playing the young teenage Amy. The woman has to diplomatically affirm this.

Amy, unable to face yet another change in her lifestyle, goes off in a huff. She spends time in solitude, musing over her past. In the end, the woman has to endear herself to the girl. "Listen to me, Amy. I know I can never replace your mother. Nobody can. But if you let me, I can be your friend. And the first rule of friendship is they have to be able to trust each other." Eve had used a similar sentiment with Lindsay Lohan in *Life-Size*. She acknowledges, "Every girl deserves to have a mother, and no one can ever replace her for you."

There seems to be one magic formula for a woman hoping to achieve acceptance from a girl: helping the child apply make-up. It was a successful method for Eve in *Life-Size* as it was for Shelley in *My Girl* (1991). Even Julia Roberts found it gained her acceptance into the life of Jena Malone in *Stepmom*. Miss Trixy, too, thought this angle might work, in *Paper Moon*, but she was wrong. Addie (Tatum O'Neal) found Miss Trixy to be a threat interposing herself between the girl and Moses, the father-figure. When Miss Trixy hones in on the man, Addie arranges a compromising situation with a hotel receptionist instead, thus keeping Moses for herself. *Paper Moon* features real life father and daughter, Ryan and Tatum O'Neal, playing a pair of drifters getting by as confidence tricksters selling Bibles to people whose spouse had just died. But in the film, the man was not Addie's real dad.

Sometimes it is necessary to oppose an interloper. "You ain't my dad. You'll never be my dad." In a moment of bravado, John Harper stands up to the scary man who that day has just married his recently widowed mother. John is trying to protect his little sister, Pearl, with her rag doll, from this imposer who has sidled his way into their lives. What John hasn't realised is his new father is the serial murderer, the Rev Henry Powell, played scarily by Robert Mitchum in *The Night of the Hunter*. What John and Pearl also haven't realised is their mother is shortly to be the next victim in his quest to get his hands on the ten thousand dollars that only the children know the location of. Rev Powell couldn't care what his new son thinks. "You poor disgusting little wretch," says the man of the cloth. "Where's it hid, boy? Speak, or I'll cut your throat and leave you to drip like a hog in butchering time."

It is not often the scriptwriter allows the man to successfully worm his way into the household and stay, as Fred Galley is able to do in *Miracle of 34th Street*. Usually there is a severe price to be paid. In *Are We There Yet*, the children are definitely not looking for a replacement father. Twelve-year-old Lindsey and seven-year-old Kevin live with their mum in Portland, Oregon. Mum is divorced from her husband who has moved to Richmond. Father refused to accept his parental rights over the children. We later discover this is because the kids are such trouble. Although the kids miss their father, they will not tolerate any other men who date their mum.

This is a comedy film so we witness the *Home Alone* style pranks the kids play on any intruding men who try to break up the happy threesome. "I feel sorry for the next sucker who tries to make a move on mum," says Kevin. But into their lives comes Nick, played by Ice Cube, who catches mum's eye. Nick's sparkling brand-new car is used to ferry mum to and from work, to the supermarket, and to the airport. Ultimately he is talked into ferrying the two kids from Portland to Vancouver. Cue a journey full of mayhem and havoc as Nick's pride and joy is gradually scratched, dented, soiled, puked-on, trashed, crashed, and incinerated. Although his possessions are destroyed, his spirit isn't. As the delivery of the two children is made, the kids who disliked him at first are now so attached to him they won't let him go.

Trying to remember Mother/Father

All too quickly the memory of dead parents seem to fade, as Julie tells her brother in *The Cement Garden*, "I can't remember how it used to be when mum was alive." And as Abigail Breslin says in *Nim's Island* after father tries to recollect, "That's all my mother is to me now – just these stories."

The passage of time only allows us memories fogged by the veiling cobwebs of the past. The single snapshot dehumanises experiences as a frozen frame devoid of context and emotion. "You have rearranged your memories, stepped around the painful ones for so long until they seemed to disappear," lawyer Kate Weston is told by her brother in *Sacrifices of the Heart*. As a seven-year-old, Kate (played by Chase Wilmot) had opened the garage door only to find mum dead from carbon monoxide poisoning, a hosepipe attached to the car exhaust. Kate had raced inconsolably to her bedroom with helpless cries of "Mummy". Now in her adult life she has flashbacks of her mother's death. But, according to her brother, the skewing of time has left her with a misinformed blinkered memory of her parent's relationship. For Chuck (Nick Stahl) in *Man Without a Face*, his dreams of his dead father are equally blurred. "In my dreams… there is always a face I can't see, beyond the edge of the crowd."

Those that were infants when mother departed have the fewest recollections. In *To Kill a Mockingbird*, ten-year-old Jem (Philip Alford), and six-year-old Scout (played by ten-year-old Mary Badham in an Oscar nominated role) live with their widower lawyer father, Atticus Finch (Gregory Peck), in the film of Harper Lee's classic novel. Scout is too young to remember her mother. She was only two when mum died, but her older brother was six at the time. "Jem," Scout asks her brother as he is dozing off to sleep, "Was mum pretty? …. Did dad love her? …. Do you miss her?" Jem is tired and mumbles an affirmative "mmm" to each question. But father sitting outside on the veranda can hear their bedtime conversation, and a fond memory catches in his throat.

Pollyanna was equally excited to learn about her mother. "You knew my mother?" she asks in surprise, demanding of Mr. Pendleton, a grumpy old man she has rescued from a ditch, "What was she like?"

"She broke a few hearts, I can tell you." Mr Pendleton had been an admirer of her mum in younger days. "When she went away from here it's like someone turned out half the lights."

Orphaned *Heidi* asks a similar question after finding a photo while rummaging in Grandfather's trunk in their hovel high on the alpine pastures. "What was he like – my father?" Yet, the life-weary old recluse can only tell of him dying in an accident, along with her mother. Not a comforting tale for a forsaken child.

Kirsten Dunst playing Judy in *Jumanji* seems to mask her real feelings by making a joke out of it when asked about her parents. "Do you miss mum and dad," asks her younger brother.

"No!" says the girl.

"Liar!" replies the boy to the girl who has a reputation for telling fibs.

Her younger brother certainly does miss his parents. Every night he stares regretfully at a picture of them before hiding it under his pillow, just as Macaulay Culkin does after the unexpected absence of his family in *Home Alone* (1990), while Keke Palmer spends time each day staring at her dead father's photograph to gain inspiration and motivation, as well as sorrowing about past regrets, in *Akeelah and the Bee*. "God bless mummy and daddy, in Heaven," chants Danielle Harris as she kneels beside her bed in *Halloween 4*.

Even Dumbledore's mirror in *Harry Potter* does not allow the whole truth to be revealed. At his Hogwarts School, Harry Potter discovers a magic mirror, which allows him to see the deepest longings of his heart. Always inquisitive about his parents who had died when he was a baby, a vision of his parents appears before him in the mirror. "Mum! Dad!" he cries as he reaches out his arm to touch the vision, and he imagines their hands on his shoulder. Day after day, he returns to the mirror to burn their picture on his mind. Noticing how this is distracting Harry's studies, Professor Dumbledore decides to have the mirror moved. "It does not do to dwell on dreams and forget to live."

HOME ALONE: KIDS IN CHARGE

This is the premature dream of all kids – the wish to escape the constrictions of family life. The den at the bottom of the garden, the tree-house, the sleepover, all provide the first taste of freedom for the adventurous child. For the runaway, the challenges are so much greater. But the prodigal always has the chance to return to the safe haven of home when the big bad wolf materialises. Movies make such a lifestyle seem an idyllic temptation, and I am sure several children make their own bid for freedom influenced by what they have seen on film. In reality, however, life away from the nest is hard and dangerous. The big bad world *is* big and *is* bad. What follows are the fictional tales of children abandoned to isolation and experiencing the life and death struggle of coping alone.

Some children are orphaned and escape the attention of the authorities (*The Cement Garden*, *The Little Girl who lives down the Lane*), some escape from foster homes or orphanages, trying their luck at independent living (*Manny & Lo*, *Les Diables*); others are just neglected by the incompetence of the parent (*Nobody Knows*, *Lilya 4-ever*). In some, we find the child stranded alone as a consequence of war, as in *The Empire of the Sun*; while in *Lord of the Flies* and *Battle Royale* clusters of children find themselves abandoned on an island in an ultimate fight for survival.

The children in *Slumdog Millionaire* are left parentless after witnessing the slaughter of their parents in a religious feud. The stark reality of life in the Mumbai slums is hammered home to us as we observe the kids scrabble for any recyclable piece of rubbish from the city's waste tip, which becomes their new home. At least the three Indian 'musketeers' are rescued into an orphanage – but even here, the motives of their adult 'rescuers' are promiscuous and abusive. Brothers Salim and Jamal need all their wits to evade a life of abused beggars by becoming petty thieves. "What the hell can a Slumdog possibly know?" the teenage Jamal is derided. Alec Guinness alludes to a similar way of life as he narrates the introduction to *Doctor Zhivago*: "There were children in those days who lived off human flesh," though we don't see this in the film, the story line taking a different direction. But they do vividly re-emerge (as flesh-eating zombies) in *Wicked Little Things*.

Yet, the children from *Slumdog Millionaire* are far removed from the romanticised adventures of their fellow compatriot immortalised in Rudyard Kipling's *Kim*. Dean Stockwell makes life as an orphan waif seem a veritable wonderland as the roguish scallywag runs errands, scampers through back alleys, duping the affluent, and making friends with horse-traders, holy men, and the British colonialists. After both his expatriate parents had died, the infant ran away from his orphan school to live life carefree. He only agrees to endure the constraints of St Xavier's Boarding School because he made a promise to his holy man.

The Blue Lagoon

This scenario of the abandoned child is precisely what was in the mind of Henry de Vere Stacpoole when he wrote the children's classic *The Blue Lagoon*, also written around the same era that Kipling scripted *Kim*. This has thrice been turned into a film, firstly in 1949, then in 1980, followed by the miss-hit, *Return to the Blue Lagoon*, a rehash of the original.

The Blue Lagoon is about a journey made in the late nineteenth century in a sailing boat, which caught fire off the west coast of South America. Two eight-year-old children, Emmeline and Richard,[42] escape to the safety of a tropical island. Although they have a sailor, Paddy Button, to help them at first, he quickly succumbs to the temptation of a barrel of rum and drowns while drunk.

So, like the orphaned infant in *Greystoke*, the two young children are left alone to fend for themselves. They learn to gather fruits from the forest, fish in the teeming coral sea, run naked through the golden strand, swimming the lagoon, building a shelter from bamboos and palm fronds. Through trial and error, they discover what is good to eat, avoiding the 'never-wake-up-again' berries (until at the end of the film they eat them in a final suicide pact).

As they mature into adolescence and realise their bodies are changing – Emmeline's breast, Richard's muscles, Emmeline's first alarming blood-stained period, Richard's secretive masturbation – they discover intimacy and the delights of kissing, and eventually sex. Richard in his confusion wishes "a big book would drop out of the sky and fall in my hands right now," which would explain about all the strange changes that are happening to them.

Although they don't understand the mechanics of how a baby is conceived, Emmeline becomes pregnant and gives birth to a baby boy. Motherhood and nurture innately take over, she begins breast-feeding, and as a partnership, they take on the joys and responsibility of parenthood. At least the film is more honest about the birth than Stacpoole's book. In the novel, the baby appeared miraculously while the pregnant Emmeline slept (so as not to alarm the young readers of the book – after all, this was a children's classic of the late Victorian era).[43]

I admire the pluck of the directors in making these films. After all, we are being voyeurs in childhood sexual development, and there is a thin line to be trod between being ethnographically didactic, and explicitly voyeuristically paedophilic. The director, Randal Kleiser, acknowledged he doubted whether the intimate kissing and intercourse scene would be permissible by today's child actors, whereas back in 1980 the censors gave it the green light.

In the 1991 remake, *The Return to the Blue Lagoon*, a mother and two infants are set adrift in the Pacific following a cholera outbreak on board their boat. They land in precisely the same Fijian island home that Emmeline and Richard had made their own. In this film, the children have a mother to nurture them until she dies of pneumonia, leaving them to discover life-skills for themselves as they mature to adolescence.[44]

Vulnerable Girls Forced to Seek Help

The concept behind *The Blue Lagoon* is that children are resourceful enough to solve life's difficulties, just as a fledgling sparrow or a fox cub would be. All they need is fear, dexterity and experimentation. The marooned children achieved a life-style more fulfilled than a generation of disaffected inner-city youngsters who whinge and riot as if they themselves are feral. In *The Blue Lagoon* the children had to cope entirely by themselves. At least in *Nim's Island* and in *Manny & Lo* the children left in a predicament attempt to seek help.

Nim's Island features a little girl trying to survive on a remote tropical island. She thought she could cope on her own. "I'm not a little girl," the eleven-year-old had reassured her father. But now she seeks help from a stranger living half a world away, the famous adventure writer, Alex Rover. She sends out an emergency e-mail: "I'm all alone. Father is lost at sea. My leg is all swollen, and buccaneers are coming to take over the island. Help! Come!" Unfortunately, the legendary Alex Rover is actually a reclusive and timid Alexandra Rover, played by the adult Jodie Foster. The little girl turns out to be far more resourceful than the successful author.

I believe *Manny & Lo* missed a trick by not exploring the emotional dilemma and the impact on the younger sister of a runaway girl who finds herself to be pregnant. Fostered Lo (sixteen) and her eleven-year-old sister Manny (played by the now immensely successful Scarlet Johansson) have run away. They have to find a way of surviving without adults. Lo has stolen a car, and steals petrol to fuel it. Daily they keep a vigilant check to make sure they are not depicted on the missing persons display on the sides of milk cartons. At night, they break into empty houses, and live a comfortable lifestyle fending for themselves. That is, until Lo realises she is in an advanced stage of pregnancy, and beyond any hope of abortion. Neither of them know anything about babies or about the process of labour, so while staking out a maternity shop they find a knowledgeable shop assistant. They abduct her and take her back to a vacant chalet they have found deep in the forest.

This is a film showing children are not always able to fend for themselves so they need adult help to get them through the birth of the baby. Emmeline in *The Blue Lagoon* of course did not need this help because she was unaware of her pregnancy, and any way there was no help available for her.

Because this film concludes with the birth of a baby boy, we do not get to see how the children coped raising the new baby – I imagine the baby would be abandoned and adopted just as they were. For eleven-year-old Manny, however, we get glimpses of her regrets at not living in a family, for she collects as souvenirs the family portraits from the houses they crash out in.

Jeliza Rose has to survive following the death of both her parents in Terry Gilliam's fantasy horror, *Tideland*. Jodelle Ferland, who plays ten-year-old Jeliza, had to help her father daily inject himself with drugs so daddy can "go on vacation", but on one occasion he overdoses and doesn't wake up. The fact that he is dead does not dawn on the girl at first, so when she checks him and he has not woken up she believes he is still 'on vacation'. Living in a remote shack on the vast Saskatchewan Prairie (Texas in Mitch Cullam's novel), she has only her imagination and her dolls to keep her company, and a jar of peanut butter to feed from. Eventually, she 'befriends' an eccentric neighbour, Dell, and her retarded grown-up brother, Dixon. In their games together, Jeliza Rose and Dixon are unaware how close to the borderline of sexual deviancy they are getting.

Depending on how the audience interpret this 'Alice in Wonderland meets Psycho' film, either Jeliza Rose has the happiest days of her childhood living in her dream-world free of parents, or they feel relief as at the end of the film a 'normal' lady rescues the girl from her insane world.

Kids Abandoned to Struggle Alone

Nobody Knows is based on the true story of a family of children left to fend for themselves in a Tokyo apartment in Japan in 1988. A single mother has to struggle raising four children while searching for work. A landlord has agreed to house only the mother with one son, so the other children have to be smuggled into the apartment in suitcases. The children have to promise to keep quiet all day long and not go outside.

While mother is out at work the oldest boy, twelve-year-old Akira, has to care for his younger brother and two sisters. Yuya Yagira won best actor prize at the Cannes Film Festival for his role as the young boy Akira. He has to go shopping, make dinner, put the young children to bed, do the washing, plus try to keep abreast of his home studies. After a while, mother goes away for a few days at a time, then for months on end, and finally mother disappears altogether, only communicating by post and forwarding cash.

So the children are left to cope by themselves. The situation seems to work adequately while they have money. Their only complaint is the boredom of being housebound. The boy pays the rent, and the water and electricity bills in a payment machine. Neighbours and shopkeepers are unconcerned or unaware of the absence of mother as Akira daily does his shopping trip.

The children spend their days patiently waiting for mother to come home. Christmas arrives but still no mother. Akira waits outside the Christmas stores for the last minute price reductions so he can bring home a bargain-priced Christmas cake. In mum's absence, they start to cherish simple gifts and cards as memories of their mother. Pretending her to be a visiting cousin, Akira takes his youngest sister Yuki outside to look at the trains and the aeroplanes flying overhead. "One day I'll take you on the monorail to see the aeroplanes" he promises her.

Then the money dries up. Their lives radically change. The water and electricity are cut off. They hide when the landlady comes to collect the rent. Their once pristine flat deteriorates. Akira goes daily to the drinking fountain to collect water in a bucket. He starts begging for out-of-date food from food stores. Their house starts to stink. Eventually they dare to go out to play, and explore the shopping malls together. They wash their clothes at the fountain, and use the street toilet. They realise they must not call the police or the social services nor get caught, for then the four of them will be split up.

On one occasion, when they are hungry and desperate for food, Akira catches his younger brother chewing. "What are you eating?" he asks in exasperation, believing he has a secret cache of food. But the little boy spits out a clod of chewed paper, probably one of the service bills, which by now they were using as drawing paper. The flat becomes a tip. It's hot and there is no water to drink, they are bored and demoralised. The older girl Kyoko hides away in the dark closet to blot out the drudgery of her life.

*Then a tragedy happens. The youngest girl, Yuki, falls off a chair and is concussed. Akira uses up the last of his coins in a desperate attempt to locate mother on the telephone but his coins are used up before getting through.

Too late, more cash arrives through the post from mum, but Yuki is already dead. They squeeze her tiny body in the suitcase that she arrived in. To fulfil a promise, they carefully take her to the monorail and board the train for the airport where they bury her in sight of the runway.

That is how the film finishes, inconclusively. Since it is based on a true story, we assume that either mum returns or the authorities are called. Either way we are not told.

2. Families, Step-kids & Orphans

A similar storyline persists in *The Cement Garden*: four children struggling on their own after their parents' death having the dilemma of what to do with a dead body. But this story is far more gritty and salacious than *Nobody Knows*, and the children are older. Based on the novel by award winning author, Ian McEwan, four children witness their father die, then one day, after a period of illness, they find their bedridden mother dead. They obviously are bereft and spend a tearful day in mourning. They become inadequately dependent upon each other. "If we tell someone, they'll take Tom into care." So they decide to bury mum's body in an upturned wardrobe in the cellar and fill the casket with cement. "Us four, that's all the family we need."

They are not short of money. Mum, knowing she was due to go into hospital, had opened a bank account for the older girl, Julie (Charlotte Gainsbourg), into which money would be paid weekly by direct debit to use for domestic items. But the children are ill-disciplined. They don't do the washing up so the kitchen quickly becomes a festering mess of staleness. Like *Nobody Knows*, they run out of food and forget to replenish essential items. The older boy, Jack (Andrew Robertson), stops washing and never changes his clothes so he starts to smell. The youngest boy, Tom (Ned Birkin), mentally regresses, wanting to act like a baby sleeping in a cot and drinking from a baby's bottle. Without parents to control them, the children start experimenting in deviant sexual behaviour.

When Julie brings back a boyfriend (a thirty-year-old man) he can sense the reek of death emanating from the cellar. As with *Nobody Knows*, we are not shown what the future held for the four children. The film ends with the sound of a sledgehammer breaking open the casket of cement, and the flash of blue lights through the window tells us their game is up. We have to assume the children are taken into care after all.

At the age of thirteen, Jodie Foster plays a child, Rynn, trying to struggle on independently by herself after the death of both her parents. The locals get to think of her, as the title tells us, as *The Little Girl who lives down the Lane*. Her mother moved out when Rynn was just three. The girl had been living with her poet father since then. Recently, father and daughter had moved from London to Nova Scotia, in what they hoped was a quiet backwater of a place, near the sea. Unfortunately for Rynn, it was not the place where people kept to themselves. It seemed to be full of do-gooders, nosy parkers, and over-intrusive neighbours.

Shortly after the move, father became sick and knew he was dying. He made plans for his very independent and intelligent daughter to cope on her own for the next three years until she came of age. Traveller's cheques were securely deposited in a safety deposit box.

"Don't give in and play their game," was the last piece of instruction father gave her before yielding to his "unbearable pain".

But neither father nor daughter had counted on the over-friendliness of the locals who intrude constantly on the hermit girl. Jodie Foster tries to be polite and tolerant, but in trying to fob off her visitors, they take offence.

"Thirteen means I have no rights, is that it?" protests the girl to the landlady.

"Since when did they let kids do what they wanted?" the woman counters.

Rynn does not go to school. "School is stultifying." She is bright enough to educate herself from the library. "School is having people *tell* you what life is, without ever finding out for yourself."

Her intrusive visitors include the obnoxious landlady, then the landlady's paedophile grown-up son, who is severely tempted by this young teen living seemingly on her own and accessibly vulnerable. Then there is the police detective who feels a need to keep an eye on the little girl.

All the while, the girl has to deflect their enquiries about her dead father – saying either he is upstairs asleep or working, or he has gone to New York for a book publication. As their visits become more invasive, the little girl has to take ever more drastic action.

The situation in *Lilya 4-ever* is even grimmer. This is a hard-hitting film, difficult to watch. It is a portrayal of a girl who gets trapped in the inescapable vice of child trafficking for the sex trade. Although in this film Lilya, played by Oksana Akinshina, is sixteen, the message is clear that this could be the fate of younger children too. It begins hopefully enough. Living in Russia, Lilya's mum has linked up with an American on an Internet dating site, and the girl is excited that at last they can escape the drudgery of the bland grimy apartment block in which they live, to escape to a land of plenty. But on the day of departure mum drops a bombshell. Lilya can't come. She'll be sent for if all is well. Lilya rips up her only photo of mum, but soon regrets it and sticks it back together like a jigsaw. She tries to pick herself up again. Mum has left some money with the promise more will be sent. The girl invites friends round to party in her flat.

Her unwilling aunt has reluctantly been designated as her guardian. The aunt moves the girl out of her spacious apartment into a small dingy and filthy flat. When Lilya protests, she is told of her other options: "It's the streets or the orphanage." Lilya has to carefully manage what little money she has.

It is not long before her money runs out. Every day she checks the mailbox for letters from mum but her landlady cruelly tells her, "You didn't get any letters today. I think your mother's forgotten you." Lilya goes begging to her aunt. "They cut off my electricity and I have got nothing to eat." But the aunt is unconcerned. "So go into town and spread your legs like your mother used to do."

Next, the girl receives a letter from the Welfare Department. She is told her mother no longer wishes to be her guardian. She burns the photo of mum. Desperate for money, she tries to sell her meagre household goods in the street but no one is interested in her junk. Finally, as her aunt suggested, she goes into a nightclub in town and becomes a whore, and ultimately is trafficked into the Scandinavian sex trade where she is batted like a piece of meat.

Boys Home Alone

When it is a girl left alone, she becomes the vulnerable target; our sympathies reach out to her as a potentially impotent victim who has to remain in hiding lest her innocence be compromised. In the case of boys, however, there is the expectation for them to be brave, to stand up to any aggression, and to assertively defend themselves. At least, that is what the child believes his role should be.

This is true of the archetypal home alone movie called, well, *Home Alone* (1990). Eight-year-old Kevin (Macaulay Culkin) is accidentally left behind when the extended family of fifteen frantically race off to Chicago Airport for a Christmas break in Paris. As soon as Kevin realises there are burglars targeting the supposedly empty house he turns on all the lights and hides under the bed. But then his male-generated bravado nags him: "Only a wimp would be hiding under the bed. I'm the king of the house... This is my house; I have to defend it." Despite his constant resorting to artificial screaming, he decides to tackle the burglars head-on with a variety of ingenious traps that only an imaginative young boy could devise.

But the boy also has to fend for himself domestically. We find him shopping in the supermarket, using the washing machine, and the house is miraculously spick and span once his family return from their aborted trip. Most importantly, he has the commonsense to dial 911 to call the cops, which allows him to witness the burglars being arrested.

Joshua Baskin gets a rude introduction to the adult world after he makes a wish in *Big* (1988). Magically turned into a man (Tom Hanks), mother does not recognise her boy when he wakes up in his outgrown pyjamas. He hurriedly finds some old clothes dad left behind, and mum chases him from the house assuming he is an intruder. Appealing to his best friend Billy, "Something really strange happened. I need your help."

Joshua is forced to check into a hotel – in the roughest seediest part of town where prostitutes ply and fights break out. He only feels safe after he has barricaded the hostel door with a chest of drawers. When his money runs out he has to find a job. He is employed in a toy business where his childlike intuition helps him progress to managerial status. But though he is managing to survive, and his best friend, Billy, thinks, "You're the luckiest guy I know," his constant yearning is to become his thirteen-year-old self again.

The Ultimate Struggle: Survival of the Fittest

The grimmest scenarios are those in which the child, buoyed by independence and anarchy reverts to a feral existence, in a primeval survival of the fittest syndrome, in which membership of a gang and selfish aspiration take precedence over respect for fellow sufferers. In both William Golding's classic *Lord of the Flies*, and *Battle Royale* (a sort of *The Running Man* for obnoxious youths), the caveman instinct that has hidden dormant inside the male gene for generations is given freedom to run amok with fatal outcomes.

These are definitely the playgrounds for boys, even though *Battle Royale* has girls taking a lead part. In fact, absence of girls helped Jack (Chris Furrh) look on the bright side of their predicament in *Lord of the Flies* (1990). "We've got it made:" he tells his rival, Ralph (Balthazar Getty), as they stroll the strand of the Jamaican inlet on which they have been marooned. "No parents, no teachers, no academy, no girls." His nemesis, Ralph, wants order and cooperation: "too many kids are screwing around instead of working," he accuses them – food has to be collected, and the signal fire maintained. "We can't have kids stealing and running wild. We're going to have stricter rules." But sadism soon rears its ugly head as allegiances divide the survivors. Geckos are speared, a wild pig brutalised, dissenters whipped, and eventually weaklings are killed. "It was dark. We were scared. It wasn't our fault," weeps Piggy (Danuel Pipoly). The whole meaning of life seems to dissipate from Piggy's and Ralph's world as anarchy prevails: "We did everything the way grown-ups would have. Why didn't it work?" For Neil Sinyard, commenting on the 1963 version of the film, Ralph's weeping at the end symbolised 'the end of innocence and the darkness of men's hearts.'[45]

Battle Royale is equally bleak, set in a futuristic Japan when civil reforms had got out of hand and a high level of truanting results in too many kids causing mayhem and engendering hatred. The authorities have selected one class of fourteen-year-old school kids to be ferried out to an offshore island. This is where the children take part in a brutal battle of elimination. "Today's lesson is… you kill each other off," until there is just one survivor left alive! Although the bulk of the actors are Japanese youths, some are as young as fifteen, including Aki Maeda who plays the ultimate heroine, Noriko. These are compellingly good actors. The desperation, passion and torment on the innocent faces is brilliantly depicted, and each actor seemed to have their own convincing way of dying.

This is a real battle for survival. The 'game' had been fool-proofed to ensure it was impossible for the children to help each other, escape, or even hide, for the irremovable collars each child wore were primed to explode if they evaded the competition. "Don't forget – life is a game. So fight for survival," is the maxim given to them, along with a haversack full of supplies, including a weapon. Yet this is what most of the children naturally try to do: they try to cooperate while retaining their classroom friendship cliques. Those targeted first are spurned ex-boyfriends/girlfriends as former jealousies determine the lottery of fatalities. One girl Mitsuko, raped as a nine-year-old and abused by her teacher when she tried to confide in him, tries to use her sexuality as a survival strategy. Others die defending friends, while others are double-crossed. "It's tough when friends die. But cheer up!" the public address system mocks.

The situation is of course far-fetched, and on its release, the movie was decried for its depiction of brutality. The release of the sequel was postponed because of a real-life slashing copycat event by a Japanese schoolgirl who had read the novel. [46] Also, a youth crime wave in Japan was blamed on the film, resulting in a parliamentary debate. [47] But isn't this just what the British public was wishing on the football hooligans of the 1980s: to lock them in a stadium to battle it out between them? Yet this is not so far-fetched. The director, having been inspired by the novel, describes the film as a fable reminding him of his own experiences as a fifteen-year-old in World War Two when he and his classmates had to work in a Japanese munitions factory. As the factory was bombed the survivors were sent back in to collect and bury the corpses – his own real life experience of Russian Roulette, whittling down the survivors.

There can be few films that have had such an adverse traumatic impact on the lives of youths, yet for the actors and actresses taking part in the film, they must have had a whale of a time, applying gory make-up, rough and tumble fights, playing war-games, and their only corruption would have been in the editor's cutting department.

ENDNOTES FOR VOLUME TWO

1 *Blended Family* refers to households comprising a child living with one birth parent and a step-parent, and maybe several step brothers and sisters.

2 *Radio Times* 7 Aug 2010 p17

3 Christine M. Williams Anchor Correspondent Catholic News Service 11 Dec 2011 [Internet]

4 Prime Minister David Cameron's phraseology in response to the UK riots in August 2011.

5 *Focus on families* (UK) by MORI, 2007 (Of the 62% quoted, 56% live with married birth parents, a further 6% live with cohabiting birth parents).

6 *US Census Bureau.* Figures are for 2004.

7 Fact Sheet FS 5 Publisher: Swedish Institute, Jan 2009. Published by the Swedish Institute on www.sweden.se.

8 SOURCE: Childstats_gov - *America's Children Key National Indicators of Well-Being*, 2011. Sourced from: U.S. Census Bureau, Current Population Survey, Annual Social and Economic Supplements. For more information, refer to America's Families and Living Arrangements 2010 detailed tables, available at http://www.census.gov/population/www/socdemo/hh-fam/cps2010.html.

9 Note, these particular figures refer to married parents and not just birth parents. The difference may amount to a negligiable difference of 2 or 3%.

10 Mary Park, *Are married parents really better for children?* [Internet]. This is from an annotated version of a Couples and Marriage Research and Policy brief published in May 2003 by the Center for Law and Social Policy (available at www.clasp.org).

11 There are several versions of *Scrooge*, based on Charles Dickens' *A Christmas Carol*.

12 Neil Sinyard *Children in the Movies* p64

13 The figure of 17 minutes refers to older children. While in the UK in 1975, fathers spent just 3 to 8 minutes per day with their children and mothers spent just 8 to 21 minutes per day, this figure had vastly increased in 2000 so that fathers spent 32-36 mins per day with their children, and mothers spent 51-86 mins per day. (*BBC News on the Internet* 7 Apr 2010). By 2011, this figure had increased still further so that fathers now spend 43-63 mins per day with their children while mothers spend between 81-155 mins per day. (Laura Donnelly Health Correspondent for *The Telegraph on line* 27 Mar 2011). The higher of each pair of figures indicates a stay-at-home parent or parent on their day off work, the lower figure indicates a working parent. I do not have figures that distinguish between time spent with infants as opposed to older children.

14 In the 1949 version of *The Secret Garden* the parents died during an cholera epidemic in India.

15 Quoted from *The Guardian on-line*, 13 Oct 2011

16 *BBC News on-line*, 22 Mar 2001 & *BBC News on-line*, 11 Nov 1999

17 About.com '*Runaway Children*' from About Wiki, for About.com.

18 *BBC News on-line*, 11 Nov 1999

19 Neil Sinyard *Children in the Movies* p20

20 Neil Sinyard *Children in the Movies* p19

21 John Conger *Adolescence* p81, 89

22 Sula Wolff *Children Under Stress* p27

23 IMDB from the internet review *Rebel without a cause* (1955), comments from pedro miguel & evan talbott

24 John Conger *Adolescence: Generation Under Pressure* p81

25 Filmsite Movie Review: *Rebel without a Cause* (1955)

26 *11th Virgin Film Guide* p212

27 Neil Sinyard *Children in the Movies* p53

The Tinman and Scarecrow in *The Wizard of Oz*, Pumpkinhead and Tik Tok in *Return to Oz*.

28a In Frank Baum's classic, Dorothy doesn't run away from home.

28b U.S. Census Bureau: November, 2009.

29 *Office for National Statistics* (2006) – quoted from Wikipedia: Single Parent

30 Only the character is obnoxious. Gaby is a delight.

31 Mackay, Ross (2005) "*The impact of family structure and family change on child outcomes: a personal reading of the research literature*" Social Policy Journal of New Zealand (accessed February 18, 2008) quoted in Wikipedia: Single Parent

32 Approx 25% of children live in single parent families, of which approx 1 in 10 live with just their father. According to the *Office for National Statistics* in 2009 there were 200,000 single fathers in UK compared to 1.8 million single mums. Quoted from *Telegraph Media Group, on-line* 10th Jan 2012, *Single Fathers: Pa excellence.*

33 See Table (i) for the categorisation of films in my sample.

34 *Telegraph Media Group, on-line* 10th Jan 2012, *Single Fathers: Pa excellence.*

35 The film *Hidden in America* comes with a blatant message: "On any given night, up to five million children in America go to bed hungry. How many of us will wake up in the morning and think about solutions?" Regrettably, this message is tagged on to the end of the credits after all the viewers have already switched off or gone home.

36 Marianne Sinclair *Hollywood Lolita* p131

37 *The Camomile Lawn* by Mary Wesley.

38 This pair, Paul Eddington and Felicity Kendal, seem inseparable since starring together in the British sitcom, *The Good Life.*

39 In Johanna Spyri's classic, the aunt Dete at first appears to be Heidi's older sister, until she is addressed by a villager in Dörfli, "I suppose it is the child your sister left?"

40 In Henry James' novel *The Turn of the Screw* the governess is not given a name. In the 1961 film version (*The Innocents*) she is named Miss Giddens. In the 1992 film the governess is named 'Jenny'. In the 1999 TV drama, as in the classic novel the governess is not named beyond being called 'Miss'. In the 2009 film version she is simply 'Ann'.

41 In *The Innocents*, Pamela Franklin plays the sweet Flora, while Miles is played by Martin Stephens. In *The Turn of the Screw* (2009) Flora's part falls to Eva Sayer. In the 1992 film, Clare Czekeres plays Flore with Joseph England playing Miles, and in 1999 Flora's part was played by Grace Robinson.

42 The parts of young Emmeline and Richard are played by Susan Stranks and Peter Jones in 1949 and by Elva Josephson and Glenn Kohan in 1980.

43 The parts of the older children are played by Jean Simmons and Donald Houston in 1949 and by Brooke Shields and Christopher Atkins in 1980.

44 Courtney Phillips and Garette Patrick Ratliff play the younger children, while Milla Jovovich and Brian Krause are the adolescents.

45 Neil Sinyard *Children in the Movies* p57.

46 *BBC News* website, 3 June 2004

47 Wikipedia *Battle Royale*

Volume Three

Tomboys, Adventurers & Talented Kids

"Kids are like sponges. They pick things up so quickly."
(Danny Boyle, director of *Slumdog Millionaire*)

"Childhood is both a very liberated place
And also a very normalised place."
(Céline Sciamma, director of *Tomboy (2011)*)

CONTENTS FOR VOLUME THREE

3. Tomboys, Adventurers & Talented Kids..........................143

Contents for Volume Three...145

Introduction..147

Crossing Gender Boundaries..148
Billy Elliot: boy breaking the mould....................................*150*
The Tomboy..*151*
Tomboy (2011): The Film...*156*
Hollywood's Tomboy Legends: Hayley Mills & Mary Badham................*158*

The Talented Child..160
Musical talent..*160*
Creative Talents..*163*
Striving against the Odds..*164*

Sports Starlets...168
The Great Pretender: girls masquerading as boys................*169*
Climbing...*170*
Soccer...*171*
Water sports..*173*
Dance..*175*
Getting the Parents' Support..*177*

The Adventurers / Just Good Fun.....................................179
The Adventure Journey as a Rite-of-Passage.....................*179*
The Amazons: Girl Adventurers...*184*
Just Good Fun...*187*

Endnotes for Volume Three..189

INTRODUCTION

History has bequeathed us a sugar and spice/puppy dog tails perception of children: the active, exploring boy, playing sports and embarking on adventures, climbing trees, catching frogs, and keeping pet spiders in a glass jar. Contrast that with the little pony-tailed girl playing with dolls and kittens in the safe haven of the living room, embroidering her sampler, not daring to dirty her smock. These are obviously antiquated Victorian conceptualisations, in which the child had rigid obsessions and expectations, and God-forbid, never were there any sexual thoughts or deviations in the mindset of the child.

A century later, film directors are at pains to show how roles can be/have been reversed. Movie makers are keen to thrust onto the stage children that buck the trend: the have-a-go independent girl, fearlessly exploring, and playing the games that have been the traditional preserve of the male: climbing trees, riding bikes, playing football, the kung-fu girl. Step forward the tomboy.

For the young actress, these are fun parts to play, and they do not even need to exert themselves to play the role, the editor's cutting room can do that for them. There is just one requirement: the girl must be pretty, slim, flat-chested and white.[1]

The director is less keen on showing the reversal of gender roles for boys. While there are many males who have retained the image of superhero, few are depicted in girlish roles, effeminate or wimpish. To gain any entertainment value as a film, such children are depicted as the subject of bullying.[2] Few boys have crossed what we recognise as the gender line, for instance, into the field of dance, or have shown an interest in fashion, make-up, or domesticated roles. Where they are presented in more passive activities, it is usually video gaming as a computer geek.

Gone are the days when movies portrayed girls as just pretty objects, like a token bunch of flowers on a trolley in the hallway; the sweet, well-behaved compliment to a family, seen and not heard – the Sandy Descher effect.[3] In many films today, the girl has a skill to perform, a proficiency to exhibit. She may be talented in dance or gymnastics, good at singing, a musician, an artist, or good at sports. The challenge for some directors is to portray the girl, not as a sweet angel, but as the tomboy, the adventurer, even the rebel, bucking the trends, crossing the gender boundaries and stereotypes. So in this book, we consider films in which girls are having fun, about talented kids and adventurous children, in particular where girlish traits spill over into rough-and-tumble games to be superseded by more boyish characteristics.

On the boys' side, we focus on their superheroic adventurous roles, but also on those few occasions when the boy has taken effeminate attributes. This is a hard act for a boy to take. Stephanie Theobold (*The Guardian*) believes, "It's easier to be a tomboy than a 'sissy', a boy who displays female traits."[4] Films depicting boys with effeminate traits are few and far between. As we shall see with *Billy Elliot*, "boys are discouraged from engaging in cross-gendered behaviour."[5]

147

CROSSING GENDER BOUNDARIES

"Most girls like to play pretty, but you like guns, do you?" Tom Chaney flinches in *True Grit* (2010) as Mattie Ross (Hailee Steinfeld) points a gun barrel at the man who murdered her father. Mattie Ross was a spirited young lady, out of character with the expected norms of her more gentile gender. As the gunman she hires (Rooster Cogburn[6]) tells her, the outback is no place for a girl.

But in modern society, the differences between what is expected of boys and girls have been blurred. The days when girls played with dolls and boys had train sets have diminished in this era of computerised gadgetry. That girls will become nurses, and boys become soldiers, has been lost from their daily play-acting. Only pink for girls and blue for boys in maternity stores remain as a visibly enduring vestige of an era of gender divide. And yet, while specific gender activities have become blurred, Stephanie Theobold, writing in *The Guardian*, claims the traditional tomboy of an earlier era – 'George, who could row a boat "like a grown man" in *The Famous Five*; Jo, who'd rather be a soldier than a seamstress in *Little Women*; and Scout who feels "the starched walls of a pink cotton penitentiary closing in on me" every time she is made to wear a dress in *To Kill a Mockingbird*' – has disappeared.[7]

You certainly don't expect to see a girl amusing herself on a metalworking lathe in father's workshop. This is the abnormal trait enjoyed by difficult adolescent Charlotte Gainsbourg in *An Impudent Girl*.[8] I guess this should not be extraordinary in this modern era but Charlotte, more out of boredom than anything else, starts up the machinery and pursues a pastime more associated with the male. Father pops his head round the door reminding the sulky girl to turn off the machinery when she's finished and return the tools. "It's me who pays," he complains, "and it hurts." *Tres Bien* to the French director who shows the girl bucking the trend.

Conversely, it is amusingly startling when Ian Colletti, playing ten-year-old Jamie in *Phoebe in Wonderland*, approaches the drama teacher and asks if he can play the part of the Queen of Hearts. It is never made clear whether he has an effeminate leaning or whether he just likes the dialogue: "Off with their heads!" This is a boy who unusually enjoys the company of his girl playmate, Elle Fanning, at an age when boys are expected to shun the dreaded opposite sex. "Why do you want to play a girl's part when every one just makes fun of you?" she asks him. The boy can't vocalise his reasons: "Just because!" But Jamie has to pay the price for his 'deviancy'. Vandals scrawl 'faggot' over his costume. But he is only aping the time-honoured tradition of the male being the Pantomime Dame. This was not viewed as effeminate among Shakespeare's acting troopers.

In more traditional societies, the modernisation of gender roles has had a greater divisive impact – causing family rifts. As we shall see shortly, *Billy Elliot* provides a remarkable example of a boy daring to break free of gender constraints in a traditionally macho mining community. Likewise, Beatrix Potter broke free of the shackles that had condemned her contemporaries to tightly fitting corsets and restraining apron strings. In *Miss Potter*, artistic Beatrix was not going to be constrained by parental expectations of marrying her off to the most eligible bachelor. "When you grow up Beatrix, you have to run a household, plan parties, have to keep a social calendar, your cheeks will glow!" her mother forewarns her. No, Beatrix was going to have none of that. She resolutely rejected suitors, instead successfully pursuing her writing career. That was early twentieth century England. Other cultures are only just going through this modernisation process.

In affluent westernised New Zealand, there are still communities where the older generation try to cling on to, and perpetuate, their traditional Maori culture while their younger progeny spurn their superstitions. Pai was born into such a 'culture in transition' in the mesmerising film by Niki Caro, *Whale Rider*. Oscar nominee, Keisha Castle-Hughes, plays the eleven-year-old heroine, the only grandchild of Koro, the Maori village elder. Pai outrivals the boys in her Maori clan to prove she has equal rights of inheritance.

Of course, Koro the tribal chief had wished for a grandson to whom he could teach the Maori customs, with the aim of becoming his successor. But in the absence of any male descendents, like the grandfather in *Alas de Mariposa*, he despises the granddaughter. Pai is a girl, and a girl may not meddle in the manly customs of tribal chants and pageantry. She attends the tribal *Welcoming* and resolutely sits in the front row with the other trainees. This makes Koro's blood boil, for females may neither talk at the *Karanga*[9] nor sit in the front row. "You're a girl. Go sit at the back." When she refuses, she is evicted from the meeting. "You don't mess around with sacred things," he angrily tells the girl. But this is the tale of a girl who strives to buck the status quo. There are no gender stereotypes in this girl's mind. Secretly, behind her grandfather's back while the boys are trained, the girl sneakily looks on taking everything in.

A day comes when a school of whales beach themselves on the strand. Koro and the male villagers call upon their Maori magic to help re-float the dying whales, but they are unsuccessful and turn away tired and despondent. But left alone on the beach with the enormous hulks of the whales, the girl Pai gently caresses the lead whale, whispers Maori chants to it, and clambers on top of its hide. In restoring life to the ailing beast, she is in essence re-establishing the lost status of womanhood, reclaiming equality for the female in traditional society. "I called to the ancient ones – and they heard me," she tells us. The whale is invigorated, flaps its tail and Pai is carried out to sea riding on its back, the equal of any male tribal chief.

According to the directors, Levin & Flackett, the character of Nim in *Nim's Island*, "transcended gender". "She was a little bit boy and a little bit girl." The part was played by eleven-year-old Abigail Breslin, a competent actress who, no doubt, was chosen for the part because she was the buzz-name in acting circles at that time, having that year received an Oscar nomination for her role in *Little Miss Sunshine*. However, in contrast to Keisha Castle-Hughes in *Whale Rider*, Abigail Breslin seemed anything but a tomboy. In the film, Nim was a girl who was required to swim with sea-lions, run along the strand, climb a rocky volcano, shin up coconut palms, play soccer on the beach, zip down an aerial runway, and pick up mealworms in her palm. The end result was a delightful amusing movie and Abigail played her part admirably, and in the words of her older colleagues, "brightening up the film".

Yet Abigail, herself, was very much a girlish girl – she was not a strong swimmer, and had to be taught over several weeks how to swim underwater and hold her breath. It took time for her to develop confidence in the water. To help her sink, she had to have weights sewn into the hem of her shorts. Abigail admitted that shooting this film was the first time she had ever been in the ocean. Her next non-tomboyish trait was that she ran like a girl. For the scene where she runs barefoot through the beach and the jungle, she had to be taught how to run like a boy "and how to not run like a girl," explains the director. Even so, the director said of her, "She can accomplish whatever you throw at her, she just lifts to the plate." She had turned "from a girl from New York into an action girl."

At least Abigail had a modicum of swimming experience. It transpired, after the shooting of *Whale Rider* had begun, that Keisha Castle-Hughes was a non-swimmer enrolled for a part which entailed swimming off-shore in the deep ocean!

Billy Elliot: boy breaking the mould

It is not unknown for a boy to become a ballet dancer. That is not what is unusual about this film. Ballet has been the pirouetting ground for the male for decades made prominent by the likes of Rudolf Nureyev and Wayne Sleep. Rather, it is that the lad came from the heart of a mining community where boxing, wrestling, and football are the only possibilities, and where ballet and theatre exist only in a foreign land inhabited by pansies and poofs. Eleven-year-old *Billy Elliot* is a rough-and-tough lad, immersed in his working class culture, in daily conflict with his older brother and father with whom swearing rants and punch-ups are common. The boy, played by fourteen-year-old Jamie Bell in a remarkable Bafta winning performance, is forced by tradition and expectation to attend the weekly boxing club. But his heart is not in it. "Jesus Christ, Billy Elliot, you're a disgrace to those gloves, to your father, and the traditions of this boxing hall." Even his girlfriend Debbie (Nicola Blackwell) tells him, "You're crap at boxing."

When the neighbouring girls' ballet class are forced to share their facilities, Billy starts sparring with the punch bag in rhythm to the dance music. A misunderstanding while returning a set of keys finds him joining in with Julie Walter's ballet class – one boy in a hall full of girls dressed in tutus.

After one session, he admits to his best mate, Michael, "I feel like I'm a sissy." Had Michael laughed and jeered at him his path may have been different, but Michael is himself secretly effeminate and encourages Billy, "You would look good in a tutu!" Even his batty grandma provides words of support. But not so the male population of Everington who are deeply entrenched in the miners' strike. There are daily running battles with the police. There is violence, rioting, and arrests. Being anything other than burly and resilient is frowned upon with intimidating cries of 'scab', and violent attacks.

"You look like a great wanker to me, son," says the pianist for the ballet class. Yet even this put-down does not deter Billy. While the boy is secretly trained by Mrs Wilkinson (Julie Walters), outside in the streets we witness the striking miners involved in their own choreographed struggle with the police.

When father discovers Billy having ballet classes, this smacks at the soul of all he and his colleagues stand for. "You! Out! Now!"

But defiant Billy Elliot needs it spelled out for him. "What's wrong with ballet?"

"It's for girls. Lads play football, or boxing, or wrestling. Not frigging ballet! You know perfectly well what's wrong with it."

"It's not just poofs, dad."

"From now on, you can forget about fucking ballet."

"I hate you," the boy yells at his dad. "You're a bastard."

Bill does not give in. As he states at the auditions later on, "When I dance I forget everything. As if there's a fire in my body." He tap-dances up the streets, dances over walls, even while sitting on the toilet, stamping out the rhythm to Jam's *A Town Called Malice*. It is only when he arrives home and slams the front door that the music in his head stops, as his home becomes an alien intimidating environment to him more daunting than the rioters in the streets outside.

Finally, father catches him dancing again. Realising the incredible talent the boy has, he decides not to quash his chances anymore. He pawns his dead wife's jewellery, then crosses the picket line to raise money to send Billy to the auditions in London, and the whole mining community gets behind him to support their local hero who like them is fighting the system.

According to Claire Monk (*Sight & Sound*), "The striking miners function as little more than a sign of the masculine class culture which initially thwarts Billy's ambitions." [10] Jamie Bell, "conveys an adult-child mix of mouthy defiance and sensitive introspection."

The Tomboy

The distinction between sports girl and tomboy is tenuous. Many critics and DVD blurb-writers classify any girl playing sports, or horsing around, as a tomboy. Even girl guides are tainted with the same tag. It is an easy label to apply. Princess Anne, being interviewed by Alan Tichmarch on BBC1, considered herself a tomboy in her childhood days, when horse riding through Balmoral and Scottish glens gave her freedom to ventilate from a starched upbringing. But many other girls would object to such a male-imposed designation. It is a label arguably given by men who don't like girls polluting their sports-right, or by armchair spinsters who daren't go out in the rain and object to their wards doing likewise.

Girls may enjoy and excel at boys' sports, as did Tatum O'Neal playing baseball in *Bad News Bears*, Mary-Kate Olsen as soccer player in *Switching Goals*, or as pugilist Melinda Kinnaman boxing with her sparring partner in *My Life as a Dog*. They may lead or tag along as one of the gang in adventures – camping and playing pirates in *Swallows and Amazons*, surfing the ocean in *Whale Rider*, or rock climbing in *Catch that Kid*. Or maybe they just adopt the laddish traits of a rough-and-tumble kid: Hayley Mills in *Whistle down the Wind* and *Tiger Bay*, Charlotte Gainsbourg in *An Impudent Girl*, Mary Badham in *To Kill a Mockingbird*, and Bertille Noël Bruneau in *The Fox and the Child*. Of course, this does not necessarily make them true tomboys. And yet, in the mind-set of some little girls, their desire to be the equal of, or even be identified as a member of, the opposite sex is as real as the sky or sea are blue. The movie *Tomboy (2011)* exemplifies this, as we shall see shortly. Not only does Laure enjoy doing boyish things, but she also adopts a boy's name (Mickäel) and actually convinces others that she *is* a boy.

What are the characteristics of a tomboy revealed by the cinema and how does one become a member of this tomboy fraternity? Does being a Girl Guide qualify, or being brought up on a farm? Does donning a cloth hat and dungarees count as an identifying uniform? Tomboyism is a way of playing, an attitude of mind, a propensity for boisterous activity and sports, a shunning of girlish ways. Several films and their critics describe their little girl characters as tomboys simply because they dare climb trees or ride a bike. Just because ten-year-old Hailey McCann clouts a perfect pitch worthy of Joe Jackson in *The Time Traveller's Wife* doesn't necessarily make her a member of the club. Lesley Burke (AnnaSophia Robb) in *Bridge to Terabithia* does qualify: she uses imaginative play inventing a land across the creek where she and her friend Jess chase, climb trees, make a base in a tree house, fight with trolls, and use pinecones as pretend hand-grenades. This is a girl who adopts masculine militarism, possessing a stoical attitude to all life's obstacles: "Nothing crushes us!" she proclaims.

"I like doing things boys do, and I can swim faster, and run faster, and sail a boat better than any boy," boasts Georgina (Jemima Rooper) in *Enid Blyton's Famous Five*. "Look at you – a teddy in bed!" she derides her roommate Anne.

Jemima and AnnaSophia's characters are displaying the typical tomboyish traits that, according to psychologist Sarah Showfety, "allow females to stand out and be rewarded for activities rather than appearance or demeanour," and characterised by an assertive competitive personality that does not want to be pigeon-holed and for whom second best does not count.[11] According to Michael Pollick, "A tomboy often chooses to adopt a more masculine lifestyle as a form of preadolescent rebellion against the strict gender roles of her society."[12] Meredith Salenger in *The Journey of Natty Gann*, epitomises Pollick's conception of the tomboy, idling her days on the streets, stealing the odd item from a market stall, and hanging out with the other lads smoking. With as much delinquency as *Candleshoe's* Jodie Foster, she hangs on the backs of trucks to sneak a ride as they screech around corners, and is caught by the police because she dares to throw stones at the bailiffs who are evicting a destitute family.

Rebecca Smart's characterisation of *Celia* (1988) verges on delinquent radicalism. As a tomboy she plays in the local quarry and has fights using soil bombs. She defaces a picture of the Prime Minister on the classroom wall. She secretes herself out of her house at night to burn effigies of the people in the community she hates. But tragically, her sense of justice overtakes her, and she is responsible for a terrible accident to the local bobby, the father of her archenemy. As she stages a mock hanging for the culprit, you can sense the little girl has a twisted sense of justice unusual for a child of primary school age.

Others are tarnished with the tomboy brush whether they want it or not, simply because they grow up a farm where muck and dirty hands are as synonymous as mosquitoes in the meadows or crabs in the creek: eleven-year-old Alexa Vega in *Run the Wild Fields* helping with chores at the family farmstead, ploughing fields, sowing seed in her bare feet, driving the tractor, fishing in the river; Hayley Mills donning her wellies around the Lancastrian farm in *Whistle down the Wind*; Becca Gardner in *An Unfinished Life* climbing trees on their Wyoming ranch, helping fix the jeep, and learning to drive the 4x4 pickup while granddad (Robert Redford) does the muck-spreading from the back. When she practises using a lasso around Morgan Freedman's feet she asks, "Are there really cowgirls?" – as if that were an adventure worth aspiring to.

Boys may pooh-pooh the tomboy as a serious competitive rival until, that is, he discovers he has met his match. At first the girl may be ridiculed as she enters the male domain: Christina Ricci derided by an onlooker in *Now and Then*, "Who are you kidding: girls can't play softball. Why don't you go play with your dolls?" Usually the tomboy is the loner on the periphery of the boy gang – Hayley Mills wanting to join the game of bandits in *Tiger Bay*, AnnaSophia Robb pushed aside at the flat race in *Bridge to Terabithia*. But the tomboy swiftly gains respect when the girl excels: AnnaSophia wins the race, Hayley purloins the revolver, Christina delivers a right hook to the boy deriding her. When the inevitable brawl begins, feline claws demonstrate the tomboy is no genteel pussycat.

The girl's respect is elevated, but only ever in contrast to the 'superior' male. One of the local lads watches on as Christina Ricci plays basketball by herself in her backyard and realises, "You're pretty good," he tells her. "I mean, not just for a girl, but for a guy." There is a similar dialogue about how girls should play with their dolls in *Life-Size*, until Lindsay Lohan hurls the winning throw to get the due praise – "You're pretty good, not just for a girl, but for anyone," the boy admits. Josh Hutcherson admires AnnaSophia Robb in *Bridge to Terabithia* after he is beaten in the race, "You're pretty fast… for a girl." This was Amy O'Neill's compliment in *Honey, I Shrunk the Kids*: "She's not bad: for a girl," says Thomas Brown as the girl coaxes the animatronic giant ant with bait from a biscuit. Always, however, this apparent praise for the achievements of the girl is made in comparison to the assumed superiority of the boy. It is now Christina Ricci should have repeated her right hook. Alas, the girl seems to take this pseudo-praise with pride. Even the Zoconian invaders are at it in *Aliens in the Attic* as the male alien mocks his female counterpart: "Decent technique – for a female!"

Hayley Mills is fed the same compliment in *In Search of the Castaways*, "You've been just fine…. for a girl." Like all girls nowadays should, Hayley Mills took this as an insult. However in the context of the Victorian era when 'normal' girls just did not go sailing the Seven Seas, climbing the Andes, sliding down glaciers, evading lava flows, escaping from Maoris, helping to defeat a gang of gun-running arms-trading pirates, shacking out for a week in an Ombu tree above the flooded Pampas frying birds' eggs, I guess the boy had a legitimate point about the bravado of this girl, Mary Grant, who was travelling the world to find her shipwrecked father. This tomboy must surely have ranked alongside the greatest of Victorian women explorers.

Perhaps the true tomboy is a breed apart, certainly not feminine though she can't escape being anatomically female. "She ain't a girl!" Buddy objects in *A Christmas Memory*. "She's a demon from Hades!" after eight-year-old Eric Lloyd is told to stop fighting with Julia McIlvaine. Nine-year-old Thora Birch is told by her mother in *Paradise* (1991), "You don't have a feminine bone in your body." And we can watch the whole movie *Tomboy (2011)* never quite certain of the actual gender of child actress Zoé Héran until all is finally revealed anatomically in the bathroom scene.

We have a veritable army of girls queuing up to raise fisticuffs to protect their non femininity: Jodie Foster in *Candleshoe*, Hayley Mills in *Tiger Bay*, Meredith Salenger in *The Journey of Natty Gann*, Mary Badham in *To Kill a Mockingbird*, Alexa Vega in *Run the Wild Fields*, Rebecca Smart in *Celia* (1988), Melissa Gilbert in *Little House on the Prairie*, Christina Ricci in *Now and Then*. Even Hermione Granger gives a bare-knuckle punch to Malfoy (Tom Felton) in *Harry Potter*. "That felt good!" she exclaims with relish.

Eileen Quinn in *Annie* (1982) single-handedly fights off a gang of five lads who have tied cans to the tail of a stray dog. After smacking one of them with her fists she humbly acknowledges, "I didn't do nothing any decent person would not have done!" Certainly Punjab, Mr. Warbuck's bodyguard is proud of her: "A child without courage is like a night without stars."

Meredith Salenger's fight with a boy in *The Journey of Natty Gann* is sparked because he called her father a *commie* (because father is a trade union rep). "I'm no red," confirms her dad. "I just fight for what I believe in." As if to compliment his daughter on her pluck he helps her to spar. "That's it, keep that left up!"

There are several other girls who are prepared to fist their cuffs in defence of their father's reputation. Scout Finch, wearing that hated school dress, fights with her classmate for calling her dad a 'nigger-lover' in *To Kill a Mockingbird*. Alexa Vega, in *Run the Wild Fields*, strikes out in the schoolyard, also attired in school dress, at a boy who has called Tom (the farmhand) a 'Nazi-lover', because Tom was not fighting in the war like all the other dads. All three girls win their fights.

But Opal is told by her inconsiderate teacher who has believed the rumours concerning Tom, "If I were you I'd be careful who I defend. If you lay down with dogs you end up with fleas!"

Adding to the roll of honour of scrapping girls defending their father's reputation is Tegan Moss playing twelve-year-old Bernice in *The Angel of Pennsylvania Avenue*. "Your father's a murderer," taunt her classmates after Robert Urich had wrongly been accused of fatally striking a shop steward in depression era Kansas. Soon, Bernice is laying into the taunting girl and the fight begins.

Laura Ingalls picks a fight with her obnoxious schoolmate, Nelly Olsen, in *Little House on the Prairie* because Nellie is mocking her for being a '*country girl*'. Melissa Gilbert, playing Laura, gets her fists exercised: "That Nelly Olsen is the meanest girl I've ever seen. She made me so mad I wanted to smack her good." Mother rebukes her, "You go to school to learn, not to fight." But Laura responds, "I won't have to do it again. Nelly is scared of me now." Jodie Foster from the roughest parts of Los Angeles in *Candleshoe*, was no country bumpkin. On arrival in England she is soon fighting with her rival, Fluny (Veronica Quilligan), ending up firstly in a chicken coop, then in the pigsty, and the brawl only finishes when they flounder in the lake together. As Jodie Foster rightly declares, "I'm not deprived, I'm delinquent!"

Another girl with a proud sense of justice is Celia Carmichael in the Australian movie, *Celia* (1988). Rebecca Smart plays "a nine-year-old tomboy with an awesome imagination and a fierce sense of justice." Celia is like Natty Gann, she stands up for the socialist principles of her hounded communist neighbours, the Tanners. The Tanners and their children are being picked on and ostracised by others in the community – including the local policeman (who should know better) and his nine-year-old daughter Stephanie. Celia remains loyal to the Tanner brood, often picking fights with the other gangs of children. Dad warns her, "You are not to play with the Tanners anymore – they are communists…. Do you think we fought the war so that people like you can be so stupid? I don't want you getting into anymore fights, is that clear?" But Celia ignores her father's instructions. "The Tanners are my friends," she protests.

Others find different weaponry to demonstrate their emancipation: Vanessa Lee Chester swinging on the rafters of the research station in *Lost World: Jurassic Park* to boot an attacking velociraptor through the window; Wendy Darling in *Peter Pan*, whisked off to Neverland to act as mother to the Lost Boys, nevertheless confronts Captain Hook and his band of pirates, which is where her tomboyish streak comes to the surface. "Don't call me Girlie," she shrieks, brandishing her sword at the pirates, as she takes on her new identity as Red-Handed Jill. "What would mother think of me," she declares, "my becoming a pirate?" And she thrusts and lunges as good as any boy, though she does admit, "I couldn't be expected to pillage!" Peter Pan is impressed. "Wendy, one girl's worth more than twenty boys," he humbly admits.

The tomboy can be recognised by the clothes she wears, and even more so, by the clothes she refuses to wear. Pink is definitely out. Scout Finch's reluctance to show her face at breakfast-time in *To Kill a Mockingbird* was because the school skirt she was constrained to wear made her feel as alien as the Negroes in Makeham courthouse. Jodie Foster's Casey Brown in *Candleshoe* was a real rough-and-tumble kid from downtown Los Angeles, scrapping with the lads, disrupting games of basketball, starting a brawl in a garage where oil spills made great slapstick. When she is to be taken to England to masquerade as the lost heiress of a posh stately home, she is told to take a bath and given some clothes to wear. "But that's a dress!" she complains as if it were some strange costume for convicts on death row.

Georgina in *Enid Blyton's Famous Five* has short-cropped hair. Meredith Salenger in *The Journey of Natty Gann* wears labourer's trousers, jacket and cloth cap just like an industrial worker in 1930s depression era Chicago. Though bushy, her hair is cut short so she easily passes for a boy. Eleven-year-old Benji (Saoirse Ronan) dresses in boy's clothes with a boy's cloth cap in *Death Defying Acts*. For her, this is a survival strategy for the streets of 1926 Edinburgh. As Benji says, "You play the game, or you go under."

It seems as if dungarees are the prerequisite to qualify as a tomboy. It was Scout Finch's preferred outfit in *To Kill a Mockingbird*, as it was Addie's in *Paper Moon*. More realistically it was the fashion for rough-and-tumble girls in the mid-twentieth century, for we find pony-tailed Alexa Vega dressed in dungarees in *Run the Wild Fields*, set in 1945 rural America.

The tomboy, despite her abhorrence of girlish attributes, is however anatomically female and cannot evade feminine traits. Veda in *My Girl* (1991) wears trousers, climbs trees, rides a bike, jumps in a lake and goes fishing. She is a tomboy because the DVD blurb tells us so, though I am sure there are plenty of girly girls who enjoy the same pastimes without being labelled *tomboy*. What Veda is, is the amazingly pretty Anna Chlumsky at eleven years of age hobnobbing with best friend *Home Alone* star Macaulay Culkin playing Thomas J. As a 'tomboy', she is certainly aware of her femininity. "My left breast is developing at a significantly faster rate than my right," she tells her father. Shelly (Jamie Lee Curtis), hired as a make-up artist at father's funeral parlour, helps her apply make-up to her already stunningly beautiful face.

Later Veda asks her friend, Thomas J, "Have you ever kissed anyone?" and they share their first kiss together. So much for tomboyishness!

At the end of the film she acquires a new friend: a girl, Judy. Off she goes bike riding, but this time wearing a dress, as if to show she has shrugged off her tomboyish days: she has had her first period, and her first kiss, and she is now a 'true girl'!

According to Michael Pollick, Veda is depicting normalised tomboy behaviour in which, '*a tomboy may simply be enjoying the last vestiges of her childhood before taking on the more challenging role of an adolescent.... A young tomboy may become exceptionally feminine as she develops physically and emotionally during puberty.*' [13]

By contrast, Amanda Whurlizer, played by Tatum O'Neal in *Bad News Bears*, is trying to throw off her reputation as a tomboy, a typical trait for tomboys as they reach adolescence. [14] Like Opal in *Because of Winn-Dixie*, she used to be a great pitcher in baseball with 'the best right arm' throw. But now, the eleven-year-old says, "I'm through with all that tomboy stuff. I'm going to take ballet lessons and be a model. I'm almost twelve and I'll be getting a bra soon," she says, sitting outside under a shady tree, while selling maps to tourists to finance her future dreams. She is reacting to the demands of her mum's former partner, coach Buttermaker, who is desperate to acquire good players for the baseball team he is coaching. Buttermaker (comic actor Walter Matthau) is an ex-baseball star who has now become a beer-swigging, cigar smoking slouch, but he has been roped into coaching a motley bunch of no-hopers. At least he has found a sponsor for his team – *Chico's Bail Bonds*. Now all he needs is decent players to lift them off the rock bottom of the junior league. Thus he desperately needs Amanda in his team. He only succeeds in changing her mind by bribery (by offering to pay for her ballet lessons), and by insulting her: "Anyway, girls reach their peak when they are nine!" The insult provokes her to a reaction.

Amanda joins the team, her pitching is spot on, and things start to improve. But training is frequently interrupted by a local yobbo, who disrupts their games. They discover he is a brilliant thrower of the ball, but he refuses to join their team. So now, the feminine side of Amanda's tomboyish talent has to be brought into play. She challenges the boy to a game of table pushball.

"If I win," says Amanda, "you play baseball in our team."

"If I win," replies the boy, eying up the pretty girl and wryly smirking, "then…"

The boy wins and Amanda loses so she has to commit herself to a Friday night date.

The horrified coach tells her "Eleven-year-old girls don't go on dates."

"I'll handle it," the preteen assures him. "I know an eleven-year-old girl who's on the pill!"

Whatever transpired on the date we never know but the boy joins the team and together they inspire the squad to victory.

The 2005 re-make of this film featured a much older-looking twelve-year-old, Sammi Kane Kraft, in place of the more slender Tatum O'Neal. "Leave me alone, Buttermaker, I'm too old to have a stalker."

Coincidentally, Tatum O'Neal also tried to throw off the idea of her being a tomboy a few years earlier, as she played orphaned Addie in *Paper Moon*. She had short-cropped hair and, dressed in dungarees, she was often mistaken for a boy. "I'm not a boy!" she would protest, and thereafter defiantly showed it by wearing a tatty dress and bonnet, and standing in front of the bathroom mirror dressed in her underwear tried to pretty herself by applying make-up and practise girly poses.

Ariana Richards was the target of the same misunderstanding in *Timescape* (1991), dressed as she was in dad's painting shirt and cap, with a paintbrush in her hand. A visitor passes her on the steps. What a helpful young lad, the visitor praises Ariana. But when Ariana protests that she is a girl not a boy, the visitor pokes her finger into each of the little girl's unformed breasts. "Don't you worry, child, the chest will be along anytime soon!"

How do these hoyden impostors compare to the real rough-and-ready lad? For David Bradley playing Billy Casper in *Kes* (1969), bashing brambles, chucking stones in ponds, chewing grass: all are actions second nature to him and he does them as an autonomic reflex. These are things a boy does because it is in his genes. It is a male tendency to subconsciously break a twig or pluck a stalk as he passes it by, and to end up grubby and covered in muck. When he arrives in the library unaware and unconcerned by his filthy state, the librarian scolds him because any volume he touches will become a dirty book. Billy doesn't appreciate the problem. "I don't read dirty books," he innocently defends himself.

Tomboy (2011): The Film

In *Tomboy(2011)*, Zoé Héran plays a ten-year-old girl, Laure, who has recently moved to a new home. When she has a chance to make friends and join in with their games, she introduces herself as Mickäel. We do not get to see the psychological reasons leading up to this desire to be a boy. The reaction of her younger sister implies she has tried this dupe before. In fact, director Céline Sciamma makes it clear (in the DVD extras) that the movie is not about *why* she is masquerading as a boy, but *how* she does this and how the dupe is finally exposed and resolved.

"The point is to raise questions, not to provide answers, which is more fair to childhood," so she says. Maybe for Laure it is an impulsive experiment to see how strangers react, or more likely she was too shy to correct the mistake made by others when they mistook her for a boy. But it *is* a mistake, as the film reveals, not because she wants to be a boy, but because she lies to her new friends about her gender. The misgivings result from the reaction of her new friends when they finally discover she is actually a girl.

Zoé Héran certainly passes for a boy: her clothes, her short hairstyle, her demeanour, her gait, her voice, her facial features and gestures. She even spits appropriately. Anyone seeing her would believe she *is* a boy: it is an easy assumption to make. Compliments must go to the casting director for acquiring such a talented young actress from the French drama agencies who conforms to the required physique and temperament.

Everything about Zoé Héran cries boy. It is possible to watch the whole movie and believe we are actually watching a boy masquerading as a girl, rather than a girl masquerading as a boy, even for the final scene when she is made to wear a dress. Director, Céline Sciamma has to resort to depicting nudity to convince the audience of Zoé's true gender. As Zoé grooms herself while topless in front of the bathroom mirror, and plays football without her shirt, we realise her nipples are beginning to poke. But the real clincher is as Zoé steps from the bath to reveal she has the genital anatomy of a girl. On the DVD extras, we also get to see the pretty Zoé with shoulder-length auburn hair before it has been trimmed for the film, every much a delightful little girl.

That we, the audience, have to be given such demonstrative prompts to prove her gender, shows what a masterly piece of casting this was, for the girl certainly dupes her new friends, who accept her as a boy without question. (It would have been amusing to have kept Zoé Héran's fellow actors in the dark about her true gender to ensure convincing performances all around. Alas, this was not possible because Zoé's acting playmates had been selected from among her real-life friends. Robin Williams was able to carry out such a dupe in *Mrs Doubtfire*, his fellow child actors at first being unaware he was a man in drag.)

Here lies the brilliance of this film. There is nothing wrong in Laure wanting to be a boy: it has been the aspiration of a proportion of girls in every generation and culture. Nor is there even anything wrong in adopting a boy's name (Mickäel), although her mother found this shameful. What is wrong is the fabrication that causes her new friends to believe she is truly a boy. This is what causes the heartbreak and tears when the truth is finally outed. Had Laure declared she is a girl yet acted like a tomboy, this would have been acceptable and she would have been happily assimilated into their play. The error of her dupe derives from the deeply entrenched prejudices that society inculcates regarding gender. In this film, this impacts in two ways.

We see this firstly as ten-year-old Lisa (Jeanne Disson) craves for Mickäel as her new boyfriend. The whole gang accept Lisa and Mickäel as sweethearts. As they share their first kiss, Lisa is believing she is kissing a boy, not a ten-year-old girl. Had Laure made it clear she was a girl, this may still have resulted in a similar romantic relationship. We even see Lisa putting make-up on Mickäel's face, and ironically, she says, "It suits you. You look great as a girl!"

But when the gang of boys discover Mickäel is actually a girl, they then accuse Lisa of lesbianism, an unwanted and unwarranted label. "If she's a girl, you kissed her. That's disgusting," accuses one of the boys. And Lisa has to agree, and she decides to disassociate herself from Laure (Mickäel). The director, Céline Sciamma is not here taking an anti-homosexual stance, for in her previous film *Water Lilies*, she seemed to promote lesbianism as almost commonplace among teenaged girls. Instead, she is highlighting a deep-rooted view that all societies treasure: that boys and girls must be nurtured within established gender strictures.

At least, Laure's mother is accepting of her daughter's tomboyism, as long as she does not hoodwink others. "I don't mind you playing the boy," says mother, but only as long as others realise you really are a girl. Even so, at the end of the film, mother forces her daughter to wear a dress, then drags her round to the apartments of each of her former friends so they can see the inevitable truth.

The second repercussion for Laure's deception lies in the humiliated reaction of the boys. These boys would have accepted her as a tomboy because there are other girls joining in their games of tig, water fights, and rough-and-tumble scraps. She does confront a dilemma when all the boys go into the woods to pee; and when they all go swimming, she has to cut up her swimming costume to make a pair of trunks, filling out the crotch with a sliver of plasticene to maintain the pretence. She has fights with the lads and wins. This has the effect of raising her up the pecking order of respect. The boys do not object being beaten up by another boy, but when they discover Mickäel is a girl, then that is an affront to their own gender status. Director Céline Sciamma states, "It's a boy who has to prove his masculinity," and their time-honoured status has been usurped by the impostor. This is the reason why the girl is ultimately shunned. The boys had accepted this impostor as one of their own gender, so that they saw no shame in spitting and fighting in 'her' presence.

For Sciamma, "the pressure is on one's gender and how others see you." As the character Laure discovered, "How you are defined and how other people see you can be liberating and empowering, but also confines you."

Hollywood's Tomboy Legends: Hayley Mills & Mary Badham

Growing up in the 1960s, Hayley Mills seemed to pioneer the role of on-screen tomboy. These were the days when kids played cowboys and Indians, or cops and robbers, and had acres of dockland or derelict sites as their playground. As an eleven-year-old in *Tiger Bay*, Hayley Mills plays Gillie who cannot join in the pistol shooting games because she does not have a toy gun. But she does have a plumb-bob bomb which when loaded with caps makes a great pistol crack. Her tomboyish streak spurs her into taking on a couple of lads on the Cardiff dockside, and starts bashing them for insulting her. Another boy breaks up the fight. "You mustn't hit a lady," he tells them. "I'm not a lady," protests Gillie, "Give me back my bomb." Arriving home late to her aunty, she is rebuked, "I don't know what next! Little girls wanting to play with guns and bombs, and dressing up like gangsters."

But this *is* a gangster movie. Gillie, peering through her neighbour's letterbox overhears one of the Polish dockworkers argue with his girlfriend. A real pistol shot rings out. The man rushes out and hides the gun. But Gillie sees where he has hidden it. So now she has a real gun with which to impress her mates. Auntie hurries her off to the church choir. While angelically singing her way through *Crimond* with the other choristers, she raises her cassock gown and proudly shows off her newly acquired gun to the boy next to her.

Like many tomboy films, Gillie shows her vulnerable side. Although there is no love interest involved as there is with *Natty Gann* or *Bad News Bears*, she does form an attachment with the murderer and has ultimately to be rescued by him.

Hayley Mills also has a tomboyish role in *Whistle down the Wind* in which, as in *Tiger Bay*, she is raised by an auntie as a substitute mother, though father is still the breadwinner (he is a farmer). Also ironically, she again confronts a gun-toting murderer. Hayley Mills plays Kathy Bostock. Being a farm girl, she naturally has what are judged to be tomboyish tendencies. Donning her boots, she is out traipsing in mucky fields, exploring old quarries, and disused railway cuttings. Like other 1950s kids, she has the freedom to roam the length of her Lancastrian village,[15] unaccompanied and without fear. When father hears of a murderer at large in the district, father feels the need to warn her about who she talks to: "I don't want you talking to strangers. You didn't talk to any strangers did you, Kathy? There are some funny people about; funny men, and that." But too late! Tomboy Kathy has already shown her feminine caring side. Having rescued a litter of kittens discarded to drown in the local slurry pool, she stumbles across Alan Bates recovering from wounds in the barn, and assuming him to be Jesus, supplies him with food, wine and snout.

The ultimate tomboy has to be Scout Finch, played marvellously by ten-year-old Mary Badham in *To Kill a Mockingbird* in an Oscar-nominated role. In the film, she plays the six-year-old daughter of lawyer Atticus Finch (Gregory Peck) and brother of ten-year-old Jem. During the balmy Alabama summer of 1932 they play out from dawn to dusk, climbing trees, making tree-houses, rolling down the street curled up inside tractor tyres, sitting upside down in a rocking chair, taking dares to creep up at Boo Radley, the local boogeyman's home. Dressed in blue dungarees and t-shirt, and with short black hair, she not only looks like a boy, she acts like one too. It's only when she pulls out of a dare that her brother riles her, "You act more like a girl every time!" The girl does not take this as a compliment.

On her first day at school Scout is reluctant to show herself for breakfast. For the first time in her life she has to wear a dress, and she is deeply embarrassed. Yet despite being in her frock she soon starts fighting with the boys once she gets to school (and she wins), and can only be restrained from continuing the fight by her brother holding her back. Yet at the end of the film a tender feminine side of her appears as she comforts the retarded Boo Radley, taking him by the hand to visit her unconscious brother. "You can pet him if you like," she offers, and then sits on the veranda swing next to the man who used to give her nightmares.

THE TALENTED CHILD

I guess all the children mentioned in this book are themselves talented because they are successful or up-and-coming actors. Many of the characters the actors represent have specific talents of their own. "Everyone has their own talent, Alice," Alyson Stoner is assured in *Alice Upside Down*. They may be dancers, musicians, singers, skilled at sports or creativity. It is the role of the actor to depict that talent, and surely the task of the casting director is to select children with at least a modicum of expertise for the skill he or she is portraying. Otherwise the child has to resort to mime and the editing cuts of the technician.

What is doubly impressive is some of our child actors display genuine talent themselves beyond just acting proficiency; this may be a sporting skill, a musical gift, or a special talent that promotes them above their peers: Jamie Bell's super proficiency at dance; George Sampson, the fourteen-year-old winner of *Britain's Got Talent*, after a spell in a West End Musical was diverted into acting roles in *Waterloo Road* and *StreetDance*; Miley Cyrus as Hannah Montana, as well as being an actress is a successful singer. Aleisha Allen sings at the end of *Are We There Yet*, as does Hayden Panettiere in *Dust Factory,* and AnnaSophia Robb sings on the *Bridge to Terabithia* DVD. Likewise, the musical improvisation by the pupils at the end of *School of Rock* is a marvel, in particular Rebecca Brown on base guitar, Kevin Clark on the keyboard.

Some children portray a modicum of sporting expertise to help them through their role: Mary-Kate Olsen's footballing in *Switching Goals*, and Dee Hepburn's in *Gregory's Girl*, Tatum O'Neal's baseball pitching in *Bad News Bears*, Anton Glanzelius and Melinda Kinnaman's boxing in *My Life as a Dog*, Charlie Ray and Josh Hutcherson scrapping and manhandling each other at karate practice in *Little Manhattan*, and Lindsay Lohan's American football in *Life-Size*. If only there had been a movie requiring athletic ability among girls: Dana Hill (*Fallen Angel, National Lampoons Vacation*) would have fitted the role perfectly, being the third highest ranked middle distance runner in America for the under tens.

Others are not necessarily talented themselves, the editor's cutting room fabricating the action, as with Kristen Stewart's rock climbing in *Catch that Kid* in which we never actually see her climb any rocks, she just dangles from a rope.

Are the talents and sporting skills depicted in the movies still allocated along traditional gender lines? Is it still girls who go horseriding, while boys kick the soccer ball? Do girls remain tied to domestic chores, singing melodiously as they look after younger siblings, while their male counterparts are bashing along adventure trails? What we can deduce from the following chapters is that the stereotypes allotted to different genders of children are gradually being eroded.

Musical talent

With sweet voices and an aptitude for singing, girls are more likely to be displayed with musical talent than boys. The universal worry among adolescent lads that their voice might break and that singing is associated with choirboys, has instilled in boys a fear of being ridiculed, along with connotations of effeminacy. TV celebrity Gareth Malone's attempt to inspire the males of this country to sing in choirs is admirable. Boys are more likely to direct their enthusiasm towards instrumentation rather than singing. As they become youths, males use the cover of more experimental musical genres to mask the tuneful clarity (or tunelessness) of their voices.[16] Of course, there *are* some boys that sing, and do so. But in films, this is where the girl is able to excel. The movie business is peppered with girls who sing tunefully, and they are given plentiful opportunities to demonstrate their talent. When it comes to playing a musical instrument, however, the level of competence is stifled.

Patty McCormack in *The Bad Seed* pounds out repetitively a one-fingered tune on the piano, and Anna Paquin sings absent-mindedly as she plays in *The Piano*. Carol Coomes repetitively hammers out *Hark the Herald* in *It's a Wonderful Life* until James Stewart in a fit of temper rages, "Must she keep playing that? Haven't you learnt that silly tune yet?" None of these actresses are accomplished musically, nor do they claim to be, and nor are their attempts necessarily genuine. Carol Coomes only lays her fingers across the keys without depressing them, as does Eddie Hodges in *Summer Magic* while singing a duet with Hayley Mills. Clothilde Baudon masquerades as a top child prodigy in her role as Clara Bauman in the French film *An Impudent Girl*. Maybe she is genuinely skilled at the piano but despite the wonderful accompaniment, we never see her fingers tap the keyboard. Nor do we see Kirsten Dunst's fingers in play as she tinkles the ivories while taking a respite from sucking blood in *Interview with the Vampire*, or Eva Sayer in *Turn of the Screw* before her nanny is driven insane. Yet we do in *School of Rock*. Here, encouraged by rock star Jack Black, we see a bevy of school kids genuinely play along on their musical instruments. As we mentioned earlier, it is a joy to watch the final skiffle as the credits roll.

Julie Richalet plays the piano in *Page Turner* as an eleven-year-old taking a practical piano exam. But her examiner, a famous concert pianist, causes a distraction, which makes Julie lose concentration, thus failing the exam. Because of this, she gives up playing the piano. But as Julie becomes an adult she gets a chance to take revenge on the piano judge.

The astonishing piano playing movie *Shine* is surely unrivalled as a musical biography, the adolescent David Helfgott bullied into excellence as he tackles the near impossible Rachmaninoff. Here, we witness a stupendously talented child prodigy at work. Yet even here we are duped, for this 'youngster', Noah Taylor playing the part of the adolescent David, was twenty-seven years of age! Unlike the brilliance of his adult counterpart (Geoffrey Rush) we never see his fingers ever touch the keyboard, though the preteen David (Alex Rafalowicz) makes more of a genuine attempt to depress the ivories.

Evan Rachel Wood was not a musician, yet the director sent her a violin in preparation for her lead role in *Little Secrets*. Having watched a video of a concert, mimicking the moves of the instrumentalists, she was able to give the impression she was an accomplished violinist herself. So convincing was the child's performance, the director Blair Treu was complimented, "Wow! You have an actress who actually plays the violin." Yet the director had to admit the girl was just miming.

We are equally misled by the angelic singing of *Suo Gan* by Christian Bale in *Empire of the Sun*. He mimes along with the other choristers in Shanghai Cathedral. And the later rendition in the concentration camp as he sings above the Japanese soldiers is stirring and magical. But another choirboy has to take the credits (James Rainbird). Bug Hall dares to serenade his girlfriend in *Little Rascals*. His singing can be categorised as sweet rather than tuneful, but at least he was willing to have a go.

We mentioned earlier the singing talents of Hannah Montana (Miley Cyrus) and Aleisha Allen. Other girls, naturally, are able to sing, and do so either during the film, accompanying the credits or as extras on the DVD: Tina Majorino and Fiona Fullerton in *Alice in Wonderland* and *Alice's Adventures in Wonderland*, Amelia Shankley in *Dreamchild*, Alicia Morton and Aileen Quinn's powerful nasal rasping in *Annie* (1999) and *Annie* (1982). Roxy Hunter and Hannah Montana have films dedicated to their singing talent. Florrie Dugger is lead singer, Blousy Brown, in a chorus line of girls in the brilliant *Bugsy Malone*, in which Jodie Foster also pouts a sexy rendition of *My Name is Tallulah*. Here, the director regretted, on reflection, not having persuaded all of his young cast to sing genuinely (most of the children mime to an adult accompaniment). In *The Five Pennies*, five-year-old Susan Gordon croons along with the famous Danny Kaye. And, of course, Shirley Temple and Judy Garland are legends. As if trying to emulate Judy Garland and Margaret O'Brien's Oscar performance in *Meet me in St Louis*, Thora Birch sings along with Lauren Bacall in *All I want for Christmas* – a pleasant-enough rendition, but not award winning.

This list is, of course, notably absent of boys who sing. To the rescue come Sean Marshall in *Pete's Dragon*, and Paul Terry in *James and the Giant Peach*. But neither of them would be wise to abandon their careers by becoming songbirds. Mark Lester's angelic rendition of *Where is Love?* in *Oliver!* was a convincing example of mime (his parts were actually sung by a girl, Kathe Green). At least Mark Lester is able to demonstrate some instrumental talent as he and Tracy Hyde strike up a duo in *Melody*. As the girl practises her recorder, the boy joins in on his cello, a prelude to love. Here the playing is genuine, warming and basic, hinting at the beginnings of improvised talent.

Alyson Stoner has the awkward task of singing out of key in *Alice Upside Down*. She takes part in an audition for the school play. She had been led to believe (by her father) that she had a good singing voice because her dead mother was a good singer. Yet at the audition she sings awfully. This is quite a hard task, as comedian Les Dawson exemplified in his humorous piano renditions. You need some degree of talent to be able to make this convincing without it sounding ridiculous. The director, however, does enable Alyson to show she is a really competent singer as she sings over the credits at the end of the film. If only director, Deborah Kampmeier, had allowed Dakota Fanning's early renditions of Elvis' *Hounddog* to have been less staged and intrusive. (I found this really jarring and uncomfortable to listen to, but I guess to make a point, the girl had been asked to sing tunelessly. It is only after Dakota has been ravaged that she is able to perform with soul and feeling.)

In *The Angel of Pennsylvania Avenue*, Brittney Irvin plays nine-year-old Lilly who accompanies her own singing of *Cockles & Muscles* by playing it on the piano. Later, she has to raise funds for a bus trip to Washington, which she does by singing Christmas Carols in the mall. Mayim Bialik plays the eleven-year-old CC Bloom in the brilliant film *Beaches* (1988). She is full of confidence, humour and pizzazz as she plays "the fantastic, world famous child-wonder." I agree with her friend, Marcie Leeds, who praised her: "I almost started crying when you sang *That's the story of Love*." [17]

That's precisely what *I* did in *The Sound of Music*. I blubbered my way through every song as the seven very talented children warble the now legendary *Edelweiss*, *Doh-ray-me*, *Goodbye*, *My Favourite Things*. "You never told me how enchanting your children are," says Uncle Max to Captain Von Trapp. The seven children – their names have to be remembered for posterity – Charmain Carr (Leisl aged 16), Nicholas Hammond (Friedrich aged 15), Heather Menzies (Louisa 13), Duane Chase (Kurt 15), Angela Cartwright (Brigitta 10), Debbie Turner (Marta 7), and Kym

162

Karath (Gretl 5). Superb! Uncle Max concurs: "Is there a greater expression of good in this beautiful country of ours than the innocent voices of our children?"

Other just-for-fun films are in a different league. *Monkey Business* (1998) is an undemanding film in which a gang of four children – who call themselves *The Cobras* – hang out together awaiting a gig for their rap band. Incredulously, these eleven and twelve-year-olds have their own rap band but we never hear them perform! This film is an affront to the talents of children. While *Bugsy Malone* celebrated the talents of the kids – even though the singing was mimed – this film, *Monkey Business* (1998), insultingly does not even allow the cast to try to display any talent (except for a ten second episode of pitiful jiving). There are myriads of musically talented actors who could have been cast for these roles (*The School of Rock* proves that), and I consider this a failure on the part of the casting director. "Janie, I'm sorry. You go on and practice," James Stewart apologises.

Creative Talents

The message here is dogged perseverance, and if a film has a purpose it is to inspire today's kids to pursue their dream. In keeping with the imbalance in academic success across the genders, in the main, this message is conveyed by the more studious girl-child. It is the girl who is depicted aspiring to be the great artist, musician, author. This is not necessarily a bad thing, either. In a society where the male seems to leapfrog the academically successful girl to attain the greater success and the top jobs, it seems worthy to encourage the girl-child to strive. Some, such as Beatrix Potter show today's child this need not just be a dream, but a reality.

Some films embody the child's desire to project talent creatively. This may be expressed as artistically or in literary writing. In *Atonement*, Saoirse Ronan playing Briony Tallis is a novice script-writer, presenting plays for her relatives, to the delight of her mother, but to the distain of her cousins who are roped in to be reluctant actors in the performances. Here the authors are projecting the creative writing talents of the academically-aspiring schoolgirl. Winona Ryder's, Jo Marsh, has a flair for writing in *Little Women*. "Reading your book was like opening a window to your heart," she is told by an admirer. Mischa Barton, in *A Ring of Endless Light*, plays Vicky, a teenager with a gift for poetry writing. "You've a light, Vicky. Don't ever hide it," encourages her grandfather. By contrast, in *My Girl* (1991), Vada (Anna Chlumsky) aspires to be a writer/poet for the wrong reasons. The eleven-year-old has a crush on the English tutor, and that is her motivation for joining the extra-curricular poetry class.

Yet, don't be fooled, as I was, by the artistic talents of Aimee in the intriguing documentary-style film *Catfish*. It took ninety minutes of being duped before the researchers informed us this was not a super-talented eight-year-old who had sold thousands of dollars worth of paintings exhibited in Chicago galleries, but her mother masquerading as a child artist.

For Josh Hutcherson in *Bridge to Terabithia*, it is artistic talent that newcomer AnnaSophia Robb encourages him to pursue while his father dissuades him with demoralising put-downs, "Get your head out of the clouds." There is an opposite response from the girl in *Great Expectations* (1987). Pip has his portraits nonchalantly rejected by the Estella of his dreams. In *Alas de Mariposa*, the little six-year-old Ami (Laura Vaquero) spends her days drawing and redrawing butterfly wings, never managing to get them right, until finally she cracks it. She makes a beautiful picture at school, and waits outside the school gates ready to present the picture to her mother in an attempt to try to mend a strained relationship with an anxious parent who is rejecting her. Alas, this is just the day mother has to be rushed to hospital to give birth to the longed-for baby boy. So Ami and her drawing are neglected, forgotten, unwanted. Not the honourable lesson other idealistic directors would have us strive for.

Emmy Clarke uses art as therapy, helping her recuperate from the loss of her parents in a bomb blast, in the drama *My House in Umbria*. Similarly, a psychological slant can be placed on Charlotte Burke's artwork in *Paperhouse*. She makes drawings of an isolated house that haunts her in her dreamworld that she drifts into as a result of her illness. In a similar, unsettling way, Jodelle Ferland draws weirdly disturbing horror pictures of the apocalyptic ghost town, *Silent Hill*, and Dakota Fanning in *Push* uses her crayoning set to predict the future.

In Orphan, Esther Coleman's artistic skills bring her to the attention of her future guardians who are visiting the institution where she lives, looking for a child to adopt. Isabelle Fuhrman plays the nine-year-old who endears herself to the visitors, but who eventually becomes their murderer. Maybe they should have realised her superb artistic masterpieces could not have been produced by a typical child.

One girl stands out among the rest as having artistic and writing talent which flourished from her childhood days, and we only have to mention her first name, Beatrix, to realise we are referring to *Miss Potter*. "There's something delicious about writing those first few words of a story," she narrates. "Those first words – you never can tell quite where they will take you." Lucy Boynton plays the popular children's author when she was aged ten, living in the stifling constraints of an affluent part of London, but whose life was enhanced and transformed following a visit to the English Lake District. "Like an animal released from its cage she fell under its spell," where her whole menagerie of farmyard tales and drawings were formulated: Jemima Puddleduck, Tale of Squirrel Nutkin, and Peter Rabbit, etc. I am sure each reader will have his or her childhood favourite. Her father sums up her resolve to be a success: "When you showed me your books all I saw was my little girl bringing me clever drawings. You're not a little girl anymore. You are an artist, the genuine article, and now I am proud of you, Beatrix."

I reiterate that, with the exception of Josh Hutcherson, and Pip from *Great Expectations*, the children playing these roles – Saoirse Ronan, Winona Ryder, Mischa Barton, Anna Chlumsky, Laura Vaquero, Emmy Clarke, Charlotte Burke, Dakota Fanning, Isabelle Fuhrman, Lucy Boynton – are all girls, white, pretty, slim, and do not wear spectacles. Perhaps the cinema is trying to redress the stigmatisation of the dumb blonde, but it does not promulgate the idealism of the successful ethnic child. Let us consider a minority of films that do.

Striving against the Odds

Various films show the child using their talent to rise above their humdrum life. Earlier, we described how the film *Billy Elliot* portrayed a preteen boy from the macho Durham minefields transcending local entrenched obstinacy and intimidation to become a Haymarket ballet star. Others escape the perceived entrapment of the ghetto[18] culture of black American hopelessness (Keke Palmer in *Knights of the South Bronx* and *Akeelah and the Bee*), while in *Little Miss Sunshine* a plump no-hoper fights against the odds to penetrate the cliquish world of child beauty pageants.

By casting Keke Palmer, the director has dared to use a black actor to show that success is not just the preserve of the middle class white child: Keke is shown rising above the constraints of her own black ghetto to prove she is the equal of her more affluent white middle class contemporaries. The inspiration that Abigail Breslin provides of a tubby girl hoping to enter a beauty pageant is negated when we learn the child herself is not actually plump, but has a specially designed swimsuit, provided by the costume department, to make her seem so.

For Jamal (Dev Patel),[19] the general knowledge assimilated while subsisting as a Mumbai orphan enabled him to become *Slumdog Millionaire*. But for Jamal, neither the knowledge nor the money were as important as the televised exposure that could regain the attention of his childhood sweetheart, Latika.

Keke Palmer in her first two films was required to demonstrate a successful black child from a poor neighbourhood, rising to success by competing against affluent white kids. In *Knights of the South Bronx*, she plays a member of a chess team from a black New York slum, a team that perseveres to become national chess champions.

In the 2005 movie *Akeelah and the Bee,* Keke plays an eleven-year-old, disillusioned with school life – a truant and a rebellious girl, a no-hoper from a poor Los Angeles slum. But she has one amazing talent recognised by the headteacher – she is a good speller. This doesn't just mean she gets few spelling errors in her essays. She has grasped the concepts of syntax, and of word derivations. Headteacher encourages Akeelah to enter a district competition. "Why would I want to represent my school when you can't even put doors on the toilet cubicles?" she protests. The headteacher puts Akeelah in touch with a previous winner of the competition to give her coaching. Her older brother taunts her: "You're going to be up against a bunch of rich white kids. They are going to tear your butt off."

Akeelah just scrapes through the district competition and reaches the regional, and ultimately, the national finals. But on the way, she witnesses the stresses and bullying that other children are put through by their over-ambitious parents.

As Akeelah experiences success for herself, she discovers the stresses and expectations imposed on her: her friends abandon her because she is always too busy to play with them; she can't cope with the local media, and people in the community where she has become a minor celebrity who expect her to win. Even mother is not fully supportive.

In the national finals, she succeeds in reaching a head-to-head with an oriental lad whose pushy father is making his life hell. So Akeelah takes pity on the lad by fluffing a question so they can share the trophy and the glory.

In Keke Palmer's second inspirational role, *Knights of the South Bronx*, Keke plays Kenya Russell. Her mother is a junkie. On one occasion, police bring her to school because they found her with her mother in a crack den. Her classmate, Jimmy, is bullied and beaten up by other youths, who demand protection money from him while his father is locked up in prison, and he is forced to do jobs for the gang such as stealing bicycles. Another classmate, Renée, has no interest in learning so never makes an effort at school. On their way to school, the children have to duck underneath cars to evade a street gun battle. So this is the type of neighbourhood they live in, and at fourth-grade they have already given up hope of escaping its clutches.

Into their school comes a new teacher – a supply teacher, Mr Mason, who introduces the children to the game of chess. "If you can win a game of chess, no one can call you stupid," teacher tells them. "Chess doesn't matter if you're poor, or black, or from the Bronx, or even if your dad is in prison." When the children discover that success in chess could be their passport out of the ghetto, Kenya dreams, "Imagine, I could go to college, and I could win a scholarship."

Obviously, they lose at first, but they are taught to use defeat to their advantage. "Losing a game is one of the best things that can happen... A loss is nothing but an opportunity – an opportunity to get better and learn something. When I lose – I study my mistakes, fix them, and come back stronger."

In time, this unruly rabble becomes a disciplined team, and starts to win tournaments. But what is pitiful is the way some children have to hide their success from their parents. When Kenya's mother discovers her trophy, Kenya quickly snatches it from mother's hands. She thinks mother might pawn it for drugs. Another boy is afraid to show his trophy to his father. His father has objected to the boy learning a namby-pamby game like chess – he should concentrate on the forlorn hope of becoming a doctor instead. But when father does eventually learn of the trophy, his pride gets the better of him. Father holds the trophy aloft to the customers in his café: "This is what my son has won – a kid from the ghetto, against posh white kids."

When the team qualifies for the national finals in Dallas they realise it will be too expensive to attend – until a generous benefactor donates the money. Being a heart-warming film, the team wins the nationals.

Despite this being about super-talented kids, none of the actors have to display any chess skills. Their moves are just a set of clips in the greater tournament. But that does not matter. It is the inspirational and motivational response that is important for this type of film. The film ends with a true comment, an encouragement, from a child who achieved the 'impossible dream' of going to college. "Chess gave me the strength to believe that if we put our minds to it, lack of money can't completely hold us down in life, and we can strive and succeed like anyone else."

I guess this is the virtuous goal for directors who make this type of film – the encouragement to strive, giving hope to the underdog, battling against adversity. These are inspirational stories, urging us to strive to achieve, despite our backgrounds or status; a sentiment repeated in *Little House on the Prairie*. "I'm scared of getting up in front of all those people," quails Laura Ingalls as she is about to read her essay to the parents' meeting. "I just know they will all laugh at me."

Mum reassures her: "As long as you do your best, we'll always be proud of you."

Striving against the odds is the explicit message of directors Dayton and Faris in *Little Miss Sunshine*. Abigail Breslin plays the seven-year-old daughter of a motivational speaker. "Inside each of us is a winner waiting to be awakened and released upon the world," he lectures to his audience. "Refuse to lose." His constant reciting of his nine-point plan to his own family however has left nothing but resentment: for the past nine months older son Dwayne (Paul Dano) has been mute, refusing to speak, not until he is goaded into a tirade of abuse against his parents highlighting their hypocrisies. "Divorce! Bankrupt! Suicide! You're fucking losers!" he yells.

But the inspirational messages have drip-fed down to the young daughter, Olive (Abigail Breslin), who is watching a beauty pageant on TV. She copies each of the triumphal motions of the contestants: holding the face in disbelief, setting the crown on her head, and she knows she can win one day, despite looking in the mirror to assess her tubby paunch and bespectacled face. When she learns of her qualification (by default)[20] to the pageant in California 800 miles away, the whole family make a frantic expedition half way across America, in a clapped out yellow Dormobile, mainly because they feel they are obliged to fit in with father's motivational never-say-die philosophy.

When Uncle Frank wishes the girl good luck, father rebukes him, "Luck is what losers give to their failings, Frank." Miss Breslin (Olive) brilliantly scurries in and out of the room making her preparations and talking off-camera. As their destination gets closer, Olive starts having doubts about her success and seeks reassurance from her grandpa. Is she going through with this out of fear of her father? "Daddy hates losers," she confides to her grandfather. But Grandpa reassures her, "A loser is someone who is so afraid of not winning they don't even try."

Now, grandpa is one almighty sex fiend, buying pornographic mags along the journey and instructing the grandson to fuck every girl he can while he's still young. This is the man who has done the choreography for Olive's performance. So, after we have watched all the prim and proper little beauty queens parade on the stage, it is Olive's turn to strut her stuff. That is when the seven-year-old begins her striptease act, to the alarm of the judges, and the family are chased from the venue and hurried back to New Mexico from whence they came.

Maybe Olive would do well to heed the advice given to Lewellen (Dakota Fanning) in *Hounddog*: "If your dreams have got to go underground for a while, bury them deep in the earth so they can survive."

SPORTS STARLETS

There are plenty of movies that depict boys infatuated with sports. This is what we expect of our sports mad heroes. John Albasiny in *P'Tang, Yang, Kipperbang* daydreaming his life away as a cricketer, Josh Hutcherson in *Bridge to Terabithia* aspiring to be the school's fastest runner, Michael Conner Humphreys as *Forrest Gump* outrunning every boy in sight, Ingemar (Anton Glanzelius) in *My Life as a Dog* trying to emulate the Swedish boxing champion. Others just enjoy the rough and tumble of the game – the *Sandlot Kids* playing baseball in the local park. Other boys loyally fulfil the expectations made of them by joining in only because parents, in particular fathers, want to live out their own glory days through their sons, as in *Little Giants* and *Bad News Bears*. Barely a girl in sight! Girls play netball or hockey or take ballet classes on the other side of life's Berlin Wall. Of course, this traditional separation of the sexes is outdated, and moviemakers have enthusiastically taken up the challenge to show this.

Several films depict girls playing what, in olden days, were generally considered to be male sports. Either they have successfully crossed the stereotypical gender boundary and play in an all-girls' team, or they are at an age where a junior league incorporates mixed-sex teams. Occasionally the girl has to pretend to be a male in order to be accepted as part of the squad to get a game – the true tomboy, the girl not just acting like a boy but actually pretending to be a boy. In films, the latter-most scenario is most likely to be a comedy. As with the bulk of the population, the director sees the girl playing in a male team as being laughable – either to berate their talent, or to make a pretence they are more talented than they actually are. Or else they dwell on the comic scenarios that can occur in the dressing rooms: girls being wary about undressing, their eyes bulging as they pass among the naked showering boys, boys kissing the female goal-scorer, or the girl impostor's team being told "you lads play in skins!" Directors like to play on comic misunderstandings. For example, when the headmaster in *Gregory's Girl* learns there is a girl playing in the boys' soccer team he sensibly asks "What about the changing arrangements?" to which the P.E. teacher naively replies, "Oh, she'll bring her own soap."

In *Wild Child*, Emma Roberts grudgingly followed in her dead mother's footsteps as lacrosse captain of the frigid girls' boarding school in which she was reluctantly incarcerated.

Hayden Panettiere ice-skates in *Dust Factory* as she also does in *Ice Princess*. Here is one girl who is not just an actress but talented in the featured sport as well.

For one girl, however, all this sports activity, in particular going to a ball game, was a big waste of time, as Jodie Foster says in *The Little Girl who lives down the Lane*. "A game is pretending. It's like going through the motions of living without ever living."

Some have been sportswomen in their own right. Patty McCormack, the award winning lead in *The Bad Seed* had been a tomboy as a kid, playing baseball among the boys in the junior league tournaments on Long Island. Dana Hill (who won a Best Young Actress Award for playing the target for a paedophile in *Fallen Angel*, and was the Griswold daughter in the *National Lampoon's European Vacation*) was at the age of ten, ranked third for her age group for a middle distance runner in the whole of America, running in the 880 yards and the mile race. Then, having collapsed on the track a few weeks later was diagnosed with diabetes, which ultimately led to a diabetic coma and her premature death.

Even Daniel Radcliffe and Rupert Grint, the boy idols in the *Harry Potter* series, admit their co-star Emma Watson regularly thrashed them at table tennis.[21]

The Great Pretender: girls masquerading as boys

We saw how Zoé Héran in *Tomboy (2011)* created the pretence that she is a boy to gain acceptance in a gang of lads. Many films introduce us to this theme using sport as a springboard, in which a girl wishing to pursue a pastime in a male dominated sphere can only do so by pretending to be a boy.

There are several films featuring girls playing soccer. The Olsen twins in *Switching Goals*, the afore mentioned *Gregory's Girl*, the very successful *Bend it Like Beckham*, a film which first saw Keira Knightley rise to stardom.[22] Most of these films, however, feature older teenagers. The actresses have some limited competence at soccer, but they are woefully shown up on the soccer pitch by their soccer playing male teammates. To facilitate the filming, the boys visibly hold back from tackles to allow the girl through; in the passes the girls make, the ball trickles just a few yards, and their shots on goal are seldom shown hitting the target without an editor's cutting and pasting job. I am not decrying girls playing soccer, but actresses are not necessarily sports stars and so the viewer has to watch without being critical of technique especially in a team where the lads most obviously out-skill the girl impostor. Alas, if you cast a super-talented soccer girl in the role they may not have the acting skills to carry the film. I appreciate the director's dilemma.

She's the Man is one such example in which a high school girl pretends to be her twin brother to get a game because her own all-girls team had to be disbanded due to lack of players. This film is great fun if you overlook the girl's limited soccer talent.[23] Amanda Bynes plays Viola, an American high school pupil, who enjoys playing soccer but cannot get a game because not enough girls are interested in raising a team. While her twin brother flies off to London for a music gig she decides to impersonate him, attending his boarding school and infiltrating the soccer team ready for a big match against her old school. Of course, this means shacking up with her new teammates in their dormitory, pretending to be a boy, avoiding the showers, explaining away why she carries a box of tampons. Frequently she has to make the rapid transition to become a girl again for various activities. This drops her in the embarrassing complications that boy-girl relationships can engender. However, the aim of the film (if any), besides being good fun, is to show that a girl can be acceptable in an all-male team, and that soccer is not exclusively a boy's game anymore. Now then boys, anyone for netball?

Another girl trying to fit unnoticed in an all-boys' team is Saga in *My Life as a Dog*. Although this Swedish film is basically about a boy, Ingemar, and his worries concerning his ill mother, running as a thread through the film is his relationship with his twelve-year-old friend, Saga. Saga played by Melinda Kinnaman enjoys playing football. She has short-cropped hair so passes as a boy in the football league in which she plays alongside Ingemar. There is the predictable amusing episode of the boys in the opposing team unwittingly wanting to swap shirts with her at the end of a game, which she defiantly refuses to do. The boys all have a communal bath, but of course, she can't join in and has to make herself scarce. She also enjoys boxing. Frequently she is sparring with her friend Ingemar.

One day Saga confides with her friend: she doesn't think she can maintain the pretence of being a boy much longer. She holds her blouse tightly against her chest so her budding boobs protrude. "They are showing," she protests to Ingemar. "Can't you see them?"

"Can't you hide them?" suggests Ingemar.

So, Saga pulls off her blouse and between them they wrap a scarf tightly around her chest to flatten her boobs. That seems to have resolved the problem for now, but Ingemar is concerned. "How fast do breasts grow?"

"I don't know," replies Saga, but they continue their boxing sparring, Saga flat-chested in her tight scarf but obviously not a boy.

But Saga has other motives on her mind besides boxing and soccer, for while continuing to box with Ingemar their sparring transposes into a prolonged embrace. Later, she seems to take pleasure in removing her wrap-around scarf in front of Ingemar, much to his embarrassment.

Finally, the girl realises she must yield to her adolescent growth spurts. After a boxing bout she sits down with the lad on some hay bales. "I've grown!" she asserts. "I don't think binding will help any more. That means no more soccer for me. Take a look." And the boy ogles at her as she unbuttons her blouse to reveal the proof. But the boy is not yet ready for her advances. When she asks, "Would you like to touch them?" he storms off, and their friendship is broken, if only temporarily.

The day arrives which the entire Swedish nation has been anticipating: a Swedish boxer taking part in the world boxing championships. Ingemar and Saga had been excited about this fight for weeks. They have made up and are friends again. Now the streets are empty as the whole nation tunes in on their 1959 radio sets. But other desires have superseded the sporting fanaticism of Ingemar and Saga. Oblivious to the commentary on the radio describing the victory bout of their boxing hero, the young boy and girl are curled on the sofa in an intimate embrace. Nothing else seems important any more.

Climbing

Another sports enthusiast who, like Saga, becomes entangled in a love affair, which almost thwarts her plans, is Maddy in *Catch that Kid*. Whereas Saga falls in love with Ingemar as a natural extension of her boxing fanaticism, with Maddy she really needs to use the carrot of a love interest with an expectant pair of boys to ensure her plans are fulfilled. Maddy, played by Kristen Stewart, is a keen rock climber. She had taken up this sport following in the footsteps of her father – a successful Everest mountaineer. Dad, however, had suffered from a near fatal fall while on the mountain and during this film he has a relapse resulting in paralysis. It is no wonder then that he tries to dissuade his daughter from climbing: "I just wished you'd do something that doesn't involve falling off." Mother also tries to deter her. The film starts with the twelve-year-old girl doing a solo climb up the flanks of a giant gas cylinder. One of her anchor points has come loose. Maddy has slipped twenty feet and is hanging precariously from the end of a rope when her mobile phone rings. "What are you doing?" asks mum on the other end of the phone. "You're not climbing are you?" Maddy denies it. "Homework," she lies.

The bulk of the film follows Maddy's attempt to raise money for dad's operation, by robbing the bank in which mum has been installing a new security system. To be successful, she needs the help of her two male friends and she has secretly promised to be the boyfriend of each of them as a reward for helping her carry out the heist. The robbery involves elaborate planning to override the security systems so that she can scale the walls of the bank to reach the elevated vaults and safety deposit boxes to gain access to the safe.

Of course, Kristen Stewart does not actually do any climbing herself. That is left to her stunt doubles. She just has to look athletic, dressed in her jump suit, and dangle from ropes while other look-alikes do the climbing and swinging from gantry. But the action is seamlessly edited, and I am sure her exploits could act as an inspiration for other girls to rock climb as a hobby – but not up gas cylinders, and not solo climbing.

Yet, the use of stunt doubles made Kristen Stewart more convincing as a climber than some of the staged action in the football movies. Likewise, Melinda Kinnaman playing Saga in *My Life as a Dog* had obviously been coached in boxing manoeuvres, and because her opponent was her own age and ability, the action looked realistic and not staged.

Like Kristen Stewart, Abigail Breslin also had a rock-climbing feat to perform in *Nim's island*, in which she had to scale the flank of a volcano. But I believe this was a climbing wall with the volcano scenery added in. She only had to cling to the wall in her harness and was not expected to do any real climbing.

Soccer

Unlike *She's the Man* and *My Life as a Dog*, the girl stars in *Gregory's Girl* and *Bend it like Beckham* are not trying to impersonate a boy. In the case of *Bend it like Beckham*, Keira Knightley does a good job as a soccer star in an all-women's team. In *Gregory's Girl*, the lead lady, Dorothy, is trying to get a place in an all boys' school team, and is standing up for her women's rights to ensure she is picked for the squad. She has seen an ad on the school notice board about a trial for a striker in the soccer team. Dorothy turns up alongside a motley bunch of incompetent boys and demands she is given a trial. "The notice said a trial for talented players," she insists. "It says nothing about being for boys." Of course, she outshines them at ball control, shooting, and running stamina tests. (Some credit can be given to Partick Thistle FC for bringing her up to scratch for the filming.)[24]

"I'm the best in the team," she asserts, but the PE teacher, a naïve Mr Menzies, just wants to fob her off. However, just like coach Buttermaker in *The Bad News Bears* had been put in charge of an underachieving bunch of no-hopers and so was determined to incorporate tomboy Tatum O'Neal into his squad, so too Mr Menzies is desperate to revive the fortunes of his hopeless team. He is already the laughing stock in the staffroom – "I heard your team were awarded a corner last week and took a lap of honour!"

So, after consulting the headteacher, Mr Menzies picks Dorothy for his team. But she also has to overcome the negativity of her peers. "Girls are not meant to play football. It's too tough, too physical," says Andy who is disgruntled at having been replaced by a girl.

"Tough?" responds a defensive Gregory who has fallen madly in love with his fourth year teammate, Dorothy. "Have you ever seen them play hockey? They are like wild animals. Even at twelve and thirteen. They'd kill you."

In sexist mode, Andy replies, "If women were meant to play football they'd have tits somewhere else. They were not designed to play football." But as soon as their team concedes yet another goal he despondently changes his mind. "We need more women in this team!"

Of course during the match, striker Dorothy scores her goal and is instantly mobbed by not just her own players, but the opposing team as well who all enjoy a celebratory kiss with her. The director is further reinforcing the stereotype of a sporting girl in a boy's team as being a joke, something to parody.

Gregory, who was besotted by the girl, had an interesting stance on tomboyism. While his mate Andy derides the girl, "Dorothy, she's too like a boy."

Gregory rebuts, "No. She's just modern."

The Bad News Bears seems to act as a kind of template for girls-in-sports movies – a team of no-hopers is transformed by a girl, a tomboy. The story of *Switching Goals* has many similarities; only the sport is soccer and not baseball. Sam, played by Mary-Kate Olsen and described on the video sleeve as a tomboy, is keen on sports. She wins the wheelbarrow race with her sports' fanatic father. Like Tatum O'Neal in *Bad News Bears* she is a whiz at table shove-ball, shocking her boyfriend by beating him. And she is star striker in her father's soccer team. The shelves in her bedroom are stacked with the sporting trophies she has won over her past thirteen years. When Sam hears the soccer league is changing from all-girls teams to go co-ed she is impressed and thinks it is a great idea to play alongside the boys. "I'm sick of being stuck in those dippy girl leagues," she says.

But the other team managers are not so impressed with the thought of having mixed teams. One manager sarcastically comments, "Girls bring a whole lot of other components into the game – tears, fashion, their mums!"

Another inadvertently says, "You know what they say about girls – they are great equalisers!"

Sam has an identical twin sister – Emma. Though Emma is a willing trier she has no sporting ambition, and is far more interested in boys and fashion, turning up to the soccer trial in shades, painted nails and arm-length gloves. "I must have missed the good athletic gene," she jokes to her twin.

So, Emma is popular with boys but no good at sports, while her twin Sam is good at sports yet, "Let's face it, when it comes to guys I'm just, well, one of the guys!" Despite all Sam's achievements she says to her sister, "I would trade all these trophies for one of the looks you get from the guys at school."

New squads have to be picked. Sporting Sam ends up in a different team, while disgruntled dad is forced to select his non-sporting daughter Emma. The film follows the tricks the girls get up to, exchanging identities by exploiting their identical looks, in the same way that Viola did in *She's the Man*. Also like *She's the Man*, there is the confusion when the one twin confronts the other twin's boyfriend.

Through all their shenanigans both teams progress to the finals. Emma discovers she is a good goalkeeper, and the winnings are shared as Emma parries the final shot from striker Sam to draw the game. "Are you ok, Em?" consoles Sam.

"I broke a nail," says the fashion-conscious Emma, " – but it was worth it!" Girls make good equalisers, after all!

Others take part because sport is on the curriculum for every schoolgirl, whether they are talented or not. Hence, Jena Malone is involved a soccer match during *Stepmom*, playing in an all-girls' team. Keke Palmer plays soccer in her girls' team in *Cleaner* (2007) and scores a goal, but her dad is too busy talking about his job to notice. In *(500) Days of Summer*, Chloë Grace Moretz also plays in a soccer team. While she is a substitute she is able to help her older brother with his dating problems. But then the coach calls her back on the field. "Hey, we haven't finished yet," shouts the boy disappointed, being more interested in his own troubles than in his sister's game.

Water sports

John Creasy (Denzel Washington) is a merciless killer. So when he is hired as bodyguard to a little girl, Pita (Dakota Fanning) in *Men on Fire*, it is only natural he uses analogies with firearms to help coach the little girl in swimming technique. "The gunshot holds no fear," he shouts at the swimming novice, and the girl has to repeat the words back to him as she hovers at the poolside waiting to dive. Pita is good in the water but hesitant when awaiting the starting gun, so the bodyguard helps her improve her initial dives, and coaches her into winning the gala. [24a] In *My Queen Karo*, Anna Franziska Jager proves competent swimming underwater and diving from high platforms as she is coached in lifesaving skills.

Christina Ricci plays nine-year-old Kate Flax in *Mermaids*. She is a keen swimmer with ambitions of swimming the English Channel. She completes a couple of lengths at the local baths but still has a long way to go! She practises by holding her breath underwater in the bathtub like a mermaid. Even so, when she falls in the local pond she has to be rescued from drowning.

Other films depict water-based sports for girls: diving in *Dive*, and synchronised swimming in *Water Lilies*.

In *Water Lilies*, Adèle Haenel pursues synchronised swimming. Whether or not the underwater ballet sequences are performed by a double, she has considerable water confidence of her own. It is out of the water where she is less secure, particularly with her boyfriend, and she develops a lesbian relationship with a girl who has a crush on her.

Both *Dive* and *Water Lilies* feature older teenage girls, so really they lie beyond the brief of this volume but I have included them because they help illustrate certain dilemmas facing many young teenagers. In *Dive* (a TV drama) we see a nineteen-year-old Aisling Loftus playing Lyndsey, a high school student training for the 2012 Olympic Games. In it, her character shows real dedication for the sport: up at dawn for a strict gymnastics and diving regime, which stretches her to the limit. But the girl is affected by the break-up of her parents, and she seeks solace among her friends – one of whom, a boy, gets her pregnant, shattering her Olympian dreams.

For thirteen-year-old Annabel Andrews (Gaby Hoffman) in *Freaky Friday* (1995) her talent is diving, too. As captain of the diving team she has been given the unpleasant task by the coach of deciding who to leave out of the team. This leads to a falling out with all her best friends. This is a crazy movie in which mother and daughter magically switch roles on Friday 13th. This results in chaos, but a diplomatic solution is found in which the team agrees to alternate the dropping of one of the team members.

In *Innocence* (2004), the boarders at the French girls' boarding school go swimming in the lake. It is the duty of the older eleven-year-old girls to teach the youngest arrivals how to swim. As the other girls bob in the water, Bianca (Berangere Haibruge) and her friends carefully corral little Iris as she makes her first attempt at doggy paddle.

We mentioned earlier how Abigail Breslin was chosen for the role of the Robinson Crusoe type girl in *Nim's Island*. Regardless of the fact that she was not a strong swimmer and had to be coached to help her swim underwater, she was nevertheless chosen for the role, which involved a lot of filming in the sea (or a wave pool). For someone who had to spend a considerable time working in the water, I hope there was more than just the assumption that Abigail could swim. I would have thought the casting director would have ensured her lead star for *Nim's Island* was a competent swimmer. At least she was not playing the part of a talented swimmer, a representative for her sport. Similar safety concerns needed to be assessed for any child involved in action in the water: Tina Majorino alone in a dinghy in a choppy sea in *Andre*, Georgie Henley on an ice flow in *The Lion, the Witch and the Wardrobe*, the Von Trapp children whose boat on the lake capsized in *The Sound of Music*, the buccaneer children in *Swallows and Amazons*. After filming, Abigail Breslin admitted having never even seen the ocean before, let alone swum in it.

At least director Niki Caro ascertained from her lead child actress, Keisha Castle-Hughes, that she was a competent swimmer, for the child was expected to swim under water and sit on a whale's back in the open ocean in *Whale Rider*. The eleven-year-old assured the film director she could swim. It was only after Keisha had been cast for the role that it was discovered she was not a strong swimmer, after all, and so a stand-in had to be used for many of the swimming scenes. Even so, Keisha was expected to ride astride the animatronic whale in the ocean scene, ten miles off-shore. The Oscar-nominated child says it was the scariest thing she had ever done and was terrified.

Vincent Kartheiser and Thora Birch, whose canoe capsizes in *Alaska* (1996), are left floundering in boiling rapids, washed away by the raging current. Although generous use of stunt doubles were used, these children had some exciting action to perform, keeping the audience clinging to their seats.

Concern over the water-competency of the child actors was raised in *Water Lilies*, as the teams of synchronised swimmers go through their training and take part in competitions. At least we do witness the aspiring actresses on their selection interview to be chosen as members of the cast. Adèle Haenel was sensational in her previous acting role as the carefree runaway in *Les Diables*. Now she is being interviewed by her casting director to play the part of swimming team leader, Floriane, in *Water Lilies*.

"How long have you been swimming?" asks the director, no doubt assuming the answer would be 'all her life'.

"I've been swimming for two years," Adèle says vaguely.

"Only two years!" Alarms must be ringing in the mind of the director. "But you've always been sporty?"

You can see Adèle conjuring up an answer. "Judo, a bit of dance, ping pong," as if that has clinched the role for a part as a strong swimmer.

But for first-time director, Céline Sciamma, this was her début film, and she seemed a novice interviewer. At the auditions, the embarrassed cast members were asked to face forwards, stand profile, turn round, as if they were part of a cattle auction. However, despite these seemingly tentative forays into casting, the director made a wise choice, creating a sumptuous, salacious movie about teenage love and angst in the context of a swimming club. There are some spectacular underwater scenes of the girls doing their synchronised routines. I may be wrong, but I assume that Adèle Haenel's swimming parts were played by a stunt double, though a lithe Pauline Acquart prowls purposely through the foreground like a playful porpoise.

No doubt, the actresses chosen for these roles of sporting stars have some athletic talents themselves – and maybe Adèle Haenel was just being modest at her interview.

Dance

Boys are becoming more prominent in the world of dance, a sphere previously perceived to be dominated by girls. The world of ballet must take credit or blame for the female bias, and for decades, dance has appeared on the school curriculum for girls' PE, as exemplified by Tracy Hyde and her female classmates becoming eye-fodder for the boy voyeur, Mark Lester, in *Melody*. Ballet lessons and frilly tutus were the little girls' domain; Ethan Randall waits embarrassed in the snowy street for his younger sister, Thora Birch, to emerge from ballet class dressed in her pink tutu and goose pimples (*All I want for Christmas*). In *Billy Elliot*, too, the ballet class was for girls only; the boys did boxing. The twenty-first century phenomenon of streetdance has allowed boys to excel in the sphere of dance in what was once the preserve of the girl. This is very much an explosive cultural revolution. While streetdance requires muscular and gymnastic skill in the way ballet does, its immersion in popularist music culture, linked to Caribbean identity, has allowed this, like Carnival, to mushroom into acceptability. Here is a stage on which the boy can shine, crossing the gender boundary of respectable consensus.

Whereas only few males became movie icons of the disco era – the likes of John Travolta (*Saturday Night Fever*, *Grease*), Patrick Swayze (*Dirty Dancing*), and Michael Jackson (*Moonwalker*), all of whom are adult actors – dance has now been given twenty-first century street-cred by the likes of George Sampson (*StreetDance*), Jamie Bell (*Billy Elliot*) and the dance troop *Diversity*. Both *Billy Elliot* and *StreetDance* must be given credit for making the world of ballet more accessible and credible to a sub-culture of males who had previously maligned this as a sport for namby-pamby Morris Men, and for little girls country-dancing round a May Pole. And yet, dance is still a theme geared towards the female adolescent. It is the adolescent girl that seeks out the venues in *Dirty Dancing*, no boys join the mass ranks of dancers on the pier for *Mamma Mia!* and boys are a scarcity in the Irish dance film documentary, *Jig*.

Unlike actors chosen as sports-playing characters, the dancing actor is likely to hold genuine skills. It is much more difficult to fake a talent for dance, and there are many films which feature girls as dance enthusiasts. Since girls tend to be natural dancers, it is refreshing watching genuine dance routines being performed without resorting to use of a double. In *Innocence* (2004) the dance consists of slow classical ballet tragedy sequences in which eleven-year-old girls perform in front of an audience to help pay for the running of their orphanage. The director, Lucile Hadzihalilovic, on purpose cast girls with no acting experience but who came from a dance/gymnastic background. In *Slumdog Millionaire*, Tanvi Ganesh Lonkar was cast because of her experience of classical Indian dance, though her dancing skills were underused on screen. Most film guides list *Children of Theatre Street* as a film but is in reality a documentary tracing the auditions, schooling and rigorous training of aspirant Russian ballerinas in the 1970s Soviet Union: eleven-year-old Angelina Armeiskaya and Alec Timoushin, and teenaged Lena Voronzova.

The boy dancer Jamie Bell in *Billy Elliot* has stupendous talent. The character of Billy defiantly chose ballet despite knowing he would be ridiculed for it in the Geordie mining community in which he lived. But daily, with Mrs Wilkinson's (Julie Walters) help, he attends the girls' ballet class and forms a friendship with Mrs Wilkinson's daughter, a fellow member of the ballet troop. Jamie Bell, aged fourteen, won a Bafta for this performance.

George Sampson, fresh from his victory in *Britain's Got Talent*, puts together an impressive routine in *StreetDance*. His role is to cause a distraction, using dance, to allow time for the ballet contingent to arrive for the streetdance championships. This is an exciting toe-tapping movie, blending opposing genres of rap-dancing and ballet. "We'll win the competition because of who we are," says Carla (Nichola Burley), not willing to fall into a copycat rut.

Beaches (1988) is a chronicle about the lives of two women who first became friends in their childhood. Mayim Bialik, as a thirteen-year-old, displays a convincing song-and-dance routine. CC Bloom's tap dancing down the hotel lobby attracts the attention of guests and staff alike. Many other girls have acted the role of dancing songsters – Aileen Quinn and Alicia Morton in *Annie* (1982) and *Annie* (1999), the great Judy Garland in *Wizard of Oz*. All these girls are super talented and have no need for miming or for stunt doubles. Margaret O'Brien had no singing/dancing experience for her role as Tooti in *Meet me in St Louis*, and yet her exuberance saw her nominated for an Oscar – although playing alongside Judy Garland she was in the presence of surely the greatest singing child actor of all time.

Lindsay Lohan dances along to the closing credits in *Life-Size*, a delightful Julie Glenn, as nine-year-old Lulu, does a splendid jive in front of a long mirror in the garden during the French film, *An Impudent Girl*, her arms and unbuttoned blouse dancing wildly with the rhythm, to the lyrics of *Sara Perche ti Amo*, while Ana Torrent dances with Conchita Perez to *Porque te vas* in *Cría Cuervos*, and there is a great acrobatic choreography performed by Eileen Quinn and the rest of her fellow orphans in *Annie* (1982). For Ayami in the Japanese horror *Audition*, classical ballet was a way of "calming and purifying ugly feelings" brought on by a childhood of abuse. In this film, we see flashbacks of when the lady was a seven-year-old child, as Ayaka Izumi performs stuttering pirouettes in her white leotard, before being brutalised by her stepfather. "When I danced, I shared my troubles with my sweat," she tells us. For Ayami, ballet was a distraction that helped her to come to terms with her past.

All the above actors and actresses share a discernable talent for both dance and acting. Where the actors lack dance skills, the directors have to find ways to mask any shortcomings. *Balletshoes* is a made-for-TV adaptation of Noel Streatfeild's novel. Lucy Boynton (from *Miss Potter*) plays Posy Fossil whose ambition is to become a ballerina. She had been adopted as a baby by a globetrotting palaeontologist, her only possession being a pair of ballet slippers left to her by her now deceased ballerina mother. Posy grows up hoping that one day her feet will fit inside the slippers and she will achieve success as a ballerina. The germ is obviously in her blood, for she is soon spotted by Madame Fidolia who is willing to personally tutor her. We get to see some marvellous dancing by Lucy Boynton who, at first glimpse, appears to be a brilliant natural dancer, until you realise all the action is performed in subdued light as a silhouette against the bright window, and that maybe a stand-in is doing all the elaborate dance moves. Her world seemingly falls apart when Madame has a stroke, and Posy arrives home inconsolable. That is, until the others discover the true reason for her tears. "I'm not crying about Madame. I'm crying about me!" All the dreams she had built up are now shattered because her tutelage has been terminated. But she is undeterred. She has the gall to turn up uninvited at a Russian dance school. "Do you speak Russian?" this impostor is asked. "No, but I dance Russian," Posy tells them. And the film ends with her setting off for Prague to train among the world's elite.

There are other dancing actors who don't quite make the grade. In *Dickie Roberts, Former Child Star*, ten-year-old Jenna Boyd has a minor role as Sally Finney. She has to perform a dance routine at a competition. The girl who precedes her in the competition is obviously a competent dancer, but because she performs her routine it in a sexy and suggestive manner (mimicking Britney Spears), she is confronted with stony-faced glares from the audience and panel of judges. But when the diminutive Jenna Boyd dances, her routine is perfunctory and elementary, yet she receives tumultuous applause. Here is a case of an actress being shown up by another successful sports-girl. I wonder if the director regretted not casting the quality dancer for the role of Sally Finney?

Chloë Grace Moretz plays a nine-year-old cheerleader, Carrie, in *Big Momma's House 2*, hoping to perform with her team at the regional competition in California. When the time comes for the competition, Carrie's dance-troop perform a spectacular dance routine. They are obviously talented preteen performers who do not need stunt doubles (though there are men on stand-by to catch any acrobat that might fall from the impressive pyramid they form together. Chloë Moretz, however, is an actress, and her role in the dance routine is simply posing in sequence – she doesn't do any of the acrobatics herself.

Amy's *Running Bear* dance in *How to Kill your Neighbour's Dog* was a way of proving a physical handicap could not defeat a disabled girl despite her over-protective mother. Suffering from a mild form of cerebral palsy, Amy's (Suzi Hofrichter) mother wraps the child in proverbial cotton wool. As a result, the girl is friendless because she has not been allowed to join in activity games or to swim. With the help of neighbourly Kenneth Branagh she performs actions to the *Running Bear* song. Despite stumbling and knocking over a precious vase, the girl and Branagh enjoy themselves and are keen on continuing. It is the stifling mother who feels apologetic and self conscious, prematurely terminating the dance.

Several DVDs are available in which children demonstrate dance routines, though they are not movies. Instead of being talented actresses, the DVDs portray talented girl dancers. Probably the most well-known among them is *Lambada* in which twelve year old Brazilian girl, Roberta DeBrito, demonstrates the dance moves alongside the professional adult performers, accompanied by the diminutive Chico Oliviera. Other dance DVD/Videos promote modern disco-style moves: *Moving n Grooving, Rhythm of Life, Party Dancing,* and *Barbie Dance Stars. Dance the S Club Way* features S-Club Juniors, who were a successful pop child-septet aping the singing and dancing routines of the chart-topping S-Club Seven. A Swedish version of a girl-child group was called BreZe.

Other dance DVDs/Videos teach little girls to dance ballet or classical moves – *Bella Dancerella*, or the beautifully made *Dance like the Flower Fairies*, which features delightful girls parading gracefully to the music. By contrast, I am unaware of such DVDs teaching aspirant boys how to dance, unless he is willing to wallow in the tutorage of writhing teeny bopping wenches.

Getting the Parents' Support

Any sport's coach involved with children's teams will probably tell you their worst enemy is the parent, particularly the father who wants to live out his own failed sporting dreams through that of his child. The cries and taunts from the touch line must be the most disheartening experiences for the confused child whose attempt to play the game naturally are thwarted by a torrent of conflicting suggestions, reprimands and swearwords from over enthusiastic parents who have inflated expectations, and who ought to know better. Keke Palmer saw this happening as she competed in the national spelling competition in *Akeelah and the Bee*. A pushy parent was making life hell for her main rival, so on purpose she fluffs and answer so the lad would not be reprimanded for failing to win.

In *My Year Without Sex*, we have Jonathan Segat about to kick for goal in Australian rules football. It is close to the final whistle. Father urges the boy to kick to touch to avoid conceding possession, instilling a win-at-all-costs mentality instead of allowing the child his moment of individual glory with a goal scoring attempt.

Chloë Grace Moretz, in *Big Momma's House 2*, wishes mum and dad would come to watch her cheerleading. But her parents always make excuses and are too busy. Chloë tells her nanny (Big Momma), "I just want to be good. If I'm good, daddy will come to watch me." Big Momma gets her to refocus her ambitions. As you practise your dancing, do it for yourself, and not just as a way to please your parents.

Lindsay Lohan in *Life-Size* has the same desire: if only her father would attend her American Football matches. Since her mother died, her sporting ambitions have been thwarted, and she squabbles with her teammates. "Go play with your dolls, Casey," one particular boy tells her.

"I hate dolls as much as I hate you," she retorts. The girl is angry because father has missed the match again.

Father, in the throes of clinching an important business deal, apologises to her when she gets home. "I should have been there, sorry," he feebly says.

But she admonishes him: "You wore out sorry a long time ago."

But the day of the seventh grade championship arrives. "You're her biggest fan, right?" Dad, realising he has been side-lining his daughter for too long, abandons the business deal at the crucial moment, and races to the ballpark to watch the game. "Go on, Casey," he yells as he arrives. The girl, so surprised at hearing her father, is instantly flattened by the opposition. But it is not long before the rejuvenated girl throws the killer pass that wins the match. "That was the best pass I've ever seen," praises her father. "I'm so proud of you."

And her antagonistic teammate joins in the adulation: "Hey Casey, nice pass."

"For a girl?" questions Casey.

"For anyone!" admits the boy.

THE ADVENTURERS / JUST GOOD FUN

Not all films have to fit into a meaningful category. Some are just good fun, entertaining for the viewer without being demanding, and enjoyable to take part in for the actors: such as Josh Hutcherson exploring the depths of the Earth through volcanic vents in a modern update of *Journey to the Centre of the Earth*, and mimicking the roller coaster ride of Ke Huy Quan in *Indiana Jones*; or Mason Gamble single-handedly thwarting the thief (Christopher Lloyd) while shattering en route the peace and sanity of his grumpy neighbour, Walter Matthau, in *Dennis* (1993); while in *Russkies*, the trio of lads (Leaf Phoenix, Peter Billinsley, Stefan DeSalle) hold as a hostage the Russian spy who carelessly marooned himself off Florida's Key West. Others, such as *The Goonies* find themselves pursued by crooks in a underground labyrinth of caves, while in *Zathura* and *Explorers* the adventures take on extraterrestrial dimensions.

The Adventure Journey as a Rite-of-Passage

Where a journey is undertaken, in most cases, the adventure incorporates a rite-of-passage in which the troubled child re-evaluates his/her life and relationships. In *Magic Island* and *The Adventures of Sharkboy and Lavagirl* we find two boys (Jack and Max) who feel neglected by their respective parents – Jack (Zachery Ty Bryan) despondent that his mother is going on yet another all night 'business' trip, Max (Cayden Boyd) distressed by the constant arguing of his parents and a fear of school bullies. According to Sinyard, it was 'dissatisfaction with ineffectual parents' that caused the children in *The Goonies* to embark on their fanciful subterranean journey.[25] These kids are following the footsteps of alarmed Dorothy, whose fear that her dog Toto may be destroyed, forces her to flee home to seek out her own Yellow Brick Road. In *James and the Giant Peach*, Paul Terry dreams of escaping his evil guardian aunties. Roald Dahl's tale takes his hero on a turbulent voyage to reach his proverbial 'Big Apple'.

The child is invariably whisked away in a cataclysm. Jack is vortexed into the pages of the book he is reading, Max's heroes arrive in a whirlwind (with an imagined spacecraft handy), and we all know how the Kansas tornado whisked Dorothy into the psychedelic realm of Oz (in *Magic Island*, *The Adventures of Sharkboy and Lavagirl* and *The Wizard of Oz*, respectively). A time-travelling tardis transports Craig Warnock in *Time Bandits*. Various portals are needed to access Narnia besides wardrobes, the eddy from a passing tube train sends the Pevensies spiralling to the rescue of *Prince Caspian*. Only Alice seems to drift serenely off to sleep before the white rabbit appears.[26]

Many of these adventures are scripted by authors with cotton wool and comfort blankets at the ready, who transport their cast into a magical world, but hey, we can't really have our children traipsing too far from the homestead, so the magic ends as the child awakes realising it was only a dream (an easy cop-out for the author). These authors are using the dream adventure-of-a-lifetime as a form of escapism from reality, hoping the child will emerge edified without experiencing the reality of trauma. When our adventurers return, nothing has actually changed in their respective households, yet somehow, the dream has magically shifted the child's psyche to make reality more acceptable. Judy Garland is asked, "What have you learnt, Dorothy?" and she realises "If I ever go looking for my heart's desire again, I won't look any further than my own backyard." Max on his return from planet Drool realises, "Dreaming prevents you from seeing what is right in front of your eyes." Neil Sinyard explains it thus: "The adventure has been a sort of temporary aberration, and the child returns gratefully to the family womb."[27] Yet, Dorothy's dreaded Mrs Scott with her pushbike and pannier still lives up the road,[27a] and Max's folks still bicker. The dream helps the child put a positive spin on his/her reaction to life's hurdles.

For any positive message to be effectual, the child has to take these adventures in the absence of parents. How else can the nurturing embrace of the welcoming family for the returning prodigal be enhanced? Where there are accompanying parents, as in *Mosquito Coast* and even *The Swiss Family Robinson*, the children are begrudging followers in the wake of their parents, so that for the child the adventure loses the dimension of fear, independence, self-reliance and self esteem. There is certainly no tearful embrace for the prodigal as he/she returns.

Perhaps the best children at having fun were those living in the middle of the twentieth century when they had freedom to roam and explore. Less danger of traffic, unaccompanied bicycle rides, outings to the sea, messing about on rivers, no distractions of television or computers – all contributed to an outdoor lifestyle for rural kids. Enid Blyton encapsulated the era with her books about the exploits of *The Famous Five* exploring the countryside and coast, when ginger beer and raspberry jelly made a veritable treat (no burgers or pizzas in those days). In *Stand by Me*, Richard Dreyfuss reminisces about the childhood trek he made in 1959 with his three boy companions, bedrolls draped over their shoulders, following the rail tracks into the Oregon wilderness to search for a dead body. "You did remember to bring food, didn't you?" demands Jerry O'Connell, as hungry-time nags his stomach. Even as late as 1970, four unaccompanied girls go off cycling to the next town and explore graveyards at midnight, in *Now and Then*. This was all possible in those days – boys and girls had freedom to explore.

There was less pressure on doing homework, no SATs tests to get het up about, no ferrying to and from school in mum's car, no curfews. Today's kids are restrained from going out of the house, let alone going to the park by themselves, and certainly not camping out on their own. Although stranger-danger was considered a problem, it was not blown out of all proportion as it is today, and there always seemed to be a Bobby around to keep an eye on things. "While going about my duties on the other side of the park I noticed some valuables had gone astray," says the constable in *Mary Poppins*, holding Jane and Michael by the scruff of their collars.

So what a spiffing piece of nostalgia is engendered when watching *Swallows and Amazons*. The premise of four children going camping by themselves on their own island in the middle of Cumbria's Lake Derwent,[27b] coping without any adults, sailing where they please, exploring the nooky inlets on the shoreline, playing pirates, setting ambushes – the idea of such freedom and fun must be looked upon incredulously by modern day kids. Although I loved this film, which brought back the magic of my own childhood, I guess in reality, modern kids will think it all rather trite, lacking in mechanical and technological sophistication. How could they have had fun without gameboys, or mobile phones to text on?

Of course, the children had to get permission from father by telegram (remember those?). His reply: "Better drowned than duffers. If not duffers won't drown." So there we are then, surely that's clear!

To prepare for their camping trip, John reads up on nautical symbols, Susan reads up on recipes, Titty reads adventure stories so she'll know how to evade capture if they get into difficulties with the natives! After all, they are in Cumberland.

They set 'orf' for their island in the lake, and pitch camp. "Oughtn't I have the telescope for keeping watch?" asks John politely.

"Yes, I think you ought," replies Titty, who surely owns the most inappropriate girl's name in history.

While they all have nice jolly fun without squabbling, the older children do feel it's their duty to boss the younger ones around. For oldest boy, John, it is obvious he must be captain. For younger boy Roger, well, "Roger it's time you were in bed."

The six children in *Swallows and Amazons*, certainly got real hands-on action. There were no stuntmen sailing *their* yachts, and when Capt. John said "Mind the painter" they all knew it wasn't an encounter with an artist, but that they needed to duck as the sail's angle was changed and the boat tacked. The four Walker children and the two Blacket girls spent their days camping, fishing, cooking on open fires and sailing their yachts around the bays, inlets and islands of Lake Derwent, culminating with a battle against Uncle Jim in which Ronald Fraser was made to walk the plank.

While the Walker and Blacket children used their adventure to role-play a game of espionage, Dean Stockwell chose to immerse himself in the real-life intrigue of the sub-continent's north-west frontier in *Kim (1950)*. Kim's whole existence seemed one big adventure, in the film based on Rudyard Kipling's yarn. The orphaned waif hobnobs with horse traders and holy men, becomes involved in spying and espionage, at the time of the British occupation of India at the turn of the nineteenth century.

Being an English boy in the guise of an Indian scallywag, he becomes the ideal pupil to be taught 'The Great Game', in which he uses observational skills to act as a spy for the British army. When he discovers the recipient for one of his messages has been murdered, he heads off by himself for the Khyber Pass to relay the message, much to the alarm of his adult supervisors. "I only think the boy has gone on a man's mission," explains Red Beard to the colonel.

For a more contemporary thrills and spills adventure seek out *Alaska* (1996), in which Thora Birch and her impetuous brother (Vincent Kartheiser) set off for the wilderness in search of their father whose plane has crashed somewhere in the glacial mountains. Theirs is a dogged pursuit in canoe and on foot into a desolate unknown. These child actors must have had great fun on their outwards bound style adventure – abseiling down rock faces, clinging for dear life on rocks in raging rivers, paddling (and capsizing) their canoes through incredible landscapes, and dropped by helicopter on top of remote mountain plateaus.

Stereotypically, the girl is portrayed with practical tomboyish commonsense, who knows her limits and assesses dangers without being foolhardy; the boy is a jump-in head first character, whose misplaced bravado finds him floundering for his life in rivers, and dangling precariously from mountain crags, his dictum bellowing from his indomitable spirit: "Keep going! Never give up!"

At least when the *Swiss Family Robinsons* took their trans-global boat adventure, they knew they were coming back eventually, had they not been shipwrecked. Alas, a different Robinson family in *Lost in Space* knew they would never return from *their* adventure. They were heading off for a ten-year journey in suspended animation to start a colony on Alpha Prime, at the far side of the galaxy. "There are no manuals on how to deal with this," complains mum, "about taking a family to a new planet."

But for teenage daughter, Jenny Robinson (Lacey Chabert) this was like the end of her life. On her final night on Earth, instead of staying in with the family like she was told, she mutinies, "I'm going out to say goodbye to the whole of my life… I'm going to blow ten years of allowance at the mall." When her brother says there will be trouble, Jenny laughs at him. "What are they going to do, ground me?"

Blast off occurs after they have all been cryostatically preserved in their space pods. But before long, a stowaway sabotages the computer robot, so that the family prematurely awake from their slumber to confront a series of implausible and unconvincing scenarios, until they eventually arrive at Alpha Prime. But the billions of dollars spent on all this space travel, the life-threatening encounters, ten years in cryostasis – all this was worth it for, "It's nice having the whole family under one roof – even though we had to cross the galaxy to find it!"

Magic Island is a wonderful tale of pirates, buccaneers, and of a neglected teenage boy who magically arrives on the island to receive a life-enhancing lesson. A boy from Los Angeles, thirteen-year-old Jack, is fed up with mum never being at home. Like in *A Never-Ending Story*, he is given a book to read by his Trinidadian housemaid.

"Stories are for kids – I'm thirteen," objects the boy (Zachery Ty Bryan).

"This is not just a book," the maid tells him, "It's a story that will change your life."

Lying on his bed, Jack disinterestedly flicks through the pages. "You want adventure? You want to rescue the princess? To save the universe…." A vortex drags the boy into the pages of the book, and he lands with a thud on a Mexican beach in 1796 where a band of buccaneers are sword fighting with Blackbeard and his pirates.

The buccaneers adopt the lad as a member of their gang and call him Mad Jack, the Sorcerer from Los Angeles. Jack has chance to impress them using the twentieth century gadgets he has in his kitbag – a water gun, torch, chewing gum, and a cigarette lighter. They are hoping Jack will guide them safely using his magic.

Jack falls into the sea. This is where we meet the remarkably wonderful fourteen-year-old actress, Jessie-Ann Friend, who steals every scene with her confident performance, her clarity, her never-wavering gestures, and her striking beauty, clad only in an oyster-shell bikini and a grass skirt, as she runs barefoot through the sand. Jessie-Ann Friend plays Lily, a mermaid who magically grows legs when on land. Lily rescues Jack from drowning, after which the couple are inseparable.

"Take me with you, Jack," the mermaid insists. "I've always dreamed of such an adventure."

Entrusted with the treasure map, the young couple lead the buccaneers along jungle paths, closely pursued by Blackbeard and his cutthroats. This is pantomime, so expect to see coconuts bonking on heads, vines to trip on, quicksand, and people buried up to their necks on the beach.

"I'm no use," despairs Jack. "I'm not a real sorcerer."

But Lily reassures him, "You've already saved your friends once, Jack, and if it was without magic, then how brave you are! You're the bravest boy I ever met, Jack," and their lips almost graze.

They arrive at the cave entrance where the treasure is hidden. Jack finds a way to open the door, and they all drool over the piles of jewellery and gold. Blackbeard claims it all for himself, while Lily suggests with feminine practicality, "Well, why can't we all just share the treasure?" Booby-traps in the jinxed cave means everyone leaves empty handed. But Lily is not despondent.

"It's the best adventure I ever had, Jack, although I'm glad to be back home." Her thank-you kiss makes the boy blush bright pink. "Goodbye, Jack. I'll always remember you," and after a final kiss, Jack finds himself waking up in his bed at home, with mum looking in his room explaining she has cancelled her appointment because she wants to be back home with her son.

Jack's adventure stemmed from resentment against his mother, who was too often away from home, causing the boy to feel neglected. Max is another boy using his dream adventures as a strategy to cope with the constant arguing of his parents. "I guess you've been noticing lately that your father and I are not compatible," explains his mother in the film *The Adventures of Sharkboy and Lavagirl*. This is another imaginative film full of rollicking good fun. The main characters, Sharkboy and Lavagirl, both figments of Max's imagination, help the young boy to come to terms with his fear of bullying at school, in particular, from one boy Linus. Max's lifeline is his dreamworld, which he records in his dream journal, lest he forget. Sharkboy is played by the energetic, tough Taylor Lautner, who pounces gymnastically into every scene with gusto. Lavagirl, played by Taylor Dooley, is "an amazing girl with purple flames for hair, and skin of molten lava rocks." She is able to shoot lava from the palms of her hands. Like Jessie-Ann Friend in *Magic Island*, both Taylor Lautner and Taylor Dooley light up every scene they are in with their dramatic action and poses.

Fearing ridicule from his classmates, Max is able to dream his heroes into life. Sharkboy and Lavagirl come storming through the classroom window in a whirlwind. "We need your help, Max. Come with us," entreats the flaming girl. "We need you to save our planet, Drool." This really impresses Max's classmates, particularly bespectacled Melissa, whose spectacles mask a twinkle in her eye for the boy.

Outside is the rocket that Max has dreamt up, and all he has to do to fly it is press 'go'. They arrive on planet Drool with just forty-five minutes to spare before darkness completely destroys the planet. The planet is full of wacky imaginative psychedelic landscapes. They have to go through the '*Passage of Time*', travel on the '*Train of Thought*', swim through the '*Stream of Consciousness*', and skate across the '*Sea of Confusion*', before reaching Mount Never Rest, all the while being pursued by snaking electric plugs which are manipulated by the evil Mr Electric.

However, all their actions are restricted by Max's dreaming. "Most dreams don't come true on their own." So, if he has not thought out the scenarios, they cannot come to fulfilment. "The '*Train of Thought*' gets easily distracted." As things start to go wrong, and time is rapidly ticking down, Sharkboy and Lavagirl persuade him to dream good thoughts and not nightmares. Nice thoughts bring them to a land of milk and cookies, where their raft – a giant chocolate chip cookie – floats down a river of milk.

Things don't begin to go right until Max learns one vital lesson. "I wanted all my dreams to come true. But I only dreamt for myself. I wanted to escape my real world. Selfish dreams should not come true." It takes positive thoughts about his enemy Linus, and about his arguing parents, before Max and his friends can fulfil their mission. "What do you do when your dreams have been destroyed? Dream a better dream."

Despite its low rating by film critics, I found this film great fun. Like most children's films it has moral messages to pursue, and this film was not reticent about revealing them. "You thought you could escape fear by running away to dreamland, but fear is in the one place you can never escape – your mind."

In *The Mosquito Coast*, Harrison Ford is the domineering father and maniacal adventurer taking his family into the heart of darkness, abandoning their American homeland for the Belize jungle. The family consists of crackpot inventor dad, compliant mum, proud son Charlie (River Phoenix), his younger brother Jerry (Jadrian Steele), and the dutiful nine-year-old twins, April and Clover (played by Hilary and Rebecca Gordon).

At first, the children loyally follow their visionary father's lead, setting up camp and building a smallholding in the leach-infested jungle. They help dad build an ice-making machine, and carry ice through the forest to impress the natives. They swim in the fishpond. But really, they are hemmed in by the oppressive forest. It is not long before the pioneering children are complaining. "I miss my old home in America." The kids have to muck in: "There was work, and more work: a routine that took up every daylight hour," complains the oldest boy, Charley.

Father taunts them saying how lucky they are to live their subsistence way of life: no TV, no homework, no pollution. "Everything we need is here." What better education do they need? They can learn all they need to know from the jungle.

It is dad's never-say-die attitude that rankles the family. "In the end Robinson Crusoe went back home, but we are staying," announces father defiantly, even though their position is seriously precarious. It is this that makes his once-devoted children start to hate him, they see he is turning crazy, and they plot their mutiny.

"I hate him. I wish he was dead," says the younger son.

"I hate his shoulders, his greasy hair, the sight of his spine, and imagine what it would be like to stick a knife in him," says the older brother.

"Think of it as an adventure," suggests German officer David Thewlis to his eight-year-old son, Asa Butterfield, as they are relocated to run a concentration camp in *The Boy in the Striped Pyjamas*. The lack of honesty on the part of the father by concealing the truth about the compound behind the barbed wire fence results in the inquisitive boy being herded up with the other Jews into the gas chamber. Maybe father's own racist beliefs and deceitful comments were his downfall: "If you ever found a nice Jew, you would become the best explorer in the world," he had told his son.

The adventures need not take place in outer space or darkest Africa. The backyard becomes the jungle, full of alien danger for the four kids miniaturised to the size of pinheads in *Honey, I Shrunk the Kids*. Here is a stage-set that all children are familiar with, where their own imaginations can run riot. Where else is riding on the back of friendly ants possible, or sparring with scorpions, or sleeping the night away with the girl next door inside a child's lego brick. "I don't think we're in Kansas anymore, Toto," exclaims the bewildered Amy O'Neill to her brother Robert Oliveri.

The Amazons: Girl Adventurers

There have always been female adventurers. The intrusion of sexist propaganda has caused us to forget that. They are, of course, a rarity. History anthologies rave about the solitary female enduring privations among 'uncivilised' natives, stalling the constant question 'Why are you travelling without your husband?' The Victorian era brought these wanderers to our attention.

Some were motivated by missionary zeal. Others, surprisingly travelled for travelling sake, to satiate a curiosity about far-flung places around the world: Freya Stark, a nomadic explorer in the Arabian peninsula, Mary Kingsley bashing through the jungles of West Africa, Gertrude Bell travelling through Biblical haunts of Syria and The Levant, Margaret Mead expressing anthropological curiosity about Samoan and Coral Sea cultures.

The screenwriter does not allow our younger travellers the same freedom to wander. Our Amazons have to travel with a mission. Hayley Mills' voyage around the world is to seek her missing father, Capt Grant (in *In Search of the Castaways*); Juliane Koepcke's solitary struggle through the Amazon jungle for nine days in *Miracles Still Happen* (1994) was undertaken only because the plane crash had left her the only surviving passenger; Jenny Agutter's *Walkabout* was necessitated by her father's suicide leaving her and her little brother stranded in the vast Australian outback. At least Jenny had previous wanderlust experience being escorted through Nubia to evade the Mahdi, in *East of Sudan*.

"Dear mother, I'm about to embark on a great adventure," writes Mattie Ross (Hailee Steinfeld) in True Grit (2010). This fourteen-year-old has hired a lawman to seek out the murderer of her pa. And she's going along, too, thinking it will be like "a glorified 'coon hunt".

This headstrong girl is more stubborn than the mule she has brought along, and she is very determined. When she is left behind by the river ferry, she makes the horse swim the current to rejoin the posse. Gunfights, hangings and thrashings can't deter her, until, in a final showdown she shoots her father's killer – she, of course, politely tells him why before doing so. At the end of the trail Le Boeuf (Matt Damon) is able to congratulate her, "You've earned your spurs, that's clear enough."

For the four girls[28] in *Now and Then*, their bike ride into the next town was, for them, an adventure into the unknown, a first tug at the strand of independence, a cementing of friendships in a joint enterprise, the tarmac stretching ahead of them was their rite-of-passage leading to encounters with strangers (the de-mobbed soldier), confrontation with issues of death (as Christina Ricci pretends to drown, and the moonlight cemetery escapade), while their theft of the clothes from the skinny-dipping boys was their way of asserting they were not fearful of the opposite sex. Even so, the journey had a purpose: to seek information from the neighbourhood library about a baffling death.

Lyra (Dakota Blue Richards) in The Golden Compass sets off to Svalbard to rescue children locked in an experimental station. "This ain't no game," she is told. Using her initiative, cunning and her magical compass she procures the help of polar bears, witches, and an underclass of drifters to perform the impossible and save the universe. "That girl's something, huh!"

In the examples we have mentioned, our young Amazons have been willing adventurers, suffering adversity without complaint and devising ways to pull themselves through difficult situations. *Miracles Still Happen* is a true story tracing the extraordinary escape of an air crash survivor, a teenage girl, who trekked for endless days all alone through the Amazonian jungle before emerging into a Peruvian logging camp.

Other travellers are dragged along as loyal accomplices: Sarah Polley's abseiling from the moon into Vulcan's volcano in the long-winded attempt to thwart the Austrian-Turkish hostilities in *The Adventures of Baron Munchausen*, under Terry Gilliam's direction. (Gilliam also dragged a lad along on far-fetched escapades in the immensely silly *Time Bandits*, schoolboy Craig Warnock, helping to purloin Napoleon's loot, among other things.) These Amazons are adventurers by accident, caught up in unforeseen circumstances. None of them planned their journeys. In the

3. Tomboys, Adventurers & Talented Kids

case of Sarah Polley in *The Adventures of Baron Munchausen*, she was literally caught up by accident, her leg being trapped by a trailing rope from the hot air balloon that whisked her off the ground, and transported her to the ends of the Earth and beyond. Even *Alice's Adventures in Wonderland* and Dorothy's journey into the land of Oz (*The Wizard of Oz*) were both reluctant travellers, only too grateful to arrive home to safety from the confusion of the obsessed dream their creators (Lewis Carroll and Frank Baum) had placed them in. Neil Sinyard ascribes their effectiveness as stories because they 'appeal more to a child's sense of fear than to his or her sense of fun."[29] In any wonderland, there is a blurred distinction in the child's mind between what is dream and what is nightmare.

"I'm all alone. I'm eleven-years-old. Father is lost at sea. My leg is all swollen, and buccaneers are coming to take over the island. "I need you, Alex Rover. Help me, please."

This is the email message received by Alex Rover, a world-renowned adventure writer, played by a comical adult Jodie Foster. The film is *Nim's Island*. The eleven-year-old is Nim, played by Abigail Breslin.

Nim lives with her oceanographer father on a remote tropical island in the Pacific Ocean. Her only other company is a pelican, a sea lion, and an iguana that sits on her shoulder for much of the film.

Dad has to go on an ocean trip, so Nim is left alone to fend for herself for a few days in her tropical paradise.

In this movie are three simultaneous adventures. First, there is dad's boat trip searching for illusive photo-florescent plankton. He is soon hit by a tropical storm, which destroys his satellite link, and immobilises his boat. Then there is Nim's adventure of climbing to the top of a volcano, and surviving the typhoon which ruins their tree-house. She has a battle of wits trying to resist the invasion of a party of tourists who come ashore, polluting the peace of the unspoilt island. Thirdly, is the amusing journey of author Alexandra Rover, as she overcomes her agoraphobic fears, leaving the sterile security of her New York apartment, and travelling around the world to rescue one lonely little girl. All the while, on her travels, she is accompanied and her conscience prodded by the imaginary hero of her own novels.

Nim's Island is humorous, delightful, and undemanding fun, the type of adventurous fun shared also by Emily Thornton (Deborah Baxter) in *A High Wind in Jamaica*. Emily climbs rigging and slides across the wet deck of the pirate ship, and is winched on the hoist from boat to boat. The captain of the vessel tells her mother, "Don't worry Madame. A ship is the finest nursery." Mrs. Thornton is alarmed at the gradual changes in her children, the result of their expatriate life in the Caribbean. "They are not like English children at all," her mother complains. "It's this place. It's turned them into savages."

Maybe Jenny Agutter's character in *Walkabout* was aware of this. She constantly cajoles her younger brother (Lucien John) to not scuff his shoes, or tear his jacket, "We don't want people to think we're a couple of tramps," despite being hopelessly lost in the middle of the outback. While the girl strides out with dubious purposefulness, the boy sees through it all: "We're lost, aren't we?" sighs Lucien John. "I don't suppose it matters which way we go."

Neil Sinyard suggests a similarity between both films, *A High Wind in Jamaica* and *Walkabout*. "Both are about British children in an alien environment searching to find their way back to 'civilization' and social decorum."[30]

Eleven-year-old Shirley Temple playing *Susannah of the Mounties* is the only survivor of a wagon train attacked by Red Indians. The Mounties muster a rescue party but they are too late – all are dead, except for little Susannah. Nevertheless, our heroine is not downhearted. She spends her days cheering up the soldiers at the fort. This was filmed in the days when Red Indians were conceived as the baddies, and a group of these natives had been seen stealing horses. But little Savannah befriends the son of the Indian chief, and by sneaking between the two camps, the girl is able to prevent a race-war, rescue the Mountie Police chief, and stop the horse thieving. They don't make such sophisticated heroes that easily, these days.

It is films like these that help redress the gender balance, and generate inspiration for the underdog girl who is usually made to feel subservient in a male-run society. For Bea (Bella Riza) living as an expatriate child in Morocco in *Hideous Kinky*, however, she declines the opportunity of accompanying her mother and sister in their quest for an Algerian Sufi. Sensibly the nine-year-old says, "I don't need another adventure, mum. I have to go to school."

Just Good Fun

The following two films, *Bugsy Malone* and *Grounded*, are films in which sets of children interact together so that as a combined cast they have terrific fun, without needing any specific message to be expounded or a rite-of-passage to be endured. They are just rollicking good fun. We could have included here *The Sandlot Kids*, *Lord of the Flies*, *Melody*, or *Cheaper by the Dozen* and its sequel, which turned into one big holiday camp for the child actors. In these films, kids are allowed to be kids: they run riot. There is a notable absence of supervisory adults in the cast, or where the adults do exist they are ineffectual at controlling the anarchy of the kids.

The cast of *Bugsy Malone* must have had a whale of a time play-acting as gangsters, driving pedal cars, dancing routines with inspirational choreography, and culminating in the most audacious bun fight in movie history – and no doubt the biggest laundry bill! We witness the children chuckling their heads off in their finale song-and-dance act, their faces and clothes caked with custard pies and foam ice cream, all miming merrily with hands waving to the rhythm. "So this is show business!" exclaims an exasperated Jodie Foster pertly wiping the smears of gunge off her plastered face. Despite the fact that the movie perpetuates gender stereotypes this is, nevertheless, brilliant entertainment, a spoof of Broadway musicals like *Guys and Dolls*.

The film is full of wonderful song-and-dance routines, the words being mimed by the children, but the dancing is brilliantly carried out. The songs are memorable and becoming legendary. "*We could have been anything that we wanted to be.*" "*My name is Tallulah.*" "*Tomorrow never comes.*" The brilliant "*So you want to be a boxer*" must surely now rank among the music hall greats.

As well as being great fun, the words of the songs are full of inspirational messages. "You can't be certain that you'll lose until you try." "Sure you've hit the bottom but remember you're starting from the ground up." "You're going to be remembered for the things you say and do."

Six children get to cause havoc at Chicago airport in the film *Grounded*. Maybe it's the children who should be grounded because of their mischief, but it is the aircraft that are grounded as "the snowstorm of the century" hits Chicago, on Christmas Eve. All six children are unaccompanied travellers – their parents having gone on holiday for the Christmas vacation and have sent their kids to stay with relatives in different parts of the US. Airport security staff are lumbered with caring for the 'abandoned' children.

To the children, the airport seems a barren boring prison. There are no Christmas decorations up, and there is nothing to do. The kids have been herded into a secure holding area away from the other passengers, where they can be supervised without disturbing the other travelling public. Hence the title of the book on which this film is based – *Babysitting*.[31]

So the first task for the children is to escape. Using ventilation ducts as escape routes they end up in the baggage area, slide on the chutes, drive the courtesy cars, and wreck offices. In the animal holding bay they release one of the dogs from its travel cage. All this, while being chased by incompetent security guards. They evade capture, decorate the passenger terminal, and dress a Christmas tree they have stolen from a nearby garden centre.

All the while, one of the mums at home is worrying, "My children are trapped at the airport on Christmas Eve. Can you imagine how bored they'll be?"

Little do they realise, at that moment, her inadequate son is being given a heavy parting kiss from twelve-year-old Quinn Shepherd.

"All adventure stories – they all end in a kiss," says Wendy, in *Peter Pan*.

ENDNOTES FOR VOLUME THREE

1 See the section *Gender Imbalance* and *Multiculturalism* in Volume One of this series: *Gender Roles and Themes*.

2 We highlight the plight of the bullied child in Volume Eight, *Children in Films: Physical & Sexual Abuse*.

3 Sandy Descher played 1950s roles of the sugary sweet child in *It Grows on Trees*, *A Gift for Heidi* and *The last Time I saw Paris*. We mention in Volume 1 *Gender Roles and Themes* how Sandy was the subject of kidnap attempts by a woman who fantasised about the child being her own daughter.

4 Stephanie Theobold *Hurrah for Tomboys!* writing in *The Guardian*, 27 Dec 2008. Internet.

5 *Tomboys Born, not Made*, KSBW.com Action News 8.

6 Reuben 'Rooster' Cogburn is played by John Wayne in *True Grit (1969)* and by Jeff Bridges in *True Grit (2010)*.

7 Stephanie Theobold *Hurrah for Tomboys!* writing in *The Guardian*, 27 Dec 2008. Internet.

8 *An Impudent Girl* also called *L'effrontée*.

9 *Karanga* in Maori culture is the calling of visitors to a welcoming ceremony.

10 Claire Monk, *Sight & Sound*, October 2000, Internet

11 Sarah Showfety, *Field Guide to the Tomboy: High Heels and Pink? No Way*, in *Psychology Today*, 1st Sept 2008, quoted from Internet.

12 Michael Pollick, *What is a Tomboy?* writing in *WiseGEEK*. Internet.

13 Michael Pollick, *What is a Tomboy?* writing in *WiseGEEK*. Internet.

14 Girls like to throw off their tomboy label as they reach adolescence. The teenaged tomboy is likely to attract accusations of being lesbian. "Gender scholar Judith Halberstam has found that while the defying of gender roles is often tolerated in young girls, older girls and adolescents who display masculine traits are often repressed and punished." Halberstam, Judith: *Female Masculinity*, Durham: Duke University Press, 1998 quoted in article on Tomboy in Wikipedia. Although there are dozens of films projecting the girl as a tomboy, I am not aware of any that dare portray the tomboy taking on homosexual characteristics after puberty.

15 Filmed in the unspoiled idyll of Downham, in Pendle, Lancashire.

16 I'm referring to rapping and punk rock.

17 Crying with admiration, not out of disappointment!

18 Some commentators decry the use of the word ghetto because of the negativity it engenders, encapsulating a scene of deprived ethnic hopelessness and entrapment. I have used the word ghetto here because that is the word used in the film.

19 Ayush Mahesh Khedekar played Jamal as a youngster.

20 Another contestant had dropped out so Olive (Abigail Breslin) is only invited to make up the numbers.

21 *Radio Times* 20 Nov 2010 p15

22 Keira Knightley had a previous role in made-for-TV drama *The Treasure Seekers* based on Enid Nesbit's novel.

23 Amanda Bynes in *She's the Man* is a talented soccer player among her own gender. It's just that she shows obvious weakness when depicted playing alongside boys of her own age.

24 Barry Norman's 101 Greatest Films, *Radio Times Supplement*, 21 Jan 2012.

24a In Quinnell's novel, Creasy coaches Pita as a sprinter, rather than swimming.

25 Neil Sinyard, *Children in the Movies*, p20

26 We are, of course, referring to *The Lion, the Witch and the Wardrobe*, along with *Alice's Adventures in Wonderland*.

27 Neil Sinyard, *Children in the Movies*, p20

27a Mrs Scott is only a neighbour in the film. Frank Baum makes no mention of her in his classic novel. Likewise in the book, Dorothy does not run away from home to prevent Toto from being put down.

27b *Swallow and Amazons* was filmed in Cumbria's Lake Derwent in the English Lake District. However, the characters in Arthur Ransome's novel were based on children he knew and taught to sail upon Lake Windermere, and upon Lake Coniston where the novelist had a lakeside home.

28 Thora Birch, Gaby Hoffman, Christina Ricci & Ashleigh Aston Moore.

29 Neil Sinyard, *Children in the Movies*, p18

30 Neil Sinyard, *Children in the Movies*, p142.

31 The novel *Babysitting*, on which the film *Grounded* is based, is by Susan Burton.

Volume Four

Childhood Friendships

"I believe that children … share a fundamental quality … a drive to connect with other human beings in positive, nurturing ways … in spite of differences in health, sexual orientation, race and culture, and levels of poverty or wealth."
Michael Tompson *Best Friends, Worst Enemies*

"No doubt you'll be our most popular student in no time,"
says Miss Minchin to new girl Sara Crewe in ***A Little Princess***.

"Wendy, one girl's worth more than twenty boys,"
(says Peter Pan)

CONTENTS FOR VOLUME FOUR

4. Childhood Friendships...**191**

Contents for Volume Four..**193**

Making Friends...**195**
The Rule of Gender...*195*
Best Friends Forever...*196*
Breaking into the Clique: On the periphery of friendship groups.............*200*
Group Dynamics: The Rejected Child.......................................*202*
Childhood Sweethearts: Overcoming the Gender Barricade.................*204*
Sharing the same frying pan: friends thrust together...........................*206*

Inter-Racial Bonding...**210**
American Segregation..*210*
South African Apartheid..*213*
Australian Aboriginal Culture..*214*
Cross culture bonding..*217*

Children bonding with Adults..**221**
The Retarded Adult Companion...*224*
Travelling Companions..*226*
The Drifter and Loner as replacement father-figure and object of first crush
....*231*

The Child's Best Friend: Animals and Children....................**237**
Animal Welfare over Child Welfare..*239*
The Pet as Provider of Unconditional Love.................................*240*
The pet as a lesson in life and death..*242*
The Call of the Wild..*246*
The Child as Rescuer of the Helpless..*249*
The Horse Lover..*252*
Let us down to the sea again: Dolphins and Whales, Seals and Sea-Lions *255*
The Pet as a Punishment..*256*

Endnotes for Volume Four..**258**

MAKING FRIENDS

The Rule of Gender

The friends that children make are determined by timeless gender rules laid down over generations: boys play with boys, girls play with girls. Once the nappy is unfastened, their upbringing – the toys they are given, their games and their role-play – cause boys and girls to grow up with different preferences. This is conflict unwittingly induced by parents and grandparents, whose initial hope is that their perfect family (with one of each kind: a girl and a boy) will live harmoniously, making friends sociably with others in the community. Yet birthday gifts and Christmas wishes provide the implements with which to perpetuate the gender divide: the doll set and pram, the necklaces and mood rings, and frilly pink outfits for girls; the gun and holster, the baseball bat and catapult, and anything except pink for the boy.

Most of the books children inherit depict boys and girls playing happily together, ever since *Janet and John* and *The Famous Five* were released into schoolrooms. In the classroom, gender harmony is expected and nurtured, boys and girls being forced to cooperate, to share tables, to interact. But as soon as the bell rings for playtime, the sexes dare not mix, neither in the schoolyard, nor when playing with the gang on the sandlot: it is a time-honoured rule, and punishments for deviancy can be harsh. Girls pair off with a bosom pal, while boys are expected to muck about with the lads. As we shall see, Josh Hutcherson highlights this succinctly in *Little Manhattan*, as he observes the situation in his own school classroom: "In first grade, the iron curtain came down: girls on one side, boys on the other."

This gender divide is a barrier that, in the main, film directors tend to ignore. The movie industry advances the parental dream that boys and girls make companionable buddies. And better still, if the idea of sweethearts can be injected into the proceedings then parents can have their nostalgic dreams reignited, and the film producers are onto a winner.

A special quality of girls is their ability to form close friendships. Girls have more enhanced communication skills, can vocalise their worries, loves and problems, and are thus better able to talk through their difficulties, mediating conflicts by consensus. In the main, their friendships are more intimate and enduring.

Boys, as a generalisation, form groups or gangs in which threats, force, initiations, competitive tests of strength, as well as communal trust leads to acceptance with the in-crowd. This is how we first meet *Huck Finn* (Elijah Wood), scrapping by the shore of the Mississippi, egged on by his ragamuffin supporters.

And yet, for both genders, finding and fostering friendships is the ultimate aim of all children. Professor Dumbledore tells Harry Potter in *The Goblet of Fire*, "Remember this Harry, you have friends here. You are not alone." Billy (Jared Rushton) says to Josh (Tom Hanks) in *Big* (1988), "I'm your best friend. What's more important than that?" Dakota Fanning playing solitary Lily in *The Secret Life of Bees* dreams, "I can't think of one thing I'd rather like than someone loving me."

195

Boys and girls do not form friendships with each other across the gender divide, unless there is an exceptional reason for doing so. Ten-year-old Elijah Wood and Thora Birch were only friends in *Paradise* (1991) because, as both acknowledge, they had no other friends to play with. "You're my best friend," says the lonely girl, only because she has no one else to play with.

Both genders have been nurtured differently with opposing interests and expectations. The preteen boy who befriends a girl is usually ousted from his social group. Not until the teenage years are reached is that social barricade lifted. Then the hormones buzz and the next few years of teenage angst is employed trying to fathom out the opposite sex that has been ever present yet never approachable.

Best Friends Forever

Michael Thompson, in his book *Best Friends, Worst Enemies*, confirms that "for children, particularly girls, 'best friends forever' is part of the rhetoric of friendship. They expect their close friendships to be of long duration, in spite of the reality that the average childhood friendship lasts a year or less." [1] Thora Birch's friendship with Elijah Wood in *Paradise* (1991) lasted just one summer vacation.

Yet films perpetuate the possibility of childhood confederacies enduring throughout teenage years and even lasting a lifetime. In *Beaches* (1988), a chance encounter between two eleven-year-old girls, Hillary and CC, under the boardwalk, resulted in a friendship lasting till their dying days, as it did between cousins, Elsie Wright and Frances Griffiths, in *Fairy Tale* (1997). The girls bonding in their adolescence in *Now and Then* made a pact to be there for each other in case they encounter difficulties in adult life. By contrast, the boys who set off on their mutual rite-of-passage in *Stand by Me* had all flit in different directions once their summer escapade was over.

Of course, it is not all plain sailing: most friendships traverse choppy waters. The trio of wizards in *Harry Potter* who remained loyal friends throughout their entire school life had occasional fallings out: Hermione having to relay messages between the two disgruntled boys, Harry and Ron, and the unpleasant shunning of Hermione in *The Philosopher's Stone* almost led to her demise at the hand of a troll. In *Beaches* (1988) the fallout between CC and Hillary lasted for years. Others, find that boyfriends interpose rifts in childhood alliances, as in *32A* and *Angus, Thongs and Perfect Snogging*, while for others, friendships come to a natural end as they move to a new home, as in *Aquamarine*. For some, as in *Me without You*, the relationship can become stiflingly oppressive, with one girl comparing it to a strained marriage. For six-year-old Andy (Alex Vincent) in *Chucky*, the promise "I'm Chucky, and I'm your friend till the end," becomes a slavish entrapment by the demonic *Good Guy* doll.

Friendships are enhanced by adventures, often a coming-of-age feat of endurance, and by the confiding of one's secrets. This also is how friendships come to a crushing end, as one partner discovers their confidences are revealed.

Several films take on this theme of enduring friendships. Let us use *Beaches* (1988) as an example. Two eleven-year-old girls meet by accident on a beach in Atlanta City. CC Bloom (Mayim Bialik), is a down on her luck aspirant singer/tap dancer, strutting the auditions circuits in her tutu and awful black stockings and her shock of straggly red hair, in the hope of the big break that will lift her and her mother out from the depths of poverty from their Bronx hovel.[2] CC (Cecilia Carol) is having a surreptitious fag under the boardwalk at the edge of the beach, when along comes a lost tearful girl, eleven-year-old Hillary Whitney (Marcie Leeds). "Don't tell me. You're lost!" pipes out CC, offering the pretty, well-dressed posh girl a drag: as with *Kamikaze Girls*, a definite case of opposites attracting.

It transpires that Hillary is the daughter of a rich businessman, mother having died when she was young. But when asked *her* name, CC finds it incredulous that Hillary doesn't know who she is. "What's my name!" utters CC with pizzazz, her already inflated ego about to pop. "I am no other than the fantastic, world-famous, child-wonder, CC Bloom. Ta-daa."

Promising to help Hillary find her hotel, the pair of girls set off, but on the way, CC is rushed off by her mother to see a talent scout at an audition, but as usual she fails the audition. Then it's off to the hotel where Hillary treats her new friend to an ice cream soda, the likes of which the poorer girl had never even dreamt. But on the way, they pass a photo booth. Their crazy twin photos are shared, addresses exchanged, and a friendship cemented forever. Before leaving, Hillary insists they write to each other. "Why do you want me to write to you so much," demands CC for whom such an enterprise seems anathema.

"Are you crazy," replies Hillary. "You just happen to be the most amazing person I've ever met in my entire life. Be sure to keep in touch, CC"

"But sure, we're friends aren't we."

And they do keep in touch, all through their adolescent years. Hillary gets a law degree, while CC continues to pursue her singing career in low-down, smoky dives, still awaiting that lucky break. Then Hillary (now played by the adult Barbara Hershey) seeks freedom from the stifling constraints of her father, and goes to share a flat with her childhood friend (now played by the marvellously vivacious and effervescent warbling red-head, Bette Midler).

Living together in a cramped squat, marked by a difference in class and education, they endure all the things that test true friendship, until their relationship is stretched too far as jealousy rears its ugly head as they both date the same man. "What a sneak," says CC. "I'd never do anything that heartless to a friend," (after Hillary sleeps with CC's musical director.)

In time, they have a bitter argument and fall out with the ultimate slagging match. "We've grown apart," explains Hillary. "It happens to the best of friends. You might as well face it."

They spend years apart, ignoring each other's letters. Both get married, and Hillary has a child. Time and regrets bring them back close again, apologies are made, Hillary develops a terminal illness, and CC becomes guardian to the orphaned child. Before Hillary's death, CC makes an intuitive remark about how firm friends really are. "I know everything there is to know about you," as if they were husband and wife.

Me without You takes the best friends forever theme a stage further, and the stifling oppression it creates if pursued into adulthood. The director, Sandra Goldbacher, has made her film loosely autobiographical, for she herself had a best friend relationship between the ages of eleven and seventeen – a Siamese twin pairing that was both dependable and welcome for her adolescent years, but as it spilled into adulthood she found this claustrophobic and repressive. This film has several similarities to *Beaches* (1988), though in this film the girls did not meet by accident. Rather, they were twelve-year-old next-door neighbours living in a London suburb – Anna Popplewell as frivolous, must try everything Marina, while Ella Jones (taking a break from her TV series *The Queen's Nose*) plays the more studious and dependable Holly.

Right from the start we see Marina as the domineering partner. "What's the matter, Holly, don't you trust me?" Holly is barefooted and blindfolded, and Marina is directing her where to tread to avoid the glass-strewn lawn, in a dare game. They make an anagram from their names *Harina*, stuff it in a bottle, and bury it in the garden pond announcing the pact: "Now we'll always be together."

Close friendship was a welcome blessing during their adolescent years, but as the girls mature into youthful womanhood, Marina becomes clingy and manipulative. Holly's attempts to date Nat, Marina's older brother, are thwarted as Marina fails to forward the letters. "You've got me, Holly. You'll always have me." Like an irritating wasp, Holly sees the prediction becoming only too true.

Both girls go off to Brighton University, and there, Marina proves to be just as controlling of Holly's social life. Just as the rift in *Beaches* (1988) was caused by two girls dating the same man, so too in *Me without You*, both girls unwittingly date the same college tutor, and it is this that causes them to tearfully split apart. Holly refuses to answer Marina's telephone calls. "I don't know who I am when it's not us," Marina complains.

Finally, in exasperation, Holly declares to her lifelong friend, "You're strangling me." And, as if they had been an unhappily married couple she states, "We're getting a divorce." Thus Marina, who sees this as a devastating loss, gives the film its title: "There is no me without you."

Now and Then features a gaggle of four girls who bond and make a commitment to be there for each other, though only two of the twelve-year-olds, Samantha and Teeny, use the phrase with each other, "*best friends forever.*" This to some extent goes against the grain of one girl having just the one best friend. The film takes place one summer, back in 1970.

Living in the small Indiana town of Shelby, the group of girls complain that nothing exciting ever happens in their community – except the murder of a boy half a century ago, and whose grave they frequently visit and puzzle over. I guess the film sets out to ape the successful *Stand by Me*. The two films have similarities – both films feature a gang of four (though this deals with a different gender), and both groups are haunted by the death of a boy. And, like *To Kill a Mockingbird*, it has a Boo Radley figure, Crazy Stephen, who comes to save the life of Gaby Hoffman when she falls down a flooded drain trying to rescue a friendship bracelet she has shared with Thora Birch.

Another way loyalties are tested to the extreme is when Christina Ricci jumps from a cliff into a lake and scarily fakes drowning. Both Gaby Hoffman and Thora Birch discuss giving the prostrate girl mouth-to-mouth resuscitation, but squirm away from actually doing so. It is only when Ashleigh Aston Moore plucks up courage to do the deed does the pretender splutter to life: "Well, it's good to know who your true friends are," she tuts, disappointed with them.

Isabel Telleria plays a similar trick on her younger sister, Ana Torrent, in *The Spirit of the Beehive*, when she convincingly feigns death. So effective is her ruse that both Ana, and us the audience, are sure she has been killed by the monster. Ana even goes back to double check that her sister is dead before going to seek help.

Returning to *Now and Then*, the film shows their unity as the four girls explore together, buy a tree house, and discuss pubertal changes with each other, and their rivalry with a gang of boys, and their taking revenge on them by strewing the road with clothes as the boys are skinny-dipping. As Christina Ricci gets to kiss one of the boys later in the film, she threatens him, "If you mention this to anyone, I'll beat the shit out of you," as if by making friends with a boy she is somehow breaking the group pact she made with her girl friends.

Sitting in their tree house, which they have communally purchased, they agree, "Let's make a pact, here and now. Whenever we need a friend we're here for each other." Although their intimate group friendship lasted only for that summer, ("What that summer actually brought was independence from each other"), nevertheless they were tied to their group pact into adulthood. For, as one of them becomes pregnant, they all rally round to help with the birth, and that is how the film both begins and ends.

The secret pact made between the two cousins in *Fairy Tale* (1997) lasted a lifetime. This is a tale of the Yorkshire Cottingley Fairies. Elsie Wright (Florence Hoath) and Frances Griffiths (Elizabeth Earl) make a pact that they will never tell how they made their clever photographs of fairies. Despite being hounded by the press, and even Sir Arthur Conan Doyle and the great Houdini, they remained true to their agreement. It was not until they were elderly ladies and one of them died that the other finally felt released from the agreement and revealed the fakery of the photographs.

With some, friendships come to a natural end. Maybe it is the course of time, or a new boyfriend, or the end of a holiday. In *Aquamarine*, it ended because one of the girls was moving away. Emma Roberts and Joanna 'Jojo' Levesque were desperate to stay together, but even the intervention of the magic wishes from a mermaid could not prevent the inevitable separation.

In *32A*, it was the new boyfriend that created a rift in the friendship circle. Maeve (Ailish McCarthy) preferred to honour a date with her boyfriend than stay loyal to her best friend, Ruth (Sophie Jo Wasson), at a time when she was needed most. Incidentally, in *He Loves Me, He Loves Me Not*, the boy takes the opposite stance: he chooses loyalty to his friends rather than to his girlfriend.

The boyfriend is often a factor causing the split in childhood friendships, as Georgia Groome discovers in *Angus, Thongs and Perfect Snogging*. Georgia and her friend Jas (Eleanor Tomlinson) try to hook some new boys at school. They pretend Georgia's cat, Angus, has gone missing. But while the search is on, Jas hooks up with one of the boys. Comments made behind each other's back rapidly spread into rumours, creating the rift (temporarily) in their friendship.

In *The Goblet of Fire*, it was a failure to trust what the partner was saying was true that caused the rift between Harry Potter and his best friend Ron Weasley. Their friend Hermione Granger had to be the go-between for them by relaying messages even though the two friends were only ten paces apart. Usually the split comes over innocuous trivialities, and the protagonists usually forget what it was they were arguing over.

Evan Rachel Wood has a great rapport with her friends in *Little Secrets*. Whenever they go away they always keep in touch by sending each other videos. Yet inexplicably, she keeps a secret from them – just like Gaby Hoffman in *Now and Then* she does not want them to know she is an adopted orphan. Eventually she is advised, "If you want to be close to someone you can't keep secrets from them." This provides the spur to help her confide.

Whereas girls make intimate lasting friendships with a solitary bosom pal, boys are more prone to team up in small groups or gangs. This is borne out by the classic bonding movie, *Stand by Me*. Rather like *Now and Then* a group of four twelve-year-old boys enjoy their last summer together before moving up to Junior High. An adult Gordie (Richard Dreyfuss) is reminiscing about that summer adventure back in 1959 in Oregon. "I never had any friends later on like the ones I had when I was twelve. Jesus! Does anyone?"

Basically, the four lads go on a three-day trek along a railway line to search for a reported dead body, then come back again! They trespass in a junkyard, cross a scary bridge, camp overnight while coyotes howl nearby, trudge through a leech infested swamp. But it is their bonding, fallouts, scraps, arguments, and complaints that no one thought to bring any food; it is these trivial incidents that the children have on their rite-of-passage that makes this a cinematic classic. Like *Now and Then*, their expedition did not cement the four-some forever, for new school and new ambitions soon split them up.

Breaking into the Clique: On the periphery of friendship groups

Thompson's book *Best Friends, Worst Enemies*, refers to the initiation tests that are requisite for entry into larger groups. Thompson refers to this as '*hazing*'. "Children long to be initiated into the secrets and privileges of older children and of adults. In most cultures throughout the world initiation ceremonies have played an important part in the lives of young people, particularly as they make the transition from childhood to adulthood. The willingness of the newcomer to be tested, and the group's feeling that membership is worth fighting for, creates the conditions for a test, a challenge."

Unfortunately, the boundary between what is considered an initiation challenge, and what is blatant unpleasant bullying, is blurred. Thompson makes it clear that "hazing involves intentional humiliation of the individual; initiation never does."[3] Pai in *Whale Rider*, by coming through her challenge, proved she was a worthy member of her Maori tribe. So too, Margaret O'Brien playing Tooti in *Meet me in St Louis* proved herself worthy of the gang by volunteering to throw flour in the face of the bogeyman, Mr Brokov with his 'frierce' dog. And Charley Boorman playing abducted Tommy in *The Emerald Forest* goes through the full tribal ritual of initiation by being covered in biting ants then dunked in the river. The tribal chief proclaims: "The boy is dead. The man is born." For Frankie Muniz in *My Dog Skip*, acceptance into the group, and the prevention of further bullying, meant sitting all night alone in the cemetery where the dreaded witch was sure to haunt.

Ten-year-old Alice Bloom, played by Eliza Dushku in *That Night*, however, was given a humiliation test, but she failed. In a huddle of girls and boys playing spin the bottle, Alice was expected to close her eyes and wait for a kiss from the boy who the bottle was pointing towards. Expecting a kiss, like the other girls before her received, she waits eyes closed and open-mouthed. But instead of a kiss, they cruelly place a toad inside her mouth. She races out in tears, spitting out the unpleasant taste, and she sobs in the garden at the front of the house. She has failed the challenge so is ridiculed by the group.

So, Alice is left on the periphery of the group and becomes the butt of teasing. She really wants her own best friend. Across the road from Alice lives a seventeen-year-old teenager, Sheryl, a hotshot for the local youths. Alice admires the older girl; copying everything she does – wearing the same perfume, listening to the same records, even buying the same pendant. "I wanted to dream her dreams, and live her life… if I could only be her for one night."

Teenage Sheryl has struck up a relationship with an older boy that her mum does not approve of. Sheryl has been grounded by her mother and needs an excuse to sneak out to be with her boyfriend. Alice suggests that Sheryl pretends to baby-sit her while going off to visit her boyfriend – but only as long as she can accompany her. So this seems a mutually satisfactory solution to both of them. After 'that night' they were inseparable; Sheryl pretending to be babysitting while smooching under the boardwalk, while Alice gets a night on the town learning about love and make-up, and going to bowling alleys and cafes, always accompanied by her special older friend.

Inevitably, Sheryl wearies of the little girl's devotion. "You're following me around as if I am your goddam princess, wearing my perfume, listening to my records." But the relationship has been an education for the ten-year-old. She has discovered some truths about love, and her self-esteem has grown.

Water Lilies shows all the hallmarks of the typical best friend syndrome – the strong relationships that form between pairs of girls, and the distress that results as the girls fall out with each other, as rivalries and jealousies between girl partners emerge. Although this is a film about older teenagers (though one of the girls claims to be 14 ½ to try to get a cheaper meal in a cafe), it illustrates the frustrations that younger girls experience as they try to hold onto their special best friend.

The film is a French movie. Pauline Acquart plays the part of Marie, a teenager who spends her time hanging out with synchronised swimming novice, Anne. Marie waits for Anne after swimming and they go off to the shopping arcade where honest Marie has to cover for her friend's petty shoplifting. They spend time together in each other's bedrooms, confiding in their sexual fantasies. There is a real contrast in their looks. Marie: slender, lithe, developing; Anne is large and well developed. But in an unfriendly jibe, Marie hurts Anne by saying she had boobs when she was in primary school, no wonder they are so fat and large now. For Marie has recently become infatuated with the star of the swimming team, an older girl Floriane (played by Adèle Haenel). Marie cruelly tells her lifelong friend, Anne, she doesn't want to see her anymore. So Marie develops a friendship with Floriane, she is smitten with the older girl, and is willing to take on the role of devoted servant, such as being her escort when visiting a boyfriend, supposedly to be ready to step in if things get out of hand.

Eventually, Marie realises she is just being used, so one evening she refuses to be Floriane's escort any more. But forgiving Anne is ready to receive her back. "We mustn't split up, Marie," Anne implores her, "I do daft things by myself."

However, it only takes a spot of kindness to endear oneself to others, as Sara Crewe found in *A Little Princess*. "You are all the best friends anyone could ask for," she says as the other girls steal back her precious locket from Miss Munchin's study that the headteacher had previously confiscated.

Regrettably, theft is a method of gaining acceptance into clique groups, as Evan Rachel Wood discovers in the teenage rebellion movie, *Thirteen* (2003). Desperately wanting to be friends with Evie, the most popular girl in the school, Tracy (Evan Rachel Wood) finds she has to join in the shoplifting spree if she is to become an acceptable member of the clique. Tracy goes away disappointed, but temptation is soon placed in her way. Tracy is sitting on a bench in the mall. A woman absorbed in a mobile phonecall carelessly dumps her bags beside her. Tracy steals her purse containing hundreds of dollars, takes it to Evie and they become instant friends, giving Tracy access to nightclubs, boyfriends, self-harm and illicit substances.

Group Dynamics: The Rejected Child

Everyone longs for friends. The greatest fear for any child moving home is the worry of not being able to make new acquaintances. (We explore this more fully in *Volume 7: Childhood Traumas*, in which the child moving home equates the experience to a bereavement.) A child's dilemma is hightened when it finds itself an outcast, on the periphery of closeted cliques. For the rejected child, this misery is like living in hell, as they become insular, the victim of abuse, and in some cases results in suicide.

A child may be rejected by the group for a number of reasons, usually related to being different from the group norm, for example, being individualistic, not adhering to the dress code of a social group. The victim becomes a scapegoat, a role which may endure for the length of a person's childhood. For Suzi Hofrichter, playing Amy in *How to Kill your Neighbour's Dog*, it was because she had mild cerebral palsy and was left out of playground games such as jump rope. This girl resorted to playing at home by herself with her dolls, a companionless loner. For Ann Carter in *The Curse of the Cat People*, it was her flights of fantasy that kept her aloof and that perpetuates her lonesomeness. Sharyn Moffett in *The Body Snatcher*, crippled by a tumour on the spine, tells us bluntly in her own words, "Of course I don't have any friends. That's because I cannot walk."

For Hermione Granger (Emma Watson) in *Harry Potter and The Philosopher's Stone*, it was because she was a swot, a know-it-all, outdoing her classmates. For this reason Ron Weasley says of her, "She's a nightmare. No wonder she hasn't got any friends." Overhearing what the boy had cruelly said, she hides away the whole afternoon in the girls' toilets crying her heart out, until the unexpected arrival of a troll causes the trio of classmates to rely on each other for mutual support. In the end, the children become best of buddies as Hermione concedes, "Me – I'm all books and cleverness. But you, Harry, have more important things – friendship and bravery."

At least Hermione's rejection was only temporary. It was not her fault she was rejected; the blame can lay in the blinkered attitude of her two friends. When Laure (Zoé Héron) falls out with her friends in *Tomboy*, the blame must be laid firmly at her own door. Laure's fault was not so much in wanting to be a boy, but in lying to her friends by untruthfully convincing them that she *is* a boy. While her friends, both male and female, were happy to integrate and play with her, they felt affronted and they shunned her once they discovered they had been duped.

This affront is related to the entrenched boundaries that exist in all cultures regarding gender. When Laure (masquerading as Mickäel) fights with the boys and beats them, that is acceptable to them as part of life's pecking order. But when the boys eventually realise they have been beaten up by a girl, a sacrosanct boundary has been crossed. Likewise, when Lisa (Jeanne Disson) shares her first kiss with her new sweetheart, Mickäel, she feels betrayed when she learns Mickäel is actually a girl. "If she's a girl, you kissed her. That's disgusting," the boys deride Lisa, and she agrees with them. This excellent film concludes by the newcomer finally admitting her real name, and Lisa is happy to re-establish the friendship.

In *Innocence* (2004), little Laura sits crunched up in the corner of her room watching the others, but unwilling to join in. She has an element of spitefulness branded into her – whether as a result of her being excluded from the dynamics of the group, or because of it, is not clarified. She shivers alone by the lakeside while the other children at the orphanage splash and swim in their underwear. She throws stones and scratches another girl's legs. Whatever her problem is, she has become a loner, depending on herself, unaided by the group, so when she takes the rowing boat onto the lake thinking she can escape the orphanage that way, the boat becomes inundated, and there is no one around to save her from drowning.

Like Laura in *Innocence* (2004), Unn in *The Ice Palace* is a loner, and that means trouble. She stands against the playground wall and watches the other little children playing. But she is alone, aloof. "Why don't you play with the rest of us?" asks Siss, her only friend.

"I told you to never ask me that," replies a guilt-ridden Unn. Unn has a hidden secret that rankles her. We are never told what that secret is, but her mother has recently died, and she does say, "I don't know if I'll go to Heaven."

On her way to her Swedish primary school, she is distracted by the weight of her anxieties and wanders off into a maze of glacial labyrinths. Hopelessly lost, she gets cold, wet, and trapped like an insect caught in amber, and she freezes to death, undiscovered until the thaw at the end of winter.

The Ratcatcher also has a lonely child: a girl, Margaret Anne (Leanne Mullen) unable to integrate with her playmates. Maybe it is because she wears glasses, or she is the only girl of her age to have reached a premature puberty. But the attentions she attracts are abusive from the boys in the slum area of Glasgow where she lives: she receives unwanted fondling; she has to be compliant, for she does not know any other way to defend herself against the bullying. It is only when her glasses are smashed and thrown in the canal that one of the lads, William Earle, makes an effort to retrieve them for her, and genteelly he declines the offer of a sexual favour as a thank you. Fortunately, the demise of Margaret Anne didn't result in her premature death, as it did for both Laura and Unn. *Welcome to the Dollhouse* takes up a similar theme, with Heather Matarazzo taking the role of the eleven-year-old misfit.

Ann Carter's depiction of Amy in *The Curse of the Cat People* portrays a little girl kept aloof by other children because of the world of fantasy she inhabits with her head in the clouds. To compensate for this lack of friends, like many children in the same situation, she invents playmates of her own. In the words of Neil Sinyard (*Children in the Movies*) this film presents 'the study of the inner life of a young girl whose loneliness supplies her with an imaginary friend.'[4] Her belief in magic is too literal, so that when she posts the invitations to her birthday party in the hole of the 'magic' tree in the bottom of the garden and consequently no one turns up for her party, she is despised still further by her classmates. Her teacher can see the problem clearly: "Amy has too many fantasies and too few friends." But her hypocritical father does not see it that way; one moment he is encouraging her girl to make a wish, and the next is scolding her for being dreamy. It takes the class teacher to quote from Robert Louis Stevenson's poem to help understand why some children are loners forced to inhabit their own private world of make-believe:

> *When children are playing alone on the green,*
> *in comes the playmate that never was seen.*
> *When children are happy and lonely and good,*
> *the friend of the children comes out of the wood.*[5]

Michael Thompson would describe these children as being '*rejected-submissive children*' and they make up approximately ten percent of the child demography.[6]

Childhood Sweethearts: Overcoming the Gender Barricade

For children under ten, the games they play are invariably gender specific, a trait reinforced by parents and grandparents, so much so that gender cliques are formed. Ridicule and other punishments are meted out for a child who dares mix/talk/play with the opposite sex. If your more powerful peers decree you will play with them, then you don't risk being shunned from one's social group by crossing gender boundaries. The jest of being called a 'sissy' can be a powerful inducement to gender loyalty. Daniel Roche discovered that when playing *Just William* in the TV series in which he denies ever playing with the detestable Violet (Isabella Blake-Thomas), even though he secretly enjoyed her company.[7]

In his study of inter-gender relationships, Michael Thompson,[8] describes how infants have a dislike for the opposite gender instilled into them through their upbringing, their play, and their education. "Boys and girls play at being enemies even as they are fascinated by one another." An infant is aware there are rules governing interaction between girls and boys. "Violation of these rules results in teasing, rejection, gossip, and other punishments."[9] Eleanor Maccoby (*The two sexes: Growing Up Apart*) asserts that this separation of the genders is universal, in both industrialised and third world communities. Boys learn to be aggressive in their play, more interested in sport or making things. Girls on the other hand spend more time on building close personal relationships.

Little Rascals' portrayal of this gender barrier is both endearing and amusing. It tries to be a spoof send-up of attitudes in the early twentieth century. A gang of infant boys have a *Woman-Hater's Club*, and jealously guard their clubhouse to ensure they are not polluted by that alien incomprehensible species, *girls*! To the boys, all that girls want to do is talk, whereas boys "stand up for themselves," and worst of all girls "smell weird!" Alas Alfalfa (Bug Hall), the gang member chosen to represent them in the forthcoming go-kart derby has been charmed by Darla (Brittany Ashton Holmes), and is currently romantically serenading her in a boat on the sultry river.

The film recognises the defiant opposition between young boys and girls, and tries to break down these gender barriers. However, this is a chasm deeply entrenched in all cultures of the world. Although in the film the boys end up welcoming the girls to their club, and there are cutesy kisses all round with the adult audience sighing with nostalgic memories, I doubt any child watched this film with feelings of remorse or intention to change.

Director, Mark Levin, was well aware of this inter-gender barrier when he made the film *Little Manhattan*. Ten-year-old Josh Hutcherson, reflecting on his time in the infants, realised "In first grade, the iron curtain came down: girls on one side, boys on the other." Referring to his own sweetheart, Rosemary, played by Charlie Ray, "She was always there from first grade. It's just that I never saw her." So the chances of having a childhood sweetheart is fairly remote, and is only likely among the more outcast members of social groups.

Jess was one such boy on the periphery of a social group, in *Bridge to Terabithia*. Katherine Paterson's book was made into a film in 2007, with AnnaSophia Robb[10] playing the part of Leslie Burke. Ten-year-old Leslie Burke was a new girl who had recently arrived in Jess' community. At last, the lonely boy (Josh Hutchinson) had a playmate, other than his four taunting sisters. By means of Leslie's lively imagination, they dream up an imaginary world that they can explore together, by swinging on a rope across a creek in their dreams. Day after day, they explore their wonderland, strengthening their relationship, until there is that romantic spark between them. Tomorrow will be a special day, for Jess and Leslie would be going off together all day. We just knew that from this point their love affair would take off and we would be voyeurs of their first tender kisses beneath the spreading boughs of the forest. But while Jess is away on an unexpected day trip, a tragedy happens. Leslie dies, by drowning in the creek, and the boy's dreams, hopes and joys are shattered in one fell swoop. The book was written to help children become aware of the possibility that some day they may lose a loved one. As well as the tragedy being so sudden, the film becomes a distressing sob story, serving as a practical lesson in life.

Childhood friendships between boys and girls, which endure into adulthood, inevitably end in either blossoming romance (the childhood sweetheart syndrome) or else end in jealousies and recriminations. In *There will be Blood*, HW (Dillon Freasier) is the eleven-year-old son of a ruthless oil prospector around the 1900s. He makes friends with the young daughter of the ranch owner, Mary Sunday (Sydney McCallister), only because they are the only children, there are no peer-group gender inhibitions to fear and they are able to play sporadically as children do. But when HW is made deaf following an explosion at the drilling rig, Mary becomes more attentive of the boy as he learns sign language from HW's tutor. The bond grows, so that by the time they become adults, the two childhood friends marry.

In *Lovers of the Arctic Circle* two eight-year-olds, Otto and Ana, become friends, bring their single parents close together, and then get to live in the same house. "You two are like brother and sister," believe the parents, hopefully, as the two children get on so well together. Both children agree that fate has brought them together, and it is additionally 'lucky' that both share palindromic names. For Otto, bit-by-bit he starts to fall in love with his new 'sister'. As they grow older, their friendship becomes a love affair, which they have to keep secret from their parents.

The whole purpose of *Slumdog Millionaire* is to show the heart-warming story of Jamal's search for Latika, his childhood friend, an orphaned girl (Rubina Ali) he befriended on the trash heaps of Mumbai slums. His brother Salim goads him, "Oh god, baby brother's in love with a flat-chested hijra!" [11] Uninterested in the twenty-million rupee prize money, Jamal's only intention is to spin out his appearance on the show long enough for his childhood sweetheart to realise he is still searching for her. "I never forget. Not for one moment," says Jamal after Latika declares, "You came back for me."

A similar scenario in which a boy and a girl become childhood friends and who dabble in romance as they mature is *Great Expectations* and, as in *Lovers of the Arctic Circle*, it is the boy who dotes on the girl, the girl being the passive tolerant partner. In the 1997 version of *Great Expectations*, an update of the original Dickens classic now transposed from the Essex marshes to the Florida Everglades, a ten-year-old Finn Ben (Jeremy James Kisner) is taken by his handyman uncle to work at the neglected overgrown grounds of *Paradiso Perduto* belonging not to Miss Havisham but to Miss Dinsmoor (played by an over exuberant Ann Bancroft), jilted on her wedding day, and the gardens left untended ever since. There, passing through the shrubs, Finn espies the angelic apparition of the stunningly beautiful blond niece, ten-year-old Estella, played by Raquel Beaudene, and he is immediately smitten. To add to his trance, Miss Dinsmoor invites Finn to visit every Saturday to be a playmate for her young niece.

But the day he first arrives to visit, Estella is standoffish, turns up her nose at the visitor, and announces him as 'the gardener'.

"What do you think of her," probes the old lady.

"I think she is a snob," is his honest reply.

"But she is beautiful, isn't she?"

The smitten boy cannot deny it. "I think she's real pretty. But I don't think she likes me."

"If you love her," the woman predicts, "she'll only break your heart."

The girl seems to show nothing but disinterested distain for her playmate, glibly discarding the portrait he has sketched, yet as she shows the boy to the door they share a very intimate parting kiss (I describe this more fully in *Volume Six: Puberty & First Love*).

On his further weekly visits, the girl shows no other interest in the lad. Finn despairs of ever attracting her love. They seem to spend their time mechanically dancing for the entertainment of the lonely spinster. It is not until they have grown up as teenagers, that Estella flaunts herself lustfully in front of the feeble boy, enough to taunt and tempt him, and the next day when he feels his dreams might at last materialise, like the teenage disconsolate Humbert Humbert in *Lolita* yearning for his Annabel, he discovers she has gone off to Switzerland to study.

They meet up again when Finn becomes a successful artist, exhibiting in New York. She still taunts him seductively but keeping him at a distance. "Why do you have no feelings?" he asks her.

And she tries to justify her unsocial behaviour as a child: she was a child shut off from the daylight of the outside world, taught to fear it, that it was her enemy. "You can't be angry if that little girl won't go out to play. We are who we are. People don't change."

Yet, Finn had lived his whole life dreaming of this girl. "Everything I do, I do it for you," he tells her. But the now adult Estella helps him to realise he was just a pawn in Miss Dinsmoor's design – he was "the mouse thrown in for the snake."

'Sweetheart' was a term post-war children heard used by returning soldiers. Some baffled boys considered having a sweetheart as a possession, a status symbol, perhaps a requisite if they were to be friends with a girl. In *Back to the Secret Garden*, Lizzie (Camilla Belle), an orphan from New York arriving at Yorkshire's Misselthwaite Manor, caught the eye of one of the other orphan boys, Stephen (Justin Girdler). "Lizzie," he asks her when he has reached a quieter part of the garden, "will you be my sweetheart?"

Not sure what this entails, Lizzie agrees. "Sure, ok I guess," and they shake hands while Stephen goes back to playing cricket. But later he is offended because Lizzie isn't interested in watching him bat. And that is how long their special relationship lasts – literally, just a short innings. Lizzie clarifies her feelings: "I like you as a friend, not a sweetheart." Yet for Rachael Bella playing young Nikki DeMarco in *The Devil's Child*, it did not even last five minutes. While sitting on a rooftop garden she is asked by her close friend, "Nikki, will you be my girlfriend?" Barely have their lips grazed before they are disturbed. And the next moment the girl has slipped off the roof, and is tumbling a hundred storeys to the pavement far below.

Sharing the same frying pan: friends thrust together

In reality, children do not get to choose their own friends. Companions are often thrust upon them by circumstance, or geography. Thrown together in mutual distress they can either tolerate their lot, or lump it.

In the cases of *Heidi*, cruelly traded into servitude, and Mary Lennox thrust as an orphan into cold Misselthwaite Manor, both have become exalted as tales of lonely children rising above despondency, to raise the spirits of the new friends they encounter. Because of the warmth engendered, these stories have elevated the success of both *Heidi* and *The Secret Garden* as well-loved classics. Unfortunately, where the tales are of abused children such as Joanne in *London to Brighton*, and Lilya in *Lilya 4-ever*, theirs are tales of gritty reality in which even the flicker of hope for an enduring outcome never materialises.

The genteel nature of the story of sweet *Heidi* masks an evil undercurrent of inconsiderate self-interest – the trading of little children like chattel, the devastating rifts that can result from a misunderstanding, and the wickedness of childhood jealousies (exhibited by goatherd Peter's kicking Clara's wheelchair over the crag). But the endearing story of compliant, uncomplaining *Heidi* is, like *Pollyanna*, a tale of bonding, of bringing people and communities closer together, even if Heidi's impact on Madame Rottenmeier was less successful than Pollyanna's melting of Aunt Polly's stubborn heart.

Heidi's aunt found the girl an encumbrance now she has found a better job, so off she jaunts to the high Swiss Alps to unload the orphan onto her grumpy grandfather. But before many days are up, the Aunt is back dragging Heidi off to Frankfurt where she is to be playmate to an invalid girl, Clara. Aunt receives cash-on-delivery for the little girl, even though the 'goods' are seemingly unrefined and uncouth.

There is a mismatch in age between the two girls, who have to become friends whether they like it or not. Heidi is eight going on nine (in Joanna Spyri's classic she is just five), Clara is eleven. [12] In spite of their age difference they quickly bond, Heidi recounting her tales of life with the goats amidst the alpine pastures, smuggling kittens into the house behind Rottenmeier's back, taking their school lessons together, and Heidi is a source of laughter for wheelchair-bound Clara. Yet, despite this bonding, Heidi is homesick, yearning for the trees and fells and her flock of goats. But she isn't sent back, not yet. For as Clara's father says, "As to the little Swiss Miss, it seems as if Clara has formed quite an attachment to her. It'll be wiser not to send her back just yet."

However, as Heidi's pining for home continues, and she starts sleepwalking, loses her appetite, and has nightmares, the doctor resolves to send her home. Later, back in her Swiss mountain hut Clara visits her in her wheelchair. Peter the goatherd becomes jealous, kicking the wheelchair over a crag. But this provides the incentive for Clara to learn to walk – her limbs being strengthened by the healthy mountain air.

This mix of fresh air, childhood rivalry and jealousy seems to be just the remedy for invalid children. Just as it healed Clara in *Heidi*, so too the same mix provided the cure for Colin in *The Secret Garden*.

The Secret Garden is a tale of three children forced by their circumstances to nurture a life-affirming friendship between them. Kate Maberly plays the lonely orphaned girl, Mary Lennox, forced to stay in a dreary mansion in Yorkshire, following the death of her parents in an Indian earthquake (by cholera in the 1949 version in which Margaret O'Brien is equally superb in the role as Mary). Mary is an obnoxious girl and neglected by her parents. She has never before had friends, and has been spoilt rotten by having her own personal servants waiting upon her. Living near her new home of Misselthwaite Manor is local lad, ten-year-old Dickon, who rides a horse across the moors, and has a menagerie of animals to show the little girl – a pet raven, a baby lamb, a ferret, cute deer and ducks.

It is hard work befriending Mary – she is belligerent, and does not know how to interact, and she assumes everyone is insulting her. Yet the boy, Dickon, dutifully perseveres. Between them, they explore the secret walled garden that had been abandoned and declared out of bounds following the death of Mary's aunt ten years ago.

In the house, shut up in solitary confinement due to his ill health, lives another ten-year-old boy, Colin, the invalid son of the master of the manor. Mary explores the house at night, because like *Jane Eyre* she hears mysterious sobbing from another part of the house. The boy is bedridden, so he never gets a chance to get out of his room. And his self-centred moping father never comes to visit him. Mary's visits to the boy have to be kept secret. Their conversations are often abrasive as they bicker with each other. "I hate you, everyone hates you. You're so selfish. You're the most selfish boy there ever was." But in time, a fondness grows between them.

With Dickon's help, they tear down the shutters from Colin's windows to allow light and fresh air into his room, and together the three-some explore the grounds together, in particular the Secret Garden. It is here where, just like Clara in *Heidi*, the boy makes his first tentative steps unaided, and collapses joyously into the arms of the beckoning girl. The fresh air and sunshine rapidly give strength to the boy's limbs so that in time the boy learns to walk. "Are you making this magic?" he asks Mary, looking fixedly into her dark eyes, and together they share their first fumbling embarrassed kiss. Now the two ten-year-old cousins are inseparable, sneaking into each other's bedroom at night, and sharing each other's bed.

But their overwhelming irk, is that the master of the house neglects them, and is always away. So, building a bonfire one night, they do an Indian spirit dance to induce the father's return. It works. As Colin plays blindfolded hide-and-seek with his friends in the walled garden, father appears at the hidden gate, mesmerised by the miracle in front of him – his bedridden son, walking and running like a normal healthy child.

The transitory friendship between Joanne and Kelly in *London to Brighton* is a result of them both being victims of a prostitute ring. The older Kelly had been persuaded to find an under-aged girl for a child-abusing rich client, and a search at a London railway station finds eleven-year-old Joanne (played by Georgia Groome). When the abuse goes too far, the guilt-ridden Kelly rescues her young charge, and fleeing from a murder scene, take refuge in a toilet cubicle before catching the early morning train to Brighton. Rather than being a close friendship, this is more like an older girl guiltily feeling responsible for a younger waif, the younger girl being totally dependent on Kelly, despite Joanne initially saying she can look after herself. Kelly is prepared to find more clients to raise money to send Joanne on her way to her grandmother's house in Devon. The alternative ending to this film shows how tenuous are the bonds of friendship binding the two girls:[13] As soon as Joanne reaches the safety of her grandmother's house, Kelly finds a new client and discards through the car window the only memory she has of the innocent frightened girl she had trapped and then rescued: a teddy bear won in the amusement arcade. Georgia Groome's depiction of a resilient girl on the surface but a terrified innocent inwardly is exceptional, and in Volume One (*Gender Roles and Themes*) we refer to the psychological impact playing this role had on the child.

The situation in *Lilya 4-ever* could not be more contrasting. A sixteen-year-old girl is abandoned by her mother and left to fend for herself in her grim and grimy flat in a uniform Soviet tenement block. When she is rejected by her schoolmates (she is called a whore having being cruelly slandered by her best friend) the only person who shows her any interest is an eleven-year-old boy, who himself has been kicked out of the house by his violent and unpredictable father. At first, the boy starts flirting with her. "Come on. I'll turn the light out," he says. But she stifles his advances, "You're too young. Cut it out." But the boy has nowhere to go so Lilya allows him to sleep on the couch. He spends his time glue sniffing, she smokes when she can afford fags, and together they share their dreams of good food, of basketball, and the freedom of heaven.

In their demise, the boy threatens to end it all by swallowing a bottle of pills, but Lilya dissuades him from doing so. But when Lilya gets into trouble the boy is less successful at convincing her. Lilya is being duped by a man who wants to take her to Sweden where he has a job waiting for her. The boy can see the outcome. "He just wants to sleep with you," he warns her. But the girl is beguiled by the tender caring nature of the man and cannot see through the dupe. The girl is eventually trafficked off to Sweden where, after a spell of being prostituted, she commits suicide. The boy re-finds the bottle of pills, and both rejoin each other for an eternal game of basketball – wearing angel wings.

INTER-RACIAL BONDING

I mentioned in Volume One (*Gender Roles and Themes*), there appears to be a general overall scarcity of children from ethnic minorities portrayed in feature films. They can be called upon to play a multicultural role, but for the run-or-the-mill parts, which are not race-specific, white kids seem to be preferred by casting directors. In this section we focus on the children who are constrained to make friendships across the racial divide, whether or not these liaisons are imposed or freely sought. This itself is a testing hurdle for children to make. Friendship groups tend to despise anything that dares to be different – the wrong trainers, wrong make-up, or tastes in music – and children will do anything to comply, especially if they are on the periphery of social groups. Colour is no exception. Friendship groups tend to exclude "anyone who doesn't fit the mould of the dominant group." [14] Multiculturalism challenges this notion.

According to Sula Wolff, it is between the ages of six and twelve – *the stage of cultural affiliation* – that the child "becomes aware of similarities and differences between social groups, sensitive to the stigma of accent, colour, social anomaly or handicap." [15] After this age, children become morally conscious of the harm that racial taunts effect, and consciously take or reject a prejudicial stance against anyone who is different. What was so pertinent about the 2012 Channel Four documentary, *Make Bradford British* was how several of the adult housemates, when taken back to their childhood haunts were still, a generation later, emotionally affected by the racist treatment they received as kids.

In the following sections, we consider films that put racial prejudice into a historical context within the eras of American partition, South African apartheid, and discrimination against Australian aborigines. Finally, we ponder movies in which friendships dare bridge cultural boundaries, in particular where actors from racial minorities are helping raise the positive image of an oppressed culture.

American Segregation

White-skinned Molly, played by Tina Majorino in *Corrina, Corrina*, is sitting on a tree branch next to a black girl. "Do you taste of chocolate?" asks Molly.

"Do you taste of vanilla?" asks the black girl. Both girls sweetly lick each other's cheeks to test out the theory.

Although children are aware of differences in the colour of skin, and may be wary over mixing with others who are physically different from themselves, yet at primary school level they only associate negative connotations if they are told about them. [16] For seven-year-old Molly, however, growing up in southern states USA still reeling from the end of partition, having a friend with different skin colour was almost unheard of. Her nanny, played by Whoopi Goldberg, has brought her young charge to visit her own family, and this presents a challenge, as the once segregated children have not previously had the chance to mix.

The same is true in *A Time to Kill*, as lawyer Jake Brigance (Matthew McConaughey) brings his little daughter Hannah (Alexandra Kyle) to play with ten-year-old rape victim Tonya (Raeven Larrymore Kelly). The lawyer had just been defending Tonya's father, Carl Lee Hailey (Samuel E Jackson), arrested for shooting two white men who raped his daughter. The trial (based on John Grisham's novel) provides a catalyst for black-white reprisals, bomb attacks, and marches by the Ku Klux Klan. The lawyer was working on the misapprehension that in some way (like Atticus Finch in *To Kill a Mockingbird*) he was a friend of the blacks, because he was endangering his own life by defending Carl Lee Hailey, and also endangering the life of his own family. (They have their house burnt to the ground, and we are told the daughter arrives home from school every day crying because the other children call her dad a nigger lover.) But his client makes it clear: he is not the lawyer's friend. That is why he chose this lawyer to represent him in court. Jake Brigance cannot be a friend: he has never even visited Carl Lee's house, never brought his daughter over to play. And that is why at the end of the film, when the lawyer has achieved the impossible by convincing the jury of Hailey's innocence, he remorsefully takes his wife and daughter to visit his client's family, and the two little girls meet and shyly shake hands, with the same confused embarrassment as the children in *Corrina, Corrina* (though we never actually see the racially different children play together: maybe that is an imposition too far).

In *Mixed Company* (1974), a newly adopted black stepbrother (Haywood Nelson) baffles seven-year-old Ariane Hellen. She tries to remove the boy's clothes to see if he is black all over. "I'm white all over and I don't care who sees it," says the girl pulling down her panties.

In *My Dog Skip*, it is the dog that provides the link between the little white boy and the black kid. "Like all dogs, Skip was colour blind. He made friends with people of all races." While whites and blacks formed separate queues for the cinema in 1940s southern USA with blacks being herded into the balcony seats, the dog helps blur the boundary in the mind of the child.

Several other films set in early twentieth century USA also refer to this barrier. White children do not play with coloureds, and if they do, any sexual innuendo is deemed to be deviant. Violet in *Pretty Baby* is scolded for flirting with a coloured boy. Violet is the twelve-year-old daughter of a prostitute living in a New Orleans brothel around the time of World War One. The black boy is the son of one of the servants, so they all live and play communally. But when Violet, played by preteen Brooke Shields, taunts the boy, their game turns sexual, and the Madame of the brothel orders the girl to be whipped. "White and coloured, they can't be together as far as that is concerned."

To illustrate this further, *The Secret Life of Bees* considers intimacy across the racial divide. The film features Dakota Fanning. She plays Lily Owens, a fourteen-year-old, who has run off with her black maid in 1964 Louisiana, at the time of the Civil Rights Movement, when Martin Luther King was coming to prominence in American politics.

Lily goes to stay with a trio of black sisters (Alicia Keys, Queen Latifa and Sophie Okonedo) who run a popular local honey-making business. A youthful black boy (Nate Parker) lives with them as a handyman. Lily and the boy spend a lot of time together, which is risky, particularly when they drive into town together and go to the movies, which were still segregated in those days. They surreptitiously hold hands, but when they are spotted together, the boy is mistreated by the white authorities in the town.

Even though this film was made as recently as 2008, in an era when multiculturalism and inter-racial marriages are acceptable, it does seem vaguely risqué even today showing white-faced Dakota kiss deep African-black Nate Parker. Despite being beautiful today, if this kiss had been witnessed in 1964 Louisiana, they would have been in deep trouble, the black boy would have been lynched and strung up on the nearest overhanging branch. As Sue Monk Kidd writes in her novel, "You have to understand, there are people who would kill boys like me for even looking at girls like you." The black boy could not court a while girl. It was a 'law of nature', as Lily Owens narrates, "Such a thing could not happen, the way water could not run uphill or salt could not taste sweet."[17]

A film representing a similar era in southern states USA is *To Kill a Mockingbird*, based on the small 'tired old town' of Makeham, Alabama, in 1932. Although the film does not depict bonding among children across the racial divide, yet it provides glimpses of the prejudicial nature of relationships during those times, of which the children become aware. Gregory Peck plays the lawyer, Atticus Finch, called upon to defend Tom Robinson, a Negro labourer unjustly accused of raping a white girl. Atticus is able to show the court what really happened. The white girl had tried to molest the black man – "she did something that in our society is unspeakable – she kissed a black man. She has committed no crime. She has merely broken a rigid and time honoured code of our society – a code so severe that whoever commits it is hounded from our midst as unfit to live with."

Although all men are created equal, "there is an evil assumption that all Negroes lie, that all Negroes are immoral beings, all Negro men are not to be trusted around our women. But our courts are the great leveller."

Scout is Atticus Finch's six-year-old daughter. As a tomboy, she is always in scraps and scrapes. But on her first day at school, she picks a fight with a boy who called her dad 'a nigger-lover'. Father has to explain, "There are a lot of ugly things in this world." In order to explain why he is defending a Negro, he tells Scout (played by the award winning Mary Badham), "You never really understand a person until you can see things from his point of view, until you climb inside of his skin and walk around in it."

This idea that all men are created equal is further questioned in *Shadrach*. Two children, ten-year-old Scott Terra and thirteen-year-old Monica Bugajski, form a brief but compassionate friendship with a dying ninety-nine-year-old former Negro slave, who has returned to their farmstead to die and be buried. The two children are the only ones who can actually deduce what the decrepit man is saying, but they are able to translate the man's dying wishes to their father. The film throws up all the prejudices that were rife in the 1920s Virginia: how in cinemas whites sat downstairs while the Negroes had to occupy the balcony, how the toilets were for whites only, blacks were forced to have their own churches, their own graveyards and undertakers, and separate baptisms in the river. This caused the children to wonder whether Negroes had to have their own separate Heaven, too, when they die.

Such a bonding between slave and white child is brought to the fore in *The Adventures of Huck Finn*. Huck (Elijah Wood) is a little bemused by the desire of his fellow travel mate, the runaway slave Jim, whose dream is to raft down the Mississippi to the Ohio from where he can reach the *Free State* and freedom. "I've never heard such talk in my life!" declares Huck. But thrown together as travelling companions, both look out for the well-being of each other.

"Why did you come to get me?" asks Jim, wasting in jail ready to be hanged. "Because you're my friend, Jim. The best friend I ever had." The man replies, "You're the only friend I *ever* had, boy."

In *The Well*, we see how quickly racial tensions in a community can rapidly escalate and turn into a full-scale riot as a result of misplaced innuendo and gossip. A little five-year-old black girl, Carolyn, played by Gwendolyn Laster, has been sidetracked on the way to school while searching for flowers. She falls down a disused uncovered well shaft, beyond the shouting range for her tiny distressed voice. She is reported missing when she fails to show up after school. This is 1940s small town USA when it was safe for even toddlers to make their own way around town.

The search parties find nothing, except reports that a stranger arrived in town and had been seen talking to the child, and had even bought her a bunch of flowers. The man is arrested but denies any involvement with the child. The man had bought the flowers as an impulsive gesture having seen the child look longingly in a shop window at a bunch of violets.

When the child's family probe the sheriff about what progress has been made, they accuse him of bias. "Maybe you have not found her because you're a white man, Sheriff."

"Be sure, colour has nothing to do with it," he asserts.

Soon reprisals break out in the town, rumours circulate, gossip intensifies, and before long a full-scale race riot has begun with vigilante groups roaming the streets, houses being burnt, people and cars attacked.

But a young white boy, a classmate of the missing Carolyn, discovers the girl's school things at the head of the well, reporting his find to the parents. The whole community are now able to rally round to rescue the little girl and the racial tensions quickly subside as the child is raised alive from the depths of the well.

As we shall see shortly, in *No more Baths* children get to learn about the era of segregation and apply lessons learnt from that time to help fight for justice for one black 'pillar of the community' about to be turfed off his land.

A quirk of the race issue is taken up in *Imitation of Life*. This features a black mother (Juanita Moore) whose daughter, Sarah Jane, has skin so fair she can pass for a white girl.[18] Sarah Jane grows up sharing the home of a white actress, her mother serving as the black housemaid. As she grows older, the pale-skinned girl is able to integrate herself in the white community, that is, until her black mother comes to collect her from school, or from a dance. This racial stigmatisation prevents her from forming deep friendships. Likewise, just as she was about to pursue a romantic relationship with a white boy, her Negroid mother turns up at an inappropriate moment, and the date is scuppered. "How do you explain to your child she was born to be hurt?" muses the parent.

South African Apartheid

In a reverse scenario to *Imitation of Life*, in the South African film *Skin*, Sandra Laing was a girl who was officially classified as white on her birth certificate. Both her birth parents were white-skinned, but Sandra had all the traits of a black child: short matted black hair, a darker skin tone, and her lips, teeth and facial dimensions pointed to there being black genes somewhere in her past parentage – a *polygenetic inheritance*. Not long after her birth, the parents realised there was something wrong, so to avoid any social complications, this being the apartheid era, they migrated to the Transvaal where they opened a shop serving the local black community. Here, Sandra grew up, happily playing and swimming in the creeks alongside other black children, and despite her paler complexion made friends easily among the locals. But when she reached the age of ten, the girl (played by Ella Ramangwane) was sent off to a girls' boarding school. Immediately the difference was obvious. She stood out noticeably among the fair-skinned whites. "I'm not black," she ineffectually cries. But this contrast in colour leads to her expulsion from the school, and for the rest of her childhood her parents are involved in legal battles with the authorities who declare her to be black. We pursue her story further in Volume Eight, *Physical & Sexual Abuse*.

As Sandra becomes a youth, she is unable to find a boyfriend because white-skinned boys dare not date her for there would be repercussions if a white and black child were seen dating. To her father's annoyance, she eventually hooks up with a black guy, and they have to abscond to Lesotho to avoid the father's murderous wrath.

In *The Story of an African Farm*, fourteen-year-old Lyndall (Kasha Kropinski) and eleven-year-old Em (Anneke Weidemann) have recently been orphaned. Both are white-skinned progeny of Afrikaans farmers. They have gone to live with their aunt on a farmstead in the Karoo, along with Waldo, the adopted son of the Uncle. Waldo is a black South African boy. Alas, the aunt does not allow the boy into the house. His job is tending the sheep, and he is often reprimanded for being lazy – he reads technical books to help his education. He has invented an ingenious contraption for sheep shearing. The girls spend time playing with the lad and sneak him into the house when auntie is not looking.

Yet the girls have to witness brutal prejudice against their young friend. When a tutor is found to educate the girls (an unscrupulous impostor played by Richard E Grant), the uncle pleads, "the boy needs a chance." But he does not get tutoring. Later, when the boy is caught helping the girls in the loft, he is given a thrashing. But, despite the prejudice of the adults, the three friends are loyal. When Waldo gets his machine patented, he promises to be able to sponsor Lyndall to go to school – which was always her dream. Here is a case of the children rejecting the alleged omniscient philosophy of the adult world in favour of unity and cooperation.

Australian Aboriginal Culture

It is often the misdirected do-gooders, the overzealous missionaries, who end up being the catalyst for heartless discrimination. This provides the premise to *Rabbit Proof Fence*. Kenneth Branagh plays Mr. Neville (the aborigines call him Mr. Devil, with some justification). He has been designated as 'protector' of the half-caste aborigine community in Western Australia.

He operates with the misconception that he is helping the aborigines by giving them a better chance in life to integrate into white man's society. His role is to implement an abusive policy formulated in 1931 and not abandoned until 1970. He personally seems to care about each individual and wants the half-caste children to be schooled, go to church, learn about hygiene and good manners, sleep inside on a bed and eat hearty meals, be given smart clothes, and generally be educated into westernised ideology. All supposedly complimentary ideas. But it is the methods of compulsion that are so heartbreaking. Children forced to leave their own parents in the outback, sent away thousands of kilometres, to be institutionalised and locked in dormitories, and ruthlessly pursued and whipped if they dare run away. The 1931 Aborigine Act gave the government power to remove any half-caste child from its parent. Half-castes had to ask permission to marry or to visit their children. "In spite of himself the native must be helped."

There was also the misconstrued belief that the culture can be ethnically cleansed. 'Protector' Neville would give itinerant lectures to white women's groups in which he would try to promote his argument that through interbreeding with white men the half-caste can be genetically eradicated by the third generation – an error vividly experienced by Ella Ramangwane as we saw in *Skin*.

Rabbit Proof Fence is not so much about aboriginal children making friends across the race boundary. They never reach that far. It is instead a frank portrayal of how prejudice has endured for much of the twentieth century in Australia. What makes this even more heartbreaking is that it is a true story. The victims survive today. We may still be unaware of the injustice, had this film not been brought to our attention through Doris Pilkington Garimara's biography.

Everlyn Sampi plays fourteen-year-old Molly. She has been raised in the outback settlement of Jigalong – a staging post along the rabbit proof fence that is being constructed between the south to north coasts of Western Australia, a distance of several thousand kilometres. Molly lives with her mother, Maud, her half sister eight-year-old Daisy (Tianna Sansbury), and their twelve-year-old cousin Gracie (Laura Monaghan). Living in the outback, young Molly is an excellent tracker and has learnt how to find food and water in this parched land.

The police capture the three girls and put them on a train bound for the south of the country. They are placed in a small cage, like animals, and taken to Moore River Native Settlement, twelve hundred miles to the south. There, the girls are placed in dormitories (with a bucket in the corner) and locked in at night. Supervised by nuns they have to say grace before meals. A tracker arrives with a runaway, who is beaten, then spends time crying in the isolation hut.

When rain clouds gather, Molly seizes the chance to run away: the rain will obliterate their tracks. Younger sister Daisy wants to stay at the mission but she is persuaded to leave. Thus begins an incredible journey walking eighteen hundred kilometres back to Jigalong following the rabbit proof fence. Along the way they have to find, steal and beg for food, all the while being pursued by the authorities, and Molly has to outwit the aborigine who is tracking them. "Just because aborigines use Neolithic tools, Inspector, doesn't mean they have Neolithic minds."

It takes nine weeks, but the two sisters (Gracie had already been captured) find their way back to Jigalong for a reunion with mother.

What is so upsetting is that Molly gets re-captured and returned to Moore River, only for her to restart her journey and walk back to Jigalong for a second time.

We are told at the end of the film that Molly eventually married, and her half-caste daughter was confiscated from her at the age of three and they have never re-met. "If they could only understand what we're trying to do for them!" yearns Mr. Devil.

We are left with the argument, which is preferable: the aboriginals' basic poverty stricken arid lifestyle, or the possessive wealth of white Australian Society? Molly's own daughter, Cherry, confiscated from her as an infant, defiantly chose her westernised upbringing and refused to have anything to do with her aboriginal mother once she discovered that she had one.

Samson and Delilah deals with aboriginal integration among older teenagers. Samson and Delilah are youths brought up in an outback aborigine community. Samson's pleasure in life seems to be lolling around in his grandma's wheelchair, glue sniffing, and hobnobbing with his girlfriend, Delilah. After altercations in their rural community, they up-sticks, moving to the metropolis (Alice Springs) where they have to confront further racial prejudice.

However, this is not so much a case of being rejected by the white community because they are aborigines. Although they are mistrusted in supermarkets, being constantly followed by the store guard, and Delilah is dismissed by tourists as she tries to sell them her artwork, they are rejected because they have become unkempt vagrants. At least the Aussie dropout who shares his spaghetti with them is more accepting of their plight.

What this film tells us is not that there is innate prejudice from ordinary townsfolk toward aboriginal youth. It is more a societal syndrome. The aborigines have been confined to a life of boredom, restricted to a lifestyle that we westerners cannot comprehend. This boredom leads to an escapist reliance on substance abuse. Samson is so stoned-out from sniffing his glue and petrol that he is unaware when Delilah is snatched by a carload of yobbish rapists, and later she is hit by a passing car. Despite these occurring just a few feet away from where he is, because he is so stoned out of his mind, he is oblivious to her dilemma.

This entrenched misunderstanding between the two cultures comes to the fore in Nicolas Roeg's classic, *Walkabout*. The aborigine, David Gulpilil, becomes the saviour of stranded Jenny Agutter and her younger brother, Lucien John. While they don't compehend each other's language, the adolescent boy understands their gestures for thirst and hunger as he guides the children to safety.

Yet, the tradition of superior white man and subservient native is perpetuated as the girl asks the aborigine to fetch her water. This young man has kept her safe, alive, providing her with survival knowledge, and now his role is relegated to that of water carrier. The children also misinterpret Gulpilil's erotic dance, explaining away the love dance as a parting ceremony. No wonder the snubbed lad resorts to suicide. Even after this ultimate sacrifice, the white girl cannot debase herself by removing her saviour from the tree.

In each of these three Australian-based films, the native aborigine is depicted as a race apart, a misunderstood culture, and the white community has not been sufficiently flexible to allow integration.

I am sure they do exist, but I have not come across a film that depicts whites and Aborigine children forming integrated friendships; though, at least in *Crocodile Dundee*, Paul Hogan treats the Aboriginal tracker as his friend and equal. Paul Krausz shares my observation in his Internet article: *Screening Indigenous Australia: an overview of Aboriginal representation on Film*. He suggests that out of one thousand Australian-made movies that he surveyed, only fifty had content concerning the indigenous Aborigines, that is, just 5% of the output.[19] His excellent article outlines the storyline of a significant number of films involving Aborigines. The website *Create Spirits* also lists dozens of films and documentaries about indigenous Aboriginal Australians.[20]

In *Storm Boy*, a ten-year-old boy, Mike (played by Greg Rowe), befriends a young Aboriginal man (Fingerbone Bill played by David Gulpilil).[21] Together, they share a reclusive subsistence living the shoreline. *Jedda* is about an Aboriginal girl born on a cattle station. Raised to learn about European ways, she naturally wants to learn about her own culture. *Yolngu Boy (2001)* follows a trio of lads brought up in the city where their outlook revolves around football, girls and music. But they are redirected to search out their ethnic roots in the outback. Alas, although these movies show Aborigines integrating into modern Australian life, they do not show cross-cultural friendships forming between children from different ethnic backgrounds.

Cross culture bonding

Most films portraying multiculturalism in the modern era feature both cross-gender as well as cross-cultural relationships, in other words, white girl and ethnic boy, or white boy and ethnic girl. A rare exception bucking this trend is *Bend it like Beckham* in which white-skinned Jules (Keira Knightley) kicks around with Asian girl, Jess (Parminder Nagra), and *Anita & Me* in which Chandeep Uppal and Anna Brewster hobnob.

It is as if directors believe the best way to raise the profile of multiculturalism is by introducing romance into the equation: eleven-year-old asian Qasim Akhtar defending and befriending arian Holly Kenny from suburban Leeds in *Mischief Night*, Keke Palmer from a deprived black neighbourhood of Los Angeles in friendly rivalry with middle class white-skinned Lee Thompson in *Akeelah and the Bee*, American Ryan thrown into reliance on Chinese girl, Ling, in *Amazing Panda Adventure*, and two displaced immigrant children (Chinese and Afro-Caribbean) provide mutual self-support in *Grow Your Own*.

Mischief Night is a film with strands relating to diversity and integration in a multiracial district of Leeds (in the UK), dealing with themes of drug taking, forced marriages, and antagonism between the Asian and white communities. But onto the stage comes Asif (Qasim Akhtar), an Asian boy of eleven/twelve, who interacts with Kimberley (Holly Kenny). Kimberley's dream seems to be discovering who her actual birth father is. Though she is a longhaired pure blond, with dazzling blue eyes, she thinks she may be part-Asian, simply because she lives in a mixed-race community. "Am I a Paki?" she asks her mum, and you can't help but be dumbfounded at the naïve impudence of this obviously arian-looking lass.

As she clambers up a climbing frame, wearing her short school dress, she notices Asif looking up at her. "Stop looking up my bum," she says. But this becomes the start of a friendship between the white girl and the Asian lad. When, one day, she gets into difficulties with an unfriendly gang – she has strayed into the Asian part of the park – Asif comes to her rescue, which further deepens their friendship. During the course of the film, they continue to hang out with each other until, in the final scene, we see them walking off hand-in-hand heading for the *chippy*, the sunset silhouetting off the sheen of her mini-skirted legs. This film paints a positive image of respect for differing cultures, and should be complimented, ignoring the minority of white people who object to members of their race being dated by Asians.

Akeelah Anderson is an ordinary eleven-year-old schoolgirl living in a tough neighbourhood in downtown Los Angeles, using the street lingo of the ghetto, despising school, sometimes truanting, and certainly street-wise. One thing she is good at, though, is spelling. After gaining top marks in spelling tests, she is persuaded to take part in the regional Spelling Bee contest. Hence the film title, *Akeelah and the Bee*, about this timorous girl who turns her ordinary life around through diligent hard work, suffering the ridicule of her peers, the loss of best friends, a rift with her mother, and the exasperation of her spelling tutor. Her brother jeers, "You're going to be up against a bunch of rich white kids. They are going to beat your butt off."

Akeelah is a pretty black girl, played by Keke Palmer. In one of the competitions, she is befriended by an eleven-year-old white boy who helps her overcome her initial shyness. He invites her to his spelling party in the posh White community of suburban Los Angeles where he encourages her in a game of challenge scrabble. He tries to test the waters by giving her a kiss on the cheek, but they just laugh together at his audacity. "Are you going to sue me for harassment!"

he jibes. Although Akeelah is offered a lift home from the party, she refuses because she does not want her new friend to know she lives in the rough part of town. Later, at the regional Spelling Bee, he risks being disqualified for time-wasting over an answer so that Akeelah, in danger of elimination if she is late, can return to the competition in time.

A positive heart-warming friendship is derived from two different cultures in *Grow Your Own*. Despite the opposition of the locals, the Liverpool social service department has designated a portion of an allotment for a group of refugees, as therapy to help them settle into their new country. Phoenix is a little Chinese girl whose father has been severely traumatised from being smuggled into the country in a container, having lived beside his wife's dead body for several days. Sophie Lee plays the girl who makes friends with an Afro-Caribbean boy, and between them, they help transform the lives of those around them. Like so many films of this cross-cultural genre, the director insists on hinting at a deeper intimacy between the children, though this is never taken above the stage of holding hands.

A similar intimacy is hinted at in *Amazing Panda Adventure*, when an American lad (Ryan Slater) travels to China to visit his naturalist father who works on a panda reserve. Hunters are stalking the protected panda, so father has to rush out to the mountains with his Chinese helper and the thirteen-year-old Chinese granddaughter, Ling, who also helps on the reserve.

"Can I go with you?" begs Ryan.

"No it's too dangerous," he is told.

"But you're taking that funny-looking girl," referring to Ling (played by Yi Ding). "If she can do it, I can do it too!"

It is not long before the search party locate the poachers. A shot is fired, and injured dad has to be helicoptered out.

The boy is left stranded with the Chinese girl, and between them, they have to make their way across the mountains, while being pursued by dangerous trappers. At first, the boy and girl are abrasive with each other. The up-start boy brags about his American heritage thinking he is invincible: "I've earned a couple of badges in the cub scouts so I think I can handle the wild." But it is not long before they meet their first obstacle – a rickety rope bridge over a gorge – and we discover which one of them has the mettle.

"You're not like your father at all," derides the girl from the centre of the bridge, beckoning the frightened boy to come along. "Your father is brave."

Alas, after a fracas with the trappers, and carrying a rescued panda cub in their arms, both children slip, fall into a raging river, and are swept away by the torrent in *Indiana Jones* fashion. And so the pair have to rely on each other to keep their wits. They end up caked in mud in a leech-infested bog. When, in their panic to get free of the leeches, they strip off all their clothes and hide modestly in the river, then insults are traded between them as they stare at each other's naked bodies. "Me seeing you in the buff will not exactly be the thrill of my life," says Ryan feigning bravado.

The episode helps them bond with mutual reliance until they are rescued, and their adventure ends tinged with sadness that they have to leave each other. (Yi Ding, who plays the part of Ling was herself a Chinese emigrant, moving to California at the age of nine.[22])

In the examples above, there are positive outcomes for the child's mixing across cultures. For seventeen-year-old Clare Danes playing Daisy in *I Love You, I Love You Not*, the outcome is a negative one, rather like Sarah Jane's experience in *Imitation of Life*. Daisy's grandmother (Jeanne Moreau) is a holocaust survivor, a fact the girl wishes to hide in the school history lessons, lest she be singled out as 'different'. She is also haunted by imagery she has seen of the holocaust. Daisy has a crush on classmate Ethan (Jude Law), and the romance between them blossoms – until, that is, the class discover her Jewish roots, and Ethan's mates persuade him to chose between them or the girl. He decides to shun her. For quiet dependable Daisy, this is devastating, and she vocally turns on her grandmother with an out of character tantrum. "Can't you see there's nothing I can do right?" And the girl races out onto the railway track oblivious to the approaching train.

Not all films have a romantic slant to them. 'Palefaced' Shirley Temple, playing *Susannah of the Mounties*, befriends the son of an American Indian chief. Between them, they learn who are the horse thieves responsible for an attack on the railroad. The boy has access to the Indian chief, the girl has freedom within the Mounties fort, and so by combining their knowledge they are able to find the culprits, rescue the Mounted Police captain, and avert the inter-tribal war! In *A Little Princess*, Sara Crewe acts out the saga of Rama and Sita with her Indian playmate, and later she makes a friendship pact with black servant girl, Becky (Vanessa Lee Chester), to always look out for each other.

In *Anita & Me*, traditionalist Punjabi parents try to deter their daughter Meena from playing with more precocious and rebellious white girl, Anita. This story is based on Meera Syal's autobiography in a clash of cultures similar to *Bend it Like Beckham*. This was more a case of Meena visualising Anita as a best friend, for the relationship was not reciprocated. "As long as I keep her laughing she doesn't punch me." Anita had other friends – white friends including boys – to distract her, and the racial barrier was as real as the garden wall that separated them. Even the Panjabi food had to be replaced by fish fingers when the white girl eventually dared visit. As in *Thirteen* (2003), the girl on the periphery felt she could be more acceptable only by stealing, in this case, the charity tin from the corner shop. "I did it for you," says Meena, presenting the piles of pennies to the older girl. But their friendship was transitory, one-sided, and terminal.

Just as we saw in *Shadrach*, both *No more Baths* and *Before Women had Wings* feature white children who seek friendship, not from kids their own age, but from a black adult; while in *Song of the South*, a white boy (Bobby Driscoll) and his playmate, Luana Patten, befriend the genial Uncle Remus (James Baskett) who makes life '*mighty satisfactual*'. But these friendships are induced for differing reasons.

In *Before Women had Wings*, twelve-year-old Tina Majorino plays Bird Jackson, a girl caught up in domestic abuse by her drunken distraught mother. Following the suicide of her father, mother seems to become ever more violent after the slightest provocation, and the girl receives a brutal beating. Living nearby is a black woman, Miss Zora (played by Oprah Winfrey). Mother has told Bird she has never to visit the woman. She says it is because the woman is a recluse, grows strange herbs, and, although this has nothing to do with prejudice (so she says), the woman is black! But as Bird receives her beating Miss Zora becomes her only sympathetic listening ear, and we learn that love can germinate beyond racial barriers. Indeed, the woman ends up being the girl's guardian while the real mother takes a therapy break.

In *No more Baths*, it is the children who go to aid the oppressed adult. Haley McCormick playing nine-year-old Millie, and her ten-year-old brother, Keagan (Andreas Michael Lamelas) are part of a gang of children who learn that Jake's plot of land, where they frequently go to play, is to be compulsorily purchased for the benefit of a heartless developer. But Jake has experienced all this before, as he explains to his young friends when they are seated comfortably. He harks back to the days of Rosa Parks, when blacks were treated as an underclass. Blacks had to sit at the back of a bus, and had to give up their seat to a white person.

Rudyard Kipling's *Kim* seems to have contradictory undertones of racism. Although the child, Kim (Dean Stockwell), acts as an Indian orphan waif, befriending both the red-bearded horsetrader MahbubAli (Errol Flynn) and the holy shaman, the boy is actually a white-skinned orphan whose expatriate British parents have both died. While the holy man is willing to accompany the boy on their travels together, the man vocalises his xenophobic stance: "Thou belongest among thy people. Thou must stay with thine own."

These latter films, in which the child is forming a special friendship with an adult, lead us nicely on to the next category, *Children Bonding with Adults*.

CHILDREN BONDING WITH ADULTS

As we saw in *Kim*, *No more Baths* and *Before Women had Wings*, it is really something especially unique when a child is not just able to confide in an adult, but can cross the race barrier to consider an adult of a different generation and a different colour as a genuine friend.

There are many examples of children who are able to take an adult as a special friend and it is encouraging when, in this era of over-protectiveness, a child can put its trust in someone older, someone who is not a grandparent, or relative, but from beyond the family unit. Of course, when such friendships are fostered alarm bells start to ring when the parents discover this liaison, and naturally they have a right to worry over such an alliance.

Such was the alarm of the parents of Eric Applebaum (Zach Mills) in *Mr Magorium's Wonder Emporium*. As mother opens Eric's bedroom door, there is a man trying on the boy's collection of hats. "Henry's my friend," Eric assures his mother. Addressing the man, "A little old, don't you think, to be playing dressing up?" quizzes mother, and the man hangs his head in shame, making a swift exit. At least the man's motives were not menacing like Mr Tumnus in *The Lion, the Witch and the Wardrobe*. "I thought you were my friend," cries Lucy (Georgia Henley) as the faun confesses his kidnapping plot.

Michael Thompson[23] focuses on the advantages of intergenerational friendships that encourage children to be more respectful and develop a 'more sophisticated repertoire'.

There may be several reasons why a child forms a relationship with an adult (or *vice-versa*).

– The child may be lonely and cannot make friends in the normal way with its peers. (This had been the concern of Eric's mother in *Mr Magorium's Wonder Emporium*. "You need to get a friend," mother had told him.)

– The child may be too mature to be hobnobbing with its intellectually inferior peer group.

– Alas, an adult may not necessarily be older and wiser, for as we shall see in a couple of films, the adult is 'retarded' and becomes a surrogate playmate for the lonely child, because the adults themselves are still infantile. In this case the child is acting out the game of 'mothers and fathers', the child having a real-life adult to add authenticity to the make-believe.

– Alarm bells should continue to ring when it is the adult themselves who are unable to make friends, the loner, preferring the company of children: the man with the Peter Pan syndrome. Lewis Carroll fits into this category, as would *Michael Jackson: the Movie*, if ever such a film were released.

– The final category includes the child groomer, the child lover, the paedophile, who befriends children for reasons beyond just friendly companionship. We are not concerned with such child predators in this volume, and the reader can pursue this further in *Volume Eight: Physical & Sexual Abuse*.

Charles Dodgson's relationship with the young Alice Liddell may or may not be a case of adult grooming of an impressionable young child. I'm sure his motives were at first innocent. For the child reflecting on the friendship in later life, this was not a case of first crush that Mathilda discovers in *Leon* or for Carlie Westerman in *Hidden Places*, nor was she aware of any abuse that causes him to be demonised in the eyes of adults such as Alice's mother or the pens of modern-day critics. I am, of course, referring to Lewis Carroll (Charles Dodgson's pseudonym) and his story *Alice's Adventures in Wonderland*. This adult-child relationship is explored in the movie *Dreamchild* in which Alice, now an elderly lady, is trying to recollect the author who made her famous.

Theirs was a relationship like an uncle with his niece: he, the teller of stories, the taker of photographs, the sharer of secrets; she, the recipient of attention and of love. But, in this film, there is no evidence to show there was ever anything sexual in their alliance. If ever there was perversion it was only ever in his mind, in his fantasies. Charles hears the delightful strains of a child singing – and there is his Alice (Amelia Shankley) singing tunefully while her sister, Lavinia, accompanies her. But their depth of companionship between man and girl was sufficient to worry the parents of the nine-year-old.

"Mr Dodgson seems to confess a remarkable number of things to you," says Mrs Liddell to her daughter.

"Every man should have someone they can trust their secrets with," replies the girl.

"But why should he say that to you?" asks suspicious mother.

"Because he loves me of course!"

Older sister, Lavinia, tries to smooth out any possible misunderstanding: "He loves us all, mother, each and every one of us."

Mother has reason to be suspicious. Mr Dodgson is often alone with her little girl and frequently taking Alice's photograph. Intently staring into the girl's eyes, he acknowledges, "I like you exactly the way you are. I wouldn't change one hair on your head."

Mother sees things a little girl cannot comprehend. "My mother tore up all his letters to me," complains Alice. "Why should she want to do that?" But when we glimpse the nude photographs that Dodgson took, that are now stored in museums around the world, our misunderstandings become demystified. For Katie Roiphe in her novel *She Still Haunts Me*, she alludes to an inappropriate relationship.[24] For Malcolm Thomson, "his intense love of little girls was the innocent affection of an uncle."[25] Authors Björk and Eriksson dismiss the accusations of his perversion as an innocent fashionable trait of the Victorian era (that of photographing nude children).[26]

The mother's sheltering protection is crucial here, as we shall see in *Shane* (*1952*). For Mrs Waterbury in *The Railway Children*, her concern, as well as protecting the innocence of her children, is also to protect the family name: "You must never, never, never ask strangers to give you things." This is after Jenny Agutter delivers a message to the genial elderly man who passes daily on the railway and to whom the three siblings are becoming endeared as a friend.

In the case of Alice Liddell, she did not go seeking the company of Charles Dodgson. He was just there and she exploited him as a playmate, whereas for Dodgson, he placed himself in the presence of the child so that a friendship could flourish. That sense of shame that so worried Mrs Waterbury in *The Railway Children* was evident a century earlier: according to Katie Roiphe, those incriminating photos of Alice meant the family name could be besmirched, and would Alice have any life at all as an adult, outside the nunnery?

She did, of course. Björk and Eriksson in their book *The Other Alice* inform us the real Alice Liddell was from an upper class Oxford family who hob-nobbed with royalty. (Alice's younger brother even had a prince as a godparent.) After an affair with the sickly Prince Leopold, Alice herself ultimately married Reginald Hargreaves, had three sons, and lived on a country estate in Hampshire, waited on by servants.[27]

Another teller of tales to bewitch the child is Uncle Remus (James Baskett) in *Song of the South*. Now, we know there was nothing crooked about this genial old Negro who mesmerised Johnny (Bobby Driscoll) with his tale of Brere Rabbit, but the man is devastated when he is mistrusted by the child's mother. "From now onwards, I want you to stay away from Johnny," the man is told. "Completely away."

The tales Heinreich Harrer told to the adolescent Dalai Lama in *Seven Years in Tibet* were as magical as Uncle Remus', about a culture and lifestyle a solitary lonely boy in the remotest kingdom on Earth could only dream about. This boy, being nurtured as a future religious icon, was not meant to play, or learn about materialistic things, but here was a stranger (Brad Pitt) from a strange land with strange tales to tell, and thus the friendship was cemented. But always, reverence and propriety were maintained. When they finally part, as the Imperialist Chinese march on Llasa, the boy acknowledges, "I am not your son, and I have never thought of you as my father."[28]

The tables are turned, so to speak, in Rudyard Kipling's romanticised tale of India, in *Kim*. Here it is the boy, Kim (Dean Stockwell), who is befriending the holy man and adopts him as a travelling companion. Theirs is a symbiotic relationship. He, as a scallywag, effectively begs the best meals for his adopted master, while the man's holy reputation provides the boy subterfuge for his misdeeds. The man instils in the boy the importance of education, and makes this a condition of their continued friendship. "Dost thou love me?" the elderly man demands. "Then go before my heart cracks," he says, sending the lad off to St Xavier's to be schooled.

The friendship that grew between the eleven-year-old Brandon de Wilde and Alan Ladd in *Shane* (1952) resulted from an accidental meeting, and its seed germinated instantly the man arrived on the homestead of the young boy and his family. The boy, Joey, is immediately smitten by this stranger riding into his ranch. The boy has had a lonely life, so any new arrival means excitement, and here is a potential source of interest, even a playmate. What consolidates their alliance is the man's instant interest in the boy and the toy gun he is playing with. This is a man who likes kids. Like Dodgson, Shane seems to relish the company of the little child, patiently talks with him, helps him arrange his holster, teaches him to shoot, puts his arm compassionately around the boy's shoulder, and leaves it there!

All the while, mum looks on, unsure what to make of this affable gunslinger. Was the woman aware of any sexual perversions in those days – a lonely man on the road, unfulfilled? Reviewers allude to a sexual attraction between Shane and the mother, but could it be mother feared a different target for the gunman's attentions?

As with Alice from *Dreamchild*, this is a case of hero worship, and that is as far as it goes. In the view of Neil Sinyard, 'cinema's most potent study of childlike hero-worship.'[29] Joey is as mesmerised by his new staid powerful role model as any football fan idolising their soccer hero would be today. Regrettably, in *Alice in Wonderland*, it was the little girl who was being idolised by a sad man whose path had led him in an unhealthy direction.

Joey's words, "Mother, I just love Shane… almost as much as I love Pa," are nothing more than a child's devotion would be, say, to a pet. He is not substituting pa. But like anxious Mrs Liddell, Joey's watchful mother gives a word of caution. "Joey, don't get to liking Shane too much," she says having watched the man and child interacting. Whatever were the worries going through her mind, her explanation was that, "He'll be moving on one day, and you'll get upset."

Which, of course, is what happens after the final shootout. "You go home to your mother and father and grow up to be strong and straight," says Shane before trotting off into the sunset.

Having just created a sort of classification system for child-adult cordiality, already I'm stepping outside it. For how can one categorise the world of make-believe in which films like *Big* (1988) feature a twelve-year-old transfigured into the adult Tom Hanks; *The Time Traveller's Wife* in which nine-year-old Brooklyn Proulx is intermittently visited by a naked man "You came into that meadow and forced yourself on the heart and mind of that little girl," (as with *Miss Potter* the child ended up married to this inter-generational visitor); or *Life-Size*, a film in which a child's doll becomes human?

Tyra Banks plays the adult Eve, a collector's doll that accidentally becomes mixed up in a magic spell meant to reincarnate Lindsay Lohan's mother. Lindsay Lohan, or rather her twelve-year-old character Casey, wakes up one morning to find this supermodel sharing the bed with her. "I'm Eve, and you're my special friend," says Eve. This must surely be every parent's worst nightmare. And for Casey, who was wishing it to be mum, it was her worst nightmare too. What must have been even more puke-inducing is when she claims, "My real purpose in life is to help girls." But for Casey, how can this intruder understand: "You have never loved someone so much then all of a sudden they are gone." But even these words come back to haunt Casey. As Eve installs herself in the household, helps the girl with her make-up and fashion, and supports her football matches, in time the woman becomes a good friend to Casey. But, just as the children in *Nanny McPhee* and *Mary Poppins* discovered, when you dabble in the world of magic, that magic has a habit of ending abruptly. Father and daughter race to the Sunnyvale studios only to witness Eve slowly transforming back into an inanimate doll.

The Retarded Adult Companion

We will consider three films in which the girl-child makes friends with a retarded adult. It is always a male adult. Girls never make friends with backward women, though boys may do so, as we discover in *Les Diables*, in which a boy has been protecting an older girl, always assuming her to be an older sister until the day he discovers she is not. Then his previously restrained masculine urges get the better of him.

But for the confused girl-child, the three adult figures we mention in this section become their friends, and in all cases the relationship is melded with a girlhood crush on the older character. Ten-year-old Evan Rachel Wood acting as Harriet in *Digging to China* has Ricky (played by Kevin Bacon) as a playmate. For nine-year-old Jodelle Ferland, Jeliza Rose makes friends with neighbouring Dickens (Brendan Fletcher) in *Tideland*. While in *Sundays & Cybele*, it is the man, Pierre (Hardy Kruger) who seeks out his young eleven-year-old friend from the French orphanage, Françoise played by Patricia Gozzi. These are all serious relationships, not like daft Chunk's (Jeff Cohen) buddy-sparring with adult ogresome Sloth in *The Goonies*.

In all cases, the relationship begins innocently enough, but it is not long until the impressionable child starts thinking of the older man as their 'cooty', their sweetheart, their fiancé, or their lover. Such is the relationship in *Sundays & Cybele*. Shortly after befriending the thirty-year-old, Cybele soon starts referring to him as her fiancé, having worked out that when she reaches marriageable age (she is eleven now), the man will still be in his thirties and not too old! It's as if all three girls (in *Digging to China*, *Tideland*, and *Sundays & Cybele*) are playing a child-like game of mothers and fathers but innocently dabble too close to the moral boundaries with their real-life guinea pigs.

In *Sundays & Cybele*, the girl's real father has dumped Cybele (Patricia Gozzi) at an orphanage and abandoned her there. The nuns at the institution insist on calling her Françoise instead of the heathen name Cybele. On the way to the orphanage, Cybele and her father had met the man Pierre from whom they had asked directions. Father failed to turn up at visiting time on Sunday and as Pierre was passing by, seeing the unattended child, he had pretended to be the girls' father. The nuns believed the dupe and the girl was happy to go with the only man who has ever been nice to her.

Every Sunday they spend the day together, usually playing games and exploring the park. Unlike Dickens in *Tideland*, and Rickie in *Digging to China*, Pierre is not exactly retarded. He is an intelligent man enjoying a sexual relationship with his adult girlfriend, but people in the community treat him as a simpleton because he is a broken man, the trauma of working as a fighter pilot in Indo China had left him with amnesia. And because he is constantly depicted on screen with a smiling untroubled face (like Chloë in *Les Diables*) we are made to assume he is simple by nature. There is never anything devious in the man's behaviour, yet the man and girl often get unusual stares from passers-by as they sit cuddled together, cheek to cheek, or as she sits on his lap staring into his eyes, stroking his face, and talking mildly, and as they run around the woods care-free like two little kids, hand-in-hand.

But this is a secret relationship, kept hidden from Pierre's girlfriend, Madeleine, so he obviously sees something wrong in his close liaison with a girl-child. When Madeleine discovers the arrangement, she starts spying on Pierre and Cybele. Pierre's brother, Carlos, treats the relationship as it is – in innocence. He warns Madeleine to be careful: "You mustn't dirty something that is beautiful." However, as things escalate before Christmas, the police are called in, misinterpret the situation, and shoot Pierre dead. So now, Cybele has lost her family, her own name, her hope, and now her only friend.

Both *Digging to China* and *Tideland* feature ten-year-old girls (though Jodelle Ferland was only nine when *Tideland* was made) making friends with retarded men in their twenties. In both films, adult and child innocently play with each other and are comfortable in each other's company, and both are unaware when they cross taboo boundaries.

Tideland's Jeliza Rose watches Dickens pee – "little girls shouldn't watch" he rebukes her. They hold hands, play adventure games "swimming" through the tall wheat Prairie fields of Saskatchewan (Texas in Mitch Cullam's novel), make a 'submarine' den from an upturned vehicle, pretend they are girl and boy friend, and they kiss (snog would be a better description) with the little girl egging the slow-witted man on. "Before she died," Dickens tells her, "My grandma used to kiss me." Dickens shows the nine-year-old actress how he had to put his tongue in grandma's mouth, and the ill-matched couple, girl and man, practise tongue kissing (though their tongues never actually touch). "I'm your wife forever," the girl giggles as they secretly watch Dickens's guardian having sex with a deliveryman. But when Dickens, in a moment of intimacy, promises to show the excited little girl his "stick of dynamite", she doesn't realise the man is speaking literally, and they never see each other again after the devastating explosion on the railway track.

In *Digging to China*, Evan Rachel Wood plays Harriet, befriending an autistic man, Ricky (Kevin Bacon), who accompanied by his mother, comes to visit the motel where Harriet lives. Their car having broken down, mother and autistic son are forced to stay for several nights while the vehicle is repaired. Ricky and the young girl talk together a lot, and go off playing together.

Once they try to make a flying vehicle from hot air balloons. Harriet even takes Ricky to school with her (the other children are tolerant of the man's childish naïvety). One night, they run away together, finding an old railway carriage to sleep in. The following morning, after Harriet has betrothed herself to the man, they improvise a wedding ceremony and kiss, even though they don't understand the significance of the actions. But soon the vehicle is fixed and so Ricky has to leave. Ricky is so overcome with grief at having to lose the only friend he has ever had, he buckles over with anguish on the floor. Harriet comforts Ricky by wrapping her arms around the foetal man, and that is how they are discovered – man and child on the floor in an impassioned embrace. Their actions are misinterpreted, the police are called, and a friendship is broken as the confused man is led away from the naïve girl.

All these relationships are seen as sweet on the cinema screen. The fact that these men are slow-witted, does that make these relationships acceptable? Though these men have child-like minds, they are physically fully-grown, with hormonal urges who, left to their own devices, may not have the self-control of restraint. Of course, in these films the child is not harmed and the relationships are stifled: Pierre's girlfriend, Ricky's mother, and Dicken's older sister see to that. But these child-adult friendships are not vastly different from the friendships endorsed by fairy tale stories such as *The Beauty and the Beast*, or *The Hunchback of Notre Dame*. Surely, that girl left alone with that Quasimodo monster is at this very moment going through hell and being cruelly molested, or that poor *Heidi* living alone with that grumpy old man above Dorfli – the imagination of the villagers have to work overtime to quash the possibilities – what with that man's reputation!

Yes, the relationships are deemed innocent, as was Beatrix Potter's when she was a ten-year-old visiting the Lake District and depicted in *Miss Potter*. Coming from a restrictive affluent family in London, whose pretentious parents were more interested in developing the girl's airs and graces than her artistic skills, her vacations in Cumberland gave her a new lease of life. "Like an animal released from its cage she fell under its spell." But Beatrix, played as a ten-year-old by Lucy Boynton, also fell under the spell of one of the local young men. How innocent and sweet was their friendship, man and girl, and not even a shimmer of inappropriateness. Yet later, as Beatrix became an adult, their friendship re-formed and they were married. I guess, with all the moralistic distrust of twenty-first century officialdom, such an innocent association would today be deemed indecent, and the man arrested for grooming.

Travelling Companions

Fellow travellers keep their distance at first: initial reserve takes time to blossom into friendship. Where the child finds him/herself as a solitary traveller in the company of strangers, their reaction can range from resigned reliance in *Alice in the Cities*, in which a man and girl are forced to stay together long after their plane journey has ended; mute withdrawal, which is nine-year-old Aimee's response after the rail crash in *My House in Umbria*; wariness, in the case of *The Journey of Natty Gann*; to antagonism (Rosetta's reaction in *Stolen Children*); and to outright animosity in *Are We There Yet*. For Ahmed (Yasser Talib) in *Son of Babylon*, he sees just the futility of the journey his grandmother takes him on across Iraq to seek the dad he never knew, in the Nasirijah prison.[30]

Invariably, where it is a girl travelling alone, her travelling companion is an adult male on whom she becomes dependent as a surrogate father-figure. Like the demise of *Leon* and Trent in *Lawn Dogs* which we shall see in the next section, this surrogate male inevitably finds his role a costly deed of self sacrifice: Korchinsky placed in police custody in *Tiger Bay* after rescuing the girl from drowning; Antonio the rookie cop who loses his job after flouting the police code of practice, as he escorts molested Rosetta and her younger brother the length of Italy; the total destruction of Nick Person's pride-and-joy vehicle in *Are We There Yet* as he dutifully takes his girlfriend's kids to Vancouver.

Fourteen-year-old Meredith Salenger travelling as a stowaway with strangers in *The Journey of Natty Gann* would by today's audience be seen as foolhardy as a lone girl hitching in the red light district of Harlem. She is making her solitary way from Chicago to Seattle in search of her father. Without money to travel, she has to find devious ways to travel West. This is the 1930s depression era in America and there are many similar vagrants travelling in her direction who sneak on to moving trains and cattle trucks. Like the three young stowaways in *The Angel of Pennsylvania* Avenue, they have to be alert to jump off as the train slows, to evade capture. For on one occasion, Natty *is* captured by the authorities and dumped in an orphanage.

Tomboyish Natty intermittently tags along with older teenager, Harry, played by a baby-faced John Cussack. The man is heading West desperate to find work. "I go alone," Harry tells her. "I take no partners, especially not a girl." But his hard heart melts.

Unlike other opportunists she travels with, this man is not out to molest her, is willing to share her company (and his beans), under the protection of Natty's guard dog that has tagged along. By the end of the journey, they have become good friends so that on arrival at Seattle they seem to want to stick together.

But Natty thinks she has located her father's logging camp inland while at the same time the man has had a lucky break acquiring a job south in California. Both ask each other to abandon their quest and travel with them instead. Though reluctant to split from one another, they both realise they have more pressing goals. As Harry boards the bus, they realise a parting smile is not good enough, and the lad comes back to place a parting memory on her lips.

Eleven-year-old Rosetta (Valentina Scalici) in *The Stolen Children* has been abused by her mother, being forced to work as a prostitute for the past two years. At last the authorities have found out, her mother has been arrested, and so the child is being sent away, along with her nine-year-old brother, Luciano, while mum is jailed. They are being accompanied by a police officer, Antonio, across Italy on the way to a children's home. The man is a rookie cop, inexperienced with kids and does not want the task, though he does try to make the best of an unwanted assignment. Respecting their privacy, he leaves the kids to sleep alone in the railway carriage at night while standing guard in the corridor outside.

At first, the children are antagonistic towards him. "It's always hurry, hurry, hurry, and now we have to wait!" Rosetta tries to be awkward avoiding getting to the station so Antonio has to manhandle her, and as they struggle, she threatens to accuse him of abuse. But as they travel south across Italy, various children's homes reject the girl because of 'her past'. So, Antonio has no option but to keep searching for a suitable accommodation for the children. As they are sent down to Sicily, Antonio is forced to take on the role of father-figure to the children, buying them snacks, taking them to the beach.

The despairing Rosetta realises she has no one to turn to for help except this man, and she collapses into his arms for comfort. "Take me away from here," she pleads (just as Emmeline demanded of Richard in *The Blue Lagoon*, after they found their guardian, Paddy, dead on the beach), and Antonio finds he has stepped outside his remit as a cop.

A similar air of resignation pervades the relationship between Yella Rottländer and Rüdiger Vogler, who play nine-year-old Alice Van Dam and thirty-one-year-old Philip Winter, virtual strangers forced by circumstance to be travelling companions together in *Alice in the Cities*. This is a marvellous study of how a childless man, at first hesitant, forms a fond bond with his companion, a compliant little girl trusting an adult stranger. And unlike most films of this genre it does not develop into a childish crush – the prudent child-adult delineation is always maintained.

Alice is at New York airport with her mother seeking a flight back to Germany. But all the flights are cancelled due to a strike. Joining the queue of travellers is a fellow German, Philip, who is in the same predicament. He helps translate for the mother at the check-in desk, and the best they can do is fly out tomorrow to Amsterdam. Since all three of them are forced to stay another night in New York, the strangers decide to economise by sharing the same hotel apartment. As she would be with any unfamiliar person, Alice is a little reticent about the relationship, but it is not long until she opens up to the stranger. The next morning, Philip finds a message from the mother, asking him to take the girl on to Amsterdam where mother will catch up with them on the following day.

So, after a bonding session looking through binoculars at the top of the Empire State Building, the man and girl amble off to the airport. The girl has to be trusting of the man and she sleeps with her head on the stranger's lap for the duration of the flight. Arriving in Amsterdam in the early hours, they find a hotel room, spending the night together, alone. In these days of stranger-danger, alarm bells should be ringing in every parents' ear, particularly as both sleep in only their underpants, and in the morning, the girl sits on the toilet while the man is naked in the bath and has just pulled out the plug! But, hey, this is Germany in the 1970s, when such behaviour was not considered as unseemly as it is today. And anyway, the trust was justified; there was never any misbehaviour to be alarmed about.

The next day, while awaiting mum's arrival, they take a boat tour along the canals of Amsterdam. Little Alice starts to irritate the compliant man with her reasonable complaints: "I'm hungry"… "You walk too fast" … "Can't we see the city?"

Phil is exasperated: "Listen, I'm in no mood to be bugged by you. Because of you I'm running round in circles."

"You'll be glad to get rid of me," needles the girl as they arrive at the airport to meet mum's flight. But mum is not on the plane. Not even on the passenger list. The tearful girl runs to the ladies' toilet and locks herself in a cubicle. Alice has a German grandmother, so Philip decides to take the girl to her, but Alice cannot remember either her grandmother's name or where she lives. After running through a list of all the possible towns from A-to-Z, when they finally get to Wuppertal, Alice, like blindly putting a pin on a map, agrees that Wuppertal is where gran lives.

And so begins the long journey by coach across Holland into Germany, then finding a hotel in Wuppertal as a base for their search. The next day finds them travelling the suspended railway around the city looking for the house that Alice remembers from her childhood, and later they resort to hiring a car, even though the man has just about spent up. It really is like looking for a needle in a haystack, yet Philip is patient with the girl, and Alice is resigned to the expedition. "Stop crying," the man shouts at her. Little does Philip realise they are searching the wrong haystack. It is not until they are sitting in a café, the girl pawing at her ice cream, that Alice delivers her thunder-bolt: "Grandma never lived in Wuppertal."

The man still does not lose his temper, though he does go to the bathroom to diffuse his anger and consider the ridiculousness of his situation. "Why didn't you say that before?" he asks the girl rhetorically. "Do you think I'm crazy about driving little girls around?"

But really, the girl is impotent in this situation. Although the viewer may consider her as exploiting the dilemma, of grabbing the affection of a surrogate father-figure, in truth she does not have the reasoning power to consider the implications. She would have had no conception of what a search for her grandmother would have entailed. For her, as a nine-year-old, a journey is from A-to-B, there is no conceptualisation of route planning, of distance, of getting lost. Those are the problems for adults, and in her limited experience, they are easily solved. She flippantly replies, "I told you. I wanted to stay in Amsterdam."

Philip feels he has no other option but to take the girl to the police station. "Take care of yourself," he says, leaving the girl with the authorities. Now this is one confused man. For the first time in his life, he has been a temporary father-figure. He cannot escape the loneliness of parting from his new dependent. Instead of going home, he goes to a rock concert, and then sits in his car, a lonely figure, cogitating over his recent loss. As for Alice, she sits bored and unattended at the police station, and it is not long before she has had enough. Like Tatum O'Neal in *Paper Moon,* she escapes from her new guardians and goes in search of her previous travelling companion. Alice finds Philip sitting his car. "The food was horrible," she tells him, and the pair laugh together, glad to be back in each other's company.

They are now together, friends reunited. Like the two girls bonding in *Beaches* (1988), they have their pictures taken together in a photo booth, which Alice fondly looks at later in the film. Then together they search around the Ruhr, visiting Essen, Duisburg, and Gelsenkirchen, until finally in Oberhausen they discover a house exactly like the photo in Alice's purse. They knock on the door, but the Italian woman now living there has lived there for the past two years. Grandma has moved elsewhere.

They are not dispirited. Instead, they decide to go swimming in the local lido. It is here, submerged in the water and playing together, they slag each other off by calling each other a string of unpleasant names, and ironically we realise the bonding is complete. "I wonder if people take you to be my father?" she ponders. The girl has the audacity to ask a stranger. "You act like you really are her father," the woman tells Philip, thus cementing the relationship they have still further.

Philip decides to take the girl to his parents' house, but on the way, the police intercept them on the ferry across the Rhine. The girl is put on a train to Munich where assumedly her mother will be waiting to meet her.

I wonder whether in *Alice in the Cities*, it did occur to Philip to report Alice's lack of a guardian to the authorities at Amsterdam Airport, particularly as the girl had said she wanted to stay in Amsterdam (or so she says later). Although he gives the impression of being burdened with an unwanted child, he has an underlying (repressed?) yearning for a social attachment or responsibility, and this subconsciously fuelled his mental choice of remaining with the girl until they had exhausted other means of finding grandma first.

In *Tiger Bay*, Korchinsky has a more sinister motive for travelling with a young girl (Hayley Mills). As a child, Hayley Mills starred in two films, both times as an impish tomboy forming a relationship with an adult male, a murderer. In *Whistle down the Wind*, she stumbles across a wounded man, and as a result of a misunderstanding of a swear word, assumes he is Jesus Christ, and brings all her friends to see this iconic figure. Ana Torrent forms a similar relationship with a runaway convict in *Spirit of the Beehive* assuming the man to be the tender monster she saw in the *Frankenstein* film. In *Tiger Bay*, Haley witnesses a Polish sailor having an argument with his girlfriend in the block of flats where she lives near Cardiff docks. She peers through the letterbox in time to see the man, Bronislav Korchinsky, shoot the woman with the gun that had been pointed at him. (It was actually self-defence, but we never get to know whether he could persuade the police of that.) The man realises that eleven-year-old Gillie is the only witness, so he seeks her out, perhaps meaning to eliminate her.

Both girl and man agree they have to get away from Cardiff. They evade the police by jumping on a ferry. Korchinsky has his opportunity to silence the girl for good when the latch on the ferry's safety gate that Gillie is leaning against comes loose. All it would take is one quick shove and the girl would be floundering in the deep water of Cardiff Bay. But instead of pushing her, he grabs her to safety, and we know that from now on their destinies lie together.

They head off to the Welsh hills to wait until a boat to Caracas is ready to set sail. This is not like *Sundays & Cybele*. We don't see much bonding, and there is no hint of impropriety, despite Korchinsky telling the girl, "Gillie, in a few years – soon – you'll be grown up, beautiful, someone will love you, want to marry you. Then you'll have all the power in the world for good or bad." According to Marianne Sinclair, "Much of the film's success rested on the ambivalent complicity that bound the girl child (a little slum kid on the verge of pubescence) and the male adult (Horst Buchholz's animal magnetism)."[31]

Gillie realises this is a parting-of-the-ways speech. "You're not coming back, are you?" But their paths do cross again. Korchinsky has just scraped his way to safety. His boat has gone beyond the three-mile offshore boundary so he cannot be arrested, despite the police coming aboard his ship, bringing along the girl to help identify the murderer. Gillie insists on denial and refuses to betray the man. But the police officer understands. "Sometimes we have to tell little lies – to help out our friends. We call this being loyal."

Korchinsky cannot now be arrested and Gillie does not betray him, so the killer is safe – so it would seem. Then Gillie falls overboard. In true self-sacrificial heroics, Korchinsky jumps into the sea to rescue her, and the bedraggled pair are hauled aboard the rescuing launch – the police launch – which takes them back to shore, and him into custody.

In *Are We There Yet*, we find Aleisha Allen, as a thirteen-year-old, and her brother (Philip Daniel Bolden) living with their divorced mother fiercely defending their independent life. "I feel sorry for the next sucker who tries to make a move on mum." Then along comes the actor Ice Cube who hates kids. "Kids are like cockroaches, except you can't crush 'em."

Yet the man ends up taking the two kids on a car trip to Vancouver in his spanking new pride and joy. Just as John Candy's interventions were not appreciated in *Uncle Buck*, so the two kids hate this man and take delight in scratching his car, denting it, puking up in it, soiling and trashing it until ultimately it gets incinerated. So now the man is forced to continue the journey with the antagonistic kids by hitching a ride in a lorry, travelling rough in a cattle truck, even riding on horseback. But what started as a hateful relationship, when it comes to say goodbye the kids cannot bear to be parted, and the man ends up marrying mum.

The Drifter and Loner as replacement father-figure and object of first crush

Mostly these are circumstances that affect adolescent girls: the father is absent (divorced, at war, or dead), and the susceptible girl needs a male figure as a source of strength and stability. Inevitably, the man becomes accessible and the confused child misinterprets her relationship as one of distanced sexual possibilities. The child develops a crush on the man, though rarely does this become physical or sexual. Films rarely depict adolescent boys having similar relationships. Brandon de Wilde's crush on *Shane* was not sexually inspired. Rather it was hero worship for a man who seemed superior to his own father. A similar adulation arises in *Nowhere to Run* in which an escaped convict (Jean-Claude Van Damme), hiding out on the farmstead, provides physical protection for a mother and her two kids about to be ousted from their land. The boy (Kieran Culkin) adores the man for his bravery and sees him as a possible father-figure. Nick Stahl seeks out the disfigured recluse in *Man Without a Face*, visualising in him a paternalism the man had spent his adulthood trying to avoid. Nicholas Hoult makes the same search in *About a Boy*, seeking out Hugh Grant for company, while the adult is determined to shun him.

Other films show a child's distrust for the stranger, particularly the recluse. In *Now and Then*, the four girls were frightened of Creepy Stephen ("Why do you hate me?" the confused man asks). The man is only seen at night-time, stalking the cemetery. In *To Kill a Mockingbird*, Boo Radley was the figure of fear – another night owl. Yet at the end of both films we are shown that these 'abhorrent characters' were in fact trustworthy citizens: Creepy Stephen secretly went to the cemetery to visit the grave of his long-lost son, and Boo Radley had a sensitivity to light. Yet nowadays, children's fear of the stranger has been reinforced. Media issues have compelled the parent to question the intentions of any adult befriending a child.

In these days of Sarah's law and criminal records checks, when every volunteer has his/her motives scrutinized, when eyebrows are raised whenever a scout leader, or a gymnastics coach gives a child a lift home, or a schoolteacher is left unattended with a pupil, it is difficult for a child to know which adults to trust and befriend. Even the friends they correspond with on their facebook pages are more likely than not to be middle-aged monsters masquerading as children. Question marks are raised over popular icons for children, Michael Jackson in the USA and Jimmy Savile in the UK, against whom severe accusations have been made, though never proven, their images tainted by mistrust even beyond the grave. "75% of school children chose Michael Jackson as the world's top ideal role model" – this was *after* the allegations against him were made.[32]

As if to justify his playfulness with kids, Michael Jackson recognized he found children 'safe'. "They can't hurt you," he announced. Kincaid adds "Yes they can, as he now knows."[33] Jackson's predilection predicament provides a salutatory warning for any adult who dares step into the eye-line of a pre-adolescent child, as Trent found to his bruising cost in *Lawn Dogs*, Korchinsky found to his liberty in *Tiger Bay*, and Jean Reno found to the loss of his life in *Leon*.

Mel Gibson playing McLeod in the film he also directed, *Man Without a Face*, shows clearly the helpless vulnerability of the solitary male befriended by a child. He lives as a recluse, the result of previous child abuse allegations. Yet when the young boy, Nick Stahl, seeks his tutoring expertise, the man becomes helplessly entangled. "He is my friend," the boy explains to his mum

– and to the cop, after he fails to return home one evening. Though the man is innocent, the community do not see it that way. Allegations of this nature do not allow mitigation.

In the next two films, the adult male reluctantly becomes friend of the child. Both are loners, the kind of person a parent should be wary about, even though neither of them was targeting the child for friendship. As in *Tiger Bay*, the adult becomes the helpless victim, further reinforcing the idea that no upstanding adult who has the misfortune to make friends with a little girl ever comes out of the relationship with his honour or his life intact. As with Korchinsky in *Tiger Bay*, the loner Trent (Sam Rockwell) finds himself under arrest (and beaten up by vigilantes) in *Lawn Dogs*, while in *Leon*, Jean Reno is forced to sacrifice his life in defence of the little girl.

In *Lawn Dogs*, Mischa Barton plays Devon Stockard, a ten-year-old girl living with her mother and father in the garden village of Camelot Gardens in Kentucky. She is a "new kid on the block", having only lived there for a couple of months, and she still hasn't made any friends. "Popular girls are never bored nor boring," dad tells her, trying to pack her off in the village to sell cookies. "The world's at your feet, Sweetheart."

Devon spends her days either fantasizing about the folk tale Baba Yaga in which she role-plays the young girl caught up under the witch's spell, or she sits playing draughts against her dolls. Every time her doll loses, she rips a limb from off its body. She has a whole box of limbless torsos and body parts. "If you lose this time, it'll cost you your head!" This, as we will discover, is the inevitable outcome of anyone daring to secretly befriend a child.

This little girl is also still suffering from the trauma of major heart surgery, and has the scars to prove it. "I'm not supposed to strain myself, you know. I almost died twice." Hence her preoccupation with blood, scars, and a willingness to strangle a chicken. Although (unusually for films) she lives in a house with mother and father, she is not happy at home. "She could at least pretend to be happy," father says to mother. The girl seems distant from her father, treating him with polite distain. She gives him reluctant kisses on the cheek. We see her rebelliously sitting on dad's car and lifting up her dress to wee down the windscreen. She discards her barbeque dinner in father's toolbox. She really needs a friend.

As Devon enters the local woods pretending to explore Baba Yaga's forest, she comes across the secluded ramshackle home of twenty-two-year-old Trent Burns, the man who mows the lawns in the village, and who is despised by the posh inhabitants of the walled garden village. The man gets a shock as he opens his door to find the young girl tying red ribbons to his tree.

As the blurb says on the back of the DVD cover, "In well-off American suburbs ten-year-old girls don't hang out with twenty-two-year-old guys... For Trent Burns, innocent young Devon turns out to be a very dangerous friend indeed." The man is not a total stranger to the girl, for she has seen him mowing dad's lawn at home. "Will you take me for a ride in your truck?" the little girl asks.

"This is private property. Go home!" The sensible man is stern, aware of consequences. But this is an impressionable young girl. She has an unfinished fantasy about Baba Yaga to complete, and the man is already unwittingly trapped just by being there. He has become a fascinating magnet, drawing the over-imaginative girl to him. She returns the following day, spying through his window and smirking as she watches him having sex with one of the village lasses.

"Don't you have any friends your age?" Trent asks her.

To get the girl out of his backyard he offers to give the girl a lift back to the village, and this is where the entangling web of entrapment begins to be spun. He knows he should not be giving the girl lifts, so he drops her off outside the village gates and not at her home.

The next day, Devon pretends she has made friends at last with another girl in the village, and tells her parents she is staying at 'Tracy's' for a sleepover. But instead, she sneaks off to the woods and to Trent's house. Again the man dismisses her, but she is too inquisitive, making him tell her about the time he was shot. When he cuts his finger, the girl sucks the blood from the wound as if that can cement their relationship, tied by blood.

The guy does his best to persuade the girl to go home on several occasions. "It's time for you to get on home." "Go home!" "What the hell do you want from me?" "I'm not good for you, d'you understand." "Go home!"

Eventually she does get the message and drifts out to the door, but only as far as the campfire outside. Somehow, the curious little girl moves his heart. While at first the girl snuggles down outside shivering beside the campfire, later we find her asleep on his bed, (and he on the couch).

Wanting chicken for breakfast, Devon's idea of raiding a chicken coop sounds exciting to the man, so between them they steal, kill and roast a couple of hens. Still thinking of Baba Yaga she asks, "Do you think if we met one hundred years ago we'd still end up friends?"

"We're not friends!" the man asserts. "What do you think your daddy would do if he found out?" asks the man, already aware of the fate that is now likely to befall him. He is trying to get the girl to see the situation from his side of the fence.

"He'd tie you to a steak and burn you," replies the girl, still in fairy tale mode, and dancing the chicken feet on his arm as if they were another of her decapitated dolls.

The trapped man has to find a way of protecting himself, resorting to the tool of paedophiles: "I'll make you a deal," he offers to the wide-eyed girl. "We can be friends if you can keep it a secret." And the hole being dug for him deepens.

"What's wrong with you and me being friends?" How do you explain to a pre-pubescent girl that the dangers of fairy tales can come grotesquely true in real life?

"Well, for one thing, I'm a country bumpkin, right," says he, trying to deflect the issue. He picks the girl up and playfully places her on the truck.

"Polish my golden slippers," says she, her princess fantasy flourishing to life.

He takes her for a ride down to the river. She mulls things over in her mind. Already her dreams are extending beyond childhood fantasy and there is the first flicker of a childhood crush. "Trent and Devon." She tests the sound of it over her tongue. "Devon and Trent." At the riverside they dance on the roof of the car, the radio booming at full blast, to the annoyance of a passing fishing boat, at whom they moon. This was Devon's suggestion. (Little did she realise the distant fishermen were the security guard and her own father!)

Back in the village, when Trent comes to mow the lawn again, Devon races out to see him, and the man gives her a turtle he found in the undergrowth. Mum is outraged. "People don't give you things without asking for something in return," and mum's suspicions are aroused.

The village's community cop goes to visit the man. "I got a report from a woman around here that you gave her daughter a turtle. Is that right? Folks are nervous these days. It'd be best if you kept to yourself when you work around here."

But Trent is now too deeply involved with the girl. On her next visit, he feels it safe to take her on a journey to visit his own parents. They know their son. They are not posh over-protective affluent people, and they see no harm in their trustworthy son bringing a ten-year-old girl with him.

"So what did you want to show me?" Trent asks on the way back home, after the girl has suggested they pull into a secluded field.

"We're best friends, right?" suggests Devon, and she starts unbuttoning her dress to reveal her bare chest.

"Whoa! Not that!" protests the man covering his eyes.

"It's not my tits I want to show you, stupid. It's my scar!" And she reveals the long scar left behind after her recent heart operation. Trent is now forced to show the girl his scars – the result of a bullet wound. And they both run their fingers to appreciate the textures of each other's scars, empathising with their past traumas.

But on their return, Trent runs over a dog. Having to bludgeon it to death to put it out of its misery, Devon gets upset and runs home. Noticing her exhaustion and distress, father asks, "Did someone hurt you, Honey?" And she blurts out the day's experiences. "Did he touch you?" he asks before summoning the local cop/security guard.

"Devon, did Trent touch you in anyway?" the cop repeats.

"Yes, but … He touched my scar. And I touched him, too! Where he was shot. We were friends. Secret friends."

A screeching of tyres, and two cars full of vigilantes lurch up outside the condemned man's yard. The cop tells the man (before thrusting his fist into his belly) "I may not be a real cop, but I can still act like one."

Father asks (before clubbing the man with a fence post), "Did you touch my daughter? She's ten years old, you piece of shit."

The gay man, whose dog was killed, adds further to his discomfort. But Devon knows where dad's gun is hidden in the cubbyhole beneath the dashboard. Soon one of the attackers has bucket loads of blood spouting from a stomach wound. While Devon assists the incapacitated Trent into his car, and with the help of Devon's magical fairy tale, Trent drives away to sanctuary as Baba Yaga's protective forest sprouts behind his departing tracks.

In *Leon*, Mathilda's unwitting friend and saviour comes to an even more gruesome end. This is another case of a disinterested man forced to take pity on a desperate girl, who had nowhere else to turn for help.

Twelve-year-old Mathilda, played in a marvellous performance by Natalie Portman in her first film role, has just witnessed her family being annihilated by a bent cop and his cronies. Mathilda knocks on her neighbour's door, desperately mouthing through the spy-hole to be let into this stranger's apartment. Mathilda had only seen Leon a couple of time before. The insular man had shown some pity on the girl when he previously spotted her on the stairwell, nursing a bruise to the face and hiding a cigarette. "Is life always this hard, or only when you're a kid?" the girl had asked him.

Leon (brilliantly under-played by Jean Reno) does not want to be involved now, though. He too had just witnesses the incredible unwarranted massacre in the corridor outside his flat, and there is no way he is going to open his door to a stranger, albeit a vulnerable little girl. But the tearful face of the desperate girl outside, persistently ringing his bell, forces a slight melting in his hard heart. Like Trent in *Lawn Dogs*, the man is unwittingly but inevitably trapped in that single action of opening the door. As in *My House in Umbria*, a terrible tragedy has entangled the lives of disparate victims so that they are irrevocably thrown together.

"What do you want me to do?" asks the girl with nowhere else to go.

Compassion spilling from the hard man's voice, "You've had a rough day today. Go to sleep and we'll see tomorrow." He throws a blanket over her, and she squeezes his fingers as a gesture of thanks.

At least this man Leon did not have the accusation of paedophilia hurled at him (though the *Time Out Film Guide* does allude to that)[34]. This man definitely did not want the girl in his house, as demonstrated by the gun he holds to her head while she soundly sleeps.

Up until now, Leon had been a loner, ("I work alone!"), an Italian immigrant with no friends, except one – a pot plant he meticulously nurtures, polishing its leaves and placing it to catch the best of the sun's rays. It's his best friend. It never asks awkward questions!

Mathilda discovers the man is a professional contract killer. "Leon, I want you to teach me how to be strong like you, and smart like you." Reluctantly, he agrees to train the girl as a 'cleaner' so she can take revenge for the death of her younger brother. The girl has to fit into his disciplined, but monotonous, routines of physical exercise, drinking endless cups of milk, as well as the basics in handling, cleaning, and the use of firearms. Yet on a lighter side, their friendship is cemented as first he cheers her up with his pig-shaped oven glove, she involves him in a game of dressing up charades, and later they have a water fight.

Yet inevitably, when a twelve-year old adolescent lives with an attractive man, the girlhood crush materialises, and Natalie Portman is not reticent in admitting this. You could see the girl had a crush on the man right from the start, from the way she happily swings on the banister after offering to fetch the man some milk from the shop. And later, he splutters on his milk when she tells him 'Leon' is a cute name.

But this crush is enhanced and not quashed. The girl is lying prostrate on the bed when she dreamily blurts out, "Leon, I think I'm kind of falling in love with you." Ironically, this comes after he has acted like a responsible father by telling her to desist from swearing and smoking.

"How do you know it's love if you have never been in love before?"

She touches her hands to her bared midriff. "I can feel it in my stomach. It's all warm."

Her romantic dreams of the man are further compounded when she tells a hotel manager, where they are staying while pretending to be father and daughter, "He's not really my father. He's my lover!"

But Leon is honourable. Never once does he usurp his trustworthiness as Mathilda's guardian. He maintains his propriety right through to the last desperate battle when he is involved in a desperate shootout trying to save the girl's life. Even his final words to the girl as he releases her down the escape shaft, tell of a paternal concern. "I love you, Mathilda," he tells the girl as any honourable father would. The incredible emotions on Natalie Portman's face show a brilliant blend of terror and heart-felt longing and love for the man about to give his life for a friend.

So many of these attributes in *Leon* are echoed in the kidnapping movie *Man on Fire*, featuring Denzel Washington and Dakota Fanning. Yet in this case, Dakota playing Pita Martin is younger and less precocious than Natalie Portman.

Pita lives happily with her mum and dad in their exclusive villa but because this is Mexico City, one of the kidnapping capitals of the world, she needs a bodyguard to take her daily to school, and to swimming and piano lessons.[34a]

The bodyguard, John Creasy (Denzel Washington) wishes to keep aloof from the little girl despite having to live in a room in the same house. But soon he is helping her with homework and improving her swimming technique and a bond between them is cemented. So that ultimately, like Leon, this man is willing to lay down his own life to protect someone else's daughter.

Once Pita is kidnapped, Creasy searches through the little girl's diary for any clue that might help lead him to the abductors. But in it, he reads entries about himself:

"Creasy is like a big sad bear."

"I hope you love me, Creasy, my number one bear."

But this is puppy love. Pita has not reached the sexual maturity of her New York counterpart in Mathilda. For Pita, hers is a love reserved for an uncle, for a teddy bear, for a pet, and any romantic undertones should be dismissed.

I acknowledge the director (Tony Scott) viewed things differently, as Karen Lury tells us. For Scott was "intrigued by the possibility of casting this 'big black man' as a compliment to this 'tiny little porcelain white nine-year-old' and believed it would make a 'fantastic, really odd love story'.[35]
[35a]

In both *Hidden Places* and *Run the Wild Fields*, a woman and her eleven-year-old child have been left on their own, the husband either having died or else gone off to war. Then along comes a drifter who helps with chores around the farmstead and gradually becomes part of the family. In *Hidden Places*, Carly Westerman grows fond of the vagrant who ends up being a replacement dad.

Tom Walker is another such drifter in *Run the Wild Fields*. Opal, played by Alexa Vega, at first is wary of the man, assuming him to be an army deserter. But he rapidly gains her affection and together they do the farm chores of ploughing, sewing seeds, driving the tractor, fishing, and he teaches her to dance.

Father is away at war, 'missing in action'. Opal no longer wants father to return, so happy is she with her new friend. As she says in her narration: "I was eleven-years-old and it was the first time I'd ever felt the weight of a full-blown crush."

In time, however, father does return from the war, and Tom knows it is time to move on. He says his adieus, but leaves his most treasured possession on her bedside table – a ring belonging to his deceased brother.

THE CHILD'S BEST FRIEND: ANIMALS AND CHILDREN

For those in movie and theatrical work, WC Field's phrase 'never work with children or animals' suggests a host of problems and bad experiences waiting to haunt directors, producers, and adult actors alike. Andrew Adamson, directing *The Lion, the Witch and the Wardrobe*, tells us "One of the things I was most terrified of was working with kids, yet at the end of the process I have to say it was the most rewarding thing." So any director who dares to include both children and animals in their film should either be recommended for an Oscar or be registered at an asylum.

Maybe for some, the indiscipline of the child has to be tamed before attempting to control an unpredictable or unmanageable animal. Yet, when both work in partnership, the director is able to exploit this cute coupling on two fronts, and is on to a winner. Both animals and children are responsive entities: Kenneth Branagh tells us in *How to Kill your Neighbour's Dog*, "Kids and dogs are the truest judges of decency and goodness."

Now that we live in an age of animatronics and computerisation, even the animal can actually be omitted, though this becomes an expensive option for the director. *Amazing Panda Adventure* successfully substituted an actor in panda costume for much of the screening, the piglets in *Nanny McPhee* were computer enhanced, as were the horses and the zebra in *Racing Stripes*, and animated glass fibre models are effectively used in films with whales, such as *Free Willy* and *Whale Rider*. In *Alaska* (1996), I was unaware the polar bear cub was an animatronic model until I scrutinised the film more closely second time around. Modern technology even solved the problem of procuring that rare species in *Jurassic Park* – the dinosaur! Although they used a real baby kangaroo in *Joey* (1997) , for some of the scenes a toy kangaroo was substituted - but this does not distract from the movie, and in many of the above films the substitutions go unnoticed.

Director Andrew Adamson uses a varied mix of real creatures (especially wolves), animatronics and digitally constructed models in *The Lion, the Witch and the Wardrobe*, so that incredibly, as well as Aslan the lion being unreal, the reindeer pulling the witch's sleigh are also animatronic. Technology today has made these to be extraordinarily realistic. When Georgie Henley's father first watched the film of his daughter playing Lucy he was alarmed that he had not been told his daughter would be acting alongside leopards and lions. He had to be reassured, after the film, that they were created artificially. Fortunately, modern design engineering has not yet found a way to replace the real-life child, though the prevalence of Japanese Manga is working towards that goal. The works of Japanese animator Hayao Miyazaki, with films such as *Spirited Away*, *Princess Mononoke* and *My Neighbour Totoro*, are trashing real-life hoydens and brats in favour of and pixels and sprites.

The child's best friend in films can encompass just about anything: from dogs (in *Because of Winn-Dixie*, *Fallen Angel*, *Lassie* (2005)), cats and kittens (*Whistle down the Wind*, *An Unfinished Life*), ponies and horses (*Dreamer*, *Little Unicorn*, *Horse Whisperer*), a pig (*Charlotte's Web*, *Uptown Girls*), a guinea pig (*Cría Cuervos*), a hamster (*The Little Girl who lives down the Lane*), a rabbit (*Celia* (1988)), and an iguana (*Nim's Island*). In other films, a whole menagerie of domesticated and wild animals has been conjured up for children to act alongside. There are geese in *Fly Away Home*, a fox in *The Fox and the Child*, a kangaroo (*Joey* (1997)), monkeys (*Monkey Business* (1998)), sheep (*The Dark* (2005)), grizzly bears (*An Unfinished Life*), and even wolves (*The Wolves of Willoughby Chase*, and that

237

turn into werewolves in *Company of Wolves*). Some films, like *So Dear to my Heart* and *Doctor Dolittle*, seem to have enough fauna to fill an ark. In *Andre*, "Any animal that had lost its way or just needed a friend was always welcome in our home," so sharing the living room with eight-year-old Tina Majorino were dogs, chickens, ducks, a rabbit, a frog, and eventually Andre the seal. Dakota Fanning in *Hounddog* has several scenes covered in snakes. WC Fields was nowhere to be seen.

Some animal-centred films endure as classics in cinematic history. This is how Elizabeth Taylor came to prominence, as an eleven-year-old in *Lassie Come Home*, and as a fourteen-year-old in *The Courage of Lassie*. Even more famously, she was the twelve-year-old upstart entering her gelding, Pie, in the Grand National in *National Velvet*. (A less successful sequel to this was made starring Tatum O'Neal: *International Velvet*).

Usually the animal is seen in a positive light in the eyes of the child, while it is the adults who are the cruel ones: Cruella de Vil who makes coats from Dalmatians, the farmer's wife who kills off the runts in a litter of pigs, or who drown the kittens in a pond, or the witch who makes a scarf from Aslan's mane, the money-grabbing racehorse owner who shoots the lame mare, the authorities who cull rabbits, the hunters who take game as trophies.[36] "Feed the birds, and what have you got?" poses Mr Daws, "Fat birds!" as the bank manager grabs the tuppence from Michael's hand in *Mary Poppins*, the tuppence that he and his sister, Jane, had wanted to use to feed pigeons on the steps of St Paul's Cathedral.

And so to gender. For the girl, the pet (even untamed fauna) is a friendly cuddly companion, something animate to add to the ranks of dolls and soft toys; an object to be cared for, domesticated, nursed on that greater road of maternal aspiration. *The Fox and the Child* is a great example of this, the little girl, Bertille Noël-Bruneau, following her inbred instincts to domesticate a feral fox.

For the boy, the pet is a confederate on the path of life's adventures, a tool, a weapon. For the boy, the animal world is black or white; the pet has a function – if not as a best friend then as bodyguard, or a status symbol. Other animate life is there for his destruction at a whim, the squashing of spiders, pulling off flies' wings, or used as target practice as in *The Courage of Lassie*. *Kes* (1969) epitomises all that is masculine in this interaction between boy and his primeval instincts. Even Joey (Brandon de Wilde), wanting to shoot the deer that had raided the newly planted kitchen garden in his homestead in *Shane*, is frustrated: "I wish they had given me some bullets for this gun." Sabu, too, playing Mowgli in *The Jungle Book* who treated all his jungle companions as fellow brothers was keen to procure the dagger to finish off his only enemy: the tiger.

Like snails, snakes and spiders, the keeping of a bird of prey is very much a male gender obsession. Ok there are exceptions; a recent TV documentary showed a preteen girl who kept and wrestled alligators as pets, while *Britain's Got Talent 2011* featured an under ten-year-old girl dancing with a live snake wrapped around her neck (Olivier Bonfield and her pet snake Lucy).

But for David Bradley, playing Billy Casper in *Kes* (1969), adopting a kestrel was part of his rough-and-tumble world. It had had precursors: a fox cub, magpies, jackdaws, even a young jay. But a kestrel fulfilled a most manly aspiration for a young teen brought up in the semi urban pit community on the Barnsley coal seam.

Only an Annie Oakley style tomboy could match Billy's dedication, as he takes pot shots at sparrows with his air rifle to provide fresh meat for his growing kestrel. He takes the bird on test flights near the edge of spoil heaps so the kestrel can fly with its tresses into his gloved hand.

Here is one child actor, so at home in his element, swinging the lure as if that has been part of his whole life.

His schoolteacher, Mr Farthing (Colin Welland), is certainly impressed. The school sees Billy as a truanting daydreamer without ambition, but as Mr Farthing witnesses the skill with which the boy handles the beast, he is intrigued. The teacher has already observed in the classroom the exhilaration with which the boy fondly talks about his bird, in the words of Sinyard "the working class schoolboy's equivalent of Henry V's speech at Agincourt."[37]

But nothing lasts. Billy is just a kid with a bullying older brother, Jud. When Billy fails to place a bet, pocketing the money instead, while Jud is down the colliery, the kestrel becomes the obvious target for a revengeful duped older sibling.

The gender difference in attitude to animate life is made only too apparent in the Austrian movie, *Benny's Video*. The fourteen-year-old (Arno Frisch) is intrigued by the slaughter of a pig that he witnessed while visiting a farm. He videotaped the action, and now re-plays it at home, fascinated. He brings a girlfriend home to watch the video, too. The girl (Ingrid Stassner) does not know how to react. She tries to avoid watching, instead side-tracking the conversation by saying, "It's starting to snow." Her failure to be impressed annoys the boy who rewinds the video to make her watch again. "It was only a pig," justifies the boy. This is a prelude to a fatal piece of role-play leading to the girl's death. If ever the reader is tempted to watch this sequence, be aware this is brutally uncomfortable viewing.

In real life, there are girls with cruel instincts, and boys who dote on their cuddly pets, yet films perpetuate the stereotypical differences in gender: that girls nurture, and boys destroy.

Animal Welfare over Child Welfare

For the past half century, and particularly since 1980 when the American Humane Unit were granted jurisdiction, the care and welfare of the animal has been paramount, and the credit listings of most movies are suffixed with the caption: "No animal was harmed in the making of this film." (*Free Willy* could be considered an exception. Concern was raised over the conditions in which this cetacean was kept, leading to an artificial model being used in subsequent sequels. The real-life hunting sequences in *Walkabout* in which we witness the dying throes of the victims of David Gulpilil's aboriginal spear, boomerang and club were filmed before the 1980 cruelty watershed.) So, as Mr McBain says to Kathie Merrick (Elizabeth Taylor) in *The Courage of Lassie*, "All he wants is to love you and have you tell him what you want him to do," we can rest assured that at least our fauna are well protected.

This serious consideration given to animal rights in acting circles can be taken to the extreme. Director John Polson highlights how excessive this has become when even angling for fish in the lake in *Hide and Seek* (2005) had to follow a humane procedure. Robert de Niro was not permitted to catch live fish. Nor could he or Dakota Fanning put the fishhook through a real beetle, despite the fact, as the director pointed out, that many beetles were probably trampled underfoot accidentally on the way to the location. A plastic toy beetle had to substitute.

In fact, so much care has been taken to show that an animal is not harmed, in order to placate animal welfare charities (and caring audiences), that the rights of the child actor may have been compromised. Kincaid, in *Erotic Innocence*, refers to a lecture about child exploitation given by Jon Provost, the boy (now an adult) who played Timmy in an early Lassie movie. He is reflecting on his childhood acting experience. The director and crew had to film Timmy and Lassie on a raft floating down the river. Without any rehearsal, as the raft approached a weir, both boy and dog were expected to jump in the water. There was a host of animal welfare agents monitoring the action and many hands were available to rescue the dog to avoid it being swept away by the river. As for the boy, Timmy, he just had to swim for it! They had not practised the scene. As the boy crashed his head on a submerged rock and was floundering in the water, the director assumed he was demonstrating brilliant method acting.[38]

To add to his protest about the way children are mistreated compared with animals: there was a stated rule that "no one on the set shall be allowed to play with, fondle, or pet the animal." Jon Provost suggests we should apply that statement to children. No doubt, the bulk of child actors have been the compliant recipient of unwanted petting, fondling and hugging all in the guise of cast and crew endearing themselves with the child.

To further highlight this difference between the human and animal cast, Andrew Collins, writing in *Radio Times*,[39] writes how ten-year-old Elizabeth Taylor was signed to star in *Lassie Come Home* for the incredible fee of $100 a week for three months of filming. In 1942, this was a heck of a lot of money for one proud little girl. However, this was peanuts (or should I say dog's dinner) compared to the animal's salary. Lassie's owner scooped up $250 a week!

And if the animal doesn't cooperate? In *Monkey Business* (1998), Marla (played by Kathren Laurents) has been kidnapped and tied up by a gang. The monkeys in the film come to her rescue. You can see them considering about untying the knots in the rope, but they do not cooperate. By means of camera trickery, the restraints magically untie themselves.

The Pet as Provider of Unconditional Love

"What possible use is a dog?" asks Aunt Polly to her niece as *Pollyanna* hugs a stray in the sitting room of their large country house hoping to be able to keep it. "Well, it makes you glad to be alive," says ten-year-old Georgina Terry in the 2002 made-for-TV version. For Daveigh Chase in *Beethoven's 5th* a dog's use is to discover buried treasure, for *Natty Gann* the dog provides protection, while *Courage of Lassie* shows how a dog can be of use to frontline troops. But for most kids the dog is just the child's best friend – the provider of unconditional love. The pet is promoted to the most important entity in a child's life, even though he/she may have loving parents, supportive siblings and a wide circle of friends. But where the child is neglected or friendless, the pet then transcends all other interactions, providing eternal companionship and undying loyalty.

"Please God, if it's not too much trouble, I'd like some friends," is the secret prayer of Opal (AnnaSophia Robb in *Because of Winn-Dixie*), a lonely newcomer to a small Louisiana town. Then along bobs a bounding French collie-shepherd dog, Winn-Dixie, as an unexpected answer to her prayer.

When a chirpy robin comes hopping around the sour, friendless Mary Lennox in *The Secret Garden* the gardener says to her, "I can't think why, but he's decided to make friends with thee."

"He has!" replies Mary (played by the splendid Kate Maberly), "I've never had any friends."

"That is the miracle of friendship," narrates Julia Roberts in *Charlotte's Web*, as the little girl Fern cares enough to adopt the runt of a litter of piglets. "All because someone stopped to see the grace and beauty and nobility of the humblest creature." So Wilbur the piglet was spared the butcher's chop and changed the fortunes of the farmer's lot.

In *Nim's Island*, an iguana spends the bulk of the film on Abigail Breslin's shoulder. Although sometimes this was a computerised mock-up, for lengthy sequences a genuine iguana could be coaxed to accompany the young girl.

But an iguana is not very companionable, and a robin even less so, and certainly not huggable, which is really what a young girl tends to crave – like a living teddy. The enormous furry rabbit became Rebecca Smart's constant companion in *Celia* (1988). Like a doll, she would take it everywhere, even as an escort on dad's fishing trips. But of course, known as man's best friend for a reason, it is the dog that makes the best huggable, lovable, dependable companion for any little girl or boy. As Elizabeth Taylor is told in *The Courage of Lassie*, "You're like a god to that dog."

Invariably, the dog adopted by the child is a stray, enhancing the child's feeling of charity, not realising it is depleting the household income and disrupting domestic life.

In *Tightrope*, two girls returning from an outing with their father (Clint Eastwood) find a stray dog rummaging in the bins. "Can we keep it, dad?" As we are led inside the home by his real-life daughter, twelve-year-old Alison Eastwood, and seven-year-old Jenny Beck, we see the soft-hearted father has yielded on other occasions too, as four dog bowls have to be filled. Caring for a dog can lead to a host of problems as Ellie Raab discovers in *Eyes of an Angel*, after nursing an injured Doberman, only to discover it belongs to a mob of gangsters.

When Winn-Dixie bounded into Opal's life (*Because of Winn-Dixie*), she saw it as her answer to the prayer she had made in the church where her father had recently become the preacher. Like Eileen Quinn's mongrel in *Annie* (1982), the dog is a stray, rampaging along the aisles of the supermarket store, knocking over displays, and creating havoc. The store-manager called for the dog pound to come and destroy the hound, so Opal out of pity tells them, "Don't call the pound. It's my dog." Then the realisation struck her: "I knew I'd done something big – and something stupid too." Contritely, she leads the flea-ridden rangy cur from out the superstore and takes it proudly home. "Daddy. I found a dog, and I want to keep him."

Dad is adamantly opposed, as is the landlord who has a no-pets rule. But bit-by-bit ten-year-old Opal wraps them around her finger until the response changes to, "He can stay temporarily while you try to find a home for him." So, translate this as 'he's permanent then', and Opal names the animal *Winn-Dixie* after the shop she found it in.

Inevitably, the dog virtually destroys the home, and leaves its excrement where the landlord can tread in it, and the dog pound has to be called out. As the officers from the dog pound are preparing to take Winn-Dixie away Opal pleads, "Please, daddy, he's the only friend I have."

The lovable dog is given a second chance, endearing himself to members of the community: the librarian, the pet shop owner, and a reclusive blind woman. Even the church congregation warm to him when the dog accompanies the hymn *Amazing Grace* with its howling. "He doesn't know the words, but he sure is moved by the spirit," notices Opal.

For Opal, "Winn-Dixie was better at making friends than anyone I'd ever known. I talked to him about everything – and he was a real good listener."

Incidentally, for the filming, two identical dogs were used, one with a loving temperament for the placid scenes, and a different dog for the more boisterous action, a method widely used in the

Lassie films, too, though you would never have guessed (*Lassie* (2005)). (In *Marley & Me*, twenty-two different Labradors were used to portray the different stages in the lovable mutt's life.)

"Almost every kid in the world needs a dog, and whatever happens, they will always love you," comments AnnaSophia Robb in the interview at the end of the film. They give "unconditional love."

Sandy, too, was a rescue dog. Rescued from a gang of boys who had tied tin cans to the tail of the stray, in *Annie* (1982), the girl proceeds to adopt it and smuggle it into the orphanage.

The theme that the dog can't stay is extended in Enid Blyton's tales of *The Famous Five – Five on a Treasure Island*. Georgina (Jemima Roper) has a dog named Tim from whom she cannot be separated. Alas, the dog constantly yaps, much to the annoyance of Georgina's obstreperous father whose work is being interrupted. Father insists the dog cannot stay any longer, so Georgina has to find a friend who is willing to look after the pet during the daytime. However, Tim is an integral member of the *Famous Five* gang. It is the dog that helps find the hidden treasure in the castle's vaults thus solving father's financial worries. The dog is allowed to stay.

The pet as a lesson in life and death

There tends to be a common theme linking films which feature animals: the secret rescuing of a doomed pet. The dog can't stay (*Because of Winn-Dixie*), or has to be sold (*Lassie* (2005)), or the horse has to be put down as in *Dreamer*, *The Horse Whisperer*, *The Little Unicorn*, or the kittens have to be drowned (*Whistle down the Wind*), or the runt to be slaughtered (*Charlotte's Web*, or rescued from the butcher's knife in *My Brother the Pig*). Then the child comes along to secrete the doomed animal away, or to persuade the owner to reprieve the condemned pet.

At least children are not usually called upon to witness harm being done to any animals – the disclaimer at the end of films ensures that the welfare of the animal is uppermost. Though I am not sure the rules were maintained in *Babel* when Elle Fanning and Nathan Gamble, both under ten, have to witness the beheading of a chicken at the Mexican wedding feast, and Dakota Fanning has her pet dog shot in *Hounddog* after it molests the turkeys. In *Alaska* (1996), when Thora Birch and Vincent Kartheiser witness the hunter (Charlton Heston) brutally shooting the polar bear cub we are horrified, only to discover shortly afterwards it was just a tranquilliser dart (and anyway, the cub was just an animatronic machine!)

Audiences can expect a message to be purveyed in films with pets: you can't hold on to something that wants to go, as in *Because of Winn-Dixie* and *The Journey of Natty Gann*. As we will reveal later in this book Tina Majorino is deterred from becoming too attached to a seal in *Andre*: "Sometimes you just have to let nature take its course." Having a pet is a way of getting a child to show love and care for something – until it dies, or disappears. Then its death provides a useful lesson, as a psychoanalyst may say, paving the way to help the child come to terms with the eventual death of a loved one. The only problem with this theory is that more often than not the child actually loves the pet as much as the parents, as we shall see in *My Life as a Dog*.

In *My Dog Skip*, the pet had grown to be more influential in a child's life than anything else. As the autobiographical memoirs of Willie Morris, growing up in 1940s Mississippi, this dog was so pivotal to the happiness and security of the child that it is Skip – not mum or dad or the heroic neighbour, nor the childhood sweetheart – that melds his memories and gives the boy a lifelong friend and a title to his book and film: "*My dog Skip, my best and most steadfast friend.*"

Deep felt emotions are shed as the dog is put down in *Marley and Me*. The whole family grieves as the pet is buried in the garden. To the three children, Marley had always been there, derived as a bonding gift soon after the parents were married. Owen Wilson reflects over the graveside about how irreplaceable a dog is: "How many people can make you feel rare or special? How many people can make you feel extraordinary?"

On the most basic level, director Shawn Levy illustrates this devotion using a frog. Mark Baker buries his pet frog Beans, in *Cheaper by the Dozen 1*. This bullied little boy eulogises to his dead pet, "For a long time, you were the only person I could talk to." When Mrs Freeling discovers the dead canary in the cage in *Poltergeist* (1982) she tries to hide it from her daughter. But five-year-old Carol Anne walks into the bathroom just as her mother is about to flush the bird down the toilet. No, the pet must be buried, insists the girl (Heather O'Rourke), in a box along with avian mementos and those items a dead canary will treasure in its afterlife. But as soon as the carcass is consigned to its garden grave the girl asks cheerfully, "Now can I have a goldfish?" Anna Franziska Jager buries her pet hedgehog, in *My Queen Karo*. The pet had died because the girl had placed it to hibernate in the freezer, to be woken up when their domestic situation is less disruptive.

Young viewers are tenderly eased into the concept of death in *Honey, I Shrunk the Kids* by means of the ant that sacrifices its own life to save the four child explorers. Even though they have only known the ant for a matter of hours, and the creature is actually just animatronic, it helps to enhance young viewers understanding of the sadness brought about by the death of a loved one.

Karen Lury suggests that viewers found watching the death of horses in *Gone with the Wind* was more harrowing that all the loss of human life in the ensuing civil war.[40] The point Lury is making here is that animals as well as children are 'perfect victims', that "their suffering was not their fault." Certainly, Hailee Steinfeld cries out in despair as she sees her faithful steed shot in *True Grit* (2010).

For Opal in *Because of Winn-Dixie*, this lesson about the loss of a loved one is learned when the frightened dog, with a phobia to thunderstorms, runs off in the drenching rain. Despite her search, Opal cannot find the dog, presuming he has run off for good. She is being consoled with a harsh but necessary lesson about life's sorrows: "You can't hold on to something that wants to go," she is told. "You have just got to love it while you've got it."

This is a family film with kids watching, so parents can be assured the dog returns at the end of the film soaking, bedraggled, but alive. This is not the happy ending for Molly and Alice, Judge Miller's daughters, in Jack London's harsh novel *The Call of the Wild*. Buck, strong-muscled and warm-coated, was stolen away to the brutal life of the Yukon, forever.

Neither is the outcome for Ingemar (Anton Glanzelius) reassuring in *My Life as a Dog*. Ingemar's pet dog is called Sickan. "I think I love Sickan as much as I love mum," the boy mopes. Having just had an operation, his mum can no longer look after the boy. Ingemar is sent to his uncle's to live, while Sickan is put into temporary kennels until the dog can be accommodated again. The boy keeps pestering his uncle to send for the dog and allow it to come and stay. The uncle keeps procrastinating, and pretending to forget to ask the sick mother about the dog. The boy is patient and hopeful, yet unaware of the real situation. One day his girlfriend in an angry outburst reveals the truth to him. "You don't get it, do you? Your dog is dead!"

Rebecca Smart also justifiably fears this outcome in *Celia* (1988). Celia Carmichael lives in a rural community in Victoria, Australia. She doted on her granny, but granny has just died. Now it's her ninth birthday. Dad knows she has been longing for the pet rabbit she has seen in the pet shop window. What's more, Celia has even told her classmate and rival, Stephanie, she is getting a rabbit for her birthday. So when on her birthday dad shows Celia her new bike, both Celia and dad are disappointed that it's not the present she wanted. What is worse, Stephanie comes round to taunt her.

The trouble is, this is Victoria in 1957. Rabbits are swarming across Australia causing devastation to crops and are breeding like – well, like rabbits. Father repeats to her what the newsreel says at the cinema: "Rabbits are vermin, like snakes and rats." The newsreel goes on to show how myxomatosis is helping to eradicate the pests – by making them blind and maimed (the children in the audience are meant to be impressed).

However, in time, Celia persuades dad to buy the rabbit, which they name Mergatroyd, and then becomes the girl's constant companion, carried in her arms wherever she goes, playing down by the quarries, or taking it fishing with dad.

As the wild rabbits march across Victoria, the government imposes a ban on the keeping of pet rabbits. When the policeman arrives to impound Mergatroyd, the parents refuse to allow him to take it. To save his own face with his superiors, the officer resorts to stealing the pet late at night to impound it at the zoo, along with all the other pet rabbits around the community. Celia witnesses him stealing the pet, so the police officer becomes a monster figure in the girl's nightmares. There is a marvellous scene in which Celia takes revenge on the bobby by throwing a lettuce smack in his face (either a lucky first shot, or the result of several rehearsals).

Celia's classroom at school has a picture of the Australian president displayed on the wall announcing the impounding of all pet rabbits. Celia defaces the picture by turning it into a devil's face. When Celia owns up in front of her teacher, the girl audaciously states, "If the president doesn't know the difference between pet rabbits and wild rabbits he should get the sack!"

A day comes when the law is repealed. Hundreds of children turn up to the zoo to reclaim their pet rabbits, but in the caged warren, Celia finds her pet drowned in the drinking pool. Any child would take resentment at such a despicable callous act of neglect. Rebecca Smart was surely no different from any other girl who came up against the state-imposed justice. The dead rabbit she clutched despairingly was obviously a sheep fleece, but the message is clear enough. This was not an unforgiving little girl who plotted revenge just for the sake of it. The seed of angry despair had been sown.

The lettuce struck in the face of the police officer was not the only piece of revenge provoked. You can blame it on the nightmares or the recent death of her grandma, yet the monster of her dreams took the form of the police officer while she was playing with her father's shotgun. It was a tragic accident, taking revenge on both the policeman, and his daughter Stephanie who had become the enemy after receiving the taunts about the dead rabbit.

There was a better outcome for Kathie (fourteen-year-old Elizabeth Taylor) after the loss of her pet puppy in *The Courage of Lassie*. She had found one of Lassie's puppies wandering in the backwoods, named it Bill, and adopted it.

Her first encounter with the puppy is when she is sitting on the lakeside pier, in her undergarments, when along comes this stray cur and runs off with her trousers! The dog runs into some scrub where a couple of hunters mistake his movements for a jackrabbit. The dog is badly wounded, and Kathie nurses it back to health. The dog proves its worth by helping to rescue some stranded sheep and their lambs when a snowstorm sets in. But the day comes when Bill the dog disappears and the girl searches everywhere for it. But she never finds it. Unbeknown to her, the dog had been run over by a passing truck. The truck driver took the dog to a vet in town and from there it was requisitioned by the army to fight in Europe where the Second World War was raging.

It is sad watching Kathie wake up one morning expecting to see the dog outside the window, but it was just a vivid dream. As time goes by, she forgets about the dog and never expects to see it again.

Years pass. The dog is now a war hero and is returning across America by train. It is deeply shell-shocked, but sufficiently aware to jump from the train just a few miles from home.

The dog has to eat, so it raids the local farms, infuriating the farmers who gang up to shoot the marauding beast. But Bill manages to locate home, running into the arms of an overjoyed and disbelieving Kathie, closely pursued by the gun-toting farmers out for revenge. So just when Kathie believes she has her long-lost friend back again, the sheriff comes along to impound the animal, until a court can decide its fate.

But when the court discovers Bill is a war hero, its death sentence is annulled, and it gets to go home with a delighted young girl again. "He's come through a bad time, but he's found a big love and a big understanding from a little girl."

The original Lassie story was *Lassie Come Home* filmed in 1943 in which the young Elizabeth Taylor first hit the limelight, and she was to become the larger than life darling of British cinema for the next seventy years. The Lassie story spawned a sequence of sequels, the most recent being in 2005 which is a rerun of the original *Lassie*. Lassie is the typical loveable collie dog owned by a little boy, Joe Carraclough, and his parents.[41] They live a tough life in a Yorkshire pit community in 1939. There is talk of the pit having to close and the men to go off to fight in Europe.

Living in the same community is a laird, the Duke, played by an aging Peter O'Toole (and by Nigel Bruce in the original 1943 version). His granddaughter, Cilla, played by Hester Odgers who easily steps into Elizabeth Taylor's shoes, has moved up north from London to Yorkshire as an evacuee – "Daddy says London isn't safe anymore" – and is trying to adjust to her new strange surroundings.

Cilla and her grandfather are following a foxhunt. Cilla, being unused to such sport, says, "It doesn't seem fair, all those hounds on one fox … I don't understand. If they don't want to eat it, why do they want to catch it?" The fox evades capture by running through the colliery. The Duke spots Lassie and realising it to be a fine specimen, orders his henchman to go buy it from its owner.

With the colliery just closed, Mr Carraclough feels he has no option but to sell the dog, now they are hitting hard times. "There's barely enough to feed the three of us," little Joe is told. "It would be cruel to keep her."

But Lassie, who is caged at the duke's house, keeps escaping, much to the delight of Cilla, who couldn't understand why the dog had to be caged up in the first place. Cilla realises the dog isn't happy here. "You just want to go home, don't you? So, that makes two of us. So do I!" When Lassie runs home to its previous owner, Joe is overjoyed too.

But now the Duke and his granddaughter are travelling up to Caithness and having retrieved the dog are taking Lassie with them. Cilla is to go to boarding school in the far north of Scotland.

Now in Scotland, it is not long before Lassie escapes again, and sets off on the long difficult journey across the mountains of Scotland, back into England, and the bulk of the film is the tale of that difficult journey. As if to make comparisons with the trapped unhappy dog, Cilla also runs away from her boarding school. It is amusing to watch her hitchhike dressed in her pyjamas, only for the first passing car to be that of the headmistress, both equally startled to meet each other.

Cilla's role in this film is not to bond with the dog. That is the role of Joe Carraclough. Rather, Cilla's role is one of empathy with a creature that has been used to freedom all its life, but is now required to be trapped and caged only to be brought out when the occasion suits. She possesses a great selfless respect for animals that does not involve possessing them. This is true both of her reaction to Lassie's being caged up, and to the foxhunt she witnessed. I imagine if this girl owned a horse she would want it roaming free over the moors instead of trapped bored and shivering in the corner of a walled-in field.

Lassie eventually arrives back in Yorkshire on Christmas Eve tired and weary, almost dead, as it trudges up to the Carraclough home. But the owners are out at church, so the dog just collapses in the middle of the street as the snow gradually blankets over her.

The Call of the Wild

For Cilla in *Lassie* (2005), the thought of an animal caged or trapped provoked an empathic response. There are many films in which a young child is thrown into an adventure to encounter wild animals. There, in the wilds, the child either appreciates the majesty of the beast in its natural surroundings, or attempts to tame it as a playmate. In the interests of ecology and conservation the director feels constrained to show nature running its course, though this may result in harsh lessons for the doting child, as Meredith Salenger found in *The Journey of Natty Gann* as her dog companion runs off towards the howls of wolves in the forest. A film which shows this all too clearly is *The Fox and the Child*.

The ambiguous message in *The Fox and the Child* is that a wild animal, no matter how cute and cuddly, should not be tamed, but should be appreciated from a distance. The message is ambiguous because the little girl who spent weeks patiently watching a fox scurrying around the incredibly beautiful forested landscapes of the Jura Mountains in eastern France, eventually felt she had earned the right to stroke and pet the wild animal. Isn't it human nature to want to tempt a squirrel or the garden robin to feed from our palms? The girl was only aping what countless nature-lovers have done through generations. She had innocently stalked the creature – not like the local pest controllers who had used traps, guns and poisoned bait – but the girl had left trails of food from her sandwich packs so that, in time, the fox had learnt to trust her and realised she was not a threat.

But the girl did not learn the first time, for when she had discovered the fox's den the alarmed vixen had to find a new hideout to take its cubs one-by-one to safety. The film concludes with a startlingly abrupt finality. Girl and fox had played trustingly together for so long that the fox had followed the girl into her home, up the stairs and into the bedroom. When the girl closed the bedroom door the vixen, feeling trapped, went berserk. Finding no way of escape, the animal bolted through the bedroom window, and collapsed in a heap, dead, on the concrete yard below.

Bertille Noël-Bruneau plays the ten-year-old. She and the fox share the entire film, yet the girl hardly has any words to say: the dialogue being narrated by the rising young star, Kate Winslett. Yet the child has a delightful air about her as she chases through the flower-strewn meadows, splashes in frog-filled puddles, clambers over rocks and waterfalls, climbs trees and explores caverns like the best of tomboys. She has a disarming smile and a delightful laugh, exuding joy as she plays with the fox cubs, and bounds over the hills with the fox.

The film shows the tragedy that can arise as a child confuses love with possession. Once the fox has trusted her and tolerates being stroked, the girl ties a scarf around its neck to lead it on a leash. She makes a pretend house and lights a bonfire, naïvely hoping the fox will play a game with her, but she is unaware of the innate fear that all wild animals have of fire. As it breaks free, the possessive child calls out, "Come back right now or I won't be your friend!"

Trying to tame a monkey had a similar fateful consequence in *A High Wind in Jamaica*. The sailors, on board the frigate taking Emily Thornton and her siblings home from Jamaica to England, capture a monkey. They are about to chop off its tail. "Its tail has gangrene," one of the sailors tells the children. They make it drink whisky to numb its senses, but the animal evades their grasp and escapes up the rigging only to lose its balance in its drunken state, and fall down dead on the deck. This, and the cockfighting, are two aspects of animal cruelty the children have to witness.

As an older girl, the young teenager, Meredith Salenger, was more attuned to the natural desire of freedom for a semi-wild creature. Although this is not based in the harsh terrain of the Yukon that Jack London wrote about in his classic novels *The Call of the Wild* and *White Fang*, the backwoods beyond Seattle make an adequate alternative for the basal yearnings of her dog in *The Journey of Natty Gann*. Her dog is part-wolf and the girl has the sense to realise this is not a pet but a temporary companion. Their partnership is symbiotic and practical. The feral animal hearing the call of the wild responds to the primeval instincts that are instilled within its genes.

In this film, the fourteen-year-old is making her way west across depression-era America in search of her father. In her desperate search for food, she comes across a group of men staging a dogfight, laying bets, and jeering at the growling curs as they scrap. One of the dogs makes a bid for freedom, snarling at the men to evade recapture. Natty, afraid for her own safety, opens the door to give the beast its freedom. She is immediately hit by one of the men for allowing it to escape.

Later, as she sneaks into a cattle truck to sleep, she finds the same dog. Too afraid, she backs off, leaving it a piece of meat she had stolen, to distract it. She heads off into the woods to sleep rough. The dog, remembering her kindness, tracks her down and deposits a freshly killed rabbit at her feet. She skins and roasts the food, and the dog becomes her good companion and guard dog for the rest of the journey (from Chicago to Seattle).

But when they reach dad's felling camp in the Rocky Mountains, the dog – which is part wolf – hears the howling of other wolves. Natty gives the animal a tearful hug, knowing the call of the wild is beckoning, and after one fleeting look back, the animal is bounding up the slope into the forest.

This implicit understanding between an animal and mankind was vocalised in *Lassie Come Home* in which the travelling peddler gives the dog due praise: "You understand some of man's language, but man is not bright enough to understand thine."

Anna Paquin is aware of the environmental requirements of the cute fluffy orphaned baby geese that she has adopted, and does all in her power to help return them to their natural habitat. Hers is an incredible feat, and the story is based on a true innovative event. A man, William Lishman, living in Ontario, trained a gaggle of orphaned geese to follow his microlight plane on their primary migration down the eastern seaboard of America. The film *Fly Away Home* is based on his autobiography.

Anna Paquin plays thirteen-year-old Amy, who lives with her father in rural Canada. When developers start ploughing through a nature reserve, the nesting geese are scared off. (*Amazing Panda Adventure* had a similar starting point: a baby panda had been abandoned after hunters trapped its mother and so the boy and girl heroes have an adventure in the Chinese mountains reuniting the cub with its parent). Amy investigates; she finds a clutch of warm eggs on a nest. The eggs are almost ready to hatch, and you can hear the chicks chirping inside the shells. The girl smuggles them home, and improvises an incubator in the barn using a lamp inside a drawer. Later that night a frantic father discovers Amy asleep with sixteen fluffy goslings crawling over her. "Can I keep them?" she pleads. "Please?"

Because Amy has imprinted herself on the birds, they see her as their mother, and follow her around. She feeds and nurtures them, sometimes on the kitchen table, sometimes in the shower. As they grow older, she races through the meadow flapping her 'wings', getting the birds to mimic her. This is great to watch. Anna Paquin is obviously having a marvellous time. Her eyes light up with delight as she plays with the little creatures, and the actress seems in heavenly bliss. This imprinting was meant to happen, of course. Evidently, so that the chicks could imprint on the girl's voice, Anna had sent a tape recording of her voice to the director while she was still in New Zealand, which could be played to the eggs for two weeks before hatching. And once hatched, the crew were surprised how quickly the babies grew, so they had to rush to keep up with filming, for after just one week the goslings were no longer small and fluffy.

Yet it is not long before they have an altercation with the local animal welfare officer who insists the birds should have their wings clipped to comply with Canadian law which will deter them from flying off into people's private gardens. The officer is forcibly removed from their land. This inclusion of the brush with the law was based on the real-life experience of William Lishman who encountered similar petty bureaucracies. In fact, the film crew also came up against crazy officialdom that wouldn't allow them to fly the geese across the American border, despite the fact that this is exactly what the birds had been doing for thousands of years.

Amy's father realised the geese should fly south for winter, but they will only migrate if they have been taught how to and where to go. "Your birds don't have anyone to show them the way," she is told. Amy's father is a microlight enthusiast, so they try to teach the birds to fly and follow the plane. Because the birds have imprinted on Amy, it is she as a thirteen-year-old who has to be taught how to fly. Soon, she is leading the birds on practice flights across the Ontario prairies ready for their autumnal migration. Just as in *Celia* (1988) when to save face among his colleagues the policeman confiscated the little girl's rabbit in the dead of night, so too in *Fly Away Home* the welfare officer sneaks in at night-time to steal the goslings, and takes them to his sanctuary ready for pinioning. So, before the migration can begin, the geese have to be stolen back again. Thus begins the eventful but successful journey across Lake Ontario, into America, and along the backbone of the Appalachian Mountains, down into the forested marshlands of Virginia where the geese would over-winter.

Naturalist, William Lishman, found the film raised the awareness of the plight of endangered bird species. Following the success of his initial experiment and the impact made by the film, he was able to raise funding to commence a programme for the reestablishment of rare migratory whooping cranes in Texas and Florida.

This realisation that a caged animal should be roaming free in its natural environment is pursued in *An Unfinished Life*. At first, Becca Gardner's relationship was with a pair of cats. They were her only friends as she moved in with her grandfather who did not welcome her arrival. But her role in this film, once she had endeared herself to her granddad, was to help release a grizzly bear that had been impounded in the local zoo. The grizzly had actually severely mauled the friend who shared Grandfather's ranch, and that was the reason the local sheriff had arranged for its incarceration. But in time, the mauled victim felt sorry for the bear, and suggested it should be secretly released back into the wild. So, it was Becca Gardner's job to help in this clandestine rescue.

This eleven-year-old had to manoeuvre the jeep while her granddad (Robert Redford) manipulates the cage to transport the beast. They prepare some chunks of meat to tempt the bear. "Don't bears like honey? Winnie the Pooh does." So, her improvised bait helps tempt the bear from its zoo cage towards the trailer on the truck. But the girl accidentally budges the gearshift at a critical moment leaving granddad exposed, facing the dangerous grizzly. Inevitably, granddad receives a mauling and Becca has to drive the vehicle to the hospital. But the bear is able to escape and roam freely back to the backwoods where it belongs.

The Child as Rescuer of the Helpless

As eggs go with bacon, so too, a little girl goes with baby rabbits or helpless kittens or little puppies or doomed piglets. Just as AnnaSophia Robb or Alison Eastwood or Elizabeth Taylor couldn't bear to see a vagrant dog harmed, so too when a child comes across a litter of kittens destined for the well, its resolve is fixed: to oppose the harsh cruelty. This tends to be the preserve of the girl, as nurse, rather than the boy, and perhaps films that feature girls as animal rescuers are perpetuating the stereotype of the female's role as that of carer.

Heidi, on hearing a litter of kittens was to be put down, volunteers to adopt the lot, knowing full well the consequence if Madame Rottenmeier found out. Kathy Bostock smuggles into the barn a sack full of kittens thrown into the quarry pond in *Whistle down the Wind*, and Fern pleads for the runt of a litter of pigs to be spared the Christmas chop in *Charlotte's Web*. It is rare that film directors entrust this role to boys. Yet boys do play a role: Bobby Driscoll tends the rejected black lamb in *So Dear to my Heart*, and ecologically-minded Billy McGregor treks across half of Australia to prevent *Joey* being separated from its kangaroo mum.

Emma Bolger as *Heidi* could not bear to see a litter of kittens put down so she volunteers to take the entire family by smuggling them into the house in Frankfurt behind the back of Madame Rottenmeier. The servants help hide the helpless creatures in the attic, where they are given an occasional saucer of milk. If only parental responsibilities were so easy. The blinkered child has no concept of euthanasia or of culling. A kitten rescued without spaying goes on to proliferate exponentially. It is easy to be a philanthropic do-gooder in the short-term when you don't have to consider the consequences or take ultimate responsibility. The child is unaware of the inadequacy of a saucer of milk, and Heidi carrying home the kittens in her pocket is not dissimilar to a boy who carries a terrapin around in his breast pocket to show off to his mates. Yet one is thought to be sweet and caring, the other harsh and brash. Despite Heidi's flippant remarks about stepping on a tortoise, she is aware of animal welfare, for as she watches her goatherd friend Peter lead his flocks among the alpine pastures she promises to give the boy her daily rations as long as the boy promises never to hit the goats again with his stick.

Hayley Mills was much more responsible in her care of the doomed kittens, for she entrusted their welfare to Jesus himself! This is the charming story written by Hayley's own mother, Mary Bell, in *Whistle down the Wind*. Hayley Mills plays Kathy Bostock, a farmer's daughter. When she witnesses the farm-hand discarding a sack-full of unwanted kittens into a pool in the local quarry she rescues them and gives one to her sister, Nan, one to her little brother, Charles, keeping one for herself. Tucking them under their coats, they sneak back to the barn to hide the kittens, and hopefully reunite them with the queen cat. They have to keep this all a secret. "Don't keep running in and out of here, else they'll know," says Hayley, deducing that adults are uncaring and hurtful to innocent animals. "I'm going to call mine Spider," says Charles. "You can't call a kitten, Spider," observes Nan, played by the nine-year-old Diane Holgate. But it is in the barn they stumble across a murderer on the run. Confusing him with Jesus, they leave the kittens in Jesus' tender care.

But all does not go well, as Charles later admonishes the 'saviour', "Jesus, why did you let my kitten die?"

Of course, the child at this age, by rescuing vulnerable unwanted progeny, is an unwitting interferer in the concept of survival of the fittest, as we discover in *Charlotte's Web*. "One Spring, on a small farm, one girl did something, something that would change everything." The little girl is Fern Arable, played by the irrepressible Dakota Fanning. The amazing something, was to rescue Wilbur, the runt of a litter of piglets. As a runt, Wilbur was destined to be Christmas dinner, but Fern begged for a chance to raise it. She was happy to munch away at one of the others in the Sunday roast: there is something about the defenceless runt that appeals to human nature. So, armed with a baby's bottle, she daily visits the barn, and soon the runt grows into a fine specimen of a piglet. The farmer complains to his wife that Fern is spending too much time by herself in the barn talking to animals. But the wife reassures him, it is a phase worth preserving for all too soon "she will grow out of it." Which is what happens eventually. Funfairs and a new boyfriend provide distractions that soon lead the girl away from the barn. But that no longer worries Wilbur, for he has found his own new friend in the form of Charlotte the spider.

So Dear to My Heart follows a similar pattern to *Charlotte's Web*, except it features a disowned black lamb rather than a runt pig. However, since *So Dear to My Heart* was released twenty years earlier, I guess it was the pattern upon which *Charlotte's Web* was based. In both films the baby animal is rejected by its mother, the child adopts the baby, the baby then goes on to win first prize at the County Fair.

In *So Dear to My Heart*, it is a boy, Jeremy (played by Bobby Driscoll), who rescues the black lamb ("black as a lump of coal," says his grandmother) rejected by the ewe because it was different from the rest of the litter. "The ways of nature seem cruel," says Gran. Although mainly about a cute boy and his cute black lamb, he is aided from time to time by his cousin, played by ten-year-old Luana Patten. Bobby Driscoll and Luana Patten also paired up two years earlier in *Song of the South* in which between them they rescued a puppy from drowning (with the help of Uncle Remus).

Made in 1948 by Walt Disney Studios, the film seems full of remarks that could be construed as inflammatory racist innuendo by modern standards (like Enid Blyton's Golliwog character), and I wonder if this has kept the musical off TV broadcasts. "Hasn't he got a cute face, Granny?" says Jeremiah, referring to his black lamb. "Wicked little face, if you ask me." And no one wants black wool. Yet, as Sister Margeritta points out in *The Sound of Music*, "The wool of a black sheep is just as warm!"

Having seen Dan Patch, the "greatest racehorse in the world" and got to keep one of its hoof nails as a souvenir, Jeremy had dreamt of owning his own colt. But his down-to-Earth Gran put paid to those ambitions. "I traded my dreams of owning a champion racehorse for a measly black ram," muses the boy. As it grows up, the ram leaves a trail of destruction in its wake, making Gran more and more irritable. "That damn boy. All he cares about is that fool lamb." The boy is given a stern warning: "You ain't thinking about that lamb. You're just thinking about yourself. Blue ribbons and awards!" But his ears are deaf to her reprimands. With the help of his cousin Judy (Luana Patten), and his uncle, the ram ends up at the Pike County Fair in Indiana and wins in a special category all its own.

At least, the film steered clear of the soapy ending in which the underdog has to win. Another underdog, Lucky the dog, also achieved a special award despite achieving second place in the sheepdog trials in *Family Gathering*. But this dog, paw heavily bandaged, had heroically rescued a bunch of kids from a forest fire.

"Animals are my passion," states Billy McGregor in *Joey* (1997). He proves his point by trespassing onto his neighbour's outback ranch in Australia where he keeps a check on a family of kangaroos. He has a camera mounted on a remote-controlled toy to help him spy on the animals' welfare, in particular, the progress of a young joey living in mother's pouch. Others think of the animals as pests, as they did the rabbits in *Celia* (1988), but for Billy, "they are not pests. They have got every right to be on the land as anyone."

One dark night the neighbours employ a sinister tracker to get rid of the kangaroos. Using a tranquilliser gun, the tracker is able to cart off all the animals, and take them to his *Kangaroo Kingdom* in Sydney. Now this sounds rather grand in conservation terms, but it is just a front for an illegal kangaroo-boxing gambling den, and an outlet for a kangaroo meat racket. But during the round-up, the baby joey falls from the mother's pouch.

Billy discovers the abandoned joey and smuggles it home, trying to feed it from a baby's milk bottle. But, like Bobby Driscoll's black lamb, the joey causes havoc in mum's kitchen. "I should have known! A house is no place for a joey. It needs its family. He'll die if his parents are not around to show him how to live." He has to find Kangaroo Kingdom. So, Billy sneaks out at midnight, carrying the joey in his backpack. He catches the night train, and arrives in the scary alien city of Sydney. He finds a place to shack up away from the other down-and-outs. "However dark it gets at night there's always going to be a sunrise," he thinks optimistically.

But by sunrise Joey has escaped. The boy searches everywhere and finds the animal in the botanical gardens. But too late! It is in the arms of a resolute authoritarian thirteen-year-old girl, Linda Ross, the daughter of the newly arrived American ambassador. Alex McKenna plays the role with confidence and comedy, treating *'stralian* to be a foreign lingo. Billy can't get the joey back from this headstrong girl. "I'm the ambassador's daughter. If you touch me it will be an international incident."

"I can't fight you for it," he protests.

But she has a modern liberal way of thinking: "Why what's wrong with fighting girls?" she demands taking up a karate stance.

Between them, and flashing her father's credit card like there was no tomorrow, they race across the city, hotly pursued by a couple of incompetent TV reporters, and half the Sydney police force who think they are dealing with the kidnapping of a diplomat's daughter. But when the boy and girl locate the illegal gambling den, where they reunite Joey with its parents, there is a sizeable police presence ready to arrest the villains.

At first father is disappointed with his daughter. "You run off in a foreign city with a scruffy lad and an oversized rat."

"He's not a rat, he's a joey," corrects the girl.

But when the ambassador realises how uncaring he has been towards his daughter he apologises. "I'm so, so sorry," says dad.

"Yes, well, you will be when you get your credit card bill!"

The Horse Lover

Like any caring human being, a child cannot bear to see an animal put down. If the dog is considered colloquially to be man's best friend, then there is one species in particular that is associated with preteen and adolescent girls – the big-faced, doughy-eyed horse.

Now having said that, I find there is a surprising dearth of films in which girls actually get to ride a horse. Obviously, I can name a few: *Angela* (1994), *Ball-Trap on the Côte Sauvage*, *The Horse Whisperer*, *Little Unicorn*, while in *True Grit* (2010), Hailee Steinfeld brushed up on her equestrian skills of horseback and trail riding once she had been cast as fourteen-year-old Mattie Ross.

Reticence to show girls actually riding is more to do with a safety issue than a lack of interest. A child falling off a horse during rehearsals or filming could have an impact not just for the well-being of the child, but would have financial implications and continuity repercussions. More usually, the child is seen seated on a horse or just a few strides may be taken. Georgie Henley and Anna Popplewell ride horses in *Prince Caspian*. Five-year-old Mara Wilson has a short pony trek in *Mrs Doubtfire*.

Most films you associate with horses have male jockeys, and there is a mad chase, or a battle with Native American Indians, until the huge beast is felled with a thud. Until 1980, it was still usual practice to use a hidden trip wire to bring down a running horse. Fortunately, recent legislation has helped in the prevention of unwarranted injury to animals. What the child *can* do in horsey films is ensure an injured horse is not put down unnecessarily, or in the case of *A Father's Choice*, the child can nurture a newborn foal to facilitate the recovery of the animal and the traumatised child.

Dreamer features a racehorse rescued from being put down after breaking its leg in a race. In this film, the girl is the unwitting saviour of the injured horse. Having fallen on the racetrack, the vet is ready to put the horse down there and then, but the trainer's daughter, Cale (Dakota Fanning), has come onto the track to inspect the damage, and so the trainer suggests delaying the fatal bullet until the girl has left. But an ensuing argument results in the life of the horse being saved. Dakota Fanning becomes its friend as it is nursed back to health in Kurt Russell's stable. But her father scolds the girl. "She's not a pet, Cale. She's what I do for work so you have got to leave her be." But the eleven-year-old ignores her father, sneaking out to the barn with popsicles as treats for the filly. It is the girl's insistence that prevents the horse from being sold on.

You can tell in this film there is a real bond between the girl and horse in real life. The horse, Sonador (Spanish for *Dreamer*), follows Dakota round in the field, even carrying her school bag in the horse's mouth. Though father sees the animal as just his business, Cale thinks of Sonador as part of the family. "She wasn't just some racehorse. She was our horse."

Although it is a team effort between father, a reunited grandfather, and daughter, it is really the girl who provides the resolve to get the horse mobile again, even though this means suspending the filly in a harness for several months until its ankle has strengthened. And the outcome? Of course, Sonador recovers to win the derby, against all the odds.

So similar are the story lines, it is almost as if *Dreamer* is based on *A Horse for Danny* released ten years earlier. Still, there is an obvious pattern if you are devising a story about a preteen girl brought up in a racing fraternity. The girl spots an under-performing sure-bet, raises cash to buy it, ropes in her guardian and a friend. An injury results in the vet decreeing the horse should be put down. The girl sees the sentimental value in the horse and not just the monetary value. The horse goes on to be a champion. So there we have it: Dreamer with eleven-year-old Dakota Fanning playing Cale, or *A Horse for Danny* with thirteen-year-old Leelee Sobieski playing eleven-year-old Danielle.

For Cale and for Danielle, the horse wasn't strictly a pet. For Polly Evans, however, her white pony in *The Little Unicorn* definitely was. She lived with it on a farm with her grandfather. Daily, she couldn't wait to get home from school to feed the animal, especially now the horse was pregnant and due to foal. But on this day, when she entered the stable the pregnant pony was lying gravely ill on the floor. The vet was called. He said there was nothing he could do for the animal except to humanely put it down, even though the pony was about to foal. Obviously Polly (Brittney Bomann) was angry that there was nothing that could be done. "Do horses go to Heaven?" she innocently asks. Her distress was short-lived, for that night the stable seemed to shimmer with magic light. There, in place of the baby foal they were expecting, was a dazzling white unicorn. No wonder the horse had felt unwell!

Polly's friend, Toby, names the unicorn *Spike*, and the boy and girl have their work cut out keeping sight-seers, journalist, and horse thieves from finding and stealing their unique unicorn.

The quandary whether to put the horse down or not in *The Horse Whisperer* resulted in what is surely one of the most amazing and inspirational films featuring an animal, and its emotional and physical impact on a family, and on one particular girl, Grace MacLean, played by fourteen-year-old Scarlett Johansson. The film, directed by Robert Redford who also played the lead man, is based on the best-selling novel by Nicholas Evans.

Grace has risen excitedly one snowy morning and met up with her best friend at the riding stables. They go on an early morning ride over the hills in New York State. But on one steep slope both horses slip on an icy bank, and tumble down onto a road and into the path of a juggernaut lorry. Grace's friend is killed outright. Grace herself has been badly injured resulting in the amputation of her right leg. Her horse, Pilgrim, has been badly cut with its face and flank ripped open, but it is able to run off from the scene. It hides shivering in a river beneath a bridge. But the horse is badly traumatised and won't allow anyone near it.

It is obvious the horse needs to be put down, but for one reason or the other the decision is put off. The horse trainer phones up the mother seeking her permission to put it down. "I've never seen a horse with such injuries and still alive," says the trainer over the phone. The officer standing with her, comments, "The animal should be put down. Anyone can see that."

Mother is a ruthless businesswoman used to making snap decisions, but she is standing beside her unconscious daughter's hospital bed. No, Grace will decide when she has regained mental strength. And so, the decision is delayed until after Grace's operation, and until she can hobble around on crutches. "I want to see Pilgrim." The girl has plucked up the courage at last. But when she sees her pet horse, she is horrified. As the trainer tells her, "Pilgrim is not the same horse as he used to be." The horse is now semi-wild, is dangerous, and has to be kept separate from the other animals. As it goes berserk mother tells the trainer, "Maybe you should give him a sedative." But she is told, "We already did."

Now that she has seen how badly injured the horse is, Grace has come to a difficult decision. It must be one of the hardest decisions a little girl has to make, even though Grace is now a young teenager. "I've decided what to do with Pilgrim. I think we should put him down. It's not fair to make him suffer."

But it's too late. Mother has been researching on the Internet and has discovered the name of a man, Tom Brooker, living in Montana who can "see into the horse's soul and soothe the wounds that are found there" – a horse whisperer. So, mother and daughter (with horse in the trailer) drive for days half way across America to see if this man can help. Really, Tom tells them, "I deal with horses with people problems," and that is really what he has to contend with. As well as the trauma experienced by the horse, daughter is fearful about riding again, and is depressed wondering how she can face a future with just one leg. And both mother and daughter are headstrong. It is their relationship that has to be healed as well as the horse's.

"I'm doing this for you," says mum to her sullen daughter.

"Bullshit! It's all about you. About you being right," protests Grace.

"I don't have all the answers," states her mother.

"No, you just act like you do!" counters Grace.

There follows a delicious period in the therapeutic Montana mountains, of Tom patiently staring into the troubled eye of the horse, while rebuilding the confidence of the young girl, and helping the mother adjust to life away from the stressful bustle of New York.

Gradually, Grace's fear of the horse is overcome. In fact, Tom tells her, "When that damned horse reared up in front of that truck I think he loved you so much that he tried to protect you. The day comes when both horse and girl have regained confidence so that Grace gets to ride her beloved Pilgrim again.

This is a wonderful film. It is not a Disney-style 'everything will be alright again as if by magic' type of film. It takes weeks of patient and realistic therapy to break down the fear in both horse and child.

Now, despite this assumed affinity that the girl gender has with the welfare of animals, the main characters actually involved in the treatment of animals are not girls at all, but are men. It is Robert Redford who is the *Horse Whisperer*, it is Eddie Murphy or Rex Harrison who is *Dr. Dolittle*, and the vet in *The Little Unicorn* is also male. James Herriot, too, has a whole series following his veterinary encounters in the Yorkshire Dales.

Males are also the main nurturers of the horses in *Black Beauty*, too. While the squire's children (Georgina Armstrong and Gemma Paternoster) get a short genteel pony ride, it is their obnoxious brother who demands a boisterous ride, yeeha, and it is the groom's assistant, Andrew Knott, (or his stunt double) who really bonds with Black Beauty, riding bareback through the paddocks.

Let us down to the sea again: Dolphins and Whales, Seals and Sea-Lions

The new holistic movement encourages a rediscovery of the mystical side of our souls. Astrology is no longer enough, as we are encouraged to make contact with our personal guardian angels, to consider the possibility of fairies, and encounter life-affirming experiences of swimming with dolphins. Dolphins are considered to have therapeutic qualities, and those lucky enough to swim with them claim to have gained mental healing, if not physical healing. Filmmakers are not remiss at exploiting this interest in creatures cetacean.

While Tina Majorino's relationship with *Andre* the sea-lion is like the faithful companionship a dog could provide, Misha Barton's bonding with dolphins in *A Ring of Endless Light* develops into a mysterious trifling with telepathy, and Keisha Castle-Hughes in *Whale Rider* transcends the entrenched sexism of her Maori community to become the personal saviour of a whole pod of beached whales. Boys don't claim any such psychic affinity: Jason James Richter's fascination for the orca whale in *Free Willy* derives from an act of bored vandalism, but ultimately both get to save the life of each other.

In *A Ring of Endless Light*, Mischa Barton plays Vicky Austin, a teenager who, along with her younger sister Suzy, has gone to stay with her grandfather for summer vacation. Grandfather lives on Seven Bay Island, which houses a dolphin research centre. Younger sister Suzy (Scarlett Pomers) is more interested in maths and astronomy so has little involvement with the dolphin. "When you study nature there are too many intangibles," she says to explain her absence from much of the film.

The dolphin research centre is concerned that the local fishing fleet is using illegal drift nets. Vicky decides to help them out, and that is where she discovers her telepathic skills. "Grandfather, would it be crazy if I told you I believe I know what dolphins are thinking, like, they talk to me... A feeling in my mind... That they are in trouble?" Fortunately, Grandfather accepts the possibility, so when the girl is able to telepathically locate the troublesome illegal fishing nets, Grandfather convinces the police launch to catch the perpetrators.

Another child who discovers she has extra-sensory rapport with cetaceans is Pai in *Whale Rider*. Keisha Castle-Hughes, in an Oscar winning role, plays the ten-year-old who finds she can bond with a pod of beached whales. As a descendant of the tribal chief in a Maori community, she is forced to prove to the disbelieving community that she is the heir-apparent of the guardianship of the Maori culture. She is a girl, so she can't be heir-apparent. But when the pod of whales beach themselves on the shoreline, the tribal chief, Koro, is unable to refloat them using his mystical chants. He and the community drift away dejectedly, unable to save the leviathans. But, like a scene from *The Horse Whisperer* in which Scarlett Johansson secretly whispers in Pilgrim's ear re-establishing the bond of trust allowing her to remount the estranged horse, Pai too tenderly approaches, caressing the largest whale, whispering gently, and then carefully climbs its flanks and clambers aboard. The whale now rejuvenates, and with a flick of its tail, heads out to sea, with Pai riding it like a horse, and the other whales following in its wake. Thus, the girl is acknowledged as the new true guardian of the Maori tribe.

Mischa Barton gets to swim with real dolphins (in a marine pool), whereas the whales in Keisha Castle-Hughes' film are all glass-fibre monoliths, propelled by animatronics.

Free Willy brings together two homeless beings: Willy, pining for the pod of whales that are basking in the bay beyond its cramped pool at the NW Adventure Park; and Jesse (Jason James Richter), an obnoxious fostered brat yearning for his long-lost mother to take him back. Unlike the girls in *A Ring of Endless Light* and *Whale Rider*, this boy has no affinity with the orca whales. He is only there to clean up the graffiti that he and his bored gang members had scrawled on the viewing tank after being caught breaking and entering. The boy finds the whale responds to him when he plays his mouth organ; and when the boy falls in the pool, the whale rescues him. "You saved my life," says Jason James Richter as his adolescence develops a new focus. The boy gets a chance to pay back for his deviancy. As the owners of the park try to sabotage the tank in a million-dollar insurance scam, the boy raises the alarm so that the whale can be rescued and reunited with the pod waiting offshore.

For a film highlighting the poor conditions that whales are kept in at adventure parks, this film itself was criticised for the poor conditions in which Willy was held, so that in the sequels, animatronic models were used instead. Jason James Richter remained loyal to his friend by appearing in both *Free Willy 2* and *Free Willy 3*.

For Toni (Tina Majorino) in *Andre*, there is nothing mystical about her relationship with a seal (actually a sea-lion) that she and her father have nurtured since it was abandoned as a weaning pup. Father makes a model of an adult seal, with nipples, to encourage the pup to suckle. "Please don't die. I'll be your best friend forever," says Toni. For Toni, the seal *was* her best friend. This is a girl who effuses joy as she plays with the tame creature, takes a bath with it, watches TV with it, and even brings it to school for a 'show and tell'.

However, seals, like dolphins and whales, seem to make enemies of fishermen who resent their precious livelihood being thieved by these marine monsters. Toni's seal, Andre, is no different, despite Toni's father (the Harbour Master of Rockport, Maine) trying to convince the fishing community differently. Seals get caught in nets and a fisherman can be financially ruined when his stocks are depleted. "Time was, you could shoot a *man* for stealing a catch," complains one fisherman after a seal ruins his nets, implying now you can't even shoot a seal.

When the little girl learns the seal would be returned to the wild, or later be sent to an aquarium, she has to resort to drastic action to try to keep her slippery friend. In the midst of an approaching squall, she sculls to the headland in her tiny dinghy to effect a rescue. Later, her parents use a little fibbing to get their own way: "Sometimes when you really love something you got to let them go."

The Pet as a Punishment

If a child loves its pet as much as he/she loves its own parent, then it becomes a cruel tool with which to threaten an uncooperative child. Although a parent may not be so mean as to deprive a child of the joy of loving its own pet, here are two films in which a child has been blackmailed by making threats against an animal to ensure the cooperation of the child. In both films, the blackmailer is a paedophile, and the child has to comply to prevent harm befalling her beloved pet.

Jodie Foster's pet in *The Little Girl who lives down the Lane* is a hamster called Gordon. Living the life of a hermit, this rodent is her only friend. Both her parents had died and she is trying to live alone by pretending her father is always unavailable because he is busy working upstairs. When the thirteen-year-old attracts the unwanted attention of the local paedophile (Martin Sheen), the man uses the pet to show her the power he can hold over her. Because the girl is continually stonewalling him, the man stubs out his cigarette on the hamster's forehead, then hurls it into the fire when it dares bite him.

In a separate film, *Fallen Angel*, Richard Masur plays another paedophile using the pet to exert his power over the child. The man, masquerading as a sports coach, hones in on the twelve-year-old girl, Jennifer Philips (played by the prematurely deceased Dana Hill), after she has had a spat with her own parents. Over time, he ingratiates himself into a position of trust. He convinces her into believing her parents don't care for her anymore. Following a visit to his gym, the man is particularly tender with her, then takes her to a rescue kennels where he buys the girl a puppy. "Just tell your folks you found it, ok." After all, like Devon is reprimanded in *Lawn Dogs*, little girls can't receive pet terrapins from men they barely know.

Soon the man is taking the girl to secluded areas in the park where he can take photos of her. "Just lift you skirt up a little bit." "Now let's try this in just your bra and panties." The day comes when he introduces the girl to other children he uses to photograph. After photographs of boy and girl kissing on a swing, the time comes for her to do a nude shot. The girl objects. The man picks up the puppy and starts wrangling its head in his hand. The girl thinks her puppy is being strangled. "The puppy is naked," the man points out to her, so there is no harm, then. So to ensure no harm comes to her pet, she slowly peels down her costume, and the man begins frantically pressing the shutter release on his camera.

Children cannot bear to see cruelty dispensed to others, and their loyalty to fellow sufferers masks the dangers life throws at them, so they become defenceless targets in the hands of those who wish to exploit them. While children may protect a pet, stand up for a friend, show loyalty to family, they can still be easily swayed by irrational argument. Used to being told what to do, they are unable to assert their personal rights, and the gangs and cliques they inhabit exert a tribalism that can exclude anyone who does not conform to the collective norm. Children themselves can be irrationally cruel to others because their immaturity has not yet allowed them the tools to recognise prejudice, or to allow inclusion for the outsider, or for those who don't conform to the recognised norm. It is not until they reach adolescence that they realise the world does not revolve around themselves, that issues do not stick rigidly to black and white, right and wrong, friend and enemy, loneliness and inclusion, that shades of grey allow a more objective rationalising of the world around them.

Michael Thompson in his book *Best Friends Worst Enemies* is optimistic: "I believe that children … share a fundamental quality … a drive to connect with other human beings in positive, nurturing ways … in spite of differences in health, sexual orientation, race and culture, and levels of poverty or wealth."[42]

ENDNOTES FOR VOLUME FOUR

[1] Best Friends, Worst Enemies, Thompson et al p62

[2] *Imitation of Life* had a similar premise: that of a girl lost on the beach bringing two families together for a lifetime.

[3] Best Friends, Worst Enemies, Thompson et al p130,132

[4] Neil Sinyard: *Children in the Movies* p60.

[5] *The Unseen Playmate* by Robert Louis Stevenson.

[6] Best Friends, Worst Enemies, Thompson et al p112

[7] Isabella Blake-Thomas plays Violet – only the character is perceived detestable, not the actress!

[8] Best Friends, Worst Enemies, Thompson et al p186

[9] Best Friends, Worst Enemies, Thompson et al p163

[10] AnnaSophia went on to perform the brilliant gum-chewing Verucca Beauregard in the Johnny Depp version of Charlie and the Chocolate Factory.

[11] *Hijra* is a derogatory term used in Urdu meaning someone of mixed gender, or having undergone a sex change. Of course, the use of this word was untrue: Latika was unequivocally a girl.

[12] Heidi is played by Emma Bolger in the 2005 film, by Katia Polletin in the TV drama, and Shirley Temple in 1937. Clara is played by Jessica Claridge in the 2005 film, and by Kathi Böhm in the TV drama.

[13] The alternative ending is shown on the DVD.

[14] Best Friends, Worst Enemies, Thompson et al p206

[15] Sula Wolff *Children Under Stress* p 26

[16] Best Friends, Worst Enemies, Thompson et al p206

[17] Sue Monk Kidd *The Secret Life of Bees* p122 & p113.

[18] The part of Sarah Jane is played by Karen Dicker as an eight-year-old, and by Susan Kohner aged eighteen.

[19] Peter Krausz: *Screening Indigenous Australia: an overview of Aboriginal representation on Film.* www.moodle.ignatius.sa.edu.au/webhost/Library/libray_staff/enhancetv/indiginousfilm.pdf

[20] *Australian Aboriginal Movies & Films* @ www.creativespirits.info/resources/movies

[21] David Gulpilil seems to be the one constant in all films depicting an Aborigine. Most famed for his role in *Walkabout*, he appears in *Rabbit Proof Fence*, Storm Boy, Mad Dog and *The Proposition*.

[22] IMDb.com, Inc

[23] Best Friends, Worst Enemies, Thompson et al p254

[24] Katie Roiphe *She Still Haunts Me.*

[25] *100 Great Books* Edited by John Canning, p377

[26] Christina Björk & Inga-Karin Eriksson, *The Other Alice: the story of Alice Liddell and Alice in Wonderland.*

[27] Christina Björk & Inga-Karin Eriksson, *The Other Alice: the story of Alice Liddell and Alice in Wonderland.* p84, 87

[28] As a 14 year old the Dalai Lama is played by Jamyang Jamsho Wangchuk, and as an 8 year old by his younger brother Sonam Wangchuk.

[29] Neil Sinyard: *Children in the Movies*, p27

[30] Because these are not strangers thrown together on a journey we do not pursue this here. See Volume Seven (*Childhood Traumas*), *witnesses to the atrocities of war.*

[31] Marianne Sinclair, *Hollywood Lolita* p120

[32] *Erotic Innocence* by James R Kincaid p 234

[33] *Erotic Innocence* by James R Kincaid p 236

[34] *Time Out Film Guide 2010*, Edited by John Pym, p600.

[34a] In A J Quinnell's novel, the action takes place in Naples rather than Mexico City, and Creasy trains Pita as a sprinting athlete rather than as a swimmer.

[35] Karen Lury: *The Child* in Film p96

[35a] Quinnell's book makes Creasy's intentions plain: "The idea of him with an eleven-year-old as a friend was about as likely as a rabbit getting on with a fox." The idea disturbed Creasy, and yet "He could not banish her from his mind and found himself not wanting to." A J Quinnell *Man on Fire* p100.

[36] 101 Dalmatians, Charlotte's Web, Whistle Down the Wind, The Lion, the Witch and the Wardrobe, Dreamer, Celia (1988), Alaska.

[37] Neil Sinyard *Children in the Movies* p90

[38] *Erotic Innocence* by James R Kincaid p 300

[39] Andrew Collins *Radio Times* 3 April 2010

[40] Karen Lury, *The Child* in Film p105

[41] Joe is played by Roddy McDowell in 1943, and by Jonathan Mason in 2005. Both films follow a similar plot, but (in my opinion) the story line seems better developed in the recent version.

[42] *Best Friends, Worst Enemies*, Thompson et al p205

Volume Five

Make-Believe, Horror & the Supernatural

"Childhood is measured out of sounds and smells and sights,
before the dark hour of reason grows."
(John Betjeman – quoted from
The Boy with the Striped Pyjamas)

"It does not do to dwell on dreams
and forget to live."
(says Dumbledore to Harry Potter. JK Rowling)

CONTENTS FOR VOLUME FIVE

5. Make-Believe, Horror & the Supernatural......................**261**

Contents for Volume Five..**263**

Introduction...**265**
Gender, Colour and Make-Believe..265
Girls With Mysterious Powers...266

Make-Believe...**270**
Alice in Wonderland...271
Folk Tales...273
Little Otik (Otesánek)..275
Santa Claus..276
Fairy Tales...278
Magic...282
The Harry Potter Series...284
Witches and Witchcraft..286

Horror **289**
Ghosts...293
Vampires...298
Werewolves...300
The Child-Killer: Children who Kill.......................................301

The Supernatural..**307**
Religion...307
Devil Possession...312

Endnotes for Volume Five..**315**

INTRODUCTION

Gender, Colour and Make-Believe

With fairy wings fixed over their shoulders, a witch's broom between their thighs, a horoscope in their palm, and a map of Narnia, Wonderland or Oz before their gaze, the world of make-believe is the adventure playground for the girl-child. Boys seem to have an excuse note-of-absence from any type of movie about make-believe. Like Barret Oliver and Zachery Ty Bryan in *The NeverEnding Story* and *Magic Island*, boys shift uneasily when romantic tales of saving princesses or of fairy godmothers are proffered. Even the world of witches and wizards were anathema to boys until JK Rowling donned Harry Potter with the same indomitability as a boy's other legendary comic-book heroes. The boy aspires to superman indestructability, and no ghostly spectre can spook his *sang-froid*, no tale of elves and fairies can compromise his assumed maturity. In this volume about ghosts and witches, vampires and werewolves, of children posssessed by devils and with murderous intent, the boy is surprisingly largely absent.

William Golding was aware of masculine bravado as he scripted his novel *Lord of the Flies*. The boys went hell-for-leather once they realised their adult-free world gave them liberty to do as they liked. Theirs was a world of frenzied hog hunts, carving and throwing spears, riots around the campfire accompanied by murderous yelps of 'kill the pig, kill the pig'. But as soon as one timid lad mentioned he had seen *the monster*, repressed primeval fears rapidly spread like a plague to match the primevalism of their newly adopted life-style. Despite Piggy[1] stating, "I don't believe in ghosts," mass consensus decreed the monster must be tracked down and hunted, but when it failed to materialise they realised it should be respected and gifts left to appease it.

You see in movie-world, boys have to be nudged, prodded and poked into believing things the girl accepts as natural. Yet the boy's bogus barrier of bravado is really a flimsy collapsible veneer of masculinity.

If a film director wishes to shock an audience, boys are not seen as vulnerable enough to be innocent victims, nor shocking enough to startle us as villainous monsters. It is the girl-child who inherits the role of the mysterious creature, the child with mystical powers. It is rare for boys to be given this tag – Harvey Stephens in *The Omen*, and Haley Joel Osment in *The Sixth Sense* being obvious exceptions. Instead, boys go on to be superheroes or super-sleuths: the young Superman, the young Sherlock Holmes. But even here, the girl has a foot in the door: *Harriet the Spy*, *Escape from Witch Mountain*, and *Spy Kids* providing a feminine grasp on the tiller.

Two young kids with supposed psychokinetic powers are holding out their hands for their palms to be read in *The Last Mimzy*. But the boy, Noah (Chris O'Neil) does not have the telltale palm print. For the tradition of the mystical girl to be perpetuated we find only young Emma (Rhiannon Leigh Wryn) possessing the cartographic lifelines on her hand. It is only the girl that the rabbit-shaped Mimzy talks to. And she can explain her powers with the total conviction that only the winsome female gender can charm: "I looked through the looking glass, mama. Just like Alice."

Like so many aspects of the movie industry, it is the white child who is seen as vulnerable victim, whose delicate ivory skin has to be protected from the blackness of a corrupting world. The likes of coloured Tyler James Williams and Aleisha Allen just wouldn't impact as alabaster-skinned Hansel and Gretel, or nacreous Kai and Girda, evidently. Steven Spielberg dared buck this trend by placing ebony-toned Vanessa Lee Chester in the path of tyrannosaurus rex in *Lost World: Jurassic Park*; and Eddie Murphy coaxed his black progeny (Aree Davis (13) and Marc John Jeffries (10)) into *The Haunted Mansion*, but these portray gothic humour, not fearful dread. It is the delicate vulnerability of the white girl-child that is perversely exploited as we shudder at the impish waif morphed into merciless killer.

"Wednesday is at that special age when girls have only one thing on their mind – homicide!" says Morticia, as bleach-face Christina Ricci is introduced to the new nanny in *Addams Family Values*.

Girls With Mysterious Powers

Why is it that girls assume this role of mystery? Is it their fairy connection, their elfin attributes? When adults are portrayed with psychic powers it is invariably the girl child who adopts the same psychic traits: the witch's spells passed from mother to daughter, the palm-reader who acquires the gift from her mother and her grandmother before that. It is the female who is more influenced by the horoscope, who uses the crystal ball to divine her future, and it is the girl (such as Mischa Barton in *A Ring of Endless Light*) who finds she can communicate telepathically with dolphins.

"When I was small I had a gift other people could not see. It was like looking into deep water," claims Benji (Saoirse Ronan) in *Death Defying Acts*.

"When I was your age I could do things other folks could not," says grandmother to her granddaughter, Carol Anne Fielding (Heather O'Rourke) in *Poltergeist II*. "Do you ever know things and you can't explain why?" The situation is confirmed when a psychic explains to her mother: "Your daughter is highly clairvoyant, as was your mother, as you are as well."

But there is little mention of any son having the same gift.

For most, being endowed with specific powers is just wishful thinking. Coincidences happen, which are ascribed to fate or to some imagined aptitude. Wishing on a star, or crossing one's fingers behind one's back, wearing a lucky charm, tossing a coin in a well, or adhering to the contradictory remarks in a horoscope: these are all ways to gamble a passage through life's adversities. And when that one-in-a-million chance eventually comes true, the recipient ascribes it to an inherent lucky gene.

Several girl characters claim to have this clairvoyant gift when really they are simply misinterpreting coincidences. Ten-year-old Eve (Jurnee Smollett), in *Eve's Bayou*, sticks pins in her doll and takes pieces of hair from father's hairbrush, to take vindictive retribution on her father. When father dies after a brawl at the bar, Eve naturally believes the power of voodoo is responsible for his death.

Another girl who thinks she has this psychic gift is Anna in *Paperhouse*. Anna (played by eleven-year-old Charlotte Burke) believes she has the power to affect the life of a disabled boy by means of pictures she draws. Her illness causes her to drift into an unconscious dreamland in which she believes she is affecting outcomes in the real world. In her dreams she visits a drab house sited atop remote moorland, similar to one she has been drawing while awake. Here she meets a boy, Marc, crippled with muscular dystrophy. When awake, Anna discovers she can affect the lot of the boy by adding things to her drawing – a pair of legs, a staircase, a bicycle. Then she discovers her doctor is also treating a real life crippled boy, who also happens to be called Marc, a boy who is severely ill, but whose improvements seem related to the amendments she makes to her picture.

Of course, as with *Eve's Bayou*, we the audience know Anna does not possess any special powers; the film shows us it is a natural child-like trait of wishful thinking, the child believing in divine influence as coincidences occur. "My children have strange fantasies – but you must not pay any attention to them," says Nicole Kidman in *The Others* (2001).

This psychic alarm is compounded when adults begin to believe their own progeny are possessed with destructive powers. In *The Children* (2008), strange things occur when children are around, and we are left contemplating whether these children created the impact using some mysterious power or whether false conclusions were related to a misunderstanding, just as we are coaxed into believing the children are possessed in Henry James' *The Turn of the Screw*.

In *The Children* (2008), two sets of parents have taken their kids on a New Year break. The adults become victims of gory attacks as they are cut by glass, run over by out-of-control sleds, and ultimately killed. When Miranda's mother finds she has become the sole surviving adult, she concludes it is her own nine-year-old daughter (Eva Sayer) who must be responsible. In a frantic attempt to escape the carnage, mother drives off in her 4x4. Ahead of her on the forest track, she sees her own daughter standing, blocking her exit. Contradictory to usual maternal instincts, she ploughs straight into the girl and crashes the car, knowing that by doing so she is destroying the conjectured source of evil. Alas, at this juncture, a whole group of forest children emerge from the woodland, as they do in *Zombies: Wicked Little Things*. Maybe, her own daughter who she has just murdered was, like the medieval witch drowned in the ducking pool, innocent all along!

In *Death Defying Acts*, the supposed paranormal powers of Benji are used in a less sadistic fashion, and we are even left wondering whether it is staged or not. Eleven-year-old Benji (Saoirse Ronan) is the daughter of a single parent who ekes out a living by duping bystanders and audiences with staged psychic scams. Mother and daughter are a double act, a bit like the double act played by itinerant Ryan and Tatum O'Neal in *Paper Moon*. Daughter Benji tries to secretly gather information from members of the audience as they queue to watch a performance, by stealing certain objects from them while their attention is diverted. Mother then performs a paranormal hoax on stage using the artefacts and information that Benji has acquired.

Along comes the famous Houdini to perform in their home city, Edinburgh. Houdini has been wracked with guilt following the death of his mother, since he was not there for her in her dying moments. So, he puts out a challenge for any psychic to come up with mother's dying word. Benji's mother (Catherine Zeta-Jones) rises to the challenge and uses devious means, including a fleeting romance with the great escapologist, to try to find the right answer to the puzzle and thus win the $10,000. But it is Benji who cracks the code by going into a trance and performing well enough to convince the great Houdini.

We reiterate: the telepathic quality of the child materialises through the female gender. Maybe the girl is a better communicator, more likely to conclude 'I know what you're thinking', or to separately blurt out something in unison with their bosom pal. It seems to be stretching incredulity when we come across girls who can, like Doctor Dolittle, converse with the animal world by influencing insects or communicating with cetaceans. (Doctor Dolittle himself possessed a rare gift for a male.)

In *Phenomena*, fourteen-year-old Jennifer Connelly has the ability to communicate with insects, using this power to help track down the location of a mass-murderer (the bee she is carrying in a jar buzzes louder as she approaches the murderer's lair!) Unfortunately, in the whole film she only uses this power once; the film does not inform us of the extent of her telepathic powers. This may have been scary in the 1980s, but it seems to have been lazily formulated. Let us snoop on the scriptwriter's meeting… 'How can we solve this crime of a girl child murdered at a waterfall? I know, why not have another girl communicate with bees and the bee can lead her there. Right, good idea!'

And yet, how does a hive, comprised of millions of individuals with no apparent means of communicating beyond buzzing, remain a regimented unified community? In our ignorance we credit their success to an evolutionary miracle. Perhaps there is some mass telepathic world to which we are not yet attuned. We are equally baffled by the mammals of the sea who intelligently communicate in grunts and squeals. So when Mischa Barton finds she can telepathize with the dolphins trapped in the illegal fishing nets in *A Ring of Endless Light*, may be this is not as far-fetched as it seems.

When finally the scriptwriter does dare to endow a boy with telepathic powers, as Alexander Seth shares with AnnaSophia Robb in *Race to Witch Mountain*, we discover they are not even Earthlings, but an extraterrestrial waiting to be beamed aboard a passing space capsule!

Where the male of the species *is* granted (by scriptwriters) with that special gift, it is more likely to be the adult male: Rex Harrison as *Doctor Dolittle*, Don Shanks as Michael Myers in *Halloween 5*. Yet Eddie Murphy in *Dr Dolittle 2* bequeaths his gift to his daughter (Kyla Pratt), while it is the girl, twelve-year-old Danielle Harris, who subconsciously clenches her fist as Michael Myers thinks evil thoughts, and her nightmares are tuned to his prowling: "He's coming," she scribbles on her slate.

As the movie industry ascribes supernatural powers to its female cast maybe that is helping rebalance the gender equation; though I am sure the feminist would prefer to be seen as equal in the commonality of life, without resorting to ethereal means.

Cassie is a thirteen-year-old girl, played by Dakota Fanning, a second generation '*Watcher*', a member of a disparate gang who have telekinetic powers and who can see into the future, in the baffling movie, *Push*. Like Anna in *Paperhouse*, Cassie draws predictive pictures with her crayoning set, which helps her be aware of any danger, and this directs her to a special serum that may revive her ailing mother. We never see her make any of the drawings, and like so many of these movies we just have to compliantly accept that what the scriptwriter tells us must be true.

Cassie's powers are psychic and intellectual. To compete in the league of male superheroes like the Incredible Hulk or Spiderman, the girl needs to be designated physical powers, such as Drew Barrymore's ability to generate conflagrations through the power of her mind, in *Firestarter*. By focusing on an object she can induce fires, and she uses this power to evade capture by the officials who are trying to monopolise her gift. (Blame Stephen King for the storyline.)

Similarly proficient at conflagrations is twelve-year-old Loren McConnell (AnnaSophia Robb), "five foot tall, blond and living out in that darn swamp with those other devil worshippers," in Louisiana's Bayou region, in *The Reaping*. The villagers of Haven have been plagued by rivers of blood which they blame on the terrified girl. As the community raises a vigilante group to kill the girl she is protected by the whole gamut of Biblical plagues, which are inflicted on those who oppose her: frogs raining from the sky, boils, maggots, death of cattle, and finally cataclysmic thunderbolts.

Fire and females seem synonymous, for as Jodelle Ferland raises her arms in *Silent Hill*, she too becomes a roaring blaze of flames. It just would not have the same effect if boys tried it.

Most children would be quietly content if they had the revengeful powers of their classmate, *Matilda*. She is an unwanted child, left to fend for herself by uncaring parents, then discovers she can do magic feats when provoked by anger. Matilda (6½), played by Mara Wilson, enjoys reading but her uneducated father thinks she should be more sociable with the rest of the family by watching trashy TV instead. The little girl glares at the screen and it explodes! At first, she is not sure if she caused this or whether it was coincidence. Later at school, when she and her classmates are being tormented by the evil ogress of a headmistress, the glass of water the woman is holding shatters. This seems to convince her she has special powers, but when she tries to prove this to her nice class teacher, Miss Honey, nothing happens.

Perhaps it only works when people rant and rave at her. She tests out this theory and lo and behold, by practicing she rapidly progresses to do amazing paranormal tricks, such as moving boxes and furniture, picking people up, making dolls and carrots fly.

Ultimately there is the battle against the bullying headteacher, Miss Trunchbull, who is no doubt, every child's idea of its worst nightmare. It is probably also every child's dream of having the spectacular powers that Matilda possesses, even if only to filch a chocolate from teacher's private confection box.

The Village of the Damned takes these extraordinary powers combined with telepathy to a group level. In a quiet rural community, all the inhabitants inexplicably fall asleep only to awake six hours later with all the women of childbearing age now pregnant. A few months later, the local clinic is overwhelmed as all the new babies are born on the same day, all displaying Arian traits: blond hair, deep blue eyes. We watch the young children grow through childhood until they reach their tenth birthday. Whenever these children become aware of any injustice or abuse towards any of their group, they use their combined telepathic powers, with their deep blue eyes glowing green and red, to cause a drastic accident. The story is based on the novel, *The Midwich Cuckoos*, and two film versions have been released, in 1960 and 1995. Though the 1995 film had potential to be a real scare, the only action demanded of the children is to walk like mechanical zombies. Otherwise, they just stand and stare, with sporadic lines of dialogue. At least in this film, the author has endowed the boys with the same mysterious powers as the girls. Psychic equality at last!

MAKE-BELIEVE

The world of make-believe is an invention fabricated and perpetuated by imaginative hypocrites. It is a world inhabited by fairies, hobbits, witches and ghosts; a world visited nightly by children tucked into their dreamworld of bedtime tales, and narrated tongue-in-cheek by parents who one moment are happy to perpetuate myths, yet the next, are berating the child for living in a dream, lying, and for not being down to earth. For, as Neil Sinyard informs us, commenting on *Curse of the Cat People*, there is a "fine line in childhood between 'acceptable fantasy' and 'untruth'." [2] Susan Walker had to contend with just such a mother in *Miracle on 34th Street*, a mother who could only believe in tangibles and never in the Santa Claus of the Christmas parade she was promoting for the toy store. "All she ever talks about is some place that doesn't exist," complains Aunt Em in *Return to Oz*.

Amy Reed has to learn the hurtful way about the inconsistencies of parental notions in *The Curse of the Cat People*. She has an invisible friend – a woman. Taking his daughter (Ann Carter) into his arms, exasperated by her continued fantasising, the father gives the girl an ultimatum. "If you say this woman is there in the garden I shall have to punish you." The girl cannot deny her imagination, so is taken upstairs to be spanked by the uncompromising parent. This is one mixed-up girl, confused by the hypocrisy of her father. Previously, father had told his little girl that the hole in the tree in the garden is magic, so Amy posts the invites for her birthday party in the hole. When no one turns up for the party, the man explains that in the tangible world magic is unreal. And yet the man has the audacity to tell her to make a wish as she blows out the candles on her birthday cake. "But you told me wishes don't come true!"

Dorothy Gale (convincingly played by Fairuza Balk) has precisely the same hurdle of disbelief to overcome in *Return to Oz*. Ridiculed for her constant talk of the fanciful land that fills her every dream, Dorothy's guardians (her aunt and uncle) resort to a visit to the doctor at the asylum to rid her once and for all of her malicious memories. Yet the hypocritical doctor tries to alleviate the girl's fear of the electrical machine that is going to eradicate her imaginative dreaming by pointing out the facial features of the machine: 'these are like eyes, here is its nose, this slot is the mouth.'

The world of make-believe exists exclusively for the infant and preteen child. "He's eleven! He has reached the age of not believing," declares Angela Lansbury in *Bedknobs and Broomsticks*. Only in religion and the spirit world is belief in such myths perpetuated among adults, though there are others who are unfairly labelled as 'living in cloud cuckooland' or 'up with the fairies'. As we discover shortly, the sudden loss of life during the First World War caused a yearning among adults to explore the world of make-believe and psychic phenomena. "Someday you'll be old enough to start reading fairy tales again," writes CS Lewis to his goddaughter, to whom he had dedicated *The Lion, the Witch and the Wardrobe*. By the time it was published, the girl had outgrown fairy tales and stories of magic, themes that have entranced generations of impressionable little children, and secretly delighted those of us who deny our dreams.

This world of make-believe is characterised wonderfully by the playful antics of Jodelle Ferland in *Tideland*. In director Terry Gilliam's words, the film *Tideland* is "*Alice in Wonderland* meets *Psycho*." Throughout the film, she play-acts with four finger puppets, each adopting a different identity, the character exhibiting a multi-faceted personality. One doll talks when she is afraid, she speaks through a different doll when she feels glamorous, happy, confident, etc. The girl "never admits she is ever frightened, but uses her doll to speak out her fears. Outside she is all joy and happiness and bounce, but inside she's quite a tragic little girl," explains Gilliam. Jeliza Rose spends her childhood living in this dreamland. Sometimes you think Jeliza is mad but she recovers her resilience. All these multi-faceted personalities are brilliantly acted by nine-year-old Jodelle Ferland in one of the most amazing child performances I have seen. I understand much of her play-acting was unscripted, but this girl has not received any credit for her performance, maybe due to the controversial nature of Terry Gilliam's film.

After the death of her mother, Jeliza Rose moves with her father into a tumbledown farmstead in the expansive Saskatchewan Prairies of Canada. There, she explores the wheat fields, animal burrows, talking to squirrels and rabbits. Her solitary life compels her into a wonder world of imaginary play. There is a large trunk in the house full of grandma's musty old clothes. She parades the prairies in the flamboyant costumes. When the radio stops working she buries it because the batteries have died, for that is what you do with dead things, she deduces.

Jeliza Rose is startled by her eccentric neighbour, Dell, who she assumes to be a ghost, but as the girl is grappled roughly by the collar she realises, "You're not a ghost, anyhow!" Dell has a retarded twenty-year-old brother, Dickens. When they meet, they play together, pretending to swim through the wheat fields. They enter Dickens' hideout that he uses as a submarine. The railway line is a shark monster, which will one day be blown up by Dickens' secret 'atom bomb'.

Scenes shift swiftly as in a dream, just as they do in *Alice in Wonderland*. After they witness Dickens' sister kissing the deliveryman, their world of make-believe broadens into playing 'silly kissing' and taboo boundaries begin to blur.

Jeliza Rose epitomises the world of make-believe of a little girl. The unquestioning trust she places in others, her endeavour to put troubles and fears behind her, the acceptance of fanciful situations as being true, and transgressing into the lives and emotions of unwitting others. Other girls follow her example: girls like Ivana Baquero in *Pan's Labyrinth* or Rebecca Smart in *Celia* (1988), whose blurred monsters take a more lifelike form, or Mischa Barton whose fantasies implicate innocent adults in *Lawn Dogs*, and others whose dreams transport them to the wonderlands of Oz, Narnia, and the realm of the Queen of Hearts.

Alice in Wonderland

Alice in Wonderland is the ultimate original fantasy that other make-believe films seem always to be compared with. Lewis Carroll's book of Alice was made for children, and specifically aimed at one little nine-year-old girl, Alice Liddell, with whom the famous author and Oxford lecturer had fallen in love in maybe more than just a paternalistic way. Yet the brilliance of his tale is exalted worldwide, and it is the exemplar for fantasy tales. Terry Gilliam described his *Tideland* as *Alice in Wonderland* meets *Psycho*, in an adult movie exploring adult themes through a child's eye. *Phoebe in Wonderland* features a child wracked by a repetitive compulsive disorder and Tourettes Syndrome, whose only escape from her troubles are in the fantasy land of Wonderland where she can confide in the characters that are through her own personal psychological looking glass. When the school drama teacher announces they are staging a play about *Alice*, Phoebe (Elle Fanning) is desperate to play the part of her heroine, yet pitifully resorts to self-harm, repetitive washing of hands, and avoidance of cracks in the pavement as her way of trying to control a baffling world and of naively procuring the part of Alice.

Several Alice movies have been made with a slight variation in title, such as *Alice's Adventures in Wonderland*. Being such a popular story the casts seem to attract an array of famous actors. The 1933 version starred Gary Cooper and Cary Grant with Charlotte Henry as Alice. A 1951 version saw Carol Marsh as Alice in the same year that Disney brought out the most popular animated version with Kathryn Beaumont voicing the lead girl. The Czech animator, Jan Švankmajer, brought a darker, more grotesque version to our screens in 1988 with Kristýna Kohoutová playing Alice as the only real-life actor in the film.

In this movie, titled simply *Alice* (1988), the white rabbit is a stuffed animal in a taxidermist's cage, which comes alive, and after running across a bare brown ploughed field it disappears into the draw of a desk, distantly followed by seven-year-old Alice. To keep a distance is the right thing to do for the rabbit is evil-looking, as are the skeletal fish and lizards, and creatures trapped in specimen bottles. As in other Alice movies, the girl shrinks and grows, swims in her lake of tears, and is squashed against the ceiling of a tiny room with her arm hanging out. The girl has little to say except constantly and infuriatingly repeating the phrase "… said the white rabbit." Fortunately the girl, Kristýna, didn't have to confront or endure the evil beings, since most of the film was animated.

The 1972 version, with an older Fiona Fullerton playing Alice, was a wonderfully colourful affair with seemingly no lack of imagination for the costumes and props, but the pace of the film was oh so slow, driving even the most impressionable child to boredom. What is tragic about this version is that the dazzling list of stars takes longer to read than the compliments about the film.[3] The same accusations can be made about the 1999 version in which Tina Majorino dazzles us in her bright yellow frock while the host of other stars twinkle slowly and dimly.[4]

It is a sultry summer afternoon. Charles Dodgson (Lewis Carroll's real name) and a friend are idly rowing the three Liddell sisters along the river to find an idyllic picnic spot. Alice, Charles' personal favourite, insists he tell them one of his imaginative stories. So he begins, "Alice was considering in her mind what to do…" and it is at this time Alice has the sense to drift off to sleep for an afternoon's daydream. She spots a white rabbit checking the time, scurries down an overlarge rabbit hole. "Curious," Alice thinks and she follows him down the hole. "Everything is queer today."

The 1999 version diverges from Lewis Carroll's opening. Alice (Tina Majorino) is expected to sing at a garden party but goes off to sulk in the orchard to escape her duty. There she drifts off to sleep. In her dreams, she confronts the array of fantastical characters that help rebuild her confidence so she can sing without anxiety after she wakes up.

The author of the Alice books, Charles Dodgson (pseudonym Lewis Carroll), was a good friend of the Liddell's, and their three daughters loved him like an uncle. But as we mention in Volume Four (*Childhood Friendships*), Alice was Charles' favourite, whom he befriended, or groomed to use the modern parlance. Dodgson had acquired the new invention, a camera, and Alice, among other pre-pubescent girls, was his favourite model. He would dress her in exotic outfits to represent a little girl from the Orient and other cultures. But as Katie Roiphe tells us in her book, *She Still Haunts Me*, it was when Dodgson proudly presented to Mrs Liddell, Alice's mother, a set of nude photographs of Alice posing for him, that he was thereafter forever shunned from their household, and Dodgson was never allowed to see Alice again.

In *Dreamchild*, Alice Liddell is now a widowed elderly woman, Alice Hargreaves, on the cusp of her eightieth birthday. The year is 1932. She has been invited to New York to celebrate the centenary of Lewis Carroll's birth. She is to be awarded an honorary degree by Columbia University. As the day approaches, the journey and the harrying by journalists bring her experiences with the author back to her. "I can scarcely recall him after all these years," she tells the reporters who mob her even before she can disembark from the liner. She is still haunted by the tale, having mixed emotions – feelings of regret, guilt and gratefulness all bombard her thoughts as the film takes us back to her childhood relationship with the man who told her tales and took photographs of her (the part of young Alice being played by Amelia Shankley).

Now Mrs Hargreaves seems afraid to be alone, left with her memories. She needs the constant companionship of eighteen-year-old Lucy (Nicola Cowper). As vivid dreams flood back she exclaims, "Someone or something just stepped on my grave." We are never shown what causes the anguish in her recollections. One assumes that due to the dubious reputation labelled at Lewis Carroll, perhaps she sees some abusive aspect in the relationship. These are certainly alluded to in the reactions of her own mother, who tore up all the letters the man had written to her daughter. But as she hears the adulation she is receiving in America and at the university ceremony, she realises the true impact Charles Dodgson made to her life. "As a child I was too young to see the gift whole, to see it for what it was, to acknowledge the love that had given it birth."

The real Alice Liddell as a child was no street waif, but the daughter of a wealthy upper-class Oxford don, dean of Christ Church College and Oxford Cathedral. As a student she courted Prince Leopold, the son of Queen Victoria. As an adult she married Reginald Hargreaves in Westminster Abbey, and became lady of a large house in the New Forest with a host of servants to wait on her.[4a]

Folk Tales

The embarrassed reactions of boys, Barret Oliver and Zachery Ty Bryan in *The NeverEnding Story* and *Magic Island*, were to switch off immediately they are offered a book of fairy tales. Billy Elliot, when told that *Swan Lake* is about a woman who is captured by a magician, immediately derides, "Sounds Crap." Yet all these boys are tempted into the various folk tales and emerge with a more-rounded character as a consequence. *Billy Elliot* culminates with the boy (Jamie Bell) taking lead role in *Swan Lake* at London's *The Haymarket*.

In *Song of the South*, the make-believe stories about Brere Rabbit as told by Uncle Remus are a moralistic parable, helping keep the lonely boy Johnny (Bobby Driscoll) on the straight and narrow. Alas, his blinkered mother doesn't see it like that. "Uncle Remus, I'm trying to bring up my Johnny to be honest and truthful, but you and your stories are making that very difficult. It may be better if he didn't hear any more." Both storyteller and little boy are devastated, and both lives become poorer when deprived of allegorical tales.

And so, tradition insists the girl-child inherits the stage in most folk tales. Folk tales are the haunts for little girls, their chance to be heroines (or desolate victims) in a male-orientated world. Director Terry Gilliam was sure to implant vulnerable girls in the forest in *The Brothers Grimm*, to scream in the right places and be carried off helplessly by ogres.[5]

Devon Stockard is obsessed by the Polish folk tale of Baba Yaga in *Lawn Dogs*. She lives in her own fantasy world in which she compares all her actions to the little girl in the Baba Yaga story. Baba Yaga is a witch "who ate little girls for dinner if they went outside the village wall." As long as she was inside the wall the girl was safe.

In a way, *Lawn Dogs* is a modern fairy tale. But instead of the witch being the dangerous ogress, it is the innocent little ten-year-old girl played by Mischa Barton who has more power to do harm and ruin people's lives than any medieval witch ever had. For today, just associating with the little girl can bring down the avalanche of false accusations, of grooming, of molestation, of perverting the innocent. That is just what befalls Trent Burns, the lawnmower man. He is aware of the dangers, constantly dismisses the girl by sending her home, but is incapable of stemming the inevitable flood of accusations.

"Don't ever go outside the village gate, Sweetheart," is the instruction from mum, packing her off to sell cookies in the village. But the wooded copse beyond the village is far too tempting for the fantasizing girl. She enters the forest and spots a ramshackle trailer – Baba Yaga's house – but in reality the home of the lawn dog, Trent.

She ties red ribbons to the tree branches as in the folk tale. She pretends she is a princess and her valet has to polish her shoes. She even believes in the power of the comb and towel which she carries with her. When fleeing from danger, "by throwing the comb in the river the waters will rise behind you to cover your tracks, and by discarding the towel this causes the forest to spring up in your wake." Thus she is invincible, so she believes. This is just what she pretends will happen as her friend Trent escapes the danger that she herself has caused. But Trent only escapes the girl's imaginery fairy tale. In reality, Trent is duffed up and almost killed by vigilantes for being the unwitting participant in a girl's deluded fantasy world.

In *Pan's Labyrinth* (El Laberinto del Fauno), Ofelia (Ivana Baquero) becomes engrossed in the imaginary underworld of fairies and fauns, maybe as her way of escaping the inhumanity of the cruel war raging around her in 1944 fascist Spain. For Director Guillermo Del Toro has incorporated elements of *Alice in Wonderland*, *The Little Princess*, Hans Christian Andersen's *The Little Matchstick Girl*, and *Little Red Riding Hood* into his mesmerizing gothic masterpiece, and Ofelia even ends up wearing the ruby slippers from *The Wizard of Oz*.

Ofelia has little to do except read fairy tales, stuck as she is in a military outpost in Franco's wooded hills. "You're too old to be filling your head with fairy tales," says pregnant mother on their way to join her hated stepfather, the General of the military units. In Ofelia's eyes the General is like all step parents that the children in *Nanny McPhee* warn us about. He is as ogre-some as the Pale Man that haunts the girl in the underground passage.

A stick insect directs her into a labyrinth where she awakens a faun, part-man part-goat with curved horns and milky eyes. But within this labyrinth her own quest for life is re-awakened, the three tasks she has to undertake becoming a rite-of-passage for the little girl. In the scene where she is chased by the ogre, even horror writer Stephen King admitted he squirmed with fear when he watched this.

Her final task to gain immortality is to offer up her baby brother, but this is something she refuses to do, sacrificing her own life instead. Yet, despite failing two of the assignments, she passes the test because she has learnt to trust herself, and according to director Guillermo Del Toro, she gains immortality by joining her mother and father in the afterlife.

The fantasy world is generated in her mind as a response to the horrors of war around her, a useful escapist ploy adopted by many a traumatized child (the boy in *The Adventures of Sharkboy and*

Lavagirl similarly invents a fantasy world to blot out a spate of bullying). "Soon you'll see that life is not all fairy tales," her mother had told her. Yet mother dresses the girl to be a princess by providing her with a new green dress and new shoes. But in the labyrinth Ofelia is a princess on the inside, a legend. As the horrors intensify so her reliance on the underworld deepens; despite what her mother says, the fairy tale grows into an all-pervading reality.

Although the Australian movie, *Celia* (1988), is mainly about the impact that the rabbit epidemic has on the keeping of pet rabbits in 1950s Victoria, it is interlaced with horror themes. Shortly after the death of her beloved grandmother, Celia (Rebecca Smart) reads a children's horror book about Aboriginal monsters called *Hobyahs*. The story gives her nightmares, and these grow so that she often confuses real life with the imaginary. When the police constable who confiscated Celia's pet rabbit, appears to her during one of her horror fantasies, she confuses him with a *Hobyah* and shoots him with dad's shotgun.

In *A Little Princess*, Sara Crewe is captivated by the tale of Rama and Sita from the exotic India where she had lived in Simla before being sent to the girls' school in New York. She cheers up the other girl boarders with her lively tales. "Magic has to be believed. That's the only way it's real," she tells them. But she goes too far when she's tries to spice up one of the literary classics in the school reading session. Miss Minchin rages at her, "From now on there'll be no more make-believe at this school. It's time you learnt, Sara Crewe, that real life has nothing to do with your fantasy game. It's a cruel nasty world out there and it's our duty to make the best of it; not to indulge in ridiculous dreams." Professor Dumbledore makes a similar comment to *Harry Potter*: "It does not do to dwell on dreams and forget to live."

Little Otik (Otesánek)

This folk tale from Eastern Europe is a blend of fairy tale and horror fable. Following on from Jan Švankmajer's success with *Alice*, this movie copies some of the techniques he had used in that film, such as the repetitive close-ups of lips, and the weird animations. But the director injects an element of paedophilia into the proceedings, either to shock us, or to make us laugh at the non-threatening dirty old man. Either way, like *Lawn Dogs* provides an initiation into the world of sex and coming of age using the tale of Baba Yaga, so too in *Little Otik* a young girl is initiated into the troubling world of adults.

The tale is about a married couple, Karel and Bozenka, who are unable to have a baby. Both adults are infertile, so their frequent visits to the clinic are futile. So neurotic has the man Karel become that he starts imagining babies on a production line and being sold in the market place.

A young girl, Alzbetka, lives in the same apartment block. She runs into the street in front of his car chasing a ball and tucks it under her blouse making her look like a pregnant pre-teen. This further upsets the despondent Karel.

Yet Alzbetka appreciates the man's demise. She wants him to have a baby: she is so dissatisfied at being the only child in the building, and the only child to get the unwanted attention from the elderly Mr Zlabek. This old man hastily fumbles for his thick-rimmed spectacles every time he spots the girl on the stairs. Conscious he is looking at her knickers up her skirt, she holds down her dress over her knees. "He wanted to touch me again," complains Alzbetka to the old woman downstairs. "I can't stand that paedophile undressing me with his eyes."

This is a girl genned up on sexual issues, for her father discovers her reading a book about *Sexual Dysfunction*, either to satisfy her growing curiosity, or as an aid to sympathise with the childless couple who share the block of flats.

Karel has been uprooting a tree in his garden. As a joke, he trims around the roots to make them look like fingers and toes, and presents the stick 'baby' to his wife. Big mistake! The woman immediately adopts the inanimate chunk of wood, dressing it in baby clothes and nappies, suckles it, and even fakes morning sickness. Bozenka the wife then joyfully announces her pregnancy, and ultimately the birth, to the neighbours.

"We'll be the laughing stock!" realises Karel. Before long, Bozenka is promenading her 'newborn' along the streets, discretely covering its body from over-inquisitive eyes. But, surreptitiously, little Otik has come alive: an ever-demanding baby requiring excessive feeding, like an overgrown cuckoo in the nest. Karel even tries to drown the monster in the bath, but you cannot drown a piece of wood! Before long, Otik has become an enormous monster consuming everything it can, including the postman and the welfare officer.

Karel locks the monster in the basement out of harm's way. This is where the girl Alzbetka finds it, adopting it as if it were a pet at the zoo. She even tempts the groping Mr Zlabek down to the cellar to provide it with its next meal. Meanwhile, the girl has been reading the parallel story of Otesánek and, she reads, the only way to destroy the monster is by stealing the hoe from the old woman downstairs, because that is what the book tells her. Like Mischa Barton who uses the comb and the towel as Baba Yaga's imaginary aid in *Lawn Dogs*, so too Alzbetka sees the need to follow the story through to its conclusion. Once the child recognises she has a role to play in the folk tale, the legend must be allowed to run its course, and Alzbetka proceeds to follow the instruction book she is reading about Otesánek.

Several commentators have tried to analyse the meaning behind the fable, dressing it up as an allegory about greed and selfish ambition. Others compare this with a virgin birth, or make parallels with *Rosemary's Baby*. According to Jason Wood (BBC Home Pages), "The director (Jan Švankmajer) describes the film as touching on one of the most basic myths of civilization: the myth of Adam and Eve and the tampering with the natural order, for which the protagonists must pay a terrible price."

Santa Claus

Every young child believes in Santa Claus, boys and girls in equal measure. The trick is to convince the adults to believe as well. Santa movies often start from the premise that adults are dumb. Of course Santa is real; it's just that somewhere in the bustle of life's distractions, adults have forgotten how to believe. After all, how on earth can all those houses receive presents simultaneously on Christmas Eve around the world if Santa isn't real?

There is a second set of movies whose ambition is to spread the magic of Christmas while implanting the thought in the child's mind that maybe, just maybe, Santa may be a collective fabrication, and then proceeds to show how real Santa actually is – the stubbing the foot approach. When Buddy (Will Farrell) arrives on his quest from the North Pole in *Elf* (2003) he is shocked to discover there are people who don't believe in Santa, his own personal friend. "You're a fake!" exclaims the boy sitting on Santa's lap in the grotto of Gimbell's toy store. This lack of faith is a serious matter, for faith is what fuels Santa's sleigh. As supplies of 'Christmas spirit' deplete, so Santa's sleigh plummets into New York's Central Park. Lift-off can only be achieved by the world in unison reviving the Christmas spirit by a communal singsong, just as Tinkerbell needed the combined faith of the audience to revitalise her flagging magic.

Miracle on 34th Street promotes the 'adults are dumb' technique, then sentimentally sets out to re-educate the world of grown-ups. Two versions of this delightful film have been made. In 1994, seven-year-old Mara Wilson was required to play a little girl who did not believe in Santa Claus. This must have been a confusing role for the child, for I am sure she, like all other boys and girls her age, still believed in the magic of Christmas. So what a disappointment her first acting role must have been. "I didn't believe in Santa last year but I still got everything I asked for," says her character, Susan Walker. But this girl has been taught by her sceptical mother to only believe in tangibles (as the 1947 movie phrases it). Kriss Kringle rebukes the mother, "If you can't believe in anything by faith then you are doomed to a life dominated by doubt." As the girl warms to Kriss Kringle, she starts to have doubts about her *dis*belief. "Do I have to not believe in Santa right away?" In the ensuing court case, Santa is proved to be real, and the placards held up by protesters in the street, "I believe!" help sway the argument in the way that the audience crying out in Peter Pan effects a reaction from Tinkerbell, "I do believe in fairies, I do, I do."

In the 1947 version, Natalie Wood plays the seven-year-old who has been taught to disbelieve in Santa, fairies, legends, and myths. At least this girl does not ask Kriss Kringle to act as God by giving her a baby brother – just a nice house with a swing, that will help convince her! "Faith is believing in things when commonsense tells you not to," says Kriss, and this is confirmed by Edward Asner in *Elf* (2003) who tells us, "Christmas spirit is believing, not seeing."

Now, what of the presents requested from Santa in our materialistic times? Is it gameboys and dolls, puppies and baseball kits? Whoa no! Part of the requisition list in both *Miracle on 34th Street* versions was for mum to team up with that "nice Mr Galley". This seems to be on the universal wish list in the mindset of screenwriters who try to imagine the most precious dreams of children (in my grandma's case this seems to have been socks). Thora Birch asks for her mum and dad to reunite in *All I want for Christmas*, while in *Single Santa Seeks Mrs Claus* the child (Dominic Scott Kay) asks for a new dad. "Daddy's in Heaven. I was thinking about asking Santa for a dad," says the seven-year-old. If only life was so compliant.

Single Santa Seeks Mrs Claus seems to copy many of the storylines from *Miracle on 34th Street*: the boy Jack is baffled by the Santa debate, and St Nick's son has his job cut out trying to convince Jack's mum that Santa is real – a matrimonial requirement. Even sitting a deaf girl on Santa's knee with the genial old man signing to her is purloined from the classic. And so are the sentiments: "The last thing Jack needs just now is to put hope and dreams in things that are not real." But of course things turn out all right. "How cool is this," declares little Jack. I'm going to have Santa for my dad."

Fairy Tales

"You do nothing but fill her head with fairy stories. She lives in a fantasy world," complains Richard Grant referring to his daughter (Elle Fanning) in *The Nutcracker* (2010). This fanciful world filled with fairies, sprites and pixies is a girls' world from which boys are definitely excluded.

Most stories labelled as *fairy tales* don't even feature fairies at all – Cinderella, Snow White, etc. Maybe Hans Christian Anderson and the brothers Grimm have to be blamed for their inappropriate misuse of the term. Yet Shakespeare gave us a glimpse of fairy realms in *A Midsummer Night's Dream*, and Kipling allowed us *Puck of Pook Hill* as our guide to the mystical legends of our history.

Fairies and little girls are as synonymous as elves and toadstools: a book of *Flower Fairies* found on many a little girl's bookshelf, and a fairy costume in her wardrobe. We have J M Barrie to thank for bringing the delight of fairies to every child's imagination as Tinkerbell hobnobs with pirates, red Indians and with Peter Pan himself. Every child who attends a pantomime knows how to close its eyes and clap very loudly chanting the timeless acknowledgement, "*I do believe in fairies, I do, I do.*" The evocation of the supernatural goblin makes a wish-granting God more accessible, just as Santa Claus makes him more tangible.

Yet it is the hypocritical adult who coaxes the child into this wishful thinking. The believing child (Drew Barrymore) in *ET The Extra-Terrestrial* is already aware of the supernatural alien, and does not need further convincing. As her mother encourages her to chant "*I do believe in fairies*" as she reads the bedtime story, the child is already aware that supernatural ET is watching through the slats in the wardrobe door, a being of which mother is oblivious. (Evidently, the infant Drew Barrymore was mesmerised by ET believing it to be a real living character, and was quite disappointed to discover after the filming had been completed that it was just a mock-up model.)

According to the director (Andrei Konchalasky) of *The Nutcracker* (2010), "Fairy Tales are based on miscommunication between parents and children. If relationships were good, there would be no fairy tale." Mary (Elle Fanning) had become involved in a 'sublimating fantasy', a make-believe world created in her mind as a substitute for undevoted parents. I wonder if child psychologists have cottoned-on to this as a clinical prognosis, that the fairy-obsessed child must obviously be showing symptoms of suffering neglectful abuse at home (if director Konchalasky's theories are to be accepted).

Like *Fairy Tale* (1997) released in the same year, and covering a similar topic, *Photographing Fairies* is not what you would perceive a fairy story to be about. It is not primarily a fantasy tale. Although fairies may take up the bulk of the film, it is the psychological impact their possibility has on a public seeking reassurance about death, the afterlife, and spiritualism, around the time of the First World War – a time when many lives had been tragically stolen by war from devoted parents desperate to make some contact with their dead loved ones. These are fairy tales for adults. Naturally, the child believes but the adult feels constrained by tragic events to grope for a god-like substitute to negate the pain of war.

Two little girls, ten-year-old Ana Templeton (Miriam Grant) and seven-year-old Clara Templeton (Hannah Bould), play in the wooded dell near the stream in their Yorkshire village of

Cottingley, between Bingley and Bradford. Here, they play with their toy theatre with cut-out characters and cut-out fairies. They take photographs of fairies standing on the palms of their hands and flying around an old oak tree. The photos are so lifelike they are published, and baffle a whole generation of Edwardian Londoners. In fact, for years and years, the truth remained a mystery, and it was not until the girls grew into adulthood and then old age and one of them died, did the other cousin feel she was released from her promise of maintaining the deception.

Charles Castle, himself a photographer, had lost his bride the day after they were married. She fell down a crevasse while honeymooning in Switzerland in 1912. He is a sceptic about spiritual matters but if only he could make contact with his dead wife! He attends a spiritualist meeting where the photos of the Cottingley fairies are being shown. "Fairies – handmaidens of nature assisting in propagation and growth," the lecturer tells the audience. "Exiles from Heaven. God's orphans straddling this world and the next." But Charles disrupts the meeting, and using his technical knowledge of photography explains why the photographs are fake. At the meeting is the renowned sleuth writer himself, Sir Arthur Conan Doyle. "We are pioneers exploring the borderland between this world and the next one," he explains. But Charles retorts, "It is a crime to offer people hope when there is none."

But the next day, Charles has a visitor to his studios. It is the mother of the two girls. She claims to have seen the fairies herself and urges Charles to look more closely at the pictures. When Charles blows up the photos in his laboratory, he notices the clear reflection of a fairy in the eyes of one of the girls and his curiosity is aroused. Ignoring his important appointments, he races up to Yorkshire to seek out the two girls and the valley where the fairies were seen.

This is how he becomes involved with the Templeton family: the abrupt scary vicar (Ben Kingsley), his two charming but evasive daughters, and his mesmerising wife who provokes him to search out the truth despite the vicar's jealousy.

The clue to seeing the spectres lies in the white flower, looking like edelweiss (and probably is wild garlic), which when eaten gives a person vivid hallucinations, reveals everything in slow motion, and creates wonderful dreams. Alas, when the victim is drugged by the flower's spell they are tempted to climb the oak tree to reach the fairies floating higher in its branches that only they can see. Little Clara eats a flower and is mesmerised by the encircling fairies that she can now see in slow motion. She is drawn to climb the heavy boughs of the oak tree, irrationally oblivious to any danger. "She's in slow time," Ana warns us, before Clara's terrible fall. During the course of the film, mother, Clara, and Charles are all enticed to climb higher which inevitably results in devastating falls with smashed blooded skulls.

But Charles has seen the vision, and he has been given a vivid sensual dream of his wife, and is convinced the fairies can provide contact with his beloved.

Charles urges his colleague up from London with all their technical camera equipment. His colleague is obstructive, "You can't capture God with a camera. It's not the proof you need – it's faith." Even so, he sets up his super speed and time-lapse equipment, eats his white flower and experiences the fairy hallucinations that are too blurred to convince his colleague.

Alas, there is a distraught and jealous vicar to deal with who smashes the equipment, fells the oak tree, but is spiked to death in the ensuing brawl. Charles, wanting a tangible reunion with his dead wife, is happy to own up to the crime, and is put on death row knowing that "death is only a change of state, is only a footfall away." Miss Gidden in *Turn of the Screw* was similarly happy to exchange the ghostly apparition she has witnessed for the gallows. Perhaps then, Kasha Kropinski was mistaken in her narration to *The Story of an African Farm*, "It's only fairy tales that end nicely."

Fairy Tale (1997) handles the same story as *Photographing Fairies* but gears it towards a children's audience. Even so, it is a thoroughly absorbing film, placing what is essentially a fantasy tale into its historical context of 1917, towards the end of World War One. The famous celebrity characters remain: Sir Arthur Conan Doyle (played by Peter O'Toole), and Harry Houdini (Harvey Keitel) the renowned escapologist, both captivated by the theosophical possibilities, both seeking psychic answers following the death of a loved one.

But in this version, the Templeton children, offspring of the local vicar, are substituted for the genuine characters in the true story: twelve-year-old Elsie Wright (played by Florence Hoath) and her eight-year-old cousin Frances Griffiths (played by vivacious Elizabeth Earl) who has come to stay with her Aunt Polly and Uncle Arthur while her own father is feared lost in the battlefields of northern France. Even references made to the location are genuine, referring to Cottingley, the Yorkshire village on the south bank of the River Aire. "In six months, twelve-year-old Elsie can start at Cottingley Mill, safe in the knowledge she has a job for life!" (Joe Cooper in his biography of the two girls tells us that Elsie was seventeen, and Frances was ten.[5a])

Yet, because this is a tale made for children, we see actual fairies, which makes it hard to explain why the story was finally unmasked as a fake when we ourselves get to witness with our very own eyes the fairies flying around the beck.

These are children who live with fairies. There is no doubt in *their* minds. "Ask any child, *'who tends our garden?'* and they will reply 'fairies'." These are kids who intuitively know that, "if you step inside a fairy ring you'll be captured and taken away forever. Everyone knows that!" says Elsie. When they make a pact together by burning hot candle wax over their hands, they are not making a promise to maintain the trickery. No, these girls are conservationists, privileged guardians of a fairy glen, fully aware of what will ensue if hordes of reporters and tourists come sniffing around. And they do. It is not long before Conan Doyle and Houdini turn up, convinced. Then the incompetent man from *The Argus* tracks them down and reports the location, so that soon lonely old widows seeking psychic contacts, families with picnic baskets, and children with fishing nets arrive, ready to capture their own fairy to keep in a jar.

Fairies are obviously real. Ask anyone who has seen Peter Pan, a character invented in the same soul-searching era. It is just that "grown ups don't know how to believe." So when father interrogates the girls, "How did you do it?" they are baffled by the absurdity of the question. "We just took the photographs, dad."

Even an expert in photographic fakery confirms the photos are genuine, "as genuine as the king's beard."

While father has his down-to-earth refusal to believe – "There are no fairies at the bottom of my garden," he tells Houdini – mother is not so sure. She wants to believe, if it will bring her close to her infant son who died. She is left with a devoted mother's dilemma: "I don't know what frightens me more: the children lying to us, or telling the truth!"

Theosophical author, Joe Cooper, has written a balanced analysis of this dupe in his book *The Case of the Cottingley Fairies* in which he explains how the two Yorkshire children were able to convince the experts, and maintain the deception almost to their dying days. Evidently the older child, seventeen-year-old Elsie, had been a talented artist for her age and attended art college. Throughout her childhood she enjoyed drawing fairies. It seems she managed to convince her impressionable cousin, Frances, who had recently arrived in England from parched South Africa. At nine years of age, Frances was enchanted by the verdant dell behind their garden. Seemingly, the older girl convinced her younger cousin that the fairies were real. The photographs were taken to try to convince mother, too, to allow them to continue playing beside the stream that made their clothes dirty and their shoes wet (mother had banned the girls from playing in the stream). From there, the dupe spiralled out of control, and the girls were trapped into maintaining the deception, even though Frances remained a believer all her life.

The Cottingley children of the films were at the age when belief in fairies was still part of their childhood fantasy. Though they were aware they took photos of cardboard cut-outs this in no way degraded their belief in fairies; they were as tangible as any child's prayer or any communicant's communion, or any psychics lucky charm. For a more fanciful tale of fairies and goblins, we have to turn to *The Fairy King of Ar*. In this film, as well as a girl (Brittney Bomann), we have a boy actor (Jameson Baltes). The boy has to put aside his male aspirations and feign interest in a tale about magic, a trait we don't expect from girls.

A happy family inherits an *olde worlde* property on the Isle of Man. The story begins with a long-winded narration of a fairy tale, being read by Kyle and Evie's grandma, describing how a realm of fairies was buried when a gold mine collapsed. "Cool!" says the boy, obviously embarrassed but pretending to be riveted. Arriving at their new home in the countryside, it is not long before a female fairy lands on Evie's hand. Though the children can see the fairies, all that the adults can see are flitting fireflies.

Evie makes friends with Thumbeleen (Leigh Greyvenstein), and the fairy even heals the cut on her finger. But can she cure father of his infuriating cough? No. It takes strenuous hard work and team effort against the opposition of the obstinate locals in order to re-open the mine and re-awaken the fairies buried there, before father can be cured by the grateful King of Ar himself.

The fairy in *Five Children and It* is not the traditional type of fairy. As Poppy Rogers playing Jane comments, "I thought fairies wore ballet dresses and wings and wands." The fairy these five children discover on the beach is encased in a giant clam shell with a monstrous reptilian head – a *Psammead*, or sand fairy – ancient enough to be sagacious but cute enough to be adored by the cast and young viewing audience alike.

In common with all fairies, the Psammead is able to grant wishes. The children are not hesitant at asking for wishes either, and the fairy is only too happy to oblige. After all, 'wishing' is a common word among children's vocabulary. They flippantly wish for household chores to be completed, for the ability to fly, or for gold, and end up with baskets of the stuff. But the wishes only create grief in the long run. Their wishes are selfish and thus none of them lasts. "What's the point of wishes that don't last?" declares Freddie Highmore. For their final wish, when they hear father is missing behind enemy lines, they selflessly wish for his safe return. As usual, the wish is only temporary, but father apparates for long enough for him to be given the compass that his son had been keeping safe.

At least the Psammead had some degree of cuteness, and the efforts of Eddie Izzard gave him humour. The depiction of the wish-granting creature in *Munchie* appeared ludicrous and infuriating. A bullied schoolboy (Jaime McEnnan) comes to terms with the enemies he can't face, the new stepdad he doesn't want, and the pretty girl he adores (Love Hewitt), all effortlessly completed with the help of a rigid scary-looking gnome-sized doll who, with the click of its fingers, can make everything right – a sort of cop-out fantasy inculcating disagreeable notions of selfishness and lethargy among our young generation.

As we have mentioned, belief in the mystical world of fairies was revived when the news of the Cottingley Fairies was publicised, and the possibility was pursued at a time when the tragedy of war compelled a nation to seek psychic contact with deceased family members. In recent times, the world of fairies has become a creative way of clinging on to a magical past that has been lost in our matter-of-fact times. As Zoë Wanamaker, who plays Martha the housekeeper in *Five Children and It*, points out: "The world is too explained, now."

In the past decade or so, there has been an epidemic of acquiring fairy artefacts. Gift shops are full of collectable models of fairies, in lead, brass, porcelain, crockery, or plastic. Many of these depict naked or semi-naked young girls dressed as fairies, as if, to put a set of angel wings on a naked figure of a girl somehow makes it more artistically permissible and less pornographic. Today, music and therapy CDs encourage people to get back in touch with their guardian angel. Newsagents are replete with annual *Flower Fairy* calendars and *Tinkerbell* stationery packs. Dance DVDs encourage infant girls to dress up as fairies (*Dance like the Flower Fairies*). This is becoming almost a religious cult as children are deified as *Earth Angels, Star Angels, Indigo Children*, souls with healing energies. Children are ready to be exploited in new mysterious ways. [6]

Magic

With children's lively imagination, they can be led to believe anything is possible. This explains the wide success of any production involving magic. The magic can be generated accidentally, the genie appearing from a lamp or an urn, inexplicably through a tornado or the arrival of a unicorn, or the child can try to generate the magic itself by concocting magic charms or incanting spells. But magic doesn't need to be so specialised. Byron Taylor, curious about card tricks, found himself in the right place at the right time when he moves next door to the ideal tutor: the twentieth century reincarnation of the medieval Merlin in *The Sorcerer's Apprentice*, but the boy was exhorted to just close his eyes and believe. "Look, you don't teach magic like you teach maths."

For David Moscow playing the young Joshua Baskin in *Big* (1988), he had only to put his twenty-five cent coin in an arcade slot machine to have his wish granted. Joshua had only wanted to be bigger so he could accompany a girl (Kimberley M Davis) on a funfair ride, but his small stature excluded him. If only he could be taller… "Your wish is granted," pronounces Zoltair, even though the machine is unplugged. Despite being magically turned into a grown up (Tom Hanks) with all its mind-bending possibilities, he spends the bulk of the film wishing he was young again. This is a film with a covert message for the child who craves to be allowed more freedom and wishing to be allowed to make adult choices: that the real world is a harsh competitive arena, full of back-stabbing, bickering and sexual innuendo. The boy, Joshua, can only survive as an adult by doing child-like things, such as inspiring new lines in a toy business.

For Lindsay Lohan playing Casey Stewart in *Life-Size* she has acquired a book of spells, which she hopes will resurrect her dead mother. Having set up her magic table for the incantation she is distracted, her doll falls on to the display, and instead of her mother appearing, the girl is lumbered with an infuriating living adult Barbie. For Casey, the magic hasn't worked (so she thinks) but instead the girl is given help to grieve for her dead mother and move on in life.

Ingenious is a TV drama about magic. Instead of a Psammead character who grants wishes, there is an *Aladdin*-style genie that grants three wishes to the children who rub the mysterious glass urn they have found among the garbage on their grandmother's Cheshire farm. "There isn't any magic in Macclesfield!" derides the sceptical Sally (Hannah Godfrey). But the benevolent genie appears. Like all their predecessors who are given magic wishes, they squander them with their indiscriminate use of the word 'wish' in their vocabulary. But instead of asking for trivialities the children ask for irreversible or impossible requests such as, "If you are a genie can you bring back my mum and dad?" In the end, Sally and her friends, Patch (Leah Sheshadri) and Spikey (Keaton Lansley), are exasperated by the prevaricating genie (Amit Shah). "What's the point of a wish if you can't wish for it?"

In all these films, as we saw with the items on the Christmas wish lists for Santa Claus, it is the altruistic wish that becomes the key. *Chitty Chitty Bang Bang* only sprouts wings when Grandpa is in danger and needs saving. Grandma in *Ingenious* needs help because her farm is about to be taken over by a developer unless she can find more funds. Now, this is more within the genie's powers, and a valuable ruby found in the ground helps save the day. The sentimental ending about grandma's farm being saved is reinforced by the maxim, "Love is the strongest magic in the world."

Others stumble into the world of magic. *The Wizard of Oz* is quintessentially a film about a good orphan girl, Dorothy, trying to get by on a planet where adults are too busy to listen and console her. She lives in the tedium of a black and white world with her Aunt Em. As her dog, Toto, strays into the garden of obnoxious Mrs Scott, Dorothy wishes she could "find herself a place where she won't get into any trouble." A tornado hits Kansas, Dorothy is knocked unconscious and ends up in a fantasy land of bright cheerful colours with its mysterious characters. "Toto, I've a feeling we're not in Kansas anymore. We must be over the rainbow."

A magic tale has to be full of morals. For the brainless scarecrow (who is already starting to think) "Well what would you do with a brain if you had one?" For the heartless Tin Man (who is starting to love), "A heart is not judged by how much you love, but by how much you are loved by others." And along with the timid lion (who is already finding his courage) they set off to confront the Wizard. This is a world of magic, yet our heroes never wield any of it for themselves. They resort solely on commonsense, purposefulness, and ingenuity. For, despite the Wizard's alleged knowledge and awe, it is the child herself who, with the click of her ruby slippers, accesses that most powerful of magic: maternal love. "If ever I go looking for my hearts desire, I won't look any further than my own backyard."

Perhaps the reason *Chitty Chitty Bang Bang* did not achieve the same phenomenal reviews as *The Wizard of Oz* is because the children, Jeremy and Jemima (Adrian Hall and Heather Ripley), were escorted to Vulgaria by adults (Caractacus Potts and Truly Scrumptious). This was not a magical tale of a child's solitary quest into the unknown. While *The Wizard of Oz* is presented as a real expedition undertaken by a runaway teen (albeit Dorothy was vortexed there in a coma), *Chitty Chitty Bang Bang* is just a story told by Dick van Dyke on the beach, rather than the flights of fancy of a child's imagination. But don't get me wrong – this is one of my favourite films of all time.

Many magical movies exist as entrapping nightmares, ensnaring its captives in a hellish sequence of events until the supernatural spews them back to reality. "What do you mean, the game thinks?" exclaims thirteen-year-old Sarah Whittle warily. This is the game, *Jumanji*, that she and her boyfriend, Alan Parrish, have just begun to play. They have just rolled the dice and are committed. There is no escape from the game. On each throw of the dice, something catastrophic happens, but they all know they can't escape until the game is completed. First, they are attacked by a swarm of giant mosquitoes with needle-like proboscides, sharp enough to penetrate doors and glass. Then a troop of monkeys are released which cause havoc in the kitchen and later drive off in the police car. Next, a lion begins to stalk them. "It's not real, Peter, it's an hallucination," cowers Judy before both of them run for their lives.

"You think monkeys, mosquitoes and lions are bad," jests Robin Williams. "That's only the beginning. I have seen things you've only seen in your nightmares."

A scary trigger-happy safari hunter pursues them relentlessly with his blunderbuss. Next is a stampede of rhinos and elephants which storm through the community. A monsoon brings floods, triffid-like plants overgrow the house turning it into a jungle, and finally an earthquake splits the whole property in two.

If only a better warning had been given by the two scared boys who had secretly buried the game one hundred years earlier hoping it would never be found. "What if someone digs it up?" asks one of the boys. "May God have mercy on his soul!" the other replies.

In *The Little Unicorn*, the magic is much tamer: a pet pony that gives birth to a magical unicorn which becomes the target for paparazzi and circus acts. Eleven-year-old Brittney Bomann and Byron Taylor have their work cut out to keep the pet from being stolen. It's magic, however, was used only once – when it instantly healed Polly's grazed knee. The magic in *ET The Extra-Terrestrial* is taken a stage further. Not only does the alien heal Elliott's cut finger, he has the power to help people fly and causes flowers to bloom.

The child actors in *Peter Pan* must have had the time of their lives flying through the air, swinging on ropes, playing pirates and Indians, and sword fighting. All children dream of being able to fly, so with the arrival of Peter Pan in the Darlings' nursery, naturally Wendy (Rachel Hurd-Wood) and her two brothers want to join him. "John, Michael, there's a boy here who is to teach us to fly!" after Pan promises, "I'll teach you to ride the wind's back."

And off they fly, lifted by magic up into the heavens, through the clouds and landing, like Dorothy in *The Wizard of Oz* or like Jeremy and Jemima in *Chitty Chitty Bang Bang*, in a magical land full of pirates, Indians, mermaids, and Tinkerbell the fairy, where they all enjoy a rollickingly good set of adventures.

In this land the weather and climate, the loves and jealousies, are all determined, like Cupid's bow, by the magical sprite, Tinkerbell, who shakes fairy dust wherever she goes. While Tinkerbell leaves Neverland, the country is cast into deep winter; when she returns, the ice melts and spring arrives, as if Aslan were returning to Narnia. When Tinkerbell sacrifices herself to save Peter Pan from poisoning, storm clouds rapidly descend, and the whole world can only be saved by the cast, crew and audience repeating the magical chant, "I do believe in fairies, I do, I do!"

The Harry Potter Series

The series of books by J K Rowling that the films are based upon really fired the imagination of Britain's children; even reluctant readers could be found with their heads in these novels. They take the reader beyond the usual formula of fairies and princesses into the magical world of wizards and wizardry, and at last, boys are allowed into the dreamworld of children. As literary works, the books are not necessarily any better than their predecessors, for example Jill Murphy's *The Worst Witch*, yet the Harry Potter series sold like hot cakes. The films likewise were an immediate success and the hype surrounding their release ensured instant stardom (and wealth) for its three principal child stars: Daniel Radcliffe, Emma Watson and Rupert Grint.

The cleverness of the books also ensured a continuum of readership. The first in the series, *The Philosopher's Stone,* was aimed at middle-school kids, and its subsequent filming was entertaining, though not scary. As the plot progressed, by the time the seventh book was published, the three child stars are now young adults, the storyline now dark and involved, and even Daniel Radcliffe himself (Harry Potter) admitted finding it scary watching some of the sequences in *The Deathly Hallows.*

At Hogwarts, their timetable consists of potions, the dark arts, divination, ancient runes, etc. They are taught, according to Professor Snape, "how to bewitch the mind, ensnare the senses, bottle fame, brew glory, and put a stopper on death."

Hagrid is the favourite teacher of the three children. He takes a personal interest in the progress of Harry Potter right from the very first day when he secretes the orphaned baby away from danger to be raised by Uncle Vernon and Aunt Petunia, "the only family he has."

In *The Philosopher's Stone*, Harry Potter uses his natural wizardry skills to rescue his friend, Hermione, from an evil troll that is destroying the girl's bathroom. His most useful possession, besides the Nimbus 2000 broomstick that ensures he becomes star of the aerial game of Quidditch, is his invisibility cloak. This helps him sneak into out-of-bounds localities and evade capture. But his greatest challenge, which he can only accomplish with the help of his friends – Hermione's knowledge and brains, and Ron's down-to-Earth practicality – is to rescue the philosopher's stone from the clutches of Voldemort, the elixir of life that will make its owner immortal.

In *The Chamber of Secrets*, the formless evil Voldemort is finding a way to gain human form through the body of Tom Riddle. Harry Potter comes up against some of Voldemort's human cronies in the guise of Lucius Malfoy who tries to arrange for Dumbledore and Hagrid's demise, and who uses his slave/servant Dobby to stifle Harry's progress. Voldemort sees Potter as his main opponent and tempts the boy wizard into the chamber of secrets where the giant basilisk will finish him off. But with the help of the phoenix, the boy is able to kill the monster and be rid of Voldemort (for the time being).

The *Prisoner of Azkaban* is a much deeper film with a different director. Here, Harry Potter has to deal with dementors, ghost-like apparitions that feed on the spirit and soul of a human and look somewhat like the Death Eaters from Mordor in *The Lord of the Rings*. The dementors are guarding Hogwarts School to protect it against the murderous Cyrius Black who has escaped from Azkaban Prison. Why are such evil creatures placed around the school when there is so much danger? It would be safer to send a pack of panthers to guard a kindergarten, or a posse of paedophiles to protect an orphanage! Anyway, their protection is inadequate as they attack Harry during a game of Quidditch, and later almost suck out all his lifeblood, and the supposed enemy Cyrius Black is able to penetrate their ineffective wall of defence. "Black could be anywhere. It's like trying to catch smoke with your bare hands."

In this film, it is Hermione who saves the day using a tool she acquired to help her attend all the classes at school: a watch that can turn back time. Using it, she and Harry can save Hagrid's pet hippogriff from execution, release Cyrius Black from the tower, evade Professor Lupin who has turned into a werewolf, and help capture Peter Pettigrew, who has taken the form of Ron's pet rat, Scabbers. Finally, she offers Harry a second chance to defend himself against the hordes of dementors that are slowly sucking his soul to death.

In the first three films of the Harry Potter series, the children are using the knowledge derived from their lessons, the wonderment of witnessing their potions and charms working before their disbelieving eyes. However, the fourth and subsequent films seem less intriguing (to me), and if you will forgive my contradictory phrase, the magic seems to have been taken out of the magic. Instead of brewing special potions, or using clever maps to ascertain where danger lies, we have bombastic blasts in which people can be transported to different places with just the wave of a wand, a feat even God might be hard pressed to perform. It becomes all too mechanically convenient, as Harry becomes a god-like superman on the par with the dark lord Voldemort.

Witches and Witchcraft

Many stories written about witches have their origins in fairy tales told to children tucked into bed, with covert warnings not to get up in the night, nor stray far from parental care. The witches are now fabled: *Baba Yaga* who eats children (yet is deified by Mischa Barton in *Lawn Dogs*), the old hag with a basket of poisoned apples in *Snow White*, the long-fingered woman in the gingerbread house in *Hansel and Gretel*, Queen Jadis in *The Lion, the Witch and the Wardrobe*, *The Snow Queen*, while in the *Wizard of Oz*, witches seem to appear from every compass point in the merry old land of Oz.

That many of these witches double as evil queens or stepmothers show how the term witch has been used to implicate a mature woman whose beauty or popularity may have waned. We can all recognise her features: a bent back, a wen on the nose, long in the tooth, and always portrayed as ugly and evil. Herein lies a prejudiced ambiguity. Pretty witches are not evil. Dorothy learns that to be so when a star apparates into pretty Glinda the Good Witch, and as the youngsters discover about *Nanny McPhee*: as a strict disciplinarian she is ugly, but her warts and buck teeth diminish as the children warm to her.

In African culture the witchdoctor is male, as is the Native American shaman, to whom *Huck Finn* visited clinging believingly onto every word uttered from the forked tongue: "Your future is drifting like the river," says the old rogue, tongue firmly in his cheek. But in white westernised communities witches are always female. So inevitably on screen, these roles are played by women and girls. The modern trend is to taunt trembling teenagers with adult horror titles such as *The Craft, The Crucible, The Witches of Eastwick, Little Witches, Suspiria*, and *The Blair Witch Project*.

But for the younger viewing public, the witch is made more personable and less frightening, having a blend of wickedness and comic goofability, exemplified by the three Henderson sisters (Bette Midler, Sarah Jessica Parker and Kathy Najima) in *Hocus Pocus*, the three aunts (Shelley Duvall, Teri Garr, and Cathy Moriaty) in *Casper meets Wendy*, by Grotbags in *Emu's World*, Miss Ernst in Roald Dahl's *The Witches*, and Grandma Frump in *The Addams Family*.

Other films have given the modern day witch an aura of normality. In the 1960s comedy series and 2005 movie *Bewitched* she is just your typical housewife. Jill Murphy's sequence of books about *The Worst Witch* (Mildred Hubble) spawned a made-for-TV film featuring Fairuza Balk, and inspired other titles such as *Sabrina the Teenage Witch, The Wizards of Waverly Place*, and even the *Harry Potter* series, in which the girl-child has equality with male wizards and can aspire to magical powers of witchcraft. Hermione Granger has restored credibility to the black art – just your typical schoolgirl but with a formidable secret. "She's just a little child! What's so special about *her*?" demands Desmond Spellman in *Casper meets Wendy*. Like *Matilda*, Hermione and Wendy are just innocuous girls who help cement the aspirations of little girls everywhere. This has coincided with the popularity of Halloween, which gives the girl-child the chance to dress up scarily, engendering a renewed interest in covens, and to be dressed as a Goth is nowadays accepted as a fashion statement.

It was not always so. Witches don't exist in distant folklore as mere fables. Both America and Britain have witches firmly associated with medieval toil and trouble: the Pendle Witch Trial in Lancashire in 1612, and the Salem Witch Trials in Massachusetts in 1692, place hubble-bubble within a historical timeframe. In practice, the medieval witch was a misunderstood ecological genius, providing herbal remedies which, alas, were seen as an antithesis to the established church who considered it 'the practice of evil magic based on a pact with the devil'. Women who practised herbology were 'reputed to have the 'evil eye' which caused wasting away or death of the person or animal on whom the witch looked'.[7] More likely, the accused was simply a boss-eyed Catholic living in a Protestant community who refrained from attending the established church,[8] and was shunned, and ultimately denounced, for being a misfit.

At least, films like *Hocus Pocus* try to fit the movie within a historical context, explaining how events in seventeenth century Salem had repercussions for Dani and her older brother Max. Ten-year-old Thora Birch plays Dani, a vivacious fun-loving younger sister to Max (Omri Katz) who, like Margaret O'Brien in the Halloween sequence in *Meet Me in St. Louis*, and like Hilary Duff in *Casper meets Wendy*, seems to steal each frame she appears in. It is 1993. Dani is hiding in the wardrobe of her brother's bedroom while the boy is passionately dreaming of his girlfriend, Alison. Dani bursts through the wardrobe door and rolls on the bed in delight taunting him, "I'm Alison, kiss me, I'm Alison!"

"I thought I told you to stay out of my room," Max rebukes her.

But tonight is Halloween night, and older brother has to escort Dani trick-or-treating through the American town of Salem. When they bump into girlfriend Alison the three of them decide to break into the Haunted House Museum. The museum has been preserved as it was left in 1693 when the three witches who lived there were hanged for abducting young children.

The witches had stolen one girl, Emily (played by Amanda Shepherd). "Come child," the witches cackle, and she is invited to sit in front of the cauldron where they are brewing the spell which will grant to them everlasting youthfulness once they have sucked the life force out from the girl. "One sip of this and her life will be ours!" But Emily's brother intervenes just in time. "You hag, there are not enough children in the world to make you young and beautiful," and with that, the spell is diverted onto the boy turning him into a black cat that never dies. The three witches are captured and hung.

Forward to 1993, Max makes the error of lighting the magic candle – the cursed candle which when lit by a virgin brings the witches back to life again. I am not sure of the message this Disney film wanted to project here. Are we meant to laugh at Max, a teenager, still a virgin at his age! Or are we meant to admire him in an age when all boys boast about their conquests, Max is admirably still a virgin?

Because his action has released a string of spooky misadventures, it's as if his two female companions are blaming him, not for lighting the candles, but for still being a virgin. So, the three medieval witches come alive again but do not seem out of place, because this is Halloween night. They pursue their original aim of capturing the child to gain everlasting youthfulness.

Being trick-or-treat night there is no shortage of possible victims, and Dani seems a perfect choice!

Casper meets Wendy is a piece of innocuous fun, a sequel for the *Casper* ghost series. It allows one preteen child (Hilary Duff) to run riot with a magic wand while finding friendship with the lonely ghost. Here, any pretence that a witch is a frightening ogre is long forgotten as Casper compliments his new young friend, "Are you really a witch? I just didn't realise witches were so cute."

HORROR

As in so many other strands of the make-believe story, it is little girls who are called upon to take a prominent role in horror movies, too. Scriptwriters and audiences empathise with the vulnerable girl trapped in the perverse arms of a monster, such as the sexualised Ann Darrow in the clutches of *King Kong*. Horror movies are made even more startling when the innocent little girl starts taking on a monstrous or demonic role herself. As we shall see, the angelic child that materialises into a vampire or a ghost or into a serial child killer is to be shunned and feared. As Henry James said, "No one will ever know whether children are monsters or monsters are children."

The fear factor is not exploited so rigorously with little boys. For Freddie Booth in *The Mummy Returns*, he was like Short Round (Ke Huy Quan) in *Indiana Jones*, just caught up in the incredulous buffoonery of it all. "Mum, dad, I can explain everything!" cries Freddie as the ancient Egyptian pillars collapse like dominos. Only in *Child's Play* is the six-year-old boy, Andy (Alex Vincent), armed with a knife ready to defend himself against his demonic doll. "You're an abomination, an outrage against nature, and you have to be stopped... Chucky's here, and he's going to kill me," whimpers the boy.

But first, the child as a vulnerable innocent: a child such as Jodie in *The Amityville Horror*, murdered in her bedroom closet by a maniacal father, but left to haunt the new occupants of her Long Island home. The girl is an innocent but she perpetuates the horror as a link between the past and the present. It is only a living girl, Chelsea Lutz, who can see her rocking in the bedroom chair and playing with the hand-me-down teddy bear. This hand-me-down doll seems to be a theme perpetuated in horror movies. In *An American Haunting* it was a doll with a cracked head that accompanied Betsy Bell (Rachel Hurd-Wood) to be rediscovered generations later to provide a catalyst for the further haunting of new arrival Jane (Isabelle Almgreen-Doré).

Two version of *The Amityville Horror* were made. In 2005 Chloë Grace Moretz and in 1975 Natasha Ryan play the living child. Jodie, the ghost, does not frighten them because "Jodie is my friend," says Natasha. When Jodie (Isabel Conner) invites the babysitter to poke her finger through the bullet hole in her head the babysitter goes berserk, driven insane with fright as she is trapped in the closet. But Jodie can't be blamed for being so scary. She is a victim herself, trapped in eternal torment, in a never-ending game of ghostly hide-and-seek with the evil man who is forever trying to track her down.

These scenarios must have been truly frightening for the child actors taking part in them. Yet while we the audience are recoiling in horror and the babysitter is freaking out, Isabel Conner is leading the probing finger into the hole in her forehead beaming with a mischievous smile. This actress is not traumatised at all by the role she has to play.

Likewise, as we shall see shortly, one would expect Heather O'Rourke to be scared witless in *Poltergeist* (1982), but instead she revelled in her role. And in *Case 39*, when confronted by the prosthetic makeup of burns covering her body, Kerry O'Malley comments on the reaction of child actor Jodelle Ferland – she took it all in her stride and was not fazed by the "really dark disturbing action."[9] Others, however, are. Delicate Jemima in *Chitty Chitty Bang Bang* claims to have been as scared as the myriads of other children viewing the evil child catcher. Trapped in the metal cage as the man cracks the whip, "They were real screams of terror," reflects the now adult Heather Ripley. "That *was* frightening!"[10] Kodi Smit-McPhee, playing Owen, the friend of the girl vampire in *Let Me In* admits "I'm going to have nightmares about it for years. Even though I'm part of the scary stuff, I'm probably going to be freaked out." In the same movie, Chloë Grace Moretz when watching the screening for the first time, actually jumped with fright as she saw the vampire pounce from the bathtub – she was startled by her own characterisation, for she was that vampire!

And yet, according to *Let Me In* director Matt Reeves, we needn't be alarmed at the traumatisation of child actors in horror movies. He states that when shooting the difficult scenes it is not a problem for kids: "It's like Halloween. The kids have fun. It's like total playtime. When you are on a movie set and there is fake blood and dead bodies it's an absolute joy!"[11]

The Birds is one of the great horror movies from that master of suspense, Alfred Hitchcock. Children are used as targets for flocks of chisel-beaked seagulls and crows that swoop down and attack the Californian fishing community of Bogeda Bay. Eleven-year-old Cathy (Veronica Cartwright) has received a pair of lovebirds as a birthday present. Soon crows start amassing on the telegraph wires. A flock of seagulls start attacking all the children at the party, so the little girls are hurriedly herded into the house to evade the sharp beaks, and to clear up the blood smears from where their legs and heads have been pecked. It is not long before windows are shattered as the sharp beaks hammer through the glass and through the panels of the door. At one point, a flock of thousands of sparrows crowd down the chimney into the living room.

"Why are they doing this... the birds?" whimpers Cathy. "Why are they trying to kill people?" But the clue is in the arrival of Miss Daniels and the caged lovebirds, just as the clue in *Urban Ghost Story* may be in the goldfish (though in that case, it is just a red herring!).

The impact is made greater because children are perceived to be vulnerable. The impact is not so succinct when it is the adults being attacked – Miss Daniel's hair is ruffled, a man gets his eyes pecked out. But the children – they are so small and innocent and thus better targets for scaring. So, when the masses of crows' wings flap like a plague of vampire bats the imagery is fixed: children running down the street, heads turned round aghast at their pursuers.

In *Resident Evil: Apocalypse*, Sophie Vavasseur is the ten-year-old who has to flee the mechanical jaws of the zombies that are ravaging her city, a genetic experiment gone badly wrong. As always, it is the girl-child caught up as victim of the horror, as it is too in *The Company of Wolves*.

Not all monsters pose a danger to the child, though it is worth being wary just in case. After watching a showing of the Frankenstein film at their village hall in rural Spain, six-year-old Ana Torrent is puzzled, not frightened, by the monster in *The Spirit of the Beehive*. She asks her older sister (Isabel Telleria) why the Frankenstein monster had been so tender with the little girl but had then gone on to kill her. Isabel explains it is a trick: that movies are not real, and the monster is not actually dead but a spirit. What is more, she mischievously says she has seen him (Frankenstein). To prove it, Isabel leads her sister across the plateau to an isolated barn to show her the monster, but the barn is empty, as is the adjacent well.

No doubt, Isabel was testing out her powers to scare her little sister, but Ana is more curious than afraid. Isabel scarily tries out her childish powers in two more upsetting ways, as she first tries to strangle the cat to see how it reacts. The frightened animal snarls and narrows its eyes as the little girl tightens her grip round its neck before releasing it from the torture. Secondly, Isabel fakes death to see the reaction of her little sister. She screams and then lies motionless on the floor. When Ana arrives she assumes the monster has attacked her sister, as in the Frankenstein film. But none of this action is vindictively hurtful. Isabel is just testing her powers and is aware of boundaries that should not be crossed. Bewildered Ana is innocently showing loyalty to her sister.

When later, Ana discovers an escaped convict hiding in the barn, it is obvious to her he must be the spirit of Frankenstein. Like Hayley Mills in *Whistle down the Wind*, she finds food and clothing for the stranger and silently tends him. But the police discover his hideout, and just as Frankenstein dies in the movie that Ana saw, so too the gunshots kill the convict. Sensing she is being blamed, Anna wanders off into the night where she has visions of Frankenstein strangling her to death.

These visions, in the opinion of Vicky Lebeau, are directly the result of the power of cinematic imagery. "Cinema has touched Ana's mind; its preoccupation of her imaginary life has driven her towards hallucination – or, more precisely, towards refracting the traumas, the enigmas of the world (the death of the soldier, the loss of her self in the woods) through a protective image borrowed from the screen (that of a monster)." [12]

The horrors of scaring children in *Jurassic Park* are much less supernatural and have been genetically engineered by their irresponsible grandfather (Richard Attenborough). Fourteen-year-old Ariana Richards plays his granddaughter Lex, and Joseph Mazzello plays Tim, her younger brother. Both grandchildren have been invited to a dummy run through the dinosaur Adventure Park that Grandfather has established on a 'secure' island off the Costa Rican coast. "We're taking extreme precautions," grandfather reassures the assembled scientists about to take their first grand tour of the park. But the human factor? Did he consider the human factor: the greedy computer expert who uses the distraction of the tour to shut down the security system so he can smuggle out some of the embryos? With the electric fences now disabled there are no security systems separating the tourists from the beasts.

"Don't scare me!" says Lex to her younger brother as they hear the thud thud of the ground shaking and a viciously hungry tyrannosaurus rex looms into view. For an hour, the children are chased from one scary episode to the next, their constant screams attracting the velociraptors that hunt them throughout the park. Both children play convincingly scared when they are on their own, and compliantly reliant on the adults from whom they seek protection.

A few years earlier, when Ariana Richards was ten, she had further monsters to endure, this time an underground version, in *Tremors*. Any vibration attracts the monster into an attacking frenzy. So when Ariana bounces on her pogo stick, Kevin Bacon has to race to rescue the girl before the monsters get to her. But unlike *Jurassic Park* the camera is rarely focused on the girl, she just has to be compliantly sheltering in the folds of her mother's arms while all hell is let loose around her.

In the sequel to *Jurassic Park* – Lost World: Jurassic Park – which takes place on a neighbouring island four years later, the obligatory scared vulnerable white girl is replaced by Kelly, the black adopted daughter of one of the visiting scientists, and played by Vanessa Lee Chester. Here, as we mentioned in Volume One (*Gender Roles and Themes*), the director Steven Spielberg is bucking a trend, a rare outing for a black girl taking the role of a vulnerable child, which up till now in movies has been the preserve of the arian white girl. Vanessa Lee does not scream when tyrannosaurus rex thunders onto the scene. Rather, she appears laid back as if to keep up the stereotype of a street-wise ghetto kid. She does hold the hand of her stepdad Dr. Malcolm, but more to assure *him* than require any comfort. So when one of the hunters tries to protect the girl by saying, "No one tell the little girl (that a man has been killed by dinosaurs)" she would be unconcerned anyway. For this girl is a gymnast. Swinging on the rafters of the research station she kicks the attacking velociraptor through the window back into the jungle from whence it came. "And the school cut you from the team!" exclaims her stepdad in disbelief.

Camilla Belle also features in this film as a ten-year-old girl put ashore on the island along with her parents. "Just let her enjoy herself for once," says the father to her over-protective mother. The girl goes exploring but then her screams alert us to the attack she is enduring from a herd of tiny sized dinosaurs, dilophosaurus, who pester like a swarm of irritating mosquitoes.

In the aforementioned films, the horror lies in something tangible: a monster/stranger in *Spirit of the Beehive*, flocks of crows in *The Birds*, and every child knows they will never confront a real dinosaur even if their fantasy explorations take them to *Jurassic Park*. But the horror for Jes (Ashley Sanchez) in *The Happening* could not be pinned down by scientists, and was defined as 'a freak of nature'. A walk in the woods, or across a meadow, give millions of people in north-east USA suicidal urges, and I hope Ashley Sanchez has not been deterred from taking country walks as a result of this horror movie. Fortunately, any frightening moments had been underplayed or tweaked out, and there is no screeching violin strings or screaming voices to scare the wits out of the audience.

While the children in *The Birds*, *Spirit of the Beehive*, *Jurassic Park*, *The Happening* and *Tremors* are depicted as being vulnerable and need protection, in other horror films the child has inherited either the physical or psychological powers to cope, as we saw in *Push* in which Dakota Fanning is able to predict the future, and in *Firestarter* or *The Reaping* in which Drew Barrymore and AnnaSophia Robb are able to use fire or plagues against their oppressors. *Silent Hill* mixes these themes.

Alessa is a vulnerable bullied eleven-year-old, but as she opens her arms she spontaneously bursts into flames. This is not a defensive mechanism. She has simply been exposed to the incinerating effects of living near a burning underground coal seam to which her body has become adapted. And anyway, she is a child spook who died a generation ago. The part is played by Jodelle Ferland who begins the movie as a sleepwalking orphan, Sharon, adopted by Christopher and Rose DaSilva. Alessa's trauma has been passed on to her descendants and is now being experienced through the subconscious psyche of Sharon who sleepwalks and makes horror paintings of her dreams. The doctor has diagnosed her condition as intergenerational psychiatric trauma. "She's getting worse everyday," complains the mother after they find her sleepwalking near the edge of a waterfall. As a therapy, mother decides to take the girl back to the deserted ghost town of Silent Hill.

In the town, Sharon sleepwalks off and enters the underworld of smouldering collieries. Mother chases the elusive girl, and in doing so encounters monsters, ghosts, walls dripping blood and crawling cockroaches. But instead of finding her own daughter, Sharon, she comes across Sharon's alter ego, Alessa, the ghost child. After mother is almost burned as a witch, she and her daughter manage to escape. But on reaching home, they find they are trapped in their time warp looking in on a bewildered husband in a parallel existence, in a scene similar to the ending of *The Dark* (2005).

The victims we have mentioned thus far have been terrorised by some animate beast or phenomenon. The *Halloween* (1978) series lays the responsibility for the terror in the hands of people, and one being in particular – that of Michael Myers. As a six-year-old, the boy returns from trick-or-treating only to watch through the window to see his teenage sister smooching with her boyfriend. Then the courting couple head for the bedroom to take advantage of the empty house, the parents being at a party.

The boy creeps up to his sister's room where she lies naked on her bed. Several thrusts of the knife and the girl lies dead. The little boy is found with bloodied knife in his hand as the parents return from their night out.

This is a boy who at his infant age is incapable of knowing right from wrong. Maybe some aspect of Halloween imagery had provoked him to play-act. Some could have praised him for his creative associations, but instead he is incarcerated in a mental institution that only reinforces his mental instability. The experience causes him to be struck mute. Instead of the asylum curing him of his actions it only serves to provoke him to repeat his offence as he escapes from the institution back to Haddonfield.

In *Halloween* (1978), the victims are mainly older teenage schoolgirls. The younger siblings – Lyndsey (Kyle Richards) and Tommy (Brian Andrew) just sit watching TV and ask about the bogeyman, but are never enticed to act really scared.

In *Hide and Seek* (2005), it is the victim, Emily, that is institutionalised, not because she has done wrong, but because her psychiatrist father believes that is the best way to help her recover from the trauma of witnessing her mother's death. When this therapy does not work, father (Robert De Niro) takes his daughter (Dakota Fanning) upstate to see if seclusion in a forest home aids recovery. But here, the ten-year-old girl becomes further insular, not wanting to befriend anyone – she even mutilates the face of a doll belonging to Ami, a neighbour who has come to visit. Instead, Emily adopts an imaginary friend, Charlie. It is this friend that gets blamed for all the unpleasantness (and eventually the murders) that occur about the house.

Dakota Fanning is brilliant in her evocation of a trauma victim, flitting from being morosely withdrawn to submissive daughter. This is a film poorly rated by other critics, but I found it deeply absorbing, always questioning who the mysterious Charlie might be. The one major flaw however is we are never given a single glimpse of father's psychosis which would justify the storyline at the end.

Ghosts

Personally, I don't think I believe in ghosts. Alakina Mann makes a healthy comment in *The Others* (2001) as she visits a cemetery with her brother in the dead of night, "Graves don't have ghosts, only skeletons." But when I hear those penetrative screeching violin notes that accompany mysterious activity while watching TV in a darkened room then I do find myself believing, and won't walk into another room without the lights on full blaze, just in case. I avoid this kind of movie like a plague, but if I have to watch I do so in the afternoon, knowing I can emerge into sunlight after enduring the torment. At any other time, I am a nervous wreck. How much more so for a child asked to take part in a ghost movie? How did seven-year-old Heather O'Rourke take to being implicit in the spooky goings on of *Poltergeist* (1982)? When even the youthful Daniel Radcliffe can admit to being scared as he watched scenes from *Harry Potter: The Deathly Hallows*, while already being aware of what goes on backstage, how cruel it must be to compel a child to take part in and witness such ghostly spectacles. Heather O'Rourke must be scared witless.

And yet Heather, as a seven-year-old, playing at first the playmate and then the kidnapped victim of ghosts in *Poltergeist* (1982) seems thoroughly absorbed in the fun of it all, as if she was the reincarnation of trick-or-treating Margaret O'Brien in *Meet me in St. Louis*. She pulls scary faces and makes genuine screams in all the right places, yet talks placidly to the TV screen waiting patiently for the spectres to appear, and there is a mischievous sparkle in her eyes as she laughs at us watching her while we are scared out of our wits, just as Isabel Conner does in *The Amityville Horror*.

However, Heather did have scared moments. Evidently, she broke down in the scene where she has to grab the headboard of the bed while being blown away in the wind tunnel. Steven Spielberg himself consoled her and assured her she would not have to re-perform the scene, finding a stunt double to play this part for her.[13] Other than this, the whole filming schedule did not faze her, and after the production she watched this movie over and over again, admitting to being scared at first, but usually just excited.

Playing Carol Ann Freeling, Heather O'Rourke's encounter with the poltergeists is at first fun, not frightening, 'a freak of nature' they just don't understand. She sits on the kitchen floor from where she is slid around the kitchen as if on a playground slide. But when a tornado arrives sucking the contents of Carol Anne's bedroom into it, the little girl is dragged into the vortex too, and disappears somewhere in the house. Her cries for help seem to emanate from within the television set.

A team of psychics are called in (they don't dare tell the police: they would not have believed the incredible story). The psychics are way out of their depth and arrive gobsmacked with awe as if they have just transferred from the set of *Close Encounters of the Third Kind*. Mother in particular, although being frantically concerned about her missing daughter, is also mesmerised by the spectres that flit and dazzle the house (they must have had one heck of an electricity bill, what with all those bright lights). And when she feels her own daughter "passing through my soul" the woman ecstatically sniffs the scent of her little girl left on her scarf.

Then a much more experienced psychic arrives. She tells them they are dealing with "souls not aware they have passed on. They linger in a perpetual dream state. A nightmare from which they cannot awake. Carol Anne must help them pass on to their destiny," she pronounces in her squeaky yet ominous voice.

As for the headstone-less corpses: they rise up in a final revenge and totally eradicate the house to the bafflement of the property developer. The family flee to Granny's house, way out in Arizona, ready for the sequel.

Ooo, scary! Switch the lights on quick.

Poltergeist II followed a few years later, casting the same actors except for the oldest daughter (Dominique Dunne) who had already flit the nest. So, slightly older Heather O'Rourke wasn't scared in this movie either? In fact, she described it as boring, by comparison. However, young girls have only a limited number of adjectives at their disposal, and 'boring' tends to be one of the most commonly wielded. A child might describe the scariest ride in Disney World as being boring if only to impress upon its friends that it has done something even scarier still.

Yet in *Poltergeist II* she is pursued by a being potentially more alarming than in the first movie, in the form of a maniacal preacher who sings his gospel song while prowling around the Freelings abode, every much as menacing as Robert Mitchum in *The Night of the Hunter*. "Are you lost sweetheart? Then why don't you come with me?" The pervert has the audacity to pretend to be helping the lost child when mother encounters them together in the shopping mall. The predator even gets a "thank you for looking after my lost daughter" from the gratefully unwitting mother.

Why the poltergeists want to pursue the Freelings to their new home in Arizona is not made clear – except that grandmother has special paranormal powers, and she discovers Carol Anne has these powers, too. The children's bedroom again comes alive so that Carol Ann and her older brother Robbie have to escape downstairs into the arms of their parents, and Heather O'Rourke makes the one liner, memorable enough to be listed in America's top 100 movie quotes, as she utters, "They're back!" The whole family know precisely what this means.

Heather O'Rourke starred in the second sequel to this film, *Poltergeist III*, the novelty having long since worn off. Tragically though, part way through filming, the twelve-year-old girl had to be rushed to hospital with an intestinal complaint and died the same day. The filming was completed using a double. It is macabre to learn that Heather's burial place is now on the itinerary for American tourist groups, and legend has it the studios are haunted by her little dead soul. Sadly too, the girl playing her older sister, Dominique Dunne, also died the following year. No one dares attempt to make *Poltergeist IV*.

Throughout this section we have stressed it is the young girl who becomes the victim of poltergeist, ghostly or other psychic events. Only rarely does the scriptwriter create a victim from a boy or an infant. Yanna McIntosh in *They Come Back* provides a reasoning behind this. When ten-year-old Marley (played by Niamh Wilson) is associated with poltergeist activity, a psychic is consulted. She diagnoses "Troubled child nearing adolescence, inexplicable physical phenomenon for which the child denies responsibility: this is classic poltergeist phenomenon. Almost always there is a disturbed child nearing puberty in the home. The belief is, that changes in the child's body free an unfocused amount of psychic energy." So, maybe all households with troubled adolescent girls should be fearful. A highly charged child could be releasing just the kind of kinetic energy needed by spooks!

It is a rare outing when a boy is troubled by psychic encounters. "I don't want to be scared any more," is the fearful cry of Haley Joel Osment in *The Sixth Sense*, one of the most highly ranked of all horror movies. As he tells his secret to child psychologist Bruce Willis, "I see dead people. People walking around like regular people. People who don't know they are dead." Why this movie is so clever is that we don't realise until the final ending twist that it is the psychologist he is referring to. The boy is able to see the past, and people who have died in the past, still trapped in the present: the convicts still hanging from the gibbet in the former schoolhouse; the girl ghost Kyra (Mischa Barton) who comes to visit him in the only place he has ever felt safe – a tent erected in his bedroom stuffed with statuettes he had stolen from the church. His freakish behaviour makes him an outcast among his peers, always attracting jeers of "freak". He even hides behind a pair of spectacles with the lenses removed.

A truly effective opening to a ghost movie is found in *The Messengers*. Someone, or something, is stalking a mother and her son in their dilapidated ranch. The boy hides in a cupboard, peers through the opening in utter terror. Then the pursuer opens the door to the hideout. A really scary scream is emitted and the child becomes a victim.

Two things are astonishing about this movie. The first is that this super-talented sequence was not played by a boy at all, but by the girl I believe to be the most talented child actress around – Jodelle Ferland (fresh from her sparkling performances in *Tideland* and *Silent Hill*). The second is that this ghost movie dies after the opening sequence as a new family move into the house and the oldest daughter, played by eighteen-year-old Kirsten Stewart, becomes the target of the hauntings and the infant boy gazes in amazement at the spooks as if he has just seen ET rather than a ghost.

In *The Dark* (2005), it is the ghost of a child that has the mysterious power to influence events. Thirteen-year-old Abigail Stone plays Ebril, a girl who had died as part of a mass suicide of a religious cult. She remained to haunt a Welsh hill farm above the cliffs. Her wish: to find her father again. Sean Bean's wife and daughter, Sarah (fourteen-year-old Sophie Stuckey), turn up at the farmstead. When Sarah disappears, probably drowned, and her mother realises the other girl, Ebril, is actually a ghost, the mother tries to manipulate the situation to get Sarah back using the cult's premise: 'A life for a life'. But Ebril won't play dead. Mother ends up living the twilight world of a ghost, while Sarah (or rather the reincarnated Ebril) is reunited with her father.

For me, *The Others* (2001) is my personal favourite of the ghost movies for it does not rely on sensational scary special effects but is a clever tale with a twist in the ending that you kick yourself for not seeing coming, because you are swept along so convincingly into the storyline. What adds to the splendour of this movie, as well as Nicole Kidman's growing neurosis, is the acting of the children, particularly Alakina Mann who plays the preteen Anne. She is able to mix scenes of fearful misunderstanding as she is spooked by mysterious activity: with playful spitefulness towards her brother as she pretends to scare him, with stubborn offence when her mother wrongly accuses her, and with hateful animosity as her mother goes berserk.

We are left clues to the reality of the situation when Anne tries to convince her mother and newly arrived house staff that something terrible has happened, but we don't learn of it until the end, and when we do, we need to place ourselves in little Victor's shoes. The only spooky action is the inexplicable drawing of curtains and occasional undefined noises. Yet the whole atmosphere is spooky: the large cold rambling Jersey mansion, lack of decorations after the 1945 war, the children with an allergy to light who must be kept in candlelit rooms, the constant fog outside the cemetery beyond the gardens, and the three elderly house staff who turn up despite mother neglecting to post the advertisement.

Anna is aware of the presence of someone else in the house, but it can't be a ghost. "Ghosts go about in white sheets and carry chains," she tells her brother, yet when her own mother sees Anne dressed in a white veiled communion dress the woman flips, violently attacking her own daughter. Then her husband turns up unexpectedly from the war, assumed dead, but his visit is hauntingly transient, and the housekeeper has to explain, "Sometimes the world of the dead gets mixed up with the world of the living," and the understanding of that is the crux to this clever film.

If *The Dark* (2005) is my favourite among ghost stories, by far the scariest is *An American Haunting*. Here, the horrors go on and on from start to finish with barely any let up. Rachel Hurd-Wood is fantastic in her portrayal of absolute terror, transfiguring from a vision of beautiful peace to anguished face contortions, frantic screams, the rolling of her eyes. Some of the ideas in this are really scary too: the blanket slowly being peeled back from her bed by the 'entity' that is haunting her. This girl is dragged violently off her bed and hung helplessly by her hair by the poltergeist demon. Although Betsy Bell (Rachel Hurd-Wood) squirms and writhes in torment, she is not possessed like Regan in *The Exorcist*. Yet she does become a ghost to haunt the next generation that dare live inside her cursed house, just as she herself was haunted by the little hooded girl (Lola Bate-Walsh) that sat silently next to her on the swing.

The father of Kathy Harvey (Christina Ricci) is actively seeking ghosts in the fun spook spoof, *Casper* (1995). Like the spiritualists in *Photographing Fairies,* he is trying to make contact with his dead wife. He has taken a job of itinerant ghost mediator, visiting haunted houses to try to establish spiritual contact. "Mum has died. She's not a ghost, dad!" says disbelieving Kathy.

Mr Harvey has found just the place to dwell: a derelict mansion in the town of Friendship. Father and daughter move in. The house is already occupied: by Casper, a friendly ghost with romantic aspirations – "Yesss! There's a girl in my bed!" – and by three more ominous spectres who are into serious haunting. Soon girl and father are terrified out of their wits; but Kat's resilience, and her father's determination to locate his wife, thwart the ghosts' effectiveness. Father is able to make his final liaison with his wife, and Casper apparates into the boy he once was, before disappearing once and for all with Christina Ricci's final kiss. The same set of four ghosts reappear in the fun clash of witches against spooks in *Casper meets Wendy* (played by the vivacious Hilary Duff).

Any message that a child need not be afraid of the dark by suggesting there are good friendly ghosts is immediately negated by Casper's three abhorrent companions. Storybook spooks are meant to be scary, either to ensure kids are obediently tucked in at night, or so adults can exert a power of control over the child's emotions. Only rarely is the child allowed a glimpse of Casper's harmless associates: Joe Jackson in *Field of Dreams*, the housekeepers in *The Others*. Even obstreperous Captain Gregg (Rex Harrison) in *The Ghost and Mrs Muir* was kept apart from the infant Natalie Wood, until it is revealed at the end of the movie the girl had been 'pleasantly' haunted by the irascible sea captain throughout her childhood.

"Are you a ghost?" asks Karin Kinsella (Gaby Hoffman) in *Field of Dreams*. The little girl is asking Joe Jackson, the legendary baseball player who died sixty years earlier, before her father inexplicably ploughed up his Iowan cornfield to build a baseball pitch in the middle of nowhere. When asked, do I look like a ghost she confirms, "You look real to me."

Doubts are also raised whether ghosts exist or not in the films based on Henry James novel *The Turn of the Screw*. Several dramas of this title have been produced: *The Turn of the Screw*, released in 1992, 1999 and 2009, and *The Innocents* based on the same book released in 1961. All are very atmospheric, all ambiguously coax the watcher into believing the two children, Flora[14] and Miles,[15] are in collusion with the ghosts of the former exploitative residents of the country house, yet nothing can be verified; it may all just be the delusion of the new governess Miss Giddens. (She is just Anne in 2009 *Turn of the Screw*, and Jenny in the 1992 version, and just a nameless governess in the book.) There is nothing in actions or speech of the children to indicate they believe in Quint, and never once do they give the game away. The children maintain loyal devotion in the face of the paranoia of their governess. As the woman continues to misconstrue what she sees, she concludes, "A man is corrupting my little babies. The children are taught depravity while the other staff look away. I must protect my little creatures from this thing." But the only way she can attack the 'ghosts' is through the bodies of her charges. As Miss Giddens sees the children frolicking in the grounds, to her eyes the innocent game of roly-poly becomes a vision of sexual intercourse between Peter Quint and the deceased governess. She sees Miles thrashing Flora as Quint molesting the governess. So, she raises her fists to thrash the boy (thinking he is the embodiment of Quint), and later as she holds him protectively in her arms, the life is squeezed from his lungs.

In *The Amityville Horror*, nine-year-old Amy also seems to be in collusion with the evil spirits that are plaguing her house. While her father, mother, and baby sister are afflicted by the evil goings on, the little girl seems indifferent to the problems. "My friend Jodie wants to play upstairs," says Amy, (played by Natasha Ryan, while in the 2005 version the character of Chelsea is played by Chloë Grace Moretz). Jodie inhabits the empty rocking chair in the bedroom that mysteriously rocks when Amy talks to it.

Her parents come to realise the house is haunted by the spirit of the previous family murdered on the property. "Jodie wants me to live here forever and ever so we can all play together." However, the evil spirit has an unwelcome way of entertaining the family. Strange smells, imploding doors and windows, black filth filling the toilet and sink, blood seeping from walls and staircases, eventually drive the family away so the spirit 'Jodie' doesn't get her wish.

According to the scientists and psychics who are treating her, twelve-year-old Lizzie Fisher (Heather Ann Foster) has attracted paranormal activity in *Urban Ghost Story*, as a result of a motor accident she had been involved in. She had been joyriding in her boyfriend's father's car when the vehicle careered off the road and rolled, killing the boy. She, too, had been dead for several minutes during which time she witnessed the proverbial bright light at the end of the tunnel. "Her spiritual aura was breached," and she has got mixed up with an entity who has died but who doesn't accept it. The furniture moves in her room (including the cabinet with a fish tank on it), water pipes rattle, there are thumps on the wall, and a glass tumbler goes flying across the room.

Lizzie is the epicentre of activity exhibiting all the hallmarks of a poltergeist: recently traumatised, an oppressive environment (in a high-rise council flat with outmoded water pipes). At least this makes a healthy change to have a haunting in a modern building and not just an old country mansion. Yet others are sceptical about the paranormal link: the medics, the welfare officer, the police, the reporter. When the mother approaches the reporter as a last ditch cry for help, "We're being terrorised by some kind of ghost. It's invisible. It smells bad too and it gets cold when it's around." The reporter still thinks it is a hoax – a family faking in the hope of jumping the welfare ladder. But the reporter is just after a sensational story to publish, and when the blocked toilet starts filling with dirty water (as in the *Amityville Horror*) he just puts it down to bad drains and noisy pipes. But not before he has managed to publish the scared girl's photo in the paper and for her to be ridiculed by her classmates.

The psychiatrist dismisses the incident as a traumatic hallucination. When she tells the welfare officer she saw the ghost, instead of taking pity the officer says, "If she sees it again I'm going to have to take her down to the hospital for a drugs and alcohol screening," adding naively, "Just remember, we're on your side!" When mother calls the police to help solve the mystery, they simply accuse her of leaving minors alone and unattended and she is arrested for child neglect.

In the end, Lizzie receives forgiveness from her dead boyfriend's mother, the family are rehoused, and the fish in the goldfish bowl is given a larger tank. Surely, the goldfish in the tank was just a coincidence, just like the caged lovebirds in Hitchcock's *The Birds*? Wasn't it?

Vampires

Vampires are often associated with sex-crazed misadventure. So there is something perverse going on when we find a twelve-year-old becoming a vampire, as does Kirsten Dunst in *Interview with the Vampire*. Adam Mars-Jones reporting in *The Independent* suggests such a film would not normally be permissible in contemporary times and only gains "licence for its own fixations on an array of modern perversions" by being performed in period costume.[16]

Of course, it is doubtful the twelve-year-old would have been aware of the sexual significance of her sensually parted lips and Brad Pitt inserting his wrist into her mouth as if it were a phallus for her to suck and gorge on while he moans with orgasmic delight.

The child's mother had recently died of plague in 19th century New Orleans, her polluted body just removed by the gravediggers, and Claudia (Kirsten Dunst) is sobbing quietly in her empty home. Along comes Louis, a tall handsome cloaked man (hungry for blood), and he comforts her. He wraps the little girl in his arms. His cuspids search out her bare neck and he takes a bite. And he enjoys her. ("Remember how you wanted her! The taste of her! Feel as you felt with that child in your arms.") Wanting to perpetuate her youth he decides to not let her die, and that is why he offers her his own blood to drink.

"I want some more," says the girl, her lips now gorged with blood.

"Gently," the man tells her, "You're so innocent."

From that day, as daylight encroaches, the girl sleeps inside the coffin with Louis, "curling her finger around my hair." Even when she was allocated her own coffin: "whenever she awoke she would crawl into mine." The girl of course is oblivious to any perversions she is awakening, and treats the man as her protector, her surrogate father.

Thirty years pass but her body remains that of an eternal child. "Her eyes alone told the story of her age staring from under her straw-like curls."

Although nothing sexual takes place, it is obvious that the vampire saw this as more than just a father-daughter relationship. "We were two of us again. So euphoric was I, I yielded to her every desire."

And for Claudia, as she plants a kiss upon his lips, "Louis, I love you still. Who will care for me, my love?"

Let the Right One In is also a tale of vampires, but not the usual lust-filled handsome male who haunts the circles of the beautiful and affluent in Victorian London. Such are usually depicted as having an almost covetous existence of longevity. No, in this Swedish tale by the blockbuster novelist, John Ajvide Lindqvist, the vampire is a helpless girl of twelve: Eli, played by Line Leandersson. She does not even have Tom Cruise and Brad Pitt who the preteen Kirsten Dunst so relied on in *Interview with the Vampire*. Eli is a helpless girl who has to depend on a mere mortal man for protection – a paedophile[17] with whom she has a relationship of mutual benefit – he supplying her with the blood of live victims.

The action is set in the winter of 1982 in a drab Stockholm suburb, where the midnight sun barely creeps above the horizon, and the wooded suburbs are leafless, bleak and snow covered. The man has found her an apartment, next door to a lonely bullied boy, Oskar. The two youngsters become friends and in time, the boy discovers Eli is a vampire – twelve years old ("but I've been twelve for a very long time"). But this does not worry Oskar for at last the lonely boy has a friend, a confidante, and protector.

Yet Oskar hears about strange killings in the local woods: a young lad hung upside down and the blood drained from his jugular. He is told of a girl who pounces onto unwitting passers-by and sucks the blood from them. When on his school outing a corpse is found submerged beneath the lake-ice, he realises that his little friend Eli is involved.

Yet, Eli is a useful ally for Oskar to have. As long as he invites her into his apartment with the crucial words ("You have to *say* 'come in'," Eli has taught him) then no harm befalls him. Eli inspires the boy to stand up to his bullies, and in an ultimate fight-out, the vampire disposes of Oskar's bullies once and for all.

But then things get out of hand. Eli's guardian bungles a string of murders and to avoid being caught pours a fatal concoction of acid over his head. A local man has witnessed Eli drawing blood and has located her hideout. It is then time for her to move on. But she needs Oskar's help putting her onto a train, which will inconspicuously translocate her to a less suspicious part of the country.

The American remake of the same movie in 2010, *Let Me In*, is equally as riveting, following closely the format and script of the Swedish original but transferred to New Mexico. Kodi Smit-McPhee is superb as the unassuming bullied wimp (called Owen in this film), and Chloë Grace Moretz is an equally effective vampire (renamed Abby). But, in the opinion of Ritchie Coster who plays the sports coach, "The true horror is not the vampire stuff but the hell kids have to go through at school!"

Werewolves

In most horror movies, the child makes the ideal victim, because the audience can be transported back to their formative memories where primeval fears mix with the unseen lurking beneath the bed. Since the 1940s when *The Wolf Man* was screened, the werewolf has invariably been a handsome hulk, as in *The Howling, Silver Bullet* and *An American Werewolf in London*, who undergoes the lycanthropic transformation to target an unsuspecting maiden, ripe into puberty. In this type of movie it is older teenage girls who are the predominant victims, though young boys do get to pet the protagonists as in *Bad Moon*, or to become one in *Teen Wolf*. Once bitten, the victim inherits the role of seductress: Katherine Isabelle in *Ginger Snaps*, or Agnes Bruckner in *Blood and Chocolate*. Perhaps this may have been the outcome for Hermione Granger had she not been aware of Professor Lupin's mutation in *Harry Potter*. However, these are young ladies. It is rare we find a werewolf targeting a child; to do so, we have to look to *The Company of Wolves*.

Filled with sexual innuendo and lessons from *Little Red Riding Hood* about the dangers of straying from the straight and narrow and not trusting men, *The Company of Wolves* is a tale of werewolves, of folk tales, and old grannies stories, the harsh frightening experience of living in a dark medieval village whose lives are haunted by wolves that attack their livestock, and are never sure whether someone is of the Devil or of God. Fortunately, this is just the nightmare of one confused adolescent girl whose dreams flit from that first escape from dependence on parents, into sexual exploration.

Sarah Patterson rocks fitfully in her sleep. She dreams of her hated older sister being chased by the sinister looking dolls and teddy bears that sit on her bedroom shelves. Outside in the forested landscape, wolves bay in the gathering twilight. Now the girl herself is transported into the forest clearing where her grandmother (Angela Lansbury) lives.

The girl dreams she is attending her sister's gothic funeral and Granny is consoling her, "Your only sister! All alone in the woods and nobody to save her!"

Grandma is always giving her granddaughter advice. "Never stray from the path... Never eat a windfall apple... Never trust a man whose eyebrows meet." Granny tells her tales of vicars meeting devilish beasts, and babies being born feet first, of women jilted on their nuptial night only for the man to reappear years later as a werewolf: the wolf's head was chopped off, fell into a barrel of milk, and instantly turned into a human head. Other tales are of men being shot and howling like a wolf as their body mutates gruesomely into the form of an animal, of a she-wolf shot and turning into a naked girl who stalks the village at night.

But when Rosaleen tells these tales to her parents, they tell her not to believe all her granny tells her. And yet, there *was* a maggot in the windfall apple Gran warned her about!

Then the cry of 'Wolf!' goes up from the forest. All the men-folk go out with their guns. "This is all these beasts understand," says father holding up a shotgun. "Kill them before they kill us." When father cuts the paw from the dead wolf as a trophy it becomes a human arm. "When I killed it, it was a wolf," sighs dad.

Granny makes Rosaleen a shawl from red wool, and the tale now becomes an elaborate version of *Red Riding Hood*. Like Beatie Edney's yellow mackintosh in *A Day at the Beach*, the little red girl in *Schindler's List*, and Hannah Pilkes' red coat in *The Woodsman*, the red shawl stands out as the only piece of bright colour in a dark dismal forest.

Rosaleen is sent into the forest to visit Granny, carrying a basket with food and drink, and wearing her red shawl, with the usual warning not to stray from the path. But on the way, this is where she meets a man whose eyebrows meet in the middle. But she is not scared, for she is still on the path. "You're not afraid of anything?" the man praises her.

He holds her to a bet: if she can reach Granny's house using the path, she can have his compass; but if he gets there first through the forest, then she will owe him... a kiss.

Arriving at Granny's house Rosaleen comments, "What big eyes you have!"

"All the better to see you with."

"What big arms you have!"

"All the better to hug you with."

The man insists on his kiss as they watch the last of Granny's hair flame up in the fire. Rosaleen realises her danger and picks up Granny's shotgun. The bullet wounds the man, and amidst yelps of pain, the man scarily transforms into a wolf – the kind with hair on the inside as well as out.

The Child-Killer: Children who Kill

I don't mean people who kill children. I mean children who kill people. Sometimes this may be the result of an accident: infant Lily Owens picking up the pistol while mum and dad are squabbling in *A Secret Life of Bees*, or Dorothy inconsiderately landing her house on the Wicked Witch of the East. For others it is a one-off reaction, a self-defence reflex they were even unaware they were doing, for instance, Emily stabbing the Dutch captain in *A High Wind in Jamaica*. With others, it may just be a false threat of retribution, as Dakota Fanning taunts in *Hounddog*, "I'm going to kill my daddy one day," showing her friend her bruised leg, or *Huck Finn* (Elijah Wood) admitting, "I might end up being a murderer myself one day." Frighteningly, for others it is part of their nature, a pretty charming waif hiding a murderous intent, exemplified by Isabelle Fuhrman in *Orphan* (2009); or the warped testing of his own powers of daring as Macaulay Culkin goads his nephew Elijah Wood in *The Good Son*.

For infant Ami (Laura Vaquero) who smothers her baby brother in *Alas de Mariposa*, she is just copying what she has watched on television. It is an unsuccessful attempt to gain the attention of a neglectful mother. There are no witnesses to her crime (except us), and despite mother's doubts, this is considered a cot death.

When a boy of the same age, Michael Myers, in *Halloween* (1978) is found with the knife in his hand that has killed his older sister, he is institutionalised as one of the most evil characters in horror movie history. Which is worse: the dagger in Michael's hand, or the smothering pillow in Ami's? The boy is vilified as the little monster, not the girl. In real life, the child killers of James Bulger are held eternally responsible; the girls who kill are not. We all know the names of Jon Venables and Robert Thompson, and these ten-year-olds will never be forgiven by vigilantes for the crime they committed at an age when their contemporaries are likewise testing their powers over life and death – pulling legs off spiders, drowning cats.[18] This is what young boys do. But few remember ten-year-old Mary Bell.[19] Isabel Telleria's testing her strength around the cat's neck in *Spirit of the Beehive* is as shocking as it is incongruous, only because she is a girl. We expect girls to be like Hayley Mills in *Whistle down the Wind*, rescuers of kittens from the drowning pool.

The Bad Seed caused controversy when it was first shown in the 1950s because it dared to make us consider sweet innocent little girls could actually be serial killing monsters. Murderous boys, whether they be fictional Michael Myers or real life Jon Venables and Robert Thompson, are left to rot in hell; their female counterparts are awarded angelic wings. And yet, as the following examples show, most child killers in the movies are little girls, not little boys.

Even after watching Patty McCormick in *The Bad Seed*, you would be forgiven for believing the child could remain sweet and innocent, for we are never shown any murders taking place. It is all just innuendo. The same is true of watching Jodie Foster in *The Little Girl who lives down the Lane*. We can't hold a grudge against her character, Rynn, for we never actually witness her committing a felony – only peppering a little white powder into the cup of tea of the paedophile predator who had come to molest her. "This tastes of almond," he tells her. "It must be the almond cookies," she replies as he starts to choke convulsively. She had earlier used the same almond recipe (potassium cyanide) on her mother – the mother that had abandoned her when she was three years old and had now dared to show up again just as soon as father was dead. The death of the obnoxious landlady who had intruded on the girl, *was* however an accident: the trapdoor crashing on her head made her fall down the cellar steps smashing her head on the concrete floor.

These murderers don't require physical strength – they are only little girls, after all. They work alone, plotting against anyone who dare oppose them. To bludgeon someone to death requires the help of an accomplice. Only with the assistance of teenager Kate Winslet could Melanie Lynskey tempt her mother to a remote spot in *Heavenly Creatures*. The stocking filled with a brick is one of the rare occasions when we actually witness the child carrying out the violence of a murder (of course, the 'child' actors were being played by older teenagers), though Eva Sayer thrusting with the crowbar in *The Children* (2008) is uncharacteristically scary.

Asami (Ayaki Izumi) has also learned how to drug her oppressors in the horrific Japanese movie, *Audition*. Abused as a young girl, Asami has stumbled across a drug that numbs her victims so she can sever their fingers, tongues, and other offending appendages, then keep them as a wounded animal in a sack. She tells her victims, "Only when you're in extreme pain do you understand your own mind." This is the tale of an abused girl who alighted on a method of taking revenge on her evil stepfather.[20] Revengeful Ellen Page follows her example in *Hard Candy*, though in her case she offers the paedophile she has just castrated a rope to hang himself with.

The trailer to *The Bad Seed* states, "The whisper of suspicion grows into the thunder of terrifying truth!" Eight-year-old Rhoda (Patty McCormick) is a child murderer. She has inherited a gene passed down through generations. Like her grandmother before her, she has become a murderer, or at least committed manslaughter, for she precipitated three accidents which all resulted in death. But none of them worried her. After Rhoda's classmate is reported drowned on a school trip, the gardener, LeRoy, observes, "You should be crying your eyes out. How come you're going skating when that poor little schoolboy is drowned in the bay?" For Rhoda, they are just the natural outcome of a spiteful girl insisting on getting her own way. "I don't feel any way at all," says the girl.

On the outside, she appears charming, immaculate, articulate and well mannered, a perfect little girl. With blond hair, long ponytails, billowing dress, happy smile and personality, she is a delight. But cross her, or deny her what she wants, and a hateful frown disfigures her face.

LeRoy pretends he can see through the girl's lies and goads her into admitting her guilt. To the girl, he says, "I've seen some mean girls in my time – but you're the meanest!" At first, LeRoy wasn't convinced of her guilt. He was just playing a wicked prank on her, by teasing her about pink coloured electric chairs, made especially for little girl child murderers. But it dawns on LeRoy that the girl really did murder the boy. So Rhoda has to dispose of the man, by locking him in the boiler room and setting it on fire.

Despite discovering her own daughter's guilt, mother does not reject Rhoda. "She's my little girl and I love her."

In *Orphan* (2009), Esther (Isabelle Fuhrman) is, like Rhoda, a delightful, pretty nine-year-old girl, surely every parent's dream of a perfect daughter. Only she has no parents. They died in a house fire, and little Esther is languishing in an orphanage, run by a group of nuns, when Mr and Mrs Coleman arrive to find a new child to help them recover from the loss of a recent tragic stillbirth. When the visiting parents spot Esther finishing off a spectacular piece of artwork, discover she is polite, articulate and highly intelligent, they are immediately smitten. And this couple of parents are exactly what little Esther has been yearning for, too. "You don't know how long I've waited for a daddy like you!"

But when they reach home, her new brother does not accept the girl. The children at her new school tease her. But Esther seems able to tolerate the rejection, instead harbouring up misdeeds in her revengeful mind. In time, she discovers cracks in her parents' relationship that she is able to exploit, gradually easing mum away so she can have sole access to dad. Esther sets up accidents so that those who have been nasty to her are hurt, or even killed, and eventually her foster mother and brother are hospitalised. At last, she can be alone with her new dad. "I love you, daddy, I really love you," says nine-year-old Esther, as she snuggles up to him on the couch, smacking him with kisses and tenderly stroking his hair. But daddy rejects her advances. "I don't love you like that," he tells the girl. Big mistake! You do not reject Esther that easily without punishment, as the fruit knife in his chest soon demonstrates.

A similar set of circumstances arises in *Case 39*, a seemingly sweet innocent child possessing an evil streak when she does not get her own way. There has to be a reason why the parents of Lilith (played by the brilliant Jodelle Ferland) bolt their bedroom door on the inside, and in desperation try to kill their daughter by shoving her in the oven. It is not just because of the selfish streak in the little girl. "She feeds on kindness and decency and sucks you dry." She is a demon, claim the parents.

But the cop who arrests the parents sees it differently: "She is a damaged child, she's a deceitful child, she's a manipulative child; but a damaged deceitful manipulative child is not a demon." But this is before the cop gets mauled by his greatest phobia: a rabid dog. Likewise, Lilith's doctor also dies from his greatest fear: hornets. As hornets appear from every orifice in his body he is tormented to death by bee stings. The parents of the boy in Lily's therapy class are also murdered. And the link between the deaths? All received a phone call from the supernatural girl in which their greatest fear is turned into reality. And the next target in line is Renée Zellweger, playing the welfare officer who has temporarily adopted this serial demon… Don't pick up the phone, Renée.

Zombies: Wicked Little Things is a 'dark fairy tale' featuring revengeful boys and girls, caught up in a fatal accident in 1913 Pennsylvania when an impatient mine manager did not give sufficient warning for his child labourers to evacuate the mine in time before igniting the dynamite. Now, generations later, they haunt the woods, targeting any person who wanders into the forest, gnawing flesh from their victims and gorging on blood, an action copied by the mutant school kids in *Resident Evil: Apocalypse*.[21]

A similar group of kids haunt the woods in *The Children* (2008). How they cause the gruesome fatalities in the two families that are having their New Year reunion ruthlessly interrupted is not clear. We are only allowed momentary glimpses of adults garrotted by spikes, shards of glass, and knife wounds, but the end product is effectively scary. Eva Sayer, William Howes and Rafiella Brookes turn into killers as a viral mutation overrides their infant bodies.

These films give a new meaning to the phrase *mass murderer*. Like *Village of the Damned*, it is a group that is infected with a killer gene, and woe betide any adult that dares oppose the will of the masses.

Other children are killers unintentionally. I have never heard anyone point a finger of accusation against Dorothy (Judy Garland) for killing the wicked witch of the East in *The Wizard of Oz*! Others are less obviously blameless, yet their crime should nevertheless be deemed accidental. Celia Carmichael (Rebecca Smart) in the film of her own name, *Celia* (1988), picks up her father's shotgun aiming at the Australian bobby who has looked in on her. She sees his silhouette, and assumes he is one of the *Hobyahs* – the monsters that have filled her nightmares. Realising her mistake, she has to cover up the crime. She and her friends hide in the quarries pretending to play as if nothing has happened. "You say anything, you'll die in Hell," she threatens her friend. "This is our secret for ever and ever." As if to prove their innocence, they stage a mock hanging in front of the daughter of the shot policeman, using another girl to deflect accusations.

It is this blurred distinction between reality and imaginative play that turns the mouse into a monster, the choirboy into the convict. "Piggy, that was murder!" declares Ralph (James Aubrey) having just witnessed the frenzied attack on the little boy in *Lord of the Flies* (1962). But Piggy (Hugh Edwards) defends the crazed mob: "It was dark. There was a bloody dance. There was thunder and lightening, and rain. We were scared. It wasn't (murder). It was an accident."

Another unintentional killer is Emily in *A High Wind in Jamaica*. Like nine-year-old Dora Szinetar who startles her pursuer into impaling his neck in *Laurin* (1988), Emily's is an act of self-defence. She stabs the captain of the Dutch schooner. He had been taken hostage by the band of pirates while the girl was asleep. The man has arrived in Emily's cabin bound with ropes, and a knife in his hand gesturing to the girl to untie the rope. But there is a language barrier. The frightened girl thinks she is going to be stabbed. In the ensuing struggle the man lies dead. But Emily does not receive any blame for this. The authorities assume the pirates are to blame. When witnessing in court back in England, the line of questioning never reaches to her involvement in the captain's death – the court is more concerned whether the pirates had molested her. The outcome is the pirates hang for the little girl's misdemeanour.

While Jodie Foster and Ayaki Izumi in *The Little Girl who lives down the Lane* and *Audition* have found a way to eliminate undesirables in their lives by using poison, Ana Torrent in *Cría Cuervos* naively believes she has found a poison and uses it to gain retribution over people in her life, whereas their deaths are really just circumstantial.

Her mother gives Ana a tin of powder to throw away because it is past its sell-by-date. Mysteriously she tells the child it's a tin of poison. It is only an offhand remark to make life more fun, but Ana believes what her mother has told her, keeps the tin, hiding it in a safe place, not realising it is only baking powder.

Later mother, dying of cancer, becomes acutely ill. Her daughter witnesses her agony and overhears mum say how she wishes she could die. Although we don't see the girl administer the poison we assume she has done so, for Ana is rinsing a glass at the sink, turning it upside down on the draining board, and mother dies shortly afterwards. It is not long before Ana's father is canoodling with an 'aunt'. The girl witnesses the couple having sex, is disgusted by it, and soon we are watching Ana again rinsing out a glass that has had 'poison' powder in it. Dad dies of a heart attack in the act of intercourse: "I can't breath. I'm choking," he cries, and the 'auntie' slinks away guiltily. Ana had blamed mum's illness on her father's neglectfulness, and that is why he had to be given the poison.

Next, Ana quizzes her infirm grandma who is wheelchair-bound asking her, does she wish she were dead? Ana interprets the nod as affirmation and soon she is delivering a glass of poisoned water to the old woman. Her final target is her Aunt Paulina, but when she discovers next day both gran and aunt well-and-truly alive she doubts the powder's fatal attributes. At the end of the film, Ana comes to realise the bottle of powder was not poison after all and that her parents had died of natural causes.

That this girl wishes others dead is rather unnerving. A little girl believing she has the wherewithal to execute that final judgement is a dangerous being, however cute Ana Torrent looks. "I want you to die," she yells at her new foster mother, Aunt Paulina. And the reason? The friendly, caring woman trying desperately to be loving, unwittingly makes the mistake of retelling *Little Almond*, the favourite bedtime story Ana's mother used to read to her before she died.

Chillingly evil is Christina Ricci's role in *Addams Family Values*. She appears more gruesome than any of the previous murderers as she attempts to kill her baby brother by dropping him out of a window, placing his head under a guillotine, and attempting to drop a giant anvil on him. And yet, this is comic spoof: all the murderous attempts are thwarted. Had this not been a comedy, this is the type of scenario of bad taste that might otherwise have got a more serious film banned. As it is, it can be equated with the cartoon humour of *Tom and Jerry*.

While the majority of child murderers on-screen are little girls – their innocent vulnerability making them ideal subjects to astound us – boys retain their psychopathic ranking. Outwardly likeable Macaulay Culkin tries to eliminate Elijah Wood in *The Good Son* (1993) in a film whose

UK release had to be postponed due to the James Bulger case. Likewise at the same time, there was furore over the release of *Child's Play 3*, also at the time of the Bulger murder. Few parents dare name their children Damien after he scared audiences witless in *The Omen*.

The murderous gene in the child has to be nurtured by experimentation and practise. Macaulay Culkin playing Henry in *The Good Son* is only at first aping Isabel Telleria's strangling of the cat in *Spirit of the Beehive* or Benny's tragic action with the stun gun in *Benny's Video*. When Henry aims the crossbow bolt at the raging dog, he is only testing out that universal curoisity that is inate in all children, of 'what would happen if…?'

But the lesson the child has to learn is where to draw the line. He needs to realise he cannot act as God. Although Henry says he is aiming to miss as he pulls the trigger, he has already acquired a lust for blood, and the yelps from the dog only add to the tally of bloodlust in his twisted mind. "Today was fun, tomorrow will be even better," he promises his nephew. When the imp dangles the dummy from the highway bridge causing a multiple pile-up, and threatens to kill his own sister and mother, his nephew's comment, "you're sick," becomes the biggest understatement of the decade.

Michael Myers must be the most famous child murderer of the horror movie genre. As a six-year-old, he attacks his older sister in *Halloween* (1978) after the boy spied on her cavorting naked in bed with her boyfriend. The child does not even have time to discard the evidence, for his parents had arrived back at just that moment – the boy limply holding a blood-stained kitchen knife, still dressed in his own Halloween costume. We don't know what provoked the child to this course of action: maybe it was the 'sinfulness' of his sister's action (this was 1963 morality), or maybe the spooky atmosphere of trick-or-treat night had provoked him to role-play. This is not like the James Bolger case. This lad is too young to be compared to that real-life event. But, like Thompson and Venables, Myers is shown neither sympathy nor mercy. The psychiatrist handling the case, Dr Loomis (Donald Pleasance), ensures he is incarcerated at a mental institution. Instead of being treated, the evil in the boy only intensifies, so much so that the doctor would only refer to Michael as '*It* '. "This isn't a man," he tells his nurse assistant fifteen years later. "What was living behind the boy's eyes was pure and simply evil." Alas, the now adult Michael Myers escapes to reek terror on the community of Haddonfield for the next seven movies in the series.

Arno Frisch's killing of Ingrid Stassner in *Benny's Video* is brutal, and makes uncomfortable watching.[22] But this was not carried out with any vindictive malice. It was just teenage curiosity. A fourteen-year-old boy, addicted to horror movies, finds he has the facility to carry out a killing. This is an impassive, detached action, like squashing spiders or pulling off fly's wings. "Why did you kill her?" asks dad. "I wanted to see what it was like." The boy had even offered the stun gun to the girl first, to dare her to pull the trigger. When the girl returns the gun to the boy and reiterates the dare, he pulls the trigger, the girl writhes in agony on the floor, and as an 'act of pity' ("please, let me help you, be quiet!") the boy feels compelled to finish her off.

This is an example of a film highlighting the potential danger of underaged children addicted to horror movies who become desensitised to reality by acting out in real life what they have seen on the screen.

THE SUPERNATURAL

Ever since the first strife in the Garden of Eden, we have been haunted by that struggle between good and evil, which the movie industry has been happy to perpetuate. While there are those that seriously depict the Christian journey, such as *The Nativity Story* (2006), *The Robe*, others taunt us with Lucifer's work and attempt to scare us witless as they portray demonic possession and exorcisms. For the latter type of film, expect a young child to be the catalyst or the target of abuse – you cannot please an audience without their sensibilities horrified by the victimisation of the innocent child (preferably six-years-old and female, as we shall see in the section on devil possession). Seldom are other religions parodied in the way Christianity is satirized (for example *The Life of Brian*), and it is a brave director who challenges Islamic beliefs on the screen, supposedly for fear of *fatwas*.

Religious belief is at the heart of every single culture. Yet the rise of atheism and the melding effect of multiculturalism have led many to question those timeless beliefs, and contemporary media has adopted this questioning stance as part of its modern role. There are several movies that have dared vocalise agnostic doubts, whether this is in our belief in God, reincarnation, or even Santa Claus, and have given rise to amusing court cases challenging belief in the supernatural.

In the *Tennessee Monkey Trials*, Scopes is tried for teaching evolution, but really God is on trial in this 'Evolution verses Creation' debate depicted in the film *Inherit the Wind* and also in the radio play of the same name (based on a real life incident). Likewise, belief in Santa Claus is put on trial in *Miracle on 34th Street*, while in *The Man who sued God* Billy Connolly tries to get the church to admit responsibilty for the destruction of his boat when it is struck by lightning – an act of God according to the insurance companies who refuse to pay compensation. "It's a lie they use to rob decent honourable people," says Connolly. The irony of this case is that the only way the church can win and not pay out the claim is if they can prove God does not exist!

In both *Audrey Rose* and *The Exorcism of Emily Rose* the possibility of possession is explored in court cases, too. In the case of Emily Rose, the justice system raises passionate debate about whether the teenager died from psychotic-epilepsy, or by negligent homicide on the part of the Catholic priest. In *Audrey Rose*, too, the belief in reincarnation is tested in court and various gurus are invited to explain their beliefs. As part of the trial, a hypnotist is called in, and the young girl, Ivy, is taken back under hypnosis to different times in her childhood. As she is taken back to the time of her birth, the soul of Audrey Rose materialises from the fitful girl, and only Elliot Hoover can calm the spirit of the child.

Religion

While some use the school nativity play as a handrail for humorous scenarios, such as *Nativity!* (2009) which amusingly compares the drama performances in two contrasting schools, others such as *The Nativity Story* (2006) hold fast to a reverential account of the Biblical events, with sixteen-year-old Keisha Castle-Hughes returning the virgin birth to the heart of Palestine.

Other than Nativity plays, there cannot be many films in which a child actor is called upon to play God, and another to play Lucifer. In the Hungarian movie *Annunciation*, Adam (Peter Bocsor) and Eve (Júlia Mérö) are tempted by Lucifer to share an apple from the Tree of Knowledge. God banishes them from the Garden of Eden. Lucifer casts a spell over the couple so that, in a dream, they are able to experience the trials and torments of mankind down the ages. Yet because this film takes the scenario so literally, with the lead child actors required to perform naked in the Garden of Eden, it is unlikely the reader will view this on terrestrial TV.

Here are three films which incorporate the Christian story as an allegory. In the case of the novels by Mary Bell and CS Lewis, this was intentional. But I am not sure Steven Spielberg intended such a religious interpretation of his movie, *ET*.

In *Whistle down the Wind* a group of children confuse a convict with the reincarnated Jesus. Kathy Bostock (fifteen-year-old Hayley Mills), her nine-year-old sister Nan (Diane Holgate), and their audacious infant brother Charles (played by the ripely-accented Lancastrian, Alan Barnes) have just rescued a litter of kittens and are taking them to their barn (they live on a farm) for safekeeping. Because the children all attend Sunday School so the teachings of Jesus are high on their agenda, particularly the second coming of Christ. So when young Charles mentions his little rescued kitten ("Spider"!), his Sunday School teacher assures him, "If you believe in Jesus he'll take care of it."

When Kathie returns to the barn to check on the kittens, that's when she discovers the almost dead body of Alan Bates. "Who are you?" she asks the barely conscious man whose stubble growth and unkempt appearance make him look like a picture of Christ in her New Testament. The man has just enough energy to raise his head, sees the outline of an adolescent girl beside his bed straw, and mutters a profanity, "Jesus Christ!" he exclaims; and so the girl is convinced the Saviour has returned to them in their very own barn.

She returns to the farmhouse to rouse her sister and brother. "I've seen him," she announces dreamily. "Jesus – he's in our barn."

The next day Cathy takes her siblings to the barn to verify the matter. "He was asleep."

"Yes!" affirms a doughy-eyed Nan who is now convinced. "Asleep in the hay."

They raid the scullery for food to give to the man: bread, a bottle of wine, and a slice of cake. The man, of course, is a murderer on the run from the police. He must be pretty confused when the children come to worship him again, adding to the misunderstanding by saying, "We know who you are, and we're going to look after you."

The children decide they must keep it a secret for if they don't, "they'll come and take him away again, like last time," referring to the Romans arresting Jesus 2000 years earlier. But these are kids. They can't keep the secret for long, so soon all of the children in the locality come to see this reincarnation in Kathy's barn.

The film is full of religious analogies; like when one of the boys is forced to deny Jesus three times and all the other children deny having seen Jesus. But when Charles's kitten dies while under the care of his Jesus, Charles loses faith. "He's supposed to look after animals but he doesn't."

In the end, the police track the man down to the barn, and the murderer is arrested. "It isn't Jesus, it's just a fella," observes little Charles. But Cathy keeps on believing. She sees the distant figure being frisked by the police, arms outstretched like a crucifix against the light of the sky.

At least, the analogies made in this film were sympathetic to Christian belief. I am not sure what to make of the TV drama *Ingenious* in which the genie seems to disappear into heaven as a god-like figure promising "I will be with you," as if he were Jesus on Ascencion Day promising an eternal supply of wishes.

I am sure, when Mary Bell wrote *Whistle down the Wind* she was well aware of CS Lewis' wonderful series of stories about the mythical land of Narnia, all allegories of the Christian faith.

As a child, *The Lion, the Witch and the Wardrobe* was undoubtedly my favourite story, as written by CS Lewis. He wrote it as an allegory of the events leading up to the crucifixion. For Christ, substitute Aslan the lion; for betraying Judas, consider Edmund, for he is in league with the White Witch; there is the comparative moment in the Garden of Gethsemane in which Lucy and Susan accompany Aslan in the dead of night; and the broken stone table signifies the resurrection itself, the rolling back of the stone from the sepulcre. Even the destruction of Mr Tumnus' homely cave could be likened to the merciless power of the Romans.

The whole tale is a delight, in which Georgie Henley playing Lucy steals every scene, and Skandar Keynes as Edmund is also compellingly competent. The two other siblings, Susan and Peter (Anna Popplewell and William Moseley) play the parts of concerned older brother and sister.

Magic is all pervasive. Even just the simple action of Lucy backing through the fur coats in the wardrobe brings a rush of tears to our eyes as the sense of imminent wonder is anticipated. The young actress Georgie Henley had not been allowed to see the set before that moment. The cameramen were ready to record the emotions on Georgie's face as she stepped from the mothballed floor of the wardrobe into the snowy winter wonderland of Narnia.

The four children are the prophesied saviours of this province "where it is always winter and never Christmas." With the help of Aslan, Peter's sword, Susan's bow and horn, Lucy's phial of healing ointment, and a repentant Edmund, the four children re-establish freedom from oppression for the creatures of Narnia (except for white stags!), but only after a major battle. Alas, as with so many modern performed battles, belief has to be suspended when the battle is won by someone using superhuman power to do the impossible. As in *Star Wars*, *Harry Potter*, *Superman*, *The Golden Compass*, or the sequel *Prince Caspian*, the battle is won miraculously, and I often think such a loss of life could have been saved by the two protagonists – Aslan and Jadus – battling it out between themselves. War is made to seem honourably just.

While Mary Bell and CS Lewis specifically set out to write their allegories of the Christian story in their books, *Whistle down the Wind* and *The Narnia Chronicles*, it is inevitable that comparisons be made when other films portray characters with supernatural powers. One such film is *ET The Extra-Terrestrial*. ET is a being who causes flowers to bloom, can make the bicycles that Elliott and his friends are riding to fly in front of the moon. His miraculous powers make comparisons with Jesus inevitable. ET has made a contraption to prayerfully communicate with his mothership in the heavens. In the forest, in the dead of night, Elliott waits patiently like a disciple in the Garden of Gethsemane. ET is captured by the hordes of government officials (all that is missing is Pontius Pilate). ET's death, subsequent resurrection, and ultimate ascension (in the spaceship) all point to an omnificent allegory. "I'll believe in you all my life. Everyday. ET I love you," worships the child. And ET points his illuminating finger to Elliott's heart, "I'll be right here," says the alien as if dispensing the Holy Ghost.

Sci-fi enjoys revelling in this uniting of cosmos and religion as scientists are at pains to repeat to Ellie Arroway (Jena Malone) in *Contact* (1997). "If it's just us, the universe seems like an awful waste of space," an empty space that is, ironically, already crowded by the parallel universe of *The Golden Compass* (Philip Pullman's *The Northern Lights* transferred to screen). This is a universe that its cohabitors are inexplicably oblivious to. "If Lord Azriel proves the existence of these other worlds, it will contradict centuries of teaching," warn the authorities. At least, Lara (Dakota Blue Richards) hits on the essence of truth. She dismisses the advice given her by Nicole Kidman, "The wise person knows there are some things you just ignore or never speak about." Instead, she pursues her quest to Svalbard to rescue the children who are having their souls harvested.

In *Alas de Mariposa*, six-year-old Ami, played by Laura Vaquero, is frightened by the framed picture of Jesus placed on her bedside table. It looks like a ghostly shroud of a scary man (the Turin shroud), and every night she turns it face down on the table. But every night father comes in to kiss his daughter goodnight and check that she has said her prayers. Always the answer is 'no' or 'not yet', and father stands the picture upright again to watch over her during the night. "If you forget to pray he'll punish you," says her father, which is not very reassuring for a six-year-old child. "If you prayed more, it would be a better world!" In the end, Ami learns to feign sleep so she doesn't have to endure this scary lecture every night.

This idea of divine punishment of a negligent child is perpetuated in cinema, and used as a threatening stick in legends, too: Santa won't bring presents to naughty kids. Nicole Kidman revelled in ensuring her children understood about Hell, in particular 'children's limbo', as she played mother to Alakina Mann and James Bentley in *The Others* (2001). Yet her daughter Anna starts to see through her argument. "Our mum says all this stuff written about ghosts is rubbish, and then she expects us to believe all that is written in the Bible." It is rare that a child of ten, who relies on a fantasy dream world 'for hope', as Elle Fanning does in *Phoebe in Wonderland*, can come out with such a dogmatic statement, "I don't believe in God!" And yet it is around this age that the absence of fairies and of Santa Claus unfogs the child's supernatural perspective.

Other films in which the misdirected fundamentalist fervour of the adults reach abusive prominence include *Oranges are not the Only Fruit* and *The Magdalene Sisters*. In Volume Eight (*Physical & Sexual Abuse*) we reveal the extent to which children were abused in the name of religion by pious nuns in the *The Magdalene Sisters*. According to Deborah Kampmeier, director of *Hounddog* (2008), "The Church has placed fear and repression on our society that represses the spirit, sexuality and creativity of women." Referring to the dogmatic attitude of the twelve-year-old's grandmother who disapproved of Lewellen's 'blossoming of body and spirit,' the "repression is what leads to abuse."[23]

In *Oranges are not the Only Fruit*, Jess is played by Emily Ashton (aged 7) and by Charlotte Coleman (aged 16), a girl adopted by Geraldine McEwan as a bigoted zealot. As we discuss in Volume Six (*Puberty & First Love*), Jess learns of her mother's strict disapproval of homosexuality, and in Volume Seven (*Childhood Trauma*) of mother's neglect for the girl's illness. Likewise, fornication seems shameful, too. Talking about her father to her mother, Jess has noticed, "When you're in bed he gets up, and when he's in bed you get up!" No wonder they had to *adopt* a daughter. While they are having a home prayer meeting with some ladies from the chapel they hear muffled banging and moaning from the house next door. "They're fornicating!" exclaims one of the ladies. Jess is hurriedly sent from the house to get ice creams, while the ladies all pin their ears to the wall, prayers abandoned. Yet the little girl innocently tells the ice cream man what she had inadvertently heard, "They're fornicating next door!" Deborah Kampmeier states, "When you cut someone from their sexuality you are robbing huge chunks of her soul."[24]

At least, these children were aware of the tenets of Christianity. Not so, the modern child who jumbles Jesus, Santa, and the Tooth Fairy into one deity. "Is that what Jesus is famous for?" expresses Portia Bradley ignorantly in *My Year without Sex*, "being born on Christmas Day?"

The child's prayer in the movies is always personal and seldom selfish. It invariably involves a plea for the child's own family. Christie's (Sarah Bolger) nightly prayer in *In America* (2003), "Mum, Dad, Christie and Ariel, altogether in one happy family," is chanted to keep her family uppermost in her (and God's) thoughts. Opal (AnnaSophia Robb) bows her head in chapel in *Because of Winn-Dixie* whispering, "Please God, I'd really like to see my mama again." Zac Fox in *Wah-Wah* offers a similar prayer, "Please make our mummy come back again, and fix our broken family. Amen." Zuzu's (Karolyn Grimes) prayer in *It's a Wonderful Life*, wrenches at the very fabric of the soul: "Please God, something's the matter with daddy. Please bring daddy back." This is a life and death plea, in the words of Frank Capra Jr, "for a desperate suicidal man saved by those who believe in him," plus, of course a little help from the guardian angel, Clarence.

It does help if the supplicant believes. Jesse James in *The Amityville Horror* (2005) is full of doubt. "Praying doesn't do any good – nobody answered me when I asked if dad could be kept alive." Only John Albasiny's request in *P'Tang, Yang, Kipperbang* can be deemed self-absorbed as he yearns a kiss from Anne Cruttenden's lips. "Please God, just one kiss; one will do." And yet this boy doesn't see the gift when it is placed right under his nose! "Sometimes you have to step back to see what's right in front of you," says Ahmin Mueller-Stahl to Ryan and Melissa," in *The Dust Factory*.

Director Rebecca Miller claims for her film *Angela* (1994) that "children have an exaggerated responsibility for the sad things in their life, such as death and illness."

Miranda Stuart Ryne, as Angela, invents a world of make-believe for herself to help her come to terms with the misplaced guilt feeling that arise as a result of mother's psychiatric illness. Though she has no reason to feel any blame or shame, I guess, the feelings of guilt haunt a child reaching adolescence. And because Angela has dreams in which a semi-naked Lucifer appears beckoning to her while dressed just in a loincloth, she is perhaps confused by the concept of sexual sin. These are not like the benevolent angels that appear to Alex Etel in *Millions* (2004), who persuade the boy to donate to worthy causes the sack of money that miraculously lands on his den built beside the railway track (it is a stolen cache thrown by bank robbers from a passing train).

Angela's beliefs are a corruption of the Catholic faith: she sees the Virgin as the ultimate purity. She assesses everyone she meets and fits them into the categories of good angels or bad angels. She interprets any unrelated occurrence as a possible sign from God. She devises ceremonies to help 'burn off sin', such as creating a circle using her toys and dolls from which she or her younger sister Ellie dare not step outside into 'the big nothing'. Another time she makes a ritual out of puncturing her finger to stain a cloth with her blood, which she then burns. (Unfortunately, later her sister copies this action, staining the curtain with her blood, setting fire to it, and almost burns the house down.)

Angela is afraid Lucifer is going to take her because of her sin. "Lucifer, what did I do?" She cries to him in her dream. "Why do you want me? If you take me, Ellie will die." Angela has become a surrogate mother to her younger sister while mother is ill. But as soon as Angela cries, "Take Mama instead," she immediately has regrets and knows now she has a sin to be ashamed of.

So in the film, Angela doubles her resolve to be cleansed of her sin, either by skinny-dipping in the river to be purified, or scrubbing her and her naked sister with wet mud. When she goes to a religious ceremony by the river, she too asks to be baptised. But after the priest has finished dunking her, she pleads, "Will you do it again?" as if the more often she is submerged the cleaner she will be of this sin.

Of course, all her rituals lead her nowhere. Mum is not cured; Angie and her sister do not have the patience to stay in their safety circles, and instead risk exploring 'the big nothing'. Even Angela's subjective defining of good angels is flawed. She decides one boy they meet is a good angel, but he ends up delivering her a black eye; and the good angel they meet at a funfair turns out to be a pervert who makes sexual advances on the girl.

Finally, Angela has the solution to their dilemmas. She dreams of Lucifer and says to him, "Take me!" She then takes her sister Ellie to the river. "The longer we stay under, the cleaner we get," she tells her, hoping to wash away all her sins. The girl continually dunks herself underwater. But soon Angela is floundering and the last we see of her is as she drifts helplessly towards the weir.

To help prepare her child cast, director Rebecca Miller says she spent two months with the girls talking about good angels and bad angels, being sure they knew it was just a game, but for them to know enough to make it convincing.

Edmonia (Monica Bugajski) also receives a baptism in *Shadrach*. As in *Angela* (1994), it is a traditional dunking in the river water, the washing away of sins. Yet in both films, I wonder if the real motive for the inclusion of the scenes was to titillate the audience with wet see-through linen clinging to a young girl, like in a wet T-shirt competition. In *My Queen Karo*, Karo's father accuses the girl's auntie (who is a nun), "Did you just baptise my daughter behind my back? I'm going to unbaptise her," he complains dunking the girl's head back into the bathtub.

Angela had certainly added her own interpretation to the baptism ceremony. So too has Olivia's father in the wacky Liverpudlian comedy, *Under the Mud*. Eight-year-old Olivia is played by Jasmine Mubory. It is time for her first communion. Father wants to outdo all the other communicants by making her a set of mechanically operated wings, which flap and flash as he presses the remote control button. The whole family seem embarrassed by this and try to make excuses for not attending the church service. Yet father seems oblivious to all this. He just wants a fun day out, with a party afterwards at the pub; God shunted to the sidelines long ago.

Devil Possession

The priests always lose in this type of film. Both Father Karras and the more experienced Father Merrin wrestling with Regan McNeil in *The Exorcist* inevitably are the losers against the forces of Hell. There is no advantage diluting a hysterically scared audience only to have good overcome evil. The same is so in *The Omen* with the demise of Father Brennon, and also in *The Amityville Horror* (2005).[25] The priest called to the Long Island home because "there is something evil in my house," is soon sent packing as a swarm of insects attack him from the ventilation duct. "Get you and your family out of that house – right away!" he warns Mrs Lutz as his exorcism fails.

In Neil Sinyard's words: "It is not simply the theme of evil that disturbs but its graphic depiction, all the more uncomfortable because the girl seems simultaneously the agent of evil and also its helpless victim." [26]   This is as true for Rachel Hurd-Wood in *An American Haunting* as it is for Natasha Ryan and Isabel Conner in *The Amityville Horror*, and AnnaSophia Robb in *The Reaping*, or for Drew Barrymore in *Firestarter*. The girl child becomes its epicentral catalyst for hauntings and inexplicable psychic phenomena, whether that be ghosts, witches, or fairies.   The young girl also becomes that innocent (virginal) victim for sacrifice in paganistic communities as exemplified in *The Wicker Man*.   Teenage harvest queen Rowan Morrison becomes the sacrificial bait to lure the gullible Sergeant Howie to the Scottish Summer Isles to make amends for the crop failures.   "In the name of God, woman, what kind of mother are you that you can stand by and see your own daughter slaughtered," accuses the devoutly religious policeman (Edward Woodward) not realising that he, himself, is about to become the sacrificial substitute.

The child is the agent of evil; this ought to be the conclusion we reach in *The Omen*, one of the few horror films in which the possessed girl is replaced by a boy – in this case, the infamous Damien (Harvey Stephens).   But this boy does not writhe convulsively like Regan, nor blurt out expletives.   He just seems a scared manipulated young boy.   He is labelled as the antichrist by prophets of doom and successive generations, yet the audience finds this as incredible as Gregory Peck discovering the '*666*' birthmark beneath the boy's scalp.   Certainly deaths occur wherever the little boy goes, but only because the evil-eyed nursemaid accompanies him, and the snarling black guard-dog snaps at the heels of anyone over-inquisitive.   This is one boy as innocent as AnnaSophia Robb's character in *The Reaping*, a scapegoat for the twisted beliefs of fanatics.   It took two sequels of *The Omen* to fully besmearch the boys' good name.

In both *The Exorcist* and *Audrey Rose* the child is possessed: by a demon in the Exorcist, and by the incarnation of another soul in *Audrey Rose*.   In both cases the host has to be purged of its parasite: by exorcism in the case of twelve-year-old Regan MacNeil, and by hypnotism in the case of eleven-year-old Ivy Templeton in *Audrey Rose*.   Both methods result in death: the death of the exorcist, while the child survives, in the former film; and by the death of Ivy Templeton, in the latter film, though the father of the incarnated child is vindicated in his beliefs.

Both girls, Linda Blair (*The Exorcist*) and Susan Swift (*Audrey Rose*), start off as normal well adjusted children, but a feeling of malais overtakes them which develop into bad dreams and nightmares, and finally into dramatic raging fits in which the child does damage to herself, though Susan Swift is not corrupted by the unprintable expletives emanating from Regan's mouth.   I guess, both girls had great fun screaming and thrashing about in the making of these films and the crew will have needed effective ear plugs!

While Audrey Rose's soul is deemed by Elliot Hoover (Anthony Hopkins) to be trapped inside another child, a sort of reincarnation gone wrong, he has trouble convincing others of this.   "When I die," says the girl's father, "I'm not going to hover around some maternity ward ready to jump into any infant."   The cops who come to arrest Hoover aren't swayed by his argument either.

The Exorcist is a much scarier affair.   This is demonic possession, and not just a lost reincarnated soul.   The lead girl, the possessed Linda Blair is terrific in her acting.   When mother witnesses the shaking bed she assumes Regan is causing this herself.   She seems unable to distinguish between a psychiatric complaint and a spooky misadventure.   The doctor diagnoses a nervous problem, perhaps caused by separation from her father, and prescribes drugs for hyperkinetic behaviour.   When these don't work Regan is taken for further gruesome invasive tests at the hospital. The doctors are far out of their depth. They misinterpret the condition but keep doing tests to eliminate possibilities. Mother seems inexplicably blind to the poltergeist forces that are moving the bed.

A rapid deterioration sees Regan going into full demonic possession, changing her facial appearance with fits, violent outbursts and a range of expletives, including words which I thought were still banned in the media.

While most movies about possession suggest the triumph of evil, *Bless the Child* endows the six-year-old with discerning powers in the struggle for good. Six seems the standard coming-of-age in horror movies: perhaps there is some recognition of the uncorrupted innocent. It was the age Alex Vincent started his apprenticeship in *Child's Play*, as did Harvey Stephens in *The Omen*. Even *Audrey Rose* had been six-years-old when she was trapped in the wreck of the burning car, before she transferred her soul into Ivy Templeton.

In *Bless the Child*, Cody's (Holliston Coleman) mysterious powers are acquired because she was born on a day when an auspicious special star appeared in the sky: the Star of Yorath. Aunt Maggie raises the child but notices she has autistic traits – repetitious behaviour and retention deficit. "It's as if she's listening to something we can't see." Maggie first notices Cody's telekinetic powers when visiting a church, Cody lighting the candles using the power of her mind.

However, a devil-worshipping cult has been searching for children born under the Star of Yorath. When they trace Cody they kidnap and try to brainwash her. But Cody insists on only using her powers for good. As a test, the cult leader tries to set fire to a tramp, and Cody dutifully uses her power to stifle the flames. On another occasion, he taunts her in the same way Jesus was tempted by the devil on the roof of the temple, goading her to jump, but she refuses. As the police search frantically for the missing girl, there is a final confrontation in which a host of devils try to attack the little six-year-old, but the girl is rescued by a host of angels. The film does try to spin us a critical message that "the devil's greatest achievement is that people don't believe he exists." At least, in this movie the balance has been redressed as forces for good win the day.

"From now on there'll be no more make-believe at this school!" says Miss Minchin shooing all the boarders off to bed, in *A Little Princess*.

ENDNOTES FOR VOLUME FIVE

1 Piggy is played by Hugh Edwards in the 1962 version of *Lord of the Flies*, and by Danuel Pipoly in the 1990 version.

2 Neil Sinyard *Children in the Movies* p61.

3 The 1992 version of *Alice's Adventures in Wonderland* featured an array of theatrical stars and contemporary comedians: Peter Sellers, Michael Crawford, Michael Hordern, Roy Kinnear, Spike Milligan, Dudley Moore, Ralph Richardson, and Flora Robson, but in my opinion all failed to lift the film above a glamorous façade.

4 The 1999 version of *Alice in Wonderland* featured Robbie Coltrane, Whoopi Goldberg, Ben Kingsley, Christopher Lloyd, Peter Posslethwaite, Miranda Richardson, Peter Ustinov, Gene Wilder, Ken Dodd, Sheila Hancock, and Liz Smith. Again, glittering stars, but a torturous plot.

4a *The Other Alice* by Christina Björk & Inga-Karin Eriksson p84.

5 Director Terry Gilliam acquired local Czech girls for these parts: the film being shot in the Czech Republic.

5a Joe Cooper *The Case of the Cottingley Fairies* p14.

6 Track titles and lyrics from *Earth Angel* CD sung by Llewellyn & Juliana (Paradise Music Ltd).

7 *Newnes Popular Encyclopaedia*, p3014.

8 This was the basis for the Pendle Witch Trials, held shortly after the Reformation, the accused women did not attend the protestant church, and when a passer-by fell dead (probably of a heart attack) while passing their house, the occupants were accused of witchcraft.

9 from the extra sequences on *Case 39* DVD.

10 *Chitty Chitty Bang Bang: After they were famous*, shown on ITV1, December 2011.

11 from the extra sequences on *Let Me In* DVD.

12 Vicky Lebeau, *Childhood and Cinema*, p54

13 IMDb Mini Biography Heather O'Rourke by Celia Foster .

14 Flora's parts have been played by Pamela Franklin (1961), Clare Szekeres (1992), Grace Robinson (1999), Eva Sayer (2009).

15 The part of Miles has been played by Martin Stephens (1961), Joseph England (1992), Joe Sowerbutts (1999), Josef Lindsay (2009).

16 Paraphrased from *Halliwell's Video & DVD Guide*, 2004.

17 From reading John Ajvide Lindqvist's novel, it is implied that Eli's guardian is a paedophile, though this is not referred to in the film. In the American remake, *Let Me In*, a glance at the girl's family photograph alludes to the man being her brother now grown up. Because Eli was ravaged aged twelve she has as she says in the film 'remained twelve for a very long time.'

18 Jon Venables and Robert Thompson were both convicted despite *doli incapax*, which 'presumes that young children cannot be held legally responsible for their actions' – Wikipedia *The Murder of James Bulger*.

19 Mary Bell, convicted in 1968 for strangling two infants while she was aged ten and eleven.

20 This movie, *Audition*, was so horrific I could not face watching the final ten minutes!

21 This is only a ten-second sequence. Most of the film features adults performing ridiculous jerky movements to let us know they are zombies.

22 "A subtly disturbing experience", "Stupifyingly horrific" according to *The Radio Times Guide of Films* 2010 p104, and as "unsettling" according to *Time Out Film Guide* 2010 p86.

23 Deborah Kampmeier, director, being interviewed for *The Making of Hounddog*.

24 Deborah Kampmeier, director, being interviewed for *The Making of Hounddog*.

25 *The Exorcism of Emily Rose* is an exception: teenager Jennifer Carpenter died, while Father Richard is charged with negligent homicide.
26 Neil Sinyard *Children in the Movies* p70.

Volume Six

Puberty & First Love

"You know, anyone who thinks growing up is easy, doesn't remember it."
(says Cher in *Mermaids*)

"She's a headache... she's an angel... she's a girl!"
(from *How do you solve a problem like Maria?*
 in *The Sound of Music*)

CONTENTS FOR VOLUME SIX

6. Puberty & First Love..**317**

Contents for Volume Six..**319**

Coming of Age...**320**
Puberty..*321*
Masturbation...*323*
Steps towards the Adult World...*325*
Body Parts...*326*
How babies are perceived to be conceived.....................................*329*

Children in Love..**333**
Just Good Friends..*334*
A Word of Advice: Rehearsing that First Kiss................................*337*
The First Kiss..*339*
Unconventional Kisses: the bizarre and audacious........................*343*
Snogging..*345*
Enduring Affairs...*347*
Spurned Love...*349*

Unorthodox affairs..**352**
Affairs with Older Men...*352*
The Penalty for Being Precocious...*355*
Lesbian Affairs..*357*
Gay Boys and the Effeminate..*360*
Hermaphrodite Children..*362*

Child Nudity on Screen...**365**
What is indecent, and are we, as viewers, breaking the law?.....................*367*

Endnotes for Volume Six...**375**

COMING OF AGE

This is the trial all children have to go through; some are severely affected by it and find it traumatic, others skip through it as if on an exciting roller coaster. We as adults all remember the awkwardness of youthful days, the pains and surprising changes in our bodies, the first pangs of love: all part of nature's design to carry us into adulthood.

Most of us look back fondly on our adolescence, but others have endured a painful road to maturity. When we dream of returning to those halcyon days, we are transported there through the lives of our junior actors and actresses.

Here we encounter an ambiguity. While our youngsters have endured the emotions of happiness and sadness, pain and friendship during their infant lives, they have a reference point for their acting. But as they approach puberty they confront new experiences, and we, the public, expect our actors to perform with the spotlight focussed firmly on their first tentative fumblings.

With today's explicit media, modern youth is far more experienced/knowledgeable sexually, and with the UK topping (or bottoming) the European table for teenage pregnancies,[1] this indicates a large percentage of our young teens, and even a proportion of preteens, are sexually active. It is however, more likely that our carefully chaperoned child actors have been steered clear of such indiscretions by their parents, and confront head-on the full truth about sexuality from the movie script presented to them by the scriptwriter. For many of our young inexperienced actors, their initiation into adult themes is approached primarily through the films they perform in.

Rites-of-passage are not confined to sexual changes and desires within puberty. It is also about responsibilities, adoption of morals, inter-personal relationships, initiation ceremonies, and orientation for the spheres of work. For the four lads in *Stand by Me*, it was the experience that "somehow made their town seem smaller," after their three-day excursion in Oregon's backwoods to search for a reported dead body. For Ivana Baquero playing Ofelia in *Pan's Labyrinth*, it was the moment when she learnt to trust herself, instead of blind allegiance to the ogre of her fantasy world. As director Guillermo del Toro commentates, "The loss of childhood is a profoundly melancholy moment in all our lives." The girl in *Pan's Labyrinth* "is at the crossroads that we have all been through. It has something to say about that moment when we put away our toys, our fairy tales, and our soul, and become just another adult."

For thirteen-year-old Gaby Hoffman in *Freaky Friday* (1995) that crossroad can't come soon enough. She complains to her mother, "(You say) I'm too young to date boys, too young to have my own phone. According to you I'm too young to live!" But the all-knowing mother has seen it all and been through it all: "Sweetheart, what wouldn't I give to be too young!"

Coming-of-age is a time of mixed blessings, the time when the parent is proud of their maturing offspring, but also reluctant to relinquish their child, their baby. "She's twelve-years-old," Robin's father explains to his wife as they discuss whether she should go off to summer camp in *Down will come Baby*. "How many more summers does she have to be a child?"[2]

Since coming-of-age covers a variety of themes that we consider elsewhere in this series, for this volume we confine ourselves to puberty and first love.

Puberty

"There's something I should tell you," says Angela Lansbury to Sarah Patterson in *A Company of Wolves*. "But maybe you're too young, too young to understand. But maybe no child is ever too young…"

Puberty is considered a trying time for children, and more so for girls. There are emotional confusions about relationships with the opposite sex. There are other more physical traumas to confront: physical changes in the body, the growth of breasts and body hair, body odour, unwanted explosions on the skin, divergent, even contradictory, instructions about sex and birth control, things made further baffling by old wives' tales, and prudish religious scruples. Alas, puberty comes at a time when the child is straining to be free of parental restrictions, and the crucial questions that the child needs to ask become awkward as the parent-child bond begins to fray. Which trusted figures can the child turn to, besides their equally misinformed peers? Conflicting information is bombarding the child from all directions, and particularly from the media. Anna Chlumsky delightfully transports us through these quandaries as she plays the role of Veda Sultenfuss in *My Girl* (1991).

Although a bit of a tomboy, Veda is becoming aware of the feminine changes taking place in her body. She is already a hypochondriac, visiting the doctor for all sorts of imagined complaints. On one occasion, she says she is dying of prostate cancer! On another afternoon, she is talking to her widower father, "Dad, I don't want to upset you, but my left breast is developing at a significantly faster rate than my right." Father is wrapped in his own troubles. Whether he even heard what his eleven-year-old daughter has just said, or whether he is not prepared to answer, all that father replies as he makes the sandwiches is, "Hand me the mayonnaise from the fridge." A single father raising a girl through puberty is like a blind man painting a landscape.

Shelly (Jamie Lee Curtis) works for Veda's father as a make-up artist. Veda is obviously becoming more concerned about her looks. "Shelly," she asks the woman, "Do you think I'm pretty?" "Yes, Veda, I think you are very pretty. You've got these great big sparkling eyes, cutest little nose, an amazing mouth." Shelly helps Veda put make-up on her already startlingly beautiful face. Lindsay Lohan, playing Casey in *Life-Size* is offered similar compliments. "You know Casey, you're a really pretty girl, and there is nothing wrong in showing it sometimes. You've got lovely eyes," says Eve as she, too, helps the girl apply her make-up.

Physical looks are an overriding neurosis for maturing girls. Abigail Breslin asks the same question in *Little Miss Sunshine*, "Grandpa, am I pretty?" Grandpa provides the stock answer of all adults. "You're the most beautiful girl in the world." This is a girl with self-belief who has travelled half way across America for a beauty pageant. She looks in the mirror doubtfully, assessing her tubby paunch and bespectacled face. But her mother says, reinforcing the argument, "You're pretty on the inside as well as outside." (The costume department had provided Abigail Breslin with a padded swimsuit to make her look plump.)

For maturing children, puberty raises misunderstandings and alarm as they are suddenly confronted by the extraordinary issues and new experiences in their young lives. For the boy, it is the baffling erection, then the unexpected ejaculation; for the girl, the alarming haemorrhaging following her first period. Returning to *My Girl* (1991), Veda (Anna Chlumsky) was rushing out of bed one morning, desperately searching for dad. Dad had gone out, and the make-up artist, Shelly, is holding the fort. "Shelly, I'm haemorrhaging," screams the desperate Veda. The adult has to comfort and reassure the girl, then patiently, in the bedroom, explain about the stages of puberty, and give a sex education talk. "My mum and dad did that!" Veda protests in disgust. "You'll come to enjoy it, someday," she is told.

Emmeline (Brooke Shields) also exhibits a similar state of alarm about her first period in *The Blue Lagoon*, but this girl has no adult to explain the changes in her body. She is bathing in a pool when she notices streaks of blood surrounding her in the water. She screams for the only one available – Richard (Christopher Atkins) – but as soon as he arrives, she yells at him in embarrassment to go away. It is something she has to face alone.

While Veda and Emmeline were taken by surprise, for Eleanore Karwien, her first period was a long-awaited joy for the thirteen-year-old, and she proudly announces its arrival to her mum in *Peppermint Soda*. But on doing so, she receives a slap around the face for divulging the fact. But the mother explains the slap: "It's just a tradition," she tells her tearful daughter while giving her a congratulatory hug.

Chandeep Uppal, playing Meena in *Anita & Me*, was concerned over other physical changes. "I'm getting hair in strange places," she observes. "What if my hair keeps growing and I end up like a werewolf?" Anne Frank, likewise, was baffled by the pubertal changes in her body, and "not only on the outside." With no one to confide in, she sobs in front of the mirror in *The Diary of Anne Frank* as Anne (Ellie Kendrick) writes in her journal, "I have this terrible urge to touch my body."

If the issues being depicted by the child actor are carefully explained to them, then instead of being frightened by the impending changes in their own body, they can be forewarned, even pleasantly surprised by their journey through puberty. What must be most disturbing for any child is the partial story, the half-truths, the hearsay, that implants dread and guilt in the mind of the child, so they become victimised by puberty rather than be rewarded by it. The child actor can gain advantage over his/her peers when the action he/she is depicting is sympathetically explained.

Despite this, the pre-adolescent child can remain ignorant of the sexuality around them. "She's going through a stage. It's her age," says mum about her daughter Devon, in *Lawn Dogs*. Mischa Barton plays a girl trapped in that transient stage between playing with dolls and living in a fantasy fairy tale world, while growing up as a ten-year-old who is unable to live up to the expectations of her affluent parents. She is becoming aware of her pre-pubertal body, but is not yet aware of its significance, using it as a form of protest and defiance. At night, she sits on the roof, takes off her nightdress, and lets the wind float it away on the breeze while she howls at the moon like a naked wolf. She unbuttons her blouse in front of her adult friend, Trent. "I'm not showing you my tits, stupid; it's my scar." In defiance to her father, she sits on his car, raises her dress, and pees down the windscreen.

When a male friend of her mother tries to molest the child by groping her chest under her blouse, she tries to fight him off. But when she reports this to her father, she is not taken seriously. "Bret put his hand up my skirt yesterday at the barbecue."

"Is that all?" replies dad. "Anything else? You mean, you let him put his hand…." Devon is made to feel the guilty party, so she deflects the seriousness of the assault by pretending it was only a tickling game." We discuss in Volume Eight this dilemma of not being believed as being a major hurdle the adolescent girl has to confront (Kristina Adamcova playing Alzbetka in *Little Otik* and Vanessa King playing Kelly in *Liar, Liar* both encountering disbelief as they describe how they are being abused).

Devon is a girl who has peered through windows to watch adults having sex, and caught a visitor with his hand up mother's dress. She is becoming aware of the desires of adults but she is still subject to her own child fantasies. We see the same traits in nine-year-old Bella Riza's portrayal of Bea in *Hideous Kinky*. "They're prostitutes," she declares as her mother waves to the women flaunting themselves on the balcony above their Moroccan home. "Where did you learn that?" Her mother (Kate Winslet) is surprised at her brazen observation. But this is a sensible child who has witnessed mother's cavorting with a naked man, and immersed in a foreign culture is a little girl who has to grow up fast.

Another voyeur of the sexual act is Anna Paquin who peers through the crack in the hut where her mama (Holly Hunter) is supposedly giving piano lessons to Harvey Keitel in *The Piano*. While playing with her Maori friends, she starts to mimic what she has seen by hugging and kissing tree trunks. Her new stepfather catches her doing this and to show his disapproval makes her scrub the trees with soap and water.

Masturbation

Puberty is a time for experimentation and deviancy for boys, too. *The Cement Garden* features sexual experimentation spilling into incest and cross-dressing. In a family of four children, the older boy, Jack (Andrew Robertson), practises kissing on his hand. He masturbates in front of the mirror at just the moment his father is dying. Mother tries, with difficulty, to talk to the boy about his pubertal urges – this would have been father's task had he been alive, mum tells him. She has noticed how big his pupils are, and the bags under his eyes, and, "Every time you, you know, do it, it takes two pints of blood to replace it!"

We are expected to see the funny side of a boy's subconscious spasm. "What does he do in his sleep!" exclaims Joshua's mother in *Big* (1988) as she inspects his pyjamas. Maybe this helps assure boy viewers that wet dreams are part of every maturing male's puberty. In the French film *Pocket Money*, a shocked woman teacher confides in her male colleague that the eleven-year-old boys in her class are "sitting at the back of the classroom playing with themselves." But the man explains it is just part of growing up. "Next year, when we go co-ed, there will be new problems!"

Renato's deviancy in *Malèna* was stealing the black lace underwear from the clothesline of the twenty-seven-year-old neighbour. This is a stunning woman that the whole Italian town of Castelcuto swoon after: the town comes to a standstill every time she passes, turning all the men's heads. Twelve-year-old Renato (Giuseppe Sulfaro) spends his days spying on this woman. If he hears anyone say a bad word against her, he secretly spits in their drink, or pees in their handbag, or smashes their shop window. Though his devotion to the woman remains secretive, the physical outpouring of his desires cannot remain unnoticed. Father hears the bedsprings violently squeaking in the bedroom above and bashes the ceiling with a broom handle. "You're going to go blind," he yells. When Renato's father finds the boy asleep with the black knickers smothering his face, he locks him in his bedroom, while mother sews up his pockets. In the words of director Giuseppe Tornatoro, "Through his secret passion for Malèna, Renato becomes a man."

Only recently have movies brought masturbation into the open as normalised (if laughable) behaviour. Brooke Shields laughs about Christopher Atkins' abnormal fidgeting on the rocks in *The Blue Lagoon*. John Albasiny in *P'Tang, Yang, Kipperbang* wears a glove in bed to placate God.

Seldom is it depicted with serious intensity. Two shepherd boys find their own crags to hide behind in *Babel* as they relive the vision of the naked girl they had earlier spied through a crack in the wall.

This activity is always secretive. Perhaps we all grow up with a guilt gene – an instinctive suppression of admitting our desire to masturbate. This secrecy seems inherent in all cultures, as every adolescent and adult, male and female, on every continent feels compelled to conceal, even deny, their masturbatory activity. In some religions, this suppression has made the action synonymous with sin, thus formalising the feelings of guilt that accompany a child's secrete action. Yet like fear, sadness, love, this feeling of guilt associated with masturbating is innate within the chromosomes of an adolescent; maybe it is nature's way of recovery, ensuring we don't over exert the throbbing protrusion. Most children are not told about guilt feelings. Mother Nature seems to impose them simultaneously, to counteract the accompanying feelings of elation. This is self-discovery, learnt from life's equivalent of a DIY store. Only through time does the adolescent learn to disassociate the feelings of guilt from the pleasure.

This element of suppression is borne out in Dorothy Allison's semi-autobiographical novel *Bastard out of Carolina*. While the film based on the book dares to depict the preteen girl (Jena Malone) squirming on her father's lap while the man masturbates beneath her, and the film graphically shows the father's attempted rape of his child; but when it comes to depicting Dorothy's growing urge to masturbate and her secret listening to her younger sister doing likewise (both are significant sections within her novel) within the film itself this is one taboo too far. The director does not dare confront this most intense feeling that possesses all of us on a daily basis. Masturbation in the movies remains where society has decreed it to be: hidden, unspeakable, *closetized*. And in the words of Dorothy Allison, she felt she was "committing a sin." [3]

By offering the word *closetization*, I refer not just to masturbation as an individualistic activity, accomplished away from the prying eyes of others. I define this as an inherent need to perpetuate both the denial and the secrecy of masturbation as a solitary act, in opposition to the current trend of exposing this as a shared activity (as depicted in contemporary salacious media). While it is important that connotations of guilt and sin associated with masturbation are removed from the child's mind, no child should be bullied into the alternative indoctrination of this being a shared experience – shared neither vocally[4] nor shared physically. This is as universal and timeless a decree as are the laws of the Medes and the Persians. Nor should a child actor be required to portray, or be seen to portray, this intensely private act just because the media wishes to break taboo boundaries. This is what Berangere Haibruge was required to do in *Innocence* (2004). The gloved hand self-massaging her inner thigh was probably not the child actor's but the hand of an adult stand-in, yet the audience associates the girl herself as being the participant in this solitary act of self-molestation.

Tarra Steele was just eleven-years-old when she was required to gesture masturbatory motions as she played the thirteen-year-old feral child in *Mockingbird Don't Sing*. As well as massaging under her skirt, the girl has to show intense pleasure on her face so that the social workers supervising her can report on their records: "Katie is fond of touching herself." This is one problem they believe has to be suppressed. Before long, the girl is being fostered out to an unfeeling fundamentalist foster family.

Steps towards the Adult World

"Totally unprepared am I to face a world of men,
Timid, shy, and scared am I of things beyond my ken,"

sings Liesl (Charmain Carr) as she was *sixteen going on seventeen* in *The Sound of Music*, *innocent as a rose*. Her boyfriend has just sung to her:

"Your life, little girl, is like an empty page that men will want to write on." Now that sounds scary!

Scary too for parents who see their little babies rapidly growing into young adults. Alan Davies sighs to his daughter (Georgia Groome) in *Angus, Thongs and Perfect Snogging*, "Why don't you just enjoy being fourteen. What's the hurry growing up so fast?"

"Sorry, dad, I must be hormonal." The girl had made a mess of plucking her eyebrows. "I wish you'd stop messing about with yourself – you're beautiful." Thinking he is just being patronising, Georgia replies, "You have to say that, you're my dad."

The process of going through adolescence is such a confusing passage, and most children think they are ill prepared for the journey. In *Peppermint Soda (Diabolo Menthe)*, introverted Anne (Eleanore Karwien) is both confused and anxious about the world of men that Liesl had sung about. She irrationally runs away from a man she regularly passes in the street, which is quite disconcerting to the poor man (as does Kristina Adamcova playing Alzbetka in *Little Otik*). Anne dislikes her mother's new boyfriend, having a distrust of any male she does not know, yet seems anxious to discover about them. Her older sister Frederique had a boyfriend but Anne does not. In her curiosity she steams open one of her sister's love letters. The film is the first of an autobiographical trilogy by director, Diane Kurys.

Adolescence is a scary time, of not knowing who to trust, and Granny's old wives tales are certainly not to be trusted, or are they? This was Rosaleen's (Sarah Patterson) dilemma in *The Company of Wolves* as her gran tells her about men: "Oh, they are as nice as pie until they have had their way with you. But once the bloom is gone… the beast comes out! Never trust a man whose eyebrows meet!"

Boys, too, realise adolescence is a staging post towards adulthood. "Congratulations on your twelfth birthday, I've got a surprise for you." says dad (Robin Williams) in *Mrs Doubtfire*.

Matthew Lawrence asks hopefully, "Is it a stripper?"

For perplexed twelve-year-old Lizzie (Heather Anne Foster) in *Urban Ghost Story*, a girl who was still dependent on her mother and had not yet had her first period, her aspirations of adulthood seemed to be set by the example of her older sister. Cradling her baby in her own Glaswegian council flat she tells her younger sister, "You wait till your sixteen, Lizzie. Get yourself pregnant. Tell the *Social* you can't live with your mama and they will have to find you a wee flat."[5]

The proud day arrives when Lizzie has her first period. "I can have babies now," she tells her mum, one foot already out the proverbial door. This, more than any other aspect of adolescence is the fear of parents of the teenage child: that sexual experimentation will lead to unwanted pregnancies. And this is hype exploited almost salaciously in the media. Yet, despite the common thought that children today are more precocious, with the age of first sexual encounters becoming younger, the reality of the situation remains that the majority of children under sixteen do not have sex.[6]

The movie industry does however have its historic wayward hoydens. Tuesday Weld claimed to have had her first real affair aged eleven, Sue Lyon on her thirteenth birthday, and Roman Polanski's 'Sandra' claimed to have started "at eight with a kid down the street."[7]

Body Parts

The changes occurring in an adolescent's body are baffling to them, even frightening. Too often, the child has to teeter on the stepping stones of self-discovery while others around them mock their ignorance, treat puberty as a joke, or pretend they are already knowledgeably informed. Honest education is too often lacking, or arrives too late, or is presented as a confusing array of indecipherable text-book diagrams. Parents are often reticent at imparting knowledge, so the facts of life have to be secretly shared between peers and siblings who may be equally ignorant. The movie industry, which lusts after these salacious misunderstandings, perpetuates this ignorance in the child viewer and the child actor. Alas, I suppose that by writing this chapter in a frivolous manner I myself am sustaining these misconceptions.

The three *Blue Lagoon* movies are genuine coming-of-age films created, like Stacpoole's novel to show how adolescent children cope with puberty. While Emmeline and Richard had to discover things for themselves, at least in *Return to the Blue Lagoon* the two children, Lily and Richard, who were stranded on a desert island, had a mother to teach them "life facts", certainly for the first part of their childhood. But a fat lot of good it did them in those prudish Victorian times (1897) for, as I am sure so many parents experience even today, there was a reluctance to confront sexual issues.

The three of them, eight-year-old Lily (Courtney Phillips), her mother (Lisa Pelikan), and her adopted son Richard (Brian Krause), are bathing in a pool. Lily asks her mother why she has different body parts to Richard. Mother, however, is too embarrassed and says she will explain about life facts later, after their spelling lesson. Mother could not even bring herself to give names to the male genitals, and behind an embarrassed snigger she says let's not mention the male parts. Yet eight-year-old Richard suggests Lily's female anatomy is like a cowry shell, and mother is relieved that's one lesson she can shirk.

Then (after spellings) comes the sex education lecture – how Richard will grow big muscles, have hair on his chest and chin, and his voice will deepen. Then Lily is told what will happen to her in a few years' time. For the actual actress, Courtney Phillips, playing the part of Lily, this must have been a bewildering lesson and during the actual filming was probably the first time she had, herself, been introduced to the concept of puberty. You can see the furrow of alarm forming on her face as mother explains how her body will change, how she will bleed from between her legs, how her breasts will form, and a baby will grow inside her if she lies close to a man. Frightening stuff for an actress so young. Yet Richard comes to her rescue again, citing how they watch the iguanas "coming close together" and thus *mating* is incorporated freely into their vocabulary – a source of secret consternation when in later years a young English lady comes ashore to visit them and hears them openly referring to 'mating' as part of everyday language.

Similarly, a prudish grandmother was horrified to discover that Anna (Nina Kervel), in the French film *Blame it on Fidel*, shared a bath with not just her brother, but her mum and dad, all naked in the same bath together. Anna's friend, Cecile, also gets a shock when she comes for a sleepover to be confronted by Anna's naked father. All this seems natural for Anna, but for Cecile, "she had never seen a dickie," so Anna had some explaining to do to her friend.

If instructional sex education is not provided because of the prudish self-reserve of their guardian, then children discover about the anatomy of the opposite sex either by self discovery which can be frightening if confronted by an unclothed adult, or by playing the "if I show you mine…" game. Otherwise, they live in ignorance. In *Hope and Glory*, a gang of boys offer Pauline (Sara Langton) some of the booty they have gleaned from bomb-damaged London, if only they can queue up to look down her drawers.

For the young boy, induction into the world of breasts and boobs is a dream come true, even a neurosis: the gang of lads spying with their telescopes in *Gregory's Girl* as the student nurse undresses in the flats beyond the bushes. "I can't breathe, I can't breathe," gasps Andy. For ten-year-old Elijah Wood, Paradise was not just the name of the village in South Carolina where he was on vacation. "Do you want to see my sister Darleen with her clothes off?" asks nine-year-old Thora Birch; and the descriptive terms *'a pair of fried eggs'* enters the boy's vocabulary as he watches the topless teenage vamp ironing, and as later he and Thora Birch spy on the young woman enjoying sex with her boyfriend, in the film *Paradise* (1991). All this makes nine-year-old Anthony Cunningham's (Lewis McGibbon) action, in *Millions* (2004), of zooming in on the woman's breasts on the computer screen, pale into insignificance, while his blissfully ignorant seven-year-old brother (Alex Etel) watching with him asks "What's a nipple?" Twelve-year-old Shaun (Thomas Turgoose) is invited by his much older girlfriend (Rosamund Hanson) in *This is England*, "Do you want to suck my tits?"

These are all ways the heuristic movie industry helps enlighten our younger generation; through laughing at ignorance, titillation and brazen remarks.

But curiosity can have its harmful qualities, as Molly (Asia Vieira) discovers in *The Good Mother*. Molly's downfall comes from a misunderstanding. "I've tried to raise Molly freely. I didn't want her to be ashamed of her body or think it was something she had to hide," says Diane Keaton, playing the girl's mother. So when the little girl intrudes on mother's boyfriend having a shower and out of curiosity asks to touch his penis, this results in a custody battle in which the courts decree the girl should go to live with the birth father, instead of the mother and her boyfriend. The actress, six-year-old Asia Vieira, of course was never exposed to any of this beyond reading a book about body parts with Diane Keaton. Nor was there any physical corruption as Alex House and Charlotte Arnold converse in *The Safety of Objects*, though the script must have reduced the child actors to uncontrolled titters off-camera. "Do you want to see it?" probes the boy. "You can touch it if you want." But the girl is not impressed. "It's soft. It's supposed to be hard!" she protests. Yet the exploitation of the child actors in *Hounddog* was greater. Cody Hanford has first to remove his shorts to "show me your thing first" before Dakota Fanning agrees to kiss him.

While the boy is the observer of change, the voyeur of others, the girl has to witness the puzzling transformations in her own body. This may lead to feelings of ecstasy or of worthless self-pity, as she becomes the object of admiration. She may flaunt this or cringe from it. Christina Ricci does both in *Now and Then*, as she at first ashamedly tapes up her new protuberances, while later flaunts them once she had gained a boyfriend.

But the girl needs reassurance she is developing correctly. Perhaps this is the reason behind the strange undressing game that Unn (Hilde Nyeggen Martinsen) and her new friend Siss (Line Storesund) played in *The Ice Palace*: the desperate desire to check if others were enduring the same metamorphosis. In *Toto le Héros*, eleven-year-old Sandrine Blancke plays Alice, the older sister of Thomas (Thomas Godet). She is becoming aware of the changes in her body. When mother is away, Alice and Thomas get the run of the house for themselves. Lying in the same bed together at night, Alice needs reassurance that she is developing correctly. "Do you like my nose?" she asks her brother. She holds out her hands and spreads her fingers. "Which hand is the prettiest?" The boy can't decide. "Are my legs too skinny? Are my feet too big?" Everything seems just right. "Do I look like a boy?" the girl asks him, but his negative reply is all the girl needs for reassurance.

He has already had chance to compare her budding mammaries, for they often share baths together. "I didn't know you had breasts," he had told her when she had recently stood naked before him. Then she had confused him. "Don't you read newspapers?"

"What? Is it in the paper?" the baffled boy replied as if he should have seen her naked picture in the press!

Now, lying in bed, she leads her brother's hands to fondle the growing buds and they share a kiss together. The boy has fallen madly in love with his sister. "Nefertiti, the Egyptian queen, married her brother," the boy tells her, justifying his feelings. And he wonders whether perhaps he could have been switched at birth in the maternity ward, thus making his love affair permissible.

In *Angela* (1994), Miranda Stuart Ryne stands open-shirted in front of the mirror. For her, her breasts appear to be growing too slowly. Using a felt pen, she outlines on her chest the position of where she would like her breasts to be, whereas in *Flickan*, the girl (Blanca Engström) opens her legs to sketch her more intimate anatomy.

Alice (Eliza Dushku) and her friends are confused about their budding breasts, in *That Night*. They had read an advertisement that implied that if they rub ointment on their breasts they would grow. So, we share the mirror as we watch the three preteens massage their nipples with ointment, but after what seems like several minutes of rubbing it doesn't seem to work.

Saga (Melinda Kinnaman) is also concerned about the growth of her breasts in the Swedish film *My Life as a Dog*. Her misfortune is that her best friend, Ingemar, has not yet reached the same stage of adolescence. Saga is a barely pubescent twelve-year-old. She loves playing soccer, but to maintain the pretence of being a boy so she can continue playing in the boys' league, she dresses like a tomboy. Her best friend, Ingemar, knows she is a girl so she confides in him. She unbuttons her blouse in front of him to show him her dilemma. Her newly budding boobs are becoming too prominent. Nevertheless, Ingemar helps her bind her chest with a scarf to make them less noticeable, as Christina Ricci does in *Now and Then*.

But Ingemar, himself, has not yet reached the stage of sexual curiosity. As part of his 'coming-of-age' he had to accompany a young lady, Berit, to her nude modelling assignment, as a chaperone, to ensure the artist didn't take advantage of the woman, "Just to make sure things stay artistic." When his uncle quizzes him about the experience later, what was she like in the nude? "How were the melons?" drools the older man.

"I don't know. I didn't really look."

Another girl invites Ingemar to a party. When all the other children are downstairs, she says to Ingemar, "Do you want to see my bedroom?" She sits on the bed with him, no doubt ready to be passionate, but all the boy wants to do is continue eating his hotdog.

On a later occasion, Saga unbuttons her blouse again, inviting Ingemar to touch her tiny breasts, "I've grown," she tells him. But the boy is disinterested. Still, if the hormones ain't ready, the hormones ain't ready. This makes Saga irate. Now she has shown him her boobs, she insists he show her his own privates. "You've grown too, haven't you? Show me. I want to check."

"No way," says Ingemar, running away out of embarrassment.

"I showed you mine," yells Saga. "What's the matter, do you need tweezers to pull it out?" A boundary has been crossed for which Ingemar had not been prepared, and he breaks off his friendship with the girl.

The trouble is, Ingemar had been bombarded with temptations before, but he never rose to the bait. He had been living with his sick mother and elder brother. His brother was explaining to a group of giggly but curious children how babies are made. His brother uses a glass bottle to illustrate the female organs. He gets his young brother, Ingemar, to demonstrate by sticking his willy into the mouth of the bottle. But of course, it gets stuck. Mum has to rescue the situation by smashing the glass and awkwardly helping to prise the organ free. "Why did you do it?" asks mum accusingly. Ingemar irrationally assumes some guilt, "I don't know. I guess it's a phase."

Later, he plays with his girlfriend/playmate Kiki Rundgren. They are in a culvert under the railway track. Ingemar is happily reading a newspaper. Kiki lies flat on the ground ready to play mothers and fathers. "Come to bed," implores the little girl. "Come on, I've taken my clothes off." But the boy is not interested and continues reading the paper instead. But just then, the girl's father comes by and innocent Ingemar again receives a rocket.

Others, of course want to protect their modesty, and rightly so. "He saw me. I know he did," complains fourteen-year-old Anna Paquin to her dad's girlfriend, as she stands naked in the shower in *Fly Away Home*. The girl had pressed the wrong tap in the shower and soapy hot water had squirted into her eyes. Her screams had caused her father to bust open the bathroom door, and that is how she was revealed, in her birthday suit, to the young man who was visiting. "No he didn't," lies father's girlfriend, trying to placate her. But this is a girl who has experienced a growth spurt, causing a visiting welfare officer to utter the overused quip: "Don't they grow up fast!"

We mentioned how Christina Ricci taped her boobs in *Now and Then*. "Whatever I do they just keep getting bigger!" She is frustrated by the unstoppable growth of her breasts and she decides to strap them up so she won't look different from her friends. (Later, when she shares her first kiss with one of the local boys, that is when she stops taping up her boobs, so she can look more attractive and grown up). Her friend, played by Thora Birch, has an opposite view. "I don't have any real ones yet," she complains, as with a flourish she pulls from her cleavage a partly inflated balloon. "You're lucky," responds Christine as if she has already had some bad experience, "Men love them when they're big. You'll get them, and you'll hate them." And as if a maturing child feels inconspicuous: "If you hadn't noticed, I'm a woman now," fourteen-year-old Georgia Groome yells at her parents in *Angus, Thongs and Perfect Snogging*. "I even wear a bra."

How babies are perceived to be conceived

"If you didn't have men, who would drive the women to the hospital to have the babies?" puzzles Mason Gamble in *Dennis* (1993).

For children conception of babies is the biggest mystery of them all, not helped by the prudish self-consciousness of some adults, still upholding Victorian attitudes. Even de Vere Stacpoole writing *The Blue Lagoon* was unwilling to divulge this mystery to his child readers. His reading audience is told that Emmeline simply found the baby in the woods – that the love affair and courtship were totally unrelated.

At least in rural communities the mechanics of the act can be witnessed by watching animals. In *Times & Winds*, Yildiz was able to watch copulating dogs and donkeys, always a source of laughter for her and her friends. But for Mitch Brenner, in Hitchcock's *The Birds*, even that was going too far. "I'd like a pair of love birds," he says to the attendant in the pet shop. "It's for my younger sister who is only eleven. I would not want them to be too…. demonstrative!" Similarly, in *Oranges are not the Only Fruit*, religious zealot (Geraldine McEwan) who has an adopted seven-year-old daughter (Emily Ashton) acknowledges, "I don't even let Jess watch wildlife programmes for fear of what she might see!"

So, "How *are* babies made?" asks Cecile in *Blame it on Fidel*.

"Haven't your parents told you?" replies Anna, her eleven-year-old friend, trying to deflect the question.

"No, when I ask they pretend they have not heard."

"So do mine," agrees Anna, "especially my grandmother." So the big important question in their young lives is never fully answered.

Now and Then is a coming-of-age film in which a gang of four girls become aware of their budding maturity, but also encompasses other aspects of rites-of-passage: the faked drowning of one of their friends (this was a practical joke), and their curiosity over a boy buried in the local cemetery who had been murdered.

One of the girls, twelve-year-old Chrissie, played by Ashleigh Aston Moore, had to receive her sex education from her self-conscious mother who was as incompetent at explaining the birds and the bees as was Lisa Pelikan's character in *Return to the Blue Lagoon*. "All women have a garden," says Chrissie's mother, "And all gardens need a big hose to water it!" And so the poor girl gets into tangles when she has to explain what she knows to her friends.

"Chrissie," the others ask her, "Have you ever been French kissed?" "You're kidding," she replies, "I don't want to get pregnant." But her comment is not as naïve as it sounds, as she clarifies, "It's common knowledge if you tongue-kiss a boy it can lead to doing the deed with him." Even so, the others laugh at her for her ignorance of how boys get a "hard-on."

Chrissie's ignorance of such a term was shared by seven-year-old Jennifer Beck in the Clint Eastwood movie, *Tightrope*. In fact, I'm surprised the scriptwriter even used this vocabulary just to get a cheap laugh at the expense of such a premature child. Clint Eastwood is driving his two daughters, when out of the blue, the younger daughter, Jennifer, asks, "Dad, what's a hard-on?" Both father and older daughter guffaw simultaneously and splurt out their Pepsi. How the question even arose I am not sure, and this was the only line of script this little girl had to say in the entire movie. I can imagine the little girl going proudly to her school and telling her teacher she was in a film with the famous Clint Eastwood. "Oh, that's nice, Jennifer, what lines did you have to say?"….

The father tries to explain, but without success, and the older sister, twelve-year-old Alison Eastwood, pretends she knows. (I assume Alison is the real life daughter of Clint.) Oh, and Jennifer Beck had just one other line of script to say, later in the film. She says to her father, "You can have a hard-on any time you like!"

The brazenness of little children is further exploited in *Nowhere to Run* as the infant girl audaciously asks the visiting man, "Are you and mum going to sleep together and have sex." This after the children (Kieran Culkin and Tiffany Taubman) had stated the man (Jean-Claude Van Damme) has a big penis.

Such an attempt to get cheap laughs through sexual innuendo is further exploited by Terry Gilliam in *The Adventures of Baron Munchausen*. As we can see in *Tideland*, this is a director who revels in pushing boundaries. The king and queen are cavorting together in bed, the queen generating audible orgasmic noises. Written into the script for the young actress Sarah Polley is the question, "Why is she making those funny noises?" The nine-year-old is told, "Her majesty is with the king, and he is, er, tickling her feet!" The only purpose of these lines in both *Tightrope* and *The Adventures of Baron Munchausen* is to exploit the child so that we can titter at her ignorance. As if to nullify the hypocrisy of the remark, the king lifts the blankets from the bed so that we can witness him tickling the queen's toes with a feather.

Similarly, in *Little Rascals*, an infant boy is asked to explain to his mates how he got rid of an annoying girl. "I whipped out my lizard!" he tells them, and to demonstrate, he takes with a flourish from his pocket a little green lizard. Compare this with the genuine laugh-induced innuendo in *The Brady Bunch Movie*. Oldest Brady daughter, Marsha, is kissing her prom date, Charlie. But Charlie in desperate embarrassment declares, "I've got to go. Something suddenly came up!" In this case, the 'child' actors were adults, so there is no case of exploiting seven- and nine-year-olds for our titillation.

In *Cría Cuervos*, Ana Torrent's housekeeper explains how she became pregnant: she had been walking past a building site when something fell from above inside her blouse, whereas ten-year-old Alice Bloom (Eliza Dushku) in *That Night* thinks babies are conceived by standing upside-down. Alice is often left on her own while the women gossip together. She mishears snippets of conversation. "If you want to have another baby," she overhears one of the mothers saying, "You have to stand on your head for eight weeks." So, Alice reports back to her friends who are all becoming curious about sex and puberty. "My parents do it on their heads," she tells them. But to add to her confusion, when she had asked her parents how she was born, they told her, "They kissed each other and breathed me into life."

Idle gossip at summer camp inevitably allow children to share notes. In *Addams Family Values*, one girl explains how her parents got her new baby sister, "A stork brought a diamond, left it under a leaf in the cabbage patch, and it turned into a baby." But Christina Ricci startles them all with her blunt appraisal: "Our parents are having a baby, too – they had sex!"

"I think it's a baby in me from kissing," says Jeliza Rose in *Tideland* when she hears her tummy rumble. This ten-year-old, played by Jodelle Ferland, had been snogging a grown man, Dickens (played by Brendan Fletcher).

So many children assume pregnancy comes from kissing. Even two girls kissing together might achieve the same result. That was the fear of the little sister in *Angela* (1994). Ellie (played by Charlotte Blythe) has just been snogged by her older sister, Angela (Miranda Stuart Ryne), and the young girl now fears she might get pregnant. Angie reassures her, "You get pregnant from boys only." They look at a stallion in the field. Angela points out the horse's penis. "You see this?" she tells her sister. "That's exactly what men have. They stick it in the woman. I've seen dad do it. It looks like it hurts." And the girls stop to watch, mesmerised as the horse's willy jiggles as it grazes. "But," she adds, showing how much influence misinformation creeps in, "If you don't do it by the time you are twenty-one you start getting smaller."

The knowledgeable youngster was even younger in *Hope and Glory*. Geraldine Muir is spying with her older brother, Sebastian Rice Edwards, watching a young couple's foray into sexual intercourse, or to use the actual words from the ten-year-old boy's mouth, "Fuck!" The infant girl states, "They don't do it right. They are still learning, that's why." It is not how *her* parents do it. "Mummy keeps still and daddy moves on top of her. That's what they do," and the little girl turns away surprised at her older brother's ignorance.

Thora Birch is able to sneak into the barn with her young friend Elijah Wood in *Paradise* (1991) and watch her older sister have sex with a boyfriend. But even here, the knowledge she learns is impregnated with ignorance. "Every month girls have a curse put on them," explains Thora to the ten-year-old boy. "I don't know who does it, but when they get the curse they don't have a baby."

In *Times & Winds*, the girl Yildiz, played by Elit Işcan, is a dutiful daughter who runs errands for her parents. As a future woman, we gradually see her becoming aware of the sexual role of the female in traditional Turkish society. Hearing strange noises from her parents' bedroom, she spies through the keyhole and is distressed by what she sees. But when she and her friend witness two donkeys copulating, and later two dogs, they both burst into laughter. Interestingly, the boys watching with her castigate her for looking at the coupling animals, yet the boys feel no guilt themselves.

In this age of explicit media saturation, we expect children to be sexually aware. But this is a fallacy perpetuated by innuendo, parental reserve, and watersheds. It has always been so. Colleen Moore, recollecting her experiences as a fifteen-year-old actress, recalls referring to the "so called facts of life", that "I and my girlfriends at the studio didn't know them, and would not have dreamed of asking anyone. We were fully as innocent as the heroines we portrayed."[8]

So, we have seen that sex education for children is a play of innuendo, half-truths and old wives tales. Child actors are exploited to perpetuate such myths, for our frivolity. I hope film directors do take time to explain the scenarios their young actors are depicting, so our screen children can distinguish the humour from the truth.

It is rare that a film dares explain the true facts to our next generation. Audiences, it seems, would prefer a cheap laugh at the expense of the kids. And yet, that is what we get in *Definitely, Maybe*. At least, ten-year-old Maya (Abigail Breslin) had been taught the facts of life in her primary school classroom. There is an excited buzz at the end of the day as the children gather in the school foyer while their parents collect them. But in this film, we are not duped into laughing at children for their ignorance, but for their brazen outspokenness. "Just when were you going to put your penis in mum's vagina?" she asks her father, and we the audience are expected to be shocked into laughter at the audacious remark. But her schoolteacher had evidently not covered everything. "If you didn't want a baby then why did you have sex?" the girl demands. And later, she wants to know what is a three-some, and what is the boy-word for *slut*. Somehow, the romance has long since been omitted.

So let us continue by injecting some romance where our memories are fondest – first love.

CHILDREN IN LOVE

"Love? I've never heard of it," protests *Peter Pan* to Wendy Darling. "We have fun don't we? I've taught you to fly and to fight. What more can there be?"

There is a programme on UK television called *You've been Framed*, a sort of candid camera style broadcast in which members of the public send in their home movies to share with the whole nation. Usually they depict calamities and mishaps to laugh at, but there are also the inevitable cute sequences of toddlers in their nappies who are giving their fellow infants a great big hug and fondly kissing each other lip-to-lip. Accompanying this from the studio audience is a spontaneous sigh of "aaah, how sweet!" Everyone seems to enjoy watching little kids playing the kissing game. As the child becomes an adolescent, however, affections are less public, and are never featured on candid camera. Except in the movies, that is. Table (ii) shows us that in one-in-every five films with child actors, the children are expected to kiss on screen, and we the public become voyeurs in what should be a very private initiation.

"What is a kiss for?" asks Wendy Darling in *Peter Pan*, and Aunt Millicent replies, "It's for the greatest adventure of all. They that find it have slipped in and out of Heaven!" Everyone harks back to their very first kiss, and stores it fondly in their memory, with occasional delightful flashbacks to jog us longingly back to our childhood. (Oh Julia, where are you now?). Those first fumbling experiments with love by the preteen, barely pubescent child. Their guidebook, their set of instructions, is what they have seen for themselves, usually from watching television. It is a tricky time, a mix of embarrassment, yearnings, hormonal urges, a fear of getting it wrong, false expectations, and exploitation.

For some children, this first kiss is not offered voluntarily. Their first memorable kiss is stolen from them (for example, eleven-year-old Jena Malone who had to endure a prolonged and enforced snog while being raped in *Bastard out of Carolina*), and we will deal with this in a different darker Volume Eight. But for now, this volume is about those first few delightful blossoming romances as portrayed in various movies about first love.

Sometimes the whole movie is about first love – *Melody*, *P'Tang, Yang, Kipperbang*, *Little Manhattan*. In others, the love scenes are just an inconsequential add-on, or bonus, depending on how charming or sickly the viewer sees it. Whichever it is, we all become voyeurs in a child's deeply moving first romantic experience, imprinting on the memory for all time in both the character's and in our own psyche. Because, for many of the children required to kiss on screen, it is their first ever boy-girl kiss, and they perform it initially in front of the director, the camera crew, and ultimately in front of the whole viewing public. As director Mark Levin acknowledges in *Little Manhattan*, for both Charley Ray and Josh Hutcherson their on-screen kiss was their first ever kiss, and he could visibly see the nerves of the performers. This is the memory society impels them to cherish or hate for the whole of their lives.

Little children do not spend their childhood in kiss-and-chase games, and yet that is what we expect of them in the movies. This intrusion by the public into a child's first foray into osculatory intercourse could conceivably be construed as being perverted, and that watching children kiss on screen is the new acceptable face of child pornography. Baring of the sexual soul rather than the bare body. Or is this too startling a concept to commence with? This is not a rare intrusion. I have compiled Table (ii) to highlight the regularity with which film directors expect us to be voyeurs of children kissing. Of the 500 films I have researched for this book, I have arrived at a figure of 19% of films requiring children to kiss on screen. That is, one-in-every-five films. Yet, we do not see one-in-every-five children kissing outside the school gates. Children are manipulated to kiss on screen to massage our memories, to satiate our senses.

The priest in *Cinema Paradiso* would agree with me. At his rural Spanish fleapit, he previews the films before his parishioners can view the screenings, ringing a bell when he wants the projectionist to cut out any kissing scenes. "I shan't watch pornographic films!" he defiantly protests.

Just Good Friends

For some children, their first romantic dream is just that, a dream; puppy love that does not even stretch to the holding of hands, let alone kissing and hugging. All it meant to Holly Kenny and Qasim Akhtar in *Mischief Night* was going to the chippy together. For Dakota Fanning and Joseph Lotesto in *Charlotte's Web*, just a day out at the county fair, the surreptitious touching of fingers providing the barest hint of ardour. For Frankie Muniz in *My Dog Skip*, it meant hobnobbing with Rivers Applewhite (Caitlin Wachs), "the prettiest girl in town," and the innocent holding of hands. And for Jaime McEnnan in *Munchie*, Love Hewitt barely became much more than a dream, while for Josh Hutcherson in *Bridge to Terabithia*, the unexpected death of Lesley (AnnaSophia Robb) meant he was left with just memories of what might have been.

Neither did it reach much further with Harry Potter or his friend Ron Weasley, who in turn shared crushes with Hermione Granger, and with Ginny Weasley and Cho Chang. For J K Rowling, the author of the Harry Potter series, steered clear of the polluting concepts of romance and sexual flirting (for the first three volumes, anyway). She was more than happy to allow her heroes and heroines to smile sweetly at each other with all the awkwardness of adolescent angst, but there was never to be any bewitching of each other's emotions. That was one magic trick lacking on the part of the superhero played by Daniel Radcliffe. "You fight dragons, Harry," says his friend Ron in *Harry Potter and the Goblet of Fire* as they prepare for the Wizards' Ball. "If you can't get a date, who can?" But the inexperienced hero cannot pluck up the courage to invite a single girl. "I'd think I'd take the dragon, right now!" he admits.

Harry has similar cold feet when coming to the rescue of Ginny Weasley *in Harry Potter and the Chamber of Secrets*. Ginny (played by Bonnie Wright) has a crush on the star wizard, but when Harry turns up to visit his friend Ron, Ginny spots him and rushes out of the room in embarrassment. "What did I do?" asks Harry as Ginny runs off. His friend tells him, "Ginny, she's been talking about you all summer." Later, Ginny is captured by the evil Lord Voldemort, and it is up to Harry to find a way to rescue her. Yet even when Harry saves her, there are no tender touches, no racing into the other's arms, nor even looking sweetly into each other's eyes, just embarrassed restraint. However, maturity does redress the balance; now a youth, Harry Potter receives his first real kiss in *Harry Potter and the Goblet of Fire* from a passionate Cho Chang (Katie Leung).

The two other co-stars have similar restraints in *Harry Potter and the Prisoner of Azkaban*. Hermione, played by Emma Watson, is developing a crush on her classmate Ron, played by

Rupert Grint. At the start of the new term, they spy each other, race towards one another ready for a hug, but there are others watching, so the closest they get is to shake hands. During one moment of fear, Hermione reaches for Ron's hand. Later, they are alone together. Hermione suggests to Ron, "Do you want to move a little closer?" But the timid boy has cold feet. "No, I'm fine!" he says missing out on the chance of his life. After that, their romantic aspirations deteriorate, so that in the next movie they verbally spar with jealous rants, finding it easier to slag each other off than to admit affection for each other. Thompson, in his book *Best Friends, Worst Enemies*, describes this as a trait of maturing childhood. As they grow towards adolescence some kids start to understand "that the game has shifted from really not liking each other to pretending not to like each other."[9]

Veda learnt this same lesson in *My Girl 2*. Played by Anna Chlumsky, Veda has been insulted at school by a boy she fancies. Veda talks this over with her father's girlfriend (Jamie Lee Curtis) ("Uh-oh! Here comes puberty!" derides one of Jamie Lee's colleagues). Veda comes to realise that sometimes boys make insulting remarks as a cover, because they do not have the confidence to say they like you. So, armed with this knowledge, she boldly strides off to see her best friend, Judy, to consult her about it, when who should open Judy's door but the boy she fancies, now Judy's new boyfriend. So much for that theory!

At least Martha Plimpton's invitation to River Phoenix was less ambiguous than Emma Watson's sidling up to Rupert Grint, and Veda's misdirection. "Charlie, do you have a girlfriend?" Martha asks the boy on the voyage both of their families are taking to the inhospitable jungles of *The Mosquito Coast*. "I could be your girlfriend if you want," she suggests. It was a take-it-or-leave-it offer. Nothing else happened, as if the scriptwriter had planned to develop the theme but the director either did not pursue this or else cut it. Perhaps there was too much friction between Martha and River's fathers. One was an eccentric missionary, the other an obsessive visionary. I guess the boy was too proud of his genius father and did not want to upset his dad by mixing with the 'enemy'.

We find a similar situation in Billy Elliot. Nicola Blackwell says to Jamie Bell, "Billy, do you fancy me, like? If you want I'll show you my fanny." But for the boy, that is one audition too far. "Nah. It's alright." He is happy to sit with her on the bed, have a pillow fight, but when he finds he is face to face with the girl, within kissing distance, that is too daunting an adventure.

In *Jumanji*, the kiss is just a token of gratitude between two children who are girlfriend/boyfriend without the complication of romance. "Alan, there's something I've been wanting to do," says Laura Bell Bundy as she leans forward to give her boyfriend a kiss. That fond peck of thanks is the result of being saved by her hero, having been given the wildest adventure imaginable from playing the crazy board game.

As in adult films, in even the most innocuous of circumstances where there is a boy lead, the director insists on including the complimentary girl, the admirer, to add that spark of brewing romance, even if it is never fulfilled. Age is no deterrent. Marc Donato is bid a fond farewell by Yana, the ethnic Costa Rican girl (Marianella Jimenez), in *Blue Butterfly*; as Ethan Randall also receives from Amy Oberer in *All I want for Christmas* (1991); Hayley Mills and Michael Anderson walk off arm-in-arm after their global adventure in *In Search of the Castaways*.

Melody is a wonderful love story that takes me right back to my own childhood. It was filmed in the early 1970s when falling in love meant holding hands and carrying each other's satchels. No horny sexual romps that children nowadays see on television and feel obliged to copy. No, through a nostalgic 1970s soundtrack, in a depressing London still emerging from the last vestiges of post-war clearance of dereliction, we find ourselves in an unruly school where teachers can barely keep discipline without resorting to "Julius Caesar", the slipper for naughty backsides kept warm on the radiator. Here, children race from class to class along echoing corridors, and clunking up and down staircases, boys in their scruffy drainpipe trousers, and girls in their ever so short chequered dresses.

Into this world slips eleven-year-old Daniel, played by Mark Lester, famous for his role as *Oliver!* in the Dickensian movie. He is a polite boy with a socially aspirant mother. In the chaotic school assembly he spots Melody Perkins (Tracy Hyde), and later spies on her in the girls' ballet lesson. When, at the monthly school dance he breaks an unwritten social rule by asking her to dance with him, the rumour circulates in school that they are in love. Melody sweetly waits for him following an after-school detention, and they walk hand-in-hand to the quiet of the overgrown cemetery where they can talk, away from prying eyes.

Melody tells him, "Some people are spreading a rumour saying you love me. I don't mind, but it's not right when you're the last to know." Daniel listens politely but carries on biting his apple, which he shares silently with his sweetheart. They sit cuddled together arm-in-arm sheltering from the rain under a briefcase. We never see them share a kiss; the love affair is convincing enough as it is.

The couple decide to take a day off school and travel to the seaside together where they spend their time on the amusements and splashing in the sea. They are infatuated with each other, and see nothing wrong in being so. Of course, when they arrive back at school it is straight to the headmaster's office for a firm, but friendly, little talking to. But when the eleven-year-olds insolently tell him they want to get married, the Head's veins begin to split.

Daniel's best friend, Ornshaw, played by the brilliant child actor Jack Wild, at first tries to break up the friendship of the two young lovers, "Girls are snotty nosed gits, they are," but eventually he helps the couple elope. The whole class skip-off lessons, head for the waste ground and hold an impromptu wedding, thwarted only by the arrival of the teachers. An anarchic fight ensues, but the two lovers escape using the manually operated railway shuttle, and disappear into the distance.

That the innocent holding of hands should conceivably progress to matrimony is further alluded to in *The Railway Children* as Phyllis (Sally Thomsett) declares, "Cor lummy, Pete, they'll have to marry now!" She has just witnessed older sister Roberta (Jenny Agutter) say goodbye to Jim with a prolonged holding of hands after a farewell handshake. (Jim had been rescued from the railway tunnel with a broken leg and nursed by Roberta. Incidentally, this same girl had earlier in the movie developed a crush on the bachelor doctor who seemed happy to encourage her, in both the film and in E Nesbit's classic novel.)

If it's not teachers, then it is parents who are to blame for the frustrated demise of courting youngsters! In *Cheaper by the Dozen 2*, interference by the fathers prevent the friendship between the two children from going any further. Alyson Stoner plays Sarah Baker, and Taylor Lautner plays Elliot Murtaugh. They catch each other's eye when the two families have a get together at a lakeside camp, both fathers being old college rivals. The two young sweethearts decide to have a boat ride together, but suddenly jealous father (comic actor Steve Martin) gets paternal instincts and insists on joining them, sitting in between the boy and girl. Later the boy invites Sarah to the cinema. Father relents, and the girl seeks out her older sister for advice on make-up etc. But mother wisely informs her, "When you like a boy, never be anybody but yourself. Elliot liked you without make-up, didn't he." (Incidentally, the production crew had expected Alyson Stoner to be dolled up with make-up and emerge from her closet wearing a halter-top and short mini skirt, but director Adam Shankman insisted she wear normal pretty clothes. He should be congratulated for not over-sexualising the young girl.)

Boy and girl sit together in the cinema, but unbeknown to them, both fathers turn up and sneak into the cinema to sit where they can keep an eye on their kids. This is a comedy film, so soon both fathers are squaring up to each other. Sarah's dad spots Elliot putting his arm around Sarah's shoulder, so Mr Baker accuses his rival: "Your son has raging hormones like any other male teenager." Then a fight ensues, the parents are ejected, and the embarrassed children's first romantic fling is foiled.

A Word of Advice: Rehearsing that First Kiss

"What's it like to kiss, you know, boys?" The gaggle of girls are squatting around *Melody* (Tracy Hyde) in the school playground. This is a new daunting life experience for them, full of dangers and pitfalls! What if they don't do it correctly? Eleven-year-old Anna gets to ask the same question in *Paperhouse*. Charlotte Burke, playing Anna, watches her best friend kiss a boy. When they play truant from school one afternoon, she asks her friend, "What's it like to snog a boy?" Her friend then goes through a list of her conquests at her last party: how she kissed so-and-so on the sofa, then someone else in the bedroom, and a different boy on the stairs. (She was only twelve!) Anna becomes curious about this new sensation, storing away the information for a later encounter.

First, you need an object to practise on: Anna Paquin and her little Maori friends use tree trunks in *The Piano*; some nuzzle against their pillow; for others, their teddy provides a nightly comforter; while others find mooching on their arms an accessible substitute. In *The Man in the Moon*, fourteen-year-old Dani, played by sprightly, Reese Witherspoon, is taught by her older sister how to practise kissing her own hand, ready for the big event (which she eventually gets to do for real with her new neighbour while skinny-dipping in the river). The two boys (Øystein and Trond) in *Sommer Jubel*[10] likewise practise kissing their own arms as a tester for kissing the real thing – two ten-year-old girls they meet while skinny-dipping in a Swedish lake. "What's kissing like?" one boy asks. "Like this," he replies and while romantic strings provide a serenade, he demonstrates kissing on his arm. "It doesn't taste of anything," says the first boy as he copies the demonstration. "No," he is told. "You have to close your eyes and think of somebody." So he tries again, this time thinking of Kåre, while his friend dreams of Åse.

Anna Chlumsky (as Veda) and Macaulay Culkin (as Thomas J) share their first kiss in *My Girl* (1991). Throughout their eleven years of childhood they have been best friends, playing, swimming, cycling, and climbing trees together. There is no romance between them, despite some of her classmates taunting her: "Veda's with her boyfriend. I bet you kiss him on the lips." She dismisses their childishness: "I only surround myself with people I find intellectually stimulating."

Veda has been watching her father and his new girlfriend sharing a kiss, and she is curious to know what it is like. She asks her friend, Thomas J, "Have you ever kissed anyone?" The answer is negative. "Maybe we should," Veda continues, "Just to see what's the big deal." First, they practise on their own arms. "Now close your eyes," says the girl, clenching her fists threateningly in case Thomas J doesn't comply. Then they purse their lips, and POW! The peck is pecked, the deed is done. But neither of them look convinced. Alas, they don't get a second attempt, for when chivalrous Thomas J goes to retrieve the mood ring that Veda has dropped near a hornet's nest, he gets attacked and dies from an allergy to bee stings.

Of course, kissing just used to be a simple peck on the lips. But youngsters have so many anxieties over such a simple act. First, there is the problem of the nose getting in the way. Next, does the girl tilt her face to the right or the left? These were just the conundrums for Aidan Pendleton and Joshua Jackson as they attempted their first kiss in *Andre*. After first trying to avoid clashing each other's nose they end up bashing their foreheads, so the attempt is aborted. Maybe the mouth should be open. And where does the tongue fit into all of this? And what does French kissing mean? The kiss is such a daunting task for a tenderfoot boy or girl.

In the Irish movie *32A*, two fourteen-year-old girls provide a demonstration for their classmates how to kiss correctly. Theirs is a girls' school so there are no boys to practise on. Maeve (Ailish McCarthy) needs to know how to kiss a boy, for she thinks she may have a date. Ruth (Sophie Jo Wasson) asks her "Have you ever rubbed tongues with anyone?" "Yes," replies Maeve, "My dog!" The gang of girls encourage Ruth to show Maeve how to kiss with tongues. So, while Maeve sticks out her tongue, Ruth licks it up and down. Then they practise kissing each other. "Keep your mouth open," she instructs. Here, the director is teetering on the verge of making a lesbian movie, but it's ok 'cos the children are only practising! And because the thirteen-year-old scriptwriter Nikki Reed includes girls kissing together in *Thirteen* (2003) then perhaps this could be misconstrued as normalised acceptable behaviour for experimenting teens![11] And anyway, these are teenage kids. Directors wouldn't dream of exploiting preteen children in similar roles. Would they?

In Rebecca Miller's début movie, *Angela* (1994), ten-year-old Miranda Stuart Ryne plays the title role. While out exploring with her younger six-year-old sister, Ellie, (Charlotte Blythe) they meet a boy about Angela's age. The older girl is expecting there may be some kissing so she needs to practise quick! So Angela takes Ellie into a separate room. "We have to practise kissing. You can't just leave it to instinct." And with that, she rolls onto the bed with her sister and they share a prolonged snog. At the end of this, Miranda Ryne looks up at the cameraman with an embarrassed glint in her eye as if getting confirmation from the director that she did it right! The trouble for younger Ellie is, her pregnant babysitter had recently told her, "You can get pregnant without a husband. A couple of kisses and you're there." Now, after being kissed by Angela, little Ellie is worried she will now be pregnant. So while they are out riding on a horse, Ellie expresses her worry to Angela. The older sister assures her "You get pregnant from boys only."

Sometimes the younger girl has to offer advice about dating to an older brother. This was a service provided by Chloë Grace Moretz in *(500) Days of Summer*, and Madeleine's role in *Gregory's Girl*. Allison Forster plays the ten-year-old Madeleine who advises her brother Gregory to not be too romantic on the first date. "Don't make her too special," she advises. "You're too romantic – it scares them off." But when Gregory asks his sister what she dreams about, Madeleine replies, "Just ginger beer and ice cream. I'm still a young girl, remember."

The First Kiss

For some, their first kiss is a horrendous embarrassment, a chore to be completed, just to see what the big deal is all about. This was the ordeal for Macaulay Culkin and Anna Chlumsky in *My Girl* (1991). Neither was convinced, the world did not move. Others, like Duckworth in *P'Tang, Yang, Kipperbang*, become quivering bags of nerves, trepid travellers about to be wrecked on the rocks of romance. And when the feat is accomplished, they are racked by self-doubt as Gabe discovers in *Little Manhattan*. Yet others are transported to a seventh heaven by the euphoria of it all, as Veda (Anna Chlumsky) finally reveals in *My Girl 2*: "Life is full of barbaric customs. I just hope they all end in a kiss like that!"

For child actors, the first kiss becomes an embarrassing performance in front of the director, film crew, and the viewing audience. As Table (ii) shows, the viewing public demand kissing kids, and directors/scriptwriters oblige us in 19% of films that involve children. The director of *Little Manhattan*, Mark Levin, acknowledged that for both his child actors, Josh Hutcherson and Charlie Ray, this was their first ever boy/girl kiss, and they got to perform it once only but in front of six cameras all filming from different angles. No chance of any rehearsals for them, either. No wonder they were nervous. This issue of camera and crew watching was a concern too for Alyson Stoner and Dylan McLaughlin in *Alice Upside Down*. Miss Stoner complains in the post-screening interview how uncomfortable she was made to feel by all the crew, who were trying to be reassuring, making such a fuss of the scene by asking, "Are you ready?" in a condescending manner. This made the child actors even more nervous. Others are obviously uncomfortable in their role: Pascale Bruchon and Geory Desmouceaux in Truffaut's *Pocket Money*, their lips politely grazing, their arms hanging limply at their sides, unsure of how to progress. The scene is obviously unrehearsed as evidenced by their awkwardness. Jonathan Lipnicki also appears uncomfortable having Amanda Alch hold him round the waist; he twice removes her hands before receiving his kiss in *When Zachary Beaver came to Town*.

In *The Secret Garden*, director Agnieszka Holland tries to inject a little romance between the two cousins: Colin, played by Heydon Prowse, and Mary Lennox, played by Kate Maberly. At first, they bicker, but in time a fondness grows between them. They sneak into each other's bedrooms at night and sleep side-by-side, cousin-by-cousin. Their relationship comes alive when they explore the secret garden together, for this is where their intimate gazes into each other's eyes result in their first kiss. But for poor Kate Maberly, this was obviously her first ever kiss, and she was left fumbling a fleeting brush to his face with an embarrassed laughing smile, and a frown to the camera as if to reprimand us all for watching.

All this kissing by children helps feed the demand from a modern viewing public. It was not the norm in former years. Shirley Temple did not receive her first stage kiss until her twenty-fifth screen role playing *Miss Annie Rooney* at the age of fourteen. Her peck was received from Dickie Moore, also a first time for him. When Anne Frank asks, "Peter, did you ever kiss a girl?" in *The Diary of Anne Frank* (1959) it seems to take an age for their novice lips to actually touch (but here the director it toying with us, for these are adults playing the part of the holocaust victims).

At the tender age of eleven, newcomer Kirsten Dunst gets to kiss the famous heartthrob, Brad Pitt, in *Interview with the Vampire*. Women and teenage girls would have queued around the block for this privilege. So what was it like, your first screen kiss with Brad Pitt? "It was horrible. I hated it," admits Kirsten. "Brad Pitt was like a big brother on the set, so it was like kissing your big brother." In the film, she had barely brushed his lips before the couple were disturbed by a band of marauding vampires.

For Øystein Offer-Ohlsen and Camilla Sletten in *Sommer Jubel* kissing was almost a chore, something to get over and done with. "Can you kiss?" asks Øystein. The misguided ten-year-olds feel they need to remove their clothes first. I am not sure what message the director was trying to impart here. Camilla gets impatient waiting. "Hurry up and do it before Jørgen comes." Bodies apart, but lips pressed together. Like Ellie in *Angela* (1994), Camilla starts to have doubts: "What if we have kids, Øystein?" she asks worriedly, but the boy is not sure himself.

What worried the parents in *A Company of Wolves* was the nameless fate lurking in the bushes for those foolish enough to stray off the path through the woods – subliminal messages are given to stay on the straight and narrow in a world filled with proverbial *men in sheep's clothing*. "Rosaleen, would you take a walk with me in the woods? After church? On Sunday?" asks the boy to Sarah Patterson. "I won't stray off the path." The good girl checks with her father first. "He only asked me to walk with him!"

"Well, one thing leads to another," warns father doubtfully. But on Sunday morning, after church, the young couple go hesitantly into the oppressive woods, watched by the parents. "That's my boy!" mutters Brian Glover, triumphantly.

When the boy forces a kiss on the little girl, "Isn't that nice?" he asks her. "No!" comes the reply.

Another stolen first kiss was received by Allison Mack in *Honey, we shrunk ourselves*. "You should have asked first," the girl tells the impetuous boy.

For the bulk of children, the first kiss is a delicacy eagerly anticipated, yet hours of anguished rehearsal can precede this momentous rite in a child's immature life. "Why don't you just kiss her instead of talking her to death," George Bailey is admonished in *It's a Wonderful Life*. "Youth is wasted on the wrong people!"

This first foray into love was a real difficulty for Duckworth in *P'Tang, Yang, Kipperbang*. The young lad (John Albasiny) is keen on a popular girl in the class and is sure he is out of her league. If only he could kiss Anne Laughton (Abigail Cruttenden). Every night he prays to God for one kiss from Anne's lips. "Please God, just one kiss; one will do." As if to placate God he wears a boxing glove in bed to avoid the temptation of idle hands. Then God seems to provide an opportunity for him, for he is selected to act in the school play alongside Anne. And the script states they kiss! He gets a chance to kiss the girl of his dreams, but on each rehearsal he is thwarted by an interruption; yet there is still the big night of the performance. But just like Hermione Granger racing towards Ron Weasley in the *Harry Potter* movie, Duckworth at the last moment draws back from the kiss, nerves getting the better of him in front of his classmates. "Kiss her," prompts the stage director. "Just kiss her." But he can't and doesn't.

Later, Anne confronts him asking why he failed to kiss her in the school play, and the boy has to explain about his nerves. "You can kiss me now, if you like," the girl of his dreams suggests, and she pouts her lips waiting. Her lips are there, just millimetres from his face – all he ever dreamed of about to come true. But the stupid fool says no! He declines. "No, it is enough knowing I *could* have kissed you. That's good enough for me." Aaagh! That's like offering a bowl of water to a man dying of thirst, and him declining – "no it is enough just to know I could have drunk if I wanted to!" Oh the fickleness of hormones! Not to be denied, the girl gives him a quick peck on the lips, following which the boy walks home with a swagger, tall and as proud as punch.

Children in Love

Little Manhattan is explicitly billed as a tale of first love. But again, the boy is left confused and baffled by the whole kissing business. Ten-year-old Gabe, played by Josh Hutcherson, and eleven-year-old Rosemary, played by Charlie Ray, develop a friendship stemming from the karate class they both attend. They practise moves together so already they have plenty of physical contact by means of tussles and scuffles. He notices how his heart pounds fast when he is with her. "I couldn't wait to get to karate class, to grapple with her, to smell her hair." When he realises he is falling in love with her, and spots her in the street the confused boy cycles in the opposite direction to avoid a confrontation. Then the girl invites him to practise karate at her home. "There I was, in the inner sanctum, alone with her," he reflects. But he acknowledges to himself, really they "were just karate friends," nothing else. Then she suggests practising at Gabe's house. In anticipation, he practises greeting her in the mirror, as Gordon John Sinclair does in *Gregory's Girl*. Finally, she arrives. "She was in my house, and we were all alone." They practise their karate, and he finds himself straddled on top of her, just as Jamie Bell does with Nicola Blackwell in *Billy Elliot*, each staring into the other's eyes. "Kiss her, kiss her," his conscience shrieks. But like Duckworth in *P'Tang, Yang, Kipperbang*, he can't, and like Jamie Bell he doesn't.

Later, Rosemary's parents invite them both to a concert. Here, Gabe plucks up the courage to hold her hand under the dining table, out of sight of the other dinner guests. As the director of *Little Manhattan*, Mark Levin, points out, "Holding hands is one of the key moments of first love." After this special evening out, they are left alone to say their goodbyes. Gabe, in now-or-never haste, takes a stab at her lips. The boy kisses her in what he feels is the most tasteful way, and after getting home, he rehearses the kiss in his mind to re-assure himself he kissed correctly.

But what did Gabe do wrong? Maybe he was too forward. Whenever he had suggested they meet up again, the girl would prevaricate. Perhaps she is dating another boy. Depressing possibilities flood through his mind so he cannot think logically. So when she phones the next day, the confused jealous boy yells down the phone, "I hate you." And soon the boy is howling in distress as he realises his error and his misinterpretation of the signs. The boy now is frantic. He seeks out the girl once more and declares, "Rosemary, I love you." And Rosemary, looking all confused, with vulnerable honesty replies, "I don't know what I think, Gabe. I'm only eleven. I don't think I'm ready to be in love." A reflective Gabe realises that though there are other girls out there, "there will never be another first love. That is always going to be Rosemary."

Perhaps Gabe should have heeded the advice of the tramp he met. "I had a girlfriend once," he tells him. "She trampled my heart and left me bleeding on the floor." Run now while you can!

Matine and Patrick needed help from their friends before they could take their first romantic steps in *Pocket Money*, a film by the master French director, François Truffaut. The young couple, Matine (Pascale Bruchon) and Patrick (Geory Desmouceaux), meet at a summer camp. They seem besotted with each other, and everyone else knows it. Together they are all smiles and eyes but too shy to go any further than that. Their friends set up an encounter. While Matine leaves the canteen to visit the bathroom, Patrick's friends tell him that Matine has just gone outside to wait for him to kiss her. The young lovers meet on the stairs, and that is where we witness their first shy kiss.

At least Patrick got a girl in the end, for he had previously made a hash of things at the cinema. He and his mate had fixed a date with two girls. They had all sat side-by-side in the cinema. His friend had sat next to buxom older Corinne and when a kissing scene commenced on the screen they too started busily snogging. Patrick was seated next to the younger Eva (played by director Françoise Truffaut's own daughter). Eva looked invitingly into Patrick's eyes, but the young boy was too shy or too polite to kiss her. So Eva flippantly reacts, referring to the kissing couple, "What idiots!" But soon the first boy is kissing both Corinne *and* Eva, leaving Patrick aloof, his chance missed, his passions unrequited.

Normally, a child's first kiss is a little more romantic than Jodie Foster's brusque offer in *Bugsy Malone*. "How about smearing my lipstick," says Tallulah to Scott Baio (Bugsy). Yet the first kiss when offered may be opportunist but is to be cherished. The preteen Marine Casto in *A Good Year* leaves a parting kiss never to be forgotten. Little Max Skinner (Freddie Highmore), staying at his uncle's château in Provence, is lying beside the pool reading his book. At the opposite end of the pool is a visitor's daughter, Fanny, with her dark eyes, sitting sweetly on a swing chair. She stands up, a vision of loveliness, strips off her shorts to stand in her dazzling white underwear at the pool's edge. She dives in, swims underwater, and emerges at the far end, face-to-face with the prostrate Max. Inexplicably, she gives him a tender kiss, then whispers an apology in his ear, "Forgive my lips; they find joy in the most unusual places." We never see the girl again. Until, that is, they are now adults, meet up, remember that brief childhood encounter, and take up the love affair where they had left off as children.

The departure lounge of an airport must be worst place for receiving a first kiss. A fond message left on the lips, but the separation of time and space mean it can seldom be repeated. Austin O'Brien walks off proud and tall after a parting kiss from Anna Chlumsky in *My Girl 2*, but the girl has a lonely confused walk through the departure gates of Los Angeles airport with only dreams to cherish; while in *Grounded*, Tyler James Williams receives a hefty lip-smack from Quinn Shepherd, before both take off in opposite directions.

Poor little Toby in *When Zachary Beaver came to Town* seems so impotently besotted with a girl who only looks ten-year-old: Scarlet, played by Amanda Alch.[12] Toby (Jonathan Lipnicki) rapidly tries to straighten his hair and readjust his glasses, as this dream spectre approaches. Scarlet is a blond-haired sweet-faced girl, but with a deep husky sexy voice like Marilyn Munro, and the boy is mesmerised in her presence. Scarlet in her slow Texan drawl asks Toby to watch over her little sister, Tara, for a while. Toby is only too pleased to oblige, until he hears the reason. The girl wants to be rid of her little sister because "Mum's out, so Ron is dropping by." Later, Toby passes by to return the sister, Tara. It is then he sees his idol, Scarlet, cuddled together with the older boy, Ron, on the doorstep.

But the next evening, when Toby bumps into Scarlet outside the dancehall, she tells him, "I broke up with Ron. Mama didn't like Ron because he's fifteen and Guatemalan. I don't want a boyfriend that's scared of my mama." All the while, she is twinkling her eyes at the dumbfounded lad. Scarlet persuades Toby to dance with her, there, in the street, outside the dancehall. This prepubescent girl is very forward. "You hold a girl like this," forcing his hands round her waist and slow-dancing under the streetlamps in a tight hug, cheek to cheek. Then the girl gives him a fond goodnight kiss on the cheek. The poor lad doesn't know what has hit him.

In *Cider with Rosie*, Laurie Lee (played by Joe Roberts) describes his first encounter with girls as a "solitary studying of maps." For him, the spread body of Jo Jenkins (played by Sally Beer) was just a tool, a voyeur's encounter with a naked body. There was no love or tenderness between the boy and girl; he just pretended he was a doctor, and Jo had to strip off before him for an 'examination'. The girl was just someone who could be "folded up and put away" like a map. Yet "so quiet was Jo, always so timorous yet eager to please, she's the one I chose first." And he takes her down the grassy bank beside the gently trickling stream.

He tells of his first day at school, his initial encounter with his desk companions, "two blond girls, already puppishly pretty, whose names and bodies were to distract and haunt me for the next fifteen years of my life."

But as a teenager, the buxom Rosie Burdock (Lia Brown) visits him during the harvesting of the hay meadow, carrying a flagon of cider. "I've got something to show you," which is more than just the cider of the title. The couple abscond under the hay wagon, out of sight, to share passionate kisses, hidden behind strands of straw. "Never to be forgotten … or tasted again."

Unconventional Kisses: the bizarre and audacious

Kissing is such a confusing adventure for young actors; their first tentative moves made in front of an unforgiving camera. Yet scriptwriters have introduced outlandish complications to confound the distorted faces of the children. Amanda Peterson and Ethan Hawke are expected to kiss while flying away together into the closing credits, in *Explorers*. No doubt, this was filmed in a wind tunnel for the children are suspended while they fly superman-style. It must have been a tricky feat to get the flying children to come together in unison to kiss each other without getting bloody noses. I guess more than one rehearsal was needed for that scene. In *Honey, the Kids Rule the World*, Anna Wilson and Blake Foster get to smooch underwater in the swimming pool, away from prying eyes so no one gets to witness it – except for us, of course! Both are kissing scenes where the participants leave their eyes wide open, to see clearly to locate the lips while maintaining balance.

Almost as bizarre is the kiss that takes place between Taylor Lautner and Taylor Dooley in *The Adventures of Sharkboy and Lavagirl*. (Is this the only movie in which both the male and female leads share the same first name?) Sharkboy lives in the icy depths of the ocean, while Lavagirl has purple flames for hair and skin of molten lava rock. You can imagine the impact this has when they kiss – Sharkboy's cheeks almost melt! Henry Thomas playing Elliott in *ET The Extra-Terrestrial* has to stand on the back of a classmate to be able to reach the lips of Erika Eleniak. Christina Ricci gets to kiss a ghost, in *Casper* (1995). "Yesss! There's a girl in my bed!" chirrups lonely Casper whose only wish was, "All I want is a friend." For a brief period, he gets his Cinderella moment by turning back into the twelve-year-old boy he was before he died which gives him the opportunity to dance and romantically kiss this intruder living in his haunt. The kiss Mikey (Sean Astin) receives from Andy (Kerri Green) is totally out of the black. Expecting the arrival of her boyfriend in the dark cave in *The Goonies*, she unwittingly kisses his younger brother instead. "I never knew you still wore a tooth brace!" she exclaims.

Bizarre turns to perverse exploitation in the next two movies. In *Fallen Angel*, a boy and a girl (Dana Hill) are sweetly kissing on a fairground ride. As the merry-go-round revolves, we see them obviously enjoying themselves and with each pass, a photographer (Richard Masur) takes their picture. But this is not the innocent sweetness it seems, for the photographer is a paedophile controlling the kids for his own perversions. The kiss shared between Júlia Mérö and Peter Bocsor in *The Annunciation* competes with *Great Expectations* and *kids* (1995) (which we will come to shortly), for sheer audacity. These twelve-year-old children perform as Adam and Eve in the Garden of Eden. Lucifer has tempted Eve to pluck an apple from the Tree of Knowledge. Adam and Eve both take bites from the apple, and while sharing an intimate kiss, the piece of apple is passed from Adam's mouth into Eve's. But being Adam and Eve, these barely pubescent kids have to perform this scene naked!

Other directors exploit the embarrassed awkwardness of their cast. "Your face, Jack," exclaims Jessie-Ann Friend to Zachery Ty Byron in *Magic Island*. "It's turning the most horrible red colour. I've never met a boy who blushed before." In *Peter Pan*, Tiger Lily (played by Carsen Gray) holds the cheeks of Wendy's younger brother, John (Harry Newell), in her hands giving him a hearty smacker on the lips. John's blushes burn purple, as he is transformed with superhuman strength. After this, he is able to take on the pirates single-handed. And the impressionable children in the audience witness the magical power that one single kiss can bring.

The story of *Peter Pan*, though a great fun-filled adventure story, is also a tale of yearnings and the first tentative adventurous steps into puppy love – where that first kiss is considered a mind-blowing danger. Twelve-year-old Wendy Darling is about to take her first steps along that dangerous adventurous path, for her Aunt Millicent has declared in front of the whole family, "Wendy possesses a woman's chin." The little girl feels her face, looks worried and steps back from her accuser. "Observe her mouth. There, hidden in the right hand corner – is that … a kiss?" Wendy feels her lips to check out this incongruity.

"But what is it for?" the puzzled girl asks.

"It's for the greatest adventure of all," replies her aunt. "They that find it have slipped in and out of Heaven!"

And that is the adventure that Wendy pursues in this rather sexy interpretation of J M Barrie's classic novel, in which Rachel Hurd-Wood plays the bewitched maiden.

Her adventure begins asleep in bed, no doubt dreaming. But where do dreams end and reality begin? For in her semi-conscious state she pictures a boy, about her own age, lying just above her, within kissing distance – every protective parent's worst fear, every adolescent girl's most cherished desire. "I should like to give you – a kiss," declares Wendy, but as it is her first kiss and she is too nervous, instead she conjures from her pocket a thimble.

The scene shifts to the classroom at school. Instead of doing her sewing, she has made a sketch of Peter hovering above her bed. Teacher finds the sketch. "If this is you in your bed," says the teacher sternly, "then what is this?" she asks, pointing to the boy lying on top of her. Girls in the early twentieth century were not expected to have such wicked dreams, and of course, to innocent Wendy she could see no wicked significance in it, anyway.

Wendy, all smiles and wanting to help, sews Peter's shadow back to his feet, and is taken in by the boy's patter, and the world's most audacious chat-up line, "I'll teach you to ride the wind's back," as they launch through the nursery window to fly out to the dream world of Neverland.

Throughout the film, Wendy and Peter get close to exploring their first kiss, but it is a tough barrier to cross. When they witness the astonishing impact of Tiger Lily's kiss on John, they decide they must share this too as they fly romantically hand-in-hand through butterbur and coltsfoot. "Peter, what are your real feelings?" smiles the alluring preteen. "Is it – love?" Peter, lost in his emotions, replies, "Wendy, it's only make-believe, isn't it?" But the fairy, Tinkerbell, knows the danger that a first kiss can bring. She is provoked into jealous revenge, thwarting any possibility of romance between the two children. The jealousy is further provoked as the pirates capture Wendy, and Captain Hook tries his winsome ways on her. "My new obsession is you," she confirms to the captain as she joins the pirate ranks.

Later, as I am sure every puzzled, spurned teenage boy has experienced, she plays hard to get. She says to Peter, "I find Captain Hook to be a man of feeling. You, Peter Pan, are deficient –

you are just a boy." But eventually, the two do get to share their first devastating kiss. Wendy tricks Hook into allowing her to give Peter Pan a dying gift – a thimble. "Brace yourselves, lads. It's a powerful thing," says John, as Wendy gives Peter a full kiss on the lips. The mind-blowing kiss revives the boy to battle Captain Hook once more. "That was no thimble!"

Snogging

While directors require their novice actors to perform a perfunctory peck on the lips, older adolescents seem compelled to show they are not romantic tenderfoots, and do so by squirming and slobbering like their adult role models. The prolonged kiss is exploited by directors who, geared up with clapperboard and egg-timer, ensure their audience and protagonists get their moneys-worth of gorging and spittle. *Angus, Thongs and Perfect Snogging* parodies this custom: Peter Dyer (Liam Hess) sets his stopwatch to thirty minutes; when he and his protégé, Georgia Groome, have completed their half hour of snogging they are left with enough spit and foam between their lips to cement Eastbourne's Grand Parade.

Dictionaries allude to the *snog* as being *an amorous kiss and a cuddle*.[13] It is this 'amorous' element that should worry parents of the actors they place on the stage: the prods and pokes by the partner's prehensile toothpick, the accompanying fumblings. "What's my auntie going to say when I kiss her at Christmas?" reflects Gordon John Sinclair after his début snog with Clare Grogan in *Gregory's Girl*. "Hey, where did you learn to kiss like that?" the rock-and-roll-loving, rebellious John Wildman asks his blushing cousin, twelve-year-old Margaret Langrick, in *My American Cousin*.

As we mentioned earlier, in *Paperhouse*, eleven-year-old Anna, played by Charlotte Burke, has seen her friend snog boys, so is obviously curious. Anna is the lead in the film. She has contracted a psychiatric illness causing her to drift into unconsciousness to enter a dream world where she meets a crippled boy, Marc, who she is able to help and share experiences with. Sitting comforting each other at the top of some cliffs overlooking the sea, Anna asks Marc, "Have you ever kissed anyone?" Neither of them admit they have, and thus begins a long deep kiss, to quell their curiosity, not the usual short peck on the cheek you see in most adolescent movies, but a real enduring smooch that both young actors appear to enjoy. As they release each other, Anna remarks, "So that's snogging!" and they sit contentedly on the cliff edge, her head resting on his shoulder.

As in *Paperhouse*, *The Dust Factory* dwells in the twilight world between consciousness and death. A boy (Ryan Kelley) has drowned in an accident but is unaware of this, emerging into a limbo land halfway to heaven. It is here that he meets Melanie (Hayden Panettiere), a bubbly vivacious girl. She too has been through a life-threatening illness. Here, they explore and learn about each other's past, gradually falling in love and kissing. "Good thing you met me, huh?" ribs Melanie.

Kissing seems to come naturally to Sam Huntington (loin cloths and Adonis figure) and Leelee Sobieski, in *Jungle 2 Jungle*. After a sleepover, the girl's father discovers them together, "That boy is putting the moves on my twelve-year-old daughter!"

What must probably be the most intensive screened snog ever between preteen children was in *Great Expectations (1997)*, a modern jazzed-up version of the Dickens's story, with Ann Bancroft playing the eccentric Miss Dinsmoor. Little boy Finn (Jeremy James Kisner) is invited to visit because he has artistic talent, and stays to make a portrait of ten-year-old Estella (played by the stunning blond, Raquel Beaudene). He shows her the picture. She glances at the portrait and with nonchalant disinterest discards it in the hallway while leading him to a drinking fountain in the foyer. Estella takes a sip of water, then stares intently at the boy. "Do you want some? It's not poisoned, you know." Little does he know about the poison about to take over him, as Nabokov would say,[14] smitten for life. The boy reaches forward to sip from the fountain, his tongue out ready to catch the cascading droplets, but what he catches is Estella's probing tongue, and the two prepubescent tongues entwine like prehensile writhing slugs, as their lips drawl and suck and circle. The boy keeps firm grip of the handrail, while the girl twists her foot involuntarily to the heart-wrenching emotions they are sharing. This is not just seconds of smooching. Their snogging goes on and on, until finally Estella wipes her lips with the back of her hand and traipses triumphantly up the stairs to her room. Is Finn tempted to follow her? He is too shocked, and makes a hasty exit, only to be devoted to, and his soul tormented by, the girl for the rest of his conscious life. Poisoned by a kiss. Who knows what would have happened had Finn followed her up the stairs?

The older children are, the more experience they seem to need to show in their intimacy. In *Wild Child*, Emma Roberts plays a rebellious teenage California girl sent to a starchy British girls' boarding school. She immediately targets the only boy on the premises, the son of the School Principal. In an outlandish attempt to be expelled from the school and be sent back to sunny California, she starts to snog the impressionable lad, and in so doing, the idea of being expelled seems less appealing.

The theme of little girl in love is taken to a higher and more sinister level in *The Little Girl who lives down the Lane*. Jodie Foster plays the just-turned thirteen-year-old, Rynn, a reclusive girl secretly trying to cope by herself following the death of both her parents. A creepy paedophile and his intrusive mother have just overstepped the mark by trying to exert power over the young girl. Rynn needs help trying to dispose of dead bodies, and this is where Mario, played by Scott Jacoby, comes in. He is a schoolboy magician who has deduced the girl's crimes, yet is happy enough to ignore them and help her cover her tracks.

A dead body has to be buried, that of Mrs Hallet, the landlady. But it is pouring with rain as Mario, unnoticed, hurriedly digs a grave under a tree round the back of the house. After the corpse is buried and leaves scattered over the grave to hide the evidence, Mario comes into the house sodden and bedraggled. "I've got a tub waiting for you upstairs," says the young teen as she dries Mario's hair. And together they go upstairs where Jodie helps scrub the boy's back in the bath. This is a girl who faces the realities of life head-on. "Mario, if you want, I can get into bed with you." Jodie Foster gets undressed then wraps her naked body within the blankets. There are kisses, and there are cuddles. "Mario, have you ever..." But the boy just taunts her with the stock answer she usually gives him to his questions: "Hundreds of times."

As brother and sister, Jack (Andrew Robertson) shares a degree of intimacy with his sister, Julie (Charlotte Gainsbourg) in *The Cement Garden*. (This is much deeper than the puppy love shared between the siblings in *Toto le Héros*.) When Julie does a handstand in front of him, he is tantalised by the sight of her legs and crotch. After a game of tickling, both children sense other urges and desires becoming prominent. As Julie sunbathes on the concrete patio, she invites Jack to rub suncream on her almost naked body, further tempting his desires. Then the occasion comes when they console each other, and it turns into an intimate naked kissing session.

"Do you think what we did was right?" asks Julie.

"Seems natural to me," responds Jack.

A similar scene between siblings occurs in the French movie, *Les Diables*, in which a brother and sister discover the joy of romance and sex. Here we have a protective brother, Joseph (Vincent Rottiers), caring for his severely autistic older sister, Chloé (Adèle Haenel). As orphans, they are on the run from the authorities and have found an underground hideaway. All her life Chloé had hated being touched, but now for the first time she is responding to physical touches. Like a cat that keeps responding to being stroked, she returns again and again to her game of fondling Joseph's face and stroking hands. This sensation of sensual touches brings out a latent emotional response from the psychologically traumatised girl. Now, bathing naked in the underground pool, the girl explores her own sexuality, and this becomes the spur to share the intimacy of kissing and fondling with Joseph.

The sole goal of Georgia Nicolson (Georgia Groome) in *Angus, Thongs and Perfect Snogging* is to practise snogging, to make her *'boylingual'*, so she will be confident dating Robbie, the new hunk in her school (Aaron Johnson). Along with her friend Jas (Eleanor Tomlinson), she has devised a seven-point scale on the path to perfect snogging. This girl is always devising lists. Their snogging scale starts innocently enough: 1. Holding hands, 2. Arms around waist, 3. A goodnight kiss. Then the delirium goes wild as they fantasise about the possibilities: 4. Kissing lasting over three minutes (without breathing!), 5. Open mouth kissing, 6. Tongues, 7. Upper body fondling.

Georgia goes to visit another boy, Peter Dyer, who holds private practice sessions in kissing. This is her first kiss, and the session lasts a full thirty minutes. But as they withdraw a distasteful sticky slither of saliva links their mouths, and she refers to the boy thereafter as *Saliva Mouth*. Unfortunately for Georgia, this boy now seems hooked on the girl, and she is forever trying to evade his unwanted attention at school. It is Robbie she fancies, and she devises a plan to get his attention using her cat, Angus. But the course of true love never runs smooth.

No doubt, the most outrageous kiss of all between children was in the film *kids* (1995), though this was not a kiss of first love. This was pure ribald passion. As the two semi-naked children kneel on the bed and embrace, the boy says, "You know what I want, don't you?" "Yes," replies the girl (Sarah Henderson, maybe thirteen), "You want to fuck me." And so begins a session of intense smooching that goes on and on and on and on.

And on and on until you see the adolescent couple simulating a sex scene on the bed. Raw, distasteful, leaving a bitter taste in the mouth, the innocence of childhood long gone.

Enduring Affairs

For the child commencing the journey to romance, he/she dreams of first love enduring a lifetime. "George Bailey, I'll love you till the day I die," whispers Mary (Jean Gale) into Bobbie Anderson's deaf ear, in *It's a Wonderful Life*. That seldom transpires, though its memory can never be adequately erased, as tormented Heathcliff discovers. For Mark Webber in *Snow Day*, "true love is all about finding someone you can stand to be around for more than ten minutes at a time." But most expect a longer taster. Mary was lucky: she lassoed childhood sweetheart, George Bailey, so that now each Christmas a nation weeps romantically into their handkerchiefs as the blockbuster makes its annual screening. In all the following examples, we find childhood sweethearts spanning the generations, for better or worse, enduring into adulthood.

In *Lovers of the Arctic Circle*, an eight-year-old boy and girl meet by chance after school in Spain. Ana (Sara Valiente) runs after a ball while young Otto (Peru Medem) is running out in the park on the way home. Ana slips, and Otto helps her up. When their parents catch up with them, Otto's mum and Ana's dad (both strangers before) become friends. So now, the children get to sit together in the back seat of the car on the way to school. Eventually the two families move in together, and the children live like brother and sister. But as they grow up a sexual bond grows between them, which they feel they ought to keep secret from their parents.

As children, their love is expressed in cute smiles, but into their teens they sneak into each other's bedrooms to kiss and make love. Throughout each phase of their lives, the story is told twice – once through Ana's eyes, and the other through Otto's eyes. As they become adults we are not sure if they remained lovers – this depends on whose version you believe: infatuated Otto's or tolerant Ana's.[15]

The Blue Lagoon is no doubt the most famous movie of children growing up to be sexual partners and ultimately siring a child. De Vere Stacpoole's classic novel, written at the turn of the nineteenth/twentieth centuries was a sweet tale in which the children grew up as innocents away from any adult influence. The book was written in such a way that makes the young reader believe the stork brought the baby. Though this deals with adult themes, it was written as a children's book. When Richard finds Emmeline holding the newborn baby, he asks, "Where did you get it?" Emmeline replies, "I found it in the forest," having become unconscious at the time of the baby's birth. That was the book. With the film, you cannot pull the wool over the eyes of the modern viewer.

The Blue Lagoon was first filmed in 1949 and featured two little children, maybe eight years old; Emmeline played by Susan Stranks[16], and Michael played by Peter Jones. The boat they were travelling in on the way to "San Farisco" caught fire and sank in the Pacific Ocean, and they were marooned on a tropical deserted island and left to fend for themselves finding fruit and berries, and going skinny-dipping for fish in the island paradise. It is as they reached adulthood, with the parts played by Jean Simmons and Donald Houston that they explore the sexual urges that have attracted them to each other's bodies, and the mystery of sex and childbirth has to be experienced without any adult guidance.

The second *Blue Lagoon* film of 1980 was a much more sexual and intimate production, though the story line and script were much the same. The actors, of course, were different: Elva Josephson as little Emmeline, and Glen Kohan as the young Richard. They must have had the time of their lives, running naked through the strand, and bathing in the warm sea. It was the intimacy of the teenage actors that was far more provocative then the earlier version. Cue Brooke Shields, who as a twelve-year-old had already shocked the world by playing the sensual nymphet in *Pretty Baby,* whose character, Violet, had grown up in a whorehouse and had gone to live with her adult lover, played by Keith Carradine. In *The Blue Lagoon*, Emmeline has now reached puberty and she has to learn to accept the physical changes that are taking place in her body – her periods, her growing breasts, her 'tingling' feelings inside. As she parades semi-naked throughout the movie she becomes a temptation to her teenage cousin Richard, played by Christopher Atkins, who is discovering for himself masturbation, the beauty of nakedness, and the joys of physical touches between them. A child is sired.

In order to cash in on the success of this movie, a sequel was made: *The Return to the Blue Lagoon*. But the format and story line had become tiresome, and this was not a success.

Emile Brontë's novel of *Wuthering Heights*, written in the 1840s, tells the stormy tale of relationships in Victorian Yorkshire. Cathy lives with her brother Hindley and father Mr Earnshaw on a lonely elemental windswept moor. One stormy night father returns from a trip to Liverpool with a present for Cathy – it is an eight-year-old Gypsy boy, Heathcliff, a playmate for young Cathy, who was a similar age.

Cathy's brother, Hindley, takes an instant dislike to him, and thus begins a feud that stretches beyond a generation. For Cathy, however, the boy is a welcome friend. They become inseparable, exploring the moors and rapidly developing a fondness for each other. "Cathy was drawn to the silent self-possessed boy, but it was not hardness but gentleness that kept him silent."

As they grow older, the fondness becomes more intimate, until the day Mr Earnshaw dies. Hindley then assumes head of the household, and Heathcliff is made a virtual slave. Only with difficulty are Cathy and Heathcliff able to meet and carry on a clandestine romance. As she becomes a young lady, Cathy is sent away to live with the Lintons at Thrushcross Grange, making Heathcliff totally isolated, trapped and tormented for love. Eventually Cathy marries Edgar Linton, but she dies in childbirth, adding to the torment of the still doting Heathcliff.

Although this story is famous as a love story between Cathy and Heathcliff, it is doubtful the love was ever consummated, and most of the tale (in the book) is of the revenge between the feuding adults after Cathy's death. There are several film versions of the story, most of which pass quickly over the childhood part of the tale. In the 1992 version, Jessica Hennell plays a preteen Cathy, but we catch only glimpses of her for the first five minutes of the film. In the 2011 version, thirteen-year-old Sheffield actress, Shannon Beer, plays young Cathy, and Solomon Glove her adolescent playmate.

The love affair between Kate and Taylor in *My Sister's Keeper* was limited by life expectancy. Sofia Vassilieva plays a teenager (Kate), racked by leukaemia all her young life, but is now on the terminal ward in a hospice. There she meets a fellow sufferer, a boy named Taylor (Thomas Dekker), and they have a romantic fling together. But in their hospital ward there is nowhere private to pursue their passion, so they seek out operating rooms vacated for the night. There they can have some degree of privacy, until Taylor rapidly deteriorates and death steals Kate's only source of comfort. Father acknowledges, "Taylor was a drug of a different sort, working his magic by building her up."

In *(500) Days of Summer*, Chloë Grace Moretz quotes Nietzsche: "There's always some madness in love, but there's also some reason to madness."

Spurned Love

When fledgling girls and boys dream of their first love enduring to eternity, they are naturally devastated when their maiden flight never even gets off the ground. Probably films that show this, inject reality into a child's perspective about love, helping a child understand that hearts can be broken, even though they don't supply the glue to fix the shattered pieces. How confusing it must have been for Jenna Malone and her boyfriend as they split up in *Stepmom*. "Poor girl, she must be devastated," comments Susan Sarandon, her real mother. But stepmum Julia Roberts rebuts her: "The point of going out with someone is so they can be dumped."

Tendres Cousines is a film by the photographer David Hamilton, whose controversial photograph books of naked girls were rapidly removed from the shelves of UK art shops when indecency laws were tightened at the turn of the twenty-first century. A little girl, Puone (Valerie Dumas), is excitedly awaiting the arrival of her older cousin, Julien (Thierry Tevini). Both are young enough to innocently play together and go off exploring and on cycle rides, but old enough for the girl to have a crush on her visitor. They giggle as they spy on a lady swimming in the nude. "How does it feel to see a naked woman?" Puone asks the fourteen-year-old. But the little girl can't tempt him, and he ends up kissing the older girls, while the little girl's love hopes are spurned.

Another example of love affair that didn't work is in *I Love You, I Love You Not*, although we have an older teenager, Claire Danes, playing the student who falls in love with one of the sports-mad lads in her tutorial group. Though she is madly in love with him, he just seems to be using her for romantic gratification. For when he discovers she is the Jewish daughter of a holocaust victim, he defiantly turns against her. In this film, however, the real eye-opener is watching the groping behaviour of the grandmother (Jeanne Moreau) whenever the two females interact!

When two members of the same family love the same guy, that complicates relationships somewhat, as we discover in *Man in the Moon* and *Little Women*. In *Man in the Moon*, Reese Witherspoon has to compete against her older sister as they vie for the attention of local farmer-boy. The younger fourteen-year-old thinks she has found heaven when she finds the boy swimming in the local creek. She joins him for a skinny-dip and later enjoy a kiss together. But when the local dance comes around, it is her older sister who is invited, resulting in bitterness between the two sisters, as the younger girl feels rejected. In *Little Women*, next-door neighbour Teddy grows up as a youth with the Marsh family, joining in their games, and watching the plays staged by the two younger sisters, teenage Jo played by Winona Ryder, and preteen Amy played by Kirsten Dunst. Jo loves Teddy's company, and their interaction is such you expect them to become lovers and marry. But when the time comes for Teddy to propose to Jo, she spurns his advances. "Why do things have to change," she objects. As they grow up, Teddy then discovers the attractions of the youngest sister, Amy. They turn up unexpectedly at a family gathering and announce they are already married! Rather late, Amy checks with Jo, "You're not upset are you?"

Whether *Gregory's Girl* comes into the bracket of spurned love is debatable since the outcome for Gregory was positive; he got his girl in the end. I remember being pleasantly amused when this film unceremoniously appeared on British television. It was released without any fanfare, yet has become one of the most popular British films about teenage angst. Gregory (Gordon John Sinclair) is a gangly-legged buffoon, a fourth-former who loves soccer, but is hopeless at it. He is swept off his feet by the beautiful teenage girl, Dorothy (Dee Hepburn), who has joined his mixed soccer team. "She's got lovely blond hair, and she smells gorgeous." He falls in love and seeks the help of his younger ten-year-old sister, Madeleine (Allison Forster), to help him procure a date. Eventually, he plucks up the courage to ask Dorothy for a date, and surprisingly she agrees. But at the allotted rendezvous time under the town clock, a puzzling succession of girls arrives as a substitute for Dorothy. Ultimately, he ends up in the Country Park with a different girl, Susan (Clare Grogan), someone from his class he had not noticed before – and they end up falling in love. Susan teaches Gregory to snog. "What's my auntie going to say when I kiss her at Christmas?" quips the boy. Arriving home after a confusing evening, his young sister asks him how he got on with his date, and he explains about his dilemma. But when his sister Madeleine asks, "So who is Gregory's girl, then?" he gives her a brotherly kiss on the lips. "You are."

Ten-year-old Madeleine had a suitor of her own. A little boy Richard (Denis Criman) regularly walks home with her after school and carries her bags. When Richard knocks on Madeleine's door, hoping to hang out with her, Gregory answers the door. Gregory rebukes the boy for wanting dates and "underaged walks" at his young age. "You'll run out of vices before you're twelve if you don't slow down."

Unorthodox Affairs

Affairs with Older Men

"Just doing my bit for the war effort," was fifteen-year-old Dawn's reply in *Hope and Glory* after she was accused, "Didn't I see you with a soldier last night, Dawn?"

In Volume Four (*Childhood Friendships*) we consider examples of where a girl makes friends with an older male, often developing into a childhood crush: Evan Rachel Wood in *Digging to China*, Natalie Portman in *Leon*, Patricia Gozzi in *Sundays & Cybele*. It is not uncommon. According to Marianne Sinclair, "A lot of very young girls are prepared to accept and even encourage the advances of older men in a position of power."[17] Sometimes the crush develops into an affair, which is exploited by the adult. We shall refer to such grooming in Volume Eight, *Child Abuse*. Here, we confine our attention to those relationships in which the child is aware of having a crush and attempts to advance this into a physical romance between an underage girl and an adult male. In most cases, the child is besotted while the adult sensibly maintains discretion, and could even be considered the victim themselves. However, we also include examples in which the adult cooperates with the child's desires.

The eyes that fourteen-year-old Ariana Richards makes at Sam Neill in *Jurassic Park* is just an innocent unreciprocated crush confused with hero worship by a teenage girl. Ariana insists on travelling in his car while they journey through Jurassic Park, but he will have none of it. And when the giant brontosaurus rears into view, still her eyes are fixed on the handsome man instead. She even trips on purpose so he can pick her up and hold her hand. After the odd chase or two with a T-rex and a volley of velociraptor, he relinquishes his frigidity as the girl, cradled in his arms for protection, nuzzles her head under his chin.

Amber Beattie's flirting with a German officer in *The Boy in the Striped Pyjamas* is also a case of a child's first unrequited crush. Any older male figure will do. Playing twelve-year-old Gretel, the girl enjoys chatting with her father's chauffeur and flirtatiously caresses his arm when father's back is turned; and the man reciprocates by bringing her magazines about the Hitler Youth. Her collection of dolls discarded in the cellar, and her bedroom wall plastered with pinups and cuttings from the donated magazines, show how her adolescent focus has shifted as she shakes off childhood shackles. Even when the chauffeur is acrimoniously sent off to the Russian front the girl, undaunted, is only too happy to butter up to the more elderly tutor who is home-schooling her.

Dora Szinetar playing the title role in *Laurin (1988)* gives her new teacher a knowing smile every time she finds him staring at her mesmerising eyes. Her male classmate, Stefan (Barnabas Toth), is equally uncomfortable. "Hey, Laurin," he asks. "Do you like Mr Van Rees?" She is not yet sure about crushes. "I don't know." Stefan, with a premonition of future difficulties admits, "He's pretty nice, but sometimes he looks at you real funny."

In *Whistle down the Wind*, a murderer (Alan Bates) on the run hides out in a barn to recover from his wounds. He is found by a family of children, who bring him food and drink to help his recovery, led by fifteen-year-old Hayley Mills. "Why are you and the other kids helping me?" asks the man.

"Because we love you!" states the girl. See it from Alan Bates' point of view. A sick man, visited by an angelic girl who says "we love you," and all sorts of perverse thoughts could flood his mind. But the adolescent girl is at that transition stage when love does not yet have a sexual dimension. For the girl, her love is a religious devotion to a man she believes is Jesus, her God.

But even when the man is trapped like a fox, surrounded by police, Hayley Mills experiences the traumatic rejection as her idol rebuffs her. "I love you, I love you," is her anguished cry through the wall of the barn. "Go away, kid," says the man, before being escorted off, and frisked by the police, spread-eagled like a crucifix.

In *The Camomile Lawn*, a story by Mary Wesley about the impact of the Second World War on a family of cousins assembling in a Cornish villa, little ten-year-old Sophie dotes on her rather obnoxious nineteen-year-old cousin, Oliver. Oliver is due to return from fighting as a mercenary in the Spanish Civil War and Sophie is disappointed she has to be in bed when his train arrives. So, she waits up all night hiding behind the curtains in his bedroom until he arrives home and gets ready for bed. They cuddle up in bed together to keep warm, though there is nothing sexual in this. She likes being in his company and later listens in as he tries to woo his older cousins. "I'll be your comforter," she naively volunteers not understanding the sexual connotations.

Barely any less innocent is Susannah York's wooing of the middle-aged Kenneth More with whom she falls in love in *Greengage Summer*. From what I remember of reading Rumer Godden's raunchy book, the children in the story had some disturbing sexual encounters. But in this 1961 film version, their only tryst is to secretly kiss on the veranda. However, further dastardly deeds were deterred as the younger siblings insisted on being taken out on all the car journeys. Miss York was twenty when she played the sixteen-year-old Joss Gray. Veteran actor Kenneth More was very, very much older (47!).

In *Great Balls of Fire*, Winona Ryder plays thirteen-year-old Myra Gale who falls in love with and becomes the child bride of her pop legend cousin, Jerry Lee Lewis. At first, the innocent play-acting between child and youth is charming, but becomes alarming as their intimacy develops into sexual deviancy. When Myra's parents discover the relationship, Jerry Lee takes the girl away for a shotgun wedding. This was the 1950s when some American states still allowed girls of thirteen to wed. The wedding did not help Jerry Lee's record sales, for as the news broke, his popularity flagged. The pop star had arranged a tour in Britain. When the London Press reported that he had married the child bride, all the concerts were a flop. Winona Ryder was eighteen when she played this part, but her childlike looks and vivaciousness allowed her to pass for a young teen.

Brooke Shields played the part of an even younger child bride in *Pretty Baby*. As a twelve-year-old she goes off to live with Papa Bellocq (Keith Carradine), her prostitute mother having abandoned her to run off with a client. "Will you sleep with me and take care of me?" the little girl pleads, arriving at his New Orleans villa with her luggage bag. She had originally met the man during a game of sardines at the brothel (a form of kiss-me-quick hide-and-seek). Bellocq had hidden in a laundry cupboard, and that is where Violet had found him. She had squeezed up beside him and they tenderly kissed. Now they are living together, and Violet (Brooke Shields) enjoys romping on the bed with Carradine. They kiss, they cuddle, he watches her in the bathtub, then photographs her in the nude. But the bored girl becomes tired of her role as pretty model. It becomes a lonely life for her, separate from the company she shared at the brothel. The girl is often left to wait alone in the house. Although they get married, the child is only too happy to return to her mother when she comes looking for her.

Melissa P, based on the book *100 Strokes of the Hairbrush before Bed*, had grown up in an abusive household, the victim of sexual abuse. This has set her on a way of life in which she actively seeks out men as sexual partners. She starts by sitting in an outdoor café, staring at an older man, blowing him kisses until he comes over and tries to molest her. This is the start of a slippery slope.

Lolita, that most controversial book of all time, which surprisingly was never banned, and which Nabokov claims he himself had tried to destroy, was twice made into a film. The first version (1961) is trivialised by the humour of Peter Sellers and James Mason. In the 1997 version, the thirteen-year-old Dominique Swain plays Lolita who is targeted and seduced by Humbert Humbert (Jeremy Irons). The young teen is a willing participant and instigator of kissing and sexual romps as they travel around the country, adding a whole new vocabulary to dictionaries of '*Lolita*' – *a seductive little girl, a lolita*. Incidentally the term *nymphet* was also first coined by the author, Nabokov.

For Marianne Sinclair, 'The cinema is a natural idiom for illustrating the magic of the Lolita myth,'[18] and is a concept that has been widely exploited through the history of cinema, right from its inauguration with Lolita's predecessors, such as Lilian Gish, Mabel Normand, and Mary Pickford.

The first time we see the true precocious Lolita at work is after Humbert has collected the girl from summer camp. As they are driving off down the country lane, Lolita says to her new guardian, "You can't really love me; you haven't kissed me yet." The man screeches his car to a halt. The girl takes out her teeth brace and the next moment is slobbering all over him.

This reminds me of the action of Stephanie Berrington in *Father Goose*. Stephanie takes off her glasses revealing a pretty fourteen-year-old face and calls out to Cary Grant, "Mr Eckland, you can kiss me if you want." Cary Grant was playing an American, "a rude, foul-mouthed, drunken beast," sitting out the Second World War on a remote New Guinea island when he is caught up with the Japanese invasion and finds himself in charge of a gaggle of refugee school kids. Having saved the girl's life once, which had aroused her hormones, she feels she can benefit from his good nature by thanking him. But the rough-and-ready man scares off the teenager's advances. Clutching her in his arms and hovering above her he sarcastically jibes, "This first burning kiss is just the beginning." And the frightened girl runs off, unkissed.

"How old are you, little girl?" asks Clint Eastwood, playing an injured Yankee soldier at the time of the American Civil War, in *The Beguiled*. Pamlyn Ferdin, playing Amy, has just stumbled across him in the woods while she was picking mushrooms. "I'm twelve, but I'll soon be thirteen," the innocent girl tells him. "Just old enough to be kissed," says the stranger, giving her a prolonged kiss on the lips, and as he withdraws we momentarily see the preteen girl purse her lips for some more, and the girl is instantly smitten with love for the stranger in uniform.

Now this kiss raises some dilemmas. Here is a full-grown man, an adult on the run, and no doubt sex-starved, and here is a compliant preteen girl yielding her lips to a stranger. To the love-smitten girl living in a boarding school full of closeted schoolgirls, whose constant chatter is about men, this is maybe her first physical contact with the male of the species. But for the man, a troop of enemy confederates was approaching as he dived into the bushes with the girl. The shrubbery made a good hideout; the kiss helped silence the girl, lest she had called for help from the passing enemy troops.

The other unusual anomaly is that older girls are called upon to masquerade as youngsters for the more raucous parts (a theme we develop further in Volume One). Yet here, in *The Beguiled*, twelve-year-old Amy is played by an even younger girl – eleven-year-old Pamlyn Ferdin called upon to kiss the older man, Clint Eastwood, just as eight and a half-year-old Jodelle Ferland was chosen to play an older girl snogging the adult in *Tideland*.

Once the coast is clear, Amy helps the wounded soldier to the school gates where many earnest hands of man-starved schoolgirls and school maams are eager to prod, poke, wash, shave and kiss the helpless invalid. "Girls, back to your beds instantly," headmistress has to command, as they each volunteer to tend to him. Several times young Amy sneaks into his room to replenish her kisses.

But the man has a dilemma. The headmistress intends handing him over to the authorities as soon as he is well enough, so he does not have long to ingratiate himself with the members of staff. Soon, he has two adults and a student drooling over him, as well as Amy. When one night he is found sharing the bed with one of the older naked schoolgirls, jealousies are compounded, and they realise he must be got rid of. In confusion, twelve-year-old Amy confronts him: "You were found in Carol's room – and she was all naked. Why? I thought you loved me." So, under the suggestion of the headmistress, the little girl compliantly returns to the woods to collect some of the 'special' mushrooms for his final feast. As the Rat Queen[19] tells us in *The Nutcracker* (2010) (referring to Elle Fanning), "Little girls in love can be very dangerous." Maybe they should all have heeded the warning from Ruby's auntie in *My Year without Sex*. The eight-year-old (Portia Bradley) is advised, "Don't you ever go for someone who is old. You want someone who is young and hot, and prepared to lick honey off your toes!"

The Penalty for Being Precocious

When first love is such a tricky path to tread, to have to cope with rejection as their first emotional experience is a harsh lesson to handle. Some children, like Amy above, who develop crushes on older men, resort to revenge when their advances are spurned. For the men who dared deter the girls in *Atonement* and in *Orphan* (2009) the outcome, like Clint Eastwood's in *The Beguiled*, was pretty scary, even fatal. In other films, *Mermaids*, or *kids* (1995) the implied message seems to be that other people's lives are in danger when the girl delves too deeply into precociousness, while *Melissa P* declares open war on the entire male population.

In *Mermaids*, Winona Ryder's intentions are innocent, wanting to convert to being a dutiful Catholic. So, she is euphoric when the family move house ending up next door to a convent. But the teenager is confronted with temptation; for working in the convent grounds is a hunky handyman. "Please God, don't let me fall in love and do disgusting things," pleads helpless Winona. But of course, she falls in love. When she should have been looking after her younger sister (an infant Christina Ricci), she runs up the bell tower to have sex with the boy. It is while they are making love that the statues of the saints seem to haunt her, racking her with guilt. It is then that she remembers her little sister whom she should have been looking after. But it's too late. The little girl is face down in the water in the convent lake.

There is a fatal penalty for snogging, too, in *Zombies: Wicked Little Things*. Instead of running from danger, Scout Taylor-Compton, dwells to snog with her boyfriend on the back seat of the car where they become an immediate target for the half-dead, flesh-eating children who surround the vehicle and destroy its contents.

In the film of Ian McEwan's novel, *Atonement*, Briony (Saoirse Ronan) has a crush on the young man, Robbie. Briony lives in a massive country house with idyllic rambling gardens where every day seems to be a sweltering summer day. Briony jumps into the pond feigning drowning in the hope Robbie will jump in to rescue her. She pretends to sink under the water. Her dupe works. A worried Robbie jumps in after her, swims under the water, wrestling with the water weeds, until he can finally grab the bust of the little girl's costume, and together they float back to the surface; a beaming Briony mischievously whispering in the young man's ear, "Thank you. I love you, Robbie." But Briony receives no sympathy from the man, just a stern rebuke.

When Robbie fails to watch a play that the thirteen-year-old is performing for her visiting cousins, she is disappointed. Later, witnessing Robbie squabble with her older sister (Keira Knightley) and then have sex with her, Briony wrongly assumes the man to be a sex fiend. So, when later that evening the visiting cousin is raped, Briony draws her own conclusions. Partly out of spite and partly out of a misunderstanding, she informs the police that Robbie is the rapist. As a consequence, Robbie is arrested and sentenced to five years imprisonment. His only crime was spurning the attentions of a little girl.

Robbie's punishment was trivial compared to the penalty nine-year-old Esther metes out in the horror thriller, *Orphan* (2009). Esther (Isabelle Fuhrman) tries to seduce her adoptive father. Soon after arriving in her new home, she witnesses her new parents having sex on the kitchen table. Her mother has to explain to her, there are some things adults do that little children should not see. One night when a thunderstorm drives the girl to her parents' room for protection, she bleats, "Can I sleep with daddy?" The girl observes and exploits weaknesses in her parents' relationship, antagonising the mother, while father only tries harder to be her protector. He is blinkered to her misbehaviour while mother is gradually getting closer to the truth. A whole spate of accidents is sparked off by Esther, culminating in mother being hospitalised. With mum out of the house, Esther dresses sexily in mother's clothes and cuddles up next to her father, whose head is woozy, having opened a bottle.

Esther strokes her father's head and tells him, "I love you, daddy," kissing his cheek, then seeking more intimacy. But daddy still has sufficient clarity of mind, and spurns her advances. But this is a horror movie. When dad rejects the girl, she picks up the fruit knife and stabs the man, sending him the way of all the others who opposed her.

Earlier, we mentioned the intense snogging in Larry Clark's New York based movie, *kids* (1995). The main character, Telly (played by Leo Fitzpatrick), was an amoral youth whose sole purpose in life was deflowering virgin girls. Their lack of sexual maturity was unimportant to him; it was safety from sexually transmitted diseases that was his concern. "Virgins, I love 'em. Just pure pleasure!" His victims had other concerns. For Sarah Henderson who we see being deflowered in the opening sequence, her fear was of becoming pregnant. For thirteen-year-old Darcy (Yajira Peguero) her worry was about the pain it would cause. The boy has to cajole his victims into having sex with him: he convinces them with an on-going patter – it won't hurt, you won't get pregnant, I love you, I care for you – anything that will get the novice child to open her legs for him. Alas, he has already impregnated another girl, Jenny (Chloé Sevigny). It had been her only attempt at unprotected intercourse, so she naively assumed she could not catch Aids. She had only accompanied a friend to an HIV clinic to keep her company. But Jenny was persuaded to take a test, too, and now she discovers she is HIV positive. She has to track down Telly to give him the news.

The whole film is uncomfortable to watch, and to call it entertainment is like saying eating puke is a delectable treat. For eighteen-year-old scriptwriter, Harmony Korine, he had no moral agenda to pursue; he was just stating street-life as he saw it. But for director, Larry Clark, there *was* a purpose: to show the inevitability of contracting AIDS for those partaking in unprotected sex, and the credits indicate that a portion of the profits from the film go towards support for sexual clinics.

If the film *Melissa P* has a purpose, it is to show that teenage girls are sexual beings in their own right, with sexual urges. But living in Sicily, surrounded by erotic images and expectations, this fifteen-year-old girl (fourteen in the book) is not sure how to marry romantic desires with profligate experimentation in group sex romps and sadomasochism. According to Geraldine Chaplin, who plays Melissa's grandmother, "From the age of twelve to eighteen all a girl thinks about is sex," citing her own daughter as her source.

Having been 'used' by a youth she admired ("Do you want to kiss me?" the boy had asked, "Then kiss my dick!"), Melissa resolves to "Avenge against all men, to humiliate them. I'll treat them all the same, not caring for their feelings. I will think only of *my* pleasure." She starts recording her desires, actions, and conquest in an explicit diary. Alas, this resolve ultimately makes things worse for her as she finds herself in an ever-deepening spiral of promiscuity; she taunts strangers in cafes, indulges in blindfolded sex orgies, and visits strangers in their hotel rooms for dressing-up games. She attracts a reputation as a slut, she sees damning graffiti written about her on the school window, and her secret diary is stolen and read aloud to other classmates.

It is not until a classmate of hers, Marco, who has always fancied her, shows Melissa an album of paintings he has made of her, that she finally unravels the romantic aspect of being in love.

It is movies like these that present the adolescent girl groping prematurely for those desires that have been triggered in her body, but for which her immaturity has not yet prepared her, and the child in her resorts to revenge as soon as her feelings are hurt. While some deem punishment of their male aggressors to be just reward for their victimisation, at least Sarah Henderson in *kids (1995)* realised her precociousness had led to Aids and had the sense to seek out the boy who had impregnated her, to order to warn him.

Lesbian Affairs

As the flood of lesbian films produced for the adult sex market proves, lesbianism has become acceptable in modern society, though it is still approached with a snigger and produced to titillate. A half a century ago homosexual activity was still a criminal offence. As far as children are concerned, several mainstream movies now tackle lesbianism as a serious issue, and the subjects are usually older teenagers.

Perhaps preteen and younger teenagers are not yet ready to consider their own personal sexual stance. I am not aware of any movies that depict lesbian issues among younger aged girls, though *Billy Elliot* daringly bucks this trend with boys. Is this because girls are not mature enough to choose their sexual preferences until their later teenage years, and that children do not become homosexual until they have passed through puberty? Is it because there would be a backlash among critics, who might decry such a scurrilous activity among our innocent kids as being scandalous? Certainly, young girls are specialists in adopting close same-gender relationships (we discuss this further in Volume Four); girls have an intimate attachment to a solitary female friend, even though this seldom lasts for longer than a year.[20] At what stage does this evolve into sexual intimacy? Or could it be that what is actually just normal interaction between two girls is misinterpreted by hormonally crazed males as being sexual activity among females.

This was certainly the case in *Heavenly Creatures*. Kate Winslet and Melanie Lynskey play thirteen/fourteen-year-old schoolgirls (both actresses were over sixteen) who develop a mutual crush which involves hugging, snogging, and sharing the bath, and neither can face separation from each other – this is what triggers the tragic murder of Pauline's mother. This is based on a true story from New Zealand in 1953. Yet Kate Winslet's character, Juliet, claims (once she had been released from prison) in reality there was never any lesbian aspect to the girls' friendship. This was all a fabrication of the sensationalist scriptwriter.[21]

We mentioned earlier the televising of infants kissing on candid camera. Such infants are not able to associate kissing with sexuality. Yet, at some stage in their development, the kiss becomes a sensual sign of affection, and this is aroused during puberty. So, two children like Anna Chlumsky and Macaulay Culkin, who kiss in *My Girl* (1991) with no sexual intent, but just to "see what the big deal is all about" cannot even be classed as having a love affair. They are just good friends. Likewise, two girls of a similar preteen age who kiss together should not be confused as being lesbian.

Even so, it is still deemed a taboo subject among children going through puberty, and because certain directors like to push at taboo boundaries, no doubt it will not be long before we are inundated with preteen girls pursuing secretive lesbian affairs on screen. Thirteen-year-old Georgia Groome mentions this in *Angus, Thongs and Perfect Snogging*: "I'm a lesbian," she says, but only in desperation to deflect unwanted attention from another boy. In *Thirteen* (2003), Evan Rachel Wood shares intense kissing with Nikki Reed, including exploring with her freshly pierced tongue. But these are sixteen-year-old girls making out as thirteen-year-olds, whose ultimate goals are the boys in their school, rather than cementing a lesbian relationship with each other. In *The Brady Bunch Movie*, Marcia, a teenage girl popular with all the boys and who finally relents to the advances of a lesbian lover, was in fact played by twenty-four-year-old Christine Taylor.

Yet even as long ago as 1961, director William Wyler was breaking ground by showing us that even very young children were aware of lesbianism – though in those early days it was frowned upon. In his film, *The Children's Hour*, ten-year-old Karen Balkin is aware of the concept, for she spitefully complains to her Gran about the "unnatural" behaviour of two of her female teachers. Little girls were not expected to know about such things so it must therefore be true, and for this reason the rumours become accusations, and the teachers (Audrey Hepburn and Shirley MacLaine) are forced to close their school. One of them commits suicide because she cannot face up to the taunts in the community.

Eleven-year-old Becca Gardner is aware of it, too, in *An Unfinished Life*, for she blurts out to the two men who are looking after her: "I had a music teacher who was a lesbian." She had tried to work out in her own mind why two adult men (her grandfather and a former work colleague) would want to live together on a ranch, so she wrongly assumes her hosts are gay. Robert Redford and Morgan Freeman burst out laughing at the audacity of the statement.

We get an inkling of an affair in *Ice Palace*. In this Norwegian movie, a preteen Unn (Hilde Nyeggen Martinsen) invites her new friend Siss (Line Storesund) to visit. Unn takes her eleven-year-old friend into her bedroom and locks the door so they can be alone. They strip off in front of each other to stare at each other's naked body and to "play". After this, Unn develops an overwhelming feeling of guilt, and the next day she dies of hypothermia by getting lost in an ice labyrinth. For those who have not read the book, the film is ambiguous: did she get lost or did she commit suicide; was her anxiety related to the stripping session or other factors relating to her own dead mother? Nor does the film depict this as a lesbian affair, but rather two friends being curious and needing confirmation that the physical changes taking place in their bodies were normal. (Incidentally the two eleven-year-olds removing their endless layers of clothes – this was icy Norway in wintertime – were actually fourteen-year-olds, further reinforcing the idea we propounded in Volume One that older children are auditioned to play the more sensitive roles.)

However, Tarjei Vasaas, upon whose novel this film is based, alludes to an infatuation between the two girls, never physically expressed, but strengthened by Siss' dreams in Unn's absence. Regrettably, in trying to replicate the poetic prose of Vasaas' novel, the pace of Per Blom's mysterious film is mesmerizingly tortuous.

Lesbianism is a topic that remains controversial. Directors like to depict the salacious aspects yet remain moralistic, perhaps to avert disparaging reviews. In the aforementioned *Heavenly Creatures*, the scriptwriter is at pains to present the opinions of the parents. "Their friendship is unhealthy and unwholesome," states Juliet's father. "It's the intensity of the friendship that concerns me." They seek medical advice to find a 'cure' for their 'malady'. "Homosexuality: this condition is often a passing phase with girls of this age. It can strike at any time, and adolescents are particularly vulnerable," suggests the doctor. How can one explain this delicately to a child? "Pauline, there's nothing wrong in having a close friend, but sometimes things can become 'too friendly'." This movie was replicating the opinions of the 1950s. Modern culture, surely, is more 'civilised'.

In the French movie, *Water Lilies*, we have a film that fearlessly depicts lesbian relationships among older girls. The main character is Marie, played by Pauline Acquart. "I don't know why I bother anyway. I'm not normal," she confides in her best friend, Anne. Marie has become infatuated with Floriane, a girl she sees in the synchronised swimming team. Marie finds a way of getting into the baths so she can watch the training sessions and hang out with Floriane in the changing rooms. But at first, the friendship is one-sided. Floriane is into boys and is unaware of Marie's passion for her. Marie has to pay a price for Floriane's friendship: she has to act as escort on her dates, presumably to be ready to step in if the boyfriend oversteps the mark. Marie also accompanies the older girl to competitions as a sort of dogs-body, to help apply make-up and lotions to her hair. Marie is so smitten by Floriane she even brings home the rubbish that Floriane has discarded so she can have a precious reminder of her idol.

Floriane has a reputation for being an easy hit with all the boys, but we discover it is all a charade – she is still a virgin. Now Floriane comes to Marie for help – she wants Marie "to do it for her first!" And so we come to the intimate scene in the bedroom with Marie caressing the genitals of her lover, under the sheets, and they enjoy a repeat of the kiss they had earlier shared in the shower together.

A lesbian love affair between two girls surfaces in the TV drama *Oranges are not the Only Fruit*. A third of this drama focuses on the upbringing of Jess as a seven-year-old, growing up in a restrictive religious family in which her own thoughts, opinions and life-style have been brain-washed into her as a devotion to Jesus. Now as a sixteen-year-old schoolgirl (and played by Charlotte Coleman, who was not sixteen but a young woman in her twenties), she sees nothing wrong in falling in love with Melanie, a girl she has met on a market stall. Further, her relationship had stemmed from bringing her friend to Jesus, for she too has become a Christian.

As part of this relationship, the girls lie naked in bed together, kiss passionately, and enjoy themselves at the funfair.

When their families and the church pastor get to hear of their 'deviancy' the girls are given an ultimatum and told to cease their wickedness. Yet, there are other church members sympathetic to their sexuality at whose homes the couple are able to covertly pursue their passion.

One day, the 'concerned' church members hold both Jess and Melanie captive. They are tied up "for their own good" so they can have their evil demons exorcised from their bodies. This involves a tormenting battle of wits in which the girls are manhandled and abused (this takes three days), until they are finally convinced of their sinful nature.

Of the other films depicting girls kissing girls – *Angela* (1994), *32A* – these are girls practising to be ready to kiss boys. The reverse is not true: boys do not practise on other boys to be prepared for kissing girls – not in the movies, anyway.

Gay Boys and the Effeminate

The reason why *Billy Elliot's* interest in ballet was so frowned upon in the Durham mining community where he grew up was that ballet was for girls. Any boy taking part must be a poof. Billy was at pains to stress, "It's not just poofs." But on the periphery of his dance world, we find Michael (played by Stewart Wells in a role he would later come to regret because of the ensuing bullying taunts). Michael shows tender feeling for his friend Billy, feelings that must be kept a secret in this very macho community. We first get glimpses of this as Michael looks longingly at his male friend. Then later, when Billy knocks on Michael's back door, he finds the boy sporting a long blue dress and wearing lipstick. "It's one of mother's," he explains, and evidently he has secretly spied his own father putting a dress on, so to him it can't be that abnormal. Michael sits Billy on his bed and helps apply lipstick to his face.

On another cold wintry evening, Billy complains of cold hands. So, Michael takes them in his own hands and puts them down his trousers. "What are you doing?" asks Billy bemused. "Nothing! Just warming your hands!" Then he kisses Billy on the edge of his mouth. Billy defends his own sexuality. "Just because I like ballet doesn't mean I'm a poof!"

Stewart Wells, who played Michael in this blockbuster film, was affected in the aftermath, receiving taunts from his schoolmates for playing such an explicit role. Here is a specific case of a child being required to act a part, which later has a psychological and socially negative effect on the actor. However, although Stewart looked like a young teen when he was cast for the role, he was in fact eighteen when the film was released.

The cross-dressing in *Little Rascals* is really just tongue-in-cheek. Like Elijah Wood donning a pink dress in *The Adventures of Huck Finn*, this is solely to evade detection. Two infant boys are chased into a storeroom. To evade capture, they dress in the ballet costumes they find there. This of course leads them into tricky situations. As nine-year-old Bug Hall woos his girlfriend (Brittany Ashton Holmes) he states, "I'm a sensitive male. I'm in touch with my feminine side," but only to impress upon the girl that he is not like the other 'women-hating' boys from his gang.

The boy alone is vulnerable, as Jonathan Segat discovers while waiting for his father in *My Year without Sex*. Sitting alone, the twelve-year-old is approached by a homosexual man who tries to chat up the lad. Fortunately, the boy remains evasive until his father arrives.

360

Fear of taunts and the need for secrecy surface in A M Homes' novel and screenplay in *Jack* (2003). The boy, Jack (Anton Yelchin), is desperate to ensure no one knows his divorced father has recently turned gay, fearing he will be tarnished with the same label. Before long, graffiti appears on his school locker. Society has a polarised opinion concerning this sexuality. Although modern society is more accepting of homosexuality, when confronted with it in the immediate family barriers are raised, resentment and conflict arise, as we will see shortly in *CRAZY*. This is borne out by Jack's reaction when his father drops the bombshell that he is gay, while boating on a lake. "I want to go home," objects the boy, feeling trapped.

"Jack, I'm still your father," appeals the man, revealing his paternal love hasn't waned.

But the boy is confused, vulnerable, as if he thinks he too might catch this 'dreaded disease' and become the butt of coarse bullying by his schoolmates. "No you're not (still my father)," asserts the boy, fleeing from his father's presence. When he is alone, he ponders his fears. "If he's a homo, what does that make me?"

Later, father attempts a reconciliation with his son, and asks how he can help. But the boy is adamantly entrenched in his opinion: "You can help me by not being gay."

Few other films about child homosexuality exist in mainstream cinema, unless subconsciously my own viewing preferences have neglected them, oblivious to their existence. There are numerous European-made movies, deemed by censors to be unsuitable for viewing by the British public; films in which boys interact with boys for the entertainment of voyeuristic homosexual males. Though I have not viewed them, I believe films fitting this category include *Barnens O* and *Genesis Children*.

The Canadian movie, *CRAZY* (2005), attempts to decipher the factors why teenager Zac (Michel Côté) was ridiculed by his peers, and even his own father and brothers, for being gay. In his late teens, we see him enjoy a straight relationship with a girlfriend. It is because others have seen him befriend other guys that the gay label sticks. His brothers make anal jokes about him. His father, in a fit of desperation, declares, "There's no way I fathered a poof. We'll clear his head of these ideas," and the boy is sent to a counsellor.

Perhaps it is because the lad enjoys David Bowie music, mocks one brother. Zac traces the 'problem' back to when he was an infant. "I'd just turned seven, and unwittingly declared war on my father." Zac had been the only one in the family who could keep the baby from crying. Mother believed he was endowed with a miraculous gift. The boy became the favoured one for pushing the pram, and so took on a motherly role by wearing mum's robes and necklace. That is how father discovers him, dressed in mum's clothes. "What have you done to him," dad complains to his wife. "He's a cry-baby. He dresses like a girl. It's not normal." Even if mother and Zac do not see this as abnormal, the rest of his childhood days are a struggle to earn respect, interspersed by scrapes and arguments with family and schoolmates.

It seems there are no films that show a boy coping with homosexuality without attracting taunts and disapproval by family, friends, and that society at large is not yet ready to cope with homosexualisation of children.

Hermaphrodite Children

In this section, we consider girls or boys going through the trauma and confusion of not knowing what sex they are, and the misinterpretations that ensue from their divergent behaviour. Surprisingly, film directors have been more brave in confronting this issue than that of intra-gender relationships. Later in this section we consider *XXY*, a film that seriously confronts the dilemma for an androgynous girl with both male and female genitalia. But firstly, on a more trivial level are the experiences of boys raised by females and who are required to adopt traits that are more feminine.

A Christmas Memory concerns an eight-year-old boy, Buddy (Eric Lloyd), raised in 1930s Alabama by three elderly women. His world revolves around domestic chores, so that all the boy knows is how to cook, sew and clean, living as he does in a woman's world and having no friends of his own age. The most domineering of the sisters decides Buddy should be sent away to Military School where he can be brought up in a man's world with other boys. At least, Buddy does not have to wear women's clothes like Tom chooses to do in *The Cement Garden*.

In *The Cement Garden*, two older sisters help their younger brother, Tom, live as a girl by wearing dresses and acting in feminine ways. Here, it is a boy (Ned Birkin) who is cross-dressing to conduct himself as a girl, though it is his older sisters who suggest the transformation. Tom is the youngest of four children. At school, an older boy is bullying him. Tom comes home and tells his older sister, "I wish I was a girl – girls don't get hit." His older brother tells him, "You can't be a girl if you're a boy." His sister contradicts him. "If Tom wants to be a girl I think we should let him be one." So the two sisters Julie (Charlotte Gainsbourg) and Sue (Alice Coulthard) dress Ned Birkin in a skirt and give him a blond wig. He helps them with their family chores dressed as a girl.

The older brother, Jack (Andrew Robertson), and sister, Julie, argue about cross-dressing. "All boys secretly want to dress up as a girl," suggests Julie. Her brother, Jack, protests saying it is degrading. "What you really mean," insists Julie, "is that it is degrading being a girl. But secretly you'd love to know what it is like." Jack argues it is not normal for a boy to dress as a girl, "It might affect him in later life." Julie retorts, "All children like dressing up."

And that is all it meant to little Tom. It was just a dressing-up game, a part of play-acting – there was no sexual dimension to it, for him. However, he persisted in this role-play; when his best friend comes round they play-act being mothers and fathers, Tom taking the assumed mother's role of sweeping the house, and laying the bed. Sometimes they pretend they are mum and dad, at other times they play being Julie and her older boyfriend, Derek. Other times they play being Julie and Jack, his older brother and sister, but all the time Tom plays the girl.

"What do you do when playing these games?" Jack asks him, curiously. "Do you get strange feelings in your willy?" But Tom denies understanding what he means. So, when we witness the two little boys lying together in bed it is pure innocence with no sexual intent.

For Tom, though, this must have been a difficult part to play, dressing up as a girl, and sharing his bed with his naked older male actor. And it must have been a headache for the casting director to find a child whose parents would permit him to play such a perverse role. However, the problem was resolved by the director, himself, casting his own son to play this part. The question then arises, what freedom did the child have in agreeing to play this controversial role? What persuasions and bribes were used?

At first, Tom had complained of being bullied at school, and that is why he wanted to be a girl. Older brother, Jack, goes to Tom's school and threatens the bullying boy. Does this resolve the issue? And was Tom right to be so judgemental about the roughness of boys and the tenderness of girls? The next day, Tom arrives home from school with a bloodied nose again – the bully's two younger sisters had duffed him up instead!

The concept of cross-dressing is encountered in *ET The Extra-Terrestrial*. To the brothers, Elliott and Kevs, it is obvious that ET is a boy. But their little sister, Girtie (Drew Barrymore), would prefer him as a girl, so she dresses the alien in girl's clothes and a wig. "This is the most ridiculous thing I've seen. You should give him his dignity," argues Kevs. What was undignified to the boys was not the sight of girl's clothing, but that their friend – a 'boy' – was dressed in girl's clothes.

There is not always a sexual motive. In the case of Anna, in *Lena My 100 Children*, the child was rescued by Linda Lawn as one of the few surviving Jewish children that managed to escape annihilation in the German concentration camps. As they remove Anna's dress ready to give her a bath, Lena exclaims, "Anna, you're a boy!" 'Anna' had been masquerading as a girl in Krakow for the duration of the Second World War because "If you're a boy, the Germans can tell if you're a Jew by pulling down your pants," to see the evidence of circumcision, whereas the female carries no such tell-tale scars.

In *Let the Right One In*, Twelve-year-old Eli (played by Lina Leandersson) looks and dresses as a girl. To the boy next door, Oskar, who has fallen in love with her, she seems like a girl, though she does have some unnatural traits. This is because she is a preteen vampire, and requires a daily dose of human blood. One evening, Eli visits Oskar in his flat next door. "Close your eyes," Eli says. She takes off her clothes and gets into bed with him. After a kissing and fondling session, Oskar asks, "Eli, do you want to go steady – to be my girlfriend?" It is then the girl reveals, "Oskar, I am not a girl," and later we get a close-up of her crotch to see she has no genitalia at all (she excretes sweat rather that urine).[22] But none of this upsets Oskar who is only too pleased to have a friend. *Let Me In* is an American remake of this film, the parts of the children played by Kodi Smit-McPhee and Chloë Grace Moretz. According to director, Matt Reeves, his interpretation of John Ajvide Lindqvist's novel is that Eli is a boy who was castrated when younger. This is ambiguous. It is not how I read the story. To me, Eli was a girl who had become asexual, her anatomical scar having healed over during the course of her ageless youth.

In the Uruguayan film, *XXY*, issues of being a hermaphrodite child are given serious airing, and we are obliged to deliberate over the distressing dichotomy an 'afflicted' child has to face. Alex is a child who has been raised as a girl, but has both male and female genitalia. When the locals discover she is a "freak" their curiosity is aroused and Alex is almost gang-raped just so they can have a peek. Although this film is about Alex as a fifteen-year-old teenager and played by an older-looking Inés Efron who was twenty-two, the story makes us think about the trials that a bi-sexual child has to endure throughout his/her childhood.

Evidently, as soon as Alex was born, the doctors could immediately see something was wrong and offered to operate immediately to remove the offending appendage. But against advice, the parents refused, preferring to defer the decision and to see how the situation developed. Now, as a pretty-looking teenage girl, Alex needs to take creams and pills to defer hormonal changes as facial hair starts to grow.

She obviously is a female, for as well as having a girl's face and hair, we see several episodes of her topless, with small breasts. And when she shares the shower with her younger girlfriend, it appears a natural girl-thing. But we also get clues to her looming manliness. She walks with a man's gait, she masturbates like a boy, she has homosexual intercourse with her teenage boyfriend, and she stands on the beach having a pee. Her father morosely acknowledges, "She'll never be a woman."

We see the dilemma from two angles. The daughter's difficulties in adolescence – her need for secrecy, her difficulty with relationships, her being bullied as a freak, people referring to her as an "endangered specimen". "You're not normal." Even her boyfriend tells her, "You're different and you know it." It is like a giant anchor always holding her down, trapped in her own body. "I've had enough of my pills," she complains to father. "Go tell everyone I'm a monster."

We also see the dilemma on the part of the parents, particularly the father. Right from the birth of the child, when the first thing relatives asked was, "Is it a boy or a girl?" he has had to deflect the truth. When Alex was younger, the parents decided to leave their home city, Buenos Aires, and move into Uruguay. "We moved on so that we didn't have to hear every idiot's opinion." But in time, the local Uruguayans realised there was something unnatural about the child.

After the attempted gang-rape of his daughter, father pulls up outside a police station to report it. But he stalls. How does one start to explain the situation, the physical examinations, the truth being revealed? Everyone will find out. Instead, father seeks out another man who was born a woman, and seeks advice from him. This provides father with assurance that he has done the right thing by not allowing the operation at birth, and waiting to allow the girl to choose for herself. He is also aware that his daughter will never be a woman, and that he cannot hide her from the outside world for the rest of her life.

And what of Alex's opinions and frustrations? It is distressing to see her tip her pills on the floor in despair. "I've had enough of the pills, the operations, the changing schools. I want things to stay the same." Alas, this tantrum solves no problems except to dissolve the current vexations, only for them to build again another day.

CHILD NUDITY ON SCREEN

In the world of adult movies there invariably seems to be a love scene. The female actor is required to take off her clothes and simulate sex with the lead male actor, who has stripped to his torso. Only rarely is the male actor required to remove his pants. Possibly, the female actor cannot gain recognition until she has been through this film-world *rite-of-passage*.

Can the morality of a nation be reflected in what is portrayed in the movies or on television? When I grew up in 1960s Britain, nudity on television was very rare, and the idea of having sex outside of marriage was still considered adulterous, as it still is in many countries of the world even today (and punishable by death in some of them). Over the following decades, the sex scene and nudity wheedled their way onto the screens, so that now on prime-time television, even before the 9pm watershed, seems to be frequent, if not the norm. Promoters would always imply "We are only reflecting society." I do not believe this, even though I have no evidence to back up my argument. No, I believe sex and nudity were falsely portrayed in the media as the norm and 'in the public interest', for that is what sells newspapers and films, and the rest of society gradually followed suit. "Familiarity breeds acquiescence."[23]

Mary Whitehouse, in 1960s Britain, was a vocal campaigner fighting against this intrusion into the nation's morality. In November 1965, she set up *The National Viewers Association* to monitor "bad taste and irresponsibility" in order to "clean up TV".[24] Almost half a century later the British Prime Minister, David Cameron concurs: "We're sleepwalking to a place where porn is the norm."[25]

So now today, children growing up in a different decade and generation, learn that to have a relationship requires compulsory undressing and physical intimacy, and not just the innocent holding of hands and discreet peck on the lips as in former years.

Because of severe censorship laws brought in during the last decade, scenes of children undressing and of nudity are again now virtually absent from British and American made movies. But in the Seventies, Eighties, and Nineties directors seemed keen to procure children who would appear naked on screen (for films such as *Pretty Baby*, *Blue Lagoon*, *Angela* (1994)), a trend that never declined in the less prudish Scandinavian, Franco, and Eastern European cinemas (*My Life as a Dog*, *Ice Palace*, *Impudent Girl*, *Annunciation*). Yet today directors seem to want, and audiences demand, cute children on stage reminding them of their loves, fantasies and dreams of their 'halcyon' childhood days. Childhood days which, according to Vicky Lebeau, in Victorian times saw a distinctly non-sexual element to the depiction of "child nakedness as source of pleasure, interest and desire. The image of the nude, or semi-clothed, child was ubiquitous in late Victorian iconographies of childhood."[26]

In the main, we are referring to girls. There are, of course, several films in which the boy is paraded naked or in his underwear: David Bradley forced into the shower by his PE teacher (Brian Glover) in *Kes* (1969), Kacey Mottet Klein cavorting naked beside the new motorway or sharing the bath with his older sister in *Home* (2008), Samuel du Chatinier in *My Queen Karo*, boys skinny-dipping in *Shadrach*, the four lads in *Stand by Me* who frantically strip off to remove leeches after wading through a swamp. Young Salim (Azharuddin Mohammad Ismail) runs naked into the shower after the little girl Latika (Rubina Ali) shoves chillies onto his groin while he sleeps in *Slumdog Millionaire*, (though director Danny Boyle deletes from the final edit a scene of a naked boy pissing). Dean Stockwell is given a prolonged scrub in the bath by Errol Flynn in *Kim* (1950). To accentuate an argument I am restricting the following discourse to girls.

As we mentioned earlier, there are today an incredible number of films featuring children who are encouraged to take part in a kissing scene, all cooing the audience back to their own forays into first love (see Table ii). And although children may not actually appear nude as adult actors do, a bath scene or a shower scene seems almost compulsory, maintaining the premise that children should not be shy of being naked on screen, even if not in front of the audience. So, in what are seemingly innocent films of the 1990s and 2000s, the sweet non-sexual child is depicted in the bath or shower, as in *Fairy Tale* (1997), *Fly Away Home*, *Whale Rider*, *The Secret Garden*.

The point I am trying to make is, that getting the child to remove its clothes for the camera is one step on the road to preparing them for more explicit roles as they grow up, and this may titillate a certain portion of the audience, whether paedophilic male or maternally yearning female. After all, when Brooke Shields ran around naked in *Pretty Baby* she was the obvious type-cast candidate to invite to play the nude role in *The Blue Lagoon*, or to have naked sex in *Endless Love*, or to hide naked in the boot of George Burns' car, in *Just you and me, kid*.

Other child actors who showed willingness to either undress or snog matured into successful adult actors – Natalie Wood (*Driftwood*), Charlotte Gainsbourg (*An Impudent Girl*), Scarlett Johansson (*Manny & Lo*).

This seems to be the place to iterate (sarcastically) that although the child is expected to undress, "it's alright!" The public won't see the nudity. It will be discreetly covered up! But the cameraman, sound recorder, parents, film crew, and a whole host of hangers on, in many cases do get to see sensitive scenes as the child prepares to bathe or shower, even though these may be cut from the final editing. Other directors use the fig-leaf approach, using laughable strips of paper taped over the 'offensive' body parts, as in *That Night*. This can look clumsy when a 'naked' girl emerges from skinny-dipping in a lake hoping the audience doesn't notice the discreet piece of towelling she is holding over her chest, as in *Man in the Moon* or *Lilya 4-ever*. There is an alternative: the scene could be omitted if it is fraught with such embarrassments.

It seems almost a compulsion for a director to portray a shower scene, as if that is part of the directing manual. Anna Paquin showers among the baby goslings in *Fly Away Home*, then is caught naked in front of the father (Jeff Daniels) and a visiting young man. *We* only get to see the rear view, though the other cast and crew get a full-frontal before a towel is hastily found. The director, Carroll Ballard, commenting on this later, says, "We had to go to some lengths to avoid showing kiddy porn," as if to justify the inclusion of the clip. If they were seriously worried about this, surely they would not have filmed the scene in the first place. After all, he wrote the script.

Likewise, in another children's favourite, *Balletshoes*, Emma Watson and Yasmin Paige share a bath together. Nothing is revealed and, no doubt, both girls were submerged wearing bikinis, and being aged seventeen and fifteen they were not exactly underage anyway, yet the director, Sandra Goldbacher, felt a compulsion to include the incongruous scene.

Several young actresses have adult body doubles for more revealing scenes. Reese Witherspoon jumping naked into a lake in *Man in the Moon*, and Brooke Shields swimming naked through the sea in *The Blue Lagoon*: both use an adult stand-in look-alike. Yet this latter young teenager has an intimate kissing scene to perform naked for which sensitive private parts are carefully masked. To film this sequence, the director had all the crew removed from the set so it was just the two actors, plus the director and the cameraman. I guess the latter two had to discreetly turn a blind eye and ignore any over-revealing action, as if they were sexually disinterested GPs.

Dwelling on this theme of underaged girls undressing in the movies, thirteen-year-old Jodie Foster in *The Little Girl who lives down the Lane* removes her blouse and trousers (she is wearing no underwear) then jumps into bed with her boyfriend, the schoolboy magician. (The schoolboy's part is played by a twenty-year-old, Scott Jacobi, so there is a massive age differential). Yet in the darkened bedroom, the bare back turned towards us and the mature-looking breasts appears to have the skin texture of an older woman, the glimpse of the face snuggling on the pillow appears fleetingly to be that of a different lady so here too, presumably, a body-double was used. Yet, the message is clearly there – thirteen-year-old girls jump naked into bed with twenty-year-old men.

Others use older-aged actresses playing the parts of younger teenagers as is the case with Inés Efron in *XXY*, Jenny Agutter in *Walkabout*, and Charlotte Gainsbourg in *The Cement Garden*. But for the bulk of movies depicting naked children, the director has invariably dared to use willing(?) child victims: Katya Berger in *Little Lips*, Line Storesund & Hilde Nyeggen Martinsen in *The Ice Palace*, Charlotte Blythe in *Angela* (1994), Berangere Haibruge in *Innocence* (2004), or Anna Franziska Jager in *My Queen Karo* (2009) to name just a few. The fact that the majority of these are foreign actresses reveals a message about the moral differences between British and European codes of conduct and laws.

Perhaps the parents of twelve-year-old Monica Bugajski got the balance right in *Shadrach* and highlighted the absurdity of the inconsistencies of current scruples. There was a skinny-dipping scene beside the millpond. All the boys and some of the adults stripped off to wash-off the day's grime, but Monica resolutely kept her petticoat on, and strode into the waters fully covered. Maybe she didn't want to strip off, or perhaps her parents forbade it. Good for them! Or maybe the director was as concerned as Carroll Ballard and realised, that to avoid legal wrangling over a pubescent preteen he should not permit the underage girl to strip to bathe.

What is indecent, and are we, as viewers, breaking the law?

So this brings us to the significant question related to nakedness on screen: "What is meant by indecent?" This can be a subjective matter; what is indecent in the eyes of one person is acceptable to the eyes of another. What may be natural conduct or mode of dress by one child or its parents may be considered outrageous by others. Customs, cultures, religion, geographical location, and historical timescale all play a part in the subjective opinions concerning decency. The British Board of Film Classification ensure, or try to ensure, consistent standards so that a modicum of decency is maintained for the UK viewer. (Australia has its equivalent, *The Australian Classification Board*, whereas in Canada and USA censorship of specific films is determined by individual states, yet operates a nationwide *Motion Picture Rating System*.)

Those charged by the British police with possessing or downloading indecent images of children from the computer are usually assessed according to the degree of indecency as defined by the Copine Scale. This roughly, in rising order of severity from one to five, is ranked as follows:

Nudist – naked or semi-naked images of children;
Erotica – surreptitious photography showing children in underwear or nakedness;
Posing – deliberate posing suggesting a sexual content;

Explicit erotic posing – emphasis on the genital area;
Explicit sexual activity – images depicting explicit activity, but not involving an adult;
Assault – images depicting sexual assault on children involving an adult;
Gross assault – images depicting penetrative assault involving an adult;
Sadistic/bestiality – sexual images involving pain.

At least this makes the issue black and white for legal purposes, though it can impose difficulties on a parent who may have to tread cautiously to avert the long arm of the law. Many parents take naked photos of their babies, continuing into infanthood, but at what age does one stop clicking the shutter release? To most parents their child is sweetly innocent, while others viewing the pictures may have perverted thoughts when confronted with the naked or semi-naked image of a child. The recent incarceration of Vanessa George, an English nursery schoolteacher from Plymouth, who exchanged images of her infant charges confirms that; and the reluctance of some schools to allow filming of Nativity plays highlights the extremity of fear of exploiting or being seen to exploit children, or of allowing children to be exploited.

Parents who take their children to naturist sites expose their child to continual photographic surveillance by eager enthusiasts promoting the naturist way of life, as they do if they take their child to most Mediterranean or Black Sea beaches.

Is a mother snapping a photo of her child playing alongside any number of strangers' children on a nudist beach any more or less guilty than a man sitting aloof in his own home clicking the save button on his computer when he finds an image he may want to view again? (The legalistic term for this is making indecent images, and the innocent mother who dares show the holiday snaps to someone else is deemed to be distributing indecent images.)

And what is acceptable in Scandinavia or Germany may not be acceptable in the United Kingdom or America. Likewise, what may have been acceptable in the 1970s may not be acceptable in 2020.

Bearing these points in mind, film directors know the boundaries of decency and indecency (or should do, though it can be ambiguous and subjective), as do the boards of classification. Yet, many of the movies we watch on television or at the cinema have been imported from countries where the laws of indecency are different, or films made in a different era. Other film directors, on purpose, wish to push the boundaries of perversion, perhaps to see what they can get away with, or else using the pretence of artistic licence. *Adolescent Malice (aka Maladolescenza/Spielen wir Liebe)* is one such film,[27] promoted under the banner of artistic genre but banned in European courts as being pornographic and abusive;[28] as has the more recent controversial *A Serbian Film*[28a] in which a child has to watch an adult couple share oral sex. So when we view sensitive material on our screens they may already have been edited, cut, or received an outright ban. The dilemma for us, the viewing public, who may be attracted by a foreign made film purchased over the internet, is that we may be in possession of video/DVD images which are decreed as being indecent according to British law as determined by the Copine scale above.

Let us now consider which, if any, fit into the Copine bracket. Fortunately, I am not aware of any films depicting images in the two most severe categories, four and five.

Child Nudity on Screen

Level 1. Nudist: Naked or Semi-Naked Images of Children.

I am not a lawyer. I guess many parents will have naked photographs of their own children at home, maybe taken when their child was a baby, or as a junior playing in the garden, or on a beach. I assume, if the photograph has not been taken for salacious reasons then the authorities would turn a blind eye to possession of such material. Whether or not this is true of possessing the pictures of other children playing alongside your own children I do not know. Possession of such photographs gleaned from the Internet probably would be deemed both pornographic/indecent and illegal. In between, are those pictures acquired through watching commercially made films. Having recorded a programme broadcast over the TV would, I assume, be permissible, since boards of censors would have passed the material. However, a programme recorded on video in 1970 might have now fallen beyond the boundary of decency. A case in point would be *The Spy Who Caught a Cold* in which a mother and her ten-year-old daughter (Isabella Nightingale Marsh) visit a nudist camp. The naked girl frolics around on the beach doing cartwheels, walks among naked men and women, sometimes spying on them with a pair of binoculars. This was broadcast on Channel Four in the 1980s in the UK. It has not been screened since, and I notice it does not appear on Channel Four's web-site of available products for sale. Yet surprisingly, the recent French movie *Tomboy (2011)*, in which the child is paraded naked before our eyes so we can determine her gender, is issued a U (Universal) rating by the British Board of Film Classification.

The purpose of the following lists is to show the extent to which children, particularly girls, are required to appear naked or semi-naked in movies. While the reader may consider some of the examples trivial, I have included them to emphasise a point. Of the 502 films reviewed for this series of books, this represents the statistic of 19%, or one in every five movies, in which the girl-child is required to remove her clothes for incongruous naked or semi-naked action. At the end of the listings we rationalise the need for film directors to include a bathing or shower scene, but also discuss how this affects the child actors.

Most of the films relate to children aged between 8 and 14. Legally, the actor remains a child up to the age of 18. There are a host of films not reviewed for this series of books that have been excluded from these statistics. If all ages of children are considered, then assume an alarming figure of at least one-quarter, and probably one-third of girl children are expected to appear naked, semi-naked, or in bath and shower scenes.

Films that have been shown on British terrestrial television, which may fall within this category, are:

Alice in the Cities in which Yella Rottländer promenades and swims topless wearing just her panties.
Blame it on Fidel: Nina Kervel appears topless while preparing to bathe, and while in the bath.
Blue Lagoon (1949): Susan Stranks is topless for most of the beach scenes.
Blue Lagoon (1980): Complete nakedness by Elva Josephson & Glen Kohan (distant views). Topless close-ups of Elva Josephson. Brooke Shields and Christopher Atkins kissing (prolonged), including naked kissing. Brooke Shields naked, though all shots of breasts were of a body double.
Cider with Rosie: Sally Beer strips off naked. Topless close-up.

Emerald Forest: Native children fully naked / topless.

Fairy Tale (1997): Elizabeth Earl topless in bath.

Genova: Filmed on Mediterranean beach where other children are bathing topless.

Hideous Kinky: Carrie Mullan topless.

High Wind in Jamaica: Karen Flack topless on deck of pirate ship.

Ice Palace: Line Storesund & Hilde Nyeggen Martinsen undress and appear naked. Full-frontal nakedness on 2 separate occasions.

Impudent Girl: Charlotte Gainsbourg appears topless while washing in sink. Julie Glenn topless on bed and dancing open-bloused in front of mirror.

Innocence (2004): Iris arrives topless in coffin. Topless bathing in lake, plus dressing & undressing scenes. Bath scene. Berangere Haibruge steps from bath revealed full-frontal in mirror.

Karma Sutra: Underwater shots of 2 topless girls during opening credits.

Jakob the Liar: Topless girl is inspected by doctor.

Lawn Dogs: Michelle Barton takes off nightdress and howls to the moon topless.

Little Girl who lives down the Lane: Jodie Foster gets undressed & appears nude getting into bed with boy (may be a stunt double).

Meet me in St Louis: Side view of topless Margaret O'Brien after taking off her robe.

Mission, the: full nudity as native girl walks to canoe.

Mixed Company: Vietnamese girl (Jina Tan) strips off nude while chased upstairs and hides naked in cupboard.

My Life as a Dog: Melinda Kinnaman lifts her pullover to reveal her breasts. Later, she unbuttons her blouse to show her breasts.

Paperhouse: Charlotte Burke sits up topless in bath.

Peck on the Cheek: Keerthana runs through bedroom topless in panties.

Piano, the: native girls fully naked.

Pied Piper: Clare Drummond topless bathing in river.

Ratcatcher: Lynne Ramsay Jr. naked in bath scene. Michelle Stewart nude in bath with William Eadie.

Return to the Blue Lagoon: Courtney Phillips continually appears topless for part of the film.

Secret Garden: Kate Maberly, topless, is dressed by her maid. In a bath scene, appears topless getting out from bath.

Walkabout: Jenny Agutter removes her blouse, revealing her breasts while the Aborigine dances, and she swims naked with her younger brother, Lucien John (though dressed as a schoolgirl, Jenny was 18 when this film was released).

Other films in this category, which as far as I am aware have not appeared on British television:

Angela (1994): Miranda Stuart Ryne appears topless while bathing in river and bathtub. Charlotte Blythe appears topless while bathing in river and bathtub. Charlotte Blythe complete nudity, including close-ups, while being rubbed with mud.

Annunciation: Prolonged nudity with close-ups, at start and finish of film.

Children of Theatre Street: several topless auditions.

Cría Cuervos: Ana Torrent is undressed to appear topless. Conchita Perez's breasts seen from side view while getting dressed. Maite Sánchez is stripped naked and lifted into bath. (The water is evidently scalding hot for she has to be immediately lifted out. The other actors are amused, except the whimpering child)

Diables, Les: Children exit naked from communal showers (distant shot). Adèle Haenel topless (several occasions).

Driftwood: Natalie Wood in prolonged bath scene.

Father of My Children: Close-ups of topless swimming by Alice Gautier.

Good Mother, the: Asia Vieira topless around the house and in bath with mother.

Laurin: Dora Szinetar watches nude father (from rear), and appears in topless bath scene.

Little Lips: Katya Berger full-frontal nakedness washing beside river (2 separate occasions). Naked views while washing in bathtub. Blanket covering her nakedness falls open for topless view.

Man on the Moon: Reese Witherspoon – Skinny-dipping using a body-double. As 'naked' Reese emerges from water a hidden bra is momentarily revealed.

Melissa P: Maria Valverde topless, strokes her breast and groin. Appears topless in shower scene.

My Queen Karo: Anna Franziska Jager naked on several occasions, including washing in bathtub, skinny dipping, swimming, sleeping and dressing.

Pretty Baby: Brooke Shields is undressed for dais scene. Topless in bath then stands up. Lies naked in bed (face down). Naked in bathtub (submerged). Totally nude photos (crutch not visible). Naked from behind when running. (This film has been broadcast on *Sky* in 2011 to British audiences)

Somer Jubel: 2 boys & 2 girls go skinny-dipping. Complete nudity (distant).

Tomboy (2011): Zoé Héran complete nudity. The film seems constrained to show her genitals to confirm the gender of this tomboy. Numerous topless scenes. Malonn Lévana emerges topless from bath.

Toto le Héros: Sandrine Blancke takes a bath with her brother, Thomas Godet. She stands topless in front of brother (close-up). Boy holds her breast.

Other films in which a naked or semi-naked child is undressing, bathing or showering though no apparent indecency is depicted (though we don't know if the child had to parade naked in front of the crew in preparation for the filming). None of this should be classed as indecent, but I have included these films to show the extent to which directors feel compelled to show a bathing scene or expect their young actress to remove her clothes:

Amazing Panda Adventure: Yi Ding & Ryan Slater undress, but no nakedness visible.

Andre: Tina Majorino submerged in bubble bath.

Balletshoes: Emma Watson and Yasmin Paige share bath, but no visible nudity.

Brooke Ellison Story: Vanessa Marano is bathed, rear view only (panties discernible underwater).

Cold Light of Day: Perdita Weeks is submerged in bath.

Company of Wolves: Sarah Patterson in tin bath (submerged)

Corrina, Corrina: Tina Majorino in bath (distant view).

Curly Sue: Alisan Porter – immersed in bath.

Dark, the (2005): Abigail Stone – naked in bath, rear view only.

Dark Water: Ariel Gade in bath with mother (submerged)

Dustbin Baby: Alexandra Hewitt in bath (submerged)

Eloise at the Plaza: Sofia Vassilieva submerged in bath.

Exorcist: Linda Blair naked in bath (submerged).
Fly Away Home: Anna Paquin – shower scene with geese – no frontal nudity visible.
Hounddog: Dakota Fanning in bath scene, completely coated in soap suds.
Innocents, the: Pamela Franklin in bath (submerged)
Let Me In: Chloë Grace Moretz emerges from shower wrapped in towel.
Liar, Liar: Vanessa King submerged in bath.
Lilya 4-ever: Oksana Akinshina sits in bath – a flesh coloured towelling just apparent masking nudity.
Manny & Lo: Scarlet Johansson in bath (submerged) plus shower scene (discreet).
Memoirs of a Geisha: Suzuka Ohgo appears naked (rear view) when given geisha clothes.
Mockingbird Don't Sing: Rear view of eleven-year-old Tarra Steele fully naked while her mother & older brother dress her.
Pan's Labyrinth: Ivana Baquero in bath.
Parent Trap: Lindsay Lohan skinny-dips (concealed).
Peppermint Soda: Girls' changing room – girls in bras. Eleanore Karwien & other girls in clinic in underwear. Eleanore Karwien in bath with older sister (concealed).
Poltergeist II: Heather O'Rourke shares bath with her naked mother (Jobeth Williams).
Rabbit Proof Fence: 3 girls shower – completely screened & probably clothed.
That Night: 3 girls topless in front of mirror (breasts masked by sheets of flesh-coloured paper).
Time Traveller's Wife: Tatum McCann emerges from bath wrapped in towel.
32A: School changing-room scene, girls in bras. Girl removes vest in changing room closet (viewed from behind).
Untamed Love: the back of Ashlee Lauren in bath is shown to highlight scars of abuse.
Urban Ghost Story: Heather Ann Foster in bath while mother helps wash her hair.
Whale Rider: Keisha Castle-Hughes topless in bath (rear view).

Level 1: Erotica – surreptitious photography showing children in underwear or nakedness

A Good Year: Marine Casto poses in her underwear before swimming across pool to kiss boy.
Ball-trap: 2 girls moon at the camera by raising their dresses.
Camomile Lawn: Rebecca Hall – naked bottom while having a piggyback
Cold Light of Day: A doctor inspects a girl in her underwear. (Doctor turns out to be a paedophile)
Eve's Bayou: Jurnee Smollett undresses down to underwear.
Great Balls of Fire: Winona Ryder strips to bra for kissing.
Hideous Kinky: Bella Riza & Carrie Mullan cavort in their underwear on several occasions.
Me without You: Anna Popplewell & Ella Jones dance in their underwear.
Now and Then: Christina Ricci appears in her bra, taping up her chest.
Paper Moon: Tatum O'Neal poses in her underwear.
Paradise (1991): Thora Birch and Elijah Wood bathe in river in underwear.
Shadrach: Monica Bugajski emerges from baptism with wet see-through revealing clothing.
Skin: Ella Ramangwane swims in her underwear.
32A: School changing room scene, girls in bras.
Water Lilies: Pauline Acquart in bra & panties.

<u>Level 1: Posing – deliberate posing suggesting a sexual content</u>

Taxi Driver: Jodie Foster parades in hot pants suggesting being a prostitute.

<u>Level 1: Explicit erotic posing – emphasis on the genital area</u>

Cement Garden: Focus on Charlotte Gainsbourg's groin during handstand (though Charlotte was 21).

<u>Level 2: Explicit sexual activity – images depicting explicit activity, but not involving an adult</u>

Adolescent Malice: Full nudity. Close-ups. Weeing. Kissing. Stripping. Bondage. Kissing of genitals & breasts. Simulated naked intercourse.
Annunciation: Prolonged nudity with close-ups, at start and finish of film with suggestion of kissing girl's genitals.
Diables, Les: Adèle Haenel & Vincent Rottiers: fondling of bare breasts.
Exorcist: Suggestion of girl masturbation.
Innocence (2004): Suggestion of girl masturbation.
kids (1995): Prolonged snogging: Sarah Henderson & Leo Fitzpatrick. Simulated sex scene in underwear in which girl's unbuttoned top opens out. Simulated sex scene between Leo Fitzpatrick & Yakira Peguero
Little Girl who lives down the Lane: Jodie Foster (blushing) washes back of boy in the bath.

<u>Level 3: Assault – images depicting sexual assault involving an adult</u>

Terminology such as assault can be construed to cover a range of actions so it is possible the following may be included at this severe level of indecency/pornography:

Bastard out of Carolina: There is no nudity in this film but eleven-year-old Jena Malone has to sit on the lap of Ron Eldard while he simulates an orgasm beneath her. Later, the girl endures a prolonged snog while being violently raped.
Great Rock & Roll Swindle: Man writes on chest of topless girl (aged 13). Topless girl poses while man (Malcolm McLaren) is in bath.
Little Lips: Man watches Katya Berger's full-frontal nakedness beside river (2 separate occasions). Katya Berger kisses man while she is naked. Man watches naked views of Katya washing in bathtub. Blanket covering her nakedness falls open for topless view while being caressed by man.
Lolita: Dominique Swaine – Jeremy Irons removes her blouse, and simulates arousal as she squirms on his lap (though in this scene a substitute actor may have replaced Dominique).
Pretty Baby: Adults undress Brooke Shields to be sold as a prostitute. Topless in bath then stands up naked while a man decides whether to buy her services. Brooke Shields kisses Keith Carradine (2 different occasions). Naked in bathtub (submerged) while Carradine watches her bathe. Totally nude (crotch not visible) as Carradine photographs her.
Tideland: Jodelle Ferland kisses adult, including tongue wagging.

This list appears endless and the proportion seems alarmingly high: of the 502 films reviewed for this book, this represents a ratio 96/502, that is 19% films in which the girl-child is required to appear naked or semi-naked, close to a proportion of one in five films.[29] The question to be asked now is how does this affect the child who is required to strip for the cameras? These are little children who have probably had little say in the matter of parading bare flesh before our eyes. Many have been coerced or sweet-talked into the role by an aspirant parent who hopes to wallow in the financial reward or the glory of seeing their child on stage. Others may have been led to believe it will open future doors for them as they enter adult acting spheres. To complain could be seen as expressing ingratitude. Once committed, the scenes cannot be un-shot, and the nakedness is there in-perpetuity.

Most actors seem compliant in their roles, except that in *Cría Cuervos* the audience can see the obvious distress as the tearful Maite Sanchez is lifted naked into the bath. Brooke Shields applied to the courts to have a set of indiscreet naked pictures of her as a ten-year-old suppressed. The US judge deemed the nude photos were 'so lascivious' they would 'result in serious injury to Miss Shields.'[30] Novelist Grahame Green was sued for daring to highlight the lascivious innuendo of Shirley Temple's preteen acting. A few days after allowing a naked photoshoot for *Vanity Fair* in 2008, Miley Cyrus confessed, "Now, seeing the photos and reading the story, I feel so embarrassed."[31] So you see, children do find a voice, but alas, not until it is too late.

A current concern among socio-psychologists is the over-sexualisation of underaged children, exposed as they are to the influences of the media, fashion, and music industry. MG Durham, in her book *The Lolita Effect*, highlights the harm this sexualisation is causing. Referring to the photos of Miley Cyrus, "A variety of adults had connived to use her body for their own commercial motives, a situation in which no young girl should ever be placed." While acknowledging that children have a sexual dimension, she stresses this "is best dealt with in a safe or private space." The harm this sexualisation is doing is making children sexually active, raising teenage pregnancy rates, and increasing their vulnerability to sex crimes; these are sexually active children who are unaware of or how to seek health care services or birth control facilities. Quoting a study in America, she shows there is a direct correlation between children's exposure to sexual content on TV and teen pregnancy rates.[32] This is a theme we pursue further in Volume Eight, *Physical and Sexual Abuse*.

ENDNOTES FOR VOLUME SIX

1 Vicky Shaw, writing in The Independent 18 Oct 2007. She quotes a report by Population Action International "Britain has the highest teenage pregnancy rate in Western Europe." However, on a global scale, UK was ranked as low risk: 18th compared to the other 130 nations in the study.

2 Robin is being played by Evan Rachel Wood, in *Down will come Baby*.

3 Dorothy Allison, *Bastard out of Carolina*, p175.

4 No, I don't mean orally. If masturbation is suppressed vocally in society, should a child actor be expected to depict this, even by gesturing?

5 Teenage Mothers : Decisions and Outcomes – Provides a unique review of how teenage mothers think Policy Studies Institute, University of Westminster, 30 Oct 1998. Reference obtained via Teen Pregnancy\Teenage pregnancy - Wikipedia, the free encyclopedia.mht, which states "There is little evidence to support the common belief that teenage mothers become pregnant to get benefits, welfare, and council housing. Most knew little about housing or financial aid before they got pregnant and what they thought they knew often turned out to be wrong." http://en.wikipedia.org/wiki/Teenage_pregnancy - cite_note.

6 Teenage pregnancies among under 16s was 0.8% in 2008, and 4.2% of girls aged between 16-18 became pregnant: BBC News Channel on Internet 26/02/09.

7 Marianne Sinclair, Hollywood Lolita p108, 116, 140.

8 Marianne Sinclair, Hollywood Lolita p24.

9 Thompson et al Best Friends, Worst Enemies, p186.

10 Summer Rejoice, also called After Spring.

11 I hope the reader read this sentence and the next sarcastically.

12 Amanda Alch was actually fourteen.

13 The Encylopedic World Dictionary: Snogging = to kiss, cuddle, behave amorously. (The Oxford Concise doesn't belittle itself by defining the word.)

14 'The poison was in the wound, and the wound remained forever open.' Vladimir Nabokov. Lolita p20.

15 In *Lovers of the Arctic Circle*, Ana as a child is played by Sara Valiente, as an adolescent by Kristel Diaz. Otto as a child is played by Peru Medem, and as an adolescent by Victor Hugo Oliviera.

16 Susan Stranks went on to be presenter in the popular children's series, *Magpie*.

17 Marianne Sinclair, Hollywood Lolita p9.

18 Marianne Sinclair, Hollywood Lolita p7.

19 Frances de la Tour plays the adult Rat Queen, and is referring to Elle Fanning.

20 Best Friends, Worst Enemies, Thompson et al p62.

21 The Virgin Film Guide (2003) p310.

22 A dummy is used to show the close up of the crotch.

23 Marianne Sinclair, Hollywood Lolita p126.

24 Chronicle of the 20th Century, Edited by Derrik Mercer.

25 Re-quoted on Radio Five Live, Sun 8th January 2012.

26 Vicky Lebeau Childhood & Cinema p92.

27 Adolescent Malice, also known as Maladolescenza (German: Spielen wir Liebe). Maladolescenza - Wikipedia, the free encyclopedia.

28a *A Serbian Film* has recently been re-released. I understand, this new release has been severely edited.

29 My total number also includes films involving boys without any girl actors. So, in reality, the proportion is probably higher. This compensates for the fact that I have included films using some over-age actresses and body doubles. In some films, more than one child may be unclothed, and I have not

allowed for this in my ratio, either. Although my statistics are not scientifically gathered, my ratio of one-in-five will be fairly accurate, and asserts the point that girl actresses are required to be willing to act unclothed.

30 Marianne Sinclair Hollywood Lolita p148-154.
31 MG Durham The Lolita Effect p2.
32 MG Durham The Lolita Effect p2, 5, 22, 48.

Volume Seven

Childhood Trauma

"Childhood is the best time of your life.
There again, childhood is what you spend the rest of your life trying to overcome."
(*Hope Floats*)

CONTENTS FOR VOLUME SEVEN

7. Childhood Trauma..**377**

Contents for Volume Seven...**379**

Childhood Trauma: Introduction..................................**381**

Separation and Divorce: Its Impact On The Child..............**382**
The Comedic Approach to Divorce...............................*384*
The Serious Approach to Divorce.................................*386*

Illness and Disability...**389**
Coping with a Disability...*390*
Contracting a Disability...*396*
Contracting a Disability: The Brooke Ellison Story..................*398*
Contracting a Disability: Lorenzo's Oil...........................*400*
When the Child becomes Ill...*402*

Underage Pregnancy...**404**
Observing Pregnancy in Others....................................*404*
Coping with Pregnancy..*405*
Pregnancy: the boy's responsibility..............................*407*

Death **409**
Platitudes..*410*
Terminal Illness...*412*
Psychological Effects of the Death of a Parent on the Child.......*414*
Misunderstanding in the Child's Mind about death.................*419*
Muteness as a reaction to the Death of a Parent...................*421*
Death of a Friend..*421*
Guilt feelings that arise as a loved one dies........................*424*
*Life After Grief: Coming to terms with and Rationalising the death of a
Parent*..*426*
Taking on the burdens of responsibility when adult carers can't cope......*428*
The Afterlife...*429*
When death is of no concern...*431*

The Impact Of War...**433**
Vulnerable Refugees *434*
Ethnic Cleansing...*437*
Resistance Fighters..*440*
Witnesses to the Atrocities of War.................................*441*
Evacuees...*444*
Keeping Home Fires Burning...*445*

Moving To A New Home...447
Fear of not being able to make new friends................................*448*
Regrets of the past...*449*
Beneficial Moves..*452*

Endnotes for Volume Seven..453

CHILDHOOD TRAUMA: INTRODUCTION

In this volume, we consider films that depict children coming to terms with a trauma, whether that be illness, death of loved ones, the separation and divorce of parents, or an unexpected pregnancy. Moving home also creates a loss in a child, in his/her eyes almost as devastating as the void left by the death of parents: in this case, leaving old friends and the fear of not being accepted into new spheres and cliques. In all instances, the child feels deprived in some way, whether that is the loss of a loved one, the loss of physical ability and strength, or the loss of friends. The trauma can impact on the child, as well as on its parents and peers; influencing the child's hopes, confidence and ambitions, and expressing itself in the pain and sense of injustice that this imbues.

Child stress has increased 70% since the 1970s. There are now 80,000 children in the UK suffering from depression, aggravated by a lack of play space, an increase in cars, academic expectations and an over-emphasis on educational testing, coupled with society's negative attitude towards modern youth, and absentee parents – one-in-five kids have both parents out at work. On average, parents spend just seventeen minutes a day with their kids. According to one commentator, "Children today are not free-range. They are battery reared."

Sula Wolff in her book *Children Under Stress* [1] reminds us of the behavioural indices of a stressed child: 'nightmares, bedwetting, temper tantrums, excessive fears,' and 'reverting to infantile clinging,' which in later years may be exhibited in shoplifting, anorexia, self-harm, and even suicide. [2] She acknowledges that 'adverse events are harmful for children when they arouse more anxiety than the child can cope with.' Home environment and parental nurturing is crucial in satisfying the child's psychological battle with trauma. The stressed child 'should be allowed to bring out in talk and in play their true thoughts and feelings about the events, even if these are aggressive, sadistic, and apparently callous.' [3]

Of course, it is the natural reaction of parents to try to protect their child from the impact of trauma. The words mollycoddle and cotton wool spring to mind. In the opinion of French author Tomi Ungerer, [4] "I do believe in traumatising children: children have to be exposed to realities." He uses as an example, parents avoiding visits to a Holocaust exhibition or to Auschwitz lest their child be traumatised by the experience. Likewise, children should be able to psychologically 'bury the dead' and not be deprived, for example, of a funeral experience. The parents successful at nurturing are the ones who steer the child through life's stresses in a caring and informative way without trying to stifle the child with bluff and half-truths. Maybe, the child actor is best placed to receive the most wholesome education compared to other children by being exposed so vividly to the traumatic hurdles that obstruct life's passage, but without the misery of experiencing them first hand.

This is the purpose of this book, to highlight those films that show children coming to terms with bereavement, ailments, with the separation and divorce of their parents, or being wrenched away from familiar surrounding by moving house, or by the evil of war. Rarely are there edifying solutions or optimistic outcomes. These are terrifying paths the child has to endure. Maybe, God supplied us with tear ducts just for this purpose.

SEPARATION AND DIVORCE: ITS IMPACT ON THE CHILD

We mentioned in Volume Two (*Families, Step-kids & Orphans*) how film directors seem to exaggerate the problem of divorced or bereaved families by over-inflating the problem, leading us to believe that the majority of families are comprised of a single mother or single father struggling alone trying to raise their kids. We are constantly expected to sympathise with the maternally impoverished child, and compliment the director for noticing problems in family structures and directing our attention to them.

But the fact that a majority of children still grow up in a unified family unit has evaded our scriptwriters, and deluded us. I direct you to Table One, which lists films according to how they depict broken homes. In reality, 66% of children live with their birth parents, yet the film world would have us believe it is just 29%. (66% is an estimate of the worldwide average. In the US, 61% of children live with both biological parents, in the UK the ratio is 62%, while in Sweden the ratio is 72%).

Of course, we must not belittle the situation, for a disunited family is a source of trauma for all involved.

Some directors tackle the issues of separation and divorce by confronting the problem head-on (as in *Child of Divorce*, *Kramer v Kramer* or *Shoot the Moon*) and this makes for hard-hitting, tear-jerking films. Others try to lighten the blows by adding humour to the 'entertainment' (such as *Mrs Doubtfire*), while others just mention a parentally-deprived child in passing (the band-wagon approach as in *Explorers*). Then there are those films that try to resolve the problem by turning the child into a matchmaker, either by bringing mum and dad back together again (*The Parent Trap* and *All I want for Christmas*), or by finding a new partner for the single parent (*Miracle on 34th Street*). Yet, seldom will a film show a daughter trying to find a replacement mother for her single dad, nor a son trying to find a new dad. It appears that as long as the daughter has her dad, and a son has her mother, all appears well in their lives – in the movie world anyway.

Divorce is a modern post-war phenomenon. Although parents did separate and divorce before the Second World War, there was widespread social disapproval of any couples who couldn't make their marriage work. (There are exceptions to everything, of course: in 1939 Cary Grant tries to escape an unhappy marriage in *In Name Only* abandoning his daughter (Peggy Ann Garner), while in *The Women* (1939) Virginia Weidler is the innocent subject caught up after divorce proceedings; in 1946 Sharyn Moffett touchingly plays the daughter of a separating couple in *Child of Divorce*, while also in 1946 Patti Brady has to alternate between each of her divorced parents in *Never Say Goodbye*).

In fact, the American film industry operated a self-censorship code in the mid-twentieth century banning the portrayal of divorce as acceptable practice. While other films covering the theme of divorce resolved themselves with a happy reconciliation, *Child of Divorce* dared to openly depict divorce as a practice having a negative, even cruel, impact on the affected children.

Although more acceptable in modern society, parents going through a divorce are even today left with a feeling of inadequacy and failure which impacts on themselves, and impinges on their children, and there is a perceived effect on the acquaintances of their offspring, too: a child will fear disapproval among its friends, and worry about being different. For Sula Wolff, "Illegitimacy and family breakdown still constitute the most serious and the most common sources of privation and anxiety for young children." [5]

The child takes the guilt on its own shoulders thinking this shameful, and hides the truth even from its best friends. It was for this reason that Gaby Hoffman refrained from confiding in her close friends that her parents were going through a divorce, in *Now and Then*; while in *Background* (1953), Jeremy Spenser was worried what his friends at school would think, now that he has become 'different' from the others; and in *Little Secrets*, Evan Rachel Wood also conceals the truth of her adoption, this despite her operating her own counselling service for her troubled peers.

In this latter film, *Little Secrets*, Evan Rachel Wood plays fourteen-year-old Emily who runs a therapy kiosk for her little friends who confide in her when any problem arises at home (It is like a confessional for kids. For instance, if a kid breaks crockery at home, he/she can confide in Emily). She promises never to reveal her clients' secrets to anyone. Yet she is afraid to confide the one secret of her own – she does not want her friends to know she is adopted, her own parents having died in a head-on collision with a drunk driver when she was 10 months old.

Sula Wolff further explores this fear of what others will think, by stating, "Families broken by divorce or separation…are still open to censure from their own families and retain feeling of resentment, guilt and failure. Moreover, because they have become single parents as a result of their own shortcomings in intimate relationships, they are…less well-equipped to cope with the resulting problems, practical or emotional." [6]

Inevitably, the child of divorcing parents will feel emotionally deprived, yearning for the missing parent, and in many circumstances, even feel guilty for the separation of the adult partners, as Matthew Lawrence does in *Mrs Doubtfire*.

A common reassuring cry from a parent to a distressed child is, "It's not your fault," a mantra Robin Williams was at pains to recite to his son. Dustin Hoffman also had to reassure his child in the tearjerker *Kramer v Kramer*. "That's why mummy left, isn't it, because I was bad?" demands eight-year-old Justin Henry. His father tries to reassure him, "She didn't leave because of you, Billy. She left because of me." Richard Compton (Nicholas Hoult) cries on his father's shoulder in *Wah-Wah* as his mum leaves. "It's all my fault," the fourteen-year-old wails, but with an alcoholic father and an adulterous mother it was the inevitable outcome of colonial life in Swaziland in the late 1960s. Even Elle Fanning in *Phoebe in Wonderland*, troubled by the impact her Tourettes Syndrome is having on her family, despairs, "it's my fault" when she sees her parents arguing. Fortunately for her, her parents were not about to separate.

Whether it actually solves the family problem if the child tries to reunite the parents is also debatable. According to Ms Wolff, a child may be equally deprived in a feuding family that tries to stay together, in which parents pursue a violent or antagonistic relationship within an unhappy marriage. The bitterness of family ties where husband and wife doggedly remain together (for better or for worse) is exemplified in The *Prince of Tides* in which family trust had broken down. To evade having an irate violent husband, the whole family colludes in keeping secret from their father that a gang of intruders raped mum and daughter, an incident witnessed by all the children but kept from the unpredictably violent father. In *Background* (1953), the feuding adults decided on reconciliation, neglecting their own ultimate happiness, "for the sake of the children." The reunification of the parents in *Wah-Wah* lasted barely one day.

The Comedic Approach to Divorce

Like Jacqueline Wilson (author of *Dustbin Baby*: a tale of a despondent orphan desperately wanting to discover the mum she never knew), Anne Fine is to be commended for bringing inevitable domestic traumas to the attention of her child-aged readership. Using her stories, they have a reference point for their troubles: to show children they are not isolated and are not the only ones going through family difficulties; and that children of divorcees are not unnatural or alien; nor are they at fault for the demise of their former domestic bliss. Further, Dyllan Christopher adds in *Grounded*, "Divorced kids are more resourceful."

Anne Fine's novel, Madame Doubtfire, was made into an immensely successful movie, *Mrs Doubtfire*, attracting $200 million at the box office.[7] By casting Robin Williams as the lead (father of three, Daniel Hillard) ensured a comically engaging film, though the focus is more geared to the effects of the divorce on him as the father, rather than the impact on the three kids: fifteen-year-old Lisa Jakub, twelve-year-old Matthew Lawrence, and six-year-old Mara Wilson.

The children had to experience the lack of fun and attention without their father. "I'll miss you," says the older daughter, Lydia.

"Can't you just tell mum you are sorry?" lisps six-year-old Natalie, who treasures the child's simplistic remedy that a kiss and cuddle always make amends.

There is the usual comic interview and rejection of suitable housekeepers that you find in equivalent films (*Mary Poppins*, *Nanny McPhee*). There is the intrusion of a new man (Pierce Brosnan), a potential interloper who unsuccessfully takes over the role of father-figure.

But two important child-related issues do surface: guilt feelings, and the inevitable loss of the father. The son, Chris (Matthew Lawrence), starts to feel guilty for the break-up of the family. After all, it was his birthday party that was the catalyst for the ultimate separation of his mum and dad. (Dad had invited a neighbourhood petting zoo to invade house and garden, leaving the kitchen floor like a mucky farmyard.) "It's not your fault," father reassures the boy. "It was an accident waiting to happen."

The most difficult part of the business was the children listening to the arguments unfold. The petting farm animals in the house and garden were the final straw for mother, Miranda Hillard. "It's over, Daniel," she tells her husband.

Daniel tries to remonstrate, "Everyone has problems. We can work it out. What do you mean it's all over?"

"We've been trying to work it out for fourteen years!" responds mother.

"Let's go to the family therapist. We can do this together."

"It's too late for that. We've just grown apart. We've nothing in common."

"Sure we do. We love each other," says the man, hopefully.

But mum is defiant. "I want a divorce."

Father has to move out, solicitors are involved, and their case comes to court. "Although it is not in the child's best interest to deprive him or her of a loving father," pronounces the judge, "but because the father has no job, and no abode, sole custody is awarded to Mrs Hillard." As a result, the children get to see their father for one day a week only. Bitterness inevitably ensues.

"I don't want to hurt our children," says mum.

"You took my children away from me," retorts the father, acrimoniously.

Although, later in the film, the mother has a slight change of heart, allowing the father greater access to the kids, there is not the predictable soppy ending: they never again become a happy family. The only enrichment in these cases is the pockets of solicitors, as Jim Carrey's boss (Amanda Donohoe) says in *Liar Liar*, "I love children: they give you so much leverage in a case like this."

Stepmom is another film confronting issues about divorce in a comic way, necessarily trivialising it to impact its message. The family counsellor is talking to divorced father and his new girlfriend. "While change is exhilarating for an adult, it can be quite a challenge for a child."

Anna (Jena Malone), the twelve-year-old daughter, is creating fantasies because of the stressful home situation. "Anna needs a home where she feels safe and loved."

She says to her divorced mother, "Sometimes I wish you and daddy would get back together." Knowing this to be wishful thinking, she adds, "I figured if I said it out loud it may come true."

New girlfriend (Julia Roberts) of divorced father arrives, and is often called upon to baby-sit as the new stepmum. The kids are resentful of this; they rebel by being obnoxious and uncooperative. Stepmum arrives with a puppy to placate the children. But Anna cannot be bribed – "I'm allergic to dogs," she lies.

Anna protests to her father. "No one asked me when you got a divorce. No one asked me when I got a new mother. No one asked if I liked her."

The reply comes back, "You know, life is full of hard things, and sometimes it isn't fair." Eventually stepmum wins Anna over by helping her with make-up and giving advice over a new boyfriend. But the ex-mother can see all this transpiring. Jena's little brother, aware of jealousies, can see how his spurned mother is feeling, and tries to placate her. The little boy, referring to dad's new girlfriend, says to his natural mother, "Mummy, if you want me to hate her, I will."

A third movie dealing with divorce in a comic way is *Hope Floats*. But unlike *Stepmom* and *Mrs Doubtfire*, this is over-tedious, sugary humour. Described as a comedy, it takes a serious subject – the impact of parental separation on the child – and treats it in a light-hearted way, dabbling with the issues instead of approaching them head-on.

Bernice's mother (Birdie) has discovered her husband is having an affair with her best friend. She discovers this, of all places, on an Oprah Winfrey style television show. So, Birdie moves out of the family home and takes her daughter to grandma's house in Smallville, Texas. Grandma is not very comforting to the mother. "Life just moves on and you've got to move along with it."

The girl (movingly played by Mae Whitman) is excited on those times when daddy phones. But mother is not. As with *Mrs Doubtfire*, the little girl has to be reassured as a letter arrives from daddy, "None of this is your fault." As mother's relationship with a new boyfriend grows, so Bernice starts to distance herself from both of them, strengthening her bond with grandmother. This of course impacts on the mother who seems to dilute the love for her own daughter when it is not reciprocated. Mother now starts to notice, and confides in grandma, "There's a wall between Bernice and me."

We see how distant the child has moved away from her mother. Instead of becoming more reliant on her own mother, she starts blaming her for the loss of her father. When mum arrives at the school playground with Bernice's forgotten lunch box, Bernice ignores her, walking into school instead of rushing to greet her mother.

But then Granny collapses and dies. Father arrives for the funeral, much to Bernice's joy. Of course, it is not long before the mother and father are squabbling again. Bernice tries to mediate: "You're not leaving until you stop fighting." As father is about to leave, she declares, "I'm coming with you, daddy." She races upstairs, throws a few items into a holdall, along with her teddy, and rushes down, futilely chasing after dad as he drives away.

Other films where the tug of love becomes an amusing game of tug of war include *Trouble along the Way* in which John Wayne tries to gain custody of his daughter Sherry Jackson, and *Trading Hearts* in which the mother of Jenny Lewis is threatened with court action. In *Rich Kids*, the parents of twelve-year-old Trini Alvarado and Jeremy Levy pitifully try to keep their infidelities a secret by pretending to live at home as a normal married couple, but are unaware their daughter keeps a daily diary of their secretive indiscretions.

The Serious Approach to Divorce

One classic stands head and shoulders above all other movies in its serious attempt to portray the cruel effect that the separation of squabbling parents has on the child, without trying to trivialise matters with distracting comedy. This film is, of course, *Kramer v Kramer*, which won a trio of Oscars: for Dustin Hoffman, Meryl Streep, and as best picture. That director and screenwriter, Robert Benton, could coax such an endearing and convincing performance from eight-year-old Justin Henry is praiseworthy.

Meryl Streep plays a mother in a strangled relationship. She thinks the only way her personal life can blossom is by leaving her husband and son. She says a prolonged final goodnight to her son with hugs, kisses, and "I love you, Billy." Then, after rearranging his duvet, she shuts the front door behind her. "I'm no good to him," she explains to her husband before leaving. "He's better off without me."

Dustin Hoffman derides her devotion: "How much courage does it take to walk out on your kid?"

Next, comes months of father struggling to raise his son by himself, handling the boy's obstinacies, tantrums, and domestic needs. Eventually after the divorce, he packs away his ex-wife's possessions and removes the family photos. But later, he discovers a photo of mum that his son has secreted away in a drawer. He carefully stands it back on the dresser so Billy can see it when he wakes. Mother writes a note of explanation for little Billy, but it is inadequate. "I'll always be your mummy, and I'll always love you. I just won't be your mummy in the house. Just a mummy of the heart." (Philip Friend uses the same drivel in *Background* (1953), as we shall see, as does Miranda Richardson in *Wah-Wah*.)

After a couple of years, the mother has a change of heart. Having now carved a career for herself, she feels she is capable of looking after her son once more, so custody proceedings begin. "Just because you sent a few postcards doesn't give you the right to come back here," objects the ex-husband.

An expensive lawsuit proceeds. Custody is awarded to the mother, because that is the norm, evidently. Since the whole film is from the viewpoint of the father, we are made to believe this decision is unjust. Now father has to explain to his little son why he has to move home to go to live with mummy. There are tears and the boy has little option but to be resigned to the decision. This little boy breaks your heart with his acting; none more so as he sits in the house with his clothes and toys all packed waiting for mother to arrive. "Are you ready?" asks Dustin Hoffman, as we weep floods of tears at the injustice of it all.

There are other films that try to take these custody battles seriously: *Table for Five* in which divorced dad John Voight battles for custody with his kid's stepdad, and *Child of Divorce* in which Sharyn Moffett sorrows through the court proceedings of her parent's break-up. The court orders the child to live alternately with each parent. Eventually, after the girl breaks down, she is packed off to a boarding school (to ease the burden on the parents!) There, Sharyn Moffett meets Ann Carter, a fellow pupil familiar with the divorce rigmarole. Ann puts Sharyn right: "First your parents come every week, then their visits get fewer, and then they just don't come." In *The Good Mother*, we find Diane Keaton being sued for custody of her six-year-old daughter Molly (Asia Vieira) following accusations of alleged sexual abuse against the mother's boyfriend.

In *Danielle Steel's Daddy*, Patrick Duffy has to cope after his wife leaves him with a handful of kids. *Enid* (2009) is a tale of the heartless author Enid Blyton who ignores her children, divorces her husband, and woos another man. "But I just want my old daddy," whines her neglected daughter, Ramona Marquez.

The cold heartlessness with which the mother betrays her child in *Kramer v Kramer* and *Enid* is replicated in Richard E Grant's semi-autobiographical coming-of-age drama, *Wah-Wah*. Miranda Richardson is saying goodbye to her eleven-year-old son (Zac Fox) at their 1960s colonial home in Swaziland. "This is the hardest thing I've had to say…" and as if she can remove herself from the impact by continuing in the third person, "Mummy's leaving…" Then comes the icy platitude we heard reverberating in *Kramer v Kramer* and in *Background* (1953)… "But I love you very, very much." Though the boy's tears are genuine enough, the mother seems to have procured them from the crocodiles basking in the creeks of the nearby veldt. At least in *Background* (1953) the feuding couple modify their squabbling 'for the sake of the children' (Janette Scott, Mandy Miller, and Jeremy Spenser).

Background (1953) effectively draws out the impact on the children of an impending divorce. It is the children who make this scene work, particularly the tearful and angry reaction of Jeremy Spenser, and the doleful confused response of Mandy Miller.

Mother and father bring their three kids together for an important talk. The children are assuming they will be discussing a forthcoming holiday, or even a celebration of the parents' silver wedding thinks Linda (Mandy Miller). But it is not about that. Instead, father formally announces the break-up of the marriage, their incompatibility, "A lot of married people do it – it's just one of those things that happen." And then, to try to placate the kids with worn-out platitudes father adds, "Don't forget, whatever happens, Mummy and I will always love you very much."

The two youngest find this hard to accept. The older girl, however, is excited that mum will be marrying her new boyfriend; a man the girl herself has a crush on. The boy, Adrian (Jeremy Spenser), starts to worry how his friends will react. "I don't want to be different from other chaps," he says. "There's a boy at school whose parents are divorced. He's different. There's something about him," but Adrian cannot vocalise what it is. He realises mum's new boyfriend is the undoing of the marriage. In a frenzied outburst, he snatches the photograph of the interloper, stabs it against the dartboard. "I hate him, I hate him, I hate him," he cries thrusting the darts into the picture of the man. All the while, the little girl Linda (Mandy Miller) rocks tearfully in the embrace of the housekeeper.

This episode sends out such a powerful message to the viewers and to the actors as well. I wonder how much of this seeps down into the psyche of the child actors so that in later years they too think twice before considering divorce, 'for the sake of the children'. [7a] Thinking about the impact on the child is such a strong concept to philosophise over, but is probably seldom heeded when push comes to shove. Perhaps, as Tomi Ungerer says, "Children have to be exposed to realities." [8]

Obviously, both genders of child are devastated at the loss of a parent. Yet in the movies, the main urgency seems to be reunification with the father, no doubt, partly because in most divorce cases custody is awarded to the mother. The reason for this is clarified in *The Good Mother*. "I thought only a mother's incompetence would be sufficient grounds for a custody suit," Ralph Bellamy accuses his adult granddaughter, Diane Keaton. That Bernice in *Hope Floats* would start hating her mother is untypical. In all cases, the child becomes resigned to the ultimate separation, and as in real life, few of the films present a happy ending. For children going through the same wrenching heartaches, perhaps watching these films help provide some degree of therapy beyond that of painful reminders, and the comedy approach of *Mrs Doubtfire* or *Stepmom* may be more helpfully healing. It is doubtful a child audience could endure or be comforted by the intellectualism of the more serious *Kramer v Kramer* or *Enid* (2009), despite their hard-hitting effectiveness.

ILLNESS AND DISABILITY

Films that focus on illness and disability are often polarised either showing how traumatic an illness or disability is, or else how naturally the afflicted is able to cope. Sometimes it is the children themselves who are depicted as sufferers, as in *Touched by Love* or *Mandy* (1952). At other times it is an ailing family member putting a strain on the lifestyle of the child, as in *My Sister's Keeper* or *No Sad Songs for Me*. Films help us empathise with the afflicted by opening our eyes to a daily struggle that the majority of us will never be subject to. Others focus on the self-sacrificing devotion of parents (*Lorenzo's Oil* or *The Brooke Ellison Story*) or relatives (*The Book of Stars* in which a thirteen-year-old Jena Malone suffers from cystic fibrosis and is nurtured by her older sister), or by dedicated members of the medical profession (such as *Sister Kenny*, an Australian nurse who seeks acceptability for her methods of treating polio, by standing up to the opposition of her superiors).

Most usually, a 'healthy' actor is called upon to pretend to be disabled or ill, and they have to do their best to empathise with the hardship – a difficult task usually outside the experience of a typical child actor. In the case of Jack McElhone, playing the part of a deaf mute in *Dear Frankie*, this is not such a difficult challenge, since the disability is not apparent (until the boy attempts a crude version of signing, or absent-mindedly responds to aural instructions). For Bobbie Anderson, playing young George Bailey in *It's a Wonderful Life*, his becoming deaf after jumping into a frozen pond to save his kid brother is included to show how 'one person's life touches so many others.' [9]

Where casting directors have selected a disabled actor there are dilemmas to be overcome: that of placing the child in the spotlight of ridicule, unnatural sympathy, or being misinterpreted as a freak. As Rinko Kikuchi, playing a sexually frustrated deaf student in *Babel* declares about a group of youths that she fancies, "They look at us as if we are monsters," she says, gesturing animatedly with her signing hands, as she and her friends are rejected by the group of boys. (The youthful Miss Kikuchi was a twenty-six-year-old playing a schoolgirl.)

The children's TV series *Grange Hill* came part way to bridging the chasm by casting Francesca Martineza, a child with cerebral palsy and a speech impediment who integrated herself into the normality of everyday life in a children's home, by playing the part of Rachel Burns. The pace of the action inevitably slowed whenever it was her turn to speak. Though the cast were patient with her and gave her the respect she deserved, you cannot prescribe the same response from the invisible audience. Regrettably, "When she left *Grange Hill* in 1998, acting work dried up because no directors wanted a disabled actress." [10] Other films feature children with Down's Syndrome, such as *Toto le Héros* or Krystal Hope Nausbaum playing the adolescent Pheobe in *The Memory Keeper's Daughter*, or deaf children who use sign language, as in *Mandy* (1952) (though like Jack McElhone in *Dear Frankie*, the lead child actress playing Mandy (Mandy Miller) was not herself deaf). This allows the disabled actor to integrate into normalised activity, bringing their disability – and more importantly, their abilities – to our attention. Undoubtedly, the most successful films in this category are those featuring a disabled actor who is able to mask their differences leaving the audience unaware.

Directors are more likely to opt for the less challenging option. Alexander Mackendrick, director of *Mandy* (1952), chose not to have a deaf child as the lead in his film: "Deaf-mute children can be extraordinarily intelligent and perceptive; but they have this terrible desire to make you feel they've understood you when they haven't really." [11] He does, however, retain the realism by casting other deaf children to be Mandy's classmates.

Where it is the mother who becomes ill, the husband and children have to rally round in sympathetic response and change their daily routines. In *My Year without Sex*, the mother of eight-year-old Portia Bradley and twelve-year-old Jonathan Segat is hospitalised with an aneurysm of the brain. The young girl is tender as she watches her mother's recuperation. Father notices his tearful son crying at mum's bedside. Dad tries to reassure him, but the boy will have none of it. "There'll always be next season," says the boy glimpsing back at the muted TV set above mother's hospital bed in which the final score for a football match is being broadcast. This brief incident reinforces the stereotype of the girl as sympathetic carer, while the boy prefers other distractions.

Coping with a Disability

Some child actors have a disability and are able to act naturally without it affecting them, as Beatrice Edney does in *A Day at the Beach*, and the singing beggar boy, Arvind, from *Slumdog Millionaire* brought on set from a Mumbai school for the blind. For others, an abled actor has to be called upon to show how they overcome an overwhelming difficulty. Patty Duke performs as the deaf blind mute, Helen Keller, in *The Miracle Worker*; Sherry Jackson playing a young deaf mute in *Come Next Spring*; Donna Corcoran playing a swimmer stricken with polio in her youth; Sybil Jason as a crippled girl in *The Great O'Malley*.

Sometimes the acting is so effective it is not possible to tell whether the actor is disabled or not, so that seven-year-old Mandy Miller in *Mandy* (1952) convinced me of her disability, so naturally did she play the role of a deaf mute. It was only later I discovered she was not deaf at all, and in fact, as a sixteen and seventeen-year-old she was a contestant on the popular music programme, *Juke Box Jury*.

These actors, Beatrice Edney, Francesca Martineza, etc. are representing other 'brave' or 'resilient' kids who have already been through the trauma of contracting their demise and we glimpse the strategies the child uses to see them through life's adversities. I place the over-used words 'brave' and 'resilient' in quotes, for these children are often patronised by the public when what they are actually doing is using coping strategies without being daunted – reacting positively to a constraint laid on them that they have to come to terms with anyway.

A second category of films are those in which an abled child is suddenly struck with a life changing disability, and we are shown the horrors as the child gradually becomes aware of the restrictions placed upon its future life, damning its dreams. For these films, such as *Pollyanna*, *The Brooke Ellison Story* or *The Horse Whisperer*, an able-bodied child is usually cast in order to portray the before and after sequences, or in the case of *Forrest Gump* to show the miraculous cure. Either way, we are being educated about a life hardship, which thankfully most of us will never have to endure.

The 1970 Roman Polanski film, *A Day at the Beach*, features Beatrice Edney, a girl wearing a metal calliper on her leg: presumably, she has polio.[12] She plays Winnie, eight years old, who is taken on a day trip to the beach by her Uncle Bernard where he gets progressively drunk, while she is left to fend for herself, neglected, in the pouring rain. That she is a polio victim is unimportant – it is never mentioned, and it neither adds to nor detracts from the story (except when uncle initially suggests the visible calliper looks shameful and tells the girl to change into trousers instead of shorts). Beatrice Edney plays a perfectly normal young girl who acts naturally. Whether or not she has polio in real life (she does not), she was the best choice of actor for this part, and it is a delight seeing her reactions and relationship to her self-abusive guardian. Winnie in her bright yellow PVC raincoat brings the only light and colour to a depressing storyline. Metaphorically speaking, the person wearing the metal calliper is the drunken uncle. It is he who has the grave disease, making him susceptible to alcoholism, and which inescapably clamps his soul in irons more rigid than the ones on Winnie's leg.

Like Winnie in *A Day at the Beach*, Mario in *The Little Girl who lives down the Lane* is also a victim of polio. In the former, we respect the director for not needing to bring attention to the disability, but in the latter film, I do not see the value of raising this as an issue. While Beatrice Edney's metal calliper was not seen as unusual, Scott Jacoby's limp was; he walks with a limp having told us that he was not inoculated for polio as a child. Unless Scott Jacoby was genuinely afflicted, I am not sure what was the point of him acting with a limp since it did not seem to enhance the storyline, except to attract empathetic attention. Beattie Edney's calliper, though noticeable at first, became congruous as the film progressed. The 'disabled child' was portrayed as a very normal little girl.

In *Forrest Gump*, Michael Conner Humphreys' wearing iron leg braces adds a touch of humour to his disability. "His back is as crooked as a politician's!" Pretence is made that Elvis Presley adopted his jiving gait from watching this disabled boy dance. There is danger here of portraying disabled children as foolish. That Forrest Gump is a seemingly gormless simpleton is only borne out *after* he has lost his disability. Mother would teach him to deflect any criticism of his disability into a positive attribute. "Don't let anybody tell you they are better than you, Forrest. You're the same as everybody else." Being chased by a gang of bullies, the young Forrest shakes off his leg irons in a bid to escape. No disabled actor was employed in this film. Yet, Forrest's apparent gormlessness leads him to become a successful decorated war veteran, hobnobbing with the famous. As his mother used to remind him, "Life is like a box of chocolates. You never know what you're going to get." This apparent light-hearted misrepresentation of a serious subject has it benefits. As we point out in Volume Eight (*Physical & Sexual Abuse*), the jovial depiction of the implied sexual abuse of Forrest's playmate, Ginny, helps raise issues that might otherwise be just swept under the carpet.

How to Kill your Neighbour's Dog conveys messages about the dilemma for a disabled child: exclusion from the normal world of child play, and over-protection by the parent. Suzi Hofrichter plays Amy, a child with mild cerebral palsy – exhibited by an exaggerated limp and a propensity to fall over. Other children exclude her from their play so she has become a loner, playing by herself with just her dolls for company. (Sharyn Moffett complains of the same lack of friends in *The Body Snatcher*: "Of course I don't have friends. That's because I cannot walk," says the nine-year-old with a spinal tumour.) Neighbourly Kenneth Branagh takes pity on Amy, proving to her own mother that she can dance, jump rope, and dive in the swimming pool.

The problem is, her mother has resigned herself to her disabled daughter being a loner, excluded and 'special'. While Kenneth Branagh allows Amy to show mother the *Running Bear* dance that she had been practising, the girl stumbles, knocking over ornaments. Amy's mother starts to apologise for her daughter's behaviour and turns off the music. But Branagh can see that she is really apologising for her daughter's disability. An almighty argument starts because mother was not allowing her daughter the freedom she needs. "Anyone can raise children," Branagh sarcastically rants, "but it takes a real genius to fuck one up." This seems a rather unfair dismissal of a self-sacrificing parent who has patiently nurtured her disabled child. But the blinkered mother can become entrenched in cotton wool routines and forget to allow her child to fly.

Phoebe in Wonderland angles in from a different stand-point: the mother trying to understand her daughter's dilemma, seeking advice from psychiatrists, and coming up against the intransigence of inflexible teachers. Elle Fanning competently plays the girl with Tourettes Syndrome and a repetitive compulsive disorder, whose only escape from the rigidity of rules is into her dreamworld of Lewis Caroll's wonderland. "I feel as if I want to jump off the edge of a roof," she tells her friend, not because the ten-year-old has suicidal thoughts, nor because of a belief in the magic of flying, but because her life is one endless battle of restraining herself from doing the opposite of normalised behaviour. Her whole body screams 'jump' simply because she knows she mustn't. Her desperate avoidance of stepping on cracks, of self-harm, of shouting rude abuse ("You're fat," she involuntarily calls to the woman on Halloween night, simply because she cannot restrain herself), are the outward manifestations of a child tormented by the constrictions of rules. In the end the girl does jump from the stage gantry believing, like Alice, she is following the White Rabbit down the hole.

In *Miracle on 34th Street*, Richard Attenborough makes sure a deaf child is not excluded from communicating with Santa. It is a joy to watch the face of Samantha Krieger light up as Kriss Kringle sits her on his lap and they share a conversation with each other in sign language. This is made to seem so normal, and is life-affirming for the audience to watch.

Aryana Engineer shares the same disability in the horror movie, *Orphan* (2009). The physical disability can easily be overlooked because the performance of the child actor is so natural. Aryana Engineer plays Max, a five-year-old deaf girl. Throughout the film, she uses sign language and lip-reads. The film cleverly helps us to empathise with her disability: when she goes to bed at night, taking off her hearing aid, all background music and sounds in the film are stopped as we enter her silent world of hand signs and gestures, a method also taken up in *Babel*, and to some extent *The Miracle Worker*.

The thought-provoking Ealing production of *Mandy* (1952) makes us reflect on the trauma of a deaf child living in a world where hearing sounds is important for survival. Mandy Miller plays the six-year-old trapped in her fenced-off London garden, unable to play with the children in the bombsite beyond the railings that confine her like a prisoner. The analogy is apt, since she *is* a prisoner, as Neil Sinyard points out in *Children in the Movies*, 'locked out' from the rest of society by her handicap.[13]

Because she is deaf she is also unable to speak. On a visit to the park, she carries her ball where other children involve her in a game of pig-in-the-middle; she does not understand the game or the instructions, and is left anguished, feeling the other children are taunting her. As a result, in a desperate attempt to reclaim her ball she starts fighting with the children. Their mother comes to break up the fight. "She's insane," the other parent rebukes, "she's not fit to be with other children." So Mandy has realised other children are too unpleasant and unpredictable to be with, for that is how her entrapment has made her feel.

On another occasion, the family dog has run onto the road, so Mandy runs outside to retrieve it, unaware of the noise from the approaching trundling lorry. The lorry driver has to brake abruptly to avoid her. He jumps from the cabin, grabs the frightened girl, and gives her a stern telling off. Of course, the deaf girl does not understand a thing, and races back into the house in floods of tears, unable to explain to her parents what the matter is. But for mother, this is the final straw. "Harry, I can't go on like this." she complains to her husband. "What we are doing to Mandy is criminal," leaving her shut up at home all day. Her resolve is made up; against the wishes of her husband, she decides to take the child to a special school for deaf children in Manchester. The mother of Helen Keller takes up an almost identical conversation with her husband in *The Miracle Worker*, but in that case the special home would mean the asylum and all the stigmas associated with it.

But first, mother rants about Mandy's grandmother. "She uses Mandy as someone to fuss over, like a spinster with a lapdog." Of her husband, she accuses him of being ashamed of the girl, keeping her out of sight, shut up in the house. Likewise, the analogy of a pet is used in *The Miracle Worker*.

There is no pretentiousness in this film. Though Mandy Miller, the child actress is not herself deaf, the children at Manchester's Clyne House, (*The Royal Residential School for the Deaf*), where this movie was filmed, are. There, the children seem so happy and natural, interacting with one another like any 'normal' child, and we are privileged to be voyeurs of a successful education system without it being freakish.

"Do they ever get to the stage when they can live a normal life?" Mandy's mother had pessimistically asked the principal while her back is turned. It is then that she realises the seemingly normal principal is also deaf herself, dependent on lip-reading, and mother's qualms are allayed. The tear-inducing moment comes, when after smashing crockery out of frustration, Mandy begins to scream her first syllables, and after further practices feeling the vibrations of her voice on a balloon, is able to utter first 'b' sounds, then 'p' sounds, and finally, 'Mama' and 'Mandy'.

But this is of no comfort to father when he travels angrily up to Manchester to reclaim his daughter. Mum desperately tries to coax the child to speak, to convince father of her progress. But the frightened, or self-conscious, child clams up.

However, to make comparisons with *A Day at the Beach*, in which I suggest it is the drunken uncle who is actually the disabled person, not the girl, for it is he who is handicapped by an addiction to alcohol; likewise commentators point out that in *Mandy* (1952) it is the parents who are blinded to the handicap of their own child.[14]

This film begins when Mandy is two year of age. Mother is anxious that her daughter has not yet started to utter her first words, whereas her friend's children at the same age have started to talk. Father says this is nothing to worry about. It is only when a metal tray falls to the floor with a loud clatter, that they realise Mandy has not heard anything.

They take the infant to a specialist. He explains that Mandy has a congenital condition in which the auditory nerve failed to develop. The specialist is almost cheerful that he has managed to diagnose a problem and tells them "in a reassuring way" there is nothing to be done about it. To the doctor, this was "an interesting case," not at all unusual. Mandy is just one of the one in every sixteen thousand children born deaf. To the doctor, she is just a statistic. To the parents, this is devastating. At least when the girl is aged six, mother makes the effort to send Mandy to deaf school, but the blinkered father wants to keep the child at home rather than allow her to be regimented and left to rot in an institution, assuming he, the father, is the best remedy for the child. It almost takes a divorce and a scandal before the man is able to see the light.

Inferred from *Mandy* (1952) is that the risk of divorce is greater among parents of disabled children. One might argue that a disability helps bind a family to mutually work through an adversity, but more realistically the strain becomes too much, one partner giving up the challenge.

Dear Frankie shows us that a disabled child (in this case a deaf mute) does not come from a perfect happy family. The abusive father has long since disappeared – "Frankie wasn't born deaf, it was a present from his daddy" (implying violent assault) – while mother stalwartly strives to raise her child alone. Yet, the mother guiltily feels the need to pretend that all is well, that his father is not neglecting the boy, fabricating a story that father has just gone away to sea, a dupe which the boy believes. The complicated arrangement of writing to father, and for mother maintaining the pretence that father has written back, was originally an attempt to get her son to communicate, "It's the only way I can hear his voice," (i.e. his written 'voice') and partly in response to grandma's nagging, "You should encourage that wee boy to speak more." But the dupe has long since got out of hand, for the child constantly tracks father's 'voyage' by sticking pins into a wall map.

Nine-year-old Frankie (Jack McElhone) has no lines to speak. He simply gives a shopping list to the woman in the chip shop, or holds up his notebook displaying a written answer to his schoolteacher. He is only partially deaf, having a hearing aid.

That disabled kids are perceived as stupid is enhanced by the comment made by the chip shop owner: "He's a smart wee cookie – for a deaf child!" At school, the class teacher primes the pupils on the day the new boy arrives: "You don't have to shout at him," she advises the class. At least this film shows the boy having a (fairly) normal relationship with two of his classmates, Ricky and Catriona. Mother warns the teacher to be careful what you say for "he's a champion lip reader," and "I don't want him treated any different."

This is a typical reaction by the public, the temptation to treat any disabled kid differently, as special. On Frankie's first visit to the library, the librarian strides after the boy to admonish him for ignoring her, but when she discovers Frankie is deaf she takes the opposite standpoint, which the boy exploits, after he is told she will move mountains to obtain whatever book he needs!

The child, Helen Keller, in *The Miracle Worker* had not just deafness to contend with, but she was blind and mute too. Having no concept of senses other than touch and smell she was left to subsist as a wild animal until her parents were driven crazily towards that final cop-out – the asylum. This film is based on a true story. Patty Duke who plays the tormented child is phenomenally brilliant. Out of all the performances that I have written about in this series of books, hers is the most convincing. She deservedly won an Oscar for her acting.

Like the film, *Mandy* (1952), ten years earlier, Helen Keller's parents discover her handicap as a baby in a cot. They go wild with anguish at the realisation. Now Helen Keller has grown into a young teenager. She has the run of the large gardens at their American home – her arms flaying to sense any danger ahead. She is a destroyer: she wraps herself in the sheets hung on the washing line, she crushes the pots and crockery, and she thrashes out at anyone in her way or opposing her. She has been spoilt as a child, and knows no better action because her parents have yielded to her every whim. Her only comfort seems to be her dolls. But now she is getting older and more difficult to handle. "You really ought to put her in an asylum, father. It's the kindest thing," says Helen's older brother. The boy thinks the girl is a disgrace as he observes the way she dresses and behaves. But mother cracks back at him: "Don't you dare complain about what you *can* see."

Father asks, "Is there some way to confine her?" as she upsets his work and his routines "Where?" asks the mother, realising they look upon the girl as an animal or at best a pet. "In a cage?" (This was the unfortunate outcome for Katie (Tarra Steele) in *Mockingbird Don't Sing*.)

As a last resort, they apply to a blind school to supply a teacher. So, arriving on their doorstep is the half-blind lass, Miss Sullivan (Anne Bancroft) on her first assignment. The parents are very sceptical about this new upstart, and are not convinced by her methods. "If a house full of grown-ups can't look after the child, how can an inexperienced half-blind Yorkshire schoolgirl manage?" Yet, this woman achieves success because she is prepared to restrain the child and teach her the meaning of 'no'. But to achieve this requires hours of patient, physically tiring and mentally draining hard graft, and not the 'miracle' that the film title would have us believe – that is to belittle her talents. As Neil Sinyard tells us, "Ann Sullivan does not really work miracles: she just works very hard." [15]

In Miss Sullivan's presence, the girl becomes almost demonic in her actions, and there is a continual physical struggle between the two, as a frightened, unhearing, unseeing girl is broken-in, like you would break-in a horse. But the first day is a success, eventually. Despite having food spat back in her face, a broken tooth, and the dining room totally destroyed, Miss Sullivan emerges victoriously but wearily announcing, "She ate from her own plate, with a spoon, and she folded her napkin!"

Aged fifteen at the time of filming, Patty Duke was considered too old to play the part of the real-life seven-year-old Helen Keller. But because she had already performed the screenplay alongside Ann Bancroft, Patty Duke was fortunately retained. Deservedly so, both actresses achieved Oscars for their performances.

For Colin in *The Secret Garden*, he made sure everyone was aware of his affliction. It provided him with constant attention from the train of servants at his beck and call, but the disability also supplied the chains that fettered him to his wheelchair or confined him to his bed. "Do you know who I am?" he demands authoritatively from the gardener. "You're the little cripple," says the man unthinkingly, disbelieving what he is seeing, as the boy explores outside the confines of his house for the first time in his life. This causes the boy to go berserk. But for Mary Lennox his playmate, she can see through his spoilt obstinacy, seeing much of his ailment to be psychological, and gradually, with the help of the secret garden, coaxes Colin to health and strength, until the day comes when he is able to stagger without his wheelchair.

In the 1949 version, Dean Stockwell is the bedridden boy whose illness is diagnosed as 'fear imparted by the father'. "I prescribe fresh air, wild animals, and children," says the doctor visiting from London. An exuberant Margaret O'Brien is his playmate. In the 1993 version, Heydon Prowse plays Colin, while Kate Maberly is the efficient Mary Lennox.

Fresh mountain air and the warmth of friendship had a similar effect on Clara (Jessica Claridge) in *Heidi*. Wheelchair-bound for the whole of her twelve years of life, she visits her friend in the mountain pastures above Dorfli. Here, the sunshine, and gentle coaxing by Heidi and her grandfather, help her limbs to gradually strengthen. The day comes when jealous goatherd Peter wickedly kicks the wheelchair over a crag, but ironically this proves beneficial as the girl, like Colin in *The Secret Garden*, learns to walk on her own limbs.

These are miraculous endings in which, against all odds, the child recovers, and the audience suspends disbelief for the sake of entertainment. It is the type of ending the audience secretly hopes for in films like *Lorenzo's Oil*, or *My Sister's Keeper*, too. But in real life, happy endings seldom occur. So the ending in *Blue Butterfly* is almost derisible, as a boy (Marc Donato), dying of a brain tumour, goes off exploring in the Costa Rican jungle, a sort of dying wish to search for the evasive *Blue Morpho*. "Even if I get eaten by an anaconda, it will only take a couple of months off my life!" he jokes. When his expedition finishes (after an Indiana Jones-style escapade), he discovers his tumour has gone! The audience accepts the story as a light-hearted flight of fancy, until the credits tell us that the film is based on a real story, and that maybe miracles can happen after all. Perhaps the clue lies in the lucky charm placed around the boy's neck, by the native girl (Marianella Jimenez).[16]

For me, one of the best studies of a disability (besides Patty Duke's brilliance as Helen Keller) was portrayed by Adèle Haenel in the gritty French movie, *Les Diables*. She plays the mentally traumatised Chloé, suffering from autism, muteness, and she has a repetitive compulsive disorder in which she constantly paces across a room and tries door handles. She always walks straight ahead until she comes to an obstacle, at which she stops and takes a side step as if her thought processes do not allow her to think beyond the obstacle. Chloé has a fear of being touched, and is afraid of anything soft. She takes consolation in handling hard objects such as a pencil sharpener and the coloured glass chips she carries with her everywhere. When she is untroubled, she glares happily with a soppy wide-eyed smile (reminiscent of those who've seen the aliens in *Close Encounters of a Third Kind*). However, a psychiatrist later informs her brother that "when she smiles it is a deception, a façade, she wants to be left alone."

Although Chloé is not handicapped physically, she has to be completely reliant on others, in particular, her twelve-year-old brother, Joseph (Vincent Rottiers). Adèle Haenel brilliantly mimics the traits of an autistic girl, and must herself have done detailed character studies of the affliction. During the course of the film, which can be both violently heart-wrenching and tender, Joseph gradually comes to understand the psychological traumas that steer the girl's emotions and reactions. Finally, as Joseph sprawls dying from a gunshot wound, he watches her as for the first time she sits unaided on a swing and discovers how to propel herself, and at last ecstatically utters the first words she has ever vocalised, "Joseph, Joseph."

Contracting a Disability

For this category of films, the casting director seems constrained to audition an able-bodied actor because they have to show the person's traits before the disability was contracted. Like acting out romantic scenes, or pretending to be drunk, performing as a disabled person is outside the experience of most child actors, and there is the danger that the victim will be ridiculed if the action does not look genuine. If a disabled actor can be cast who can also portray being able-bodied then the director could be on to a winner. Alas, I am unaware of such a circumstance. Meanwhile we have to pretend along with Georgina Terry and Scarlett Johansson as they hobble along with their crutches, and feign the odd stumble.

These actresses, along with Vanessa Marano in *The Brooke Ellison Story*, are depicting the lives of some determined girls who have had to endure privations beyond anything most of us can imagine. As Morgan Freeman says to Robert Redford in *An Unfinished Life*, "I can't lie here every day and watch you mourn for a life you think you should have had. There are people everywhere who think they got dealt a bad hand." Well, here are some examples of those who did.

We mention in Volume Four (*Childhood Friendships*) the emotional and physical stress endured by Grace MacLean (Scarlett Johansson) in *The Horse Whisperer*. Out horse riding one snowy day with her best friend, both horses slip on an icy slope into the path of a lorry. Her friend is killed outright, the horse severely injured and traumatised, and she is hospitalised. As a result of the accident involving her horse, not only does she lose a leg, but also the life of her best friend. It is bad enough going through the pain of the accident, waking up in a hospital ward and being told your leg has to be amputated. This fourteen-year-old girl has to make life and death decisions of her own: whether to have her horse put down or not.

Several weeks later, on her first day back at school following the accident, Grace assumes she could carry on just the same with her old friends, exacting sympathy for her dilemma. But her old friends ostracise her. Her classmates had also suffered the loss of the same friend and in some way, Grace is held responsible for that, despite this being an accident. So now, she has lost her friends and cannot face up to the struggle of living life with one leg missing. She bunks off school. Mum finds her squatting against a wall. "Well, you're not staying at home all day feeling sorry for yourself," she rebukes the girl.

The girl needs to recover her confidence at doing things for herself, yet the father is too patronising by wanting to help her over every hurdle. "You've got to stop helping her all the time," the wife admonishes him, "Running to her all the time, anticipating her."

Father tries to counter by saying, "This didn't just happen to you," as if the trauma of the accident affects not just the victim but also the whole family.

The girl tries to visualise her future. She has to come to a decision about having the horse put down. In her depressed state she murmurs, "I think you should put me down too. I'm not much use anymore." Contemplating her artificial leg, and what will happen about future boyfriends, she adds, "Whoever is going to want me like this?"

What seems like a selfish action on the part of the mother (and probably was, initially) – to take the horse and daughter across country to Montana to visit a horse whisperer (Robert Redford) – in the end turns out to be the best therapy for all of them, as it helps both mother and daughter to re-bond and helps the girl regain the confidence to remount and ride her horse once more, and face the future.

Fed up with being the continual focus of attention, Grace finally confides in her mother, "I used to pray every night that you and dad would have another kid so I wouldn't have to be so special."

Pollyanna, like Grace MacLean, had to face up to the loss of the use of her limbs. This was an infectious girl who had a knack of tackling life's adversities head-on. Two versions of this story exist: the film version featuring Hayley Mills, and a made-for-TV version starring Georgina Terry. Pollyanna had an effective way of responding to illness in others. She provided words of optimism for the sick folk in her community, inspiring them to better health with her 'glad game', though for some this was also infuriatingly annoying. Bed-ridden Mrs Snow was given a new zest for life; grumpy Mr Pendleton who broke his leg was nurtured back to spirited health by the girl's compelling enthusiasm.

But when Pollyanna herself is run over by a motorcar and paralysed, her spirit is depressingly doused. "She's a remarkable girl, but even the strongest spirits can crumble in the face of such a cruel blow." Pollyanna was the ward of Aunt Polly, a self-obsessed woman who had a disgruntled relationship with other people in the community. So, when they all rally around expecting to provide comfort to the little girl to raise her spirits, the miserable old woman puts obstacles in the way, so the little girl does not receive any visitors. "Sadness is a poor healer."

Pollyanna has become a classic of English literature, and likewise Nicholas Evans' novel *The Horse Whisperer* received wide acclaim. So it is natural the films based upon those books were eagerly anticipated. Other films such as *My Sister's Keeper* and *The Brooke Ellison Story* tackle issues of trauma sensitively without being overly sensational. These are not literary classics, so critics seem to berate them. I believe the criticisms are unfair.

Contracting a Disability: The Brooke Ellison Story

The Brooke Ellison Story is a life-affirming story about a comatose girl left in a vegetative state, whose life was given re-hope through the dogged determination of her parents. This is a true story, the autobiography of one girl from when she was eleven-year-old, whose fate, to some extent, was mirrored in the similar demise of the director, Christopher Reeve (the hero of *Superman*), who had himself been paralysed as the result of a horse riding accident.

Miracles Happen was the title of the autobiography upon which this film was based, though it was not so much a miracle of divine intervention than the inspired determination and self-sacrifice of the parents: of the father, who had to spend his days fighting for justice and hope for the invalid girl; and of the mother whose daily routine revolved around the care and education of the young child. "This is not about changing what is, it's learning to live with it." That is the miracle that was achieved.

Where this film hits home, is not just portraying the adjustments the child has to make to her dreams, her lifestyles, friendships and the never-relenting pain; it also shows the impact that the tragedy has on the parents, the siblings, school friends, work colleagues, the education and welfare systems, and in overcoming the negativity and pessimism of the medical profession.

It is the first day of term at a new school. Eleven-year-old Brooke Ellison (Vanessa Marano), a caring, pretty girl is more concerned about her mother's nervousness at starting a new job on the same day, than she is about attending her own new school. Her older sister makes it clear to Brooke which bus she has to catch at the end of the school day. On her first day at school, Brooke quickly makes friends, and one of the boys suggests they walk home instead of catching the bus. Alas, this is the last time we see Brooke walking, for she is involved in a road accident which leaves her in a coma, paralysed from the neck down, with brain and spinal cord damaged, and with no sign of brain activity.

We are introduced to the first impact of the tragedy. The parents, hearing about the accident, are racing to the scene only to be held off by the police. Without being over-sentimental, the parents realise the overwhelming dimensions of the tragedy, with their only comfort being the words of the hospital chaplain, "Where there's life there's always hope." This is all they have to cling to.

Next is the blunt honesty of the medical staff: "She will never walk again – she is paralysed."

There is the faint flicker of hope as Brooke momentarily opens the eyes on her smashed-up face, only to fade back into unconsciousness again. "Come back, Brooke," cries a despairing mother.

But gradually, Brooke inches her way back to consciousness, her memories recurring in slow motion, and she wakes up in the hospital to the sight of the saline-drip keeping her alive. She has (temporarily) lost the ability to speak, so communication with her parents is painfully slow, and on the basis of one blink for yes, two blinks for no.

Next, we see the impact on the older sister who has an unwarranted guilt complex. She needlessly feels blame for Brooke's demise. "If only I had made sure she knew which bus to catch," she reflects. The sister arrives at Brooke's hospital bedside not sure what to say or how to react to her paralysed sister. She keeps looking away, seeking reassurance from mother. Later on, she sits in Brooke's wheelchair to try to empathise with the girl. Then she becomes anorexic as if that would help her come to terms with her sister's trauma.

Father has to overcome the negativity of the medical staff. After one negligent consultation, father warns the doctor and nurse, "If ever you speak in front of my daughter in anything but a positive fashion it is you who will need surgery." When the impatient nurses have difficulty in persuading Brooke to take her medicine, mum decides it is time to take over the caring of her daughter, full-time.

At the rehabilitation centre, mother discovers the future trials she has to face. She meets other mothers who have given up hope on their paraplegic children. She discovers many of the mothers end up divorced. And we witness mother tearfully breaking down at the clinic while on the phone to her husband. "You've got to realise your daughter is a quadriplegic on a ventilator for the rest of her life," says a pessimistic (but realistic) nurse.

While mother spends her time at the rehabilitation centre having given up her new job to care for Brooke full-time, father has to stay at home looking after his other two children. He has to face mounting expenses as the medical bills arrive, whilst at work he is at his wits end. But colleagues rally round, each donating one day of their holiday allocation so that father can take a week off work.

As Brooke's condition improves, father seeks help from the welfare department to make his house accessible for wheelchair and other equipment. But all they do is put further obstacles and refusals in his way. Fortunately, friends and neighbours turn up to assist with the renovations.

At last, Brooke has recuperated. Though paralysed and wheelchair-bound, she is both ready and looking forward to going back to school. "More than anything in this world, my daughter wants to return to school," the Head is told. But the school board refuses her on the grounds that they cannot provide a medical service, and they believe other students would be "disturbed" by the presence of a paraplegic in the classroom. However, this obstacle is removed by mother being approved by the doctor as a qualified caregiver, to the annoyance of the school board.

Then, living at home, the girl has to have all her bodily functions carried out for her. She has to be bathed, dressed, fed, her teeth brushed – all while Brooke has a breathing tube attached. On one occasion when she is older, Brooke appeals to mum when she is being seemingly over-finicky. "Stop torturing me," says the girl.

"Stop torturing you!" exclaims the exasperated mother. "Hey, I've got to get out of my bed every two hours just to turn your butt like a baby." And this is how mum's life has proceeded throughout the child's adolescence.

"How do I look?" Brooke asks her father on the first day back at school.

"You're the most beautiful girl I've ever seen in my life."

Mum has to attend school along with her daughter. Whenever Brooke wants to answer a question in class, mother has to raise her hand.

The film then fast-forwards seven years. Brooke is now optimistically applying for Harvard University. Throughout her disabled life, she has had problems to overcome and therefore she expects further battles with her university application. So she is pleasantly surprised when the interviewing panel assure her, "Harvard are confident they can accommodate your needs."

As with everything else, Brooke excels at student life in lecture theatres, though she knows she could not do anything without her mother. But socially, she finds she is an outcast. She looks on longingly as she sees two students snogging. "Ah!" she yearns, "It seems like everyone already has a boyfriend."

"You'll see," replies mum, "Your time will come. There is someone out there for everyone."

Soon Brooke makes friends with a fellow student and gets her first kiss. "How do you control your wheelchair?" he asks, and she explains how she has a retainer in her mouth and can manipulate the controls using her tongue. Then she mischievously adds, "I have a very talented tongue!" Alas, her boyfriend is in his final year and soon goes off at the end of his course. To Brooke's despair, she receives an e-mail from him saying he is now engaged to another girl.

In a moment of dejection when she realises she is a social outcast, she confides in her mother. "What man is ever going to want me? What company is ever going to hire me, or put me on their insurance plan? Who but my mother will ever do this for me? There is no place for me out there, mum."

But her stalwart mother replies, "You belong in this world, but you have to find whether you are going to contribute to it, or be paralysed."

However, this girl has no escape from her mother's protective wing, as she acknowledges on her graduation speech: "A mother's presence can create a whole host of social problems for those seeking more than just academic enrichment… None of us would be here if it wasn't for those who have helped us and cared for us along the way."

And what of the girl's dreams? Threaded through the film is a sequence of a ballerina. This is our peephole into the disabled girl's dreams. Whenever Brooke dreams she is never in her wheelchair. At least she is able to aspire to freedom in her subconscious mind.

The young actress playing Brooke's part, Vanessa Marano, helped drive home the film's deliberate message. She was an able-bodied girl, who had to learn immense self-control while acting as a paralysed person, taking care not to flinch even a muscle except for the movement of her face.

Contracting a Disability: Lorenzo's Oil

The undaunted devotion of Brooke's parents in *The Brooke Ellison Story* is replicated in another true story, *Lorenzo's Oil*, in which a mother and father give up all their days, their sleepless nights, and almost their sanity in a desperate search for an effective treatment for their son's incurable wasting illness.

Lorenzo first becomes ill aged six while living in the African Comoros Islands in 1983. His expatriate parents (Italian father Nick Nolte, and American mother Susan Sarandon) at first assume he has picked up an obscure tropical disease causing the child to become unpredictable and violent at school.

The Washington specialist (Peter Ustinov) diagnoses ALD (adrenoleukodystrophy), an incurable disease that destroys the myelin coating of the nervous system. The illness has only been recognised in the previous ten years, there is no known cure, and funding for research is virtually non-existent because it is such a rare illness, which only affects boys. The doctor informs the parents that all boys with ALD die within two years of diagnosis. "I'd like to offer you some hope, but…"

The frantic parents realise their only way forward is to by-pass scientific protocol if their child is to have any chance of recovery.

Zack O'Malley Greenburg plays the young Lorenzo (though five other child actors also appear as the character ages), at first a happy-go-lucky lad, who develops temper tantrums, loss of coordination in which he falls off his bike, or off a chair. He begins to portray the symptoms father has read up about: deafness, hyperactivity, progressive withdrawal, mutism, visual loss, dementia. Zack's portrayal of seizures, and his whimpering as his body degenerates effectively touches the viewers' hearts.

Yet, mother remains constantly vigilant, nursing her child on her lap throughout the night, foregoing meals, dismissing nurses who are not totally attentive to the boy's needs. She even falls out with her own sister who had only tried to suggest she needed a break. The husband tries to point out to his wife what she has become: "Only a crazy woman would shun church, her husband, her family, depriving herself of everything – food, sleep, love."

The parents of other children with ALD try to get through to her, as the bed-ridden boy is in constant agony, a breathing tube up his nostril and deprived of all dignity: "Hasn't it occurred to you that maybe he doesn't want to be around anymore?" Mother thinks this is a heartless thing to say, but later, as the boy has yet another agonising seizure while cradled in her arms, she whispers in his ear, "Fly as fast as you can to baby Jesus."

Mother and father try to rigidly follow the fat-free diet the doctors have recommended, but they lose patience with the clinical trials because of the time-scale involved. Father realises "the doctors are groping in the dark. We have to put our son blindly in their hands."

He sacrifices his career and savings to research all possible avenues. After months of research, he deduces the child needs to replenish the oils the body has been over-compensating for. Sponsoring a British chemist to crack oleic acid from rapeseed oil provides the break-through that stabilises his son. But alas, the boy is already in a vegetative state. It is hard for the parents to come to terms with the fact that "all this struggle may have been for someone else's kid." In other words, it did not save Lorenzo in time, but the oil is today prescribed all over the world for other boys with ALD. Sadly, unlike Brooke Ellison, Lorenzo never achieves any sense of consciousness beyond the blinking of eyes and the imperceptible movement of his little finger.

This dilemma of a parent grieving a dying child has added distress in *Nicholas' Gift* as they are asked if they are willing to donate the boy's organs when he finally dies.

When the Child becomes Ill

Here, the focus is not on disablement, but on a child contracting an illness, and their response to the trauma on a temporary timescale.

"I remember coming down with the fever," says Laura Ingalls (Melissa Gilbert) as the child makes a speech in front of the parents' meeting in *The Little House on the Prairie*. "Ma sat up next to me all night long. Every time I opened my eyes she'd be there smiling, putting a cold cloth to my head."

The parent's need to nurture, and the child's total dependence on the guardian, are exemplified in the little girl's speech. In fact, this close relationship perhaps is the greatest placebo in helping the child recover and maintain health. The syndrome of hugs, "kissing it better", and the showing of overriding concern over the pettiest of complaints seem to be the pattern in a little child's life. The child reciprocates as well, for instance, by tying a bandage around a pet dog's paw, or Patricia Gozzi kissing the finger of Hardy Kruger after he has grazed it in *Sundays & Cybele*.

This placebo effect is propagated by the warmth of the heart, though it didn't work for Durga (Uma Das Gupta) in *Pather Panchali*, as her Bengali mother lays cold compresses on her daughter's head. Laura Ingalls' mother had the patience of a saint in a happy household; Durga's scolding, sullen mother was fret with worries of poverty, debt, and an overdue absent father. Father, on his return, presents his tearful wife with a new sari for Durga, unaware his daughter is dead. Of course, the comparison is specious because *The Little House on the Prairie* is a cheerful children's classic, while *Pather Panchali* is a rueful rendition of realism.

All the patience in the world seems to be needed for Veda Sultenfuss, as she believes she has contracted every illness under the sun. Anna Chlumsky plays this hypochondriac in *My Girl* (1991). Veda is a perfectly healthy eleven-year-old, but she frequently visits the doctor in case she has developed an illness. Living above a funeral parlour has exacerbated this psyche, her father being a mortician, she has learnt that people disproportionately become ill then die. She often peeps at the death certificates that are in father's office, so she discovers what people have died of, and needs reassurance she isn't going to suffer the same fate. The latest cadaver died of prostate cancer, so Veda writhes on the floor wondering if she has prostate cancer too!

At least Veda was able to attract interest in her well-being. This was not the case for Jess in the TV drama, *Oranges are not the Only Fruit*. Religious dogmatism prevents Jess' mother (Geraldine McEwan) from recognising her illness. Seven-year-old Jess, played by Emily Ashton, is brought up in a fervently fundamentalist Christian family. She is mother's pride and joy, though mother never shows the girl any love. Her role in life is to mirror the religious devotion of the mother. Mother often clips the dutiful girl around the ears, not because she has done anything wrong, but because mother wants to emphasise a point.

One day, mother has been ranting on about evil in the world but Jess has not heard what she said. "I can't hear very well," protests the little girl. But mother, instead of being sympathetic, turns this to her own advantage. "It will be the Lord blocking your ears to the words of evil spirits." She mentions this to the pastor at church who makes an example of the little girl, seating her at the front in sight of the entire congregation. "This is a miracle," says the pastor. "Jess has been so blessed by the Lord, she can't hear a word of evil." Then he invites the congregation to come and touch the girl to be blessed by Jesus. "No harm can come to her. She is protected by angels." While members of the congregation dance out their religious perversions, one lady checks Jess' forehead and adenoids, declaring her to be very ill."

"Why didn't you tell me you were ill?" demands the uncaring mother.

"I didn't know I was ill," comes the reply.

"Well, I'm sure Jesus has his reasons," states the intransigent woman.

In *kids* (1995), Jennie (Sarah Henderson) had contracted AIDS from having unprotected sexual intercourse. She had been so careful, or thought she had, ensuring she had only one sexual partner, a youth named Telly. But Telly had been in the habit of targeting virgins and had multiple partners, and thus had passed the disease on to Jennie, previously a virgin. In fact, Jennie knew she was safe. She was only accompanying her friend to the AIDS clinic, and only took the AIDs test to keep her friend company. But now she is horrified to discover she has contracted the disease herself and is aware of the outcome. "I don't want to die," she cries. But she is a responsible girl too for, during the film, she seeks out the boy, Telly, who made her pregnant to warn him that he is a carrier of the disease.

By its very nature, trauma has a significant impact on the psychology of the child. When this trauma is of a psychiatric nature a host of consultants appear, sometimes unwanted, at other times at the beck-and-call of the worried parent. In Volume Five (*Make-Believe, Horror & the Supernatural*) we consider several examples of the psychiatric demise of the child – *Audrey Rose*, *The Exorcist*, *Poltergeist* (1982), etc. I found the quip made by Haley Joel Osment very pertinent in *The Sixth Sense*. "They don't call meetings about rainbows," he says as he is referred to a child psychologist. His naturalistic artwork was of no concern to the therapists, not until he drew a man stabbing someone. Only then did the child psychotherapists hold a meeting. Perhaps the child is sick.

UNDERAGE PREGNANCY

The United Kingdom and the United States have the highest rates of teenage pregnancies in the Western World.[17] Several films have been produced to show the impact a pregnancy makes on the underaged child, on her own parents, and how this affects her interaction with school friends. *Precious*, *Mom at Sixteen*, and *Juno* handle conception from the standpoint of the 'victim', but in *Manny & Lo* and *That Night* we also see the impact of a pregnancy from the viewpoint of a sibling or a friend.

Giving birth to a baby while under sixteen can result in an array of traumatic problems. Underaged girls invariably keep their pregnancy secret, only soliciting help late into their pregnancy. They are often children from poorer socio-economic backgrounds who have an inadequate diet. They receive insufficient prenatal care, are likely to suffer health issues, and be hospitalised. An underdeveloped pelvis leads to difficulties in childbirth. Teenaged mothers are more likely to drop out of school, which affects career opportunities. Most teenage mothers live in poverty, and have a higher risk of suicide. Their offspring are statistically more likely to exhibit behavioural problems, and are three times more likely to end up in prison as the child reaches adulthood.

Rarely are these pregnancies the fault of the underaged child. It is a fallacy that teenage mothers become pregnant to gain welfare benefits, despite the quip made by Ann Heather in *Urban Ghost Story*.[18] Invariably, the young teen is pressurised into having sex by an older male to whom the child does not know how to say 'no'. Sometimes, the influence of drugs or alcohol lowers inhibitions. Many girls at that age are too embarrassed to acquire or insist on using contraceptives, and when they do, they may use them incorrectly.[19]

Often, it is the media that is at fault by expressing as normal the sexualisation of dress-codes and relationships, as depicted in newspapers, magazines, TV, films, music culture, and the internet. Where the media tries to make redress by producing films that tackle the subject in an honest fashion, alas, the professional critics become sceptical, by deriding the attempt as being too sugary, too moralising, too off-putting.

Observing Pregnancy in Others

Manny & Lo are two fostered sisters who decide to escape from their respective American foster families. They travel the countryside in stolen cars, stealing from food malls, and breaking into empty homes that are for let or for sale. Sixteen-year-old Lo discovers she is pregnant. Her younger eleven-year-old sister Manny (Scarlett Johansson) waits for her in the car while Lo goes to a clinic to have her condition confirmed, and hopefully to arrange for an abortion. But she is told the foetus is too well developed and the birth is imminent. Lo is unwilling to be treated by the clinic, lest she and her sister be taken back into care. Already they have a daily routine of checking milk cartons in supermarkets to check they are not among the displays of missing children, and they do not want to be caught now. They find a remote unoccupied holiday home deep in the woods, which they decide to use as a base until after the birth.

Next, they stake out a maternity shop to try to filch items that may be useful. They notice how knowledgeable Elaine the shop assistant is about the birth of babies, so they decide to abduct the woman and take her back to their hideout. It is pitiful watching the woman tolerantly inching her way around the chalet, her legs strapped to prevent escape. In time, a bond of trust grows between the naïve ignorant children and the knowledgeably helpful Elaine. They unstrap her legs. When later their cover is blown by the return of the house owner the three-some have to flee, set up camp beside a creek, which is where the baby is born.

The film is described as a comedy. Although it was fun to watch, with comic episodes, it was more like a tragic drama, showing one method that a panic-stricken child chose to deal with an unwanted pregnancy, trivialising a serious issue. Maybe it was described as comedy because the producer was unwilling to explore the real emotional dilemma that faced the pregnant Lo and the demands placed on the eleven-year-old Manny, who had to be compliant with the wishes of the older sister. We never know the outcome following the birth. It is most likely Lo's baby was abandoned and adopted by someone else.

If such films are to have a message for underaged girls who become pregnant, then the film needs to be created without an age restriction. I suppose directors do not set out to educate, they set out to entertain. If there are to be any subversive or ethical messages regarding underage sex and childhood pregnancies then they have to be disguised, otherwise the target audience would be put off from watching it. Audiences are more likely to enjoy salacious activity rather than be warned of dangers. How do you explain to a child that sweets are bad for it? And how, after bombarding the youth of today with drama, advertisements and pop songs that constantly bear undertones of sexual messages and imagery, do you stand up and say drool at the apple but don't take a bite?

Sheryl, the seventeen-year-old neighbour of Alice (Eliza Dushku) in *That Night* became pregnant. Sheryl had been in collusion with the ten-year-old Alice, pretending to baby-sit for her when instead she was being sexually active with the guy from the bowling alley. The man, Rick, agreed to be the father to the baby. He would do his best to find a good job so he can support the family. This is 1961 when people had a conscience, if not morals. "It's my whole life, Rick; that's what you're asking for."

Level-headed mum, however, realised the relationship would not work out. "If you really do love him, then let him go. He'll support you for the rest of your life, but will hate you for it." Mum decides it is best to secrete her daughter to a hostel for pregnant girls run by nuns, and after the birth, find a foster parent. However, the young Alice discovers where the girl is hiding out, informs Rick, and he sneaks off to reclaim his gal, no doubt to be parents together.

Coping with Pregnancy

I am unaware of a film that dares to tackle pregnancy among preteens or younger teenagers. Usually the character is fifteen or over, and the actress at least eighteen. The pitfalls and traumas are shown through the eyes of more experienced adolescents. The nearest the young actress gets to portraying a pregnant teenager is as Mary in the school Nativity Play. Considering many scholars believe Mary, the mother of Jesus, became pregnant aged twelve or thirteen (an occurrence more likely in those Biblical times when a daughter was an encumbrance, an extra mouth to feed, and better to be married off as soon as possible), most schools are blithely forgetful that they are performing a drama about the anguish of teenage pregnancy. The reality is restored in the movie *The Nativity Story* (2006) in which Keisha Castle-Hughes plays the girl betrothed to Joseph. For Mary, her dilemma is in trying to convince her relatives that she had become pregnant due to divine intervention, a massive hurdle to overcome in a society that considered pregnancy out-of-wedlock as being adultery, punishable by stoning.

In *The Annunciation*, a partial retelling of the Genesis story, a pre-pubescent Eve (Júlia Mérö) announces to Adam that she is going to have a baby, while Lucifer stands in the distance with a satisfied smirk on his face.

A film more pertinent to our millennium is *Juno*. As with *Manny & Lo* and *That Night*, the character is aged sixteen, as if the director wishes to steer clear of using underaged actors. In fact, in *Juno*, the part of the sixteen-year-old is played by twenty-year-old Ellen Page, an accomplished actress whose looks pass her for a sixteen-year-old, just as they helped her be believable as a fourteen-year-old in *Hard Candy*. Ellen Page was nominated for an Oscar for her role in *Juno*. Like *Manny & Lo*, *Juno* is also described as being a comedy, which is a shame if it trivialises such a serious issue.

Juno (Ellen Page) has had casual sex with her boyfriend, but this is not a sex movie. There is no kissing, fondling, or bonking. We are just told that this nerdish guitar-playing fellow-classmate, almost unwittingly, has made the girl pregnant.

Juno's first consideration is abortion, but she is so casually and unhelpfully treated at the clinic, (dare I say it:) she aborts the abortion. "Maybe they'll canonise me for being so selfless," she says to her friend. Instead, she opts to give the newborn to a childless couple, but that is several months away. "That's a tough decision to take," her parents (father and stepmum) tell her, once she has plucked up the courage to tell them she is pregnant. Their only reprimand as she discloses to them is from father saying, "I thought you were the kind of girl who knows when to say when." As Juno was about to make her announcement, stepmum had hoped she was going to tell them she had been expelled, or was into hard drugs, instead of saying she is pregnant; the alternatives seemed preferable.

Juno has found a wonderful couple to take her baby, and she often visits them to keep them informed of the progress of the pregnancy, bringing them pictures of the ultrascan. "You want to know how your kid is cooking," Juno tells them. Alas, the wife, Vanessa, is usually out when Juno visits, so she starts getting suspicious of her husband and the girl's friendly liaisons. In the end, the happy couple split – the man, surprisingly, is not ready to be a father, while Vanessa is happy to adopt the baby as a single parent once Juno has done all the heaving and straining on the hospital bed.

Unfortunately, the film does not focus on the qualms a surrogate mother may have when relinquishing her newborn to someone else. We do not see the girl grappling with social and emotional issues influencing the pregnancy – relationships with friends, family, clinicians, or social workers. This is something that *Mom at Sixteen* does well.

Juno was credited with awards because it takes a humorous stance without making the audience feel uncomfortable, whereas the more serious movie, *Mom at Sixteen*, hard-hitting in its pertinent tackling of underaged pregnancy issues, received no credit from professional critics, despite being slick, tear-inducing, and with brilliant confrontational acting.

Jacey (Danielle Panabaker) is starting a new school following her pregnancy. To allow her to complete her education and avoid stigma, mum has agreed to pretend to be the parent of the newborn. We become voyeurs into the daily squabbles between parent and daughter, the sleepless nights, the agonising classroom discussions about sex and pregnancy in which Jacey has difficulty maintaining her deception, the trauma of deciding whether to allow her baby to be adopted. As the guilt haunts her, Jacey cries in despair, "I didn't kill anyone: I just had a baby." After Jacey finally admits to her classmates that she is a teenage mother, she imparts the moralistic message, "The world tells us that sex is part of our lives and that movies and magazines say the same thing. But the world lies to us. Sex is a big responsibility, a responsibility that we are not ready for."

In *Riding in Cars with Boys*, Drew Barrymore was twenty-two when asked to play the role of a pregnant fifteen-year-old, but in this film she was required to age to thirty-five, so the older age of the actress was appropriate. Though a comedy drama, at least the drama sends a message by alluding to how a young mother's life can be devastated and how hopes of college and a career appear to have been ruined.

Pregnancy: the boy's responsibility

Science, and not even science-fiction, has yet found a way for boys to conceive, so their role in these movies is either to face up to the music, or find ways to evade their paternal duties. Where the 'father' is of similar age to the underaged girl, he does not have the emotional maturity to fulfil the role of fatherhood. *Mom at Sixteen* features a debate among classroom students in which the boys vocalise what they think their responsibilities should be, though usually they naïvely throw the blame back at the girl. *Too Young to be a Father* takes seriously the moral issues of a fifteen-year-old lad who has made a classmate pregnant.

In *A Boy Called Dad*, fourteen-year-old Robbie (Kylo Ward) is distressed that the mother of his child doesn't allow him to see the baby. Robbie, it seems, was 'used' by the girl to get pregnant: "Hurry up and do it," she tells the boy, then after the birth goes off with an older man. Only on one occasion does the girl relent by allowing Robbie to hold the baby. "Who was that boy?" the man asks her incredulously, never assuming the wimpish lad could be the actual father.

Now, Robbie is not some irresponsible lad out to lay every girl he meets. He is seen as the class underachiever. The others jeer at him when he won't dive in the swimming pool. He is the sort of lad who is made goalie in sports lessons because no one else will. When he looks in the bathroom mirror he is still not ready to shave.

It is because Robbie feels sidelined that he makes an impulsive action. On a chance encounter he meets the new stepfather of his child. He sees the man lose patience, yelling in frustration at the baby. While the man is in the urinals, Robbie kidnaps the baby, stealing it away from his Liverpool home to North Wales. But before long, he too is feeling helpless, immersed in the terror of fatherhood, tearing out his own hair, as the baby never stops crying. Wherever he runs he can't escape the sound of the baby's wails. Realising he has to change the child's nappy, the process almost makes him puke.

Robbie's paternal instincts stem from his relationship with his own estranged father. The boy is responding to his own father's apology: "Fucking hell, I failed as a dad. Give me another chance to prove I can be your dad." Evidentally Robbie took this plea to heart, for we see him ten years later as a responsible dad, himself, playing with his now adolescent child.

However, the peers of the pregnant girl are seldom the problem. Most young teens are coerced into having sex by partners much older than themselves whom the girl does not know how to resist. 77% of teenage pregnancies are caused by older men of whom 66% are over the age of twenty-five. In the age group of 13-15 year old girls, 51% of the 'fathers' are aged over twenty-five, which leads to the consideration of the criminal issue of statutory rape.[20]

DEATH

Numerous films feature the death of a loved one. "In the midst of life we are in death," says Mrs Crawley ambiguously in *Downton Abbey*. Mortality is a pertinent theme for all of us, but for the child, who sees life stretching out endlessly before it, it becomes a cruelly heart-wrenching experience when someone they love is suddenly snatched from them, even when the child is expecting a death.

Referring to the Dashwood sisters, Hugh Grant consoles in *Sense and Sensibility*, "They have just lost their father. Their lives will never be the same again." Grandfather prepares Mischa Barton for his imminent death in *A Ring of Endless Light*, telling the girl, "Death is as natural as that storm out there." Ben Kingsley, playing Rev. Templeton in *Photographing Fairies*, is the vicar leading the service for the funeral of his recently deceased wife. "Don't think of death as a distant world," he tells the congregation and his two confused daughters, "for it is as quickly found as the blink of a man's eye. Death is merely a change of state. It is only a footfall away." Headstrong Wendy Hiller, about to embark on a foolhardy voyage is told, "In less than a second you can get from this world into the next." (*I Know Where I'm Going*).

This is depicted forcefully in Nicolas Roeg's classic, *Walkabout*, as images of father's suicide are interspersed with the death throes of Australia's fauna, all caught up in that desperate striving to survive. Decaying fruit, the daily grim battle of predation between the desperately hungry and its next victim, all portray death as routine. Nature mercilessly abandons it casualties, carcasses are wantonly slaughtered and strewn uncaringly by hunters, the nomadic aboriginal family are indifferent to the burnt-out corpse of the children's father. Even the girl (Jenny Agutter) leaves their aboriginal guide hanging on an acacia, used, misunderstood, and abandoned to the vultures whose function is to decay the lifeless back into primordial dust, nature's callous recycling of rejects and the defeated. Despite this constant drama of death accompanying them, the protective girl is nevertheless unwilling to admit death to her younger brother. Referring to her dead father, "He'll catch us up later." Her denial is exposed eventually as the little boy (Lucien John) realises, "He's dead, isn't he?"

Some people believe the blow can be softened for those children who have pets; the death of a pet can be a sad introduction to the real world of living and dying. Yet, does it really ameliorate the impact? A dying pet that has grown up with the child can be as much part of the family and as important to him/her as any sibling, parent or relative, as Ingemar (Anton Glanzelius) showed us in *My Life as a Dog*. In some cases, the pet may be the only source of unconditional love for the child. And a child who has been through the traumatic loss of a pet will have an enhanced sense of anticipated fear when they see a family member become seriously ill.

Cathy (Kristy Swanson) seems to take a different point of view in *Flowers in the Attic*. Distraught following the death of her father, she shares her regrets with her brother. "If we'd had a pet and it died we would have learnt something about death. Somebody should have told us that fathers die, too." (We consider more fully the child's relationship with its pets in Volume 4 *Childhood Friendships*.)

The film producer depicting the trauma of death may, on the one hand, be painting a realistic picture of life as it confronts us. The death may be slow and lingering as in *My Sister's Keeper*, so the child gets used to the inevitability of death, and thus the blow may be cushioned somewhat, but still devastating when the last breath is expired. In other films, the impact is shockingly unexpected; a loved one, who just yesterday was a fit and healthy playmate, sibling, or relative, is inexplicably snatched from them. This must be the most devastating scenario of all, though the child does not have to endure the pain of seeing a loved one in an excruciating fight for survival. It was child actor Abigail Breslin's role to confront both circumstances as she played Anna, the sister of terminally ill Kate in *My Sister's Keeper*, and had to handle the sudden impact of her grandfather's death in *Little Miss Sunshine*, and later, her mother's fatal crash in *No Reservations*.

Katherine Paterson purposefully set out to describe this traumatic impact in her novel, *Bridge to Terabithia*, to help a child confront an unexpected death. The book was written following the death of the childhood friend of her own eight-year-old son. She admits having felt impotent; not knowing how to console her son, and this is what inspired her to pen her novel, which was later made into the film. *Charlotte's Web*, too, helps introduce the child to the concept of death without making a devastating impact on the viewer, using the demise of a self-sacrificing spider that spreads her offspring, perpetuating her memory.

Death itself is unlikely to have a long-term effect on the child. More likely, according to Sula Wolff, it is "the emotional impact of the surviving parent" that prolongs any psychological demise.[21] Widowers, in particular, find it hard to cope as they try to hold down a job and raise the family simultaneously, needing to rely on female relatives or housekeepers. Children of bereaved fathers are more likely to be taken into care. Widows, however, tend to withdraw emotionally from their offspring, and the children are expected to assist with household chores and caring for younger siblings. It is these changes that can affect the child more than the death itself. Professor Michael Rutter observed a gender difference in a traumatised child's reaction. A girl who lost her mother in infant years may present a psychiatric disturbance at the onset of puberty, whereas for a boy, this is more likely to materialise within six months of the parent's death.[22]

Children under the age of nine are less likely to understand the finality of death, perceiving the deceased in the same bracket as someone gone away on a journey or to hospital. This is why children frequently ask questions like, 'when is mum coming back?' (See *Corrina, Corrina* and *Flightplan*). Only after the age of nine do children "accept death realistically as a biological fact," and react (as any adult would) with fits of crying, and becoming withdrawn, apathetic or hostile.[23] It is then, that the plethora of platitudes is assailed at the child under the pretext of lessening the grief.

Platitudes

When a death occurs, the immediate response is to put a brave face on the situation, to try to find the bright side in a tragedy, to offer a platitude of optimism. In most cases, an attempt is made to placate the child with a religious or supernatural hope: 'your mother is still with us in spirit', 'God has taken her to do his will', 'you'll still have your dreams!' or as Freddie Booth is told in *The Mummy Returns*, "She has gone to a better place." Dumbledore tries to placate his student in *Harry Potter and the Prisoner of Azkaban*, as the boy searches the mirror for the reflection of his dead parents, "The ones that love us never really leave us."

This is what Alyson Stoner's character is told in *Alice Upside Down*, as she and her father are about to move home. "Wherever we go she'll be with us," says dad about mother who died when Alice was five. Or Tom Oakley standing over the grave of his wife and son in *Goodnight Mr Tom*, "I didn't lose them really. They are still here, inside my head, and always will be." Maybe to hit this kind of message home, *Jack Frost*, killed in a road crash, returns to his son (Joseph Cross) in the guise of a snowman as a last gasp chance to redress all his failings as a father. "I will always be there," he says to his twelve-year-old. "As long as you hold someone in your heart, you can never lose them."

In *Stepmom*, Susan Sarandon, dying of terminal cancer is asked by her young son Ben (Liam Aiken): "Are you dying?" Cuddled in her dying mother's arms, Ben enquires, "Then I won't see you anymore?"

"You won't see my body," replies mum, "but you know how a caterpillar becomes something else…" This must be even more difficult for mother trying to put a gloss on her own imminent death. "Just because you can't see something doesn't mean it's not there… You'll still have our dream."

For some, these platitudes represent a sick wallowing in falsity, evading the inevitable hardships of life's future pathway. Not for them the sticking plasters of comfort. Although *That Night* is mainly about a ten-year-old girl, Alice (Eliza Dushku), it also features a seventeen-year-old Sheryl (Juliette Lewis) who has a good relationship with her father. One evening, a police officer comes to the bowling alley where she is enjoying herself, to inform her that her father has died of a heart attack. After the funeral, she seeks solace from her boyfriend. "What did they say to you?" he sceptically asks. "Time heals all wounds… God has his reasons? It doesn't make any goddam sense!" For Jesse James in The *Amityville Horror* (2005) he too is inadequately comforted with the words, "Sometimes things happen in life that can't be explained." This is after he complains, "Praying doesn't do any good – nobody answered me when I asked if dad could be kept alive."

What of the impact on the surviving relatives? Progeny who have not found the time to visit their elderly relatives somehow always seem to find time for that final send-off, where sad thoughts blend with precious memories, and the vicar can gen up on his anthology of eulogies. "We ought to have funerals while we're still alive," observes Laura Ingalls in *The Little House on the Prairie*, "so we can say goodbye to everybody." Her elderly neighbour overhears this comment. Her own children and grandchildren have not been to visit her in years, so the elderly woman pretends to die, announcing the funeral, so she can re-establish contact with her relatives at the funeral wake. Dressed in her black veil, she mingles with the funeral guests, listening to their platitudes, the false niceties, and the good-riddances.

Others, knowing their own death is imminent, make plans to provide solace for their children in the future. Thinking she was dying of a brain aneurysm, Sacha Horler writes a letter to her two children in *My Year Without Sex*, to be read when the children are older and after she has died. This seems a well-used idea. The mother of *Billy Elliot* chose to do the same, knowing she was shortly to die, to be read when the boy reaches eighteen. "But I opened it," says Jamie Bell playing Billy. Here, mother seems to be writing her own platitude, hoping that his life has gone well without her. She writes: 'I know I seem like a distant memory to you, which is probably a good thing. I would have missed seeing you grow, missed you crying. I would have missed telling you off. But please know I was always there with you through everything, and I always will be, and I am proud to have known you and proud that you were mine.'

"She must have been a very special woman, your mother," says Julie Walters to the boy dancer.

"She was just me mum," says Billy modestly.

Terminal Illness

My Sister's Keeper effectively conveys the trauma of a girl dying of cancer, and its impact on the various family members, without going sensationally over-the-top. Sofia Vassilieva plays Kate Fitzgerald, a girl in her mid-teens. She has leukaemia, and is gradually dying of cancer. She is usually confined to bed. She has considerable pain, which manifests itself through nosebleeds, being sick, incontinence, and hair loss. Kate is aware she is going to die. There is no cure. She should have died long ago, but her younger sister, Anna, had given her a new lease of life.

When Kate was first diagnosed with leukaemia, the doctor had told the parents that death was a certainty, unless the parents give birth to a genetically-modified baby – a designer baby – who could intermittently supply blood, bone marrow, a kidney, and other body parts and fluids. So a new child, Anna, was conceived.

During her childhood, Anna would undergo numerous painful and distressing operations as a donor, to help keep her older sister alive. She had no real say in the matter. Yes, she was asked if she consented, but it was all beyond the comprehension of a young child. The pain and intrusiveness of the procedures were never explained to young Anna and she would not have understood, anyway. She had no option but to concur. (Sarah Bolger playing Christie in *In America* (2003) alludes to a similar intervention. Mother has given birth prematurely, and the baby is placed in an incubator needing an immediate blood transfusion. On learning she has the same blood group as her baby sister, Christie immediately volunteers to provide the transfusion.)

While in *My Sister's Keeper* the mother's persistence had managed to prolong the life of her older daughter, she had been so absorbed in her maternal duties she had never stood back to consider the divergent wishes of her two daughters. Kate has now come to terms with her own illness, she sees the detrimental impact it is having on her family, and she is now self-assured: "I suppose I know now I am going to die. I had just never known before. I'm ok with it now." For Anna, now eleven and played by Abigail Breslin, she had suffered and sacrificed all her childhood as a donor, keeping her sister alive, and now she wants rights to her own body. She even takes her parents to court to preserve those rights.

Mother's difficulty is that, at all cost, she must try to keep Kate alive, and she cannot face up to the fact that her daughter is dying. "Kate's dying," says her husband, "and you don't want to know about it. You love her so much you just won't let her go... There's no shame in dying."

Kate's gradual deterioration is treated sympathetically in the film without being too overwhelming. Kate's younger sister, Anna, asks as she is cleaning up her sister's incontinence, "Are you in pain?" Kate realises the anguish she has to face, almost like Jesus in the Garden of Gethsemane coming to terms with his imminent crucifixion. "This is the end," she says to her sister. "It just gets scary from here on up," and she mumbles something about her becoming a vegetable.

On her final night, mother comforts Kate in bed. Dying Kate has kept a brave face, serene, and selflessly saying things of encouragement to the other members of her family. Anna narrates,

"I wish I could say she made some brilliant recovery. But she didn't. She just stopped breathing."

What shines through in this and other films about death is the selflessness of both carer and patient even though, on occasions, altruism strains to a breaking point. This is particularly evident where the carer is trying to prolong the patient's life while at the same time allowing them to die with dignity. There tends to be a rallying round of the whole family as they watch helplessly the gradual fading of the one they love as in *Little Women*, though sometimes, as in *Beaches* (1988), it is a close friend who assumes the altruistic role as carer. This gradual fading may be a painful struggle as in *My Sister's Keeper* or *Lorenzo's Oil*, or a peaceful drifting off as in *The Cement Garden*. What seems imperative is that an honest approach to death is pursued as in *Stepmom* instead of trying to conceal the truth from the kids in *My Life as a Dog*.

While *My Sister's Keeper* concentrates on the debilitating circumstances of an illness, *Stepmom* focuses on how the different individuals are preparing for the future – after death. Divorced mother of two, Jackie (Susan Sarandon), has contracted terminal cancer. This provides a distraction for the feuding protagonists (the divorced couple, and live-in girlfriend, Isabel, played by Julia Roberts) as they realise this parent is dying. "What are we going to tell the kids?" Jackie asks her ex-husband.

"The truth," says her ex-husband. "I think they can handle it."

As Jackie deteriorates, she moves back into the family home in which they share their final Christmas together, and where they tearfully say their goodbyes.

"Mum, are you scared (of dying)?" asks her young son (Liam Aiken). Mother nods. But I believe she is only afraid of the physical suffering. She has already been able to picture her role as mother beyond the grave.

As ex-wife Jackie heals the relationship with new stepmother Isabel, referring to the children, she says, "I can have their past, and you can have their future."

To hide the truth of a terminal illness only acerbates the trauma for family members. This is what twelve-year-old Ingemar (Anton Glanzelius) discovers in *My Life as a Dog*. He is spared the torment of watching his terminally ill mother suffer, but only because the truth seems to be withheld from him. Ingemar has been sent to the south of Sweden to stay with his uncle so that his mother can recuperate following an operation for cancer. "Mum needs some peace or we'll be the death of her," older brother tells him. Yet, while he was living at home, his inconsiderate squabbles with his older brother were making mum's illness worse. He ponders to himself, "Why didn't you want me, Mummy?" not realising he was aggravating his mother's condition.

The boy seems to have many regrets, as he says to himself, "I should have told her everything while she had the strength." Now he can only contact mother occasionally by telephone, and since this is Sweden in 1959 phone calls are expensive and must be kept brief. Christmas is coming up and Ingemar wants to buy mother a special pop-up toaster and asks his brother to go halves with him. But his brother refuses, and after Ingemar's continued nagging, Ingemar is told the blunt shocking truth: "She's going to die. Hasn't that got through to you yet?"

The loyalty that family members exhibited in *My Sister's Keeper* is shared in *Little Women*, too. The children have to watch the painful wasting away of older sister, Beth, played by Clare Danes, who contracts scarlet fever. This is a close-knit, harmonious family, and this makes the hurt even deeper to bear. Younger sister, Jo (Winona Ryder), tearfully visits her sister on her deathbed. As

413

in *Stepmom* and *My Sister's Keeper* the dying person selflessly utters words of encouragement: dying Beth whispers some courageous parting words, and while Jo looks through the window to ponder them, Beth passes away. Jo is inconsolable as she hugs her dead sister and weeps.

In *Beaches* (1988), it is the loyalty of a friend who responds to the dying wishes of a patient. Grace Johnson plays seven-year-old Victoria who watches her mother, Hillary (Barbara Hershey), gradually become frailer. As Hillary is diagnosed with a terminal heart virus, she sends for her lifelong friend, CC Bloom (Bette Midler). Loyally, CC helps look after the child as mother becomes increasingly incapacitated. "I'm so scared, CC," says Hillary, fully aware she is dying and that her daughter will be left parentless.

Then the daughter, Grace, finds her mother collapsed on the floor. Reluctantly the child has to leave her own home to live with mum's lifelong friend, CC. It is heart-breaking watching the little girl looking reflectively through the car window, clouds flooding her eyes, as she stares back at all her past memories.

For the two boy and two girls in *The Cement Garden* the death of their mother was not anticipated, even though she had been ill. The grieving of the children is tinged with the humour that comes from an unexpected action. Father had recently died; he had been choking on his pipe then died suddenly from a heart attack. Mother had been tearful at her husband's death, and the children had been stunned, but they showed no emotion. Mother tells them, "Father had found it hard to show his feelings." She had said this, perhaps to excuse some hidden past behaviour, for during the course of the film, we see flashbacks of the children flying a kite on the beach, with mum having to drag the oldest girl, Julie, by the hand to keep up with dad, but the girl had wanted to seek comfort from her brother instead, who had also kept his distance.

Not long after this, mother becomes unwell. Knowing she will be spending several weeks in hospital, she arranges monetary matters to enable the children to fend for themselves during her hospital stay. But she does not get the chance to go into hospital. One day, the children find mother dead in bed. Horrified, they sadly comfort each other. "Did it hurt her?" young Susan (Alice Coulthard) asks. "No, she just drifted off – like in a dream," replies Jack (Andrew Robertson).

As older sister, Julie (Charlotte Gainsbourg), shifts the sheet to cover the face of their dead mother, the feet get uncovered. So, Jack, the older boy, restores the sheet to cover the feet, revealing mother's face again. This causes the children to burst into a titter of laughter beside the bed of their dead mother.

For a few days after mum's death, the children just mope around playing games. They realise they will be split up and taken into care if others find out about mother's death (a dilemma also experienced by the children in the Japanese movie, *Nobody Knows*), so they bury her secretly in cement in the cellar.

Psychological Effects of the Death of a Parent on the Child

"Grief over the death of a loved one can lead people to do the strangest things," Nicole Kidman is told in *The Others* (2001) as her family forlornly wait for the father (lost, presumed dead) to return home from war in 1945. This is a constant theme running through films about death: on the one hand, the surviving adult tries to suppress the past, either by running away or going through a state of denial; whereas the bereaved child wanting to reflect on the past, is denied a source of comfort by an intransigent parent. The child deprived of this may resort to devious behaviour. This may be psychological trauma as in *Hide and Seek*, intense feelings of remorse as in *Genova*, resorting to the occult to regain contact with the loved one as in *Life-Size* and *Fairy Tale*, or delving into revenge (*Cría Cuervos*) or promiscuity as in *The Cement Garden* or *That Night*. Others become mute, either as a psychological imbalance or as a way of deflecting the truth: we shall pursue this malady in a later chapter.

Keke Palmer is searching through her deceased mother's artefacts in *Cleaner* (2007). Like Veda (Anna Chlumsky) in *My Girl 2* she is doing a school project about her dead mother. Father admonishers her, "You can't spend your life looking through this box. It's just you and me now."

But the girl is not consoled. "You just don't get it, dad," she cries through sobs of tears. For Keke Palmer, her best therapy for coming to terms with her mum's death is to reflect on the past, to reminisce, to think of the good times. For the father (Samuel L Jackson), the urge to suppress the past, even denial seems to be the way forward.

This prevarication over talking about the death of a loved one is perpetuated in *Alice Upside Down*. Alyson Stoner playing the title role demands from her dad, "How come you never talk about mum? I think about her all the time even though I can't remember her." Alice was five when mother died. She finds a box of old videos about mum in the basement. Alice had previously been told not to watch them, for dad is still unwilling to face up to his past memories. When Alice is caught watching one of the videos she objects. "You never want to talk about it!"

Mr Hoover tries to deflect the conversation when his daughter, Olive (Abigail Breslin) asks about her uncle's attempted suicide in *Little Miss Sunshine*. "Why did you try to kill yourself?" she asks her Uncle Frank. But father buts in, "I don't think this is an appropriate conversation for a seven-year-old."

This concept of suppression and denial seems to be a constant theme in death-related movies. "Charlie, dad died a year ago," says mother to Joseph Cross in *Jack Frost*. "You just got to accept that." Similar denials had to be confronted by characters played by Alakina Mann (in *The Others*), by Anna Chlumsky (*My Girl* (1991)), Alison Stoner in *Alice Upside Down*, and by Keke Palmer (*Cleaner* (2007)), and as the following films also illustrate.

Genova is a film that effectively confronts the psychological trauma that a child may go through following the death of her mother. Escaping from America to a foreign land (Italy), the family are hoping for a fresh start. But while father (Colin Firth) is out at work (he has a lecturing job teaching English), and older sister, Kelly, is off gallivanting with boyfriends, ten-year-old Mary is left alone too often to grieve by herself. No wonder she has nightmares, wets the bed, and visualises mum walking beside her down the street, and comforting her while she sleeps.

Mary (played brilliantly by Perla Haney-Jardine), blames herself for the death of her mother. This seems to be a typical reaction among grieving children, and we will explore these guilt feelings later in this chapter. In this film, *Genova*, Mary is justified in blaming herself. Mum had been driving a car, while the two girls were playing a game of I-Spy. Just momentarily, as part of the game, Mary had covered mum's eyes with her hands. This is what caused the fatal crash that has left a traumatised child to howl in her sleep. "I want Mummy to come back!"

There is a funeral. "It is a terrible shock when a life is cut short," preaches the vicar. "In her beautiful daughters, perhaps, a bit of the mother lives on with us today." Mary misinterprets this last phrase, as her dreams of a living mother become tangible. Mary hears mum talking to her in her sleep. Like Jodelle Ferland in *Silent Hill*, she draws weird pictures using dark pastels, all with a common theme: a car, a ghostly figure of mum. (In *Hide and Seek* (2005) the drawings made by Dakota Fanning after mum's death are of a monstrous man becoming more hideous and darker as time progresses, as well as pictures of her mum with blood dripping from her wrists – the consequence of a 'suicide').

In *Genova*, Mary feels her mother holding her hand; she visualises her mother walking beside her down alleyways. As she lights a remembrance candle in church, mum's caring face flickers into view. No wonder then, that Mary wanders off by herself when she thinks she sees mum walking along the cliff top path to the monastery in the hills, or crosses a busy road to catch up with mum's apparition on the other side, or follows her parallel path through the scary alleyways of downtown old Genoa.

Mary's problem is, there is no one to listen to her grieving. Father can comfort her with hugs, and has taken the family to Italy to try to forget. But this does not tackle the root of the trauma. It is not until Barbara (a friend of Mary's father) starts listening to the girl, that the truth begins to be exorcised. Barbara is helping Mary to light a candle in a church, when Mary's defences suddenly crack.

Mary: "I was in the car when my mother died."

Barbara: "I know. It must have been awful."

Mary: "She comes to me sometimes… She comes to forgive me."

Barbara: "You have nothing to be forgiven about. It was not your fault. You didn't do anything. It was an accident, a terrible accident."

Mary: "I did. It was my fault."

But Barbara cannot understand how this could be. Mary wanders off by herself heading for a monastery and gets lost in the hills, seemingly following the apparition of her dead mother. A frantic search for the lost girl ensues. Barbara has to explain to the father how Mary went missing after they were lighting candles in the church. Father, who is still so wrapped up with his own grief that he cannot understand the desperation of his own daughter, replies, "Maybe, lighting candles for dead people is not what she needs right now."

Barbara, diverting the criticism, admires their stoicism: "It must be incredibly hard for you. You are all incredibly brave." But father responds, "Well, we don't really have much choice." The lady tries delicately to press home the problem to the blinkered man. "Mary feels guilty. I think she needs help."

Here is an anguished family in a state of denial, because they have not faced talking about mother's death with each other. Instead, father had just tried to run away to Italy hoping that would solve the problem. Father is admonished: "If you don't talk about mum it's like pretending she never existed."

The film is open-ended. The grief is not resolved. But the film does give us a heightened focus on the tragedy besetting the child, and steers the viewer towards the pathway for healing a troubled soul.

Just as Perla Haley-Jardine sees visions of her dead mother, Ana Torrent in *Cría Cuervos* struggles to come to terms with the death of her mother. She often sees apparitions of mother in her dreams. Sometimes she calls out "Mamma" in her sleep. Her sister, Irene (Conchita Perez), has to put her straight: "Mummy is dead, Ana!" James Nesbitt takes on a similar duty as the father of Alex Etel in *Millions* (2004). After the boy claims visitations from his dead mother, father brings him down to Earth. "Mum: she's dead, Damian. You'll never see her again. And neither will I."

This running away to another country to try to forget a loved one is reinforced in *Hide and Seek* (2005) in which psychiatrist Robert de Niro takes his daughter Dakota Fanning up-state to the seclusion of a forest home, and also in Jim Sheridan's autobiographical film, *In America* (2003), in which Paddy Considine and Samantha Morton play Irish parents, Johnny and Sarah, who are crossing the Canadian border on the way to New York to start a new life. Their two daughters, Christy (Sarah Bolger) and Ariel (Emma Bolger) are sitting on the back seat.

"How many children have you got?" asks the guard at the border crossing.

"Three," is Johnny's instinctive reply, forgetting that his youngest boy, Frankie, has recently died.

Memories of Frankie keep popping into his head. During a game of blindman's bluff with his daughters, Johnny starts searching for Frankie, only to realise his little boy is not here anymore. As Paddy Considine comments later, "You can move anywhere in the world, but you can't run away from grief."

Mum blames herself for not being there to catch the child when he fell down the stairs. Then later mum blames the father for building a gate at the top of the stairs that Frankie was able to climb over and go tumbling down. Christy has to tearfully remind her parents, "He was my brother, too." Regardless of which characters feel the pangs of guilt, this was the director's own personal story, exorcising the loss of his own baby brother when he, himself, was a child.

At least Christy has a camcorder which she carries with her constantly, and plays back sequences to remind her of her little brother. (These tangible reminders seem very important, as *Cleaner* (2007) reminds us.) Christy holds her father's hand as they stare at the full moon. While they help Ariel say goodbye to Mateo, a black friend who has just died of AIDS, Christy forces her father to let go of his own grief for his dead son. "Say goodbye to Frankie, daddy," she insists, drilling her stares deep into his conscience.

It is interesting that the moon provides a tangible possible resting-place for an object of grief. In *Contact* (1997), Jena Malone used other celestial bodies to visualise communication with her dead mother. For this is where Heaven lies, in the troubled spaciousness of our celestial minds.

The parents of Elsie Wright (Florence Hoath) in *Fairy Tale* (1997) had a similar barrier of denial to face up to. Their son Joseph having died of pneumonia, they have left his room exactly as it was, untouched. "You can't even say his name, can you?" the mother, Polly, challenges the father. Yet this does not help their relationship: in trying to deflect the trauma, the father can no longer even picture the child in his mind. Like others in that era of people losing loved ones in World War One, mother is desperate to seek out the occult for answers. That is where she meets the famous Sir Arthur Conan Doyle who confides in her, "There are no words to describe the loss of a child." Doyle himself had been seeking help from mediums to contact his son recently killed in the Battle of the Somme.

As in *Genova*, it appears to be the child who is most traumatised in *Hide and Seek* (2005) until it gradually dawns on the viewer it is the father who has been equally psychologically scarred. Following her mother's 'suicide', Emily (Dakota Fanning) turns insular and cannot be motivated. Placing her in a psychiatric hostel for traumatised children does not bring her out of her shell; so father (Robert de Niro) decides to move up-state to see if seclusion aids the healing process. "Trauma causes pain. Eventually the mind will find a way to release it." But these comments are directed to the father, who releases his own bottled-up trauma in the most inappropriate of ways.

These are modern sociological approaches to the suffering associated with death. In wartime, when everyone was surrounded by the death of loved ones, the bereaved were expected to snap out of it. "I hate you God," shouts young Nick Robinson in *Goodnight Mr Tom* as he mourns the loss of his best friend. But he is reprimanded, "Do you think you're the only person who ever lost anybody?"

A child's wish to maintain contact with a deceased parent, as in *Genova*, is a recurring theme. In some films a child might dabble in occultist practices or magic to reincarnate a lost love one, as Lindsay Lohan does in *Life-Size*. Or in *Ingenious*, Sally (Hannah Godfrey) asks, "If you are a genie, can you bring back my mum and dad?" In *Contact* (1997), Jena Malone's passion is astronomy. When she and her father make contact on the radio with a radio ham in Florida she asks whether they could tune in to someone in Alaska, or China, or the moon. "Dad, can we talk to mum?" she asks, but is told, "I don't think even the biggest radios can reach that far!"

In *Genova*, Mary was convinced her spiritual mother was still with her in the visions she saw, and in the physical sensation of her hand being held. Bob Cratchet tells of the same feeling in *Scrooge* (1951), the anguish of memory transforming into a comforting pleasantry: "As I stood there I felt his (Tiny Tim's) hand slip into mine as if he was beside me and comforting me." The same is true of Celia Carmichael in the film of her own name. In *Celia* (1988), it is these visions that start a tragic spiral of events. Granny had been a constant source of comfort for the nine-year-old Australian girl (Rebecca Smart). The film commences with Granny's death, and we see the child giving the cadaver a final goodbye kiss before the funeral.

Soon, Celia starts imagining seeing her gran, and wistfully chases after fleeting apparitions. She races down to the bottom of a local quarry calling for her gran, thinking she saw her there. To help her remember her gran, Celia spends time sitting in Gran's vacant room, and laying on her bed, until dad discovers her in there and bans her entry by locking the door. After Celia breaks back in through the window, father heartlessly empties the room, disposing of Granny's possessions and burning her books.

"I hate him," murmurs Celia under her breath about her father. It is not made clear why dad is so disapproving of Granny, unless it is because she shared the socialist sympathies of the neighbours – "the Dirty Reds!"

Now without her one source of comfort, Celia starts imagining monsters everywhere, the *Hobyahs*, characters from the storybook she is reading. When the policeman who impounded her pet rabbit appears at her house, Celia pictures him in the gloom as a *Hobyah*, picks up father's shotgun which had been left lying around, killing the 'monster' with one bullet.

Although Lindsay Lohan playing Casey in *Life-Size* does not see visions of her dead mother, nevertheless she still want to conjure her back to life again, resorting to an occult game for help, at the expense of neglecting her friends. "Mum: she just went in for a check-up, and before I knew it she was gone. Just like that!" Her friends taunt her behind her back: "Here comes the loner. Ever since her mum died she has totally ignored us." Casey finds a book about the occult that has a spell that could bring mum back to life – *How to resurrect lost life forces*. She sets up a magic table ready for the incantations, but just at the wrong moment, her doll gets in the way, and it is her doll that is reincarnated instead of her mum.

Witnessing the death of a parent can lead to thoughts of revenge. For Celia it was the confused annihilation of the *Hobyah*/policeman. In the French classic *Jean de Florette/Manõn de Source*, Ernestine Mazurowna playing Manõn, daughter of hunchback Gerard Depardieu, takes revenge on neighbouring farmers Cesar and Ugolin whose cruel callous greed led to the death of her own father. Ana Torrent in *Cría Cuervos* secretly blamed her father for the death of her mother by not acknowledging how seriously ill she had been. The girl deludes herself that she has the power to avenge her mum's death by using a poison compound. When the father dies, Ana is led beside the open casket where his dead body is laid. Kiss your father, she is urged. But Ana refuses.

For other children, the death of a beloved parent leads to the path of promiscuity. Just as Sheryl becomes sexually rampant after her father's death in *That Night*, so too in *The Cement Garden* the four children regress into sexual deviancy once the shackles of parental restraints have been broken. The youngest boy begins dressing as a girl, the younger girl helping him in his games, while the older boy and girl explore an incestuous relationship, perhaps mimicking the role of their now dead parents, for mum had instructed them before she died, "You two will have to be like mum and dad to the younger children till I get back from hospital."

Misunderstanding in the Child's Mind about death

Earlier in this book, we cited Sula Wolff who stated that children under the age of nine had little concept of the permanence of death. To the young child, death is a temporary state, like a loved-one going away for a while: they can be reborn. Guilt feelings are often associated with the death: the child believing their misbehaviour has somehow led to the death of a parent. This can often be followed by a period of good behaviour, the child hoping the punishment will come to an end, and the parent will be restored.[24]

"We're saying goodbye to Mummy," appeals seven-year-old Hannah Bould as she and her sister are confronted by Charles Castle, to them an interfering photographer, in *Photographing Fairies*. But these are girls who have glimpsed a little of Heaven themselves through the fleeting illusions of the fairies that visit their Yorkshire dell. To them, Heaven is a transitory world that can be reached by consuming a white, edelweiss-like blossom. Mummy will never be far away.

Ambiguous religious sentimentality confused Mary, in *Genova*. This need to discuss plainly with a child, whose uppermost desire is to grasp at any slender hope that their parent may yet return, is further pursued in *Flightplan*. Julia Pratt (Marlene Lawston) is just six years old. She had been living in Berlin with her American parents, when her father mysteriously dies, having fallen from an apartment block. Now mother (played by Jodie Foster) is taking the girl and the coffin back to New York.

"Mummy, I'm scared," admits the little girl, and mother comforts her. They are sitting together on the aircraft awaiting take-off from Berlin International Airport. Distressingly, mother watches through the aircraft window as her husband's casket is towed across the tarmac to the cargo hold. The infant is obviously very confused.

"Will daddy be there (in America)?" asks the girl.

Mother, watching the coffin of her dead husband being loaded onto the plane replies, "Yes, daddy will be there, too." And the child's worries seem to dissipate with this latest piece of good news.

A similar misunderstanding occurs in *A High Wind in Jamaica*. After Anthony Quinn's pirate ship pulls into Tampico, John falls from an upstairs window and dies. "Is John not coming back?" asks Emily (Dorothy Baxter). "No, he's not coming back," states James Coburn guiltily and expecting floods of tears from the girl. But Emily simply replies, "It's only that Ed wants to know if he can have his blanket." The true significance of death is misunderstood by the child.

Molly is a little girl whose mother has recently died in the film, *Corrina, Corrina*. The little seven-year-old (Tina Majorino) hides under the table at the reception dinner following Mummy's funeral. Within earshot, she overhears the funeral guests commiserate, "Poor kid! Thank goodness she's so young. Maybe she'll forget." When the father and daughter are left on their own, father consoles her, "We're going to be fine, Molly, just you and me." But in time, father becomes too busy to comfort her.

Rather like Scout Finch in *To Kill a Mockingbird* asking her older brother what he remembers of mother, Molly asks father, "What colour were Mummy's eyes? What did she smell like?"

Father prevaricates. "We'll talk about her later," he says.

"Liar!" exclaims the girl. "You're forgetting her, daddy." (Charlotte Gainsbourg, too, admits in *The Cement Garden* how after just three weeks she can no longer picture her own mother.)

To try to remember her mother, Molly spreads one of mum's dresses out on the lawn, and she lies beside it, looking up to heaven. Molly now has a black nanny, Corrina (played by Whoopi Goldberg). "I think your Mummy is looking down on you from Heaven, right now," says Corrina, trying to cheer the girl up.

"When is Mummy coming back?" the little girl asks.

"She's not coming back," Corrina has to tell her. "When you die, the angels take you up to Heaven." Later, Molly tells her father, "Don't be jealous of the angels, daddy."

Although this is basically a light-hearted film, and a vehicle for comedy actress Whoopi Goldberg, it handles the distress of a bereaved daughter sympathetically, though occasionally the comedy is intrusive at the wrong times.

But Corrina is able to help the girl come to terms with her despair: "You will always miss your mummy, and that is ok."

Jeliza Rose had an unconventional reaction to the death of her parents in the weird fantasy, *Tideland*, for she neither let it trouble her, even took advantage of it, and certainly she mistook it when it arrived. Her chocoholic sluttish mother, who hoards chocolate bars and will not share them, dies suddenly. "Don't be upset, dad," says Jeliza (played by Jodelle Ferland), "Now we can eat all the chocolate bars ourselves." Dad has been fanatical about the Vikings; his Canadian house is full of Viking paraphernalia. Not knowing what else to do, father starts wrapping his dead wife in the bed sheets to create a funeral pyre to give her a Viking send-off. He is only prevented from lighting it by his daughter who explains there may be a danger of them being trapped in the burning house.

So, father and ten-year-old daughter abandon the dead mother and flee to the Prairie wheat fields to rediscover grandma's dilapidated farmstead. Unfortunately for the girl, or fortunately (depending on how you view the poor girl's circumstances), the father dies from a drug overdose. Each time he injected himself he would tell his daughter, "Daddy's going on a vacation." So when he dies, the girl pitifully believes he is still on vacation and carries on playing around her decaying father's body, oblivious to his death. She often talks to his corpse and curls up beside him for comfort.

The strange neighbour is a taxidermist. She stuffs the dead father, preserving him like a mummy, so that father can be seated at the head of the table for mealtimes. (She does this for religious reasons: so at the time of the second coming of Jesus there will still be a body to resurrect.)

Muteness as a reaction to the Death of a Parent

Psychologists tell us that above the age of nine, grieving takes the form of mourning, crying, or becoming withdrawn, apathetic, even hostile.[25] Filmmakers have added a new trauma to the traits: that of muteness, and this is evident in several modern films.

"People don't just stop talking. These things are the result of some sort of trauma," says Nicole Kidman in *The Others* (2001), referring to the muteness of her new maid.

In *My House in Umbria*, Aimee loses both her parents in an explosion on a train while travelling across Italy. Nine-year-old Aimee is hospitalised, along with other occupants of the railway carriage, including Emily Delahunty (played by Maggie Smith). Emmy Clark plays Aimee, shocked into mute silence by her devastating trauma. When the physical injuries are healed, the surviving occupants of the railway carriage require a period of convalescence, so Senora Delahunty invites the injured to her idyllic retreat in nearby Italian Umbria.

In this wonderfully literary drama (based on William Trevor's novel), a reaction is patiently coaxed from little Aimee by the diverse characters that share her retreat. Ultimately, Aimee starts to talk again, and this lightens up the lives of the adults at the retreat: "She gave us life, and spirit, and new hope for the future."

In *A Father's Choice*, two sisters witness their mother and stepdad being murdered as they interrupt an armed robbery at their Beverley Hills home. Thirteen-year-old Kelly (Michelle Trachtenberg) screams as she hears the shots and sees her parents lying dead. Younger ten-year-old Chrissie (played by Yvonne Zima), actually witnesses the shooting. She is so horrified she cannot emit a scream, but just stands there unable to react. Throughout the film this plays on her conscience; like so many other children put in similar situations, in her emotional distress she adopts guilt feelings for not being able to react, and bottles up the experience for much of the film.

Yvonne Zima drifts around the ranch in a morose state of listlessness. She seems helpless, and robotically follows the lead of her older sister. Kelly finds too much of the responsibility for her sister is falling on her shoulders. She complains, "Chris is only ten. I don't want to take care of her. I don't want to be her mother. I'm supposed to be a kid!" Later, we discover Phoenix (Sophie Lee) having a similar rant in *Grow Your Own*.

"Is she going to come out of this?" Chrissie's father asks a counsellor.

"Yes, when she's ready. If she doesn't talk about it, then she feels she's protected from it somehow," the counsellor reassures him.

Several other films, which we refer to elsewhere in this book, also depict the victim of trauma becoming mute: Tina Majorino in *Corrina, Corrina*, Ryan Kelly in *The Dust Factory*, and Kung Sang in *Grow Your Own*.

Death of a Friend

Having a special friend is the ultimate goal for all children. When that friend is cruelly snatched away so suddenly, the shock is immense. In all the following cases, the death of a friend follows an accident; there is no enduring illness to allow the bereaved to become used to the concept of death. Yesterday, two friends were merrily playing together; today, one of them has gone. Three of the incidents are by drowning (*Bridge to Terabithia*, *Ratcatcher*, and *Down will come Baby*). In *My Girl* (1991), the boy dies from a bee sting.

Although all are accidents, the bereaved child assumes an unwarranted guilt, taking up the argument, 'if only…' In all cases, the child (and the audience) responds with sadness and tears, and the film allows us to listen in on the therapy offered to the mourning child. In *Ratcatcher*, however, the child (James) is haunted by the experience and is spooked by the thought of the dead body.

As well as providing morbid entertainment for the audience, these films have a specific purpose: that of providing consolation and therapy. As we mentioned at the start of this chapter, this was the explicit purpose of Katherine Peterson as she scripted her children's novel, *The Bridge to Terabithia*. Mrs Peterson herself was challenged to write the book following the death of her son's best friend when the boy and girl were just eight years old. At the time, she says in the preview to the film, she felt helpless and did not know how to help her young son grieve for his friend. So, she wrote this book to try to remedy the situation, in the hope that her experiences could be of value to others. The book is now used in schools both in the US and in Britain as a tool to help soften the impact of a sudden death, and also to assist in empathising with those who are suffering grief.

The film, *Bridge to Terabithia*, stars AnnaSophia Robb as Leslie, and Josh Hutcherson as Jess. In Volume Four (*Childhood Friendships*), we describe the special relationship Jess and Leslie shared in their imaginary world in the forest. Knowing Jess was keen on art, his teacher invites him to visit a gallery one weekend. As they drive past Leslie's home, he has a moment of regret: maybe she should have been invited too, "Leslie would have loved to come." But there is always tomorrow…

Arriving home later that night, dad informs the boy that Leslie has died. She drowned in the creek when the rope-swing broke. The impact on Jess is sudden and devastating. Jess blames himself for not being there to play with her. Father comforts him: "She brought you something special. That's what you hold on to. That's what keeps her alive (in your memory). She loved you. You were the best friend she ever had." Even one of his hated teachers finds a kind word for him after he misbehaves. Instead of punishing the boy, the teacher patiently shows that she understands his grief, sharing her own experience of when her husband died.

Yet the film does not finish with a weepy ending. It shows Jess rising above his grief with a "moment of transcendence" as he builds a proper wooden bridge across the creek to share his magical kingdom of Terabithia with his little sister, with Leslie's life-affirming motto blazoned across its ramparts: "Nothing crushes us."

Veda, Anna Chlumsky's character in *My Girl* (1991), has grown up surrounded by death, for her father is a funeral director. Her childhood home is above her father's funeral parlour, and there she develops the fear of contracting a fatal disease from one of the dead bodies. There is a chapel of rest next to the sitting room, and a large basement where dead bodies are prepared for funerals. She is so used to the physical presence of death, having coffins and cadavers pass through the house, she even charges other kids to come for a sneak view of a dead body. Yet for herself, she is still spooked when left alone with a dead body. For, one day her ball bounces down the cellar steps to where the dead bodies are prepared. As she goes to fetch the ball, the cellar door closes behind her, trapping her in. She has a panic attack, going berserk, until her father's assistant (Jamie Lee Curtis) rescues her. "I think she's confused about death," the assistant tells Veda's father.

It is true; widower dad has always been too busy to bother to spend time talking heart-to-heart with his daughter. Veda sees a child-sized coffin delivered to the parlour. "Why is that coffin so small?" she asks, but dad brusquely replies that it is for a small person. Veda, throughout her eleven-year-old life has had a guilt complex, thinking she killed her own mother. Mother actually died in childbirth, but no one had properly explained to the girl that what had happened was an accident, and was no one's fault.

Veda has one special friend she spends all her time playing with: Thomas J, played by Macaulay Culkin. One day they are playing in the woods when they come across a hornet's nest. Veda drops her mood ring as they run away to escape. Later, knowing it will please his friend, Thomas J goes back to retrieve the ring, but he is attacked by the hornets, and his allergy to bee stings causes his death. Father has the task of explaining to Veda about the death of her best friend. In a most moving scene, played sympathetically by Anna Chlumsky, the latent realisation of the fateful news slowly dawns on her:

"Something happened to Thomas J last night. He trod on a beehive," dad tells her.

"I told him not to tease those bees," responds the girl, bravely amused. "Maybe I should go over and yell at him."

Father explains how he had an allergy to bee stings.

"He's ok isn't he?"

It slowly dawns on the girl that her friend has gone.

Heartbroken, Veda races from the house and scrambles up the tree overhanging the lake where they used to hang out together. She stays out till late, and a search party looks for her. Fortunately, she returns home safe, and locks herself in her bedroom, obviously distraught. She only comes down on the day of the funeral. Ignoring the seated grievers, she moves to the front and weeps inconsolably over the open casket of her dead friend, until she is led away.

Later, the mother of Thomas J meets her, and they comfort each other. His mother hands Veda the mood ring that was found in the hands of the dead body. "Veda, I'd like you to have this."

"Every time I see our climbing tree, I'll think of Thomas J," weeps the girl.

"I know it's crazy," says the bereaved mother, "but sometimes I think he's just away at summer camp."

Veda reassures her. "Thomas J will be all right. My mother will take care of him," referring to her own mum who died in childbirth.

In *Ratcatcher*, William Eadie plays twelve-year-old James, a boy wracked by guilt feelings for the death of his friend who drowned in the Glasgow canal where they played, though we are never told why or how this friend died. James seeks solace by walking the canals or taking a bus ride to the wide-open spaces of an unpolluted wheat field.

Mother tells him, "James, don't go near that canal, d'ya hear me?"

The grieving dead boy's mother wants James to have a brand-new unworn pair of sandals, bought for the boy before he died. James is sent into the house to fetch the footwear. But James is haunted by the ordeal. He races into the gloomy flat, finds the shoebox, and races out as if his life depended on it, bundling over objects in the process, but avoiding the ghost of his dead friend.

Like James, Robin (Evan Rachel Wood) also has a depressingly deep feeling of guilt over the death of her friend Amelia, who, like James' friend also died by drowning. The film is *Down will come Baby*. The accident occurred during summer camp. Robin had tempted Amelia to take a moonlight swim in the lake. Amelia had told her she was not a confident swimmer, but nevertheless, Robin had persuaded her into the water with taunts of last one to swim to the platform is a silly so and so. Amelia, out of her depth, had drowned as Robin tried frantically to keep her afloat. Then Amelia slips under the water, and in a blood curdling scream of desperation by Evan Rachel Wood, Robin realises her friend has gone. Now, like so many grieving children, she morosely blames herself.

"It was my fault," she confides to her father.

"Honey, it wasn't anybody's fault," reassures dad.

"It was my idea."

"You didn't make her go in the water."

"I talked her into it."

"You did everything you could. It was a terrible accident that happened to someone you care about. It was not your fault."

Talking to a boyfriend Kevin, the girl explains how she starts crying for no reason. "I just feel like my whole life is jinxed. I just don't care about anything anymore."

And then a strange woman, Dorothy, comes into her life who seems like a skilled psychotherapist, maybe just the answer to the little girl's problems. But as we see in Volume Eight (*Physical & Sexual Abuse*), her problems are exacerbated as her relationship with the manipulative Dorothy develops.

Guilt feelings that arise as a loved one dies

This seems to be a recurring theme: the child feeling some degree of guilt for the death of (or the splitting up of) parents, and the surviving adult having to reassure the child that it was not his/her fault, when all the while the adult themselves are wrangling with their own bottled-up emotions, trying to come to terms with their own grief. This feeling of grief is universal. In the words of Susan Wallbank, *Facing Grief*, for the adult "guilt can be a way of clinging on to the idea that we are in control of everything in our world… Sometimes it is easier to feel guilt than to move on and begin to understand the full impact of what we have lost from our life forever." [26] Invariably this guilt is embodied in the mantra, 'If only…'

Yvonne Zima, playing Chrissie in *A Father's Choice*, is riddled with guilt for being an impotent bystander as she watched her mother's murder: "It's all my fault. I didn't do anything. I didn't scream. I just stood there." This is a common complex among children who only wish that somehow they could have prevented their parent's death. (Of course, there was nothing the girl could have done in the face of armed robbers.) This complex is made doubly worse when false accusations are laid against a child.

"You're so stupid, Bird. You make me sick! With your god-awful ways you made him kill himself." This must be the most heartless comment of any mother made in history. Bird's mother, in *Before Women had Wings*, is cruelly passing the blame of her own drunken failures onto her innocent, devoted, and confused daughter, played with passionate emotion by twelve-year-old

Death

Tina Majorino. After a drunken argument with his wife, leaving the woman badly bruised and toothless, Bird's father has gone off with his gun and shot himself. And now, rankled by her own guilt and failures, and resorting to the whisky bottle herself, the mother is needlessly passing the blame onto her own innocent daughter. Bird is left crying at night confused by her mother's comment, and in her sleep defiantly whimpers, "I didn't kill daddy, I didn't."

Gordie endured a similar torment from his father in *Stand by Me*. While most adults need to reassure a child that the death was not their fault, the opposite seems to be the case here. Gordie (Wil Wheaton) had idolised his older brother. But now he is dead. Yet father seems to blame Gordie, suggesting it should have been Gordie that should have died, not his brother. This accusation embitters the boy throughout the film, until at the end of the expedition with his three buddies, his stiff upper lip breaks and he finds himself weeping on the shoulder of best friend Chris (River Phoenix). "Why did Danny have to die? It should have been me. Dad said I'm no good. He hates me." Chris is unable to help except as a listening ear, a sharer of burdens.

As we have seen, Veda (Anna Chlumsky) in *My Girl* (1991) has grown up for eleven years believing she is responsible for her mother's death. It was really just a complication in childbirth that caused the death of her mother three days after she was born. But as with Dakota Fanning's character in *The Secret Life of Bees*, if a child is only given the barest elements of the circumstances, she will grow up with misconceptions and develop a guilt complex as she fills in the gaps in her own mind.

Veda is haunted by the fear that she may have killed her mother, and this has been troubling the girl as she bottled it up for the eleven years of her life. As with *Bridge to Terabithia*, it takes the tragic death of her best friend before she can vocalise her worries with her father. It is only the first time her father has shown any concern for her feelings. "Did I kill my mother?" Veda asks. Father at last can reassure her. "Things like that are not anybody's fault. It just happened."

Jess in *Bridge to Terabithia* has the same regrets when his best friend, Leslie, drowns in the creek. He blames himself for not being there to play with Leslie. Father, who like Veda's dad had given his child insufficient attention before the accident, tries to console him, "It's a terrible thing. It doesn't make any sense. But it is not your fault, Jess."

For Dakota Fanning's character, Lily Owens, in *The Secret Life of Bees* the reality that she killed her mother haunts her throughout her childhood. She was only four years old at the time. Mum and dad had been quarrelling for the final time. Mum had returned home to collect her belongings and was finally moving out. During a scuffle, a gun had been dropped. The infant Lily had picked up the gun and accidentally shot her mother. *Genova* also deals with a guilt-ridden girl coming to terms with the death of her mother, but as we discussed earlier, although this was a tragic accident, it was, like *The Secret Life of Bees*, a direct consequence of the action of the child.

"I didn't kill her. Tell me I didn't kill her," is Ingemar's secretive anguished cry in *My Life as a Dog* as he reflects on his inconsiderate behaviour while his mother was terminally ill.

In *Because of Winn-Dixie*, AnnaSophia Robb's character, Opal, asks her preacher father about the mother who left when the girl was just three. "I don't even remember what she looked like. Can't you tell me ten things about my mama," demands the little girl, "One thing for each year I've been alive?"

Father has explained to her that mother was perfect, was beautiful, had lovely blond hair and big eyes, "just like you, Opal." But mother had a drink problem.

"Did she drink because I was bad?" Opal is confused and unnecessarily guilt-ridden. "Was it my fault she left?"

"Mama loved you – she loved you very much," is the inadequate unconvincing reply.

Her preacher father is taking the service at the chapel. Opal bows her head for the prayers. She whispers under her breath her own secret prayer, "I miss my mama. Please God, I'd really like to see my mama again." But, like Jesse James in The *Amityville Horror*, her prayers go unanswered. Zac Fox in *Wah-Wah* has a similar prayer, "Please make our mummy come back again, and fix our broken family. Amen." But in this case, mum has not died but has left a disastrous marriage.

In the film *Angela (1994)*, it was neither the death nor the divorce of a parent but her mother's illness that gave Miranda Stuart Ryne guilt feelings. Mother is in and out of hospital with a psychiatric illness. Angela is just reaching an adolescent age in which her dreams of a semi-naked Lucifer appear in her room beckoning to her. Maybe this is part of her inner wickedness that is causing mother's illness! She sees anything unusual as being a sign from god, and tries different methods to help release her from sin, and thus heal Mummy.

Life After Grief: Coming to terms with and Rationalising the death of a Parent

The mourning child, as well as grieving for their parent, has invariably to face a new start in life, often with estranged relatives or foster parents, and in some instances this may involve a fresh start in another part of the world. In both *Fly Away Home* and *No Reservations*, there is a car accident, and the leading girl has to come to terms with the sudden death of the mother.

In *No Reservations*, Zoe (played by Abigail Breslin) is travelling with her single mother to visit an aunt, when the accident occurs killing the mother. The girl has to move in with auntie who becomes an instant surrogate mother to her. In *Fly Away Home*, mother too dies in a car crash (in New Zealand). Divorced father is now living in Canada, so Amy (played by Anna Paquin) has not only to contend with the sudden loss of her mother, she has to fly half way across the world to start a new life in a different country.

Initially, Amy had woken up in a hospital bed after the car crash in New Zealand. She knows something is wrong when she sees her estranged father leaning over her bed. Slowly it dawns on her, "Mum died, didn't she?" In her new home in Canada she spends a lot of time brooding in solitude, remembering her past life with mum, and trying on mum's old clothes. Anna raises goslings from a clutch of eggs, then flies with the imprinted geese down the American seaboard. Now her father tries to reassure the girl: "Your mum, she's right next to you. She's in the geese. She's in the sky. She won't let you down."

Yvonne Zima playing Chris in *A Father's Choice*, witnessed the murder of her parents in a bungled raid by burglars. Eleven-year-old Chris witnessed the whole incident and this caused the girl to clam up mute, as it did with Aimee in *My House in Umbria* and Molly in *Corrina, Corrina*. Like Anna Paquin, it was the opportunity to care for helpless animals that helped Chris come to terms with her grief. When a foaling mare develops complications, Chrissie is put in charge of the motherless foal. Slowly her perspective about life starts to change. Eventually her muteness is uncorked as she breaks down emotionally in front of her father and blurts out the circumstances of the shooting that had been bottled up inside her.

For the three girls in *Father of My Children*, uppermost in their thinking was the need to rationalise the unexpected suicide of their father, a French film producer facing bankruptcy and the liquidation of his film company. But it is not just the death they have to come to terms with; it is the bitterness that comes from reflecting on the needless waste.

Despite his success and reputation, the father takes his gun and shoots himself. The suicide may have brought finality to his own personal dilemma, yet his action left a family devastated, and they still had the same financial worries to overcome.

Obviously, the three children take it hard. For oldest sister, Clémence (Alice de Lenequesaing), she had the bittersweet pill of having to offer emotional support to her younger siblings. She also could rationalise the action of her father, and as a result, concludes his death was an unnecessary waste, and she becomes embittered towards him. "He renounced us!" she complains. "He preferred the void."

Mother tries to jivvy her up. "Don't forget how much he loved you. Draw strength from that love. Remember how good and sensitive he was. How lucky we were to have him so long. His death doesn't nullify his life."

For middle daughter, Valentine (Alice Gautier), she was really daddy's little girl. Her tearful, reflective distress was also hardened by the bitter pill. A visiting uncle tries to give her a sense of importance and self-worth. "You have to think of your mum and your sisters. They need you."

"But he didn't think of us (when he killed himself)," she objects. "Why didn't he tell us he was so sad?"

For youngest daughter, Billie (Manelle Driss) she would just look glum and reflective as the rest of the family moped around her.

In time, mother decides to make a new start by returning to her motherland, Italy. Clémence is further distressed that there is no time to visit father's grave, though they are encouraged to find other ways to remember their father. "Dad will live on through his films," they decide, and Valentine adds, "Not just through his films, through us!"

Abigail Breslin seems to encounter so many dead relatives in her various film roles that maybe the FBI should be alerted! Her resolution to provide no more bone marrow for her ailing sibling in *My Sister's Keeper* results in her sister's death. Then her mother dies in the car crash in which Abigail was the passenger in *No Reservations*. Next in *Little Miss Sunshine* Grandfather is travelling with her to the pageant in California. Sharing the same motel room as her grandfather, Olive (Abigail Breslin) alerts her parents, "Grandpa won't wake up."

Later, she asks, "Mum, is grandpa dead?"

"Yes Honey, he passed away."

This for a seven-year-old girl is a very ambiguous comment. It was the phraseology I was given at the age of eleven when my grandmother died, and it took a long while until I became sure what 'passed away' actually meant. "Is Durga asleep?" asks Subir Banerji in *Pather Panchali*. The affirmative is the most convenient reply for a grieving mother to give to her infant son.

But Olive did not let grandpa's death thwart her ambition, for the show must go on, and the family have a beauty pageant to get to. After drying her eyes, she is able to prance on the stage, dedicating her performance to her grandpa ("He's in the boot of the car," she tells the audience). Then we see the dance the sex-crazed grandpa had secretly taught the little girl. Muffled protests grow louder among the prim and proper audience as this seven-year-old begins her striptease act.

Taking on the burdens of responsibility when adult carers can't cope

In most cases, the child has a parent or guardian who can steer them through the grieving process. But as we considered in *Genova*, the surviving parent will be equally traumatised. And as Bert (Dick Van Dyke) says to Michael and Jane in *Mary Poppins*, "Who does your father turn to when he is sad?"

In the exceptional film, *Grow Your Own*, it is the father who is severely traumatised following the death of his wife. Kung Sang is a refugee from China. He had smuggled his two children and his wife in a container, along with a number of other immigrants all of whom were crushed together for weeks while being transported from the Far East to the United Kingdom. Kung Sang witnessed his wife getting gradually weaker. After she died, the family had to stay with her decaying body for several days, trapped together in the container. Just like the children we referred to in *A Father's Choice*, *My House in Umbria*, and *Corrina, Corrina*, so too the adult Kung Sang was left mute as a result of his trauma. His two children, Phoenix (Sophie Lee) and her younger brother, Dragon, seemed more able to cope with the trauma, perhaps because they have to take responsibility for their now impotent father.

"You seem strong," the welfare officer says to Phoenix.

"Well, someone has to be," Phoenix replies.

"People have tried all sorts of things to get through to your dad."

"Can't you just give him a tablet or something... to make him like he used to be!"

"When a man is completely broken you have to put him together again bit by bit."

The family is allocated an allotment plot as a form of therapy and there the children help the father grow some crops, in particular, some squash seeds that the man has carried over from China. There is a container in the allotment grounds. Because it reminds him of the tragedy with his wife, he always steers clear of it.

In time, the girl becomes exasperated by having to look after her father as well as her younger brother and herself. Coming home from school one day and finding no food in the house the girl complains: "I'm not the cook. I'm not your mum. I'm not your secretary. I'm not your servant." And with bewilderment and hopelessness in her eyes she echoes the words of Michelle Trachtenberg in *A Father's Choice*, "I'm just a little girl."

In *Nobody Knows*, mother has abandoned her Japanese family of four children so they have to cope by themselves. The youngest girl dies following a fall, though at first they are not sure of the difference between being unconscious and dead. The family is in such a trying situation – there is no food or water and their money has run out, and their secret apartment is now a stinking disgrace – they have no opportunity to grieve. As with *The Cement Garden*, if they report the death to the authorities the family will be split up and taken into care. When they realise their sister won't recover – "Her body felt so cold this morning," – they squeeze the tiny body into a suitcase along with her favourite squeaky shoes and bury it in sight of the airport, fulfilling a promise they had made to the little girl, to take her to see the aeroplanes.

The Afterlife

Besides missing loved ones who have passed away, the main characters, Ryan and Melanie, in *The Dust Factory* have also themselves died, or at least have been through a near-death experience, visiting a strange sort of transit land of their unconscious mind half way between Earth and Heaven. The film tries to emulate the great classics, such as *A Matter of Life and Death*, in which a premature death creates a problem for St Peter and the Archangels. At least these films allow us a hope of an afterlife, more than just being "dead and buried" which was the extent of the children's belief in *The Blue Lagoon*, and transports us beyond the thoughts of Marie (Pauline Acquart) in *Water Lilies*, "The ceiling is the last thing most people see when they die," she observes, it being imprinted on dead people's eyelids for eternity!

Teenager Ryan Kelley has a succession of deaths to confront in *The Dust Factory*. He is still affected by the death of his father. Ryan has literally been left speechless after the trauma of watching a train plough into father's car after it had stuck on the railway track. That was some years back. Then there was the death of his grandfather. Now Ryan is standing in an endless line of relatives waiting to toss soil on grandmother's coffin. When it is Ryan's turn, he cannot face it, spilling the soil on the grass. "Tossing the dirt – that was too final," he thinks.

Now the boy feels he has nothing to live for as he moodily contemplates his memories. His friend offers to take him fishing to lift him out of his trance. But there is an accident. Ryan falls into the lake and drowns. As he swims out for the shore, he discovers he is in a different world, a sort of mystical half paradise, en-route to the afterlife. Here, he meets up with his grandfather who is also in this halfway house. Suddenly, flitting into the movie dances Melanie (Hayden Panettiere), a delightfully natural, happy, chirpy girl. Melanie has also had an accident, a near-death experience – an aneurysm on her brain. Melanie and Ryan bond and a romance blossoms.

The central focus of this world is the Dust Factory, a circus marquee on top of the hill. It is here where visitors are sorted into those who return to Earth to recover from their illness, and those who progress onto 'Paradise'.

The only way to return to Earth is to plunge off the trapeze into the dust, leading to a portal back to the real world. But this will hurt like the pain that has brought them to this world. "You're afraid of a little pain?" comments Grandfather. "That's an overrated phobia."

After weird adventures, Ryan and Melanie make it through the portal, recover and meet together back in the real world, but without any recollection of their near-death experience. But at least Ryan has been cured of his dumbness.

The curious incidents in *The Dust Factory*, suggesting a belief in a halfway stage to Heaven, a parallel universe after death, can be shared with the occultist aspirations expounded in *Photographing Fairies*, and the transient staging post for Saoirse Ronan in *The Lovely Bones* ("Susie's in the *in between*," states her fearful younger brother). The great detective, Conan Doyle, himself was keen on learning about afterlife, and once he had learnt of the possible existence of fairies was keen to pursue occult beliefs through the medium of spiritualism.

The Yorkshire folk-tale of the Cottingley Fairies provided a spur to his searches, as it did for photographer, Charles Castle, who was seeking a psychic link to his own dead wife, stolen from him by an accident on a Swiss glacier on his wedding night. Two films were made based on the Cottingley Fairies: *Fairy Tale* (1997) geared at younger viewers; and *Photographing Fairies*, which delves more quizzically into the mystical apparitions. That the whole episode was kick-started by two girls who had taken fake photographs of the cut-out fairy shapes they had made, made no difference to the deluded endeavours of these respectable academics who were seeking a higher meaning of life following the carnage of the First World War. Sir Arthur Conan Doyle is told, "Heaven is not a physical place. It is a spiritual condition we can aspire to – no more than that." And yet the great detective had seen the fake photographs of the fairies and was convinced, like Charles Castle, that they were genuine.

Thinking the occult and spiritualism may have some clues about the afterlife, Castle has sped by train from London to Yorkshire to investigate the possibility of fairies which could provide him with a link to his own sorely missed bride. He has been told that fairies are "exiles from Heaven, God's orphans, straddling this world and the next." This is where he has encountered the two girls who took the fairy photographs, seven-year-old Clara, played by Hannah Bould, and ten-year-old Ana played by Miriam Grant. The world that he discovers, once the children have allowed him to feed on the hallucinatory blossoms, is one of slow motion, one in which the effects of the drug tempt its consumers to scale the branches of the tree either to share the heights with the illusive fairies, or send him crashing to the ground in an unconscious stupor.

For Saoirse Ronan playing fourteen-year-old Susie Salmon in *The Lovely Bones*, a film in which she has been murdered by a neighbouring paedophile, the afterlife is a brightly-lit exhilarating and beautiful wonderland of exotic landscapes which merge into the inescapable nightmare of floundering through swampland in which nothing remains fixed for any length of time.

"I have to go home," says Susie in despair, feeling a need to return to Earth to inform father who the murderer is. But always she is thwarted by the ever-shifting scenes of Heaven. She does succeed in a limited way. Her sleepy little brother walks into his father's bedroom: "I just saw Susie. She came into my room. She kissed me on the cheek." On another occasion, her ghostly face appears in a window.

But, as in *The Dust Factory*, this first Heaven is a staging post, a place where the struggle between life and death is fought and lost. "You can't go back," Clarissa, her dead companion, tells her. "You have to let go of Earth. You are dead, Susie. You have to leave."

Her final release is made as the paedophile topples over the edge of a cliff. (What we are not shown is how she copes sharing eternity with her earthly killer.)

For some, the afterlife is a goal, a reward for a lifetime's achievements (and sacrifices), an eternal armchair for resting weary souls. It is filled with the spirits of the faithful. For others, those spirits are to be feared, as death is to be feared, with its accompanying baggage of ghosts and ghouls. It was the fear of an encounter with the ghost of his dead friend that causes James to flee so rapidly from the house in *Ratcatcher*. Yet for Harvey Keitel in the 1988 movie *Shadrach*, "Death ain't nothing to be afraid of. It's life that is fearsome."

Shadrach is a ninety-nine-year-old Negro, a former slave, who has returned to the farmstead on which he was raised as a child. After a long life of hardship and abuse he has returned to rediscover his childhood innocence – the only time in his life he had ever really been free. The dying man whispers in the ears of twelve-year-old Monica Bugajski and ten-year-old Scott Terra he has come back here to die and to be buried on the farm of his birth.

The problem is, this is 1920s Virginia, when racial segregation was heavily enforced. Negroes could not sit with the whites in the cinema, they had to have their own churches, and they could not use the toilets that were for whites only. The children even wondered if blacks had their own separate Heaven! The sheriff comes to visit. He tells them they cannot bury the man on the farm. A black undertaker has to be found, and a plot in a Negro cemetery purchased.

When Shadrach dies, a startled Monica Bugajski describes what happened. She was holding the old man's hand, when suddenly it fell limp, his head rolled back and he stopped breathing. That night, the children would not sleep in the house where the dead body was stored, prompting the reassurance from the father.

Harvey Keitel (the father) has to resort to a piece of duping. He fills the casket with earth, and then sends the coffin off to be buried in a Negro cemetery to fool the sheriff. Meanwhile, they dig a secret grave on the farm where Shadrach's dead body is placed, thus fulfilling the old man's wishes.

When death is of no concern

The death of someone close to them should be a sad time for a child. But for those children who have had a poor relationship with their seniors, the death may be a release for them. This was the situation for six-year-old Laura Vaquero playing Amy in *Alas de Mariposa*. Her grandfather had rejected her at birth because she was not the longed-for grandson. There was never any fondness between them. Whenever Amy drew a picture of her family, the live-in grandfather was always omitted. So, when Grandfather died, Ami had no tears to shed for him, and took no flowers to put on his grave.

Natalie Portman showed what could be considered disrespectful unconcern over the death of her parents in the violent thriller, *Leon*. Here is a girl who has lost all her family, but her only real distress is over the death of her infant brother. Her parents were killed during a drugs raid on her family's apartment by the New York police, led by a corrupt cop, Stansfield (Gary Oldman). Mathilda (Natalie Portman) is sitting on the banisters when the police raid begins, and all her family are shot dead. Yet she had no respect for her parents, so was not distressed when she discovered their bodies. "If someone else didn't do it someday, I probably would have done it myself," she reflects (a sentiment shared by Dakota Fanning in *Hounddog*). Likewise, she was always squabbling with her older sister. When she discovers her sister's dead body, she flippantly remarks, "She wanted to lose weight, anyway. In fact she never looked better!"

For others, the death of a parent rapidly becomes a distant memory. In *The Cement Garden*, the younger sister, Sue (Alice Coulthard), keeps a diary. Jack (Andrew Robertson) says to her, "I wish you would let me read those bits you have written about mum."

"Dear mum," she reads, "You have been dead for twenty-one days. No one mentioned you today." And they realise they are starting to forget mother already, and the grief is evaporating.

Julie (Charlotte Gainsbourg) confides, "I can't remember how it used to be when mum was alive."

Lewis McGibbon found he could exploit his mother's death. By entering shops and announcing "our mum's dead", he found himself plied with free sweets, a situation he and his younger brother (Alex Etel) used to their advantage in *Millions* (2004).

In other films, it is the callousness of unconcerned adults that further distresses the child. Evil schoolteacher, Mr Squeers, cruelly tells *Nicholas Nickleby* of the death of his mother while cramming his own face with cake. Equally as cruel and uncaring is the owner of the geisha house in *Memoirs of a Geisha*. Chiyo (Suzuka Ohgo) had been sold by her parents as a nine-year-old to train as a geisha girl, so when her 'owner' read to her the official letters telling of the deaths of her parents she seemed justifiably unconcerned. But the letter was read to the girl as a punishment.

At least Mr Poe, in *Lemony Snicket's A Series of Unfortunate Events*, was more civil when confronting the Baudelaire children. "Children, I'm afraid I must inform you of an extremely unfortunate event – your parents have perished in a fire that has destroyed your entire home." The children are farmed out to a succession of greedy relatives, keen to get their hands on the Baudelaire inheritance. Uncle Olaf rubs his hands with glee. "Why are you so glum, children?" he asks. But the children put him in his place. "Our parents just died!"

Miss Minchin also seems to rub her hands with glee, though she does not do so in front of the child in *A Little Princess*. Sara Crewe's father has just been (supposedly) killed in battle in 1914 and the greedy headmistress of *Miss Minchin's Seminary for Girls* has dismissed all the other girls off to bed and sent sister Amelia to fetch a black dress, by way of indicating the nature of the bad news she is about to give to the little girl.

"Why do I need a black dress, Miss Minchin?" asks Sara (Liesel Matthews).

The headmistress takes all of Sara's personal belongings using them to pay off unpaid fees and reduces the girl to the role of a servant girl who has to earn her room and board. "Don't you understand what I am saying? You are alone in the world!"

It is regrettable that in today's computerised world of twenty-four hour news, children become blasé as they are surrounded by stories of death. For them, every day is a playful routine of annihilating the enemy on video games. The child lives in a world of blood, gore, and violence. These have removed the child from the emotional realism and horror of tragedy. Susan Wallbank sees this as a positive attribute: 'It is through such games that they (children) are able to explore the complexity of the world about them and gradually learn how to deal with it.' [27]

The medium of the movie is maybe the best introduction for any child to the concept and heartbreak of death – a gently immersion into the theory without needing to live out the emotional turmoil. And perhaps the child actor experiencing the pretence of death on the stage is best placed of all to accept its horrifying finality when it arrives.

THE IMPACT OF WAR

If a film is depicting warfare, I'd like to ask whether it is highlighting the evil of war, its necessity, or glorifying it; is the child actor made to be complicit in the perpetuation of war as an ideal, or is he/she there to show up the inadequacy of war as a means of resolving the world's wounds? The child is usually portrayed as innocent, a victim caught up in the horrors of war (Dakota Fanning in *The War of the Worlds*), sometimes he/she may have a heroic act to perform (Jane Withers in *The North Star*), but the questionable indoctrination of warfare as a productive means of solving problems succeeds when the actor and audience becomes blasé or even excited over the concept of killing to achieve goals.

This glorification of war is seen at its gut-retching worst in *Johnny Mad Dog*. Like *kids* (1995) and *Audition*, *Johnny Mad Dog* becomes very uncomfortable to watch. This is not entertainment. If by watching it we confront a realistic picture of the life of child soldiers caught up in African guerilla warfare then it has done its job but this is a hell I would not wish on anyone.

Yet no boy-child touting his replica toy colt or water canon, whose whole existence seems to be play-acting as a war hero, is immune from the buzz and drama absorbed from generations of yarns about Custer, Wellington, Douglas Baden or even Private Ryan.

This was certainly the case in *Empire of the Sun*. Here we find James (Christian Bale) fascinated by the Japanese aircraft and pilots, occupiers of China where he was living as an expat. He was so impressed by the honourable kamikaze pilots, the boy salutes them as they partake in their final ceremony before embarking on suicidal missions. But he also experiences first hand the horrors of warfare. He proudly iterates the day's new word '*Atom Bomb*' – "It was like God taking a photograph."

Ronnie (Alistair Haley) also had a feverish fascination for the perversion of war in Pied Piper, as did Asa Butterfield who stretches his arms as a Luftwaffe pilot believing he is careering above the rooftops of Berlin using his two-fingered gun to assail the imaginary enemy in *The Boy in the Striped Pyjamas*. Then there is Billy (Sebastian Rice Edwards) in *Hope and Glory* who complains to his mother as he and his little sister embark for Australia. "We're going to miss this war and it's all your fault."

Hope and Glory is a film that seems to relish the fun of playing in bombsites, in the camaraderie and excitement of watching the blitz, all written through the autobiographical eyes of director, John Boorman, who himself had lived through the horrors as a child, without being burdened by adult responsibilities. Even when his family's house caught fire, it was a problem for one night only – they can go live on granddad's island in the River Thames, instead. Mum had seemed more concerned about the loss of her ration coupons that would take months to replace, rather than the loss of the family home.

There is a distinct gender bias in the mentality of childhood, particularly in play. It is invariably the boys who dream of guns, cowboys and Indians, and the violence of war games. The closest a girl might get, is to sit down to a board game of Risk or Diplomacy, though Hayley Mills bucks this trend in *Tiger Bay*, when she gets her hands on a real gun enabling her to join in the boys' war games. Yet, in *Hope and Glory* it was the older sister who persuaded Billy to stop hiding under the stairs during the air raid and come watch the tracer fire and explosions amidst a hail of shrapnel. For her, the fireworks from the dogfights added to the buzz of war. What caused this fifteen-year-old more distress than the bombed-out streets, was her Canadian soldier boyfriend (whose baby she is carrying) being sent away on a secret mission. Likewise, caught up in the propaganda of war, Amber Beattie as twelve-year-old Gretel, in *The Boy in the Striped Pyjamas*, decides it is time to relegate her dolls to the basement and plaster her bedroom wall with posters of the Hitler Youth instead.

Vulnerable Refugees

Invariably the child is the victim, trapped in the midst of advancing enemy troops, and has to be protected or rescued. This is the typical pattern whether it is orphaned kids escaping danger in *The Inn of the Sixth Happiness*, children being marched to safety in *Pied Piper*, driven in *The Sound of Music*, ferried in *Father Goose*, or trying to evade capture by aliens in *The War of the Worlds*.

Mr Howard (Peter O'Toole) had only gone to France for a few days of quiet fishing when he finds he is caught up in the German advance towards Paris at the outbreak of the Second World War. He reluctantly becomes the *Pied Piper* leading a small party of children across France, in this made-for-TV drama based on the novel by Nevil Shute.[28] At the hotel where he is staying are the two Cavanaugh children, Sheila (a confident and eloquent Clare Drummond) and her brother, Ronnie (Alastair Haley). Their parents insist Mr Howard help evacuate the children to England before the Germans arrive. He objects: "It's out of the question. I have a weak heart. It would be safer if you sent the children with someone more robust."

"Surely you could put up with two children for just twenty-four hours," the woman pleads. Despite his protests, he finds he has boarded the crowded train for Dijon with the two charges. The boy constantly hassles Mr Howard, asking him questions about how his son died in the war as a fighter pilot, and intrigued by the military manoeuvres going on around him: the aeroplanes, tanks and explosions. Throughout the journey, the boy asks annoying questions such as "Are those dead bodies?" and "What is it like to feel pain?"

Mr Howard rebukes him: "Ronnie, you have a perverse notion of war."

The journey is fraught with difficulty. Trains are cancelled. The bus they catch is overcrowded and eventually breaks down. Sheila becomes sick (scarlet fever suggests one of the passengers). Fuel and food are both hard to come by, and the arrival of the German troops adds to their problems. Resorting to walking with hundreds of other refugees, they come under attack from German bombers maiming and killing indiscriminately. Finding a boy, Pierre, traumatised by the dead bodies of his parents, they realise "We can't leave him here to bury his parents." Another refugee boy is being abused by villagers, who accuse the boy of being a German. Mr Howard and his party rescue him, only to find he is a Dutch lad.

Every time they hear an explosion, the children grimace with fear, leading Peter O'Toole to cry in despair, "Bloody War!" In the end, the children inadvertently betray Mr Howard as they talk together in English in front of a German officer, and he is arrested as a British spy.

With *The Inn of the Sixth Happiness*, Ingrid Bergman plays Gladys Aylward, a real-life missionary who, in the 1930s, found her way to China under her own steam, because the *China Missionary Society* didn't believe her to be qualified enough. This doggedly determined woman gained the trust of the Chinese peasantry due to her caring concern for their welfare and they fondly called her *Jen-I*, the lover of people.[29 & 30]

When the Japanese forces invade China, their town of Yang Cheng is bombed, and Gladys is left as 'mother' to fifty displaced or orphaned children. Their only chance of safety is a one-week march over the mountains to Sian. Just as they are departing, another mission sends a further fifty children to her, so now she has a hundred children to escort on the difficult march. "Be brave," Ingrid Bergman exhorts the children. They soon run out of food, the children complain of being hungry, tired and having sore feet. Villages where they had expected to supplement their rations had been bombed out. They make detours to evade Japanese troops, and only avert capture by one of the aids sacrificing his life by acting as decoy to distract some enemy soldiers. After three weeks, they finally tramp wearily into safety, making a true heroine out of the humble 'small' woman from Liverpool.[31]

Another group who have to make it over the mountains to safely evade the pursuing Nazis are the Von Trapp family in the enduringly sumptuous *Sound of Music*. Father has been called up to serve in the Nazi navy. This is against his loyal Austrian principles, so he has no choice but to escape with his family of seven children after their musical rendition at the Salzburg Folk Festival. First, they hide among the tombs at the convent where the children's new mother, Maria (Julie Andrews), had trained as a nun. As they freeze rigid in their hideout with gun-toting German soldiers nearby, youngest girl, Gretl, asks, "Mother, would it help if we sang about our favourite things?" Their escape bid is helped by the 'wickedness' of the nuns who remove the distributor caps from the vehicles of the Nazi army. This enables them to escape to the frontier and 'climb every mountain'.

In *Father Goose*, a group of seven expatriate schoolchildren are picked up with their teacher by Cary Grant and taken to 'safety' in an overloaded rowing boat to a neighbouring island near New Guinea during the Second World War. The children are occasionally bombed by Japanese warplanes but the film never actually focuses on the fear and deprivation impacted on the children. Rather, this is a comedy dealing with the amusing interaction between an American 'beach bum' trying to shirk his wartime duties, and a staid school maam supervising a group of prim and proper boarding schoolgirls – daughters of diplomats.

Fairy Tale (1997) is set in 1917 near the end of World War One. Injured soldiers are returning home from war on the continent of Europe. Others are de-mobbing to return to their loved ones. Not so for Frances Griffiths (Elizabeth Earl). Her father is missing in action in France, presumed dead. "She must be terrified," assumes her cousin awaiting her arrival in Yorkshire. "Travelling all the way up Africa by herself." But Frances has befriended the soldiers on the train, even getting one man with a badly disfigured face to help her play her cat's cradle string game. "My dad is a soldier like you, and he's in France," she says, still living in hope. When a few weeks later a package with French perfume arrives this reassures her, but secretly her Aunt Polly dismisses it: "These packages can be delayed by months," (implying the girl's father must be dead). But when one evening months later a car pulls up outside the house and a door slams, Frances has a premonition and knows exactly what this means, races down the stairs into the enfolding arms of the man waiting there: "It's my daddy! It's my daddy!"

We witness an equally provoking reunion at the end of *Empire of the Sun* as Christian Bale clenches his arms around his mother as if they could never be prised apart again. The twelve-year-old boy is playing Jamie, a British expatriate schoolboy living in Shanghai in 1941 at the time of the Japanese occupation of China. He is mollycoddled, affluent and has a small army of Chinese servants to help raise him. The boy is curious about war, playing with a toy airplane. "I was thinking of joining the Japanese airforce, says the expat Brit flippantly to his father. The boy is unaffected by the cruelty of war, cocooned in the Rolls Royce as he is ferried around the streets crowded with desperate hounded locals. Traffic police even whip any bystanders who find themselves in the path of these 'honourable' westerners.

Things change after Pearl Harbour. American and Brits have to leave, their homes requisitioned by the Imperial Japanese Army. Fleeing from their vehicle that is about to be squashed flat by an advancing tank, Jamie and his family are caught up in the bustling crowd of fleeing refugees. It was only one second of negligence. Jamie had stopped to pick up his toy aeroplane, and in that moment is separated from his parents caught up in the dense current of terrified civilians. Now isolated from his family, he seeks protection by other means. His surrendering to the Japanese invaders is humorously pathetic as they just ignore him as an inconsequential inconvenience.

Jamie breaks back into his villa where he stays until supplies run out. He hits the streets again, but eventually submits to a concentration camp. Even here, the boy's spirit is not broken as his survival instincts take over, despite living on starvation rations of a potato a day. He survives by being a runner, trading and exchanging cabbages/cigarettes/shoes. He even collects weevils until he has a spoonful to shovel into his mouth. All around him, fellow prisoners are either sick and dying or being brutalised by the guards. Yet despite the suffering, the boy remains enterprising and exuberant, admiring the courage of the Japanese.

As we witness his crazed attempt to resuscitate his young friend crying, "I can bring anyone back," we realise his fight for survival has turned him into a crazed feral who thinks he is invincible. When the Americans finally arrive on a bombing raid, we cannot be sure whether the boy is joyful at the reprieve this brings or whether he is relishing in the power of the gunfire and destruction.

In *Peck on the Cheek (Kannathil Mutthamittal)*, we find a child caught up in a war zone as she seeks to satisfy her curiosity about her mother. This is an effective movie in which director Mani Rahman deliberately sets out to highlight the on-going crisis in the Tamil districts of Sri Lanka in the hope his film might in some way encourage peace talks between the warring factions. Civil war is raging in northern Sri Lanka as the Tamil guerrillas fight for a homeland.

Keerthana plays nine-year-old Amudha, living a carefree life in India. When she learns she has been adopted, the child of a Tamil refugee, she gives her parents no peace until she has a chance to meet her birth mother. This involves a trip to Sri Lanka, but the parents are not aware they have to travel into the war zone in the north. Amudha wanders the street alone and starts up a conversation with a disabled man in a wheelchair. But he turns out to be a suicide bomber. As soon as a military convoy passes by, the man blows himself up and Amudha is hurt by the flying glass. The poor girl is freaked out. "I'm scared to close my eyes," she tells her father. "I keep hearing the blast."

As they travel further into the military areas, they are caught up in army bombing raids. Amudha comes across child soldiers in the jungle, father is beaten up by guerrillas, and they become trapped in the middle of a gun battle between the army and the insurgents.

The battle being fought in *The War of the Worlds* is an invasion by the Martians. HG Wells, in his classic novel, writes in 1898 about the Martian attack on London and the Home Counties. Orson Welles serialised this as a radio play. This play created genuine alarm as it was broadcast in the early twentieth century, because some of the listening public believed the invasion to be real.

The play was followed by two movies, which transferred the action to America. The 2005 film focuses on the devastation of New York.

The Martians had buried pods beneath the Earth's surface thousands of years ago (evidently!), where they lay dormant, choosing only to explode to the surface on just the weekend that divorced Tom Cruise is lumbered with looking after his two kids (Dakota Fanning and Justin Chatwin).

The first half of Steven Spielberg's film is gripping with brilliant effects of lightning bolts, pavements being lifted, flyovers collapsing, crashes, and all three characters being suitably terrified. Just as the action seems to ease off, all hell is let loose. For Tom Cruise and his kids, escape seems impossible.

The father's only concern is to get his two children to safety by driving out of New York city, travelling parallel with the Hudson River to find a bridge or ferry that could take them east to where mother was staying with the grandparents. Not only has father to battle against the Martians, he has to keep his grown-up son in check who insists on joining the battle. All father can do is entreat his son to think of his ten-year-old sister who is scared out of her wits.

Ethnic Cleansing

The United Nations was set up at the end of the Second World War in the hope that the cruel concept of eliminating a race of people would never happen again. But the relocation of the surviving Jews to a homeland in The Levant has only resulted in prolonged bitterness in Judaeo-Arabic relations. The Jewish holocaust was a criminal tragedy of such magnitude that seventy years later it is still impossible to take in the horrors. Regrettably, this incredulity of man's inhumanity has been exploited by those who have mistranslated disbelief in the atrocities into actual denial of the holocaust.

Alas, the Second World War was not the war to end all wars, and the past half century has seen the holocaust repeated over and over again as in different parts of the world races have been decimated: Marsh Arabs and Kurds in Iraq, Tutsis and Hutus in Rwanda, Bosnians in former Yugoslavia.

The Diary of Anne Frank is on the required reading list of every teenage school kid, the moving record of the daily drudgery of one thirteen-year-old Dutch Jewess forced into hiding in a cold cramped attic with her sister, parents, and two other families. At first, her regrets seem trivial: she cannot go to the movies, travel on the streetcar, or ride her bike. She had to leave her school friends and endure the indignity of wearing a yellow star. Twenty-one-year-old Millie Perkins plays the teenaged Anne in the 1959 film version, while in the made-for-TV serial (2008) the part is played by Ellie Kendrick.

Life soon turns stressful as strong-willed individuals live together in such close proximity in which animosity and resentments disrupt any hint of conviviality. Their's is a daily routine of lying silently, motionless, taking no footsteps, feeding on watery kale and potatoes, living in fear every time a police siren passes lest this is their turn to be carted off to concentration camp. The bombing raids provide mixed hope, but the families are sitting targets in their rooftop hideout. Occasionally, their spirits are raised as there is good news on the crackly radio, or a tray of strawberries arrives. Although they are secretly locked-in behind a bookcase, Anne's father, Otto

Frank, assures her "There are no doors, no bolts that anyone can put on your mind," and this encourages the girl to record all her experiences and thoughts. "No one will be interested in the musings of a thirteen-year-old schoolgirl," thinks Anne.

Steven Spielberg helps refocus on the Jewish ordeal in the project he felt he had a duty to record "in memory of more than six million murdered Jews" – *Schindler's List*. The awful cruelty of the Nazi regime is depicted as Polish Jews are summoned to leave their affluent country abodes and dwell in the oppressive confines of the Krakow Ghetto. With tens of thousands of Jews arriving, inhuman ill-treatment ensues as the refugees are forced into slave labour and eventually to the 'final solution' in the Auschwitz death camp.

Into this scene of degradation comes Oskar Schindler, a German industrial entrepreneur who at first uncaringly exploits this readily available workforce as a way of boosting his own affluence. He notices how all the academic Jews are being rejected for the Nazi work parties, so he saves them from annihilation by putting them to work as skilled labourers in his own factories (his initial motive is that Jewish labour is cheaper than Polish). With a piece of ironic foresight he lies in bed with his wife thinking up his own epitaph, an epitaph that ultimately comes true: "*Oskar Schindler. Everyone remembers him. He did something extraordinary. He came here with nothing and built a bankrupt factory into a major manufacturing industry.*" But he is remembered for something far, far more honourable.

At first, when the Nazis interfere with his work-targets by purloining his labour force to shift snow or assign them for transportation to Auschwitz, his annoyance is more related to the loss of production rather than the welfare of his labourers. But in time, he becomes attuned to their plight and their own humanity. His change of heart comes as he witnesses the sickening indiscriminate slaughter and mistreatment of the Jews with the arrival of a new Nazi administrator, Amon Goeth (Ralph Fiennes). Till now, he has blandly seen the Jews in black and white, but now one little girl comes into his vision wearing a red coat, and the first flicker of humanity colours his own soul. From now on, he becomes the defender of his Jewish workforce, a task he has to perform with delicate tact mixed with audacity. In a factory across the border in Czechoslovakia, Schindler is able to provide a safe haven of retreat for a community of eleven hundred Jews until the end of the war.[32]

Eight-year-old Bruno (Asa Butterfield) in *The Boy in the Striped Pyjamas* confronts the stark horrors of the Holocaust, but in his childish naivety at first assumes the concentration camp's fenced-off compound to be a farm.

Bruno and his twelve-year-old sister Gretel (Amber Beattie) are the children of a German officer living in Berlin during World War Two. Father is transferred to the countryside to run a concentration camp for Jews, and so the whole family relocates. The real function of the camp – the extermination of the Jews – is kept hidden from the children, and even from their mother. Bruno's conceptions are further misconstrued by the propaganda film his father has commissioned depicting the prison as a holiday camp. But when Bruno sneaks out to the wire fence for his daily meeting with Schmuel (Jack Scanlon) his confusion is compounded. Eight-year-old Schmuel, dressed in striped concentration camp clothing is unwilling to play the ballgames over the barbed wire fence. Like a feral animal, he gobbles up any piece of food Bruno brings him. "I'm a Jew," explains Schmuel but Bruno still cannot work it out. And why did the Jewish doctor working in their kitchen give up his practice to peel spuds all day?

Even when Bruno digs under the fence into the camp, the boy is still ignorant of the truth. He is too respectful of his own father to consider the possibility he has been misled. Alas,

Bruno's entry into the camp coincides with a round up of the next contingent of Jews, and the two boys are herded with the other men into the dank confines of the gas chamber. Only too late does it dawn on his father where his missing son could possibly have gone.

Lena My 100 Children focuses our attention on the dilemma of Jewish refugees in the aftermath of the World War Two, highlighting ongoing Semitic enmity. This is based on the true story of Lena Kuchler-Silberman, a Polish Jew who survived the war by pretending to be a Catholic. "There is no sin or shame in surviving," she justifies herself. She is living in Krakow. The Germans have already decimated their country, and now the liberated Polish citizens are creating civil unrest as they rebel against those they consider the catalyst of the war: the Jews.

Lena is passing the Refugee Agency when she spots four child orphans resting helplessly against the wall. She persuades them to follow her into the Agency where she had intended to reprimand the agents for being unconcerned about the refugee problem. But she is overwhelmed by what confronts her as she enters the building – a heaving crowd of homeless despondent refugees, all dirty and starving – and with inadequately few staff to assist them. Upstairs is a whole storey filled with dozens of zombie-like children, all hungry and without hope. "The children have no one," she realises, as she is told the Polish orphanages will not take Jewish children.

She returns the next day with enough bread to feed all the children. Her first task is to bathe the dirty kids. This is how she comes across 'Anna' who is reluctant to be undressed because 'Anna' is actually a boy wearing girl's clothes. Lena is told, "If you are a boy, the Germans can tell if you're a Jew by pulling down your pants." The circumcised boys would have been shipped off to Auschwitz. So for 'Anna', it was advantageous to masquerade as a girl.

Before long, the Refugee Agency is attacked by a mob, so Lena arranges a nighttime escape for all the children to a country retreat at Zakopanem, in the mountains. These are Jews who survived the concentration camps, who lived for years in holes and attics with no light and no human warmth, and now here, in Zakopanem, the children can breathe and recuperate, and each has their own bed with sweet-smelling sheets. But their security is short-lived. Lena tries to get the children incorporated into the local school, but there is resentment and opposition, not just by the students, but by the prejudiced teachers as well. The Headmaster tries to resolve matters with his speech: "It is time to stop being ruled by hatred. It is time to stop this obsolete backwardness." But his exhortations fall on deaf ears.

At least a local doctor can be persuaded to attend to their medical needs – though he only does so under threat. Yet, when the refugee children see the injection needles they are terrified, for they are aware of needles being used in the concentration camps as part of the 'ultimate solution'.

In time, roving mercenaries learn of the refugees' hideout. In the dead of night, they arrive on horseback to attack the Jewish children. But the refugees have been forewarned and provided with machine guns, which the older children are happy to wield to defend themselves.

Lena realises their only hope is to leave Poland to escape to Palestine and help set up the new Jewish state. So, in the early dawn, the party of children are led through the forests towards the Czechoslovak border, often hiding among the trees to evade the pursuing mercenaries, just as Gladys Aylward had to do in China with her convoy of kids in *The Inn of the Sixth Happiness*. Border guards have to be bribed. "Shoot us right here at the border," says one of the older boys to the border guard, "But we won't go back to the place where our parents were killed." A train shunts its way to France where they spend two years waiting until finally, in 1948, they arrive in the Promised Land.

Resistance Fighters

Others are able to stand up for their principles in heroic acts against the opposing forces. *The North Star* is a black and white movie, a propaganda film brought out by the Americans in 1943 when the Second World War was raging in Europe. Two years earlier, the German army was bulldozing its way through Eastern Europe towards the Soviet border. Villagers in the Ukrainian community of North Star were oblivious to this. It is the end of school term. Six children are planning their holiday in Kiev, a six-day walk away. Everyone is bright and cheerful, singing patriotic songs and performing Russian jigs. The group of kids set off, "We'll be back soon," they proclaim saying their farewells to the parents. Only seven-year-old Olga (Ann Carter) cannot go with them. "I'm always too young. I'm too young for everything," she moans.

After the first night sleeping rough on the open road, the expedition is attacked in a raid by German bombers. The convoy of horse and carts has no escape. As seventeen-year-old Claudia (Jane Withers) sees the carnage around her she realises, "We are not young anymore." On their route back to their village, they encounter a freedom fighter smuggling guns. He is fatally wounded, so the children assume responsibility for smuggling the guns to the guerrilla fighters from their village. This proves difficult as convoy after convoy of German military vehicles pass them on the road. They only succeed by Claudia making the ultimate sacrifice, distracting the Germans while the gun carriers make their escape.

Back in the village, little Olga does not fare any better. She and all the other village children are rounded up by the German invaders, and forced to provide blood transfusions for the enemy's wounded. Often the Nazi doctors take too much blood, resulting in the children's deaths. The film concludes with the freedom fighters attacking the occupying invaders, stifling the German invasion, temporarily at least.

In other films, children are just caught up in the horrors of war as they flee one community only to be confronted by the revolutionaries somewhere else. There seemed no escape in *Doctor Zhivago* as Omar Sharif flees with his son, and Julie Christie with her daughter, to Yuriatin in the region beyond the Urals.

The pointless futility and ugliness of war is bludgeoned home to us in the sickening *Johnny Mad Dog*. I mentioned earlier, watching this cannot be considered entertainment. Almost every frame composes a sickening trashing of humanity by callous Liberian freedom fighters who have coerced children to join their ranks. As a village is raided for young recruits, each new conscript has to perform his initiation by shooting his own parents dead. For the children, life becomes a starved routine of loyal obesience to the commander, of yelling the meaningless chants of indoctrination that become their password and their watchword. The child soldiers are taught to be pitiless, ruthless and unforgiving.

The film director, Jean-Stéphane Sauvaire, tries to inject moments of surreal humour – one fighter wears a looted wedding dress, another dons angel wings, one carries a live pig writhing on

440

his shoulders, another hangs on to a ghetto blaster larger than himself – but none of this makes the film any easier to watch. It is full of gore, rape, and the evil exploitation of terrified refugees.

Most films have us empathising with its 'heroes' however vile they are made out to be. But not so this movie. We all raise a cheer as Laokole (Daisy Victoria Vandy) finishes off Mad Dog (Christopher Minie) with the butt of his own rifle.

Witnesses to the Atrocities of War

In *Pan's Labyrinth* and *Spirit of the Beehive*, the child is a witness to the atrocities of killing. Others are caught up as prisoners of the enemy as in *Tenko*, *A Town Like Alice*, *Empire of the Sun*. Most wars create victims among those with the 'wrong' ethnicity, political affiliation, or religious faith, as the Holocaust of the Second World War bears out in films such as *Jakob the Liar*, *Lena my 100 children*, and *The Diaries of Anne Frank*. The aftermath of war can be as agonizing as the actual conflict. *Son of Babylon* shows us the horror of war does not end with the last missile, for following the final signing of treaties lie days, months, years of heart-wrenching sorrow as displaced refugees search despairingly for news or graves of lost loved ones.

Ten-year-old Lina Kronstein (Hannah Taylor Gordon) had been herded into the cattle truck along with her parents and thousands of other Jews, and the steam train was hauling them indelibly closer to Auschwitz. An unexpected stop brings them adjacent to the Warsaw ghetto. Lina's parents sense their opportunity: they lower their daughter through the narrow trapdoor in the floor of their railway carriage, and after tearful protestations and *shaloms*, the train shunts away over the prostrate body of the little girl cowering between the lines. It is here, in the winter of 1944 that Robin Williams, playing the title role in *Jakob the Liar*, stumbles across her. The Nazis have transported all other children out of the ghetto, so Jakob has to secrete the girl to the safety of his attic room. Here, like Anne Frank, she has to remain hidden.

There is barely enough food to eat. Even so, the man foregoes his meagre supplies to feed his young guest. All modern comforts of life have been removed, they are restricted by curfews and cannot leave the ghetto, whose high walls and barbed wire fences are heavily guarded by Nazi soldiers with machine guns and searchlights. The Jews are severely mistreated by the Nazis, brutally beaten with truncheons, forced to work in the warehouses, and the bodies of the disobedient are left hanging on gibbets in the square. "We learn to live without firewood, without potatoes, or decent clothes," gripes the man.

Yet Jakob, like the other Jews, learns to survive on a day-to-day basis by taking delight in the most trivial of things, and taking a cheerful stance on the ridiculous nature of their plight – "a dark joke, a sunny day, a hopeful rumour." In fact, Jakob finds that circulating encouragements from an imagined radio helps raise the spirits of the entire ghetto. "It's a wonderful medicine you have, Jakob," the Jewish doctor tells the optimistic Jakob. He even tells the little girl he is sure her parents are coming back.

But soon his ruse gets him embroiled with the Nazi commandant, and to save the lives of the ten hostages taken by the Nazis as a reprisal, he has to explain the misunderstanding about the illegal radio to the Nazis. As her guardian, Jakob, is shot before her eyes, Lina realises, "I'm not going to see my parents again, am I?" Lina and the other Jews are put back aboard the train to continue their fateful journey toward the concentration camp. War is seldom endowed with happy endings.

Pan's Labyrinth was deliberately written and directed by Guillermo del Toro to focus on the cruelty of the Fascist regime in Spain in 1944. Written to favour the guerrilla resistance movement it intertwines the horrors of war with a fairy tale in which the ruthless General becomes the real life ogre. "You're too old to be filling your head with fairy tales," says mother to her daughter Ofelia (Ivana Baquero) not realising she is herself involved in the elements of a traditional folk tale. Mother has recently married the General and she is pregnant with his child. For Ofelia, the General is her new stepfather but she has witnessed his harshness and makes it plain to everyone she meets that he is not her real father. But truth to this girl is a fantasyland; maybe fantasy is her only psychological escape mechanism from the horrors of the war around her (for she is the only one who can see the fairies and faun that she encounters).

The General cannot tolerate any form of dissent, as the two rabbit hunters, his personal doctor, and his maid Mercedes all discover by the fatal loss of their own lives at the hand of the trigger-happy General. Even his own wife is vulnerable; for Ofelia is hiding under the bed when she overhears the General instruct the doctor that he would rather his unborn son be saved than the life of his new wife. Del Toro tells us that one-quarter of a million people in Fascist Spain were killed passively, that is, outside of combat, by summary execution. With her mother now dead, Ofelia steals her newborn baby brother. Pursued by the gun-toting General into the labyrinth, the twelve-year-old girl's own life is stolen from her by the final bullet from the demonic man.

Spirit of the Beehive also deals with the same Franco regime in 1940 Castile. For Spanish director, Victor Erice, he had the added dilemma of having to face the ongoing fascist censorship when he wrote the screenplay in 1973, though the full horrors of the civil war were not made as apparent in his film as they were in *Pan's Labyrinth*. Six-year-old Ana Torrent had watched a Frankenstein movie at the village cinema and had learnt from her older sister, Isabel Telleria, that the monster was a real spirit living in a deserted barn across the plateau.

When a Republican soldier, a deserter or an enemy combatant, escaped from a passing train and took to hiding in the barn, little Ana confronts him there, and assuming him to be the spirit of Frankenstein delivers him food and her father's clothes. The fascist military track the escapee down, and a round of gunfire leaves the soldier dead. When Ana goes to investigate, she finds her monster friend gone but there are marks of blood left on the stonework.

Billy (Sebastian Rice Edwards) ought to be exhibiting all the signs of trauma as he endures the destruction of his suburban neighbourhood in John Boorman's World War Two autobiographical masterpiece, *Hope and Glory*. But for this nine-year-old and his neighbouring gang members, this was the best fun in their young lives. For his parents, theirs was a world of desolation, of rationing, of the death of loved ones, and the departure of others to the front. They cannot enjoy their usual diet, they have to seek out second hand clothes, fight over scraps from a parachute, and generally make do and mend. They had a nightly routine of being rudely awakened by the air raid siren and traipsing outside in the freezing winter cold to the flooded Andersen shelter at the bottom of the garden.

But all this washed over the head of young Billy. For him, the war created an endless playground of smashing glass and breaking mirrors as they clambered over bomb craters collecting pieces of shrapnel. He and his gang would make dens in the ruins of a terrace house, making a swing on the landing above the chasm of a collapsed staircase.

The cruelty of childhood is also brought out in their play. Billy is held captive by a gang, and stood in front of an unexploded bullet clamped in a vice, ready to be struck with a nail unless he complies by uttering a string of swear words. The gang also take advantage of older girl Pauline (Sara Langton), captured and bribed to allow the queue of boys to look down her drawers. Pauline had recently lost her mother in a bombing raid. Kids uncaringly come up to her asking 'has your mum just died' as if it were a fascinating fact devoid of any emotional impact.

Then, when an enemy bomb destroys the school, all the children dance for joy. "Thank you, Hitler!" cheers one lad. No more reciting the nine-times table while wearing a gas mask.

We witness the irony of war. Billy and his family are in the crowded cinema watching a war film when an air raid siren summons them all to leave. "Can't we watch the end?" complains Billy.

"You've got the real thing outside," mum retorts.

The most devastating impact of the war on Billy seemed to be not the destruction of his neighbourhood but the melting of his lead soldiers in the fire that destroyed their home. Ironically, in a bombed-out street, their house caught fire through negligent causes, nothing to do with the war at all!

Sinyard stresses the insensitivity of this film "to those people who lost loved ones, and to those who regard war as an obscenity that might sometimes be necessary but can never be an occasion for rejoicing." [33] Yet Boorman is simply making an honest portrayal through the irresponsible eyes of a nine-year-old, excited by the impact on his humdrum suburban life.

Son of Babylon is a film in the same vein as *A Peck on the Cheek (Kannathil Mutthamittal)* and *Pan's Labyrinth* in that the director, Mohamed Al-Daradji, set out with specific ethical goals: to foster forgiveness and reconciliation among the surviving Kurds and Iraqis in the aftermath of the death of Saddam Hussein. The film comes with a distressing message: '*Over the past forty years more than one million men, women and children have gone missing in Iraq. Three hundred mass graves have been found, the majority of which still remain unidentified.*'

A grandmother and her twelve-year-old grandson, Ahmed, set out on a six hundred kilometre trek to visit her son (the boy's father who he has never seen) assumed to be a prisoner in Nasiriyah jail. There is civil unrest, roadblocks to be negotiated, confusion and fear, and distrust between the Kurds and Iraqis. Grandmother instils in Ahmed, "When people hurt us we need to forgive them." This is an easy glib statement to make, for when they encounter a fellow traveller, Musa, who humbly admits how he was forced to kill Kurds, the grandmother rants at him and orders him away, with cries of "Murderer!"

When they eventually arrive at the bombed-out shell of the prison, they are told to search for the body among the myriads of mass graves. This is both futile and soul-destroying and has a distressing effect on both the travellers as they finally break. "I do not understand your language, but I feel your sorrow and pain," says one grieving woman to the refugees. Yasser Talib is effectively emotional as the son searching for the dad he never knew. The films attracts added poignancy, for Shazada Hussein who plays the grandmother was the only female witness in the actual trial of the despot Saddam.[34]

Evacuees

The Lion, the Witch and the Wardrobe was set during World War Two. There is a bombing raid over London. The four Pevensie children and their mother are awakened in the middle of the night and race outside into the air-raid shelter in the garden. Edmund rushes back to the house – he must get father. But what he actually means is the photo of father from the mantelpiece.

Like tens of thousands of other children, the Pevensie family is sent into the country to live with strangers. They end up in a large mansion near Combe Halt, the abode of reclusive Professor Kirk, and his housemaid Mrs McCreadie. And it is here where the adventure of their lives begins.

Five Children and It works along the same lines, but the evacuees are enduring World War One in this film based on E Nesbit's novel. The five Butterworth children are being sent off by steam train to live with reclusive mad Uncle Albert (Kenneth Branagh). Father is a pilot on bombing raids over France; mother has to stay in the city for her wartime ancillary nursing responsibilities.

The Lion, the Witch and the Wardrobe and *Five Children and It*, and the trio of children deposited with Angela Lansbury in *Bedknobs and Broomsticks*, all involve children being sent from the city to the countryside. In the former two instances, they are to live with an aged professor, a writer who must not be disturbed, in a rambling old country mansion, which would be more appropriate in a ghost story. Also, both houses contain a portal that leads into a world of magic, either Narnia through the wardrobe, or to the magic beach reached through the cupboard door in the conservatory. In *Bedknobs* the magic is provided by the reclusive Miss Price, a novice witch.

In the latter two films, the links with the war are pursued. In *Five Children and It* the children learn that father is missing behind enemy lines and they need the help of the Psammead to magically conjure a compass to help him escape. In *Bedknobs and Broomsticks* a mobile bedstead and magic charms conjure up a ghost army to help get rid of a band of German invaders. None of these films are actually war films: the wartime evacuation of children was coincidental, a coathanger on which to allow children to have adventures in a stranger's house. *Goodnight Mr Tom* tackles the ordeal of the evacuee in a more realistic, if sugary, fashion.

The real trauma of wartime evacuation is the separation of children from the love and nurture of parents, to be billeted at the countryside address of often-abusive uncaring strangers. An adventure for some maybe but for most, a scary journey of the resigned and impotent into the unknown.

On 31st August 1939, over one and a half million British children assembled at their various urban schools at 5.30am, labelled, and clutching their gas mask, toothbrush, comb, handkerchief, a spare set of clothes, and a packed lunch, and then ferried in a fleet of buses and trains to total strangers.[35] The whole exercise was repeated on July 11th 1944, as a further 41,000 were evacuated from London.[36] Although there have been several social documentaries highlighting the horrors of this migration, few films tackle this in anything but a heart-warming way.

Goodnight Mr Tom follows the billeting of one such child, William Beech, offloaded at the picture-postcard rural idyll of 'Weirwold'. The film begins with families listening to Churchill's declaration on the radio, "Consequently this country is at war with Germany," then soon parents are waving goodbye to their children. The billeting officer meets one such group of evacuees off the train at 'Weirwold'. One young lad, William, is left over with no one to house him. The ten-year-old boy, played by Nick Robinson, is forced upon Mr Tom Oakley, a grumpy widower reluctant to be involved in the proceedings. But because his cottage has a spare room and "the Home Office says it is obligatory to take one," he has no choice.

"I'm not having him," insists John Thaw playing the old man. "What do I know about kids of that age?"

"You've got him whether you like it or not," replies the officer. "I wasn't happy about leaving the lad with you, either, but it's a case of needs, must..." Not an auspicious start for a lonely frightened lad. But it turns out to be the best move for the boy who had previously been abused by his parents at his London home. The neglected boy even arrives with the strap used to inflict the welts on his back, to ensure discipline is sustained.

The man helps the boy to read and ride a bike, takes him fishing, and patiently weans him out of the stresses and nightmares that caused the bed-wetting. And the impact upon the "lonely embittered old man facing a lonely old age" is that the man ultimately adopts the boy after the death of his own parents, so that now he can declare, "I love him as if he were my own flesh and blood, I do."

Keeping Home Fires Burning

While war is raging overseas, we see how that impacts on communities left devoid of its male labourers, as mother has to assume the role of breadwinner. Such was the case in *Run the Wild Fields*, set in the spring of 1945 in an American farming community. It focuses on the events impinging on a mother and her ten-year-old daughter while father is away in the Pacific, fighting in the Second World War. Every night, as Opal Miller (played by Alexa Vega) is put to bed her mother comes to say goodnight, and together they wind father's pocketwatch as if to keep him alive. But father has not been heard of for three years, missing in action. Mother has let the farmstead run down, refusing to do the ploughing and other chores until her husband has safely returned home from war.

Others in the community stoically go to church each week where they proudly express their pride in their heroic, but absent, loved ones. We witness the grim dread as the congregation stands outside the chapel aghast as the telegram boy pulls up with bad news for one of their members.

So when a stranger turns up in their midst, a vagrant Tom Walker, all assume him to be a draft dodger, a deserter, while their own husbands are sacrificing themselves in the war. The whole village is antagonistic towards him, calling him a 'Yellow Belly'. However, Opal and her mother, desperate for a farmhand, take him in and he becomes useful around the farm – ploughing the land, sewing seeds, and doing odd jobs. But mother lays down the rules to him: "I don't want you filling my daughter's mind with pacifist theories."

"I am not a pacifist," retorts the man.

Later, as Tom is embroiled in various fights (all related to him being a 'yellow belly', Opal's mother probes him, "Tom, you never talk about the war. Why is that?" But the man modestly maintains his secret (he is a decorated war hero).

Further, Tom is cut up about his brother who had recently been unnecessarily killed as a mercenary in the Spanish Civil War: "You get killed for people you don't even know."

In time, a bond grows between mother, Opal, and Tom Walker. The girl now sees Tom as a substitute father. "I want you to be my daddy." Opal loses interest in winding her father's watch, and assumes her own dad to be dead.

One day, Opal finds a letter in the mailbox, which she reads. It explains how father has been found and is returning home. "I didn't want daddy to come home, not now." She realises if her father returns then Tom will have to leave. So, the girl hides the letter, keeping the news secret from her mother.

This film is not a tearjerker, but rather demonstrates in a realistic way the impact that an absent father fighting in the war has on the domestic arrangements of a family.

As the real father is arriving home along the lane, Tom learns about the letter, sensibly packs his bag, says his farewells, and heads off, as he realises, "Sometimes you got to lose a battle to win the war."

MOVING TO A NEW HOME

Moving home can be a trying time for a child. Though not as fraught with trauma as the death of a loved one or pet, he or she is still experiencing the death of an endeared way of life, the loss of friends, and social spheres. Moving to a new home involves the hassle of breaking into new cliques, falling in with new routines, learning new strategies for survival, where to be safe. A child's mental map has to be redrawn, and social boundaries relearned. The child moving home lacks the assurance that new friends can ever be re-made, and carries the added fear of being bullied. Mikey's (Sean Astin) appealing speech to his fellow treasure-hunters in *The Goonies* was a last gasp attempt to salvage his own treasured memories: "The next time you see the sky it'll be in another town. The next time you take a test, it'll be in another school." This is the outpouring of despair of a child who sees a precious way of life dissipating before his eyes.

For others, what alarms them is the loss of social status and comfort as they downsize. This was the annoyance for Anna in *Blame it on Fidel*, and for the Waterburys in *The Railway Children*. For Mary Lennox in *The Secret Garden* and Sara Crewe in *A Little Princess* it meant being uprooted from an exotic culture to the misery of a cold mansion or an unfriendly boarding school.

In the case of *Flowers in the Attic*, the childhood home is where dreams have taken root, where the memory of father resides. Moving home involves the shock of being wrenched from the familiar into a frightening unknown. This is what so alarmed the Gilbreth's in the 1950 version of *Cheaper by the Dozen* (1950) as they flit from Rhode Island to New Jersey, and the Smith's in *Meet me in St Louis*. They might as well be moving to another planet, so anarchic is the rumpus. This is what actually befell Lacy Chabert. On her final last night at her old home she disobediently blows "ten years of allowance" at the mall. But her family are not moving to a new town but are pioneers to a new planet in *Lost in Space*. "What are they going to do?" she asks her little brother (Jack Johnson). "Ground me?"

Yet there are those for whom shifting home is a positive step: moving away from an abusive environment, as Lily Owens escapes a violent father in *The Secret Life of Bees*; as *Harry Potter* exchanges the Dursleys for Hogwarts; and as Rosetta in *Stolen Children* crosses Italy to be safe from her pimping mother; while for Shawn Hatary and Skye McCole Bartusiak in *Witness Protection*, their move is to evade fatal repercussions. In *Ratcatcher*, James does not actually make the move, but his dreams are of escape from the grim Glaswegian tenements he currently slums in, to an idyll surrounded by golden wheat fields.

When the anticipated move is actually made, the destination doesn't always live up to expectations, as the evacuees discovered in the stage play *Pretend you have Big Buildings*. Dreaming of the buzz of city life, of high rise apartments, Rukhsana and her mixed race son found suburban life in Romford a disparaging letdown. Yet movies have to have their happy endings. As Cary Grant up-wrenches his family from the cramped claustrophobic confines of his New York apartment into a rickety ramshackle ranch in backwoods Connecticut, in *Mr Blandings builds his Dream House*, he tells his wife and daughters (Sharyn Moffett and Connie Marshall), "It is not a house we're building but a home."

Fear of not being able to make new friends

"Ma, do you think they will like us?" asks Mary Ingalls (Melissa Anderson) on the first day of going to her new school at Walnut Grove in *The Little House on the Prairies*.

"What sort of question is that?" replies mother. "Of course they will like you. Be friendly and mind your manners."

Despite being a wonderful mother, she was wrong on this score. The two new girls, Mary and her sister, Laura, are picked on and derided for being 'country girls'. However, life is not harsh for them for too long as ten-year-old Laura (Melissa Gilbert) retaliates by picking a fight with Nelly Olsen. After dusting herself down again, Laura declares, "I won't have to do that again. Nelly is scared of me now."

At least the Ingalls only had to move once, and after their initial skirmish, they became well-adapted and popular members of their community. Damian (Alex Etel) thought he could fit in at his new school in *Millions* (2004) by enthusiastically answering all teacher's questions about who their heroes are. While all his new classmates are suggesting the names of footballers, Damian reels off a list of medieval saints. So, at playtime he finds himself friendless. "Keep off the weird stuff," his older brother advises him. "Don't be conspicuous or you won't fit in."

This is an on-going fear – that of not fitting in, of being rejected by a new set of friends and the fear of bullying. It is a problem that Mae Whitman had to face too, playing Bernice, in *Hope Floats*. "What if my new friends don't like me, here?" asks Bernice. Yet the ten-year-old shows bravado by going into her new school alone, without mother accompanying her, insisting she can stand on her own two feet. "Maybe I can go in alone," she decides.

Like the Ingalls, Bernice did have grounds to worry. Because she wears spectacles, she was the butt of bullying by one girl who shouts, "She's got pop-eyes!" On another occasion, the bully has told her mates she is out to 'git' her. A crowd assembles as the taunt of "four eyes" is hurled. Bernice ignores the bullying girl, but not for long. Not wanting to lose face, the other girl picks a fight and both girls end up scrapping on the grass.

Bullying seems to be an ever-present fear for children who have moved home. For Cage Dobson in *Munchie*, when his teacher asks him, "Have you made any new friends here yet?" he feels he has to lie to deflect his bullying issues. "Yes, lots of them," he fibs.

For others, such as Anouk (Victoire Thivisol) in *Chocolat*, she has to re-start every time the wind changes direction.

"How does Anouk handle it – all this moving around?" Vianne, her mother, is asked.

"She makes friends easily," lies mother (played by Juliette Binoche). As she reflects on the question, she realises her eleven-year-old daughter hates it.

Vianne and Anouk move around (taken by the north wind) to continue a Mayan legend regarding cacao. They set up a chocolaterie in all the villages they dwell in. At the end of the film, they pack up ready to move on again. "The next town will be better won't it, Mama?" suggests Anouk. But as they pack up, Anouk finally resists. "I hate you," says the girl, as mother tries to make her move on yet again.

Kathy Hardy (Christina Ricci) had a similar itinerant lifestyle in *Casper* (1995). As she travels from one boarding place to the next with her father and all their belongings loaded in the car, she complains, "For once, I would just like to be in one place long enough to have a friend." Her words are almost echoed in AnnaSophia Robb's prayer in *Because of Winn-Dixie* having just moved to the tiny town of Naomi: "Please God, if it's not too much trouble I'd like some friends."

This too is the greatest fear of Alice McKinley (Alyson Stoner) in *Alice Upside Down* as she leaves her old home with her father and older brother, leaving behind memories of her dead mum and saying goodbye to her friends. "Before you know it, Silver Spring will seem like home," father tries to reassure her.

Alice tries to imagine what it might be like in her new school. In her dreams, she dresses in fashionable clothes and breezes into her new schoolroom attracting compliments from all her peers and becoming the most popular girl in class. But she finds reality is not like that. "I want to go home now," she says to dad. "I don't know anyone. I feel like a freak."

But father uses the oft-quoted phrase: "This is your home now."

On her way to her new school, Alice is accompanied by next-door neighbour Elizabeth, a fellow sixth-grader. Alice appeals to her, "I don't know anyone else at school. I'm really scared." But being so wrapped up in her own anxiety, she has not realised that Elizabeth is also a new girl.

While modest Elizabeth seems to make friends quickly, anxious Alice tries to make out she is someone she is not. She tries too hard to be popular, and tries to outdo other classmates in a theatrical audition. It is only when she makes a humble apology to her peers that she discovers she has been accepted.

Like Alice, eight-year-old Bruno (Asa Butterfield) relocating from Berlin with his family to the countryside during World War Two in *The Boy in the Striped Pyjamas* is missing his friends from the city. "I want to go home," he whimpers to his father.

"Home is where the family is," father tries to reassure him.

The child who makes the mistake of trying too hard to make an impression, or by living a lie, finds integration with new friends an unhappy ride. Damian found this to be so in *Millions* as did Alice in *Alice Upside Down*. Laure's (Zoé Héran) attempt to pass as a boy has a negative outcome, too, when her new friends discover her true gender in *Tomboy (2011)*. Laure had recently moved to a new neighbourhood. To make friends quickly with the bunch of boys playing football, she tells them her name is Mickäel, to be accepted as 'one of the lads'. But she cannot maintain the dupe forever. Soon, Laure has to accompany her mother to visit her new friends to tell them how they have been hoodwinked, and that is when she curls into a corner to mope, wanting the family to return back to the old home they moved from.

Regrets of the past

Moving home means leaving behind the past. "I just want to stay at home where daddy's memory is," sighs Kathy (Kristy Swanson) in *Flowers in the Attic*, as her family are about to move into her cruel grandmother's mansion.

For some, the move to a new home triggers regression in their psychological health, aggravated by a recent loss. For Mary (Perla Haney-Jardine) in *Genova*, her distress is exhibited through nightmares, bedwetting and visions of her dead mother, following the move from America to Italy. Like *Heidi*, Jennifer Connelly resorts to sleepwalking after being sent away to an exclusive boarding school in the film *Phenomena*. In *Hide and Seek* (2005), Dakota Fanning seems to develop a split personality, sharing her life with the imaginary Charlie, after moving home with her father following the death of her mother.

Margaret O'Brien, playing Tooti in *Meet me in St Louis*, is aware of the unsettling upheavals in moving home. As her father decides to move his whole family to New York, everyone objects. "I prefer to be poor and stay here. I prefer to go to the orphalans home," gripes Tooti before storming out into the snowy garden in her bare feet and destroying the snowman she had made to honour father. It is only when the father sees the bare discoloured walls where the paintings had hung, and the grandfather clock wrapped in a blanket ready for the removal van, along with the dozens of other packing cases, and the resentment of the other family members, that he has a change of heart.

Another family resolutely opposed to moving was in the French film, *Home* (2008). They were aware of a new motorway being built beside their home, which would completely cut off any access to their property. It took many years for the motorway to be completed so they failed to be concerned, using the empty carriageway as their private playground and driveway. But suddenly, overnight, the motorway opened, cutting them off completely from the outside world.

For Nina Kervel playing Anna in *Blame it on Fidel*, what worried the girl was the change in lifestyle, a down-sizing of home and nutrition, as their socialist family exchanged their affluent way of life with a more principled one, in sympathy with the socialist Allende regime in Chile. But nine-year-old Anna was unaware of these political reasons; she was only drip-fed information, all beyond her comprehension. She laid the blame on Fidel Castro, because that is who her housekeeper kept blaming, having been forced out of Cuba.

Anna had been a happy-go-lucky child in a nice French house, with nice food, and "a hot bath before dinner". But all that changed when her parents became socialists in 1970, the year of General de Gaulle's death. "Communists in the family!" moans the housekeeper.

The family moves into a cramped flat with no garden. She has to share a bunk bed with her younger brother. "Why can't we go back to our former home?" she demands. The parents try to explain their new political views about the importance of living frugally. Yet, Anna misinterprets this. She thinks that by economising they will be able to save up to return to their grand house again, so she switches off lights and the emersion heater, an action she regrets when it comes to her weekly bath time. She even steals money from the school changing rooms to add to the housekeeping.

The Waterbury family have a similar reaction to their downsizing in *The Railway Children*, though for them they hope their move is only temporary. From being one happy affluent family of city kids, they are whisked off to be country bumpkins (in Yorkshire in the 1970 version, near Sheffield Park, Sussex in the 2000 version, and in rural Kent in the classic novel by E Nesbit). "We've got to play at being poor for a bit," says mother, after father is escorted away to be the 'guests' of the official 'gentlemen' who visited their London home.

They arrive in a cold dark house with only candlelight to comfort them. Here they eke out a living "simply and in reduced circumstances" by mum writing stories to make sufficient money for buns for tea. Yet, despite their new lifestyle, their life is enriched by the adventures they have beside the railway, by the people they meet in the community, and they realise that by comparison with others, they are not really impoverished.

A similar girl, put in her place by her change of circumstances is Mary Lennox, played by Margaret O'Brien and Kate Maberly in the two versions of *The Secret Garden* (1949 and 1993). Mary was used to being waited upon by servants in her posh villa in her native India, the daughter of diplomats. But an earthquake had killed her parents (in the 1949 version it was a cholera epidemic). Despite their affluence, hers was a neglected childhood. She never cried when her parents died, since she had really grown up in the care of maids, who fed her and dressed her. Now, removed to Misselthwaite Manor in Yorkshire to be the orphaned ward of her uncle, Lord Craven, she stands, arms aloft in her underwear, waiting for someone to dress her. "No one's going to carry you around, my girl," says Mrs Medlock (Maggie Smith), the housekeeper. Gradually, the stubborn reserve of the obnoxious girl is broken down, and by mixing with Colin and Dickon in the secret garden she learns to make friends, to love, and to cry.

Sara Crewe is similarly disenchanted in *A Little Princess*. From her richly exotic childhood in Simla, India, bewitched by the story of the *Ramayana*, Sara (Liesel Matthews) grows up believing she is a little princess. "All women are princesses. It is our right," Myra the Maid had told her.

This being 1914, father is called up to fight in the war raging in Europe. "I shall miss it here," says Capt. Crewe. "India is the only place that stirs the imagination."

"I wish we could stay here, father," dreams his daughter. But she cannot. Instead, Sara is sent to a girls' school in New York, *Miss Minchin's Seminary for Girls*. Father sends to the school all her toys, dolls and belongings, and a silver locket reminding her of her father and dead mother.

But soon the girl is embroiled in the humdrum of institutional life: "Sara, there's no talking at the table."…"Sara, from now on there'll be no more make-believe at this school."…"I expect you to remember, Sara Crewe, you are not a princess any longer."…And neither is she allowed to wear her silver locket.

Father receives Sara's morose letter, smudged by her tears and soiled by the muck of the trenches where he is reading it. "Dear Papa, I miss you already. I never imagined there would be so many rules at school."

Yet Sara is able to cheer the lives of the other girls at the seminary, including the little servant girl, Becky, by bringing alive her stories of Rama and Sita.

Like Mary Lennox and Sara Crewe, *Heidi* (Emma Bolger) also made an impact on her new friends. Duped away from her grandfather in the Swiss Alpen village of Dorfli, she constantly yearns for her old life among the high pastures, the peaks that turn fiery at sunset, the eagles, grumpy Grandfather, and Peter with his flocks of goats. "Are there not any trees at all in Frankfurt?" she despairs. In her new city home, where she has been 'acquired' to be a playmate for wheelchair-bound Clara (Jessica Claridge), Heidi is looked upon as useless and uncouth by the housekeeper Madam Rottenmeier. The girl has nightmares, sleepwalks, and goes off her food. The only remedy is that "Heidi must be returned to her grandfather at once before she pines away altogether," prescribes the doctor.

Before she took the lead role in *Heidi*, Emma Bolger also created the fun happy-go-lucky daughter in the thought-provoking *In America* (2003). She plays Ariel, younger daughter of Sarah and Johnny Sullivan – an Irish family who have sneaked their way across the Canadian border to settle in New York. As we learnt earlier, the parents are still suppressing grief for a lost child. As Paddy Considine playing Johnny says, "You can move anywhere in the world, but you can't run away from grief."

The only apartment they can find is a rundown grimy flat at the top of a block in Manhattan, in a street full of junkies and transvestites. That is where the parents move in with their two children. Mum finds a job at an ice cream parlour while dad searches for auditions as an actor. Little Ariel complains, "I have no one to play with, and no one to tell my secrets to," while her older sister Christy (Sarah Bolger) has a camcorder that she uses for reminiscences.

In their daily life, they come across a variety of oddball characters including black artist Mateo who becomes an important part in their lives. They first meet him as the two girls go trick-or-treating. Like Tooti in *Meet me in St Louis*, they dare each other to knock on his door, and the scary man opens it. "When luck comes knocking at your door you can't turn it away."

Earlier the two girls had won a prize at the school fancy dress competition. Except it was a sort of consolation prize – they were the only ones wearing a homemade Halloween costume. The girls complain, "We got the prize because we were different. But we don't want to be different. We want to be the same as everybody else. As newcomers, they did not want to be seen as different just as the Ingalls sisters resented being the country girls attending school in town in *Little House on the Prairie*.

Beneficial Moves

Moving home can have its advantages and is sometimes eagerly sought by an unsettled child. This is the case for Lily Owens (played by Dakota Fanning) in *The Secret Life of Bees* who runs away with her black maid from her abusive father, and is welcomed to a new home by a family of bee-keeping women.

Daniel Radcliffe similarly escapes the constrictions of his muggle foster parents in the *Harry Potter* series. His inseparable companions, Rupert Grint and Hermione Granger, join him and together their new life at Hogwarts is a roller-coaster adventure of wizardry and friendship.

A third movie featuring children escaping from an abusive childhood is the Italian drama, *Stolen Children*. But in this film we never see the girl, Valentina Scalici, and her younger brother reach their destination.

In *Ratcatcher*, a move to a new home was the dream of James (William Eadie) and his family, but the move is thwarted by the negligence of the parents. Picture a rum housing estate of dreary tenement blocks, strewn with rubbish left uncollected in black bin bags, grim forecourts and backyards overrun with rats, the children breaking out in sores and scabs, constantly scratching at their nit-infested scalps. This is not some apocalyptic drama, but the time of the deeply entrenched dustman's strike in 1970s Glasgow.

Twelve-year-old James is one of three children in an impoverished grubby family who cannot pay their rent, but who dream of being rehoused to a better part of the city. One day James hops on a bus and ends up in a rural area of new-build opposite a golden wheat field, and his dreams are made. His younger sister, Anne Marie (Lynne Ramsay (Jr.)), is not yet old enough to question her lot and seems happily oblivious to the poverty around her.

To their joy, the welfare services come to visit, offering the possibility of rehousing. The officials see the awful way the family looks after their existing apartment, so any chance of being rehoused is scuppered, and James unfairly gets the blame for this. It is only in their dreams that they get to walk with their possessions across the heavenly wheat fields to the new-build at the edge of the city.

ENDNOTES FOR VOLUME SEVEN

1 Sula Wolff *Children Under Stress* p11, 13 & p25

2 These are my additions, not Sula Wolff's.

3 Sula Wolff *Children Under Stress* p217

4 speaking on the *Today* programme Radio 4, 3 Oct 2011

5 Sula Wolff *Children Under Stress* p103

6 Sula Wolff: *Children Under Stress* p103

Halliwell's Video & DVD Guide 2004

7a Evidently, as adults, Mandy Miller remained in a stable relationship with her architect husband, while Jeremy Spenser divorced then re-married his wife. Perhaps responsibilities about relationships had touched their psyche in their childhood, after all.

8 speaking on the *Today* programme Radio 4, 3 Oct 2011

9 Frank Capra Jr in a commentary to his father's most famous movie, *It's a Wonderful Life*.

10 Grange Hill Online

11 Mark Duguid, BFI Screen Online

12 I have searched for references to Beatie Edney's disability but can find no reference to it either way. And why should there be? A disabled child's wish is be be accepted as normal. Either she has learnt to live with it, or else her acting as a polio cripple was exemplary.

13 Neil Sinyard, *Children in the Movies*, p77

14 *Time Out Film Guide*, & Neil Sinyard, *Children in the Movies*

15 Neil Sinyard: *Children in the Movies* p87

16 *Blue Butterfly* is based on a true story. The credits at the end of the film inform us: 'In 1987 an entomologist fulfilled the last wish of a terminally ill young boy by taking him to the rain forest to find a blue morpho. After his return the cancer had disappeared.'

17 In the UK in 2009, 3.8% of females aged 15-17 had a pregnancy of which 49% were aborted. For girls aged 13-15 the conception rate in 2009 was 0.75% of which 60% were aborted. Source: Office for National Statistics & DFE 2011. According to Wikipedia, "Among OECD countries the US and UK have the highest levels of teenage pregnancies, while Japan and S Korea have the lowest." In developing countries, pregnancy rates are much higher, but are more likely to occur within marriage where the trauma of social stigma is lessened. *Teenage pregnancy - Wikipedia, the free encyclopaedia*.

18 "You wait till your sixteen, Lizzie. Get yourself pregnant. Tell the Social you can't live with your mama and they will have to find you a wee flat."

19 Paraphrased from *Wikipedia Teenage pregnancy - Wikipedia, the free encyclopaedia*

20 *Wikipedia Teenage pregnancy*: Sourced from Gracie Hsu, Statutory Rape Family Research Council

21 Sula Wolff, *Children Under Stress*, p86

22 Sula Wolff ibid p94-102

23 Sula Wolff ibid p88, 97, 98

24 Sula Wolff ibid p88

25 Sula Wolff ibid p97, 98

26 Susan Wallbank, *Facing Grief: bereavement and the Young Adult*, p20 (The Lutterworth Press, ISBN 0718828070).

27 Susan Wallbank, *Facing Grief: bereavement and the Young Adult*, p28.

28 In the 1942 film version, Peter O'Toole's part is played by Monty Woolley.

29 James E. Kiefer, Biographical Sketches Website

30 In the book by Alan Burgess, *The Small Woman*, Gladys Aylward is referred to as *Ai-weh-de*h, 'The Virtuous One'.

31 *The Small Woman* was the title of the biography by Alan Burgess.

32 Besides the girl in the red coat, two other girls who survived the war are able to tell their story as surviving adults: Danka Dresner (played by Anna Mucha) the bespectacled girl who had to endure the hardships along with her parents, and Niusia Horowitz (played by Magdalena Dandaurian) who received a kiss from Schindler as she presented the man with a birthday cake. This in itself was very daring. To kiss a Jew was something to be frowned upon, but Schindler dared to do so surrounded by German officers.

33 Neil Sinyard *Children in the Movies* p52

34 According to Emm7, writing on the IMDb review of *Son of Babylon* 2009, 'Shazada was actually the only woman to have testified in Saddam Husseins trial so this film must be very personal for her.'

35 *Chronicle of the 20th Century* p515

36 *Chronicle of the 20th Century* p606

Volume Eight

Physical & Sexual Abuse

"There can be no keener revelation of a society's soul than the way it treats its children."
(Nelson Mandela)

CONTENTS FOR VOLUME EIGHT

8. Physical & Sexual Abuse..**455**

Contents for Volume Eight..**457**

Child Abuse: Introduction..**459**

Physical Abuse...**462**
Making a Stand against Abuse..*462*
Neglect...*463*
Bodily Harm..*466*
Violently Abusive Parents...*468*
Racial Abuse / Prejudice..*470*
Kidnapping and Abduction..*473*
Slavery / Child Bondage...*478*

Bullying...**483**
Name-Calling...*483*
The Bully and Victim...*484*
Cyber-bullying...*485*
Bullying: Passive Resistance..*486*
Standing up to the Bully...*489*
Ill-Treatment by Adults..*490*

Sexual Abuse..**495**
Paedophilia...*495*
Little Girls Loved: Salacious Relationships with Children...............*498*
Boys and Older Women..*502*
Paedophilia: Seeking Justice and Revenge...............................*503*
Empathy with the Perverted..*506*
Adults Targeting Children / Grooming....................................*508*
Molestation...*514*
Child Prostitution...*515*
Therapy for Abused Victims..*518*

Endnotes for Volume Eight...**521**

CHILD ABUSE: INTRODUCTION

Despised by the public, hounded by vigilantes, reported lasciviously by the press, and condemned in the courts, the perpetrators of abuse against children receive short shrift from society. It is because the child is small, defenceless, and vulnerable they become easy targets both for a sex-crazed pervert or for a frustrated parent who cannot cope. That children love role play and games, can be persuaded to keep secrets, are in essence trustful of those they love, have great sense of loyalty, and can be bribed, these make them susceptible to manipulative adults who target them, groom them, and abuse them.

As we shall see, abuse may be physical, perpetrated either as punishment or as a way of asserting control over an underling. When abuse is psychological – as in neglect, bullying, or racial prejudice – it leaves no visible scarring, but the trauma can be equally as effecting. Abuse that is sexual can leave its evil imprint in the child's mind only to resurface decades later as the victim confronts the suppressed abuse in adulthood.

These are all important themes for the media, including the film industry, to highlight and address. While we, the audience, are 'entertained' by the harassing of the child, few films are willing to delve into the emotional wranglings the victim has to endure. Of the 130 films about child abuse reviewed for this volume, I have found none that focus on the therapy requirements of the child victim (with the exceptions of *Prince of Tides* which considers therapy for a child who suppressed his abuse until he himself was a father, and *Mockingbird Don't Sing* which dwells more on the bickering between the social workers who have divergent theories about how the child should be helped).

What I have found equally disturbing is when those films which do dare confront these important issues, handling the subject matter sensitively, they are then berated by critics who claim the film to be too sensational, too serious, or 'making an emotional meal' of the topic.

In this volume we meet Winnie (Beatie Edney) neglected by her drunken uncle as he staggers through his pub-crawl in *A Day at the Beach*; Ami with a smashed skull ignored by her mother in *Alas de Mariposa* because the baby is crying; Bird (Tina Majorino), whipped to submission by a mother who can't cope in *Before Women had Wings*. Sandra in *Skin* is thrown out of her apartheid school because her colour is wrong; Pita in *Man on Fire* and Filippo in *I'm not Scared* kidnapped for ransom because their whole community is corrupt; Chuyia and Malia thrown into a life of drudgery and servitude in *Water (2005)* and *I am Slave* because they are defenceless girls whose only fault is to live in a society that permit child brides and child slavery. Others suffer in silence as their contemporaries humiliate them by degrading bullying: Oskar in *Let the Right One In*, Dina in *Shattered Silence* (a rare attempt at highlighting the recent phenomenon of cyber-bulling).

When it comes to the sexual abuse of children, some confront the issues with a hard-hitting, but distasteful approach, as in *Hounddog* or *Bastard out of Carolina*. There are others, with salacious content like *Pretty Baby* or *Little Lips*, that barely acknowledge the abuse of the child; while the most pertinent – *Liar, Liar* or *Fallen Angel* are often dismissed as being too honest and informative.

We begin by considering the opinion of three leading film directors – the French classicist Françoise Truffaut, the British pusher of boundaries Terry Gilliam, and controversial American Nicole Kassell – who are being sounded out for their views on the depiction of abuse in the cinema.

Speaking in the prologue to his film *Pocket Money*, Françoise Truffaut states, "It's terrible to think of the way kids are in danger from morning to night." He opens his film with a cascade of children symbolically running headlong into the trials of the new day. Terry Gilliam contradicts this viewpoint in the commentary to his film *Tideland*. "There is hysteria in the media that there is danger awaiting little girls in the big wide world – abuse, kidnappings, etc. This is bullshit," (he says). "This is a sentimentalised version of children – of children as innocent victims." Rather, Gilliam emphasises the resilience of the child. The child is aware of the oppressions in the world, of the dangers and taboos, and is usually street-wise enough to avoid the dangers.

Yet both directors would agree about the existence of child abuse; they just diverge on its intensity and its depiction in the neurotic alarmist media. Truffaut continues in the DVD extras to his film *Pocket Money*: "Of all of mankind's injustices, child abuse is the most revolting, the most unbearable. The world is not fair and never will be, but we can fight for more justice."

For Gilliam, it is all a matter of the stance taken by the onlooker. He does not see victims and perpetrators, but defines abuse in the eye of the beholder – that is us, the viewer. His child character, nine-year-old Jeliza Rose (Jodelle Ferland), is aware of boundaries when she befriends Dickens in *Tideland*. The retarded twenty-year-old Dickens was as innocent as a child, despite incorporating 'silly kissing' as part of his play with the little girl. In Terry Gilliam's words, "It is only us as voyeurs who see the sexual side of the relationship." The sexual element was beyond the comprehension of both child and retarded adult (Jeliza Rose and Dickens); it is only we, who have a sexual dimension, who point an accusing finger of disapproval (though the adult Dickens must have had adult sexual feelings even though he may not have understood them – potentially a greater threat than a sexually aware male, in my opinion). Likewise, Gilliam does not acknowledge the victimisation of his child actress where drugs are concerned, either. A child might be required to assist an insulin-dependent diabetic with daily injections, and adapt to the world of drug taking without needing to become part of that world itself. Gilliam says this to justify Jodelle Ferland's assisting her father as he injects himself with heroin.

Gilliam continues, "Women aren't frightened in the way men are frightened," (referring to the sexual innuendo in his film). "Women have been through potentially disturbing situations and have come out fine. Women are aware of their own sexuality as a child but men don't want to face this." I am not sure how female readers react to Gilliam's comments, though I can imagine both an outcry by some, while others nod reflectively.

The adult character, Vickie, played by Kyra Sedgwick in *The Woodsman*, takes a similar stance. In full knowledge of his past crimes, she has befriended Walter (Kevin Bacon), a paedophile recently released from a twelve-year prison sentence for molesting two preteen girls. As well as helping him rehabilitate and protect him from vigilantes, she becomes his lover and is willing to forgive his past misdemeanours – as long as they really are past. Evidently, she herself had been 'poked about' by her three older brothers when she was a child, but she still loves them. "They are now grown-up strong gentlemen, with families of their own."

As a man, I find this a difficult standpoint. To my male viewpoint, it is almost excusing abuse as just a triviality to be tolerated, sweeping it under the carpet. But of course, Nicole Kassell, the director of *The Woodsman*, did not share this viewpoint, else she would not have made the film. She tells us in the introduction to her film, "Every child, particularly girls, have had a moment of discomfort (in their lives) when they just can't tell what the intentions of the adult are." There are people who criticised this director for making *The Woodsman* by showing it through the offender's eyes. Kevin Bacon, who plays Walter the child abuser, answers those critics: "Sweeping it under a rug or pretending the problem doesn't exist is not going to work."

This hypocrisy can be contrasted with an audience addicted to horror movies that seem to lap up abuse and violence. In *The Exorcist*, this audience is 'invited to be entertained or gripped by the visual spectacle of a child's suffering.' This, despite the director of the sequel, John Boorman, saying he found the story 'extremely tasteless, cruel and sadistic towards children.'[1] He was willing to go ahead with the project, nevertheless.

However, there are certain films that aim to portray these abuses, and the purpose of this volume is to highlight them, at the same time considering the effect this has on both the viewer and the child actor, and the degree of cognitive awareness required by the child actor when depicting these scenes.

PHYSICAL ABUSE

A large number of films handle the concept of the vulnerable child – in particular, the defenceless little girl who has no resistance to exploitation or abuse. The child may be unwanted, neglected, and despised as in *Jane Eyre*, *Melissa P*, or *Enid (2009)*. They may be the victim of kidnapping as in *Cold Sweat*, *Man on Fire*, or *The Rag Nymph*, or abduction in *Down will come Baby* and *Heidi*, sold into slavery as in *Memoirs of a Geisha* and *I am Slave*, or the victim of bullying, as in *Munchie*, or *Buddha Collapsed out of Shame*. Sometimes it is necessary for a child to endure a measure of torment or bullying to gain acceptance into a clique by means of an initiation task, but this should still be considered a form of physical abuse imposed on a child by a societal quirk (we explore this further in Volume 4: *Childhood Friendships*).

The argument in favour of bringing back corporal punishment such as the use of the cane in schools, or an acceptable clip round the ear, is endorsed by the sentiment, "Well, it never did me any harm!" For we tend to raise our children as we were raised, and abusive practices become entrenched as a sub-cultural norm. Society is naturally a copycat culture in which we learn standards by observing others. Humanity only evolves out of primevalism as it learns to question its blinkered actions, considering the impact its actions have on others, particularly our children. The medium of film provides an effective mirror to confront our previously unquestioned inadequacies.

Alas, cinematic images also provide a tool of acceptability for a minority who justify their perversions from what they see depicted on screen. The film director plays a critical role in ensuring the nation's morals do not regress to the 'good old days' of the dark ages.

Walter Matthau (playing Mr Wilson in *Dennis (1993)* tells us, "When my old man had something to say to me, he told me with his belt." At least this American version of *Dennis the Menace* is a comedy, and we take his quip as tongue-in-cheek.

Making a Stand against Abuse

The definition of abuse is hard to define because its boundaries are blurred. A perpetrator may feel justified in considering abuse is necessary to be kind, taking the viewpoint that something that is hurtful does not always mean it is harmful. I am sure everyone would agree that forcing a reluctant child to the dentist or for an operation may hurt in the short term but is beneficial in the long term. This was Mr Neville's (Kenneth Branagh) misdirected abusive stance in *Rabbit Proof Fence*, in which the Australian Government decreed that all half-caste Aboriginal children should be removed from their parents: "In spite of himself, the native must be helped." These boundaries (between what is harmful and beneficial) are powerfully tested in thought-provoking films, such as *My Sister's Keeper*.

Cameron Diaz and Alec Baldwin play the Fitzgeralds who conceive a child, Kate. Kate develops leukaemia and is slowly dying of cancer. They have only one lifeline: to genetically engineer a child who can supply blood, bone marrow, and a kidney to the ailing child. This is not an unrealistic movie spectacular. The concept has its real-life counter-parts in 'designer babies'. So, for true altruistic and loving motives the couple give birth to Anna, who during the span of her infancy is the reluctant provider of blood and spare body specimens.

The infant Anna really has no conception of refusal, because the life of her sister is at stake (so she is told). But when Anna (Abigail Breslin) reaches eleven years of age she says she has had enough of being a designer baby and refuses to provide any more spare parts for her older sister (in particular, the painfully intrusive harvesting of bone marrow). The only way she can take a stand against her parents is to take them to court, to recover her rights to her own body.

As an eleven-year-old, she states she only agreed to help when she was younger. She was then too young to understand. Throughout her upbringing, the emphasis was on her sister, Kate, and standing up for Kate's right to life. Now, as the lawyer asserts in the court case, "The question is, who stands up for Anna?" Mother asks why Anna didn't say earlier that she did not want to donate. Father responds by saying, "She told us a million times. You just did not want to hear it."

This film, based on the story by Judy Piccoult, is not far-fetched. In 2011, a six-year-old boy from Yorkshire (in the UK) was praised on TV for being "so brave" by being a provider of body parts to a sibling. I wonder what objective options the little lad was offered?

Parents don't offer objective options to their children. The child is expected to obey, and what is considered a reasoned choice is, in magician's parlance, 'forcing' the freely chosen card on you. As we discover in *Water (2005)*, if an eight-year-old girl is offered a sweet if she will marry that dirty old elderly cousin, she'll ignorantly take the sweet, not understanding the implications of her commitment.

In the eyes of the uncompromising parent, the child is always in the wrong, as Alakina Mann discovers playing Anne in the spooky movie *The Others* (2001). Forced to sit on the steps for three days as punishment for allegedly scaring her brother, the girl resolutely objects, "Mummy, I won't ask forgiveness for something I didn't do." Such an unwarranted final judgement on the part of an unwavering parent causes no end of damage in the child's psyche. "I told you there was someone in the room and you punished me. Now I don't know what to say." Soon after this, the little girl is escaping through an upstairs window down a drainpipe to evade a mother going berserk.

Neglect

Compared to actual physical hurt, neglect may seem a trivial form of abuse. But if it adds to a child's sense of rejection and worthlessness, and leads to the desire for self harm and other forms of anti-social attention-seeking, it can leave emotional scars as deep as those of actual bodily harm, and in the case of *Lilya 4-ever*, based on a real tragedy in Swedish Malmo, leads ultimately to suicide.

"It's not ok to leave a child all alone," objects Keke Palmer to her widower father (Samuel L Jackson) in *Cleaner (2007)*. Although the girl is fourteen-years-old she is understandably still upset over the death of her mother, and with her father being a private cop – a cleaner – "What if you came home dead, dad?" This is a child with a fear of isolation, with a desire for paternal love from a father who is too busy or self-absorbed to provide it.

This takes up the theme that you should educate the parents before tackling a child's problem, and is echoed even in *Mary Poppins.* Her role was not so much that of entertaining and nannying the kids, as refocusing the mother and father onto their parental duties. "When your little tykes are crying you have not time to dry their tears," sings Julie Andrews to the self-possessed George Banks who can't understand why his family is breaking apart. It is not until little Michael and Jane (Matthew Garber and Karen Dotrice) are flying their kites under the playful gaze of their parents, does Mary Poppins feel it safe to reopen her umbrella and drift away. If only Mary Poppins had looked in on the household in *Enid (2009)*, too! (We explore further the neglect of Enid Blyton's daughters, Gillian and Imogen, in Volume Two: *Families, Step-Kids and Orphans*).

"Dear mum," writes Jack (Zachery Ty Bryan) in *Magic Island* as he packs his bags ready to run away, "I'm sure you'll be too busy to miss me." Mum is going out on yet another date – 'a business meeting', mum calls it. His housemaid intercepts the boy before he leaves home: "Who knows, maybe your problems won't seem so bad come tomorrow." This is a boy who needs a boost to his self-esteem, and he finds it as he is whisked into a magical dreamland where he meets a beautiful young mermaid, Jessie-Ann Friend. There he accompanies a prince, the leader of a band of buccaneers, who confides in him that his mother, too, "never seemed to have enough time for me."

The above film is a fun-filled action movie turning the initial premise of parental neglect into a triviality, almost an excuse for an adventure. Roman Polanski's *A Day at the Beach* is a much more seriously intense film about the selfishness of an adult leading to the neglectful abuse of a ward in a man's care; in my opinion, one of the most powerful yet underrated films about child abuse, made even more forceful by the acting of the infant Beatie Edney. Mark Burns plays the uncle promising to give his niece a fun day out at the seaside, when instead he neglects her, preferring to get progressively drunk during the course of the day.

Uncle Bernard goes to collect his eight-year-old niece, Winnie, from his brother's house. Both his brother and his brother's wife are wary about leaving their daughter in his hands – they are aware of his alcoholism and seem to know what will happen. But still, both are busy parents and have to rush off to work.

While their backs are turned, Bernard is into their drinks cabinet and has downed a couple of gins, so the slippery slide has already begun. Even little Winnie, who loves her uncle, seems aware of what will be the outcome of the day. She has experienced it before. "You've been drinking again, Uncle Bernard," she exclaims as they leave, heading for the railway station in the pouring rain, "but I didn't tell mum, else there would be a row."

They arrive at the rain-soaked (Danish) seaside, wending their way along the wooden duckboards across the sandy beach, from one café to the next, on a seaside equivalent of a pub-crawl. Winnie sips her lemonade through a straw, while Bernard drinks beer after beer, trying to be philosophical with the café owners, but usually ending up insulting them, by which time they have to move on to the next café. There are few other places to shelter. Winnie waddles along in her bright yellow PVC hooded raincoat, Bernard strutting oblivious to the drenching rain.

As the day progresses and Bernard visits more and more bars, the little girl is left to fend for herself, waiting outside in the pouring rain. On one occasion, she gets desperately entangled in a fishing net, but her cries for help go unheeded, though thankfully she manages to free herself. When he does try looking for her he thinks, "You don't lose a child like a handkerchief."

She finally persuades him to take her to the funfair, but he just dumps her in a bumper car and leaves for the bar. The poor girl is helpless. She can't even reach the pedals. She is left motionless while all the other bumper cars drive around her having fun.

Bernard meets a poet friend, so while they go to get drunk on whisky and gin, Winnie has to sleep bored in the poet's sixties-style bubble car.

By the end of the night Bernard is totally sloshed. A passer-by finds Winnie shivering with cold and wet, and goes into the bar to admonish Bernard for neglecting the child. "What are you up to with that poor child?" he demands.

Bernard is now so inebriated he cannot walk straight and is seeing double. But Winnie has seen this before. The little eight-year-old knows it's her duty to find a taxi to get them home. So, while Bernard is spread-eagled in the town square lying dead to the world, Winnie desperately cries for help – but by this time of night the town is deserted.

In Volume Two, we referred to the neglect of six-year-old Ami in *Alas de Mariposa*. She could have been a happy child had it not been for her grandfather who desperately wanted a grandson, and had instilled in the mother that nothing but a boy would be welcomed. So the girl was raised unwanted and unloved. But dismally, the situation did not improve when mother finally gave birth to the baby boy that had been so longed for.

The girl was sent from the room whenever it was time to breast-feed the baby. Mother had unwarranted visions of Ami trying to kill the new baby by dropping it over the balcony. On one occasion, mother arrives home, sees the empty cot and sees Ami standing by the balcony, irrationally assumes the worst and brutally starts thrashing the little girl. "Where's my baby? Where's my baby?" And then the father appears from another room carrying the baby to see what the commotion is all about.

Then Ami has quite a bad accident, smashing open her skull. She seeks help from her mother, but the baby is crying and the baby takes priority. So the little girl is left, neglected and unloved.

There is a fine line between abuse and neglect. Françoise Truffaut, in the French film *Pocket Money*, gives us a glimpse of how these boundaries can be fogged. A mother ascends to her eighth floor flat with her toddler child, having just returned from a shopping trip. She realises she has left her purse at the shop. In her alarm she races back out, leaving the child alone to play with the kitten by the open window. Kitten climbs out of the window, the child follows it, and falls eight storeys down to the shrubbery below.

An older child, Sylvie Grezel, is left alone in a different apartment, her parents having gone to a restaurant for Sunday lunch (Sylvie stroppily had not wanted to join them). Sylvie picks up dad's megaphone and announces through the open window. "I'm hungry!" Her neighbours take pity on the girl, rustle up a hamper of goodies for the child to eat. "It's incredible leaving kids alone," decries one neighbour. "What if something happened to her?"

But Truffaut's premise is that kids are resolute and unbreakable. "They are like rocks. They bump into everything. They stumble through life." The boy who had fallen through the window bounced straight back up, none the worse for his fall, and started laughing, while mother, when she saw what had happened, fainted. The girl with the megaphone had spitefully manipulated the concept of abuse to her own gain. She had been left behind because the parents refused to allow her to carry her grubby handbag to the posh restaurant.

But Truffaut dabbles deeper into the theme of abuse. A new boy arrives at school, Julien, wearing tatty clothes and from an impoverished home. Julien resorts to shop lifting, rustling through coats in the school cloakroom, and searching at the funfair for dropped coins and other valuables. When it is his turn for the school medical, Julien refuses to strip out of his clothes. The nurse is only too aware of what this means. He is hiding burn marks and bruises where his abusive mother has beaten him. The nurse explains to the headteacher that an abused child always goes on the defensive. "I fell down... I ran into something." The police are called, the parents are arrested, and the child taken into care.

The class teacher uses this opportunity to help Julien's classmates empathise with his dilemma. An abused child "feels unhappy – but he can't put a name to it. Deep inside himself he can't challenge the adults... An unloved and battered child feels guilty... An unhappy adult can start again from scratch, but an unhappy child is helpless."

Controversially, the teacher adds from his own experience, "Those of us who had a difficult childhood are often better equipped for adult life than those who were over-protected or had a lot of love."

For Oksana Akinshina, playing sixteen-year-old Lilya in *Lilya 4-ever*, life in Estonia was one of drudgery, of bland dirty apartment blocks and uninteresting shopping malls. Mum befriends an American on the Internet and the girl becomes excited at their imminent move to the Big Apple. But on the departure date, Lilya is told she is being left behind (supposedly to be sent for later). She is left in the charge of a reluctant aunt. The aunt does not want this teenager living with her, so places her in a small filthy apartment where she has to fend for herself. Mother fails to send the promised maintenance money from America. Lilya is unable to support herself or pay any bills. She goes begging to her aunt, "They have cut off my electricity and I've got nothing to eat."

But the disinterested aunt replies, "So go into town and spread your legs, like your mother used to do."

The most heart-wrenching cases of neglect are those in which the parent is unable to cope, abandoning the child to savagery. Based on a true event reported from Los Angeles in 1970, *Mockingbird Don't Sing* brings out the neglect suffered by one thirteen-year-old girl (Katie, played by eleven-year-old Tarra Steele) locked away for all her childhood, tied to a commode, whose whole existence was that of clawing, scratching and spitting like a feral animal. "The worst case of child abuse they've ever seen," claim the LA authorities. "Wilful, gross neglect of a child," declares the judge, before the disgraced father takes a gun to his head and kills himself.

Bodily Harm

Physical hitting, slapping, being caned, stubbed by cigarettes, burnt by an iron; these are what are usually conjured to the mind when physical abuse is mentioned. While emotional and psychological abuse leave no physical scars, actual bodily harm does, and this kind of abuse is thus easier to diagnose.

"You're wicked!" protests Alakina Mann as her mother (Nicole Kidman) physically lays into her as a result of a misunderstanding in *The Others* (2001). "God help me! What's the matter with me?" cries the mother as the deed in done.

A child being physically punished may bear the evidence, but the abused child can usually be persuaded to cover up this evidence, trivialise it, deny it or lie about it if it is discovered; for a child's loyal love for its parents endures beyond the acceptance of physical pain, as we discover in *Before Women had Wings*, a forgiving child is willing to be a punch bag if it means he or she won't be taken into care.

When asked did her father abuse her, eleven-year-old Becca Gardner in *An Unfinished Life* is evasive, "No, it was mainly my mum he hit." The denial is made in the fairy tale hope that stories have a happy ending. "She is still at the age when she believes everything is going to turn out right!" says her mother as they flee from their hometown in Iowa to the grandfather's ranch in Wyoming. When the mother is asked why she stayed so long with an abusive partner, guilt feelings from a former relationship resurface: "You stay with someone because you don't feel you deserve any better."

The child may be brought up to believe that physical punishment is good for them, particularly when the iron grip of religion takes hold, as Emily Ashton experiences through constant clips around the ear in *Oranges are not the Only Fruit*. Likewise, Sydney McCallister, playing preteen Mary Sunday in *There will be Blood*, lived in a perversely religious family that used thrashings to 'help believers'. Though we never see the abuse of the little girl, it is implied.

When the stepfather in *Bastard out of Carolina* violently straps eleven-year-old Jena Malone, he justifies his actions to his wife, "Someone's got to love her enough to care how she turns out." This is a power-crazed man whose mantra, "he loved me so much," knew no distinction between physical and sexual abuse. "I hid my bruises as if they were evidence of crimes I had committed," reflects the child.

Similarly, we realise something pretty severe is up in *Prince of Tides* when the children dive into the river and remain submerged, holding their breath, whenever their father comes home in his shrimping boat. Even so, Tom, who we see cringing in fear cowering beneath his mad dad, in later life forgivingly reflects, "I guess my dad would have been a pretty good father if he hadn't been such a violent man."

Mrs March (Susan Sarandon) explains how abuse is perpetuated: "If you hit a child, the lesson she learns is to hit and humiliate," she says to the headteacher as she withdraws her child from the school in *Little Women*. Her daughter, Amy (Kirsten Dunst), had come home from school with her hands red raw from a thrashing by a teacher. Her wicked crime? She had dropped her writing slate in the snow, which had obliterated her homework. As we discover later in this volume, Patrick Brontë similarly removed his famed children from an abusive school.

This remark is echoed in the words of Papa Bellocq (Keith Carradine) in *Pretty Baby*. "You can't beat a child. It'll only teach her to beat others." This comes after twelve-year-old Violet (Brooke Shields) had been caught canoodling with a black boy. "I can do what I want," she had protested. "Everybody does that with everybody!" But she is flogged anyway: several thrashings enough to tear her dress and reveal her bare cheeks.

Even the police authorities use physical thrashing to exert control and supposedly achieve 'respect'. But no respect was received from Mrs Tanner in the Australian film, *Celia* (1988). "Don't you ever victimise my children again, or I'll make sure you are reported," says the defiant mother to the rural police constable. There had been another soil-throwing fight in the quarry between the nine-year-old children. "Dirty reds," shout the Burke children to the three Tanner children and their next-door neighbour Celia Carmichael (Rebecca Smart). With little else to do, the policeman discovers the fight. The protagonists have already scarpered (including the constable's own daughter, Stephanie Burke, played by Amelia Frid). The police constable takes it out on the Tanner children, who were really the victims. No questions are asked, only assumptions are made. The Tanners are despised because their parents have communist sympathies. The policeman takes off his belt and thrashes the Tanner children. Summary justice inflicted.

Such corporal punishment is the norm in many cultures. When asked what her first day was like at her Moroccan school, Bea (Bella Riza) tells her mother in *Hideous Kinky*, "Well, a little girl wet herself. The teacher brought her to the front of the class and beat her with a cane until she stopped crying." When mum suggests withdrawing Bea from the school, which will mean separation from her new found friends, the girl has to pretend she fabricated the story.

Sometimes the child is hurt in the rough-and-tumble of daily games, particularly where a survival of the fittest mentality is maintained, as abused victims in *Lord of the Flies* or *Battle Royale* can testify. These films portray not so much vindictive bullying as a real-life tussle to aspire to the top of a social pecking order. In *Killer of Sheep*, child actors are visibly hurt during stone-throwing games, real stones being thrown at real targets, and they hurt. Children wince genuinely and painfully as they are struck by the missiles in the black ghetto 'play' fights. These children are playing destructively because they are bored, and not out of a bullying instinct. There is no friendly or co-operative play.

For children who witness the suffering of others, the solution may be to take things into their own hands, to eliminate the abuser. This was the ideal of recently orphaned fourteen-year-old Lyndall (Kasha Kropinski) and her younger sister (Anneke Weidemann) as they lived on a kraal in the South African Karoo in the 1890s with their guardian (an aunt), in *A Story of an African Farm*. They witness their black friend (and adopted half-brother, Luke Gallant) being whipped for trivial reasons by a confidence trickster (Richard E Grant) who has wheedled his way into the family home by making romantic advances on their auntie. The cunning children get their revenge by setting up the flirtatious man with another woman so he can be discovered in a compromising position by the jealous auntie. "Adults will never hurt us again," states Lyndall.

Violently Abusive Parents

"Look at this, Mama. Look at what you have become."

Before Women had Wings is an emotionally powerful film about an abusive household, with parents being violent towards each other when drunk. Yet despite the abuse being passed down to the youngest child, Bird, the girl remains loyally loving to her violent drunken abusers.

Twelve-year-old Tina Majorino plays the younger sister who regularly sees her parents squabbling: mother with bruised face, beaten up by a threatening gun-toting husband. "Mummy and daddy don't care nothing about us," says her older more rational sister, Phoebe.

"That ain't true," the little girl protests, ever ready to forgive her violent mother.

Yet the day comes when the father so badly beats up his woman that in a desperate fit of remorse he goes out and shoots himself. "When your daddy shot himself, he shot our future off to hell," mother reflects, trying to deflect the responsibility from herself. Although this has removed one violent partner, the mother continues to fuel the hole in her life with whisky. Bird observes, "Mother wallows in that bed of nails called widowhood."

"She has a husband who died too soon. Love is eating her up on the inside, so she can't treat anyone right, not even her own children." That is the verdict of neighbour, Miss Zora, played by Oprah Winfrey. "By the looks of things your mum must be in a world of trouble," she says to Bird.

It only takes the slightest provocation for mother to blow her fuse. When she discovers older daughter, Phoebe, is dating a boy, the girl gets a brutal thrashing, leaving her badly bruised. This makes the older daughter really despise her mother. Yet little Bird remains loyal.

As mother gets deeper into her breakdown it is pitiful having to watch the devoted young daughter caressing her own mother who is sobbing on the little girl's lap. Yet Bird's troubles deepen when mother cruelly tries to place the blame for father's suicide on the little girl. Bird's only source of comfort is from the neighbour, Miss Zora, a woman that mum has banned Bird from seeing (because she is reclusive, grows herbs, and she's black!). So Bird has to make her visits to Miss Zora in secret.

When mother eventually finds out Bird has been seeing the woman, Bird is aware of what is going to happen. "She's going to beat me, and she's going to beat me bad," she confides to Miss Zora.

Mother does go berserk. The girl is clouted around the head, bundled into a closet, and thrashed endlessly with a whip until she can no longer cry for help.

As mother flees in a huff, Phoebe helps her younger sister hobble to Miss Zora's house, their only place of refuge in an era before social services. Mother, of course, in her drunken state was unaware of the damage she had caused. She is enraged again when she returns to find her daughter hiding next door. It is only when she is shown the deep weal marks on her daughter's back and the bruises on her face that she is able to conceive her uncontrolled actions. "Look at this, Mama. Look at what you have become," says Phoebe.

Miss Zora refuses to let the daughters return to the violent mother, but diplomatically defuses the problem by suggesting the mother has a break to recuperate while the girls and Miss Zora head south.

In the Japanese horror movie *Audition*, Asami Yamazaki sought comfort in classical ballet to ease the pain of her abusive childhood. Most of this abuse is related verbally as the character reflects on her past, but for one horrific sequence, we witness Ayaka Izumi playing the part of the seven-year-old. Dressed in her white leotard she has just completed her ballet practice and rests on the floor, legs apart, taking a breather.

Then evil stepfather crawls up to her, a red-hot branding iron clenched in his fist. She widens her legs submissively as he approaches her groin. Surely he won't be so cruel. But the audience gasp as the iron is thrust into her upper thigh, and the screams ring out.

Asami relates the tale of how her parents were divorced when she was small, so she was sent to live with an uncle. It was terrible there. All the girl can remember is the abuse by the uncle's wife. She was made to take cold baths in winter, and was pushed downstairs. The doctor, alarmed at her bruises, arranged for her to move back with her mother who had now married a disabled man. As a seven-year-old, she hated her disabled stepfather. Every day after school she would sneak silently into the house and hide in a dark room until mother arrived home.

That was how she learnt to take revenge. She discovered a poisonous drug that can render a victim paralysed while still conscious. In that state she could wreak pain on those who abused her, they being helpless to resist her amputation of their tongues, ears, fingers, feet.

This was not the swiftly dispatched revenge for selfish motives of Patty McCormick in *The Bad Seed*; rather this was premeditated revenge on an exploitative male population, designed to inflict maximum pain and distress. "All words are lies. Pain does not lie," she tells her victims.

In The *Amityville Horror* (2005), the abuse was more psychically charged. Stepdad George is becoming more deranged as he hears muffled voices that he cannot explain. He takes revenge on his stepson, Billy, for the inexplicable occurrences, assuming them to be hateful pranks against his authority. The most alarming is when Billy is forced to help chop wood as a punishment. Made to hold the log between his hands, Billy (in a piece of brilliant terrified action by Jesse James) quakes with fear, resigned to a fateful end, while his stepfather crashes the axe violently onto the slab of wood.

Ten-year-old Lilith is brought to the attention of the Oregon Family Services Department. She has become withdrawn at school and physical abuse inflicted by the parents is suspected. For already overworked Renée Zellweger this is yet another burden: her *Case 39*. She is right to be concerned, for in the middle of the night she receives an SOS call from the little girl. "They're going to kill me!" The social worker races in her car to the rescue.

Meanwhile, the girl is being shoved in an oven by her parents. The oven door is sealed shut using duct tape. Now the gas is ignited. We see the girl frantically crashing against the oven door as smoke fills the furnace. In her desperate dilemma she conjures up enough strength to stay alive until her rescuers arrive to free her from the oven, just in time.

Not only is this piece of action horrific and alarming to watch, the panic and anguish on the little girl's face is so realistic, and the psychological trauma for the child must be overwhelming. Surely, this child actor will have years of nightmares having been confined in such a claustrophobic and potentially dangerous situation.

Of course, this is why directors are so skilled. Firstly, the casting: the child actor was none other than Jodelle Ferland. I believe her to be the most competent and underrated child actress around. Her depiction of terror was brilliantly believable. It is only when watching the extras on the DVD that we discover she wasn't trapped in an oven at all. It was just a façade in the middle of a room. Behind the oven door was a Narnia-sized room filled with furniture, recording equipment and a smoke machine. Jodelle herself acknowledged how much fun she had making the movie.

Likewise, one would expect the effect on child actress Asami Yamazaki must have been devastating in *Audition*. She must have had nightmares throughout her youth about a red-hot poker being thrust in her groin. But of course, films are collated in the editor's cutting and splicing room. The little girl would have had no inkling of the victimised role she was depicting.

For us the audience, we need to be made seriously aware of the abuse of children, but we need not be concerned about the traumatic effect upon these actresses, for the depiction of horror is all an illusion, thankfully.

Racial Abuse / Prejudice

The time-line of racial prejudice stretches as far back as history itself. From the dawn of humanity, Neolithic Shell people have been distrustful of Rock people, battling it out on our screens with grunts and cudgels in *One Million Years BC*, and *When Dinosaurs Ruled the Earth*, and later in *10,000 Years BC* (as the scantily clad Raquel Welch, Victoria Vetri, and Camilla Belle bear witness). Since Biblical times, migrant Phoenician warships have confronted Assyrian warriors, Trojans have sparred with Spartans (*Troy*), and flotillas of gladiatorial Spartacus's have slavishly rowed their galleys across the Mediterranean Sea. Even Jesus Christ was criticised for soliciting with Samaritans. That Crusaders would trek thousands of miles across Europe to attack Saracens, and that Moors would sweep into Iberia, shows how deeply entrenched hatred for other peoples and their customs has always been. The imperialistic trading of slaves by European bigots, aided by Arab traders, has left a legacy of displaced cultures who, by daring to raise their status from guttersnipes to freedom fighters by arriving as immigrants or claiming their rights to a parcel of land, have received a tirade of abuse and prejudice from white-skinned homesteaders who see anyone different to themselves as intimidating and threatening.

Prejudice derives from fearful ignorance of the unknown and from what is different. After all, what is more strikingly noticeable than the colour of someone's skin? This bias is gradually being demolished in multicultural societies, yet deeply entrenched prejudices are hard to break down. Racist chants still occur in soccer matches, though FIFA are trying hard to eliminate these. Xenophobic groups such as Ku Klux Klan still exist as underground organisations. The medium of movies is helping to highlight the issue of racial abuse and show us the trauma this inflicts on the victim, whether that be white lawyer adopting an orphaned black boy in *The Summer of Ben Tyler*, a basketball coach adopting three ethnic orphans within a bigoted neighbourhood in *Mixed Company* (1974), anti-Japanese sentiment arising in an American community in *Snow Falling on Cedars*, or swarthy gypsy-looking Heathcliff being persecuted by Hindley in *Wuthering Heights*. In *Chasing Secrets* we find a negative reversal, as a white girl is sheltered by an elderly black couple.

Whites have a culture of believing themselves to be supremacist (until the Black Power movement dared to fist a challenge to this arrogance). In the mid-twentieth century, this notion of white superiority was expanded with the concept of the Arian race, promulgated by Hitler and his Nazi followers. Prejudice is not entirely related to skin-tone, as the attempted extermination of the Jews, Bosnians, the Marsh Arabs, or Hutus and Tutsis bear witness. (We consider further films dealing with Ethnic Cleansing and the Holocaust in Volume Seven: *Childhood Traumas*, while in Volume Four: *Childhood Friendships*, we focus on how children have formed friendships across the racial divide). Here, we are concerned with those films that confront the traumas that are encountered when victims are racially abused with regard to their colour.

Rather cleverly, *The Grinch* surreptitiously confronts children (and accompanying adult viewers) with this issue in a thought-provoking manner. The audience is unaware of being subtly swayed by the movie's subtext of highlighting prejudice, yet are happy to decry the injustice meted out to a monster because he is coloured green.

Jim Carrey, playing the green hairy yeti, is rejected by the townsfolk of Whoville for being so different from everybody else. Written into the Whoville Council's constitution is the precept that "No matter how different a Who may appear he will always be welcome." All very laudable, but they don't live that out in practice. With the whole community despising the Grinch, he is shunned and has to dwell apart living on the refuse the townsfolk discard. It takes the persistence of a little girl, Cindy (Taylor Momsen), to point out the hypocrisy to the Mayor, for the Grinch to be reaccepted (reluctantly) into the activities of the town.

Alas, the Grinch is made to act and look so repulsive and frightening that analogies made with integrating ethnic minority groups may be counter-productive. Despite the racist subtext, the Grinch is rejected, not because he was green, but because he is horribly obnoxious and anti-social (though of course, one may have caused the other).

Our empathies are likewise challenged in *Samson and Delilah*. We are shocked at the Australian rejection of their aboriginal way of life, yet we too are caught up despising the young couple in the film, not because they have a different skin tone, but because they become glue-sniffing unkempt dropouts caught, through no fault of their own, in a downward spiral that keeps them firmly placed on the bottom of the heap.

The South African film, *Skin*, highlights the incongruities of the South African apartheid system that existed in the second half of the twentieth century.

Ella Ramangwane plays eleven-year-old Sandra Laing. As the daughter of white Afrikaans parents she is described as white-skinned on her birth certificate. But she is obviously coloured – her skin is darker, she has matted short black hair, her lips, teeth, and facial dimensions are more similar to members of the coloured community. Her parents are aware of this and decide to move to the Transvaal, opening a shop in a coloured community where Sandra will be less conspicuous. She happily plays and swims in the creeks alongside other coloured children.

But the day arrives when her parents decide it is time to send her off to boarding school – for white girls only. Throughout her childhood, the little girl had always been told she is white. She has grown up believing she is white, with all the privileges that accrue. But now, alongside all the other white girls at the boarding school, it is obvious that Sandra is very different. The white girls stare at her as if she is an alien. "I'm not black," she pitifully states. But the others are not convinced.

Other parents complain to the headteacher. The Head, fed-up with the 'disruption' this is causing, calls the girl to the front of the class and beats her with a stick in front of all the other children. The police are called to escort Sandra home, and she is reclassified as 'coloured' by the courts.

It is a shame the film director did not focus more on the distress this caused to the young girl, who seemed to take the abuse passively. Instead, the film focuses on the impact on the parents. "To be slapped in the face by your own people is very poor," her father tells the Press after the court decreed: "The definition of a white person is someone who, in appearance, is obviously white." The Press take photographs of the girl for publicity purposes, but it becomes more like a freak show. This provokes the father into buying some skin-lightening lotion. But when Sandra slaps too much on, her skin burns and blisters.

Sandra has to tread a delicate path as the coloured daughter of white parents. However, her father's persistence in taking her cause to the government eventually results in a reversal in the ruling: "Descent, rather than appearance, will be the determining factor in all classification cases."

So Sandra reverts to being officially white again. But now she is no longer a little girl. She is a teenager wanting dates. White boys won't date her (or if they do, this provokes problems when going to restaurants – the black-looking girl and white boy cannot share the same eating-places).

Sandra is naturally attracted to coloured boys. But this is illegal. She has to keep her tryst with deliveryman, Petrus, a secret. When father discovers this, he threatens to shoot Petrus. So, Petrus and Sandra flee together to Lesotho where they are accepted as a coloured couple and raise a family together. Father, however, thinks Sandra has been ungrateful for all the political fighting he has done on her behalf. He angrily burns every last relic, memory, and photograph of his daughter.

"You can't help what you were born, but you can help what you become," is the conflicting moral behind this true and tragic tale.

I am including the incidents from *A Time to Kill* in this section under racial abuse rather than later in this volume under sexual abuse. The film relates the rape of ten-year-old Tonya Hailey, a black child targeted by two white men exploiting their supremacist beliefs, in the state of

Mississippi. The two drunkards were whooping it up in a black community, being abusive to locals throwing beer bottles at windows, and walking from the local shop without paying for the crates of beer. If this had been a white girl that they had spotted they would have driven by. It is only because Tonya was black, walking alone carrying her father's groceries, that she was targeted. "You know what they say," says one of the vulgar thugs. "If they are old enough to crawl they are in the right position." Now, this is one repulsive remark that jars: offensive to us the audience, insulting to the child actress required to read the script.

Fortunately, we do not get to witness the rape scene, nor any of the abuse, and the actress (Raeven Larrymore Kelly) is not required to act out being a victim. The trauma is made real enough in the aftermath as we witness the despoiled ten-year-old being brought into her father's arms and apologising, "Daddy, I'm sorry I dropped all the groceries." The cruelty of the incident is made explicit as the lawyer defending Tonya's father at court describes the horrific circumstances of the abuse, resulting in the lifelong irreparable damage to the girl.

Kidnapping and Abduction

A child, particularly a girl, is an easy target for a kidnapper: the child held to ransom for monetary gain, for status, or for sexual favours. In the past decade, a whole library of books has been published featuring abusive crimes committed against little children so that bookstores now have a whole section devoted to the theme, such as *The Natasha Kampusch Story* featuring the ten-year-old *Girl in the Cellar*, *Never on a Sunday*, or *The Little Prisoner*; all traumatic to read, unimaginable for the child who endured it, yet when transferred to film has to be made entertaining. Fortunately, few of these stories have been twisted for our titillation.

Most tales of kidnap on the screen are more related to gangsterism than actual child abuse. For example, in *Cold Sweat*, hard man Charles Bronson is abducted along with his wife and eleven-year-old stepdaughter, Michelle (Yannick Dululle), by gun-toting gangsters and confined to a remote shack in the limestone hills behind the French Riviera. Despite being edge-of-seat, nail-biting drama, with the child convincing in her portrayal of fear, the film has no real message to dispense about the trauma of childhood kidnappings.

The Western movie, *The Missing* (2003), injects a degree of trauma for Lilly (Evan Rachel Wood) who is bound and gagged by a gang of Indians from the frontier home where she had been living with her mother and preteen sister (Jenna Boyd) in New Mexico in 1855, though mainly the film focuses on the search. There is a frantic chase to rescue the girl before she is sold across the Mexican border. "These girls are going to market," says the outlaw, maliciously. In *Don't Say a Word*, Michael Douglas seeks out his daughter (Skye McCole Bartusiak) who is being kidnapped until a stolen ruby is recovered by Sean Bean and his gang of crooks. "If you want to see your daughter alive, don't say a word." Instead of being afeared, the little girl uses her ingenuity to help her be located.

In *Panic Room*, Kristen Stewart plays a level-headed twelve-year-old forced to retreat with her mother (Jodie Foster) into a special secure room built into their flat when a trio of burglars invade their exclusive apartment. In *Bless the Child*, Holliston Coleman is kidnapped by a religious cult because they believe the girl had been endowed with telekinetic powers. This is a horror tale and never dwells on the torment of the kidnapped child.

Likewise, *Waterworld* focuses on the bravado of the kidnapped Enola rather than the trauma of her capture by sea pirates. Plucky Enola is played by ten-year-old Tina Majorino. She is a precious commodity on account of the coded map tattooed to her back, though one passing trader has more basal motives in mind offering to trade with Kevin Costner for her, even just for forty-five minutes of the little girl's time, no doubt for 'an intimate study of maps', as Laurie Lee would phrase it.

Alarming exceptions to the gangster theme are *Flowers in the Attic*, in which a deluded mother, motivated by greed for her father's inheritance, colludes with the grandmother to lock her children out of sight and out of mind in the upstairs rooms of the rambling mansion; *Babel*, in which two children, Elle Fanning and Nathan Gamble, are dumped in the middle of the desert, without water, and in the searing sun as their captor evades Mexican border guards (both children acted suitably scared and both attracted nominations for Young Artist Awards for best performance in a feature film of a young actor under the age of ten); and *Down will come Baby* in which, as we will see shortly, a manipulative woman wants to live out the life of her dead Amelia through another abducted child, Robin.

In *Along came a Spider* twelve-year-old Megan Rose, played by Mika Boorem, is kidnapped from her exclusive school. She is the daughter of an American Senator, watched over constantly by the Secret Service, knowing she is a potentially valuable target. And yet she is abducted, from under the noses of her protectors by her school computer teacher who manages to dope her, and cart her away inside a computer trolley, and ferry her off to his waiting yacht where she is imprisoned in a tiny room in which the teacher has installed a CCTV camera. "What do you think of me now?" asks her former teacher.

"I think you're a sick pervert," she replies.

The teacher had been planning this abduction for two years. "Imagine the patience, the dedication," suggests the investigator (Morgan Freeman). "He's like a spider," waiting for months and years for the right opportunity to come along. Police recognise this excessive patience to be a trait of the modern day groomers who target children to molest.

Boys are not kidnapped in movies with the same regularity as girls. But when a syndicate of Italian villagers decide to bury a boy (Mattio di Pierro) in an underground bunker for monetary gain in *I'm not Scared*, the true horror of a child kept in cruel captivity is brought to light. The child can barely whisper 'aqua' to the 'guardian angel' (Guiseppe Cristiano) who stumbles across the squalid hideaway. Being deprived of light for days, the pitiful lad remains half blind for most of the film.

Man on Fire captures the violent ruthlessness of the organised crime gangs rife in Third World countries. Though the incidents in the novel take place in Italy, the film transposes the action to Third World Mexico. Dakota Fanning plays Pita Ramos, a primary school child of rich parents – father is Mexican, mother American. Securely based in their Mexico City villa, a bodyguard has to be hired to protect the child on her daily journeys to school and to her swimming and piano lessons. You can never know who to trust in this crime-ridden city, for the police are often implicated in many of the crooked deals. Ex-American cop, John Creasy (played by Denzel Washington), appears to be as hard and as honest as they come. But the man is haunted by a past failure, and has resorted to alcohol, which may have steadied his nerve but not his aim.

This film begins by highlighting the scale of the problem: "There is one kidnapping every sixty minutes in Latin America. 70% of the victims do not survive. Mysteriously, the kidnapping of Pita takes place when her mother and father have to go away on a trip. Creasy has escorted her to her piano lesson in a different part of town when two cop cars arrive blocking both ends of the road, and a third car cruises past. There is a shoot-out. Creasy is badly injured trying to protect his young charge, and Pita is bundled into the boot of a car and whisked away. Creasy, in his hospital bed, is placed under arrest for killing four police officers.

Soon, evidence shows the cops were crooked, and ultimately we learn her father was in on the kidnapping scam, too, as a way of securing some of the insurance money. Since the kidnapping attempt is bungled, assumptions are made that Pita has been killed; especially after a bag of the ransom money paid to the organiser is fake. But the recuperating Creasy carries out a sequence of violent raids to discover the whereabouts of Pita and secures the release of his young ward. Throughout the film, Dakota plays convincingly scared, and the whole film effectively illustrates the callous disregard for life where kidnapping is concerned.

Evidently, the novel upon which this film is based dwells also on the repeated rape of the nine-year-old girl, an issue that would have taken this film beyond the bounds of credulity. And yet, the closing credits hint the drama was adapted from real events. In the book there is no happy conclusion, for the girl is not released alive.

Mexico also provides the location for the disturbing kidnapping of Aidan Gould playing Tom in Erick Zonca's movie, *Julia (2008)*. It is not often the director focuses on the kidnapping of a boy. It begins with low-life alcoholic Tilda Swinton playing an evil Julia, tempted into snatching a boy from his father and delivering him to the separated wife across the border in Mexico. That is gritty and realistic enough, but the real difficulties begin as they encounter rival gangs within Mexico itself. An equally alarming movie involving a kidnapped boy is in Clint Eastwood's masterly direction of *Changeling* in which Angelina Jolie's kidnapped son is returned to her, but the incompetent cops bring the wrong child!

The kidnap of a child inevitably results in a lifelong search on the part of the parents, particularly where the infant mysteriously disappears without trace, and with no ransom demands. The recent case of the headlines-hitting disappearance of Madeleine McCann in Portugal in 2007 brings home the deeply emotional impact on the parents, the accusations unjustly made against them by the Portuguese police, the press bandwagon that relentlessly pursued them, the bugging of their intensely personal phone calls by opportunist paparazzi. If only the Greek police and the British Foreign Office had been diligent over the search for missing infant Ben Needham in 1991. Bafflingly, it took twenty-two years for the British Foreign Office to finally interview the distraught parents.

Until a child is recovered we don't get to hear the child's side of the story; and even then, children like Shannon Matthews, kidnapped in Dewsbury, England, in February 2008 (by her own parents hoping to claim reward money), are carefully sheltered by social services away from the glare of the media, so their story is not revealed, until they are ready.

We do get to hear the child's side of the story in *Heidi* as the little girl is abducted from her grandfather's mountain hut. (In Volume Seven: *Childhood Traumas*, we explore the emotional trauma that *Heidi* went through after her aunt had duped her into coming to Frankfurt, the gradual deterioration in her health, her constant pining for her old home in the mountains.)

The motive for the kidnapping of the infant Tommy (William Rodriguez) in The *Emerald Forest* is as obscure as the misty rain forest into which he vanished. One moment he was standing next to his father, mother and sister in a clearing where the father is supervising the construction of a dam in Amazonia, the next, he has been silently snatched into the lush dense foliage and taken to live among a group of tribal Indians, known as the *Invisible Ones*. Ultimately we learn from the Indian chief, "One day I was hunting at the edge of the world when Tommy came and smiled at me; the light of the forest was in his eyes!" (Not a mitigation that would sway the Metropolitan Police!)

Father spends the next ten years hunting for his boy, risking his life exploring the jungle, and visiting unfriendly forgotten tribes. Mother looks after lost children "in the hope that someone somewhere will be looking after her lost boy." The film tells us there are more than two million abandoned children roaming the streets of Brazil.

When father and son do eventually come face to face at a remote jungle waterfall, although each recognise one another, Tommy confirms the fear of all parents seeking their long-lost child, by stating he has a new father now (or in the case of the Baader Meinhof gang who kidnapped Patty Hearst, the daughter of a wealthy businessman, the girl now has new political allegiances and sympathises with the cause of her abductors). Tommy has adapted to his new way of life in the primitive village and has no desire to revert to his old ways. How long it took the boy to form this attitude we don't know. Undoubtedly, he would have been afraid at first, but his fears now are of the old world that he left as an infant.

So the father has to confront the tribal chief. "You stole my son from me," he accuses. But the boy intervenes, "Daddee, that was long ago." Father then tries to persuade the boy to return to see his old home and mother. But Tommy replies pointing to the surrounding canopy of trees, "This is my home, and my children's home." Natalie Wood makes a similar treatise as she is rescued by John Wayne and Jeffrey Hunter in John Ford's classic, *The Searchers*. Brought up for so many years by the Comanche tribe that had kidnapped her as a ten-year-old she declares, "These are my people," gesturing to the tepees, squaws and Indian warriors.[2]

In a Stranger's Hand tries to shift our attention to considering the blame the parents may lay on themselves for not taking care of their child. Yet even here, the mother did everything right. "I'm going to be late home," she tells her infant daughter, Carla (Erica Dill). "You know what to do. You stay at school and wait for me." But in the foyer of the apartment block, mother (Megan Gallagher) realises she has forgotten the lunch packs. "Wait here. Don't talk to anyone, I'll be right back." Mother leaves the child alone, races upstairs, phones her workplace to tell them she is now running late, picks up the lunch packs, and races back to the lobby. But too late. Carla has been abducted to join the thousands of other missing children in New York. But then this potentially serious film gets side-tracked and focuses on a total stranger, Jack (played by Robert Urich), who happens to see the child in the subway, and the lengths he goes to, to help find a stranger's child.

A compelling film dealing with child abduction is *Down will come Baby*, featuring moving performances by child actress Evan Rachel Wood, and solid support from her abductor played by Meredith Baxter. This might well help convey why some adults snatch babies, though in this film it is a twelve-year-old, Robin, who is taken. Robin is grieving for her friend, Amelia, who drowned at summer camp, a tragedy for which Robin feels partially responsible.

Robin is sitting alone in the park, looking down-in-the-mouth. Along comes a woman, Dorothy, who starts to talk confidently to her, raising the girl's spirits, and offering some breadcrumbs to help feed the birds. "You seem bothered," the woman says gently. This woman would pass as a capable psychotherapist, so understanding is she as she calmly coaxes the child to air her problems.

By 'coincidence', Dorothy has moved into an apartment in the same compound as Robin, and her window overlooks Robin's bedroom. At first, Dorothy is kind and interested. They often seem to meet accidentally. Dorothy is soon visiting the girl at Robin's house, helping with her homework, babysitting when Robin's parents are out. Mother starts noticing that Dorothy comes practically every day and starts to worry about it, but father is only too pleased to have this woman around, taking the pressures of raising a child from off his shoulders.

But soon, Robin herself starts worrying. Once when the woman is showing the girl how to bake cakes, perfectionist Dorothy momentarily goes manic. Later, we see how Dorothy has helped Robin rearrange her bedroom, with the bed beside the window (where she can easily be seen from Dorothy's flat). Then the woman takes endless photographs of the little girl. "You took my picture yesterday, and the day before," complains Robin, (just as Violet had done to Papa Bellocq in *Pretty Baby*). The woman has also surreptitiously hidden a baby talker in the girl's bedroom so she can overhear the conversations Robin has with her parents.

Robin shows the photographs to her mother. "She likes taking pictures of me… she tickles me… she takes me to dance classes… she's starting to make me kind of nervous… I just want to get away from her… every time I turn around she's there." Mother overhears an argument outside between the girl and the woman. When mum intervenes she is told, "I just came down to bring you some brownies. I didn't know it was going to cause a problem." Alarm bells are now ringing in mum's minds. Had this been a man, the police would have been called and the intruder charged with grooming, but since it is a woman, the situation seems acceptable. Even so, mother bans the woman from visiting the house.

Father sees things differently. "If you were home more (mother is often away on business trips) you would see this is not a problem. Dorothy is nothing but helpful. I think you're over-reacting." Alarmingly, father has invited Dorothy to baby-sit again while mum is away. It is during this evening that sulky Robin cannot evade the attentions of the intrusive woman. As the woman becomes more domineering, and the girl more disobedient, there is a struggle in which Robin is knocked unconscious.

Robin wakes up in a different house, somewhere out in the Arizona countryside, locked in a room whose windows are barred and that is filled with the pictures of Dorothy's dead daughter, Amelia. Many of these pictures have been replaced with photos of Robin. Only now does it dawn on Robin that Dorothy is the mother of her dead friend, and that Robin is to be her substitute daughter. The woman tries to get Robin to call her "Mama". Then we see how the dead daughter was branded with hot candle wax whenever she was disobedient, and Robin is about to get the same treatment. Fortunately, the police arrive along with the parents, and the woman is carted off, either to jail or to an asylum.

The case of a family of children unwittingly abducted by pirates ends in the ultimate hanging of the perpetrators even though the children were not mistreated. In *A High Wind in Jamaica*, the five Templeton children are being escorted through the Caribbean on the way back to England when a gang of pirates take over their boat. The children are puzzled why they had to change boats. "Grown-ups never do tell us anything," complains Emily (Deborah Baxter). The children were a surprise to the pirates, too. The kids had been playing in the ship's hold as the pirates set off, unaware they were carrying this "precious cargo." It is the kids that did more harm to the pirates, obstructing them, accidentally letting down the anchor, climbing the rigging, destroying their figurehead. When asked at court how the pirates had mistreated them, the children could only answer about Capt. Chavez (Anthony Quinn). "He was terribly brave – he ate a big spoon of pepper and didn't cry!"

Alarmingly, like *The Pied Piper of Hamlin* who bewitched a town-load of children into his mountain dungeon only to be heralded as a legendary hero through succeeding generations, the evil kidnapper in the next example has come to be a revered figure in children's literature. It is the popular children's fantasy, *The Narnia Chronicles: The Lion, the Witch and the Wardrobe*. The seemingly pleasant faun, half-man half-goat, Mr Tumnus, who first met Lucy in the land of Narnia, was a child abductor. He had befriended the little girl (Georgie Henley), had taken her to his own private home, fed her with tea and cakes, and finally serenaded her until she fell into a magical comatose sleep. This is a salutatory lesson for little girls to learn, about who can and who cannot be trusted, and about the danger of talking to strangers. You can almost hear Scotland Yard rattling their handcuffs. Wisely, in *Millions (2004)*, Lewis McGibbon warns his younger brother (Alex Etel), "Look! People are weird. You've got to be more careful. You shouldn't really talk to them." Yet the lesson goes unheeded in Narnia. Tumnus' intent, having captured the 'daughter of Eve', was to hand the girl over to the evil witch.

"How would you like to have tea with me?" the semi-naked man asks her.

"Well, I really should be getting back," replies the sensible girl, but the bribe of toast, cakes, and a warm snug fire change her mind. "Well, I suppose I could come for a little while." The single male bringing the girl-child back to his bachelor pad admits, "You have made me feel more that I have in a hundred years."

Fortunately for Lucy, Mr Tumnus has a change of heart and allows her to go free after confessing to her his motives and acknowledging what an evil man he is. He is wracked with guilt as Lucy protests, "I thought you were my friend." This child predator was later to become a hero and favourite among child readers the world over, once Aslan had turned him back from a block of stone! Mr Tumnus remains a genial (bare-chested!) man, and his perversion forgiven, and lessons about stranger-danger papered over. 'Oh, it will be alright!'

Slavery / Child Bondage

Wilberforce and his cronies, despite what history books tell us, did not exterminate slavery. It is still practised the world over in the twenty-first century. Young women and children, particularly girls, are kidnapped from or sold by their families in many African and Asian communities, and even in Eastern European countries, to be reared as free kitchen help or as maids, or even cast into sexual servitude. This has been endemic for centuries (notably in Arabic countries) and continues to this day. Alarmingly, the practice has become evident in Britain and other European cities.

It is not exclusively children, however: in September 2011, a group of adult males were released by police from enslavement in a rural compound, Greenacres in Bedfordshire, England. These included down-and-outs; picked up from the streets of London, offered a bed, food and free booze as recompense for manual labour, but some had for fifteen years been literally locked into an exploited way of life. Documentaries have also highlighted the plight of Chinese labourers duped into working for a pittance by digging for mussels on the dangerous mudflats of Morecambe Bay.

Two films effectively thump home the message of abuse of children on British soil: *I am Slave*, and *Stolen (2011)*, while *Memoirs of a Geisha* and *Water (2005)* clarify this as an on-going exploitation on a global scale.

Rob Marshall's movie, *Memoirs of a Geisha*, highlights the problem of slavery or child bonding in 1930s Japan. Nine-year-old Chiyo (played by Suzuka Ohgo) and her sister are sold by their parents to train in the 'leisure' industry of Kyoto. For her sister, this means working as a prostitute, while Chiyo is taken to an *okiya* where she has to train to be a geisha girl.

This is not slavery in the traditional sense of backbreaking menial tasks. Rather she has to spend much of her childhood in training so that as she becomes a geisha she will be able to earn sufficient money to pay back her owners for her original purchase price and for the debts and expenses she has subsequently incurred. She is bonded for life.

Her owners are strict with her, punishing her severely for misdemeanours, and the older geisha girls bully her. There is no chance of escape. "Like water, she has to make her own path in life." Her training involves learning to make graceful movements, etiquette, looking beautiful like a porcelain doll, so she can be judged as a "moving work of art."

The film is beautifully filmed in the culturally unique ancient Japanese back streets and ornamental gardens, and the actress Suzuka Ohgo is both confident and delightful as the confused and abused little girl who has been thrown like a lamb into hot coals.

Just as Chiyo's rights as a child were abused – the parents had total control over her fate – so too in Hindu India during the same era, the 1930s, children were directed by the whim of their parents. That could mean little girls being married off at the immature age of eight!

This is the state of affairs in *Water (2005)*, in which eight-year-old Chuyia (played by child actress, Sarala) becomes the bride of some faceless older man. Her only possessions seem to be her trinkets and jewellery – she certainly does not possess independence. She had been passed from the control of her parents (who would have been glad to be rid of her upkeep) to submit to a domineering adult husband and his in-laws. This could be considered legalised child prostitution and slavery.

When Chuyia's husband dies you may think she is now free and she could return to her parents. She certainly has no tears for her dead husband, but she does find it an imposition when she has to return her jewellery and trinkets to the in-laws. So now she has nothing. Her parents are unable to welcome her back; they are too familiar with the religious strictures of the Hindu *Laws of Manu*.

Father takes the little girl to an *ashram*, a home for widows. She is eight-years-old! There she is restrained so she cannot escape, and her hair is shaved off. She has to live out the rest of her life, without luxuries, in purity, and with a bunch of other frail widows. "We must live in purity, and die in purity," she is told. "Learn to live like a lotus, untouched by the dirty water it grows in." Religion fastens its evil grip: to reach Heaven the girl must spend the rest of her life in chastity. But if she is unfaithful, "she is reborn in the womb of a jackal."

In contradiction to this virtue, some of the younger women maintain the upkeep of the *ashram* by prostituting themselves. One particular man "has an unnatural concern for widows." The day comes when little Chuyia is told she is going home to her father, so she compliantly gets ready. But instead, she is taken to the home of the abusive man where she is raped. This destroys her will, her innocence, and her health.

But in 1938, Gandhi is spreading his revolutionary message across India. There is a glimmer of hope for Chuyia and the other widows. Gandhi says, "Widows are a stranger to love – no one should be a stranger to love." In this film, Chuyia escaped to Gandhi's entourage as he toured through the region. But according to the caption at the conclusion of the film, the majority of India's widows are not so lucky. Even today in the twenty-first century, there are over thirty-four million widows in India, still living in conditions of "social, economic and cultural deprivation as prescribed by the ancient sacred texts of Manu." In fact, so deeply entrenched are these views that even in 2005 when *Water (2005)* was being made, according to *Halliwell's Film Guide*, filming had to be abandoned due to riots by Hindu Fundamentalists assumedly opposed to the depiction of the subject matter.[3]

The TV drama *I am Slave* brings the reality of slavery into the twenty-first century. It states bluntly: "There are five thousand slaves in London," either working as housemaids, nannies, cleaners, or prostitutes – all working for a promise of money to send back home, but usually earning only a pittance or nothing at all, invariable ill-treated and often locked up all day. This play, based on a true story, follows one such girl, Malia, of Sudanese origins.

As a child, Malia is played by Natalie Mghoi. She seems a happy, contented girl, having a strong bond with her loving father, as she grows up in her Nubian village. But as part of the civil war, her village is raided and burnt. Malia is one of the children kidnapped, taken to Khartoum, and put on podia to be exhibited to potential buyers. One wealthy Arabic woman, after prodding and poking her, and checking her teeth, buys her and takes Malia to her home in Khartoum where she is to act as housekeeper/slave.

Malia is confronted with a mountain of washing up in a dirty kitchen. An endless list of chores is reeled off to her. The slight girl who is dwarfed by the matriarch is made to feel grateful for her lot in life. "A slave is nothing. You will miss nothing."

Her life is one of drudgery. On the occasion when she tries to get a little joy by playing with her 'owners' daughter, she is told off and told to never touch the daughter again. Malia does try to run away, but when caught the pointlessness of escape is explained to her. Where will you go in Khartoum? "Nowhere is safe."

Malia's father does not give up hope. He migrates to Khartoum where he finds work as a bin-man. Daily on his rounds, he searches for his lost daughter, asking the local children playing in the street if they have come across her. It is sad to see the day a few years later when Malia recognises her father and chases after the dustcart. But too late! The girl is caught, restrained, and reprimanded for trying to run away. The slave owner decides to send the 'ungrateful' child to London where she can be a slave to another relative.

The bulk of this film deals with the trials that Malia has: the threats of what might happen if she tries to leave subserviency. Ultimately, with the help of the family chauffeur and a passer-by, Malia finds a way to escape to a refuge centre in London. And that is how her story gets to be heard by the wider public.

Stolen (2011) is another made-for-TV drama, which sets out specifically to highlight the reality of children trafficked into Britain almost daily, under the noses of the police. The authorities are so overwhelmed they are virtually impotent at keeping track of the problem. We are confronted with a caption that starkly informs us of the scale of this problem, how each year there are 1.2 million child victims of trafficking around the world. Children may be trafficked for domestic servitude or into the sex trade. The traffickers (or slavers) seem immune to criticism. They firmly shift any accusations back to us, where demand lies. One slaver coldly counters his accusers saying that it is the English and other Europeans who "gladly pay money to abuse African girls."

This drama focuses on three immigrants from contrasting cultures: Rosemary, an eleven-year-old Nigerian 'imported' to work as a housemaid; Georgie, an Eastern European teenager employed to keep a hostel clean (his sister has already been hurried off to the sex industry); a Vietnamese youth smuggled by container and kept locked in a cannabis factory. All are expected to work for nothing, and have no freedom. This is twenty-first century Britain!

Rosemary is played by Gloria Oyewumi. Like a stream of Nigerian girls before her she has arrived at the airport (Manchester). Immediately, she flushes her passport and documents down the toilet as she has been told to do. She is picked up by immigration police, the girl clutching her two coins (to telephone her slaver). The stage-play *His Teeth*, highlights the similar plight of Nigerian boys (youths) "imported" into the country.[4]

The police place her with a foster mother. Despite being given a cosy bed the frightened girl sleeps on the floor, and she can make no sense of the fish fingers she has been given. The authorities are aware that "traffickers know the house of every carer in the borough." It is not long before the slaver has tracked her down. So afraid is she of the *juju* placed on her and her family that the girl makes a bid to escape from safety so she can report to the slaver. She is sold for £5000. Soon she is working as a housemaid for a family and later is mopping floors in an ethnic supermarket. It is made clear that as she gets older she will be transferred to the sex trade.

One immigration police officer, Anthony Carter, is assigned to her case. To the annoyance of his wife, he 'uses' his own young daughter Ellie (a delightful Jessie Clayton) to befriend Rosemary. This is a mistake, for as the slaver becomes aware of Ellie she becomes a potential target, too.

What is shocking about Rosemary's case is how distrustful she is of the British police and her carers. So deeply ingrained are the *juju* threats drummed into her, she feels duty bound to run away to the men who are exploiting her, and even warns them when the police arrive. It is only when another older bonded slave explains to Rosemary the danger she is in that she agrees to point out her slaver on a police identity parade. Alas, just as Rosemary's case comes to a conclusion we watch yet another Nigerian preteen arriving on her own at the airport terminal, clutching her two coins.

For Eastern European Georgie, he is thrilled to be arriving in England, punching the air with delight, gawping at the buildings, and relishing the thought of his future dreams. But soon he is escorted to a harsh landlord of a grim hostel filled with European men. His job is to try to keep the slum clean, sweeping floors, cleaning tables, doing the laundry, and he is even taken to a covert food-packing factory. He enthusiastically gets to grips with his tasks on the promise of wealth, but he is never paid for his efforts. After being accused of sabotage by the landlord, he is thrown out onto the wintry streets where he is stabbed by a gang of youths and left to die all alone.

As for the Vietnamese lad, he makes a bid for escape from the cannabis factory by smashing a hole in the roof, but is soon bundled off in the boot of a car by his captors.

The point the drama makes is that the problem is to do with economics: "It begins with demand" as if the three victims have been brought into the country to satiate the demand of affluent British. Yet in all three examples, the victims are exploited by members of their own culture: Rosemary by the Nigerian community, Georgie by the Eastern Europeans, and Kim Pak by South-East Asians.

It is eye-opening reading the *Internet* comments of viewers regarding these dramas, polarised from being either alarmed and upset, to those who deny it as a problem, claiming this to be sensationalist fabrication. My thoughts do not tally with the latter group who I believe are as blinkered as holocaust deniers.

This need to convey a believable message to our manipulable children is encountered in the update of Mark Twain's classic The *Adventures of Huck Finn*. Jim, the runaway slave befriended by Huck (Elijah Wood) informs us, "Selling slaves ain't right, Huck. All men should be free."

But Huck, who has been inculcated with white man's intransigence, dismissed the Negro's argument: "That's the way it is, and the way it's always been."

"Just because everyone says something is right, doesn't make it right, get my meaning?" But not until Huck witnesses the brutal beating of his special friend and, like Doubting Thomas, sees the weal marks on his back, does the boy become convinced.

BULLYING

Name-Calling

Name-calling might seem a minor theme to include in a chapter about child abuse. But psychoanalysts have considered this to be a significant staging post on the downward spiral towards lack of self-esteem leading to the child being isolated with suicidal thoughts. In recent times, the increased access to texting on mobile phones and computer-use has resulted in an explosion of cyber-bullying. Cases of suicide among youths have been reported as a result of cyber-bullying.

Several films have featured children who have heard their fathers being spoken of in derogatory words, the child has taken offence at the name-calling and retaliated. Girls who have struck back in their father's defence, invariably described as tomboys include Meredith Salenger in *The Journey of Natty Gann*, Mary Badham in *To Kill a Mockingbird*, and Alexa Vega in *Run the Wild Fields*.

As well as defending farmhand Tom when someone had called him 'Nazi Lover', Alexa Vega playing Opal Miller had her own name-calling to contend with. Her nickname had always been 'Pug', but now the ten-year-old arrives at school wearing spectacles, so her classmates taunt her 'Pug the Bug' because the glasses make her look goggle-eyed like a fly. This was a girl who took control of the situation by fighting back. (In *A Kiss at Midnight*, wearing spectacles was projected as a positive attribute: Jadin Gould being told she looks assured, intelligent, and beautiful.)

Mark Baker (Forrest Landis) was one of the boys in the large household in *Cheaper by the Dozen 1*. His siblings call him 'Fed X' because dad (Steve Martin) laughingly told them he was brought home in a delivery van. But the boy hates the name, and throughout the film tries to deflect the taunts directed at him. There seems no escape from such a label that sticks. Piggy (we never get to know his real name) in *Lord of the Flies* made the fatal mistake of confiding his worries to the one new friend he believed he could trust, Ralph. "I don't care what they call me as long as they don't call me Piggy," confides the bespectacled boy (played by Hugh Edwards). Too late! The nickname sticks, and the bullied boy has to lump it. At least it is better than being called Fatty he is told.

"Satan's helper," is what the other children call Anouk (Victoire Thivisol) in *Chocolat*. The priest had turned the villagers against her mother for daring to sell chocolate during Lent, and the child is receiving the same stigma from the villagers.

A more severe episode of victimisation is in *The Night of the Hunter*. "Hing-hang-hong, see what the hangman's done." These are the cruel uncaring taunts children in the village make to John and Pearl (Billy Chapin and Jane Bruce), whose father had just been hanged in depression-era America.

Similarly evil are the taunts made to Alessa (Jodelle Ferland) in the horror movie, *Silent Hill*, drumming home the isolation of the eleven-year-old girl. Alessa, alone in the world with just a single mother: "You know what can happen to little girls when they are left alone?" her classmates try to frighten her. She did not have a father like other children, "So she must be bad!"

For most of these instances, the child takes the name-calling passively. In *Song of the South*, Bobby Driscoll is the butt of jeering for wearing a frilly outfit. "Look at the little girlie wearing a lace collar," they laugh, and the mocking refrain thumps through his mind long after the bullies have gone. He can only get the haunting accusations out of his head by hurling a stone into the millpond. Yet he does not retaliate. Rarely do films show the child retaliating. There are exceptions: Alexa Vega uses her fists to fight back, while Jodelle Ferland is able to open her arms and they burst into flame, just like Drew Barrymore in *Firestarter* and AnnaSophia Robb in *The Reaping*, and Barney Clark dives in with his fists as *Oliver Twist* (2005) when he can no longer bear any more taunts about his dead mother from the undertaker's assistant.

More likely, the child introverts into moroseness, or the film even uses the bullying to feed us, the audience, making us impartial collaborators of the humour of the scriptwriter, which perpetuates the problem. Personally, I too was drawn into admiring the nickname Fed X until we, the audience, were shown how this was just another broken rung in Mark Baker's ladder of unhappiness causing the boy to run away from home. And no doubt, others joined me in a round of applause during *A Little Princess* as Sara Crewe (Liesel Matthews) faces up to Lavinia (Taylor Fry) and calls her "a two-faced bully." Name-calling has its victims, but also has its ignorant assenters.

The Press may be the worst at perpetuating the crime. In their quest to clinch the most tenuous of salacious stories, any hint of titillation will do in order to berate a young actor who has no ability to respond outside the law courts: Tuesday Weld plastered with slanderous jargon – 'pubescent bad girl', 'teenage sex-kitten', 'Bobby-soxer with a difference', 'Shirley Temple with a leer' – all headlines that perversely smear and stick to haunt or obliterate a career.[5]

The Bully and Victim

Any child who stands out as different, who does not conform to the norms of the clique, is likely to become the butt of the bully's taunts.

Michael Thompson explains that we have a stereotypical view of bullies: the oversized child, 'the big, swaggering, loudmouthed boy', with 'no real friends, only followers', who makes a beeline for the weakling, to exert his authority. But our perception of this archetypal bully 'is an oversimplification'. 'Most bullies are temporary bullies. And they don't operate without the unspoken, and often unconscious, support of the non-aggressive majority.'[6] Usually, we discover that the bully himself has been the victim at some stage in his past, and that bullying is his mode of response to that victimisation. (The bully may have been neglected at home or the target of physical or sexual abuse, and he/she may be using bullying to deflect his/her own troubles. See *Untamed Love*, below.)

The opening sequence to the film *Hoot* shows all the indicators of this bully-victim syndrome. The boy Dan (Eric Phillips), who is different from the others because he is bigger, has been forced into the role of bully as his attempt to be noticed. After gaining attention, he is forced to perpetuate that role, delighting in his power and ability to inflict pain. Then along comes the new boy, Roy (Logan Lerman), just arrived in Florida from Montana, who is immediately noticed and becomes the victim of the bully, being forced to submit as his face is crushed against the window of the school bus.

On the second day of school, the new kid sees a different boy being bullied so he, like the other children on the bus, instead of coming to the victim's defence, are just relieved that today they are not the victim themselves. This self-preservation is influential in maintaining the bully-victim roles and maintains it in perpetuity. In *Hoot*, it is when the new boy becomes victim a second time, that he breaks the trend by giving the bully a broken nose. This, of course, gets the new boy, Roy, into trouble for daring to retaliate. For, to maintain the status quo, the authorities (teachers, bus drivers, etc.) are aware of bullies and make allowances for their deviancy. Those who 'should know better' are assessed on a different judgement scale, so the victim is often more harshly treated, thwarted by the injustice of the system.

So how should one react to the bully? Should the victim strike back, the typical exhortation of fathers to bullied sons? "Learn to stand up for yourself, laddy!" This is easier said than done, but we all cheer on this type of hero. Alan Parrish chose this approach in *Jumanji*, and failed abysmally, though Hermione Granger landed a right hook on the warlocks taunting her (Malfoy and his cronies) in *Harry Potter and the Prisoner of Azkaban*. Ralph Macchio as *The Karate Kid* adopted this stance, too, gaining a generation of disciples as children the world over joined martial arts groups. Yet this particular role model is not actually a bullied child, but a twenty-three year old young man.

Should the example of Gandhi be followed, the passive resistance; or the Christian treatise of turning the other cheek, of giving one's cloak as well? This was Kåre Hedebrant's preferred option in *Let the Right One In*, while Byron Taylor in *The Sorcerer's Apprentice* concludes that if "he pushed me around because he was twice my size and he likes it," it would be better to submit. This, of course, only perpetuates the problem. The boy is urged, "If you don't stand up to him he'll never leave you alone." The children in *No more Baths* felt they should take their stand from the example of passive Martin Luther King. Or maybe the bully's victim should just slink behind the newspaper while awaiting divine intervention? This was Max' method in The *Adventures of Sharkboy and Lavagirl*, as was Cage Dobson's in *Munchie*.

The most persistent message for the child is to not flee from adversity, but stand and face life's hardships. "Don't you know you can't run away from trouble," says Uncle Remus in *Song of the South*. Although said during the tale of Brere Rabbit, its message was blatantly clear for Bobby Driscoll playing the bullied boy left lonely after the departure of his father. The boy ends up brawling with his assailants which somehow eases his troubles. Elijah Wood is given a similar exhortation in *Paradise* (1991) "Don't run away from things just because they scare you." Yet he wasn't up against Jesse James in *The Butterfly Effect*. Demonstrating an admiral piece of acting, here is one violent and vindictive bully to run a mile from, should you ever encounter him.

Cyber-bullying

I hope it won't be long before the movie industry brings to the forefront the recent epidemic of cyber-bullying among teenagers. Although both sexes are victims and perpetrators in this activity, girls tend to be the main targets. According to *fairfaxtimes.com* this can begin in the child's preteen years, with kids as young as seven becoming targets.[7] Research by Hinduja and Patchin revealed 17% of respondents claimed to have been victims of cyber-bullying at some time, and 10% had been victims in the past month.[8] Other media quote a higher ratio of victimisation. A report by ABC News stated that among students in grades four to eight, 42% of kids claimed to have been bullied on-line, and 35% threatened, and that 58% had received hurtful comments on the Internet.[9] Despite being victimised, children are reluctant to report this abuse, fearing they will have their computer/mobile phones confiscated by their parents.

The added worry of this new form of bullying is that usually the culprit remains anonymous. The attack becomes an intrusion right into the home of the victim, leaving them isolated with nowhere safe to turn, and fearing the whole world is watching them. No wonder the child turns its thoughts to suicide as an only means of escape.

Some films are beginning to address this problem. *Shattered Silence* and *Cyberbully* confront us with suicidal older teenagers. *Adina's Deck* and *Odd Girl Out* focus attention upon a younger age group. *Adina's Deck* is an American TV series about eighth grade students that raises contemporary issues such as plagiarism, inappropriate on-line grooming, as well as cyber-bullying. In *Odd Girl Out* Alexa Vega plays an eighth grade child who receives malicious messages on her computer. The stress causes her to truant, mutilate her hair, and she tries to overdose on mum's sleeping pills. Reconciliation lead to a happy ending.[10]

Shattered Silence (2012)[11] dares to confront this issue among high school students. Typically it is girls who become the victims of this twenty-first century problem. When Dina (Jenn Proske) sends a nude photograph of herself to her boyfriend over her mobile phone she soon finds it has 'gone viral', the whole school having received a copy. The girl is jeered at by her fellow students, quickly loses face, finds graffiti about herself written in the girls' bathroom, ends up losing her place in the school hockey team, as well as losing out on a scholarship, due to her disgraced reputation. When she tries to complain about the bullying, she is told, "It's high school. It's what everybody does." The assumption is made that she has to just bear it. "These days, most people's dirty laundry is posted up for public consumption (on the Internet)," suggests one of her colleagues. The victimised girl receives no sympathy from friends, and no support from the school staff, either. Wounded beyond despair Dina hangs herself.

The film explores the dilemma from the standpoint of Dina's mother, who seeks retribution from the culprit. If only the movie had concentrated more on the devastating hurt this caused to the victim, and its impact among her friends; instead the film is a whodunit, concluding by offering a ridiculous scapegoat, thus wasting a potentially powerful impact.

Teenager Taylor Hillridge (Emily Osment) also attempts suicide after being the victim of on-line bullying in *Cyberbully* (2011) but only fails because she cannot remove the cap from the bottle of pills.

Bullying: Passive Resistance

The film *No more Baths* has a blatant message that bullying can be overcome by non-violent persuasion. Although it highlights the problem of bullying among children its main focus is the bullying of an adult – a solitary elderly black man, named Jake, whose family plot is being targeted by an unscrupulous developer. At first, the developer's son grazes his knee while playing on

Jake's land, and so by exploiting some finicky technicalities the developer persuades the authorities that the land should be compulsorily purchased, and Jake's house condemned. The children in the village realise "What they are doing to Jake may be legal, but it is morally wrong."

Jake is old enough to remember the time of the Civil Rights Movement when Rosa Parks influenced the Montgomery Bus Boycott, when passive resistance instigated changes. Likewise, in this film, the children help to protest by refusing to wash! Ten-year-old Keagan (Andreas Michael Lamelas) suggests the protest, aided by his nine-year-old sister, Millie (Haley McCormick). When bath-time comes around, Millie says to her brother, "Mum wants me to take a bath. Can you not take a bath first, so mum won't be mad at me!"

The protest works as none of the children in the village take a wash for several days, including the children of the mayor and other council officials. The Press are alerted and they castigate the council for their bureaucratic incompetence. After a communal shower for all the children in the town square, supplied by the firemen's hoses, Jake is reinstated into his home. The bullying developer is undermined by passive resistance.

But the film also pursues bullying between children. A pleasant game of frisbee is interrupted by a bully who disrupts the game. The children decide, "If we don't play his game, maybe he will go away." This was the moralistic stance expected by the sponsors of the scriptwriter, for the film had specific goals to project, and to foster the idea that passive resistance works.

This may work in the smug minds of adult do-gooders, but I am not convinced it really solves the traumas that bullied children are enduring.

As Kåre Hedebrant stands before his Stockholm tenement window, dressed only in his underpants, he looks a strapping young lad of twelve who could take care of himself. But he is playing Oskar, a wimpish blond-haired victim of bullying, in the horror movie, *Let the Right One In*. We see the pitiful boy at school locking himself in the toilet cubicle to avoid a trio of tormenting lads. The bullies squeeze him by the nape of his neck, and make him squeal like a pig. They press his upturned nose to make it look like a snout. Once, after gym class, he finds his trousers have been left dunked in the urinals. But always he is submissive, but that doesn't cause the bullying to stop.

On another day, the bully gets his two lackeys to whip him with a birch switch. Oskar silently endures this. The bully takes the stick and swipes him on the face, leaving a visible cut. The boys are now worried they will get in trouble with his mother, but back at home, Oskar humbly says it was an accident. Maybe he realises that telling would not resolve his problems.

His family situation does not help things: living at home with just his mother, and making occasional visits to his father. In the blockbuster novel by John Ajvide Lindqvist, the author dwells on the boy's regular wetting of his bed – a reaction to both his bullying at school, and lack of father-figure at home.

Then, into his life comes a girl his own age, Eli (Lina Leandersson), who has moved into the apartment next door. When she probes him how his face was cut, she tells him, "Hit back. Hit back hard. Hit harder than you dare." I am not sure a psychiatrist would compliment that suggestion, but Oskar enrols for the weightlifting class after school.

When the three bullies approach him again while skating on the lake, Oskar picks up a stick to defend himself. As they threaten him again, Oskar thinks back to Eli's advice. The once timid boy gives the bully a heavy clout around the ear, so severely that the ear bleeds, and the boy is permanently deafened.

Now the bullying boy leaves him alone. Alas, matters have evolved beyond a simplistic stage. A phone call from school to Oskar's mother is not a worry for the boy. What is a worry, is the bully's older brother who seeks him out at the swimming pool. This boy plainly tells Oskar what he is going to do: "An eye for an ear." While holding Oskar's head underwater for a couple of minutes, an eye is about to be gouged out.

But the bully had not reckoned on Oskar's special friend, Eli, who turns up just in time and resolves the problem once and for all!

The American remake of this film, *Let Me In*, gives us an insight into the reason for the bully's action – the bully himself is being goaded on by an older brother who frequently calls him a girly in front of his mates. No doubt his bullying phase was a way of asserting himself in the eyes of his cronies.

At least, Oskar did resort to retaliation, even though it exacerbated his problems. Without the 'angelic' intervention, he would have been one miserably scarred target. Other films use this 'cop-out' clause, in which divine or unexpected intervention causes the bullying to miraculously stop, without requiring a change of attitude or stature of the victim, but just requiring a lucky break.

This was the fate of Cage Dobson (Jaime McEnnan) in *Munchie*. As a new boy at school, he is bullied by a couple of lads. His teacher shows concern for him, enquiring whether he has found any friends yet. He has the smugness to assure her that he has made "lots", even though he has made none. But this boy worries about his being bullied but never confronts the issue. Instead, along comes a magic gnome, the Munchie, who seems to miraculously make everything right just by clicking his fingers: an infuriating character with an unedifying philosophy.

In The *Adventures of Sharkboy and Lavagirl*, it is recoiling into a fantasy world that seems to make a bullying problem evaporate. I agree that this could be useful as a coping strategy, but it should not be seen as a panacea for solving problems.

The victim of bullying is a boy, Max (Cayden Boyd), who can call upon the superheroes in his imagination to ease his worries, but he still has to come to terms with his bullies in the real world. "Please don't make me go to school," he pleads to mum. Like so many fearful kids, arriving at a new school or a new year-group: "They'll make fun of me, I know it." The boy's stupendous flights of fantasy help him through a phase of bullying, but do not resolve the problem. This was only a diversion, as Lavagirl tells him, "We didn't come to Earth to save *you*, Max." He thought he could escape fear by running away to a dreamworld. But this is precisely where fear dwells – in the mind – a point made once in the film, though was never dwelt on.

Both the previous two films included a concerned class teacher who pitifully exhorts the child to make friends instead of giving in to the bully. The authority figure sees counselling as part of his role, but only as a listening ear; to become involved would mean taking sides. Megan (Ramona Marquez) is frequently sent to the headteacher (Kevin Doyle) for disruptive behaviour in the British TV drama *The Crossing*. Ironically, the headteacher has a poster fixed to his office wall 'Say No to Bullying', yet he fails to notice the bullying when it occurs. Megan's crimes always occur as she takes a stand against the classmates who are bullying her, yet the class teacher and the head are both blinkered to the facts. Their only suggestion is to involve Megan in the school play. "Why do grown ups always let me down," sighs the girl.

Standing up to the Bully

The above films seem to be making the point that bullying will just go away if you ignore it – the pacifists' approach preferred by blinkered teachers and other adults who want to shelter in a trouble-free world. Anti-bullying campaigns require inclusion of innocent bystanders; a positive stance that does not rely on hope and good luck, but that recognises and tackles the issues of the bully and his (or her) passive adherents. Modern cases of cyber-bullying are directed towards girls, but the movie world has not caught onto this yet (with the exception of *Shattered Silence* which tackles the impact of cyber-bullying among high school students), so that the main subject of bullying on screen is the boy.

Like many films that handle the subject of bullying, the bullying is usually directed towards a boy, but there is a girl at the ready to comfort or console the lad, as in *Let the Right One In*, or *Munchie*, *The Sorcerer's Apprentice*, *Little Manhattan* or *Song of the South*. This is the case in *Jumanji*, too. Although this is a wild adventure taken by an adult Robin Williams, his escapades are the result of a spate of bullying as a child, and his positive resolve to take his father's advice by facing up to one's fears.

The film sees a boy, Alan Parrish (Adam Hann-Byrd), frantically pedalling his bicycle to evade a gang of bullies who are chasing him on their bikes. He manages to flee to his father's shoe factory where he takes refuge. This of course may be the unwarranted cause of the bullying – him being the privileged son of the influential employer for the New Hampshire town of Brantford. "That's it, Parrish, run to daddy!" the bullies taunt him. "We'll be waiting."

Father finds his son cowering in the factory. "Look!" says Mr Parrish. "If you're afraid of something you've got to stand and face it." As I mentioned earlier, this is easier said than done, and maybe even suicidal.

Even so, the boy boldly takes his father's advice and swaggers out to collect his bike and face the bullies. But the boy is immediately set upon, duffed up, and his bike is stolen. So that didn't work! However, later that night father reveals how proud he is of his son. "I want you to know how proud I am of you. You faced them even though you were outnumbered." Maybe that went some way to healing his wounds, to lessen the hurt, to camouflage the scars?

Then Alan's girlfriend turns up (Laura Bell Bundy) returning the stolen bike. She is obviously impressed by Alan's foolhardy bravado. Together they open the *Jumanji* game that Alan has recently found; the boy is vortexed into the game, and for the next twenty-six years he has a daily battle evading danger, but still confronting his fears like his father advised him, until he is finally released from the entrapment by Kirsten Dunst, and her little brother.

I guess the unfortunate message this film sends out to the victim of bullying who can rationally analyse the predicament, is if you try to stand up to bullies you may be in for twenty-six years of hell!

Others had better success in their resolve to stand up to the bully. *Harry Potter* as an orphan is forced to live in the tiny cupboard under the stairs and is often abused and bullied by Dudley, who happens to be the apple of his parents' eyes. Hagrid tells Harry (Daniel Radcliffe) to use magic on the bully if he causes any more trouble. "But Hagrid, I'm not allowed to use magic outside Hogwarts," Harry complains.

"Yes, but Dudley doesn't know that!" Soon Dudley is finding himself shut in the zoo the wrong side of a python's cage, or squirming around with a pig's tail, and his auntie rising ignominiously into the sky like a barrage balloon.

But when Harry's classmate Hermione is provoked to retaliation against Malfoy, she is sorely tempted to wave her magic wand, but finds her clenched fist reaches a better target. Malfoy (Tom Felton) constantly calls Hermione (Emma Watson) "Mudblood". This causes the girl to lose her cool and foolishly she raises her wand to his chin. "It's not worth it," her friends warn her, and she thinks better of it. Just as she starts to walk away, she turns and strikes the bully with a right hook to the gob. "That felt good!" she says, and her troubles are over. Yet when Elle Fanning dared retaliate by spitting at her tormentors in *Phoebe in Wonderland* she only ended up in deeper water inside the intransigent headmaster's office.

Hermione still had the taunts from her teachers to confront, who should have known better. "Do you take pride in being an insufferable know-it-all?" snaps Professor Snape to the clever girl wizard in *Harry Potter and the Prisoner of Azkaban*.

Another punch, a karate chop this time, sees off the bully in *Little Manhattan*, too. Ten-year-old Gabe (Josh Hutcherson) has taken up karate to be better prepared for one particular bully who he tries to avoid. Rosemary (Charlie Ray) has just joined the karate club, as well. "Are you scared of him beating you up?" she demands.

"No!" lies the boy. "I just want to be ready for him when the time comes!"

Later, the pair meet the bully in a local park. The aggressor tells them to clear off, for this is his patch. But Rosemary won't be bullied and immediately starts laying into the guy using her karate skills, which provides the spur for Gabe to join in.

Perhaps Willie Morris got the balance right in his autobiographical novel *My Dog Skip* about growing up in 1940s Mississippi. Frankie Muniz plays the nine-year-old in the film version, musing on past events. "I was so small and puny I was the perfect target for all the neighbourhood bullies." The boy seems to wallow in his isolation. He overcomes the problem simply, by joining in with the bullies. Instead of running away from torment, he joins them in games of baseball and football, helping to prove he isn't a puny nobody. He is, of course, helped by the sweetheart (Caitlin Wachs) admiring him from the distance, just as Alan Parrish had his Sarah, Oskar had his Eli, and Cage Dobson had his Andrea. But it was his dog Skip that helped draw him completely out of his scrawny shell.

There is strength in numbers. In the bulk of these films, it is the solitary boy, the loner, who has attracted the bullying taunts of others. Alliances with a friend, with a gang, or even with the bullies themselves, seem to melt away that insubstantial wall of fear.

Ill-Treatment by Adults

While Professor Snape had it in for Hermione Granger in the *Harry Potter* series, we find other adults slip into the bullying mode at a more detrimental level – the do-gooders who religiously believe they are educating the whole child but are depriving them of nourishment, humour, independence and love. We saw this in *Rabbit Proof Fence*, in which the native aborigine children were taken into care "for their own good". It seems a trait in strict Catholic schools as Catherine Cookson's *The Rag Nymph* discovered, as did the teenagers incarcerated with *The Magdalene Sisters*.

Other institutionalised children also receive their dosage of ill treatment, as Liesel Matthews can bear witness in *A Little Princess*, as can Aileen Quinn in *Annie (1982)*.

Jane Eyre is a film in which children are being abused by a perpetrator who has the deluded notion he is doing some good – the evil of the religious zealot, who believes he is doing God's will. By doing so, he commits the worst kind of bullying.

Firstly, Jane Eyre is an orphan kept cruelly by a selfishly blinkered aunt, Mrs Reed. The aunt's son exploits her aunt's dislike for the girl, so that any misdemeanour that occurs is always unjustly blamed on the little girl. She is needlessly punished. However, Jane is given the chance to escape from the cold cruelty of Gateshead Hall when Mr Brockelhurst, the proprietor of *Lowood Institution for Girls*, comes to visit.

Mrs Reed tells Mr Brockelhurst that Jane is a wicked child. The man asks Jane what happens to wicked people when they die. "They are sent to burn in Hell," she tells him.

"So what must you do to avoid going to Hell?" he asks the little girl, expecting to be told she must not lie, she must be good and change the error of her ways.

But instead, the innocent child chirps up, "I must keep in good health and not die!"

Jane jumps at the opportunity to go to Lowood. Anything to get away from horrible Mrs Reed and her son, unaware of what she is letting herself in for. "You have made a wise choice," Brockelhurst tells her. "Wiser than you may know."

On leaving, Jane blurts out a tirade of insolence at Mrs Reed: "I hate you… The very sight of you makes me sick." There have been so many versions of this film, that a host of child actors have said these words, ranging from Peggy Ann Garner in 1944, Anna Paquin in 1996, Laura Harling in 1997, Ruth Wilson in 2006, and most recently in 2011 by Amelia Clarkson.

On arriving at the cold depressing school, Jane is hauled up before all the other girls, made to stand on a stool all day as punishment, has a label placed over her neck saying "Liar", and demeaned in front of the other children. "I wanted people to love me," the disgraced girl sighs.

The harsh religious strictures of the school cause the scholars to endure food unfit for pigs, windows kept wide open in the harshest of weather, and the girls made to parade outside in the teeming rain. "Punish the body to save the soul," is Mr Brockelhurst's maxim. That Jane Eyre endured the hardship, graduated, and left to pursue a career as a governess, is remarkable.

What is saddening, is that this story, written in the 1850s by Charlotte Brontë was partly autobiographical. Although Charlotte was brought up in a loving household by her minister father, the Rev Patrick Prunty (Brontë), vicar of Haworth in moorland Yorkshire, her mother having died, yet she and her sisters, including the famous Emily Brontë, were sent away to a school very similar to the Lowood Institution. She attended a school for children of 'churchmen of limited means' at Cowan Bridge in Lancashire. There, she was poorly treated, nutrition was poor, conditions harsh, and disease was rife. When Charlotte's two older sisters, Elizabeth and Maria, both died of an illness while at the school, Mr Brontë withdrew his surviving daughters to be home-tutored instead, just as Mrs March does in *Little Women*.

Charlotte Brontë also had harsh treatment while acting as a governess at Stone Gappe, and she visualised the horrors of that first job when describing Gateshead Hall, the residence of Mrs Reed.

The abusiveness of religious zealotry and bigotry are brought to our attention in The Magdalene Sisters. The Magdalene asylums were established in Ireland to help care for vulnerable girls who had dabbled in sexual deviancy. The credits tell us that thirty thousand Irish women had at some time been incarcerated in these institutions. With the intention of setting the teenager back on the straight and narrow, using the power of "prayer, cleanliness and hard work" they were instead sweat camps of abusive slave labour, as a myriad of girls worked in the nunnery laundries adding to the coffers of the Roman Catholic Church, but not into the pockets of these girls, abandoned without hope.

The lives of three teenagers are highlighted. Margaret (Anne-Marie Duff), a girl molested then raped by her cousin; her cries for help muffled out by the music of the wedding reception down below. The morning after she reported the rape to her parents, she was carted off to the asylum to 'regain her purity'. The second child, Bernadette (Nora-Jane Noone) had been boarding at an orphan school. While she is in the school playground, some local boys come to the school railing to try to chat her up. The teachers notice this. Bernadette does nothing to encourage the boys, yet the teachers deem it wise to send her off to the Magdalene asylum, too. The third girl, Rose (Dorothy Duff) has just given birth to a baby boy. Shortly after the birth, Rose's parents bring a priest who persuades the girl to relinquish her baby. She is then whisked off to the asylum, where the nuns give her a different name, because there is already another Rose. (The same thing happens to Cybele in *Sundays & Cybele*, who has to change her name to the more Christian sounding Françoise.)

All three girls arrive together. All their personal possessions are taken from them, so Rose has lost everything, her property, her baby, and now her own name. There they are greeted by the harsh regime, led by Sister Bridget (Geraldine McEwan, in yet another brilliant role as a religious bigot, as she played in *Oranges are not Only Fruit*). The girls share a dormitory with the other internees. No talking is allowed. Nor can they fraternise. Even acts of kindness towards each other are frowned upon. Beatings are used for the most trivial of reasons. The girls are often humiliated, for instance when they are told to strip naked so that the nuns can taunt them over the size of their breasts, nipples or fannies. And yet the hypocrisy of this is that at all other times they have to dress and undress while wearing their nightgowns, to protect their modesty! When two girls are caught trying to run away, they receive severe beatings and their hair is cut off. One girl, Una, who had run away to her father, is returned and whipped by her father who cruelly tells her, "You've got no home. You've got no mother. You've got no father."

Daily, they work in the laundry without recompense, strictly supervised to ensure they do not talk or collaborate. Even their food rations are meagre compared to the hearty feasts the nuns enjoy. In despair, Bernadette cries out, "What in God's name have we done to deserve this? All the mortal sins in the world would not justify this place. I'd commit any sin, mortal or otherwise to get the hell out of here."

It is not just religious institutions that have taken over the role of the workhouse. As Aileen Quinn and her fellow moppets belt out, "It's a hard knock life," while scrubbing the toilets and polishing the floors at New York's *Hudson Street Home for Girls* run by weary Miss Hannigan, whose reliance on alcohol is her only means of escape. This is the wonderful tear-inducing musical, *Annie* (1982). While the kids are forced to greet the old hag with the refrain, "We love you Miss Hannigan," the children are verbally abused as "My little pigs' droppings." So used is little Annie to being forced into slave labour that when she is invited to stay at the billionaire's home of Mr Warbucks she is asked, "Now Annie, what would you like to do first?" The girl ignorantly replies, "The windows, then the floors!"

The seemingly kind men in *Slumdog Millionaire* scouring the Mumbai slums in search of homeless children to place in an orphanage had, unlike Mr Warbucks, ulterior motives. Their mission has to be funded, and their innocent charges make ideal begging fodder. The three child heroes of the film, Jamal, Salim, and Latika, have all been earmarked as potential little earners. In the case of Latika (played as a seven-year-old by Rubina Ali, and as a young teen by Tanvi Ganesh Lonkar), "Have you any idea how much this little virgin is worth?"

The two boys are given a singing audition to assess who will be rewarding as beggars. When Salim witnesses another boy being drugged and having his eyes gouged out with a spoon to make him more appealing as a beggar, Salim realises it is time to escape with his younger brother.[12]

Earlier, we suggested that bullies are themselves victims. *Untamed Love* is based on a true story by Torey Hayden, *One Child*. Behind every bully is a questionable background, often more extreme than the bullying being executed. Six-year-old Caitlin Eldridge has behaviour putting her in the bracket of psychotic bully, a 'menace to society'. She had tied a child to a tree and set fire to it. Caitlin is placed in a special needs class at school until she can be permanently placed in a psychiatric asylum. "She never cries," the authorities notice. "A child that never cries: that's inhuman." Of course, we don't have to dig far to discover a history of abuse perpetrated by the parents. Her mother had physically pushed her from the car onto the highway while driving. And father, now her only guardian, suggests a game to play: "We could play house. You could be my dolly."

Hidden behind this abuse, and the consequent façade of disruption, lays a clever girl with an IQ of 168, genius level. This is the message behind this film as we watch an over-worked classteacher (Cathy Lee Crosby) gently coax the menace from the girl, to become a normalised mainstream kid. The part of Caitlin is played by Ashlee Lauren, a child who can scrap with other kids, play sullen, viciously stab her teacher, and cry on cue. A remarkable performance from one so young.

When an adult asks a child to do an unpleasant task, can that be construed as being a form of ill treatment, of child abuse? This is the controversy that arises in Terry Gilliam's film based on Mitch Cullam's novel, *Tideland*. This treads precariously over several taboos, one of which is drugs.

Jodelle Ferland plays Jeliza Rose, a ten-year-old daughter of a failed rock star, Noah, played by Jeff Bridges. Noah is a drug addict. Every day, he straps a belt to his arm, fills a syringe, and injects himself, telling his daughter, "Time for daddy's vacation." Jeliza Rose has to help him by taking the needle from him and re-arranging his arms as he falls into unconsciousness. This is all routine to Jeliza; she does it every day, and is not fazed by it. The director, Gilliam, realises the audience may be uncomfortable with this. Being interviewed at the Hay Literary Festival, he is asked by a member of the audience whether he felt a ten-year-old child (Jodelle was actually nine and a half at the time) should be exposed to drug culture. Gilliam responds by saying, if the father was a diabetic and daily injected himself with insulin with the daughter's help, would that be acceptable?

One day, Noah overdoses and never wakes up. In her innocence, Jeliza Rose carries on regardless playing her fantasy games as her father's body gradually decomposes. From time to time she checks if father has woken up yet. "No, still on vacation," she says as she lifts his sunglasses.

A child may not just depict abuse: just by acting, it is possible they themselves are being victimised. We mentioned this in Volume One as we considered the roles children are asked to portray, and the pushy parents who force them into those roles. In the 1940s, parents were often backstage to ensure the compliance of their progeny. Marianne Sinclair tells us that to get Judy Garland to act on demand, her mother would threaten her with abandonment. Judy claimed to have been psychologically affected by this throughout her life.[13] In *The Mystery of Natalie Wood*, the infant Grace Fulton (playing the part of the young legend) has to watch her mother rip a butterfly to shreds 'to encourage' the daughter to cry genuine tears. This little girl is deprived of friends, lest her commitment is sullied, and when she breaks her wrist in a filming accident mother won't allow it to be tended to, lest that deprive her of the vital movie contract.   The girl has to wear a bracelet on her arm for the rest of her life to hide the deformity.

Ill-treatment of children was rife in Victorian days, as exemplified in films such as *The Water Babies* in which boys were sent as sweeps up soot-filled chimneys (Michael, in *Mary Poppins*, was also keen to join this occupation!). There is a whole compendium of Dickensian stories – *Oliver Twist*, *Nicholas Nickleby*, *Bleak House*, *A Christmas Carol* – which all paint bleak pictures of abusive childhoods in nineteenth century Britain. Mark Lester pitifully raising his empty food bowl to Mr Bumble in *Oliver!* "Please sir, may I have some more?" or Barney Clark (as Oliver) sold for a fiver to be abused by Sourberry's wife and assistant at the undertaker's in *Oliver Twist* (2005).

Exploitation of the child worker continued into the twentieth century so that in *Zombies: Wicked Little Things* we find a group of children working in harsh conditions down a coalmine in 1913 Pennsylvania. An unscrupulous mine manager forces a little girl to hurry as she is laying a stick of dynamite but doesn't allow her and the other youngsters enough time to escape from danger before releasing the charge. It is these dead children who come to haunt the forests decades later as flesh-eating zombies. Chloë Grace Moretz has the sense to make friends with these spooks and so she and her family are spared. With all these abuses, once doled out, they are never forgotten or forgiven, and the child can harbour bottled-up revenge until he/her has the rationale to respond.

SEXUAL ABUSE

There cannot be any other crime so despised in all society than the crime against the child, nor can there be a person so reviled as the perpetrator of a crime against a child. However trivial the action is perceived in the eye of the accused, he/she is held to be more wicked than a murderer.

Fortunately, there are many films that treat this subject with the seriousness it deserves. *Liar, Liar* and *A Shadow of Doubt* are two powerful dramas approaching the issue of abuse within the family with laudable intensity. Others revel in salaciousness: *Lolita, Little Lips* and *Pretty Baby* seem to exalt the paedophile as a hero, misdirecting our empathy. While some try to angle in from a humorous direction, as *Forrest Gump* describes his young girlfriend's (Jenny's) father, "He was a very loving man. He was always kissing his daughter and touching her." Others try to show the full horror of rape, expecting the child actor to draw on supposed life experiences to portray the anguish of the physical violation: Dakota Fanning raped in *Hounddog*, the girl had agreed to undress on the promise of tickets to an Elvis concert but ends up brutalised; Oksana Akinshina prostituted in *Lilya 4-ever*; Chloë Grace Moretz in *Let Me In* imagining the pained horror and intrusion of molestation. In *Bastard out of Carolina* Jena Malone haunts our complacency with her ever so vivid depiction of agonised rape.

Several movies seem to treat this subject matter salaciously. As we discuss in the final chapter, the trauma of the victim and their need for therapy are invariably ignored.

Paedophilia

The word paedophile, literally 'child lover', has now become a word in daily use in the media. In the past, its sporadic use may have referred to a genial old gentleman, a childless uncle or aunt over-generous with the tin of Quality Street, a kindly benefactor: the solitary adult who dotes on children. Today, the term encompasses the predatory priest, child murderers, pornographers, flashers, and Internet misusers. 'Paedophile' is a catchall that tarnishes the child-lover with the same brush, irrespective of his crime. Had Lewis Carroll practised his photography today he would have been discredited, as would John Ruskin, that great art critic and philosopher, who brought the pre-Raphaelite movement to the forefront of the art world, but who would dance naked in his garden with his children.

Ruskin is a man who has schools dedicated to his name yet who asked child illustrator, Kate Greenaway, to make drawings of little girls for him. "Will you draw her for me without a cap and without shoes and without her mittens and without her frock and frills, and let me see exactly how tall she is and how round." And later (when it still hadn't titillated him)… "You really must draw her again for me without any clothes." [14][15]

Anyone accredited with this label can expect the same degree of respect from vigilante groups whether they be the Soham murderer of Holly and Jessica, or of Sarah Payne, or someone caught taking indecent photographs of under-aged girls and posting them on a web page, or even a professional who is inadvertently caught up in the hysteria of the protestations by having the name-plate of 'paediatrician' fixed to his office door and misunderstood by an ignorant public. I ask you! That is as bad as Mrs Hayes calling her daughter 'Lolita'. Whatever was she thinking using such a suggestive name?[16] Yet all these vindictive actions have occurred since the year 2000.[17] It is an easy label to apply, and the hole it digs can be inescapably deep, as illustrated by the revengeful taunt used by the deposed Santa to get his own back over Kriss Kringle (Richard Attenborough) in *Miracle on 34th Street* (1994): "Is there a darker side to all this? – a lonely old man hanging around with kids!" or as Hugh Grant is accused by Rachel Weisz in *About a Boy*: "I was wondering why a single childless man would want to hang around with a twelve-year-old boy."

Surely an old man is incapable of harming a child. That is the opinion taken in Jan Švankmajer's clever fairy tale horror, *Little Otik*. Kristina Adamcova plays Alzbetka, a maturing primary school-aged child. She is not so much afraid of the elderly man, Mr Zlabek, she passes on the stairs to her apartment, just resigned to his quirks. She knows she must get away quickly whenever he is around. If ever the man sees her on the steps above, he hurriedly fumbles for his thick-rimmed spectacles to focus more clearly to look up her dress. The girl is aware he is looking. She holds her skirt down protectively as she imagines a lump growing and throbbing at the man's crotch. At this point, the man has a seizure, collapses, struggling for his pills.

"He wanted to touch me again," she complains to a neighbour.

"Don't keep making things up, Alzbetka," says the woman. It is hard for a child to be believed when accusing an elderly man. "He's too frail. His legs can hardly carry him."

The girl goes on to complain to her parents. "I can't stand that paedophile. Undressing me with his eyes."

In time, the girl learns how to cope with the man as he comes groping towards her, arms outstretched. "Stop it, or you'll have another bad turn!"

The coping strategy, however, does not solve the problem, nor make it acceptable. All she learns to do is what myriads of females before her have learned to do: to turn a blind eye, to tolerate unwanted sexual attention as part and parcel of life. Perhaps this is what Nicole Kassell, the director of *The Woodsman*, meant when she stated all girls have periods of discomfort in their lives.

The idea of childhood extending beyond the age of ten is a twentieth century concept. In some other countries ten has been the age for matrimony. In the film *Water (2005)*, the widowed girl is just eight years old! Some scholars would suggest that Jesus' mother conceived at the age of twelve, and that arranged marriages between older men and preteen girls were not uncommon, though they are outlawed in the majority of countries today. Ten-year-old Nujood Ali describes in her book (*I am Nujood, Age 10 and Divorced*) how as recently as 2008 she was married to a Yemeni man three times her age, and was the first child bride brave enough to sue for divorce in the Yemeni courts. Even the revered Gandhi married his sweetheart, Kasturba, who was just fourteen; and Aisha, Mohammed's bride was nine years old (her husband was fifty-two!). Nabokov writes of Dante, and of Petrarch whose Beatrice and Laureen were both aged below twelve. Child brides make paedophilia acceptable in corrupt societies.

It is at this preteen age that most boys begin to notice girls, not just as beings to tease and pull their ponytails. At this age, hormones hone in on the physical changes taking place in the girl's preteen form. The same physical beauty is obvious to every grown man as well as every gangling teenager. Nabokov's claim for his Humbert is, that if not fettered, the older man is haunted by unnatural desires for the child imp. The psychiatrist says to Richard E Grant in *The Cold Light of*

Day, "Most people manage to suppress their paedophilic tendencies." According to Marianne Sinclair, the sight of teenager Caroll Baker cavorting in *Baby Doll* turned 'audiences of all ages into Dirty Old Humberts gloating at forbidden fruit,' a nymphet 'provocative yet passive, unkempt yet desirable, a doll to drive much older men mad.' [18]

The male frequently misinterprets precociousness as provocative, and that the flaunting girl should know better. "I don't try to look sexy, really I don't," sighs Brooke Shields after a magazine declared her the sexiest eleven-year-old. Deborah Kampmeier, director of *Hounddog*, questions why is twelve-year-old Lewellen (played by Dakota Fanning) "in the blossoming of her body, spirit and sexuality, seen as 'asking for it' when she is simply and innocently experiencing the aliveness of her being, the life-force pulsing through her body, the power and creativity of her sexuality?" [19] The trouble with the male perspective is that he sees the adolescent as ripe for exploitation.

Paedophilia is not uncommon. Even schoolteachers unwittingly express their perversions in the highly praised *Gregory's Girl*. Two teachers have been joking about receiving gifts of cakes from their third-year girl pupils. "Are you still getting those poems from Julie?" one teacher asks. "You are dealing with the emotions of a sensitive … red head!" the other replies, biting the cherry off his bun. Here, the children are not being exploited, but the awareness of child/adult desires are noted.

The pervasiveness of paedophilia has filtered down to our TV and cinema screens, and the Internet is awash with images. Most adult males are mesmerised by the naked female form, and a certain proportion of them wish to admire children in their birthday suits, too. In the movie, *Annunciation*, twelve-year-old Júlia Mérö, barely pubescent, was required to perform her role as Eve, alongside Peter Bocsor playing Adam. Both girl and boy are entirely naked at the beginning and end of the film. Today, this can be perceived as a case of child exploitation and abuse, though at the time people may have justified it because it was filmed in 1983 in Hungary at a time and European locality when attitudes to nudity were more relaxed and were not seen as exploitative. Nudity was condoned, placing the film under the label 'arthouse'. In Volume Six (*Puberty and First Love*), we consider the prevalence of child nudity on television and films. The recent censorship of such material demonstrates how the depiction of nakedness in movies is now perceived as sexual exploitation of children.

A man barges into after-school detention in *32A* and exposes himself to the girls. The teacher-nuns instruct the girls to avert their eyes, but none of them do. Children are genetically programmed to absorb any new experience. It is the responsibility of the adult world to filter those experiences in regulated measures. Despite a profusion of old wives tales, I guess Angela Lansbury did impart some sound advice to Sarah Patterson in *A Company of Wolves*. "If you spy a naked man in the wood, run as if the devil himself were after you." Alas, the twelve-year-old did meet a man in the woods and forgot to be cautious. "At least you've got your clothes on!" she says to the man whose eyebrows meet between his eyes.

Little Girls Loved: Salacious Relationships with Children

This was the predilection of Humbert Humbert, the nympholept with designs on his "*enfants charmante et fourbe*",[19a] in the scandalous Nabokov book *Lolita*, turned into a film in both 1961 and 1997. Humbert was a professor of English searching for digs. He harks back to when he was a teenager infatuated with a young girl, his Annabelle, whose misfortune (typhus) did not allow him to 'possess'. But he states that the seed had poisoned his blood as a result of that teenage relationship; so that when he reached his twenties he was still searching for that same child nymphet (Nabokov first coined the word) in the parks and beaches he went to frequent as an idle watcher of little children and their games.

Now in his thirties, Humbert is being shown around digs in Ramsdale, a sleepy rural town in upstate New York, by a clingy landlady he has already decided to reject. But just as he is about to leave this viewing, he is introduced to the landlady's twelve-year-old daughter, "This is my Lo!" lying semi-naked on the lawn: Sue Lyon in 1961; and in the 1997 film, featuring Dominique Swaine wearing alluring sunglasses, the lawn sprinkler coating her thin blouse with a fine spray. Hum is immediately smitten, and pays the rent up-front, there and then.

The book has for half a century been considered a masterpiece of English literature, despite English not being Vladimir Nabokov's mother tongue. But even today, it is not a volume proudly displayed on bookshelves. In the viewpoint of Karen Lury, "the novel and the film's conceit is that the story is presented entirely from Humbert's obsessed, intellectualised and romantic point of view."[20]

The first film, which was also scripted by Nabokov, was treated as a comedy, perhaps to soften the impact of such a controversial subject matter – with English comedian, Peter Sellers, playing a lead role as Quilty, Humbert's rival for Lolita's affections.

During the early part of the film, Lolita (or Dolores Hayes) and Humbert gradually come closer together to share tender moments. Lo teases Humbert while Hum is sexually tormented in her presence. She sits on his knee, they brush heads, play foot games. All the while, Humbert is planning how they could get away together.

However, Humbert's plans to get alone with the twelve-year-old are always thwarted by 'that Hayes woman'. Finally, unannounced, the mother packs her girl off to summer camp. But before she leaves, Humbert gets an affectionate smack on the lips (in the first film version this is only a hug). Having now lost the girl that reminded him of his first love, Annabelle, he must find a way to retrieve her. He realises the only way to get to his sweetheart is to marry her obnoxious mother.

The marriage takes place. Every day, Humbert feigns headaches to avoid intimacy with the new wife. The new wife discovers the explicit diary where Humbert has declared his love for the little nymph and writes lucidly of his hatred for the wife. The new wife races out of the house in disgust with letters written to those who need to be told (including the authorities), but in her frantic haste is accidentally run over and killed by a neighbour before she can reach the post-box. Humbert feigns grief and takes his now unprotected 'daughter' away 'to grieve' as a pair.

At the first lay-by, the girl intimately snogs her new father. They then search for a motel. Father has planned to drug his new daughter while she sleeps so he can have his evil way with her, but the sleeping pills don't work and the girl keeps waking in the night, to the utter despair of Humbert. But in the early hours of the morning, Humbert finds himself being seduced by the girl of her own volition, and so the age-discrepant couple make illicit and incestuous love with each other.

Thus begins a happy, fulfilled, but frustrating few months travelling around America. Humbert becomes aware of being followed by another man, Quilty, the scriptwriter of one of Lolita's school plays, who had already got to the girl and deflowered her before Humbert had (though he wasn't aware of that at the time). When Humbert finally learns the truth, he finds Quilty, and dramatically shoots him. (This scene is turned into a comedy by Peter Sellers, and is spectacularly dramatised by Frank Langella in 1997). Thus, the book *Lolita* is being written in a prison cell as a memoir where Humbert is on trial, not for the rape of a minor, but for murder.

The story of *Lolita* seems to be seen worldwide as a benchmark for westernised depravity. A book was published in 2003 called *Reading Lolita in Tehran* demonstrating how radical the perceived conservative and restrictive regime of Iranian Muslim culture has become, for now even Iranian universities study *Lolita* as a literary text.

Michael Palin, in his list of greatest jokers compiled in 1980, ranked Vladimir Nabokov sixth, behind Peter Cook and Eric Morecambe, but ahead of Spike Milligan and Peter Sellers. Obviously, Nabokov was well revered in the literary world, having written several masterpieces besides *Lolita*. "Nabokov is so arrogant, but he's very funny. Every sentence is worth reading four times," says Palin.[21] This helps us appreciate there is a different stance taken by some that *Lolita* is not just a book about a child rapist, but it presents a work of great literary value and humour.

It is rare that a book and film have such an explicit account of paedophilia in which the whole book is salaciously devoted to the subject matter (though cleverly never in the text is any terminology used regarding genitalia or the sexual act). More usually, there may be either an undercurrent of implied paedophilia or else just a small part mentions the exploitation of underaged girls. *Lolita* almost excuses the concept of child abuse; Humbert is treated as a likeable hero in the story. The same is true of the following film, *Little Lips* (*Piccole Labbra*).

Similarities between *Little Lips* and *Lolita* are numerous. A bachelor man in his thirties, of European extraction, an academic, a writer, becomes infatuated with an eleven-year-old girl approaching her twelfth birthday; the nymphet becoming aware of her blossoming beauty, being willing to tease the man – "Capable of arousing instincts without feeling them herself."

Eva is played by Katya Berger (actually aged fourteen). Eva lives on a large country estate with her aunt who is housekeeper, tending the household while the owner is away during the war. The owner is Herr Paul, gravely wounded, then nursed back to mobility. He can finally convalesce in the solitude of his chateau and its grounds. (There is a similar premise in *Sundays & Cybele*, in which yet another European who has been war damaged, Pierre, befriends an eleven-year-old orphan, Cybele.)

Through constant flashbacks of the horrors of war, which has left him impotent, Herr Paul has lost the will to live. He loads his pistol with a bullet, but cannot bring himself to pull the trigger. He hears young footsteps around his large house, and catches an eye watching him through his keyhole, and, just like Humbert, he is besotted by the girl when he first sets eyes on her.

He is walking by the river. There, kneeling like a water nymph, is the semi-naked figure of the little girl washing herself, dress unbuttoned and open, her private parts mesmerising the gaze of the man. "All of a sudden, as if in a fable, my guardian angel placed in front of my eyes a small peasant Venus."

His suicidal thoughts vanish, his writing gains inspiration, so he is able to finish his book. Daily through that summer, the girl accompanies him on walks through the woods, beside the river, and dances on the lawn. He takes her riding into town, and boating on the lake. Tenderly, he leads her by the hand, holds her close, and hugs her whenever he can.

One day, they are caught in the rain, so Eva takes Herr Paul to her secret hideout – a disused lodge on the edge of the estate. "Look, you're soaked from head to foot," he tells the girl. "We'll get you dried off right now." He lights a fire in the grate, Eva sheds her wet clothes to dry in front of the fire. She wraps her naked body in a skimpy blanket, and reclines into his arms to keep warm. In the cosiness of his caress, the blanket falls open, and he is drawn to her little lips. But he does not graze. "She tempts me with that seductive ambiguity that smoulders in her eyes. She invites me to take part in revels that are forbidden to me, only because of her child's body."

On her twelfth birthday, Paul takes her into town for an ice cream treat. There, she is serenaded by a gypsy musician who starts to flirt with the girl, and later the gypsy impresses her with magic tricks. Herr Paul becomes jealous and reprimands Eva for paying too much attention to the gypsy man. "Today you are my own little princess, and I've no intention of sharing you with anyone."

Herr Paul has to visit Vienna for the publication of his new book. He is only away for a few days, and comes home early because he is missing his young sweetheart. But as he arrives back at the chateau grounds, he stumbles across Eva in the secret hideout with the gypsy man embracing her, the girl compliant in his arms. Paul's suicidal temptations come flooding back. He reloads his pistol, shooting himself in the head.

Now, for us the audience this was a shock, a shame. I guess we were willing the man on. We wanted to see him have his girl, to share that first tender kiss. As with *Lolita*, we were made to empathise with the man – with the paedophile. Whereas Humbert wanted to have his evil way with *Lolita*, the impotent Herr Paul was much more restrained in his desires – he just wanted companionship, beauty, a tender touch, and his ultimate target – those little lips that always just evaded him. Was Herr Paul any less the paedophile?

When *Pretty Baby* was released at Leicester Square in London, it had banner-waving protesters parading outside the cinema complaining of the obvious depiction of child abuse. The story revolves around a New Orleans whorehouse in 1917. Now today, the DVD is on open sale, and even advertised in The Radio Times list of bargain nostalgic must-haves,[22] and aired on Sky Movies.

Violet, played by long blond-haired and lithe twelve-year-old Brooke Shields, is the daughter of one of the prostitutes (played by Susan Sarandon). She doesn't have a father. Her days are filled running around the grounds playing with the other children, dressed in her linen knickerbockers. She seems happy enough, that is, until one day she is caught pretending to simulate sex with one of the black children, like she has seen the other women in the brothel do with their clients. Her punishment for this is a good hiding. Later, she has her legs painted by the rice-throwing voodoo lady, who assures her, "Violet, you is goin' to have so many mans, you won't know what to do!" The girl often loiters in the reception lobby for the whorehouse guests. One 'gentleman' sits Violet on his knee. "Are you trading little girls, now?" he insolently asks the Madame of the house. As he is about to kiss her, the proprietor deters him, "Do you want to put me in jail?"

The day comes when Violet is deemed old enough to join the ranks of the other prostitutes. She is still only twelve, and not yet pubescent. They dress her in a see-through robe, and parade her around the room where the onlookers place their bids for this new "virgin, *bona fide.*"

"How old is she?" one man calls out.

"Just old enough!" comes the reply from Madame.

The bidding spirals higher and higher until one 'gentleman' hands over four hundred dollars (these are 1917 prices!) and takes his winnings to one of the available bedrooms upstairs. "Please be gentle with me," pleads Violet. Not long after, there is a scream of pain, and the man slinks off, probably not comforted.

The bulk of the film dwells on a quiet photographer, Papa Bellocq, played by Keith Carradine, who eventually takes Violet off to live with him in his own house. Here, he uses her as his photographic model. She waits for him, naked. He loves watching her bathe. They kiss and they cuddle. Her exposed breasts are so tiny and barely budding, she is definitely not pubescent, yet she is living as the child-lover of a grown man.

Eventually, her mother links up with a man and they are married. Mother returns for Violet, so the girl is taken away from her lover to go to live in her own house with her own parents for the first time in her life. In the film, we are not told what becomes of Bellocq, the child lover. In William Harrison's novel based on the film, he becomes a morose, vacuous man, haunting the streets of New Orleans until he just wastes away. He is not condemned in the movie as a child molester. Maybe this is why the film generated so much protestation. The film did not treat child prostitution as abusive, but rather as the normal practice for children of prostitutes living in the early twentieth century.

An American Haunting takes us back in time a further one hundred years to Tennessee in 1817. A fourteen-year-old schoolgirl, Betsy Bell (played outstandingly by Rachel Hurd-Wood) is playing with a boy in the school courtyard. Her teacher looks on jealously through the school window.

At a Christmas party Mr Bell, Betsy's father, comes across his daughter standing under the mistletoe with the teacher. "Now Betsy, it is not appropriate to put a teacher in such a compromising situation."

When later, the girl becomes tormented by a poltergeist the teacher feels it his duty to stay overnight with the family to keep an eye on his pupil. But mother notices everything.

"You care for her, don't you?" probes Mrs Bell. "More than the normal care of a teacher for a student."

The teacher is defensive. "Why would you say that?"

"I've seen you look at her."

But this is nineteenth century Tennessee. What is unacceptable today was permissible then. "Can she love me?" he asks.

"She will!" states the mother emphatically, as if marrying off her daughter to any eligible bachelor was one of life's priorities.

This schoolteacher, whose wedding photo shows he married his fourteen-year-old pupil in 1817, would in today's society have received instant dismissal and hounding from both the police and the press.

The propaganda these films seem to be implanting, is that sexual relationships with children has its acceptability in a historical context, when the phrase 'underage' had a different interpretation. The children playing the parts in these films – Brooke Shields, Katya Berger, Rachel Hurd-Wood, Dominique Swaine, Sue Lyon – were not being exploited as actresses for the child they were representing any more than a child playing a bullied victim or a murder victim in a gangster movie. What is arguably exploitative, however, is the physical intimacy, the kissing, the nakedness, that comes with playing the role of a vamp.

Boys and Older Women

There is not a male equivalent of *Lolita*. Sure, there are films in which the youthful boy is dressed up (or dressed down) to look sexually provocative in the eyes of depraved adults, but the boy does not hanker after the mature female in the way Nabokov's Lolita seduced the older Humbert, and his nemesis Quilty. The bare-chested Mark Lester in *Oliver!* is instantly mothered by Nancy (Shani Wallis), as is ten-year-old Elijah Wood by Melanie Griffiths in *Paradise* (1991), while the bathing of little boys in *Lena My 100 Children* has altruistic motives. 'The male nymphet does not have the same impact on grown women: the cute little boys of the screen have inspired a less ambivalent, maternal adoration in their lady fans, though doubtless some have been the secret darlings of male homosexuals.' [23]

"Miss, you don't fancy me, do you?" asks *Billy Elliot* of his ballet teacher, after the woman (Julie Walters) offers to give him free private tuition.

Yet there are films that depict teenage boys expressing a sexual curiosity over older women, as in *Malèna*; while in *Tendres Cousines* the fourteen-year-old boy (Thierry Tevini) ignores his young playmate to seek the lips and fondle the breasts of the older women. It is when his mother discovers him cavorting naked with a maid that father is sent to have a chat with the boy. But all the embarrassed father can do is offer his son a cigarette and warn him, "Next time, try not to get caught."

It is where the woman reciprocates, that sexual abuse becomes apparent. Like the above two films, you will notice that none of these films are English! In the French film, *Clément (2001)* a thirty-year-old woman falls in love with her thirteen-year-old toyboy (Kevin Goffette). After good-natured horseplay they share a kiss. The woman thinks this is just a game at first, but in time their relationship gets more serious. They spend time together, take a holiday together, and eventually share sex. The boy then falls in love with the woman, runs away from home, arriving at the woman's home intending to move in. The woman has the sense to dismiss the boy, who is naturally crestfallen.

A woman endures the same dilemma of sexual desire and fantasy in the Mexican film *Las Mariposas Disecadas*, when a boy who reminds her of her former lover moves into her life. Likewise, in another French film, *Kung Fu Master*, there is a scandalous love affair between a fifty-year-old woman and a fifteen-year-old boy.

English speaking women are not exempt from this intergenerational avidity. *Tadpole (2002)* is an American tale in which fifteen-year-old Aaron Stanford falls in love with his stepmother (Sigourney Weaver).

Paedophilia: Seeking Justice and Revenge

An effectively hard-hitting film confronting paedophilia in a raw, blunt manner is *Hard Candy*. In this drama, a fourteen-year-old girl, Haley (played by Ellen Page), is targeted on the Internet by a grown man, Jeff. The girl agrees to meet at a café, and later they drive off together to his house, where, because he is a photographer, he has suggested she might like to pose in some photographs. Haley has come forewarned, however. She knows she must not accept drinks because there is the danger of them being spiked. So, she mixes the drinks herself and cunningly spikes Jeff's drink, instead. When Jeff falls unconscious, she is able to tie him up and strap him to a chair. After he regains consciousness she then berates him for his evil intentions. She bombards him with arguments of how evil and warped his alleged 'innocent' motives are, and how helpless and susceptible all under-aged victims are. "What the fuck are you doing in a house filled with pictures of semi-naked teenage girls?"

For the rest of the film she torments and abuses him. She has brought with her a veterinary manual describing, step-by-step, how to castrate an animal. "It can't be much different on a human," she proclaims. Having shaved his private parts, she then proceeds to castrate the paedophile. With each cut of the blade she states, "I am every little girl you ever watched… touched… hurt… screwed… killed," interrupted only by howls from the tortured man. Finally, she sets up a rope so the man can hang himself.

When a director creates a film handling the difficult subject of child abuse, he has to do it in a sensitive way, but also be entertaining to the filmgoer. That is why *Hard Candy* succeeds where other films do not. It ably seems to handle the psychological arguments and distressing signposts of paedophilia, and sensationally deals with the problem by depicting the man being castrated. For the sake of entertainment the director has had to pad out the ending. This causes the film to lose conviction when we see the man walking around after his castration, barely the worse for wear.

At least the audience is given opportunity to give a final cheer as the pervert is finished off. In *Lolita*, revenge is paid out on the pervert Quilty who is shot in an equally over-dramatic fashion to satisfy the revengeful. Yet, alarmingly, the initial perpetrator, Humbert Humbert, is about to go free, a hero. Almost as an apologetic after-word we are told, by the way, Humbert died in prison.

A similar dastardly fate awaits others who dare take advantage of the defenceless. In *A High Wind in Jamaica*, the ship's captain is hung for his alleged illicit relationship with the girl-child he was transporting back from Jamaica, dabbling in piracy on the way. But the charges are ambiguous, and based upon misunderstandings and innocent declarations of young children who had been asked to account for actions beyond their comprehension.

More is made of the sexual innuendo in Richard Hughes' novel; in the film, the trial focuses more on the death of the Dutch naval captain. But certainly, eyebrows are raised in the courtroom over innocuous incidents, as lawyers interrogate Emily Templeton: "When you were with all those men, did any of them do anything you didn't like? Anything nasty?"

"He talked about our drawers," replied Emily, referring to her underwear. The court was shocked when they heard Capt. Chavez (the pirate played by Anthony Quinn) had kept the girl in his cabin. The girl wasn't able to vocalise how he had been tenderly caring for her after she had been badly gouged in the thigh. Even an innocent comment about being given medicine is misinterpreted: "He gave me medicine to make me sleep."

Nor in the courtroom had it been revealed how Capt. Chavez had lain on top of the tiny girl staring into her eyes. The girl had prophetically exclaimed, "Hell… You'll go to Hell," as she thumps the man. "You're a wicked pirate. You're going to be hanged and go to Hell." But the incident that led to this outburst was a scuffle in which the man had simply tried to get back his hat, which the children had stolen as part of a teasing game. But this is a man who had been forewarned by his second-in-command, Zac (James Coburn). "If we get caught with these kids aboard our ship…" Zac had warned, gesturing being hanged.

Both Emily's and Zac's prophesies come true. For you cannot mess with little girls and live to tell the tale, as the coastguard in *The Camomile Lawn* could testify (had he been alive to do so).

The coastguard loses his life for committing indecent exposure. In his case, he was pushed over the cliff by ten-year-old Sophie (or so we surmise – it is confirmed in Mary Wesley's book). The girl occasionally explores the clifftop path near her Cornish home, but she is afraid to go near the coastguard's house because he regularly flashes at her. When Sophie's family hold their annual 'terror run' along the same cliff path, Sophie returns from the run out-of-breath and screaming, "Pink… a man… pink snake." Her cousins misinterpret what she is saying and no action is taken.

Later, the cousins amusingly suggest another game – who can kill someone first? The Second World War had just been declared, and they would all soon be going off to war to kill the enemy. Sophie misunderstands the flippancy of the remark. She again tackles the clifftop path past the coastguard's house, and the next day the coastguard is reported dead, having fallen from the cliff.

In Eve's Bayou, ten-year-old Eve Batiste holds her father in high regard, until she catches him groping and kissing another married woman. Father is a doctor. While accompanying him on his rounds, Eve notices her father dwells overlong at certain houses where pretty ladies live. "Some sickness is hard to put a finger on," explains dad to justify his dallying. When Eve's older sister, fourteen-year-old Sicily confides in her that daddy has been kissing and molesting her, Eve loses faith in her father. "I hated him for you," she says later in the film.

Eve visits a voodoo woman, carrying with her strands of hair from father's hairbrush, and pays the woman to have him punished by voodoo. She also sticks voodoo pins in her doll. Then dad is involved in a brawl involving his lover's husband and is unexpectedly killed. So Eve really does believe she was responsible for dad's death.

An incestuous relationship is alluded to in *Forrest Gump*. The boy's girlfriend, Jenny (Hanna R Hall) is afraid to go home to her daddy (her mummy having "gone to Heaven when she was five"). "For some reason Jenny never wanted to go home." Some viewers might criticise this film for approaching child abuse in such a flippant way. (The "father was a very loving man. He was always kissing and touching his daughter.") Yet a potential victim watching this film sees the outcome of all this – Jenny having to hide in the cornfield, sneaking out at night, throwing stones at her father's derelict house in anguished retribution.

Out of all the movies I have referred to in this book that sets out to specifically bring a theme to our attention, and tackle its subject matter with serious depth, I believe *Liar, Liar* to be the most successful (don't confuse this with *Liar Liar*, the Jim Carrey comedy). Alas, this film has not attracted great critical acclaim, maybe for just that reason, that it sets out with an educational mission. This harrowing drama investigates the dilemma of a child living in a household with an abusive father, but no one seems willing to believe she is a victim.

Although she is popular at school, her friends see eleven-year-old Kelly (Vanessa King) as a fibber. Kelly is often squabbling with her younger brother, as well as her older and younger sisters. One evening, she spitefully traps her little brother in the bathroom. The little boy screams to be let out. This gets father annoyed and he comes upstairs to punish her. The faces of the rest of the family seem to drain as Kelly, desperately asking for forgiveness, is dragged into the bathroom to receive punishment. Some time later, a tearful and fearful Kelly emerges from the bathroom.

Her little sister asks, "Did dad hurt you much?"

"I hate him," Kelly replies. "He's not going to hurt me again."

At school, Kelly has been learning in PSE classes to always say 'no' if someone touches their body, to not be afraid to confide in a teacher if they are being sexually abused.

She tries to confide in her mother, but her questions are awkward. "Mum, what would you do if dad was doing stuff to me?"

Mum, who is used to Kelly telling fibs and making trouble, replies, "I don't know what story you are cooking up, but I don't like it one bit."

Next day, Kelly tells her teacher that her father is having sex with her. This, then, begins the traumatic cycle of being interviewed by social workers, having an invasive medical examination, police arriving at her home to arrest the father to the embarrassment of the whole family with the whole street watching, mother being completely baffled. Then, her friends at school ostracise her. She is left distraught, friendless, unloved and her family doesn't believe her. It's as if she, as the victim, is being punished. (Margaret (Anne-Marie Duff) went through a similar humiliation in *The Magdalene Sisters*. Her cousin had raped her during a wedding party; her cries for help being drowned out by the frivolity below. She complained to her parents, and the next day the 'defiled' girl was packed off to the Magdalene Asylum where the nuns subjected her to four years of abuse and virtual slave labour.)

Liar, Liar effectively takes us through the torment that an abused girl must be experiencing, the impact and repercussions that occur when she informs on her father – the disbelief on the part of family members, denial by the perpetrator, the splitting up of the family unit, ostracism from friends, the crime being splashed across the newspapers, the intimate details that have to be revealed in court. All these obstacles, no doubt, deter many victims from disclosing their abuse. This film provides a warning of what happens when paternal boundaries are breached.

In the film, the evidence for Kelly is very slim. It is basically her word against her father's. Her case would have failed if her two reluctant siblings had not come forward to acknowledge they had been abused as well. (They had not come forward previously, simply because their father had told them not to, and they were too frightened to tell.)

In summing up, the judge tells Kelly, "The strength and courage you have shown in this trial is to be commended and admired in a person of such tender years." To the guilty father he announces, "Your conduct towards your daughter was beyond the standards of decency and morality. That you should use your child for your own sexual gratification is both repugnant and depraved."

This film highlights the awful truth about the implications of sexual abuse to the victim and the victim's family. As an instructive film, it provides warranted messages for adults that a perpetrator could easily be that wonderful loving partner you have lived with happily for the past twenty-two years and that your child needs to be believed despite their reputation for deviousness.

However, for a child watching this film, I guess it so honestly portrays the obstacles and points out the repercussions of informing on an abuser, that only the strongest-willed victim sees the process through from start to finish.

The French movie, *A Shadow of Doubt* effectively follows a similar storyline: that of an eleven-year-old girl (Sandrine Blancke) who claims she has been abused by her father. She is often left alone with her father till mother arrives home from work at midnight, yet mother never notices the girl won't undress ready for bed while father is around. She discontinues swimming because that provides painful reminders, and becomes anorexic.

When her teacher becomes suspicious after the stories she writes at school ("If your father is doing something you mustn't keep it a secret," she tells Alexsandrine) the father simply removes her to a different school. The girl bravely takes her accusations to a police station. Complications are added when the disbelieving mother slaps her daughter and forces her to retract the accusations. "Do you realise what you've done? I can't believe a daughter of mine could do such a thing!" This cruelly places the guilt firmly in the mind of the victim. Again, it becomes just the girl's word against the father's. Fortunately, the social worker believes her, and the girl perseveres with her accusations to court. The social worker reassures her: "A forty-year-old has had forty years to practise lying, but a twelve-year-old has little experience." But the film comes with a solemn afterword: that only two out of every fifty child abuse cases actually make it to court. This film adds an element missing from *Liar, Liar* as it is revealed the father himself was abused when he was a child.

This notion of reporting an abuser to a responsible adult such as a teacher was initially included in *The Woodsman*. Kevin Bacon, acting as Walter, tells a little girl to report her abusive father to the police, but the director decided to cut this scene – it would have been a step too far for the reforming character of Walter to take.

If only all potential victims of child abuse had the physical capabilities of Evan (Logan Lerman) in *The Butterfly Effect*. As a seven-year-old playing with his neighbour's daughter, Kayleigh (Sarah Widdows), he is coerced to take part in a pornographic video with Kayleigh's father's new camera. "This will be our little secret," the father tells him. But as the boy reaches adulthood, he finds he has the mental power to revisit his past and confront issues as they occurred. He is able to succinctly state the outcome for all abused children. He stands up to Kayleigh's father. "Fuckbag," the seven-year-old begins. "You'll forever traumatise your own daughter. It will change your beautiful daughter into one empty shell. She was betrayed by her own sick paedophile father. Ultimately, it will lead to her suicide. Nice work, daddy."

Empathy with the Perverted

Why the film *The Woodsman* was criticised was the same reason it was praised: because it dared to see the world through the eyes of a child abuser, getting us to empathise with the perpetrator, focusing on the trauma of being released from prison back into the community.

Walter is now on probation following a twelve-year stint for abusing a girl of nine and a girl of fourteen. Now back in the community, living in an apartment in Philadelphia, he tries to be invisible, just going to work, doing his job, keeping out of trouble, remaining anonymous. But he finds he cannot escape children. They jostle him on the bus, they play in the playground opposite where he lives, and they are in the shopping mall and in the park where he walks. He finds temptations all around and has to find strategies to resist them.

He has a therapist with whom he can discuss his tribulations. He has also found a lady friend from work who is willing to forgive his past misdemeanours and helps him to start afresh. And there is a police officer who watches over him, aware of his movements. This officer makes it clear to Walter that, like all paedophiles, he has a problem that will afflict him for the rest of his life. "I don't know why they let freaks like you out on the street," says the officer. "We just got to catch you all over again."

Walter concurs: "Most people say the odds are against me. Most of us end up back in prison."

The film focuses on the grief, the struggle, the torment that Walter goes through; putting aside the loathing and disgust we may have for the crime, helping us to empathise with him.

Maybe Walter's first mistake is choosing an apartment overlooking a school playground. From here he can daily watch the children come and go, and play. The few visitors he has – his brother-in-law and the police officer – comment on this ambiguity: "Is that where you stand and jack off?" says Sergeant Lucas, looking through the window at the playground opposite. It is from this window that Walter sees another man arrive daily with sweets to tempt little boys into his car – a scene that fills him with horror and murderous intent.

His paranoia rises as his brother-in-law comes to visit. The visitor is eager to tell Walter about his twelve-year-old daughter, and brings him photos of her birthday party. He says he wished Walter had been there; except his sister will have nothing to do with him anymore. The visitor describes how ravishingly beautiful his daughter has become as she and her friends now wear provocatively revealing clothing. Is this brother-in-law baiting him, or is he a potential sex offender himself? As in the film *The Offence*, it is his own issues, his own guilt, that drives his actions and that sees the guilt in others.

Walter's attempt to be anonymous at work backfires. His greatest worry is being 'outed' as an ex-offender, and fear of vigilantism. His wariness at being sociable causes the factory secretary to check up on his background. As suspicions are raised, someone writes inside his locker, "We are watching you." When it is discovered he is a sex offender he is violently attacked at work.

Nichole Kassell, the director, cites this as a problem for all ex-offenders trying to go straight – the implementation of Megan's Law in USA makes it possible for enquiries to be made concerning the whereabouts of past sex offenders living in the community. Thus they become reclusive, go underground, out of the police radar, exacerbating the problem. This same fear is now being expressed as Sarah's Law is being introduced in the United Kingdom.

Walter goes through the typical denial stage with his therapist. Although he committed an act of indecency with the children, "I never hurt them," he claims. "Never!"

A girl in the locality is abused, of which Walter is innocent. But the police's immediate reaction is to call on Walter and view him with suspicion.

Walter's psychiatrist suggests he make a journal of his daily encounters and temptations. Walter is reluctant to do this, lest it becomes evidence in the hands of the police. He is uncomfortable as the therapist encourages him to look back to his past for any clues to his adult deviancy. When he was eight, and his sister was six, he enjoyed laying with the girl, but only to innocently 'smell her hair'. But as the therapist probes what happened when they were older children, Walter can only tearfully try to reject the memory and deflect the answer.

Kevin Bacon, without whom the film would not successfully have gone ahead, plays Walter effectively. Without the director's suggestion, at one stage in the filming, he improvises a despairing sobbing fit as Walter grapples with a memory that haunts him, and as he thinks about the almost impossible minefield he now has to tread. Although he believes he is not a monster, he is faced with the fact that everyone views him as one.

So he has to prove he is reformed. This is where we meet eleven-year-old Hannah Pilkes, who plays Robin. Daily, Robin gets on the same bus that Walter uses to travel home from work. One day, curiosity and temptation get the better of the man and he decides to follow her into the park where she goes bird watching. Walter catches up with her and strikes up a conversation, and a spark of friendship is ignited.

The next day, Walter waits for her on the park bench in a secluded part of the forest, and the regressive spiral of grooming has begun. For, as they share the park bench with polite conversation, Walter boldly asks, "Robin, would you like to sit on my lap?" It is only as Walter witnesses the tearful response by the girl and discovers she is being abused at home by her father that he starts to glimpse the emotional damage that abuse does to a child.

As film director Kassell says, "The pivotal point in the picture is when he realises he is hurting his victim. A key kind of rehabilitation for these men is when they realise they are hurting their victims."

Walter's resolve is further tested. Robin does not want to offend her new found friend, so says she is willing: "I will sit on your lap… if you still want me to." But with the audience's relief, the man tells her, "Go home, Robin, go home."

Robin and Walter, in this film, had built up a bond. Just like the father-daughter relationship in *Liar, Liar* and in Eve's Bayou, and stepfather-stepdaughter in *Lolita*, "the tragedy of the sexual abuse of minors is that they are put in a predicament of loving the person who is hurting them. In order for the hurt to stop, they have to hurt the person they love." [24]

Just as Vladimir Nabokov had an input into the first film of his book, *Lolita*, perhaps to justify its publication, to lessen its controversy, so too Jerry Lee Lewis had an input in the biopic about his life, by playing the piano soundtrack to the film, *Great Balls of Fire*, to make it jolly entertainment, perhaps to deflect criticism.

Winona Ryder plays Myra Gale, the thirteen-year-old cousin of Jerry Lee. When the rock legend comes to stay at his cousin's house, they start up a relationship with each other, just play-acting at first, but then snogging, and ultimately progressing to intimacy that is more sexual. Then they elope for one day, get married without informing the parents, and she becomes his child bride at the age of just thirteen. After this, several sex romps ensue on screen. Although Gerry Lee Lewis remains a revered rock legend to his die-hard fans, when the wider public hear about this wedding there is revulsion (even though at the time it was legally permissible in some US states). There is also antagonism towards him when he visits London. Just like *Lolita* seems to require a British comedy actor to soften the blow, so also in *Great Balls of Fire*, comedian Peter Cook is drafted in to play the British journalist.

Adults Targeting Children / Grooming

The mistreatment of children by their abusers if often a drawn-out affair. A vulnerable child may be targeted as a victim. The abuser then spends time (this may be years in some cases) befriending the child, gaining their trust, buying them presents, taking their photographs. This is the grooming process. The child gently coaxed into what seems at first insignificant activity, which gradually progresses into sexual deeds. For some, the groomer may be apprehended or frightened off, as in *Angela (1994)* or *The Little Girl who lives down the Lane*, while others may have to travel the long path of abuse before their abuser is brought to justice as in *Fallen Angel*.

Dana Hill looks only ten, maybe eleven, as she plays the role of twelve-year-old Jennifer Philips in the 1981 made-for-TV drama *Fallen Angel*. This is a very difficult and controversial role for any child to take – playing the victim of a predatory paedophile. Although children of that age should be aware of potential dangers, to expect them to place themselves in such a suggestive role is above the call of duty, and way beyond their life experiences. That Dana Hill was in fact seventeen at the time is a credit to the casting director, but should not detract from the competent performance she made playing the vulnerable victim. This is a clever and powerful film, effectively confronting the issues of paedophilia and of child pornography. Yet, as with *The Woodsman* and *Liar, Liar* it attracted unnecessarily harsh critiques. All these three dramas provide salutatory lessons in the dangers of paedophilia and the vulnerability of minors, yet inexplicably, they have disappeared into the vaults as irrelevant to today's entertainment demands.

Jennifer Philips is playing on the pinball machines in an amusement arcade. Along comes a stranger, Howie Nichols (played creepily by Richard Masur). Throwing some loose coins on the machine to gain her attention he says, "You look like someone who's having fun and wants some more."

He waits outside for the girl to leave, and takes her photograph as she mounts her bicycle. He compliments her on looking as beautiful as Farrah Fawcett. "You should really be in movies… That's the secret of all you movie stars, isn't it, the eyes?" And he introduces himself as "Howie." The man is able to probe her home background, convincing her that she is not really loved at home, that her mother has no time for her, being more interested in her new boyfriend. He makes her believe she is really just a love-child, an accident, unwanted at home.

Howard is a sports coach. That first meeting made an impression on the girl, for she turns up to his sports ground. He offers to buy her an iced cream and they sit in the car licking it. It's Jennifer's birthday in two days time, so Howie takes a photo of her licking the ice. "We'll take one now, and another in two days, to see the difference between twelve and thirteen." He buys her a teddy bear – she calls it 'Howard'.

On her thirteenth birthday he takes her to the park. In a secluded area within the trees he starts taking more photos. "Now just over the knee… no one's watching." Then he lowers her blouse to reveal her shoulders. "You know, the body is really a beautiful thing." He shows her a magazine of child pornography. "You know, other people your age do it all the time." Then comes the patter that all predators make to the child they are grooming: "By the way, I think we should keep our real friendship a secret, ok."

At home, just as mum's boyfriend turns up, Jennifer suggests, "Let's go to the zoo today. Just you and me." When this idea is rejected, she realises that maybe what Howard says is true. Maybe mum doesn't really love her. She goes inside and smashes the family photo of her mum, her real dad and herself. Then Jennifer goes off to the sports hall where she waits for Howard to attend to her. Tenderly he lifts her off the trampoline and takes her by the hand into his office, and sits her on his desk where he dresses her grazed hand. He confirms to the girl, "Sometimes parents don't care if you're alive or dead."

Next, he takes the girl to the animal sanctuary and buys the girl a puppy, which she calls Fred. "Just tell your mum you found it, ok." The gift is made, the girl is delighted, and victim, perpetrator, and gift walk back to the lake for another photo shoot. This time, although reticent at first, the girl is grateful and more amenable. "It's ok. You know I'd never do anything to hurt you. I'll give you a full set of prints just like a real movie star. Fred will pose with you. Fred's naked!" The girl obligingly peels off her clothes and the pornographer starts clicking rapidly.

On another occasion, Jennifer is introduced to some of the other children that Howard is photographing. There is David, a boy about her own age. The young couple have to kiss while the man takes photographs. They enjoy this so much, they carry on kissing whether the photographer is ready or not.

The day comes when Howard wants David and Jennifer to pose naked together. The girl tearfully objects at this. So the man gets Jennifer's puppy and uses it as a threat. He says he will have to send the dog back, and it will have to be put down. With tears rolling down her cheeks, she compliantly yields, and the man gets his way.

Eventually, the girl feels she is unloved at home and runs away to live with Howard and the other boys who share his flat. Now the paedophile is much more demanding. "I want you very much," he tells her. "As a lover. You and me." Just as he starts to kiss the little girl, there is a knock at the door. Mother has traced her child. All the children are freed, and the man arrested. The pitiful man pleads with them. "I've given them love. I never hurt any of them"

In his prison cell a lawyer visits him before his trial. The typical traits of the paedophile are revealed in Howard's personality: uncomfortable with adult women, he feels he is a victim, the desire to be loved by a child, becoming an unwitting father-figure.

Next is the difficulty of persuading the victim to testify in court. We saw this as a negative experience for Kelly in *Liar, Liar*. Likewise, Jennifer's mother does not permit her to testify, assuming it will destroy her girl. The defence lawyer tries to convince her: "You and I know he's done wrong. He's sick. He needs help. Is not getting him help the right thing to do, Jennifer?" But the girl still has a sense of loyalty. Although she has been wronged, she still does not want to betray her friend.

Jennifer bumps into Howard who has been released on bail. He tries to ensure she doesn't testify. "They will call me sick. They will call you a whore." But when she visits the zoo with her mother and notices other little children being photographed by men, who may or may not be their fathers, she is finally convinced. So the case can come to court.

The film then leaves us with a pertinent message. "There are a million runaways today in America. Many children rarely relate to their parents or the adults in their community. And into this void walks the paedophile, the child lover. We don't want to suggest that every coach or every teacher that a child comes into contact with is a paedophile, but it is possible that he might be." This film helpfully raises our awareness of this issue.

Millie Forrester spends the bulk of her childhood trying to evade sexual abuse in the gripping drama adapted from Catherine Cookson's historical novel, *The Rag Nymph*. Perdita Weeks plays the very pretty, and culturally refined, fish-out-of-water, Millie Forrester. She had been brought up in a fine home in London in Victorian England until mother fell on hard times after the father died. Somehow, the pair made their way to Newcastle, a coal-mining community in the northeast of England. Mother, forced into prostitution to make ends meet, is arrested by the police and destitute ten-year-old Millie finds herself homeless.

A warm-hearted rough-and-ready Geordie woman, Mrs Wincovsky, known locally as Raggie Annie, has witnessed the arrest and kindly takes Millie home for protection. Another man has also witnessed Millie's desolation – a local pimp named Boswell, who runs a whorehouse. "Did you see that youngster?" he whispers to his partner, pointing to the ten-year-old girl. "I've not seen such a valuable item for a long time."

Mrs Wincovsky is aware that Millie's prettiness and refinement makes her an attractive target to kidnappers. She predicts, "She'll go the same way as her mother one day, poor little bitch." Raggie Annie has her work cut out trying to keep the little girl safe from harm.

One day, Boswell finds Millie waiting in the street. "We're going to the fair," he tells her. "Do you want to come, my little Rag Nymph?"

Sensibly, the girl resists and shouts to her guardian, who comes to rescue her. "Half the police are in the pay of the criminals," so she cannot expect any help from that direction.

Mrs Wincovsky realises Millie must be sent away to somewhere safe, so they find a convent school where she can be boarded in relative safety. This works for a while, but Millie is already too well educated for her age and the nuns cannot tolerate her clever answers, her story writing, and handwriting beyond her years. After many rapped knuckles, she is dismissed back to the rag trade with Mrs Wincovsky.

Years pass. Millie becomes a teenager (now played by Perdita's older sister, Honeysuckle Weeks), but she cannot be constantly supervised. Eventually, Boswell does catch up with her, and kidnaps her, locking her up in the whorehouse to await clients. (Her mother had been locked in this same brothel and hung herself.) Fortunately, a rescue party is raised and Millie is released.

Had Mrs Wincovsky not rescued Millie when she was a child, then her most likely destination would have been the workhouse. Conditions at the workhouse are put into perspective when you hear one of the prostitutes claim she started whoring when she was just eleven. But that was better than being in the workhouse!

Perdita Weeks starred in two consecutive films in which she played the victim of a paedophile. Two years before playing the eloquent ten-year-old Millie Forrester in the *Rag Nymph*, she appeared in the gripping thriller, *Cold Light of Day*, in which she was the delightful, playful, but tempting bait placed to trap a serial killing paedophile. I wonder what this preteen girl thought men were all about when her two successful screen roles involved both evading and cavorting with predators.

Richard E Grant plays a detective from 'an Eastern European country' who quits his job because he knows the chief of police has convicted the wrong man for the string of child murders. "He's innocent as a choirboy, and you know it," says Victor Marek to the police chief who has his eye on becoming mayor, and who wants to wrap up the case quickly.

Marek decides to pursue the killer privately. He consults his psychiatrist friend to seek a profile of the paedophile, to know what clues to look out for. The psychiatrist tells him that the paedophile prefers the company of young children. "Generally, these people are fixed in their own childhoods. They can't deal with adult sexuality. But a child is safe. They can all be children together. Children are pure, adults are defiled. Sometimes the paedophile turns into a killer because he thinks by doing so he is saving the child from the horrors of adulthood. In wartime, mothers sometimes kill their children to escape the worse horrors of being captured by the enemy. It's the same with paedophiles. They murder children because that is preferable to growing up." He seems to imply that all men have the potential to be a paedophile – but most people manage to suppress their paedophilic tendencies. "But it doesn't take much to change a man into a beast – a few malfunctioning cells, a slight change in metabolism."

Knowing the serial killer travelled a certain route, Marek decides to rent a petrol garage on a lonely stretch of road where he can keep a check on passers-by. Now, living nearby in a derelict railway shack is an immigrant woman and her eight-year-old daughter, Anna. Marek insidiously plans to use the little girl as bait to trap the paedophile killer.

Marek persuades Anna and her mother to move in with him, the woman to act as housekeeper and Anna to be the unwitting bait for the paedophile by using the swing that Marek has set up on the garage forecourt. Anna is given strict instructions. "Listen, Anna, if anyone talks to you or gives you anything you're to tell me immediately."

The bait works. The child murderer is a surgeon, a doctor who regularly passes by on the road. We see the surgeon at home playing with child-sized mannequin dolls that he has clothed in the polka-dot dresses of his previous victims.

He espies the girl and sets about making his own trap to tempt her into the woods. The paedophile surgeon has a hand puppet dog. He cleverly leads Anna away along the woodland path by claiming the puppet to be magic, so the man and little girl start to play games with each other. But then there is the paedophile's secret: "If you tell your mummy about me, then all the magic is over. If you break the magic your mummy will disappear forever."

When Anna catches her mother having sex with Marek, she knows what this now means. She tells her own teddy bear, "Now we're all alone except for our little friend in the woods." So now, Anna is more inclined to go with the paedophile from whom she thinks she may get more love.

The paedophile tempts her once more into the woods. She is sitting quietly on his knee. Behind her back, he is getting his surgeon's knife ready to cut the throat of the little girl. But Marek gets him first, pistol in his hand, bullet to the head, just in time!

We have so far considered the paedophile as having two distinct profiles. The first, as in *Fallen Angel*, is targeting the child for sexual gratification. In the second scenario, *The Cold Light of Day*, the paedophile is a murderer not necessarily intent on his own sexual gratification, but rather wishing to snuff out a child's life in the mistaken belief he is protecting the child's innocence. That there is no rape or molestation involved, does this mean he is not a paedophile, just a murderer? His targets are children – is this because they are easier victims to handle or because they fit his deluded theories?

Motives are not clear in *The Lovely Bones* either. Mr Harvey has targeted a string of victims, all girls, mainly adolescents, though his youngest was aged six. In all cases he murdered them, though we are never made aware of any sexual motive. In the case of the youngest, "He'd only wanted to touch her – but she screamed," narrates Saoirse Ronan.

Fourteen-year-old Susie Salmon (vividly played by rising star and Oscar nominee Saoirse Ronan) is targeted because she is the near neighbour of Mr Harvey. He can observe the girl's movements from across the road. Why he should devise an underground bunker in the middle of a cornfield is not clear, rather than tempt the girl into his own home. Maybe Susie was not the intended target for his perversion. But she crosses the cornfield on a shortcut home from school. Harvey tempts her to inspect the bunker as a suitable den for her friends. Here she is mesmerised by candlelight, fluffy animals, games and figurines. He invites her to take off her coat and have a drink. The girl is not allowed to escape with her life, the murder (confusingly) being finished off in his own house where he is seen frantically mopping up the blood in his bathroom.

When Mr Harvey realised he has got away with this crime too, he begins to target Susie's younger sister, Lindsay, until, with Susie's supernatural help and an icicle, the murderer is teased off the edge of a cliff.

An equally creepy paedophile appears in *The Little Girl who lives down the Lane*. Martin Sheen plays the pervert, who taunts and haunts the new arrival in the village, Jodie Foster. It all starts on her thirteenth birthday.

Martin Sheen plays Frank Hallett, a thirty-something man with a history of past abuses. The community is aware of his predilections, but seems rather dismissive when more severe action needs to be taken. Frank Hallett is the son of the landlady, whose house Rynn (Jodie Foster) and her father had leased.

Rynn (whose parents have both died but the community are not aware of this) is now secretly living on her own. It being her birthday, she has baked herself a cake with thirteen candles on it. Knocking on her secluded door is Frank Hallett, pretending to be out trick-or-treating with his two sons. He wheedles his way into her house, "I'm just going to make sure there are not any real goblins hanging around," he tries to justify himself to the girl. "No dirty old men trying to give pretty little girls some candy."

Jodie cuts some cake for him to take to his children. But as she holds the slices out for him, instead of the cake he takes hold of her hands to stroke. "You're a very pretty girl, do you know that? Pretty eyes, pretty hair." But after he smacks her bum he becomes defensive and realises he should leave. The next day, as Rynn is walking down a quiet lane, she spots a car parked in a lay-by with the car door wide open and Hallett waiting for her. She gives the pervert a wide berth.

When the landlady rudely barges into the girl's home she warns Rynn, "If my son should come back and your father is not in, it would be better if you don't let him in," alluding to his past misdemeanours. But it's too late for that. Jodie tells the woman what happened previously, "Your son says I've pretty hair." But the woman just treats her as an insolent brat.

Later, the girl befriends the local police officer who has called round to see her father. Rynn tells the officer about Mrs. Hallet's son. "He says I'm a pretty girl. What is he, a pervert?" But officer Miglioriti has no power to do anything.

The pervert, having deduced there to be a vulnerable girl all alone in the house, can't keep himself away, and is able to force himself in. Rynn asks him, "What to they call guys like you who hang around little girls? Perverts?" Filmed in 1976, the term paedophile had not yet reached everyday prominence.

Like Ellen Page in *Hard Candy*, Rynn can also cope and has prepared herself for dealing with unwanted intruders. Her library reading has directed her towards potassium cyanide which has a hint of almond smell. She has baked almond cookies just for this scenario, and the taste of the white powder sprinkled in her visitor's cup of tea is masked by the biscuits he is now crunching.

During the course of the film, Jodie Foster is befriended by Scott Jacoby who becomes her collaborator against the oppressive adults. She gets to scrub his back in the bath, strip naked in front of him and get into bed with him for a kiss and a cuddle, and for a "have you ever.... (done it before?)." Yet, although playing the part of the schoolboy magician, in real life Scott Jacoby is actually twenty years of age, and just the type of boyfriend parents warn their little girls about. But although she has just turned thirteen and he is twenty, it's alright, 'cos he doesn't act creepy and doesn't have a perverted reputation!

Molestation

Sometimes, abuse is perpetrated on a victim by an opportunist encounter, rather than by specific grooming, as in *Angela (1994)* or *An Impudent Girl*. Of course, this is still sexual molestation, made even more abhorrent when there is a large age difference between victim and abuser. But when the child is the same age, or even older than her abusers, this may cause a moral dilemma, particularly when the girl shows passive consent to her peers as in the case of *Ratcatcher*.

In *Angela (1994)*, Miranda Stuart Ryne plays the title role of a ten-year-old girl who has become aware of the concept of sin. She plays a game that helps her recognise good angels and bad angels. When she goes to the funfair with her little sister, Ellie, they meet a man who offers to pay for them at an arcade game and he helps them win. "That man is a good angel," Angela tells Ellie.

It is not long before they meet the man again. "Would you like to go for a walk?" the man invites them. When they find a secluded spot, he beckons, "Come here, Angela. I like you," and he starts kissing the girl.

In her naivety, Angela, still thinking him a good angel, says to him, "I know who you are!" This spooks the pervert, assuming authorities are on to him, and he makes a rapid retreat.

An Impudent Girl is an example of a film in which child abuse creeps in, more as a side issue instead of the whole film targeting the topic. The steamy summer holidays have just begun, and a bored twelve-year-old (Charlotte Gainsbourg) is hanging around the dreary French town where she lives, dressed in an ever so short skirt, unaware her bronzed legs are an alluring temptation to the drifting engineer, Jean, who has recently found work in the town. He buys her a drink in the café. As he drops her off at home, he tells her, "I'm going to kiss you now." He is the first person to show her any attention or affection, so Charlotte is delighted with her new found friend.

But when, later, he takes her to his room in the basic hotel where he is staying to show her the revolving light-up globe he is so proud of, he can no longer resist her, grasps her round the waist, and slumps on the bed with her. Charlotte, now aware of the danger she is in, picks up the globe and smashes it to smithereens on his head, and assumes she has killed the man. Jean however does survive, but realising his guilt sneaks away on the train the following morning.

In *Ratcatcher*, bullying and sexual abuse seem synonymous. Margaret Anne is a teenager (played by Leanne Mullen). She doesn't seem to have any female friends her own age. Wearing spectacles, she is the object of ridicule by the boys in the neighbourhood who rip the glasses from her face and chuck them in the canal. This is Glasgow at the time of the 1970s dustmen strike. Everyone is scratching at the nits in their hair, and they are covered in scabs. Margaret is no different.

Because Margaret doesn't fight back she becomes easy prey for the gang of boys who take turns leading her into the outside toilets to touch her up or cop-a-feel, or lie on top of her in her flat, while she is stripped to her underwear. She seems resigned to this and doesn't resist, so we get the impression she is enjoying the abuse, though she never actively seeks interaction. Not until she meets twelve-year-old James. James is not out to exploit her. He is invited to share the bath with her, and to jump into bed with the girl. "James, do you love me?" "Ey," he replies.

In *Birch Interval*, Susan McClung, as twelve-year-old Jessie, is tied to a tree while other boys look up her dress and 'cop a feel'. These are both examples of girls being molested, not by adults, but by children their own age.

The molestation that Bone (Jena Malone) endures in *Bastard out of Carolina* may at first have been opportunist – her stepfather sits the eleven-year-old on his knee while they wait in the car outside the hospital where mother is giving birth to a stillborn boy. This is a child actress who has to demonstrate her awareness of sexual molestation, by screwing her face in anguish as her abuser strokes and fumbles beneath her, while his orgasmic moans rise to a crescendo. Her face betrays her bewildered emotions: how long is this painful intrusion going to endure? [25]

This one scene alone may explain why this movie never reached British cinemas or the counters of UK DVD stores, and was initially banned by the Canadian Board of Censors. [26] But, for the long-suffering child this incident is just the start of a painful childhood of physical and sexual torment of a stepdaughter, culminating ultimately in her enduring a prolonged enforced snog while being raped. The actions and their implications are depicted vividly, in a performance by a child that cannot be surpassed, and that arguably a girl so young should never have been allowed to perform or even be aware of. Although this girl, Jena Malone, won best young artist award[27] for her superb performance by a child way beyond her years, yet the role she was depicting did not receive the credit it deserved.

Even more distressing is the disbelief this engendered. Based on an autobiography published in 1992 by Dorothy Allison, her novel, *Bastard out of Carolina*, was declared too horrific and banned from American schools and libraries, as if there is a national denial that such extreme abuse can be acknowledged. Even the original sponsor of the film, Ted Turner, deemed it too graphic to be broadcast on his TV channel. [28]

Child Prostitution

Jodie Foster plays twelve-year-old Iris in Martin Scorsese's seedy film, *Taxi Driver*. She, herself, was only thirteen at the time, and had to be aware of and listen to base sexual language. Of course, we all know Jodie Foster now as the hard gritty adult actress/director, but then when she was barely a teenager she had to endure such a perverse role but seemed to take it in her stride. That she also had to play the target for a paedophile in a subsequent film, *The Little Girl who lives down the Lane*, means that, like Perdita Weeks who also had to play sexually uncomfortable roles in successive films, and like Brooke Shields, either she had been type-cast when a child or had been provided with emotional guidance from parents and counsellors.

Although the film is about a taxi driver, Travis Bickle (played by mesmerising Robert de Niro), who has a personal mission to clean up the scum and filth from off the streets of New York, yet when he comes across this young girl he has a shift in his vision, spending his hard-earned cash to purchase armoury to eliminate the pimps who are trading this underaged girl for sex.

Travis first encounters this girl when Iris, dressed in blouse and hotpants, jumps into his taxi. Immediately a man comes to grab her by the arm and forces her back on the street, leaving $20 as a tip to the driver for the inconvenience. Realising something is wrong, Travis cruises the streets until he comes across this girl again. When he finds the pimp, he arranges for a session with the young girl, by paying his $15 for fifteen minutes. "Do what you want with her," the pimp tells Travis, "She's twelve and a half years old. You ain't never had no pussy like that." [29]

In the rented flat, Iris immediately starts undressing, but Travis is not interested in that. "I want to get you out of here," he tells her. The girl is adamant she is not in any trouble. "I can leave any time I want to," she says. When Travis starts talking about the manipulative pimps, she defends them: "They just protect me from myself." I guess this is a defensive patter she has invented over time to deflect other seemingly moralistic clients.

"Girls should live at home," he tells her. "You should be dressed up, going out with boys. (Instead) you sell your pussy for some low-life pimp. He's the worst scum in the whole world."

Travis leaves, makes an appointment with a gun dealer. He buys the dealer's entire stock, then dresses himself from shoulder to toes with weaponry. He returns to the pimp, all guns blazing, eliminating the scum and filth from this part of town.

In *Stolen Children*, Valentina Scalici plays eleven-year-old Rosetta living with her mother and younger brother in a block of flats in Milan. Mother is trying to get the boy to play outside because she is anticipating a visitor. "Stop hanging onto my apron strings like a girl," she tells the boy before finally bribing him to go outside and buy sweets from the shop. Then the male visitor arrives and is led into Rosetta's bedroom, where, sitting on the bed, he takes the eleven-year-old's hand.

Shortly after this, the police arrive, having been tipped off. Both the man and the mother are arrested. This is because Rosetta has for the past two years, since the age of nine, been prostituted out by her mother.

The child is taken to a children's home in Rome but, on the excuse that there is no medical certificate, she is not accepted. This is just the start of being rejected by institutions on account of her past defilement. (We also came across this shame of being a rape victim in *The Magdalene Sisters*, too.)

"What will happen to my mum?" Rosetta asks her escort. She is blatantly told she will go to jail. "I keep dreaming she dies!" says the despairing corrupted child.

If *Hard Candy* and *The Little Girl who lives down the Lane* feature girls who can handle themselves, *London to Brighton* has a girl who thinks she can, but cannot. Georgia Groome plays the eleven year old ("I'll soon be twelve") runaway found begging at a London railway station by Kelly, a professional prostitute. Kelly has been persuaded to scout around for a suitable target who can provide 'favours' for a rich client seeking a young ten/eleven-year-old girl.

After being offered fags and a hot meal, Joanne agrees to accompany Kelly to meet the pimp. Her naive bravado forces herself to pretend she is experienced.

The eleven-year-old is asked, "Why the fuck did you run away?"

"Because living at home was shit. Mum's dead and my dad is a bastard. He beat me, just because I nicked his fags."

"Are you a virgin?" Joanne pretends she is not, not knowing what she is about to let herself into.

"Do you want a hundred quid?"

"Yer. Why? What have I got to do?"

The girl is led off to the millionaire's house. Lorraine Stanley, the actress who plays Kelly, tells how she had to apply makeup to Georgia Groome in the taxi on the way to the paedophile's house, and had to imagine what might be done to the little girl. She admits that after the filming of this scene, she had to go off by herself to have a cry because she found it so upsetting. Yet she was the adult! Joanne still says 'thanks' to the paedophile when he gives her a drink, retaining politeness to the person with status, whereas she is swearing when among the 'riffraff'. The pervert leads her by the hand upstairs and into the bedroom where she is tied to the bed and the man begins cutting off her clothes with a knife.

But her screams are heard by the guilt-ridden Kelly, who rushes to her aid, the knife ends up in the client's groin and the bloodied man drifts slowly off to death.

"Are we going to go to jail?" asks Joanne as they seek refuge in a toilet cubicle in the city. "Don't worry, that man won't find us."

The rest of the film shows the frightened girls fleeing to Brighton pursued by the dead man's defiant son, the vicious pimp and his obedient sidekick. Once they are recaptured, the kidnapped girls are forced into a car boot and taken to a Sussex field to witness two graves being dug. "Please, what are you going to do to me?" asks the quivering eleven-year-old to the violent men. But the dead man's son has a disloyal sense of justice: the two graves are filled by the pimps who had dared seek out the underage girl in the first place, while the youngsters are allowed to go free. In Volume One (*Gender Roles and Themes*), we describe the traumatic impact the making of this film had on the preteen Georgia Groome.

Swedish director, Lukas Moodysson, set out to specifically highlight the reality of child trafficking for the sex trade in his grim tale, *Lilya 4-ever*. The caption at the end states, "This film is dedicated to the millions of children around the world exploited by the sex trade." The movie concerns a sixteen-year-old girl, Lilya, played by Russian actress, Oksana Akinshina, who has been abandoned by her mother and left to fend for herself in a grimy flat in a morbid tenemented suburb of Estonia, though the director acknowledges this could have been any Soviet city.

When her money runs out, the girl is forced to sell herself for prostitution. This is what her uncaring aunt suggests she does when Lilya turns up at her door begging for help. "Go into town and spread your legs like your mother used to do." Lilya does know the ropes, for she had previously accompanied and watched a friend of hers at a nightclub.

The film paints this as a bleak picture, but allows us a ray of hope because she now has money and merrily fills her supermarket basket. So at least she has some degree of control over her life, no matter how unpleasant. She is also befriended at the nightclub by a Swedish tourist. He seems to care for her as a person and is not out to jump into bed with her. The man, Andrei, takes her to the funfair and buys her meals. Soon Lilya has fallen in love with him. So when Andrei offers to take the girl to Sweden where he can find her work, she jumps at the chance to get away from the drudgery of Soviet life.

But on the day of departure, Andrei tells Lilya his grandmother is gravely ill. Presenting her with a false passport with the promise of joining her in a couple of days, Lilya is despatched on a plane to Sweden where she is met at the other end by 'the boss'. But still Lilya seems content, anticipating her new life. It is only when she is driven to her new apartment and locked inside that her dilemma dawns on her. She has been trafficked to a stream of men who pay the boss to use her for sex.

We are offered gruesome images of horny men humping on top of her and we are made to feel what it is like for a slip of a girl being so cruelly abused by men in the affluent and 'permissive' West.

She never sees Andrei or Russia again. When the boss inadvertently forgets to lock her apartment door she sneaks out and jumps off a road bridge onto the motorway.

Director Lucas Moodysson tells of his difficulty filming these sex scenes. The cameraman had to lie under the stream of men who arrived to rape the girl. After a while, the cameraman found this so depressingly hard to endure, the director himself had to be a replacement cameraman. He too, tells of how he found this to be an emotionally difficult experience. Yet he admits he wasn't the one being raped. How horrendously worse this must be for the actual victim.

Therapy for Abused Victims

I guess the inclusion of the following film, *The Prince of Tides*, is not warranted in this book for the cast are almost entirely adults, and we catch only a glimpse of Tom and his twin sister Savannah when they are thirteen-years-old, and see only a brief clip of them as seven-year-olds. But its inclusion is a must for it deals with the emotional aftermath of the trauma and abuse which they repressed as children, and has only come to light now that Savannah is an adult who has attempted suicide. This film focuses on the danger of suppressing and ignoring childhood abuse.

Three little children grow up in an idyllic tidal shrimping community in South Carolina. But they live with a violent father, in a loveless family. As seven-year-olds, the twin boy and girl, and their older brother resort to running into the river to hide by holding their breath under water to avoid the rages of the feuding parents. Although we never witness any physical abuse of the children it is implied, and reveals their lack of security, so that when in later years they need to confide in their father, they do not have sufficient trust in him. Instead, they sweep their dilemma under the carpet (or actually bury it in their backyard), only for it to re-emerge as psychological trauma in their adulthood. Only the older boy dares stand up to his father: once, he picks up a shotgun and shoots the television in order to quell a domestic spat. Mother and the younger twins are rigidly fearful of the father.

The real problem comes when the twins are thirteen. One day when father is away at work, three strangers barge their way into the secluded family home. One rapes the mother, another rapes thirteen-year-old Savannah, while twin brother Tom helplessly looks on. Older brother again finds the shotgun and shoots all three intruders dead. However, instead of calling for help, or waiting for father to return home and incur his wrath, mother instructs the children to remove the bodies from the house and bury them, while she clears up the mess and puts the house to rights. When father comes home from work, nothing is said. The silence at the meal table was as bad as witnessing the rape, reflects Tom.

Mother, in later years, mulls over her actions: "When I say goodbye to something, I close the door and never think about it again." (Not an attitude admired by psychotherapists.)

The bulk of this film is about the aftermath of Savannah's attempted suicide as an adult. Her psychiatrist calls Tom to be interviewed to try to shed light on the reasons for his sister's suicide attempt. But in the psychiatrist's chair, Tom turns out to be the patient as he reluctantly, bit-by-bit, hints at the trauma that he and his siblings had to suffer in their childhood, which he has bottled up all these years, and about the misconceptions he held about his mother. *Prince of Tides* is a powerful recounting of childhood trauma, vocalised through the recollections of an adult.

We are shown flashbacks of this type of trauma in *The Butterfly Effect*. Kayleigh has become a morose girl with low self-esteem and suicidal tendencies. Her former boyfriend tries to jivvy her up, "You can't hate yourself because your dad's a twisted freak."

The news these days is riddled with similar stories of adults coming forward to disclose their abuse as children – often at the hands of care-home workers or priests – children who were too afraid to make a stand as kids, and only now twenty or thirty years later have the mental strength to confront the issues that have been tormenting them. At least, Kayleigh is ultimately able to stand up to her paedophile father. "Don't you ever touch me again," says Sarah Widdows.

Mockingbird Don't Sing is the true tale of a 'feral' child, neglected from birth by a mother who has gone blind and a father who cannot cope. The girl, Katie, spends her formative years tied to a commode, and is verbally and physically abused when she fails to cooperate.

Aged thirteen, she is rescued and taken into care under the surveillance of a variety of welfare agencies all with divergent opinions on how the girl should be raised. On the surface, they claim to have the interests of the child at heart; but when one therapist states how she is going to become famous as the next Annie Sullivan (the woman who nurtured Helen Keller) we realise love has been omitted from the equation. Each department treats the girl as a prized project to provide continuity for the funding of their unit.

While the girl makes startling progress at first, she is shared around so many different foster families she soon regresses back to an unloved 'feral', hidden away from society forever.

Alas, although there are plenty of films depicting child abuse, including its salacious portrayal, I am not aware of any others that focus on the rehabilitation of a child victim.

In this volume I have referred to 130 different films that cover the theme of child abuse, yet none address the aftermath of the problem, and only *Prince of Tides* addresses the problem belatedly now that the children are adults. Some films do consider the seriousness of child abuse – *Liar, Liar, Fallen Angel, Hard Candy, The Cold Light of Day, The Woodsman, The Rag Nymph* – but once the abuse has ceased there is no reference to the therapeutic follow-up for the child. Some films do show children receiving some form of therapy – *The Sixth Sense, A Father's Choice, The Horse Whisperer, My Sister's Keeper, The Brooke Ellison Story* – yet these are related to recovery from an illness or a loss, rather than abuse, while in *CRAZY (2005)*, Zac (Michel Côté) is sent to therapy to attempt a 'cure' for his homosexuality.

Other films such as *Pretty Baby, Lolita,* and *Taxi Driver* are salacious and, with the exception of *Taxi Driver*, do not even identify the child as a victim of abuse. That each actress, Brooke Shields, Sue Lyon, Dominique Swaine and Jodie Foster had to endure a traumatic aftermath later in their teens reveals the exploitative and callous nature of the movie industry. At least, Jodie Foster was offered counselling prior to the filming of *Taxi Driver*, and I admire the way that directors Nicole Kassell (*The Woodsman*) and Rebecca Miller (*Angela (1994)*) went through a nurturing scheme with their young charges (Hannah Pilkes, Miranda Stuart Ryne, Charlotte Blythe) before filming commenced.

Probably child actors need to be protected from abuse more so than other children. Child actors are away from home for long periods of time. Certain adult behaviours are normalised for them, such as kissing, undressing, scripted swearing, and using inappropriate vocabulary and innuendo, all for our titillation. The child actors place themselves in a greater position of abuse by working alongside a host of strangers (the cast and crew for a film can amount to hundreds), in unfamiliar locations, and as we discussed in Volume Six (*Puberty and First Love*), the requirement for them to strip off to bathe or shower is heightened. While 75% of abuse is perpetrated by adults known to the child victim, the child actor has more than the average number of grown-up friends and colleagues.

Michele Elliott of *The Child Abuse Prevention Programme* tells us that abuse is not just intercourse or rape but may range from "obscene telephone calls, voyeurism, fondling, taking pornographic photographs, and indecent exposure" [30] (highly likely in a bedroom film set-up or shared changing rooms, and in numerous films a child is required to work alongside a naked man, e.g. *Lauren*, *Blame it on Fidel*, *Paradise* (1991), *Hideous Kinky*).

If young actors have been made to feel uncomfortable while on set, then assume they have entered the realm of sexual manipulation. The extras on several DVDs show young actors invited to sit on the lap of other adult actors in between takes, or are manhandled in a 'playful' way while off-screen, or are patted on the head (an action most children dislike). [31] Is a child who recoils from petting likely to be rejected for subsequent roles? We know that many child stars of the early twentieth century were sexually targeted by their older work colleagues (the Gish sisters, Lilita McMurray, Joan Collins and Nastassia Kinski. In *The Mystery of Natalie Wood* we watch the adolescent legend over-nighting with her director, Nicholas Ray). Decades have passed in which autobiographies have revealed the scandalous truth. Hopefully those seedy days are long gone, or perhaps insufficient time has elapsed for our modern day child actors to come to terms with their past, though today the paparazzi are able to swiftly sniff out any scandal.

The tool of child abusers is secrecy. Children are easily coerced into silence. Child therapists teach that children should not be allowed to keep secrets, and to tell if they receive inappropriate touches or are bribed. At least the child actor is trained to be vocally assertive and should not be reluctant to voice a 'no' to improper suggestions. If it is estimated that one in ten adults have been molested as a child then it is statistically evident that at least one in ten of our child actors are objects of abuse. The risk is not just to girls. According to Michele Elliott, boys are almost as much at risk of being molested as girls. Regrettably, there is no support system such as Rape Crisis Centres for male victims. [32]

While abuse of children is recognised, such is their line of work that once they reach the age of consent their protection seems to dissipate overnight as certain elements of society expect them to strip off to appear naked in glossy magazines and to be filmed in rampant bedroom scenes. Naked photos of Hannah Montana and *Harry Potter's* Emma Watson abound on the *Internet*, all snapped as soon as the 'child' comes of age. Assumptions are made that the actor who was a child yesterday is overnight miraculously mature enough for any sexual demand placed upon him or her, once they have 'come of age'.

ENDNOTES FOR VOLUME EIGHT

1 Neil Sinyard *Children in the Movies* p70.
2 The role of the kidnapped Debbie is played by Natalie Wood's younger sister, Lana Wood.
3 *Halliwell's Film & DVD Guide 2004*.
4 *His Teeth*, scripted by Ben Musgrave.
5 Marianne Sinclair *Hollywood Lolita*, p108.
6 Michael Thompson et al *Best Friends, Worst Enemies*, p121, 122.
7 fairfaxtimes.com/cms/story quoted in Wikipedia: *Cyberbullying*.
8 *Bullying Beyond the Schoolyard: Preventing and Responding to Cyberbullying* by Sameer Hinduja and Justin Patchin, 2008.
9 ABCnews.co.com quoted from Wikipedia: *Cyberbullying*.
10 I have not viewed either *Adina's Deck* or *Odd Girl Out* and acknowledge the entries from Wikipedia for information about these films.
11 *Shattered Silence* is also known as Sexting in Suburbia.
12 Salim is played by Azharuddin Mohammad Ismail and Jamal by Ayush Makesh Khedekar.
13 Marianne Sinclair, *Hollywood Lolita*, p67.
14 Vicky Lebeau *Childhood & Cinema* p86, 88 from Rodney Engen: Kate Greenaway: A Biography.
15 John Ruskin is a man who gave Alice Liddell private art lessons, once her mother had dismissed Alice's other admirer, Charles Dodgson (i.e. Lewis Carroll) from ever seeing her again. Christina Björk & Inga-Karin Eriksson, *The Other Alice: the story of Alice Liddell and Alice in Wonderland*. p31.
16 Though my phraseology is tongue-in-cheek it is not such a wild statement. It is suggested that Nabokov corrupted the name from Charlie Chaplin's underaged bride, Lilita. Marianne Sinclair *Hollywood Lolita* p31.
17 Shortly after the murder of Sarah Payne, a paediatrician living in the SW of England had his property vandalised, because the uneducated perpetrator mistook the business plaque 'paediatrician' for 'paedophile'. The report of the incident was broadcast over the national media.
18 Marianne Sinclair, *Hollywood Lolita*, p100.
19 Deborah Kampmeier, director, being interviewed for The Making of *Hounddog*.
19a Translates as 'Charming and cheating child'.
20 Karen Lury *The Child in Film* p73.
21 Hunter Davies's *Book of British Lists* p 100.
22 The Simply Entertainment guide of offers for *Radio Times* customers.
23 Marianne Sinclair, *Hollywood Lolita*, p125.
24 Nicole Kassell, Director of *The Woodsman*.
25 The action for this molestation scene lasts precisely two minutes. This may not sound long, but in reality the child, Jena Malone, had to act continuously showing a reaction to being sexually molested. This was actual screening time, and does not include time spent rehearsing or editor's cuts. And this is just one incident in a string of sequences that this eleven-year-old child had to depict in her debut film performance. A distasteful introduction to the world of exploitable young actresses.
26 Wikipedia, *Bastard out of Carolina*.
27 In 1996 Jena was nominated for Best Performance by an Actress in a Mini-Series or Motion Picture Made For Television. And the Saturn Award for best performance by a young actor in 1997. Wikipedia, Jena Malone.
28 *Bastard Out Of Carolina* Essential Edition - Dorothy Allison - Book Clubs - Penguin Group (USA).mht.

29 The full statement made to Travis by the pimp was "Do what you want with her. You can come on her, you can fuck her in the mouth, fuck her in the arse, but no rough stuff… She's twelve and a half years old. You ain't never had no pussy like that." This is the script the minor, Jodie Foster, would have been presented with.
30 Michele Elliott, *Preventing Child Sexual Assault* p1.
31 Michele Elliott *Preventing Child Sexual Assault.*
32 Michele Elliott, *Preventing Child Sexual Assault* p39.

Curtain Call

9. Curtain Call

CURTAIN CALL

Have I succeeded in what I set out to do? Nowhere near! I thought I could view all the child focused films by watching one a day for a year. But now, three years and three months later, I have barely brushed the surface. I had expected to be able to construct a comprehensive all-inclusive catalogue of films featuring children. The more I researched the more films I discovered. For every one film I was able to watch another two would come to my attention to join the ever-lengthening queue of features to be viewed. No doubt, you have a favourite child-focused film that I haven't included in this book. It seems an increasingly daunting task. Several more films are being released around the world every single week, adding to the existing ones, and making the task impossible. Neil Sinyard states that 'films about childhood will continue to proliferate... no theme is more stimulating to the imagination nor more universal in appeal.' [1]

I thought I could categorise all the films under eight broad headings. In doing so, some groupings may appear contrived, and there are vast omissions.

For one thing, in recent years the role of grandparents has become an important aspect in a child's life, something which was outside my own personal experience a generation ago. I have failed to focus on this important relationship in a child's life. Likewise, I have omitted a major social aspect of teenage identity – that of clothes and fashion, and the idolisation of music stars and other celebrities; and by only concentrating on children and younger teens, I have ignored a complete genre of films aimed at or featuring older teenagers. On the boys side I have omitted the rough-and-tumble rogues, the pranks that characters like *Dennis the Menace* or *Just William* typify, the gang culture that absorb the vulnerability of impressionable youth such as Thomas Turgoose in *This is England*.

Another major omission is that of runaway kids. In Britain alone, 100,000 children (under sixteen's) run away from home each year. That is one every five seconds, according to *The Children's Society*. Of these 25% are thrown out of the home. 70% of these runaways are never reported to the authorities (police or welfare agencies) mainly because the parents realise the family tiff is a temporary affair. Either parents are aware where their child has gone (e.g. to a friend's house) or because it has happened before and the child has returned home safely. [2] In America, the problem is deemed to be worse, with a million child runaways, and with the teenaged girl more likely to run away than her male counterpart over the age of fourteen. Then there is the rest of the world: in poor countries, many children are homeless, having to fend for themselves with all the accompanying dangers of exploitation and abuse. Some films, like *Slumdog Millionaire*, treat this issue seriously. Others, like *The Magic Door* or *The Little Unicorn*, introduce the concept to the child as an exciting adventure.

I had expected to write separate volumes about the divergent influences on boys as opposed to girls, but so vast is the subject matter and also so interconnected, that I had a shift of focus part way through my research, deciding instead to combine everything into one mixed gender book. The original title for this entire book was going to be *Children in Films: Gender Roles and Themes*, until I decided to devote that name to just Volume One. And yet, the topic of gender gets its toehold in the text of every volume.

Because this theme of gender is such a significant thread running through each volume, it will be useful to summarise our findings here.

A large portion of Volume One referred to gender issues. Most revealingly we noticed that while there are more girl-child actors than boys, the movie industry is still dominated by men. Most directors (86%), scriptwriters (74%) and actors (70%) are male. These men wield a power that can perpetuate and reinforce gender stereotypes that we the viewing public witness on the big screen, in particular in promoting the sexualised image of the role of the female. Success in the movie industry is still awarded to slim white-skinned good-looking actors. Any adolescent Oscar nominees are more likely to be pretty white girls than gangly spotty teenaged boys.

In Volume Two, the girl is shown taking a nurturing role, caring for her younger siblings, whereas the boy avoids this domestic role, or participates only grudgingly. The male is shown as less compassionate than his female counterpart. The boy is typically seen as the aggressor, the girl as the victim. In fact, the mission of the movie industry in the twentieth century has been to show the delicate girl-child as lost and needing to be brought back to the safety of the homestead. The boy who is stranded home-alone is expected to be resourceful and brave, while the girl is perceived as vulnerable, and has to be protected or seek help. Would *Lord of the Flies* have been as effective if a planeload of girls had crash-landed on the tropical island instead of boys?

This sexist gender strand is enhanced when we note that in the movies orphans are invariably girls. Boys are not careless enough to lose their parents! When the lost girl does finally find parental comfort it is usually into the care of a man. It is the teenaged girl that yearns for a father: the boy needs mothering, and it seems to be the girl's role as matchmaker to find the ideal parent. These traits have their roots fixed firmly throughout time and cultures, stemming from the days when the birth of a girl child was an unwanted encumbrance, shunned and married off as soon as she reaches puberty, whereas pride was placed in the son who would continue the family name. Subversively, these traits are perpetuated even today with phrases bragging "So that's my boy!" and "That's my little girl!" – hinting subconsciously at the brave boy as opposed to the noticeably developing girl. "Don't they grow up fast," is only ever said with reference to the sexualised daughter.

Where (in Volume Three) children are shown crossing gender boundaries, the change becomes positive for girls who transcend into tomboys, while conversely boys are depicted regressing into bullied wimps. The tomboy has the whole realm of boyish pursuits at her command, yet rarely does the boy take on girlish traits and pastimes. As Stephanie Theobold says, "It's easier to be a tomboy than a 'sissy'.[3] The bulk of Volume Three outlined how the movie world is depicting these cross gender transgressions. In the years before reaching puberty, the tomboy is embraced into integrated childish games. Only when she persists with tomboyism into adolescence is she seen as abnormal, and then accusations of lesbianism are hurled at her.

While boys remain kings of the sports arena, the girl usually retains top billing in films featuring music and dance. Alongside sporting prowess, adventure seems to be the boy's sole purpose in life. And yet inevitably, there is a girl tagging along as inspiration, just one pace behind.

In Volume Four we reported than the girl makes more enduring friendships, the boy having more tenuous relationships involving gangs. Only in films do we find boys and girls playing good-naturedly together, despite the reality that beyond the schoolroom boys and girls do not mix. This separation has been inculcated from birth as children in every generation and in every culture across the world are nurtured along rigid time-honoured intra-gender strictures.

It is adolescent girls that seek out (or get drawn into) relationships with older men. This invariably develops into a first crush (as we discovered in Volume Four) or into an illicit romantic affair (which we explored in Volume Six).

When it comes to keeping pets, we found the girl chooses cuddly creatures that she can domesticate and nurse, while for the boy the pet has a function – as a status symbol, a confederate, a fellow adventurer.

Even the world of make-believe is divided into distinct gender lines, as we showed in Volume Five. We never see boys fantasising over fairies, or dreaming of rescuing the desolate princess. These are tales exclusively for the preteen girl. It is only since the recent success of *Harry Potter* that boys have dared show any interest in the world of witches and wizards. Previously, Halloween had provided the girl-child with an opportunity to dress up. Boys like vampires and werewolves, and superheroes to aspire to. Boys are expected to be brave, so cannot be seen being spooked by trivialities such as ghosts. No, it is the girl-child who takes up psychic traits, influenced by lucky charms, horoscopes, crystal balls, telepathy and clairvoyancy.

Even the victim in horror movies is most likely to be a girl, especially when it comes to devil possession. In the movies, girls are vulnerable, and need protecting, and have a more piercing scream! And because the little girl is seen as innocent and wouldn't hurt a fly, who better to scare us witless than to have a little girl turn into the cruel monster herself. The angelic girl who materialises into a vampire or a serial killer is to be shunned and feared. Only as werewolves have boys been allowed exclusive rights to haunt our screens.

When puberty is reached (in Volume Six) it is inevitable that sexual differences will be highlighted in the movies: the girl coming to terms with an unexpected period, and the growth of body parts; the boys being embarrassed by uncontrollable urges and erections, and the deepening of his voice.

Alarmingly, it is the girl-child who is called upon to undress before our eyes. Despite strict indecency laws, one in every five girl actors are still required to expose some part of their intimate anatomy to our gaze. This is not a requirement for the boy actor.

Girls are exploited in the movies in other ways, too. Scenes in which two boys kiss each other are never shown, whereas girls are more likely to be shown kissing each other. Lesbianism among our adolescents is evidently far more entertaining than male homosexuality. Similarly, boys are seldom shown having romantic relationships with older women, while quite frequently girls are shown courting an older man.

Childhood trauma (Volume Seven) appears to be one sphere in which gender does not play a role. Boys and girls alike are afflicted with illnesses and disabilities, affected by death, divorce, the horrors of war, and the distressing disruption caused by moving home. Yet even here, the girl-child is vulnerable when it comes to pregnancy, and there are several films which highlight the devastating effects that underaged sex has on the girl – a trial that the youthful boy is luckily able to evade.

Even so, we highlighted differences in gender responses when a parent dies or is divorced, as boys and girls come to terms with their grief in their own distinctive way.

Again (in Chapter Eight), to capitalise on cinematic effect, the vulnerable girl-child is usually chosen to depict the victim of cruelty, abuse and kidnapping. The girl being spanked, enslaved, or sexually targeted (as in *Bastard out of Carolina*, *Memoirs of a Geisha*, or *Lilya 4-ever*) is far more likely to evoke empathy from an audience. The majority of this volume (sexual abuse) is related to the distressing issues that more typically affect girls. Even the most recent form of child abuse – cyberbullying – is more likely to affect girls than boys. Only less than a handful of movies have yet been filmed to depict this form of trauma. Perhaps when this book is ready for re-editing maybe by then a few more films will have been created to refocus our minds.

In researching this book I feel I have been duped as a victim, mesmerised by the cuteness of the child, and from doing my studies have I found myself wallowing in that same mire that James Kincaid warned us of: that children are cute, and that spotty teenagers are not.[4] In writing this book, maybe I have been trapped into perpetuating this fallacy.

Children are pretty in real life, especially when dolled up by the make-up artist. What is rarely depicted on screen is the real child – with its tantrums, its smells, its obnoxiousness, its over demanding selfishness, its spitefulness and greed. When these things *are* depicted, it is more usually to engender empathy with the child – the cruel world exploiting the child. Always, the cute nature of the child who has to be mollycoddled has to come through, the hug-a-hoodie syndrome.[5] Those that do dare dwell on the evil child, such as Halloween's Michael Myers (*Halloween* (1978)), dwell only fleetingly on their childhood focusing instead on what they have become as adults.

Reflecting in her adulthood, Ana Torrent from *Cría Cuervos* states, "I can't understand how some people say childhood is the happiest time of one's life. It certainly wasn't for me, and that maybe I don't believe either in a childlike paradise or in the innocence of children. My childhood was a long interminable and sad time filled with fear – fear of the unknown." As a child the only time we see Ana happily relaxed in this film, or in her former film *Spirit of the Beehive*, is as she listens and dances to the theme music *Porque te vas*. This contradicts the comment made in *Hope Floats*: "Childhood is the best time of your life."

Having written this book, I can appreciate the terminal point that Wim Wenders refers to in *Alice in the Cities*, that by watching so much inhuman TV I lost touch with the world. Now I need proof I still exist. Maybe Alfredo, the projectionist for the *Cinema Paradiso*, arrived at the right conclusion as he steers us back to reality: "Life is not what you see in films." But, still, if I believed that, there would be no point in this book.

1. Neil Sinyard Children in the Movies, p119.
2. The Children's Society, from an interview on BBC Radio 4, 15th November 2011.
3. Stephanie Theobold Hurrah for Tomboys! writing in The Guardian 27 Dec 2008. Internet.
4. James Kincaid Erotic Innocence.
5. This was a slogan of politician David Cameron, and derided by the press, before becoming UK Prime Minister.

Tables, References and Appendix

TABLE (I): FILMS DEPICTING BROKEN HOMES V FAMILIES WITH BOTH PARENTS

This table has been compiled to show how family structures are misconstrued in the movies. While in reality 66% of children live with both birth parents, the movie world would have us believe the proportion is only 29%. It is more sensational to depict a child from a broken home or as an orphan. A child living happily with mum and dad is less likely to draw customers to the box office. Audiences prefer to see disorder, chaos and domestic conflict. Alas, while this is reducing the stigma for a child growing up with a single parent, this is also normalizing the concept of divorce in society's perception, making it more inevitable.

Where a film is listed more than once, it may be because there are different characters living in different circumstances, e.g. in *Down Will Come Baby*, Robin lives with birth mum and dad, but her friend Amelia lives only with her mother.

Total No of Films in Sample: 436 (this does not include the 65 additional films listed at the end of Table (i) for which family structure is unclear (these additional films make the total number of films reviewed for this series total 501)).

No. of Films depicting Broken Homes: 307 71%

No. of Films with both Birth Parents: 129 29%

Living with Mother only (or mum + stepdad)

112 films = 26% of sample

32A, 2012, (500) days of Summer, About a Boy, Akeelah and the bee, Alice in the cities, All I want for Christmas (1991), Amazing panda adventure, American Haunting (Jane), Amityville Horror (mum+stepdad), Angus Thongs (Robbie), Are we there yet?, Bad News bears, Bad seed, Beaches (CC Bloom), Bedtime Stories, Before Women had Wings, Blue Butterfly, Boy called Dad, Buddha collapsed out of shame, The Butterfly Effect, Cement garden, Child's Play, Chocolat, Cider with Rosie, Cinema Paradiso, Cold Light of Day, Cold Sweat (Mum + stepdad), Dancer in the Dark, The Dark, Dear Frankie, Death defying acts, Digging to China, Down will come Baby (Ame), Dr Zhivago, Dust factory, E.T. The Extra Terrestrial, Enid, Exorcist, Explorers, Fallen Angel, Father of My Children, Flightplan, Flowers in the attic, Forrest Gump, Ghost and Mrs Muir, The Good Mother, Greengage summer, Hidden places, Hideous Kinky, Hope and Glory, Hope Floats, How to kill your neighbour's dog, Imitation of life, In a Stranger's Hand, Jack (2003), Jack Frost, Joey (boy), Jungle 2 Jungle, Kes, Knights of the South Bronx, Let Me In, Let

Table (i): Films Depicting Broken Homes v Families with Both Parents

the Right One In (Oskar), Liar Liar (1997), Little women, Lolita, The Long Day Closes, Lovers of the Arctic Circle, Magic Island, Man who sued God, Man without a Face, Melissa P, Melody, Mermaids, Miracle on 34th Street, Mischief night, The Missing, Mom at Sixteen, Mrs Doubtfire, Munchie, My Queen Karo, Night of the hunter, Nobody knows, Now & Then (Gaby), One Fine Day, The Others, Our first Christmas, Panic Room, Pan's Labyrinth, Paradise (1991), Peppermint Soda, The Piano, Pretty baby, Rabbit Proof Fence, Roxy Hunter, Run the wild fields, Russkies, Safety of Objects, Schindler's List, Sense and Sensibility, Shattered Silence, Single Santa meets Mrs Claus, Son of Ranbow, That Night (Sheryl), Thirteen, This is England, Toto le Heros (father dies), True Grit, An Unfinished life, Urban ghost story, War of the worlds, Zombies: Wicked Little Things.

Living with Father only (or father + stepmum)

79 films = 18% of sample

Alaska, Alice Upside Down, Aliens in the Attic, Bastard out of Carolina, Beaches (Hillary), Because of Winn-Dixie, Billboard dad, Billy Elliot, Borrowers, the (2011), Casper, Cheaper by the Dozen 2 (Jim), The Child, Chitty Chitty Bang Bang, Cleaner, Contact (1997), Corrina, Corrina, Cría Cuervos, The Crossing, Definitely, Maybe, A Father's Choice, Firestarter, Fly away home, Genova, Grounded, Grow your own, Harry Novak's The Child, Hidden in America, Hide & Seek, Hounddog, Imagine That, Impudent Girl, Joey (girl), Journey of Natty Gann, Julia (2008), Juno, A Kiss at Midnight, Kramer v Kramer, Last time I saw Paris, Leon (dad + stepmum), Life-Size, Little princess, London to Brighton, Lost World: Jurassic Park, Lovers of the Arctic Circle, The Magic Door, Me without You (Marina), Millions (2004), Munchie (Andrea), My father the hero, My girl, Nanny McPhee, Nim's Island, Parent trap, Perfect Teacher, Phenomena, Push, Que la Bête Meure, Resident Evil: Apocolypse, Sacrifices of the heart, Secret life of bees, Shadow Man, She's the man, So Dear to my Heart (girl), Sound of Music, Stepmom, Super 8, There will be Blood, Tideland, Tightrope, Timescape, To kill a mockingbird, Treasure Seekers, Untamed Love, Wah-Wah, When Zachery Beaver Came to Town, Whistle down the wind, Wild child, Wuthering Heights, Yours, Mine & Ours.

Living with other Relatives

39 films = 9% of sample

Balletshoes, The Birds, Bless the child, Blue Lagoon, Camomile lawn, Casper meets Wendy, Children's hour, A Christmas Memory, Fairy Tale (Frances), Five Children and IT, Game Plan, Great expectations, Heidi, A Horse for Danny, The Ice Palace, Ingenious, Jacob the liar, Jane Eyre, Jumanji, Lassie (girl evacuated), Lion the witch & the wardrobe, Little lips, Little unicorn, My life as a dog, No reservations, Pollyanna, Return to Oz, Return to the Blue Lagoon, Secret garden, Series of unfortunate events, So Dear to my Heart (boy), Son of Babylon, Stormbreaker (boy), Story of an African Farm, Tiger Bay, Under the Mud, Whale rider, Wizard of Oz, Wuthering Heights (Heathcliffe).

Fostered, Living in Orphanage, or having No Guardians

77 films = 18% of sample

Adventures of Baron Munchausen, Aliens, Ann of Green Gables, Annie, Back to the Secret Garden, Bedknobs and Broomsticks, The Beguiled, Candleshoe, Conspiracy of hearts, Curly Sue, Driftwood, Dustbin baby, East of Sudan, Eloise at Christmastime, Eloise at the Plaza, The Golden Compass, Goodnight Mr Tom, Greystoke: the Legend of Tarzan, Halloween 4, The Happening, Harry Potter (6 films), Huck Finn, I am Slave, In search of the castaways, Inn of 6th Happiness, Innocence, The Innocents, Interview with the Vampire, James and the Giant Peach, Johnny Mad Dog, Jungle Book, Lena: my 100 children, Leon, Les Diables, Les Miserables, Let the right one in (Eli), Lilya 4-ever, The Lion, the Witch and the Wardrobe, Little Girl who lived down the Lane, Little Secrets, Magdelene sisters, Manny & Lo, Memoirs of a Geisha, Mixed Company, Mockingbird don't Sing, Moonfleet, My house in Umbria, Oliver Twist (2005), Oliver!, Oranges are not the only fruit, Orphan, Paper Moon, Peck on the cheek, Pete's Dragon, Pied Piper, Prince Caspian, Push, Race to Witch Mountain, Rag Nymph, The Reaping, Samson & Delilah, The Searchers, Seven Years in Tibet, Shattered Family, Silent Hill, Slumdog Millionaire, Stolen, Stolen children, Sundays & Cybele, Susannah of the Mounties, Taxi Driver, Turn of the screw, Lilya 4-ever, Walkabout, Water, Water babies, Waterworld.

Living with both Birth Parents

129 films = 29% of sample

Addams Family, Addams Family Values, Adventures of Sharkboy & Lavagirl, Alas de Mariposa, Aliens in the Attic (Pearsons), Andre, Angel of Pennsylvania Avenue, Angela, Angus Thongs & Perfect Snogging, Anita and Me, Atonement, Audrey Rose, Ball-Trap on the Cote Sauvage, Beethoven's 3rd, Benny's Video, Big Momma's House, Blame it on Fidel, Boy in the Striped Pyjamas, Brady Bunch, Bridge to Terabithia, Brooke Ellison Story, Case 39, Catch that Kid, Celia, Charlie & the Chocolate factory, Charlotte's Web, Cheaper by the Dozen, Cheaper by the Dozen II, The Children, Christmas Box, Company of Wolves, CRAZY (2005), Curse of the Cat People, Day at the Beach, Dennis (1993), Diary of Anne Frank, Dicky Roberts former Child Star, Doctor Dolittle, Down will come Baby (Robin), Dreamchild, Dreamer, Elf (2003), Emerald Forest, Empire of the Sun, Enid Blyton's 5 on Treasure Island, Eve's Bayou, Fairy King of Ar, Field of Dreams, Five Pennies, Freaky Friday, The Goonies, Great Balls of Fire, The Grinch, Hand that rocks the Cradle, Haunted Mansion, Heavenly Creatures (divorce is due), A High Wind in Jamaica, Home (2008), Honey, I Shrunk the Kids, Horse Whisperer, I'm not Scared, In America, It's a Wonderful Life, Killer of Sheep, Last Mimzy, Lawn Dogs, Liar, Liar (1992), Little House on the Prairie, Little Manhattan

Table (i): Films Depicting Broken Homes v Families with Both Parents

Little Miss Sunshine, Little Otik, Lorenzo's Oil, Lost in Space, Lovely Bones, Malèna, Man in the Moon, Mandy, Mary Poppins, Matilda, Me without you (Holly), Meet me in St Louis, Mermaid, The Messengers, The Miracle Worker, Miss Potter, Monkey Business, Mosquito Coast, Mr Blandings builds his Dream House, The Mummy Returns, My American Cousin, My Brother the Pig, My Dog Skip, My Sister's Keeper, My Year without Sex, North Star, Nutcracker (2010), Page Turner, Paperhouse, Pather Panchali, Peter Pan, Phoebe in Wonderland, Photographing Fairies, Poltergeist, Poltergeist II, Prince of Tides, Railway Children, Ratcatcher, Rebel Without a Cause, RV: Runaway Vacation, Scrooge (1951), A Shadow of Doubt, Shadrach, Shane, Skin, Snow Day, Song of the South, Sorcerer's Apprentice, Spirit of the Beehive, Swallows & Amazons, Switching Goals, Tendre Cousins, Time to Kill, Time Traveller's Wife, Times & Winds, Tomboy (2011), Uncle Buck, Under the Mud, The Well, XXY.

The following films are among the 500 films viewed for this series of books but are not included as part of Table (i), because the family structure is unclear.

There are several films mentioned in this series of books for which we are not informed of the family structure, it is irrelevant, or it is unclear to me, so these films have been omitted from the statistics. Their exclusion does not affect the proportions of broken homes/birth parents:

Alice, Alice's Adventures in Wonderland, Along came a Spider, Annunciation, Aquamarine, Audition, Babel, Battle Royale, Beethoven's 5th, Big, Black Beauty, the Body Snatcher, the Brothers Grimm, Bugsy Malone, Children of Theatre Street, Courage of Lassie, Curious Case of Benjamin Button, Devil's Child, Don't Say a Word, The Drum, Family Gathering, Father Goose, Fox and the Child, Free Willy, A Good Year, Great St Trinian's Train Robbery, Gregory's Girl, Hard Candy, Hocus Pocus, Hoot, I love you, I love you not, I know where I'm going, Jean de Florette (although girl lives with both parents at first, father dies), Journey to the Centre of the Earth, Jurassic Park, kids (1995), Lassie come Home, Little Rascals, Lord of the Flies, Lost in New York, Man on Fire, Mr Magorium's Wonder Emporium, Mystery of Natalie Wood (as a child, Natalie lives with both her parents, but as an adult is often a single mother), Nativity! Nativity Story, No more baths, The Omen, Pocket Money, Ptang Yang Kipperbang, Ring of Endless Light, Sandlot Kids, School of Rock, Sixth Sense, St Trinians, Stand by Me, Station Agent, StreetDance, They come Back, Time Bandits, Tremors, Village of the Dammed, Water Babies, Water Lilies, Wicker Man, The Woodsman.

TABLE (II): FILMS IN WHICH CHILDREN ARE REQUIRED TO KISS.

Earlier in this book (under the heading *Children in Love*) I pose the question is kissing the modern acceptable face of child pornography? This list has been compiled to illustrate the compulsion for child actors to be involved in kissing scenes.

Of the 502 films I have reviewed for this book, children are expected to kiss in 95 of them, which is 19%, reinforcing the argument that audiences demand nostalgic reminders of their childhood dreams. Yet in doing so, we become voyeurs and abusers of a child's romantic development.

A Good Year: Marine Casto poses in her underwear before swimming across pool to kiss boy.
Addams Family Values: Christina Ricci kisses Peter MacNicol through the wire fence of the summer camp.
Adolescent Malice: Kissing. Kissing of genitals & breasts.
Akeelah and the Bee: short boy/girl kiss
Alaska (1996): Thora Birch gives Ryan Kent a peck on the cheek.
Alice Upside Down: Alyson Stoner kisses boy.
All I want for Christmas: Ethan Randall receives kiss on cheek from Amy Oberer.
Angela (1994): Intimate snog between the two preteen girls: Miranda Stuart Ryne & Charlotte Blythe.
Angus, Thongs and Perfect Snogging: Georgia Groome & others – several snogging scenes.
Annunciation: French kissing between naked boy and girl. Kissing between several other characters, including cheek licking.
Bad News Bears: Sammi Kane Kraft kisses boyfriend.
Bastard out of Carolina: Jena Malone is forcefully kissed while being raped by her stepfather, played by Ron Eldard.
Bedtime Stories: Jonathan Morgan Hett receives peck from Annalise Basso.
Beguiled, the: Pamlyn Ferdin is kissed by adult Clint Eastwood.
Billy Elliot: Boy on boy kiss.
Blue Butterfly: Marc Donato given parting kiss on cheek by Marianella Jimenez.
Blue Lagoon (1980): Brooke Shields and Christopher Atkins kissing (prolonged), including naked kissing.
Butterfly Effect: 13 year old Evan & Kayleigh kiss (John Patrick Amedore & Irene Gorovaia).
Casper (1995): Christina Ricci kisses boy.
Cement Garden: Brother & sister in naked kissing scene.
Cider with Rosie: Lia Brown and Joe Roberts kiss.
Company of Wolves: Sarah Patterson kisses boy & werewolf.
Dennis (1993): Natasha Lyonne & boy.
Devil's Child: Rachael Bella kisses on rooftop.
Diables, Les: Adèle Haenel & Vincent Rottiers snog (several occasions).
Diary of Anne Frank: Millie Perkins in kissing scene (though she was 21 playing the 13 year old).

Table (ii): Films in Which Children are Required to Kiss.

Digging to China: Evan Rachel Wood kisses Kevin Bacon.
Dust Factory: Hayden Panettiere & Ryan Kelley kiss.
East of Sudan: 12-year-old Jenny Agutter is kissed by Anthony Quayle. Although this is the kiss-of-life to revive the girl from drowning it is a prolonged series of kisses, seemingly more intimate than the kiss he gives lead actress Sylvia Syms.
ET The Extra-Terrestrial: Henry Thomas kisses Erika Eleniak during classroom anarchy.
Explorers: Amanda Peterson & Ethan Hawke kiss (while flying!).
Fallen Angel: Dana Hill kisses boy on swing and merry-go-round.
Firestarter: Drew Barrymore kisses father on lips.
Goonies: Kerri Green kisses Sean Astin, and later, his older brother, Josh Brolin (on 2 occasions).
Great Balls of Fire: Winona Ryder snogs Jerry Lee Lewis actor (several occasions). Strips to bra for kissing.
Great Expectations: boy & girl (Jeremy James Kisner & Raquel Beaudene) prolonged kissing with tongues.
Greengage Summer: Jane Asher kisses Elizabeth Dear on lips (as sister).
Gregory's Girl: Allison Forster kisses Gordon John Sinclair.
Grounded: Quinn Shepherd kisses Tyler James Williams.
Harry Potter & Order of the Phoenix: Daniel Radcliffe kisses Katie Leung (Cho Chang).
Heavenly Creatures: Kate Winslet & Melanie Lynskey kiss as 13 year old lesbians (though both actors were over 16).
Honey, I Shrunk the Kids: Deep kisses shared by Amy O'Neill and Thomas Brown (though both actors were over 16).
Hounddog: Dakota Fanning and Cody Hanford lip-kiss on two separate occasions.
I Love You, I Love You Not: Claire Danes snogs twice with boyfriend.
Impudent Girl: Charlotte Gainsbourg kisses older man.
Interview with the Vampire: Kirsten Dunst kisses the adult Brad Pitt.
Jack (2003): Anton Yelchin brief kiss on lips from Britt Irvin.
Journey of Natty Gann: Meredith Salenger kisses John Cussack.
kids (1995): Prolonged snogging.
Last time I saw Paris: Sandy Descher kisses father on lips.
Let Me In: Kodi Smit-McPhee and Chloë Grace Moretz share two kisses.
Let the Right One In: Kåre Hedbrant & Lina Leandersson kiss (with bloodied mouth).
Lilya 4-ever: Oksana Akinshina kissing scene.
Little Lips: Katya Berger kisses man.
Little Manhattan: Charlie Ray & Josh Hutcherson kiss.
Little Rascals: Bug Hall kisses Brittany Ashton Holmes several times. There is a kissing free-for-all at the end of film when all the infant boys and girls kiss each other.
Little Secrets: Evan Rachel Wood kisses David Gallagher.
Lolita: Dominique Swaine – Snogging with Jeremy Irons (several occasions).
Lovely Bones: Saoirse Ronan kisses (the actual moment of kiss is masked by a shadow). Rose McIver (as her younger sister) kisses boyfriend.
Lovers of the Arctic Circle: the adolescent Kristel Diaz and Victor Hugo Oliviera kiss.
Magic Island: Jessie-Ann Friend kisses Zachery Ty Bryan.
Man on the Moon: Reese Witherspoon kisses older boy.
Melissa P: Maria Valverde kissing older men with tongues.
Mermaids: Winona Ryder snogs handyman.

My American Cousin: Margaret Langrick kisses older cousin.

My Girl (1991): Anna Chlumsky kisses Macaulay Culkin.

My Girl 2: Anna Chlumsky kisses Austin O'Brien.

Nativity!: The characters of Mary & Joseph kiss.

Now and Then: Christina Ricci kisses boy.

Paperhouse: Prolonged snog between Charlotte Burke and Elliot Spiers.

Peter Pan: Carsen Gray kisses John. Rachel Hurd-Wood kisses Peter Pan.

Pocket Money: Pascale Bruchon kisses Geory Desmouceaux. Phillipe Goldman kisses Corinne Boucant & Eva Truffaut.

Pretty Baby: Brooke Shields kisses Keith Carradine (2 different occasions).

P'Tang, Yang, Kipperbang: Abigail Cruttenden kisses John Albasiny.

Sorcerer's Apprentice: Byron Taylor and Roxanne Burger kiss.

Secret Garden: Kate Maberly's first fumbled kiss with Heydon Prowse.

Secret Life of Bees: Prolonged kiss between Dakota Fanning & Nate Parker.

Single Santa Meets Mrs Claus: Dominic Scott Kay receives peck on cheek from Mackenzie Fitzgerald.

Somer Jubel: Both pairs of children kiss, one pair first taking down their pants while doing so.

Son of Ranbow: Girls queue up to snog with Jules Sitruk.

Snow Day: Mark Webber kisses girl on skating rink.

Stepmom: Jenna Malone kisses older boy.

That Night: Girl/boy kissing during spin the bottle.

32A: Ailish McCarthy & Sophie Jo Wasson lick each other's tongues, then kiss. Ailish McCarthy kisses Shane McDaid (long snog) on 2 occasions.

Tideland: Jodelle Ferland kisses adult including tongue wagging.

Thirteen (2003): Evan Rachel Wood & Nikki Reed snog each other including tonguing & kiss boys.

This is England: Thomas Turgoose snogs older girl, Rosamund Hanson.

Tomboy: Zoé Héran and Jeanne Disson kiss on two occasions.

Toto le Héros: Sandrine Blancke kisses Thomas Godet on lips.

Water Lilies: Pauline Acquart prolonged lesbian snogging with Adèle Haenel.

When Zachery Beaver Came to Town: Amanda Alch kisses boy on cheek after close dance.

Wild Child: Emma Roberts snogs son of headmistress.

Yours, Mine & Ours: In a family of 18 children it is the older kids who do the kissing, but the message it sends is clear: schoolkids are expected to kiss.

XXY: Inés Efron kisses boyfriend while topless.

Zombies Wicked Little Things: Scout Taylor-Compton kisses boyfriend.

REFERENCES & FURTHER READING

The following books have been consulted in researching this and the other volumes in this series:

Allison, Dorothy; *Bastard out of Carolina*; ISBN 0006544975

Best, Marc; *Those Endearing Young Charms: Child Performers of the Screen*; ISBN 0498077292

Björk, Christina & Inga-Karin Eriksson; *The Other Alice: The Story of Alice Liddell and Alice in Wonderland*; ISBN 9129622425

Conger, John; *Adolescence: Generation Under Pressure*; ISBN 0063180995

Davies, Hunter; *Book of British Lists*; ISBN 0600202674

Durham M G; *The Lolita Effect*; ISBN 9780715638040

Elley, Derek (Editor); *Variety Movie Guide*; ISBN 0600583309

Elliott, Michelle; *Preventing Child Sexual Assault*; ISBN 0719911443

Kincaid, James R; *Erotic Innocence: The Culture of Child Molesting*; ISBN 0822321939

Lebeau, Vicky; *Childhood and Cinema*; ISBN 9781861893529

Lury, Karen; *The Child in Film: Tears, Fears and Fairy Tales*; ISBN 9781845119683

Nabokov, Vladimir; *Lolita*; ISBN 0140108084

Pym, John (Editor); *Time Out Film Guide*; ISBN 9781846701306

Radio Times Film Unit; *Radio Times Guide to Films*; ISBN 9780955588624

Roberts, Chris; *Scarlett Johansson: Portrait of a Rising Star*; ISBN 9781844423996

Roiphe, Katie; *She Still Haunts Me: a novel of Lewis Carroll and Alice Liddell*; ISBN 0747265577

Sinclair, Marianne; *Hollywood Lolita*; ISBN 0859651304

Sinyard, Neil; *Children in the Movies*; ISBN 0713466324

Thompson, Michael & Catherine O'Neill Grace with Lawrence J Cohen; *Best Friends, Worst Enemies: Children's Friendships, Popularity and Social Cruelty*; ISBN 0718144317

TV Guide Online; *The Eleventh Virgin Film Guide*; ISBN 0753507293

Vesaas, Tarjei; *The Ice Palace*; ISBN 9780720613292

Walker, John (Editor); *Halliwell's Film & Video Guide*; ISBN 0007167121

Wolff, Sula; *Children Under Stress*; ISBN 0140215484

APPENDIX: LIST OF FILMS

The following is a list of films mentioned in all the volumes in this series. This naming of film directors and writers acts as an acknowledgement for the quotes referred to in the text.

Each entry comprises:

- Title of film
- Date of Release
- Director
- Writer/Screenplay/Scriptwriter
- Author/Storywriter/Conceptualisation
- Significant Child Actor(s)/Actresses
- Film star rating on a scale of one to five. This comprises an average of ratings provided by *Radio Times Guide to Films*, *Halliwell's Film Video & DVD Guide*, my own personal rating, and also includes my rating of the child actor's screen appearance and contribution to the film. (This may have the effect of demoting a classic such as *Doctor Zhivago* or *Jean de Florette* in which the child takes a minimal role, whereas a child's acting may enhance an otherwise second rate film as in *Eloise at the Plaza* or *Casper meets Wendy*.)

This list also includes some TV dramas that are not categorised as films, and as such do not carry a star rating from *Radio Times Guide to Films* or from *Halliwell's Film Video & DVD Guide*, for example, *The Borrowers (2011)*, *Ball-Trap on the Côte Sauvage*, *Enid (2009)*, *Cider with Rosie*.

(500) Days of Summer (2009); Director: Marc Webb; Writer: Scott Neustadter & Michael H Webber; Actor: Chloë Grace Moretz; ★★☆
10,000 Years BC (2008); Director: Roland Emmerich; Writer: Roland Emmerich & Harold Kloser; Actor: Camilla Belle & Victoria Vetri; ★★
2012 (2008); Director: Roland Emmerich; Actor: Lily Morgan & Liam James; ★★☆
About a Boy (2002); Director: Chris & Paul Weitz; Writer: Peter Hughes + Chris & Paul Weitz; Actor: Nicholas Hoult; ★★★☆
Addams Family, the (1991); Director: Barry Sonnenfeld; Writer: Caroline Thompson & Larry Wilson; Story: Charles Addams; Actor: Christina Ricci & Jimmy Workman; ★★★
Addams Family Values (1993); Director: Barry Sonnenfeld; Writer: Paul Rudnick; Actor: Christina Ricci & Jimmy Workman; ★★★☆
Adolescent Malice (aka Maladolescenza/Spielen wir Liebe) (1997); Director: Pier Guiseppi Murgia; Writer: Pier Guiseppi Murgia; Actor: Martin Loeb, Eva Ionesco & Lara Wendel; ★★☆
Adventures of Baron Munchausen (1988); Director: Terry Gilliam; Writer: Charles McKeown; Story: Rudolph Erich Raspe; Actor: Sarah Polley; ★★★
Adventures of Huck Finn (1993); Director: Stephen Sommers; Writer: Stephen Sommers; Story: Mark Twain; Actor: Elijah Wood & Laura Bundy; ★★★
Adventures of Sharkboy and Lavagirl (2005); Director: Robert Rodriguez; Writer: Robert & Marcel Rodriguez; Actor: Taylor Dooley & Taylor Lautner; ★★★

Akeelah and the Bee (2005); Director: Doug Atchison; Writer: Doug Atchison; Actor: Keke Palmer; ★★☆

Alas de Mariposa (Butterfly Wings) (1991); Director: Juanma Bajo Ulloa; Writer: Juanma & Eduardo Bajo Ulloa; Actor: Laura Vaquero; ★★

Alaska (1997); Director: Fraser C Heston; Writer: Andy Burg & Scott Myers; Actor: Thora Birch & Vincent Kartheiser; ★★★☆

Alice (1988); Director: Jan Švankmajer; Writer: Jan Švankmajer; Story: Lewis Carroll; Actor: Kristýna Kohoutová; ★★★☆

Alice in the Cities (1973); Director: Wim Wenders; Writer: Wim Wenders & Veith von Fürsterberg; Actor: Yella Rottlander; ★★★★

Alice in Wonderland (1999); Director: Nick Willing; Writer: Peter Barnes; Story: Lewis Carroll; Actor: Tina Majorino; ★★

Alice upside Down (2007); Director: Sandy Tung; Writer: Sandy Tung & Meghan Heritage; Story: Phyllis Reynolds Naylor; Actor: Alyson Stoner; ★★☆

Alice's Adventures in Wonderland (1972); Director: William Sterling; Writer: William Sterling; Story: Lewis Carroll; Actor: Fiona Fullerton; ★☆

Aliens in the Attic (2009); Director: John Schultz; Writer: Mark Burton & Adam F Goldberg; Story: Mark Burton; Actor: Ashley Tinsdale, Carter Jenkins, Ashley Boettcher; ★★★

All I Want for Christmas (1991); Director: Robert Lieberman; Writer: Thom Eberhardt & Richard Kramer; Story: Richard Kramer; Actor: Thora Birch & Ethan Randall; ★★★

Along came a spider (2001); Director: Lee Tamahori; Writer: Marc Moss; Story: James Patterson; Actor: Mika Boorem; ★☆

Amazing Panda Adventure (1995); Director: Christopher Cain; Writer: Jeff Rothberg & Laurice Elehwany; Actor: Ryan Slater & Yi Ding; ★★

American haunting, an (2005); Director: Courtney Solomon; Writer: Courtney Solomon; Story: Brent Monahan; Actor: Rachel Hurd-Wood; ★★★

Amityville Horror (1979); Director: Stuart Rosenberg; Writer: Sandor Stern; Story: Jay Anson; Actor: Natasha Ryan; ★★

Amityville Horror (2005); Director: Andrew Douglas; Writer: Scott Kosar; Story: Jay Anson; Actor: Jesse James, Chloë Grace Moretz & Isabel Conner; ★★

Andre (1994); Director: George Miller; Writer: Dana Baratta; Actor: Tina Majorino, Joshua Jackson & Aidan Pendleton; ★★★

Angel of Pennsylvania Avenue (1996); Director: Robert Ellis Miller; Writer: Rider McDowell & Michael de Guzman; Actor: Tegan Moss & Brittney Irvin; ★★

Angela (1994); Director: Rebecca Miller; Writer: ; Story: ; Actor: Miranda Stuart Ryne & Charlotte Blyth; ★★☆

Angus, Thongs and Perfect Snogging (2008); Director: Gurinder Chadha; Writer: Gurinder Chadha, Paul Mayeda Berges, Will McRobb & Chris Viscardi; Story: Louise Rennison; Actor: Georgia Groome; ★★★★

Anita & Me (2002); Director: Metin Hüseyin; Writer: Meera Syal; Story: Meera Syal; Actor: Chandeep Uppal; ★★★

Annie (1982); Director: John Huston; Writer: Carol Sobieski; Story: Thomas Meehan; Actor: Aileen Quinn; ★★★☆

Annie (1999); Director: Rob Marshall; Writer: Irene Mecchi; Story: Thomas Meehan; Actor: Alicia Morton; ★★★☆

Annunciation (Angyali Üdvözlet) (1984); Director: Andras Jeles; Story: Imre Madach; Actor: Julia Mero & Peter Bocsor; ★★☆

Aquamarine (2006); Director: Elizabeth Allen; Writer: John Quaintance & Jessica Bendinger; Actor: Emma Roberts & Joanna 'Jojo' Levesque; ★★

Are We There Yet? (2005); Director: Brian Levant; Writer: Steven Gary Banks, Claudia Grazioso, J David Stern & David N Weiss; Story: Arthur Loew; Actor: Aleisha Allen & Philip Daniel Bolden; ★★

Atonement (2007); Director: John Wright; Writer: Christopher Hampton; Story: Ian McEwan; Actor: Saoirse Ronan; ★★★☆

Audition (1999); Director: Takashi Miike; Writer: Daisuke Tengan; Story: Ryu Murakami; Actor: Ayaka Izumi; ★★

Audrey Rose (1977); Director: Frank de Felitta; Writer: Frank de Felitta; Story: Frank de Felitta; Actor: Susan Swift; ★★★

Babel (2006); Director: Alejandro González Iñárritu; Writer: Guillermo Arriaga; Actor: Elle Fanning & Nathan Gamble; ★★★

Back to the Secret Garden (1999); Director: Michael Tuchner; Writer: Joe Wiesenfeld; Story: Frances Hodgson Burnett; Actor: Camilla Belle & Florence Hoath; ★

Bad News Bears (1976); Director: Michael Ritchie; Writer: Bill Lancaster; Actor: Tatum O'Neal; ★★★

Bad News Bears (2005); Director: Richard Linklater; Writer: Bill Lancaster, Glenn Ficara & John Requa; Actor: Sammi Kane Kraft; ★★☆

Bad Seed (1956); Director: Mervyn LeRoy; Writer: John Lee Mahin & Maxwell Anderson; Story: William March; Actor: Patty McCormack; ★★★★

Balletshoes (2007); Director: Sandra Goldbacher; Story: Noel Streatfeild; Actor: Lucy Boynton; ★★★☆

Ball-Trap on the Côte Sauvage (1989); Director: Andrew Davis; Story: Iris Rainer Dart; Actor: Amy Melhuish & Katherina Hadjimatheou; ★★☆

Bastard out of Carolina (1996); Director: Anjelica Huston; Writer: Anne Meredith; Story: Dorothy Allison; Actor: Jena Malone; ★★★☆

Battle Royale (2000); Director: Kinji Fukasaku; Writer: Kenta Fukasaku; Story: Koshun Takami; Actor: ; ★★★

Beaches (1988); Director: Gary Marshall; Writer: Mary Agnes Donoghue; Story: Iris Rainer Dart; Actor: Mayim Bialik; ★★★☆

Because of Winn Dixie (2004); Director: Wayne Wang; Writer: Joan Singleton; Story: Kate Di Camillo; Actor: AnnaSophia Robb & Elle Fanning; ★★★☆

Bedknobs and Broomsticks (1971); Director: Robert Stevenson; Writer: Bill Walsh & Don Da Gradi; Story: Mary Norton; Actor: Cindy O'Callaghan; ★☆

Bedtime Stories (2008); Director: Adam Shankman; Writer: Matt Lopez & Tim Herlihy; Actor: Laura Ann Kesling; ★★☆

Beethoven's 3rd (2000); Director: David Mickey Evans; Writer: Jeff Schechter; Story: Edmond Dantes & Amy Holden Jones; Actor: Michaela Gallo & Joe Pitchler; ★☆

Beethoven's 5th (2003); Director: Mark Griffiths; Writer: Cliff Ruby & Elana Lesser; Story: Edmond Dantes & Amy Holden Jones; Actor: Daveigh Chase; ★☆

Before Women had Wings (1998); Director: Lloyd Kramer; Writer: Connie May Fowler; Story: Connie May Fowler; Actor: Tina Majorino; ★★★☆

Beguiled, the (1970); Director: Donald Siegel; Writer: John B Sherry & Grimes Grice; Story: Thomas Cullinan; Actor: Pamlyn Ferdin; ★★★

Benny's Video (1992); Director: Michael Haneke; Writer: Michael Haneke; Actor: Arno Frisch & Ingrid Stassner; ★★☆

Big (1988); Director: Penny Marshall; Writer: Gary Ross & Anne Spielberg; Actor: Jared Rushton & David Moscow; ★★★

Big Momma's House 2 (2006); Director: John Whitesell; Writer: Don Rhymer; Story: Darryl Quaries; Actor: Chloë Grace Moretz; ★★☆

Billy Elliot (2000); Director: Stephen Daldry; Writer: Lee Hall; Actor: Jamie Bell; ★★★★★

Birds, the (1963); Director: Alfred Hitchcock; Writer: Evan Hunter; Story: Daphne Du Maurier; Actor: Veronica Cartwright; ★★★☆

Black Beauty (1994); Director: Caroline Thompson; Writer: Caroline Thompson; Story: Anna Sewell; Actor: Freddie White, Gemma Paternoster & Georgina Armstrong; ★★

Blame it on Fidel (la faute à Fidel) (2006); Director: Julia Gavras; Writer: Arnaud Cathrine; Story: Domitilla Calamai; Actor: Nina Kervel; ★★★☆

Bless the Child (2000); Director: Chuck Russell; Writer: Tom Rickman, Clifford and Ellen Green, ; Story: Cathy Cash Spellman; Actor: Holliston Coleman; ★☆

Blue Butterfly, the (2003); Director: Léa Pool; Writer: Pete McCormack; Actor: Marc Donata & Marianella Jimenez; ★★☆

Blue Lagoon, the (1949); Director: Frank Launder; Writer: Frank Launder, John Baines & Michael Hogan; Story: Henry De Vere Stacpoole; Actor: Susan Stranks & Peter Jones; ★★★

Blue Lagoon, the (1980); Director: Randal Kleister; Writer: Douglas Day Stewart; Story: Henry De Vere Stacpoole; Actor: Brooke Shields, Christopher Atkins, Elva Josephson & Glenn Kohan; ★★★☆

Body Snatcher, the (1945); Director: Robert Wise; Writer: Philip McDonald & Carlos Keith; Story: Robert Louis Stevenson; Actor: Sharyn Moffett; ★★★

Borrowers, the (2011); Director: Tom Harper; Actor: Aisling Loftus; ★★

Boy Called Dad, a (2009); Director: Brian Percival; Writer: Julie Rutterford; Actor: Kylo Ward; ★★★

Boy in the Striped Pyjamas (2008); Director: Mark Herman; Writer: Mark Herman; Story: John Boyne; Actor: Asa Butterfield, Jack Scanlon & Amber Beattie; ★★★

Brady Bunch Movie, the (1995); Director: Betty Thomas; Writer: Laurice Elehwany, Rick Copp, Bonny & Terry Turner; Story: Sherwood Schwartz; Actor: Olivia Hack & Jesse Lee; ★★

Bridge to Terabithia (2007); Director: Gabor Csupo; Writer: Jeff Stockwell & David Paterson; Story: Katherine Paterson; Actor: AnnaSophia Robb & Josh Hutcherson; ★★★★

Brooke Ellison Story, the (2004); Director: Christopher Reeve; Writer: Camille Thomasson; Story: Brooke & Jean Ellison; Actor: Vanessa Marano; ★★☆

Brothers Grimm, the (2005); Director: Terry Gilliam; Writer: Ehren Kruger; Actor: ; ★★

Buddha Collapsed out of Shame (2007); Director: Hana Mackhmalbaf; Writer: Marziyeh Meshkini; Actor: Nikbakht Noruz; ★★

Bugsy Malone (1976); Director: Alan Parker; Writer: Alan Parker; Actor: Jodie Foster, Scott Baio, Florrie Dugger & John Cassisi; ★★★★☆

Butterfly Effect (2003); Director: Eric Bress & J Mackye Gruber; Writer: Eric Bress & J Mackye Gruber; Actor: Jesse James & Sarah Widdows; ★★☆

Camomile Lawn (1992); Director: Peter Hall; Writer: Ken Taylor; Story: Mary Wesley; Actor: Rebecca Hall; ★★

Candleshoe (1977); Director: Norman Tokar; Writer: David Swift & Rosemary Anne Sisson; Story: Michael Innes; Actor: Jodie Foster; ★★★

Case 39 (2007); Director: Christian Alvart; Writer: Ray Wright; Actor: Jodelle Ferland; ★★★☆

Casper (1995); Director: Brad Siberling; Writer: Sherri Stoner & Deanna Oliver; Story: Joseph Oriolo; Actor: Christina Ricci; ★★★

Casper meets Wendy (1998); Director: Sean McNamara; Writer: Jymn Magon; Story: Joseph Oriolo; Actor: Hilary Duff; ★★☆

Catch that Kid (2004); Director: Bart Freundlich; Actor: Kristen Stewart; ★★☆

Celia (1989); Director: Ann Turner; Writer: Ann Turner; Actor: Rebecca Smart; ★★★

Cement Garden (1994); Director: Andrew Birkin; Writer: Andrew Birkin; Story: Ian McEwan; Actor: Charlotte Gainsbourg, Alice Coulthard, Andrew Robertson & Ned Birkin; ★★★☆

Charlie and the Chocolate Factory (2005); Director: Tim Burton; Writer: John August; Story: Roald Dahl; Actor: Freddie Highmore, AnnaSophia Robb & Julie Winter; ★★★★

Charlotte's Web (2006); Director: Gary Winick; Writer: Susannah Grant & Karey Kirkpatrick; Story: E B White; Actor: Dakota Fanning; ★★★☆

Cheaper by the Dozen (1950); Director: Walter Lang; Writer: Lamar Trotti; Story: Frank B Gilbreth Jr & Ernestine Gilbreth Carey; Actor: ; ★★

Cheaper by the Dozen I (2003); Director: Walter Lang; Writer: Sam Harper, Joel Cohen &Alec Sokolow; Story: Frank B Gilbreth Jr & Ernestine Gilbreth Carey; Actor: Alyson Stoner; ★★

Cheaper by the Dozen II (2005); Director: Adam Shankman; Writer: Sam Harper; Story: Frank B Gilbreth Jr & Ernestine Gilbreth Carey; Actor: Alyson Stoner & Taylor Lautner; ★☆

Child, the (Harry Novak presents…) (2006); Director: Robert Voskanian; Actor: Rosalie Cole; ★

Children of Theatre Street (1977); Director: Robert Dornhelm; Writer: Beth Gutcheon; Actor: Angelina Armeiskaya; ★☆

Children, the (2008); Director: Tom Shankland; Writer: Tom Shankland; Story: Paul Andrew Williams; Actor: Eva Sayer; ★★★

Children's Hour, the (The Loudest Whisper) (1961); Director: William Wyler; Writer: John Michael Hayes; Story: Lilian Hellman; Actor: Veronica Cartwright & Karen Balkin; ★★★

Child's Play (1988); Director: Tom Holland; Writer: Don Mancini, Tom Holland & John Lafia; Story: Don Mancini; Actor: Alex Vincent; ★★☆

Chitty Chitty Bang Bang (1968); Director: Ken Hughes; Writer: Roald Dahl, Richard Malbaum & Ken Hughes; Story: Ian Fleming; Actor: Adrian Hall & Heather Ripley; ★★★☆

Chocolat (2000); Director: Lasse Hallström; Writer: Robert Nelson Jacobs; Story: Joanne Harris; Actor: Victoire Thivisol; ★★★☆

Christmas Box (1995); Director: Marcus Cole; Story: Richard Evans; Actor: Annette O'Toole; ★

Christmas Memory, A (1997); Director: Glenn Jordan; Writer: Duane Poole; Story: Truman Capote; Actor: Eric Lloyd & Julia McIlvaine; ★

Chronicles of Narnia: Prince Caspian (2008); Director: Andrew Adamson; Writer: Andrew Adamson, Christopher Markus & Stephen McFeely; Story: C S Lewis; Actor: Georgie Henley, Skandar Keynes, Anna Popplewell & William Moseley; ★★★

Chronicles of Narnia: The Lion, the Witch and the Wardrobe (2005); Director: Andrew Adamson; Writer: Ann Peacock, Andrew Adamson, Christopher Markus & Stephen McFeely; Story: C S Lewis; Actor: Georgie Henley, Skandar Keynes, Anna Popplewell & William Moseley; ★★★★

Cider with Rosie (1998); Director: Charles Beeson; Writer: John Mortimer; Story: Laurie Lee; Actor: Joe Roberts; ★★★

Cinema Paradiso (1988); Director: Guiseppe Tornatore; Writer: Guiseppe Tornatore & Vanna Pauli; Actor: Salvatore Cascio; ★★★★☆

Cleaner (2007); Director: Renny Harlin; Writer: Matthew Aldrich; Actor: Keke Palmer; ★☆

Cold light of day (1995); Director: Rudolf van den Berg; Writer: Doug Magee; Story: Friedrich Dürrenmatt; Actor: Perdita Weeks; ★★☆

Cold Sweat (1970); Director: Terence Young; Writer: Shimon Wincelberg; Story: Richard Matheson; Actor: Yannick Dululle; ★★☆

Company of Wolves (1984); Director: Neil Jordan; Writer: Angela Carter & Neil Jordan; Story: Angela carter; Actor: Sarah Patterson; ★★★☆

Contact (1997); Director: Robert Zemeckis; Writer: James V Hart & Michael Goldberg; Story: Carl Sagan; Actor: Jena Malone; ★★★

Corrina, Corrina (1994); Director: Jessie Nelson; Writer: Jessie Nelson; Actor: Tina Majorino; ★★☆

Courage of Lassie (1946); Director: Fred M Wilcox; Writer: Lionel Houser; Actor: Elizabeth Taylor; ★★

CRAZY (2005); Director: Jean-Marc Vallée; Writer: Jean-Marc Vallée & François Boulay; Story: ; Actor: Michel Côté & Emile Vallée; ★★☆

Cría Cuervos (1975); Director: Carlos Saura; Writer: Carlos Saura; Actor: Ana Torrent & Conchita Perez; ★★★

Crossing, the (TV drama: Secrets & Words Series) (2012); Director: Reece Dinsdale; Writer: Arthur Ellison; Actor: Ramona Marquez; ★★★☆

Curious Case of Benjamin Button (2008); Director: David Fincher; Writer: Eric Roth; Story: F Scott Fitzgerald; Actor: Elle Fanning; ★★☆

Curly Sue (1991); Director: John Hughes; Writer: John Hughes; Actor: Alisan Porter; ★★☆
Curse of the Cat People (1944); Director: Robert Wise & Gunther V Fritsch; Writer: DeWitt Bodean; Actor: Ann Carter; ★★★☆
Dancer in the Dark (2000); Director: Lars von Trier; Writer: Lars von Trier; ★★
Dark, the (2005); Director: J Fawsett; Writer: Stephen Massicote; Story: Simon Maginn; Actor: Abigail Stone & Sophie Stuckey; ★★★
Day at the Beach, A (1970); Director: Roman Polanski; Writer: Heere Heeresma; Actor: Beatie Edney; ★★★
Dear Frankie (2003); Director: Shona Auerbach; Writer: Andrea Gibb; Actor: Jack McElhone & Jayd Johnson; ★★☆
Death defying acts (2007); Director: Gillian Armstrong; Writer: Tony Grisoni & Brian Ward; Actor: Saoirse Ronan; ★★☆
Definitely, maybe (2008); Director: Adam Brooks; Writer: Adam Brooks; Actor: Abigail Breslin; ★★
Dennis (1993); Director: Nick Castle; Writer: John Hughes; Story: Hank Ketcham; Actor: Mason Gamble; ★★☆
Devil's Child, the (1997); Director: Bobby Roth; Writer: Pablo F Fenjves; Story: Laurence Minkoff & Pablo F Fenjves; Actor: Rachael Bella; ★
Diables, les (2002); Director: Christophe Ruggia; Writer: Christophe Ruggia & Olivier Lorelle; Actor: Vincent Rottiers & Adèle Haenel; ★★★☆
Diary of Anne Frank, the (1959); Director: George Stevens; Writer: Frances Goodrich & Albert Hackett; Story: Anne Frank; Actor: Millie Perkins; ★★★☆
Dickie Roberts, Former Child Star (2003); Director: Sam Weisman; Writer: Fred Wolf & David Spade; Actor: Jenna Boyd & Scott Terra; ★☆
Digging to China (1998); Director: Timothy Huton; Writer: Karen Janszen; Actor: Evan Rachel Wood; ★★★
Doctor Dolittle (1998); Director: Betty Thomas; Writer: Nat Maudlin & Larry Levin; Story: Hugh Lofting; Actor: Raven-Simoné & Kyla Pratt; ★★
Doctor Zhivago (1965); Director: David Lean; Writer: Robert Bolt; Story: Boris Pasternak; Actor: Lucy Westmore; ★★★☆
Don't say a word (2001); Director: Gary Fieder; Writer: Anthony Peckham & Patrick Smith Kelly; Story: Andrew Klavan; Actor: Skye McCole Bartusiak; ★☆
Down will come Baby (1999); Director: Gregory Goodell; Story: Gloria Murphy; Actor: Evan Rachel Wood & Katie Booze-Mooney; ★★★
Dreamchild (1985); Director: Gavin Millar; Writer: Gavin Millar; Story: Dennis Potter; Actor: Amelia Shankley; ★★★☆
Dreamer (2005); Director: John Gatins; Writer: John Gatins; Actor: Dakota Fanning; ★★★
Driftwood (1947); Director: Alan Dwan; Writer: Mary Loos & Richard Sale; Actor: Natalie Wood; ★★★
Drum, the (1938); Director: Zoltan Korda; Story: AEW Mason; Actor: Sabu; ★★☆
Dust Factory, the (2004); Director: Eric Small; Writer: Eric Small; Actor: Ryan Kelley & Hayden Panettiere; ★★☆
Dustbin Baby (2008); Director: Juliet May; Writer: Helen Blakeman; Story: Jacqueline Wilson; Actor: Dakota Blue Richards, Alexandra Hewitt & Lucy Hutchinson; ★★★
East of Sudan (1964); Director: Nathan Juran; Writer: Jud Kinberg; Actor: Jenny Agutter; ★★
Elf (2003); Director: Jon Favreau; Writer: David Berenbaum; Actor: Daniel Tay & Lydia Lawson-Baird; ★★☆
Eloise at Christmastime (2003); Director: Kevin Lima; Writer: Elizabeth Chandler; Story: Kay Thompson; Actor: Sofia Vassilieva; ★★★
Eloise at the Plaza (2003); Director: Kevin Lima; Writer: Janet Brownell; Story: Kay Thompson; Actor: Sofia Vassilieva; ★★★

Emerald Forest (1985); Director: John Boorman; Writer: Rospo Pallenberg; Actor: Charley Boorman, Yara Vaneau & William Rodriguez; ★★☆

Empire of the Sun (1987); Director: Steven Spielburg; Writer: Tom Stoppard; Story: J G Ballard; Actor: Christian Bale; ★★★★☆

Enid (2009); Director: James Hawes; Writer: Lindsay Shapero; Actor: Ramona Marquez, Alexandra Brain & Sinead Michael; ★★★☆

ET the Extra-Terrestrial (1982); Director: Steven Spielberg; Writer: Melissa Matthison; Actor: Henry Thomas, Drew Barrymore & Peter Coyote; ★★★★★

Eve's Bayou (1997); Director: Kasi Lemmons; Writer: Kasi Lemmons; Actor: Jurnee Smollett & Meagan Good; ★★★☆

Exorcist, the (1973); Director: William Friedkin; Writer: William Peter Blatty; Story: William Peter Blatty; Actor: Linda Blair; ★★★☆

Explorers (1985); Director: Joe Dante; Writer: Eric Luke; Actor: Ethan Hawke, River Phoenix, Jason Presson & Amanda Peterson; ★★★

Fairy King of Ar (2002); Director: Paul Matthews; Writer: Christopher Atkins & Paul Matthews; Actor: Brittney Bomann, Jameson Baltes & Leigh Greyvenstein; ★☆

Fairy Tale: a true story (1997); Director: Charles Sturridge; Writer: Ernie Contreras; Story: Ernie Contreras; Actor: Elizabeth Earl & Florence Hoath; ★★★★

Fallen Angel (1981); Director: Robert Michael Lewis; Actor: Dana Hill; ★★★

Family Gathering, a (2010); Director: John Bradshaw; Actor: Kristina Miller & Maya Lowe; ★

Father Goose (1964); Director: Ralph Nelson; Writer: Frank Tarloff & Peter Stone; Story: SH Barnett; Actor: Jennifer & Stephanie Berrington, Laurelle & Nicole Felsette, & Sharyl Locke; ★★★

Father of My Children (le Père de mes Enfants) (2009); Director: Mia Hansen-Løve; Writer: Mia Hansen-Løve; Actor: Alice Gautier, Manelle Driss & Alice de Lenequesaing; ★★★☆

Father's Choice, a (2000); Director: Christophen Cain; Writer: Richard Leder; Actor: Michelle Trachtenburg; ★★☆

Field of Dreams (1989); Director: Phil Alden Robinson; Writer: Philip Alder Robinson; Story: WP Kinsella; Actor: Gaby Hoffman; ★★★

Firestarter (1984); Director: Mark Lester; Writer: Stanley Mann; Story: Stephen King; Actor: Drew Barrymore; ★☆

Five children and It (2004); Director: John Stephenson; Writer: ; Story: ; Actor: Freddie Highmore, Jonathan Bailey, Jessica Claridge & Poppy Rogers; ★★

Five on a Treasure Island (1996); Director: Michael Kerrigan; Writer: Helen Cresswell, Julia Jones & Alan Seymour; Story: Enid Blyton; Actor: Jemima Rooper, Marco Williams, Paul Child & Laura Patela; ★

Five Pennies, the (1959); Director: Jack Rose; Writer: Melville Shalveston & Jack Rose; Story: Robert Smith; Actor: Susan Gordon & Tuesday Weld; ★★

Flightplan (2005); Director: Robert Schwentke; Writer: Peter A Dowling & Billy Ray; Actor: Marlene Lawston; ★★

Flowers in the Attic (1987); Director: Jeffrey Bloom; Writer: Jeffrey Bloom; Story: Virginia Andrews; Actor: Jeb Stuart Adams, Ben Granger, Kristy Swanson & Lindsey Parker; ★☆

Fly away Home (1996); Director: Carroll Ballard; Writer: Robert Rodat & Vince McKewin; Story: Bill Lishman; Actor: Anna Paquin; ★★★★

Forrest Gump (1994); Director: Robert Zemeckis; Writer: Eric Roth; Story: Winston Groom; Actor: Michael Conner Humphreys & Hanna R Hall; ★★★☆

Fox and the Child (2007); Director: Luc Jacquet; Writer: Luc Jacquet; Story: Luc Jacquet; Actor: Bertille Noël-Bruneau; ★★★☆

Freaky Friday (1976); Director: Gary Nelson; Story: Mary Rodgers; Actor: Jodie Foster; ★★☆

Freaky Friday (1994); Director: Melanie Mayron; Story: Mary Rodgers; Actor: Gaby Hoffman; ★★

Free Willy (1993); Director: Simon Wincer; Writer: Keith A Walker & Corey Blechman; Actor: Jason James Richter; ★★★

Game Plan, the (2007); Director: Andy Fickman; Writer: Nichole Millard & Kathryn Price; Story: Nichole Millard, Kathryn Price & Audrey Wells; Actor: Madison Pettis; ★★★

Genova (2008); Director: Michael Winterton; Writer: Michael Winterton & Lawrence Coriat; Actor: Perla Haney-Jardine; ★★★☆

Ghost and Mrs Muir, the (1947); Director: Joseph L Mankiewicz; Writer: Philip Dunne; Story: R A Dick; Actor: Natalie Wood; ★★☆

Golden Compass (2007); Director: Chris Weitz; Writer: Chris Weitz; Story: Philip Pullman; Actor: Dakota Blue Richards; ★★☆

Good Mother, the (aka Price of Passion) (1988); Director: Leonard Nimoy; Writer: Michael Bortman; Story: Sue Miller; Actor: Asia Vieira & Mairon Bennett; ★★★

Good Year, a (2006); Director: Ridley Scott; Writer: Marc Klein; Story: Peter Mayle; Actor: Freddie Highmore & Marine Casto; ★★☆

Goodnight Mr Tom (1998); Director: Jack Gold; Story: Michelle Magorian; Actor: Nick Robinson; ★★

Goonies, the (1985); Director: Richard Donner; Writer: Chris Columbus; Story: Steven Spielberg; Actor: Sean Astin, Jeff Cohen, Corey Feldman, Ke Huy Quan, Martha Plimpton & Kerri Green; ★★★★

Great Balls of Fire (1989); Director: Jim McBride; Writer: Jim McBride & Jack Baran; Story: Myra Lewis & Murray Silver; Actor: Winona Ryder; ★★★★☆

Great Expectations (1997); Director: Alfonso Cuarón; Writer: Mitch Glazer; Story: Charles Dickens; Actor: Jeremy James Kisner & Raquel Beaudene; ★★★

Great Expectations (TV Drama) (2011); Director: Sarah Phelps; Story: Charles Dickens; Actor: Oscar Kennedy & Izzy Meikle-Small; ★★☆

Great St Trinian's Train Robbery (1966); Director: Frank Launder & Sidney Gilliat; Writer: Frank Launder & Ivor Herbert; Story: Ronald Searle

Greengage Summer (1961); Director: Lewis Gilbert; Writer: Howard Koch; Story: Rumer Godden; Actor: Jane Asher & Susannah York; ★☆

Gregory's Girl (1980); Director: Bill Forsyth; Writer: Bill Forsyth; Actor: Gordon John Sinclair, Dee Hepburn, Clare Grogan & Allison Forster; ★★★★☆

Greystoke: the Legend of Tarzan (1984); Director: Hugh Hudson; Writer: PH Vazak & Michael Austin; Story: Edgar Rice Burroughs; Actor: ; ★☆

Grinch, the (2000); Director: Ron Howard; Writer: Jeffrey Price & Peter S Seaman; Story: Dr Seuss; Actor: Taylor Momsen & Landry Allbright; ★★☆

Grounded (2006); Director: Paul Feig; Writer: Jacob Meszaros, Mya Stark & Paul Feig; Story: Susan Burton; Actor: Tyler James Williams, Dyllan Christopher, Brett Kelly, Quinn Shepherd & Gina Mantegna; ★★☆

Grow Your Own (2007); Director: Richard Laxton; Writer: Frank Cottrell Boyce & Carl Hunter; Actor: Sophie Lee; ★★★★

Halloween (1978); Director: John Carpenter; Writer: Debra Hill & John Carpenter; Actor: Kyle Richards & Brian Andrews; ★★☆

Halloween 4: The Return of Michael Myers (1988); Director: Dwight H Little; Writer: Alan B McElroy; Story: Dhani Lipsius, Larry Rattner, Benjamin Ruffner & Alan B McElroy; Actor: Danielle Harris; ★★☆

Hand that Rocks the Cradle (1992); Director: Curtis Hanson; Writer: Amanda Silver; Actor: Madeline Zima; ★★★

Happening, the (2008); Director: M Night Shyamalan; Writer: M Night Shyamalan; Actor: Ashley Sanchez; ★★☆

Hard Candy (2005); Director: D Slade; Writer: Brian Nelson; Actor: Ellen Page; ★★★

Harry Potter (1) and the Philosopher's Stone (2001); Director: Chris Columbus; Writer: Steve Kloves; Story: JK Rowling; Actor: Daniel Radcliffe, Emma Watson, Rupert Grint & Bonnie Wright; ★★★★

Harry Potter (2) and the Chamber of Secret (2003); Director: Chris Columbus; Writer: Steve Kloves; Story: JK Rowling; Actor: Daniel Radcliffe, Emma Watson, Rupert Grint & Bonnie Wright; ★★★★

Harry Potter (3) and the Prisoner of Azkaban (2004); Director: Alfonso Cuarón; Writer: Steve Kloves; Story: JK Rowling; Actor: Daniel Radcliffe, Emma Watson & Rupert Grint; ★★★★

Harry Potter (4) and the Goblet of Fire (2005); Director: Mike Newell; Writer: Steve Kloves; Story: JK Rowling; Actor: Daniel Radcliffe, Emma Watson, Rupert Grint & Katie Leung; ★★★☆

Harry Potter (5) and the Order of the Phoenix (2005); Director: David Yates; Writer: Michael Goldenberg; Story: JK Rowling; Actor: Daniel Radcliffe, Emma Watson, Rupert Grint, Evanna Lynch, Katie Leung & Bonnie Wright; ★★★☆

Harry Potter (6) and the Half-Blood Prince (2005); Director: David Yates; Writer: Steve Kloves; Story: JK Rowling; Actor: Daniel Radcliffe, Emma Watson, Rupert Grint, Tom Felton & Bonnie Wright; ★★★

Haunted Mansion, the (2003); Director: Rob Minkoff; Writer: David Berenbaum; Actor: Aree Davis & Marc John Jeffries; ★☆

Heavenly Creatures (1994); Director: Peter Jackson; Writer: Frances Walsh & Peter Jackson; Actor: Kate Winslet & Melanie Lynskey; ★★★☆

Heidi (2005); Director: Paul Marcus; Writer: Brian Finch; Story: Joanna Spyri; Actor: Emma Bolger, Jessica Claridge & Samuel Friend; ★★★

Hidden in America (1996); Director: Martin Bell; Writer: Peter Silverman & Michael de Guzman; Actor: Jena Malone, Shelton Dane & Allegra Denton; ★★

Hidden Places (2004); Director: Yelena Lanskaya; Writer: Robert Tate Miller; Story: Lynn Austin; Actor: Carlie Westerman; ★

Hide and Seek (2005); Director: John Polson; Writer: Ari Schlossberg; Actor: Dakota Fanning; ★★★

Hideous Kinky (1998); Director: Gillian MacKinnon; Writer: Billy McKinnon; Story: Esther Freud; Actor: Bella Riza & Carrie Mullan; ★★★☆

High Wind in Jamaica, a (1965); Director: Alexander Mackendrick; Writer: Stanley Mann, Ronald Harwood & Denis Cannan; Story: Richard Hughes; Actor: Deborah Baxter, Karen Flack, Martin Amis, Viviane Ventura & Roberta Tovey; ★★★★

Hocus Pocus (1993); Director: Kenny Ortega; Writer: Neil Cuthbert & Mick Garris; Story: Mick Garris & David Kirscher; Actor: Omri Katz, Thora Birch & Jodie Rivera (as Amanda Shepherd); ★★★☆

Home (2008); Director: Ursula Meier; Writer: Ursula Meier, Antoine Jaccoud, Olivier Lorelle, Gilles Taurand, Raphaelle Valbrune & Alice Wincocour; Actor: Madeleine Budd & Kacey Mottet Klein; ★★★☆

Home Alone (1990); Director: Chris Columbus; Writer: John Hughes; Actor: Macaulay Culkin; ★★★

Honey, I Shrunk the Kids (1989); Director: Joe Johnston; Writer: Ed Naha & Tom Schulman; Story: Stuart Gordon, Brian Yuzna & Ed Naha; Actor: Thomas Brown, Jared Rushton, Amy O'Neill & Robert Oliveri; ★★★

Hoot (2006); Director: Will Shriner; Writer: Will Shriner; Story: Carl Hiaasen; Actor: Logan Lerman, Luke Wilson, Brie Larson & Cody Linley; ★★

Hope and Glory (1987); Director: John Boorman; Writer: John Boorman; Actor: Sebastian Rice Burrows, Sammi Davis, Sara Langton & Geraldine Muir; ★★★★

Hope Floats (1998); Director: Forest Whitaker; Writer: Steven Rogers; Actor: Mae Whitman; ★☆

Horse for Danny, a (1995); Director: Dick Lowry; Writer: Remi Aubuchon; Actor: Leelee Sobieski; ★☆

Horse Whisperer, the (1998); Director: Robert Redford; Writer: Eric Roth, Richard LaGravenese; Story: Nicholas Evans; Actor: Scarlett Johansson; ★★★☆

Hounddog (2008); Director: Deborah Kampmeier; Writer: Deborah Kampmeier; Actor: Dakota Fanning & Isabelle Fuhrman; ★★★☆

How to Kill your Neighbor's Dog (2000); Director: Michael Kalesniko; Writer: Michael Kalesniko; Actor: Suzi Hofrichter; ★★

I am Slave (2010); Director: Gabriel Range; Writer: Jeremy Brock; Story: Mende Nazer; Actor: Natalie Mghoi; ★★★

I Know Where I'm Going (1945); Director: Michael Powell & Emeric Pressburger; Writer: Michael Powell & Emeric Pressburger; Actor: Petula Clark; ★★☆

I love you, I love you not (1996); Director: Billy Hopkins; Writer: Wendy Kesselman; Story: Wendy Kesselman; Actor: Claire Danes; ★

Ice Palace, the (Is-Slottet) (1987); Director: Per Blom; Story: Tarjei Vesaas; Actor: Line Storesund & Hilde Nyeggen Martinsen; ★★★

I'm not scared (Io non ho paura) (2003); Director: Gabrielle Salvatores; Story: Niccolò Ammaniti; Actor: Guiseppe Cristiano & Mattio di Pierro; ★★★

Imagine That (2008); Director: Karey Fitzpatrick; Writer: Ed Solomon & Chris Matheson; Actor: Yara Shahida; ★★

Imitation of Life (1959); Director: Doug Sirk; Writer: Eleanor Griffin & Allan Scott; Story: Fannie Hurst; Actor: Karen Dicker & Terry Burnham; ★★☆

Impudent Girl, an (L'effrontée) (1985); Director: Claude Miller; Writer: Claude Miller, Luc Béraud, Bernard Stora & Annie Miller; Actor: Charlotte Gainsbourg, Clothilde Baudon & Julie Glenn; ★★★★☆

In a Stranger's Hand (1991); Director: David Greene; Writer: Matthew Bombeck; Story: Matt Benjamin; Actor: Drica Dill; ★

In America (2003); Director: Jim Sheridan; Writer: Jim, Naomi & Kirsten Sheridan; Actor: Sarah & Emma Bolger; ★★★★

In Search of the Castaways (1962); Director: Robert Stevenson; Writer: Lowell S Hawley; Story: Jules Verne; Actor: Haley Mills & Michael Anderson Jr.; ★★☆

Ingenious (2009); Director: Brian Kelly; Writer: Jeanette Winterton; Actor: Hannah Godfrey, Keaton Lansley & Leah Sheshadri; ★★

Inn of the 6th Happiness (1958); Director: Mark Robson; Writer: Isobel Lennart; Story: Alan Burgess; ★★★

Innocence (2004); Director: Lucile Hadzihalilovic; Writer: Lucile Hadzihalilovic; Story: Frank Wedekind; Actor: Berangere Haibruge, Lia Bridarolli, Zoé Anclair & Ana Paloma Diaz; ★★★☆

Innocents, the (1961); Director: Jack Clayton; Writer: William Archibald; Story: Henry James; Actor: Martin Stephens & Pamela Franklin; ★★★☆

Interview with the Vampire (1994); Director: Neil Jordan; Writer: Anne Rice; Story: Anne Rice; Actor: Kirsten Dunst; ★★★

It's a Wonderful Life (1946); Director: Frank Capra; Writer: Frank Capra; Story: Philip Van Doren Stern; Actor: Bobbie Anderson, Jean Gale, Karolyn Grimes, Carol Coomes & Jeanine Ann Roose; ★★★★★

Jack (2003); Director: Lee Rose; Writer: A M Homes; Story: A M Homes; Actor: Anton Yelchin & Britt Irvin; ★★☆

Jack Frost (1998); Director: Troy Miller; Writer: Steve Bloom, Jonathan Roberts, Mark Steven Johnson & Jeff Cesario; Story: Mark Steven Johnson; Actor: Joseph Cross & Mika Boorem; ★★

Jakob the Liar (1999); Director: Peter Kassovitz; Writer: Peter Kassovitz & Didier Decoin; Story: Jurek Becker; Actor: Hannah Taylor Gordon; ★★☆

James and the Giant Peach (1996); Director: Henry Selick; Writer: Steven Bloom & Jonathan Roberts; Story: Roald Dahl; Actor: Paul Terry; ★★☆

Jane Eyre (1943); Director: Robert Stevenson; Writer: Aldous Huxley, Robert Stevenson & John Houseman; Story: Charlotte Brontë; Actor: Margaret O'Brien, Peggy Ann Garner & Elizabeth Taylor; ★★★★

Jane Eyre (1997); Director: Robert Young; Writer: Richard Hawley, Kay Mellor & Peter Wright; Story: Charlotte Brontë; Actor: Laura Harling, Gemma Edlington & Timia Berthome; ★★

Jean de Florette / Manon de Source (1986); Director: Claude Berri; Writer: Gérard Brach & Claude Berri; Story: Marcel Pagnol; Actor: Ernestine Mazurowna; ★★★☆

Joey (1997); Director: Ian Barry; Writer: Maxwell Grant & Stuart Beattie; Actor: Jamie Croft & Alex McKenna; ★★

Johnny Mad Dog (2008); Director: Jean-Stéphane Sauvaire; Writer: Jean-Stéphane Sauvaire & Jacques Fieschi; Actor: Daisy Victoria Vandy; ★★☆

Journey of Natty Gann (1985); Director: Jeremy Kagan; Writer: Jeanne Rosenberg; Actor: Meredith Salenger; ★★★

Journey to the Centre of the Earth (2008); Director: Eric Brevig; Writer: Michael Weiss, Jennifer Flackett, Mark Levin; Story: Jules Verne; Actor: Josh Hutcherson; ★★☆

Julia (2008); Director: Erick Zonca; Writer: Aude Py & Erick Zonca; Actor: Aidan Gould; ★☆

Jumanji (1995); Director: Joe Johnson; Writer: Jonathan Hensleigh, Greg Taylor & Jim Strain; Story: Chris Van Allsburg; Actor: Kirsten Dunst, Adam Hann-Byrd, Bradley Pierce & Laura Bell Bundy; ★★★☆

Jungle Book, the (1942); Director: Zoltan Korda; Writer: Laurence Stallings; Story: Rudyard Kipling; Actor: Sabu & Patricia O'Rourke; ★★☆

Jungle 2 Jungle (1997); Director: John Pasquin; Writer: Bruce A Evans & Raynold Gideon; Story: Hervé Palud, Thierry Lhermitte, Igor Aptekman & Philippe Bruneau de la Salle; Actor: Sam Huntington & Leelee Sobieski; ★★☆

Juno (2007); Director: Jason Reitman; Writer: Diablo Cody; Actor: Ellen Page; ★★★★

Jurassic Park (1993); Director: Steven Spielberg; Writer: Michael Crichton & David Koepp; Story: Michael Crichton; Actor: Ariana Richards & Joseph Mazzello; ★★★★☆

Kes (1969); Director: Kenneth Lloyd; Writer: Kenneth Loach, Tony Garnett & Barry Hines; Story: Barry Hines; Actor: David Bradley; ★★★★☆

kids (1995); Director: Larry Clark; Writer: Harmony Korine; Story: Larry Clark & Jim Lewis; Actor: Leo Fitzpatrick, Sarah Henderson & Yajira Peguero; ★★★☆

Killer of sheep (1977); Director: Charles Burnett; Writer: Charles Burnett; Actor: Angela Burnett; ★☆

Kiss at Midnight, a (2008); Director: Bradford May; Writer: Anna Sandor; Actor: Jadin Gould & Abigail Mavity; ★★☆

Knights of the South Bronx (2005); Director: Allen Hughes; Writer: Jamal Joseph & Dianne Houston; Story: Jamal Joseph; Actor: Keke Palmer; ★★☆

Kramer v Kramer (1979); Director: Robert Benton; Writer: Robert Benton; Story: Avery Corman; Actor: Justin Henry; ★★★★

Lassie (2005); Director: Charles Sturridge; Writer: Charles Sturridge; Story: Major Eric Knight; Actor: Jonathan Mason & Hester Odgers; ★★★★

Lassie Come Home (1943); Director: Fred M Wilcox; Writer: Hugo Butler; Story: Major Eric Knight; Actor: Roddy McDowell & Elizabeth Taylor; ★★★☆

Last Mimzy, the (2007); Director: Bob Shaye; Writer: Bruce Joel Rubin & Toby Emmerich; Story: James V Hart, Carol Skilken & Lewis Padgett; Actor: Chris O'Neil & Rhiannon Leigh Wryn; ★★★☆

Last time I saw Paris (1954); Director: Richard Brooks; Writer: Philip & Julius Epstein & Richard Brooks; Story: F Scott Fitzgerald; Actor: Sandy Descher; ★☆

Laurin (1988); Director: Robert Sigl; Writer: Robert Sigl; Actor: Dora Szinetar & Barnabas Toth; ★

Lawn Dogs (1997); Director: John Duigan; Writer: Naomi Wallace; Actor: Mischa Barton; ★★★★

Lemony Snicket's A Series of Unfortunate Events (2005); Director: Brad Silberling; Writer: Robert Gordon; Story: Lemony Snicket; Actor: Liam Aiken & Emily Browning; ★★★

Lena: My 100 children (2004); Director: Ed Sherin; Writer: Jonathan Rintels Jr, Yabo Yablonsky & Maurice Hurley; Story: Lena Kuchler Silberman; ★★

Leon (1994); Director: Luc Besson; Writer: Luc Besson; Actor: Natalie Portman; ★★★★☆

Let me In (2011); Director: Matt Reeves; Writer: Matt Reeves; Story: John Ajvide Lindqvist; Actor: Kodi Smit-McPhee & Chloë Moretz; ★★★☆

Let the right one in (2009); Director: Tomas Alfredson; Writer: John Ajvide Lindqvist; Story: John Ajvide Lindqvist; Actor: Lina Leandersson; ★★★★

Liar Liar (1997); Director: Tom Shadyac; Writer: Paul Guay & Stephen Mazur; Actor: Justin Cooper; ★★★

Liar, Liar (1992); Director: Jorge Montesil; Writer: Nancy Isaak; Actor: Vanessa King; ★★★☆

Life-Size (1999); Director: Mark Rosman; Writer: Mark Rosman & Stephanie Moore; Story: Stephanie Moore; Actor: Lindsay Lohan; ★★★

Lilya 4-ever (2002); Director: Lukas Moodysson; Writer: Lukas Moodysson; Actor: Oksana Akinshina; ★★★

Little Girl who lives down the Lane, the (1976); Director: Nicolas Gressner; Writer: Laird Koenig; Story: Laird Koenig; Actor: Jodie Foster; ★★★☆

Little House on the Prairie (1974); Director: Michael Landon; Writer: John Hawkins, Juanita Bartlett & Ward Hawkins; Story: Laura Ingalls Wilder; Actor: Melissa Gilbert, Melissa Anderson & Alison Arngrim; ★★

Little Lips (Piccole Labbra) (1978); Director: Domenico Cattarinich; Writer: Daniele Sánchez; Actor: Katya Berger; ★★★

Little Manhattan (2005); Director: Mark Levin; Writer: Jennifer Flackett; Actor: Josh Hutcherson & Charlie Ray; ★★★★

Little Miss Sunshine (2006); Director: Jonathan Dayton & Valerie Faris; Writer: Michael Arndt; Actor: Abigail Breslin; ★★★

Little Otik (Otesánek) (2000); Director: Jan Švankmajer; Writer: Jan Švankmajer; Story: Jan Švankmajer; Actor: Kristina Adamcova; ★★★

Little Princess (1995); Director: Alfonso Cuarón; Writer: Richard LeGravenese & Elizabeth Chandler; Story: Frances Hodgson Burnett; Actor: Liesel Matthews, Vanessa Lee Chester & Camilla Belle; ★★★★☆

Little Rascals (1994); Director: Penelope Spheeris; Writer: Paul Guay, Steven Mazur & Penelope Spheeris,; Story: Penelope Spheeris, Robert Wolterstorff, Mike Scott, Paul Guay & Steven Mazur; Actor: Bug Hall & Britanny Ashton Holmes; ★★☆

Little Secrets (2001); Director: Blair Treu; Writer: Jessica Barrondes; Actor: Wood, Evan Rachel; ★★

Little Unicorn (1999); Director: Paul Matthews; Writer: Paul Matthews; Actor: Brittney Bomann & Byron Taylor; ★☆

Little Women (1994); Director: Gillian Armstrong; Writer: Robin Swicord; Story: Louisa May Alcott; Actor: Winona Ryder, Claire Danes & Kirsten Dunst; ★★★

Lolita (1997); Director: Adman Lyne; Writer: Stephen Schiff; Story: Vladimir Nabokov; Actor: Dominique Swaine; ★★★☆

London to Brighton (2006); Director: Paul Andrew Williams; Writer: Paul Andrew Williams; Actor: Georgia Groome; ★★★★

Long Day Closes (1992); Director: Terence Davies; Writer: Terence Davies; Actor: Leigh McCormack; ★★☆

Lord of the Flies (1962); Director: Peter Brook; Writer: Peter Brook; Story: William Golding; Actor: James Aubrey, Tom Chapin & Hugh Edwards; ★★

Lord of the Flies (1990); Director: Harry Hook; Writer: Sara Schiff; Story: William Golding; Actor: Balthazar Getty, Chris Furrh & Daniel Pipoly; ★★★

Lorenzo's Oil (1992); Director: George Miller; Writer: George Miller & Nick Enright; Actor: Zack O'Malley Greenberg; ★★★

Lost in New York (1989); Director: Jean Rollin; ☆

Lost in Space (1998); Director: Stephen Hopkins; Writer: Akiva Goldsman; Actor: Lacey Chabert & Jack Johnson; ★☆

Lost World: Jurassic Park (1997); Director: Steven Spielberg; Writer: David Koepp; Story: Michael Crichton; Actor: Vanessa Lee Chester & Camilla Belle; ★★★

Lovely Bones, the (2009); Director: Peter Jackson; Writer: Peter Jackson, Fran Walsh & Philippa Boyens; Story: Alice Sebold; Actor: Saoirse Ronan & Stephanie Owen; ★★★

Lovers of the Arctic Circle (1998); Director: Julio Moden; Writer: Julio Moden; Actor: Peru Medem, Sara Valiente, Victor Hugo Oliviera & Kristel Diaz; ★★★

Magdalene Sisters (2002); Director: Peter Mullan; Writer: Peter Mullan; ★★★☆

Magic Door, the (2004); Director: Paul Matthews; Writer: Paul Matthews; Actor: Liam & Alix Matthews; ★

Magic Island (1995); Director: Sam Irvin; Writer: Neil Ruttenberg & Brent V. Friedman; Actor: Zachery Ty Brian & Jessie-Ann Friend; ★★☆

Malèna (2000); Director: Guiseppe Tornatoro; Writer: Guiseppe Tornatoro; Actor: Guiseppe Sulfaro; ★★★

Man in the Moon (1991); Director: Robert Mulligan; Writer: Jenny Wingfield; Actor: Reese Witherspoon; ★★★

Man on Fire (2004); Director: Terry Scott; Writer: Brian Helgeland; Story: A J Quinnell; Actor: Dakota Fanning; ★★★

Man who sued God, the (2001); Director: Mark Joffe; Writer: Don Watson; Story: John Clarke & Patrick McCarville; Actor: Emily Browning; ★★☆

Man Without a Face (1993); Director: Mel Gibson; Writer: Malcolm MacRury; Story: Isabelle Holland; Actor: Nick Stahl & Gaby Hoffman; ★★★☆

Mandy (1952); Director: Alexander Mackendrick; Writer: Nigel Balchin & Jack Whittingham; Story: Hilda Lewis; Actor: Mandy Miller; ★★★★

Manny & Lo (1996); Director: Lisa Krueger; Writer: Lisa Krueger; Actor: Scarlett Johansson; ★★☆

Mary Poppins (1964); Director: Robert Stevenson; Writer: Bill Walsh & Don DaGrady; Story: P L Travers; Actor: Matthew Garber & Karen Dotrice; ★★★★☆

Matilda (1996); Director: Danny Devito; Writer: Nicholas Kazan & Robin Swicord; Story: Roald Dahl; Actor: Mara Wilson; ★★☆

Me without you (2001); Director: Sandra Goldbacher; Writer: Sandra Goldbacher & Laurence Coriat; Actor: Ella Jones & Anna Popplewell; ★★☆

Meet me in St Louis (1944); Director: Vincente Minnelli; Writer: Irving Brecher & Fred Finklehoffe; Story: Sally Benson; Actor: Margaret O'Brien & Joan Carroll; ★★★★★

Melissa P (100 strokes of the brush before bed) (2005); Director: Luca Guadagnino; Writer: Barbara Alberti, Christiana Farini & Luca Guadagnino; Story: Melissa P; Actor: Marie Valverde; ★☆

Melody (1971); Director: Waris Hussein; Writer: Alan Parker & Andrew Birkin; Actor: Mark Lester, Jack Wild & Tracy Hyde; ★★★☆

Memoirs of a Geisha (2005); Director: Rob Marshall; Writer: Robin Swicord; Story: Arthur Golden; Actor: Suzuka Ohgo; ★★★☆

Mermaids (1990); Director: Richard Benjamin; Writer: June Roberts; Story: Patty Dann; Actor: Winona Ryder & Christina Ricci; ★★★

Messengers (2007); Director: Danny & Oxide Pang; Writer: Mark Wheaton; Story: Todd Farmer; Actor: Kristen Stewart & Jodelle Ferland; ★☆

Millions (2004); Director: Danny Boyle; Writer: Frank Cottrell Boyce; Actor: Alex Etel & Lewis McGibbon; ★★★★

Miracle on 34th Street (1947); Director: George Seaton; Writer: George Seaton; Story: Valentine Davies; Actor: Natalie Wood; ★★★★☆

Miracle on 34th Street (1994); Director: Les Mayfield; Writer: John Hughes; Story: Valentine Davies; Actor: Mara Wilson & Samantha Krieger; ★★★

Miracle Worker, the (1962); Director: Arthur Penn; Writer: William Gibson; Story: Helen Keller; Actor: Patty Duke; ★★★★☆

Mischief Night (2006); Director: Penny Woolcock; Writer: Penny Woolcock; Actor: Holly Kenny & Qasim Akhtar; ★★★☆

Misérables, les (1998); Director: Billy August; Writer: Rafael Yglesias; Story: Victor Hugo; Actor: Clare Danes & Mimi Newman; ★★

Miss Potter (2006); Director: Chris Noonan; Writer: Richard Maltby Jr; Story: Beatrix Potter; Actor: Lucy Boynton; ★★★

Missing, the (2003); Director: Ron Howard; Writer: Ken Kaufman; Story: Thomas Eidson; Actor: Jenna Boyd & Evan Rachel Wood; ★★☆

Mixed Company (1974); Director: Melville Shavelson; Writer: Melville Shavelson & Mort Lachman; Actor: Haywood Nelson, Jina Tan & Ariane Hellen; ★★

Mockingbird Don't Sing (2001); Director: Harry Bromley-Davenport; Writer: Daryl Haney; Actor: Tarra Steele; ★☆

Mom at Sixteen (2005); Director: Peter Werner; Writer: Nancy Silvers; Actor: Clare Stone; ★★☆

Monkey Business (1998); Director: Paulette Victor-Lifton; Writer: Ted Fox & Jimmy Lifton; Actor: Kathren Laurents; ★

Moonfleet (1955); Director: Fritz Lang; Writer: Jan Lustig & Margaret Fitts; Actor: Jon Whiteley & Donna Corcoran; ★★☆

Mosquito Coast (1986); Director: Peter Weir; Writer: Paul Schrader; Story: Paul Theroux; Actor: River Phoenix, Martha Plimpton, Jadrien Steele Hilary & Rebecca Gordon; ★★★

Mr Blandings Builds his Dream House (1948); Director: H C Potter; Writer: Norman Panama & Melvin Frank; Story: Eric Hodgins; Actor: Sharyn Moffett & Connie Marshall; ★★☆

Mr Magorium's Wonder Emporium (2007); Director: Zach Helm; Writer: Zach Helm; Actor: Zach Mills; ★★

Mrs Doubtfire (1993); Director: Chris Columbus; Writer: Randi Mayem Singer & Leslie Dixon; Story: Anne Fine; Actor: Matthew Lawrence, Lisa Jakub & Mara Wilson; ★★★☆

Mummy Returns, the (2001); Director: Stephen Somers; Writer: Stephen Somers; Actor: Freddie Booth; ★★☆

Munchie (1992); Director: Jim Wynorski; Writer: Jim Wynorski & RJ Robertson; Actor: Jaime McEnnan & Love Hewitt; ★☆

My American Cousin (1985); Director: Sandy Wilson; Writer: Sandy Wilson; Actor: Margaret Langrick; ★★★

My brother the pig (1999); Director: Erik Fleming; Writer: Matthew Flynn; Actor: Scarlett Johansson, Nick Fuoco & Alex D Linz; ★☆

My Dog Skip (2000); Director: Jay Russell; Writer: Gail Gilchrist; Story: Willie Morris; Actor: Frankie Muniz, Caitlin Wachs & Elizabeth Rice; ★★★

My Girl (1991); Director: Howard Zeiff; Writer: Laurice Elehwany; Actor: Anna Chlumsky & Macaulay Culkin; ★★★☆

My Girl 2 (1994); Director: Howard Zieff; Writer: Janet Kovalcik; Actor: Anna Chlumsky, Austin O'Brien & Lauren Ashley; ★★☆

My House in Umbria (2002); Director: R Loncraine; Writer: Hugh Whitemore; Story: William Trevor; Actor: Emmy Clarke; ★★★

My Life as a dog (Mit Liv Som Hund) (1985); Director: Lasse Hallström; Writer: Brasse Brönnstöm, Pelle Berglund & Reider Jonsson; Story: Reider Jonsson; Actor: Anton Glanzelius, Melinda Kinnaman & Kiki Rundgren; ★★★★☆

My Queen Karo (2009); Director: Dorothée van den Berghe; Writer: Dorothée van den Berghe; Actor: Anna Franziska Jager; ★★☆

My Sister's Keeper (2009); Director: Nick Cassavetes & Jeremy Leven; Story: Judy Piccoult; Actor: Abigail Breslin, Sofia Vassilieva & Evan Ellingson; ★★★

My Year Without Sex (2009); Director: Sarah Watt; Writer: Sarah Watt; Actor: Jonathan Segat & Portia Bradley; ★★★

Mystery of Natalie Wood, the (2004); Director: Peter Bogdanovich; Writer: Elizabeth Egloff; Story: Suzanne Finstad & Warren G Harris; Actor: Grace Fulton, Elizabeth Rice; ★★★

Nanny McPhee (2005); Director: Kirk Jones; Writer: Emma Thompson; Story: Christianna Brand; Actor: Thomas Sangster, Eliza Bennett, Jennifer Rae Daykin & Holly Gibbs; ★★★☆

Nativity Story, the (2006); Director: Catherine Hardwicke; Writer: Mike Rich; Actor: Keisha Castle-Hughes; ★★

Nativity! (2009); Director: Debbie Isitt; ★★★

Night of the Hunter (1955); Director: Charles Laughton; Writer: James Agee; Story: Davis Grubb; Actor: Billy Chapin & Jane Bruce; ★★★☆

Nim's Island (2008); Director: Mark Levin & Jennifer Flackett; Writer: Mark Levin, Joseph Kwong, Paula Mazur & Jennifer Flackett; Story: Wendy Orr; Actor: Abigail Breslin; ★★★

No more Baths! Kids stand up for a friend (2003); Director: Tim Nelson; Writer: Forrest S Baker III; Actor: Andreas Michael Lamelas & Haley McCormick; ★

No Reservations (2007); Director: Scot Hicks; Writer: Carol Fuch; Story: Sandra Nettelbeck; Actor: Abigail Breslin; ★★

Nobody Knows (2003); Director: Kore-eda Hirokazu; Writer: Kore-eda Hirokazu; Actor: Yuuya Yagira, Ayu Kitaura, Hanae Kan & Momoko Shimizu; ★★★

North Star (1943); Director: Lewis Milestone; Writer: Sergio & Lorenzo Donati, Paul Ohi; Story: Heck Allen; Actor: Jane Withers & Ann Carter; ★☆

Now and Then (1997); Director: Lesli Linka Glatter; Writer: Marlene King; Actor: Thora Birch, Gaby Hoffman, Christina Ricci & Ashleigh Aston Moore ; ★★★☆

Nutcracker, the (2010); Director: Andrei Konchalasky; Writer: Andrei Konchalasky & Chris Solimine; Story: Tchaikovsky; Actor: Elle Fanning; ★★☆

Oliver Twist (1948); Director: David Lean; Writer: David Lean & Stanley Haynes; Story: Charles Dickens; Actor: John Howard Davies; ★★★☆

Oliver Twist (2005); Director: Roman Polanski; Writer: Ronald Haywood; Story: Charles Dickens; Actor: Barney Clark; ★★☆

Oliver! (1968); Director: Carol Reed; Writer: Vernon Harris & Lionel Bart; Story: Charles Dickens; Actor: Mark Lester, Jack Wild; ★★★★

Omen I, the (1976); Director: Richard Donner; Writer: David Seitzer; Actor: Harvey Stephens; ★★☆

One fine day (1996); Director: Michael Hoffman; Writer: Terrel Selzer; Actor: Mae Whitman; ★★

Oranges are not the Only Fruit (1989); Director: Beebon Kidron; Writer: Jeanette Winterson; Story: Jeanette Winterson; Actor: Emily Ashton & Charlotte Coleman; ★★

Orphan (2009); Director: Jaume Collet-Serra; Writer: David Leslie Johnson; Story: Alex Mace; Actor: Isabelle Fuhrmann, Ariana Engineer & Jimmy Bennett; ★★★☆

Others, the (2001); Director: Alejandro Amenábar; Writer: Alejandro Amenábar; Actor: Alakina Mann James Bentley; ★★★☆

Our First Christmas (2008); Director: Armand Mastroianni; Writer: Edithe Swensen; Actor: Maxim Knight, Grace Fulton & Cassi Thomson; ★☆

Page Turner (2006); Director: Denis Dercourt; Writer: Denis Dercourt & Jacques Sotty; Actor: Julie Richalet; ★★☆

Panic Room (2002); Director: David Fincher; Writer: David Koepp; Actor: Kristen Stewart; ★★★

Pan's Labyrinth (El Liberinto de Fauno) (2006); Director: Guillermo del Toro; Writer: Guillermo del Toro; Actor: Ivana Baquero; ★★★★☆

Paper Moon (1973); Director: Peter Bogdanovich; Writer: Alvin Sargent; Story: Joe David Brown; Actor: Tatum O'Neal; ★★★★

Paperhouse (1988); Director: Bernard Rose; Writer: Matthew Jacobs; Story: Catherine Storr; Actor: Charlotte Burke; ★★★☆

Paradise (1991); Director: Mary Agnes Donoghue; Writer: Mary Agnes Donoghue; Actor: Elijah Wood & Thora Birch; ★★★☆

Parent Trap (1961); Director: David Swift; Writer: David Swift; Story: Erich Kästner; Actor: Haley Mills; ★★★

Parent Trap (1998); Director: Nancy Meyers; Writer: Nancy Meyers, Charles Shyer & David Swift; Story: Erich Kästner; Actor: Lindsay Lohan; ★★★☆

Pather Panchali (1955); Director: Satyajit Ray; Writer: Satyajit Ray; Story: Bibhuti Bushan Banerji; Actor: Uma Das Gupta & Runki Banerji; ★★★☆

Peck on the Cheek (Kannathil Mutthamittal) (2002); Director: Mani Rahman; Actor: Keerthana ; ★★★

Peppermint Soda (Diabolo Menthe) (1977); Director: Diane Kurys; Writer: Diane Kurys; Actor: Eleanore Karwien & Odile Michel; ★★☆

Perfect Teacher, the (2010); Director: Jim Donovan; Writer: Christine Conradt; Story: Gregory Henn; Actor: Keeva Lynk; ★☆

Peter Pan (2004); Director: P J Hogan; Writer: P J Hogan & Michael Goldenberg; Story: J M Barrie; Actor: Jeremy Sumpter, Rachel Hurd-Wood & Carsen Gray; ★★★★

Phenomena (aka Creepers) (1984); Director: Dario Argento; Writer: Dario Argento & Franco Ferrini; Actor: Jennifer Connelly; ★

Phoebe in Wonderland (2008); Director: Daniel Barnz; Writer: Daniel Barnz; Actor: Elle Fanning; ★★★☆

Photographing Fairies (1997); Director: Nick Welling; Writer: Chris Harrald & Nick Welling; Story: Steve Szilagyi; Actor: Hannah Bould & Miriam Grant; ★★★☆

Piano, the (1993); Director: Jane Campion; Writer: Jane Campion; Actor: Anna Paquin; ★★★★

Pied Piper (1989); Director: Norman Stone; Story: Nevil Shute; Actor: Alastair Haley, Clare Drummond, Dorothée Boeuf & Henriette Baker; ★★★

Pocket Money (L'Argent de Poche)(aka Small Change) (1976); Director: Francois Truffaut; Writer: Francois Truffaut & Suzanne Schiffman; Actor: Geory Desmouceaux, Phillipe Goldman, Pascale Bruchon, Sylvie Grezel, Eva Truffaut & Corinne Boucant; ★★☆

Pollyanna (1960); Director: David Swift; Writer: Frances Marion; Story: Eleonor H Porter; Actor: Haley Mills; ★★★★

Pollyanna (2002); Director: Sarah Harding; Writer: Simon Nye; Story: Eleonor H Porter; Actor: Georgina Terry; ★★★☆

Poltergeist (1982); Director: Tobe Hooper; Writer: Steven Spielberg, Michael Grais & Mark Victor; Story: Steven Spielberg; Actor: Heather O'Rourke; ★★★☆

Poltergeist II: the other side (1986); Director: Brian Gibson; Writer: Mark Victor & Michael Grais; Actor: Heather O'Rourke & Olver Robins; ★★☆

Pretty Baby (1977); Director: Louis Malle; Writer: Polly Platt; Story: Al Rose, William Harrison; Actor: Brooke Shields; ★★★★☆

Prince of Tides (1991); Director: Barbra Streisand; Writer: Pat Conroy & Becky Johnston; Story: Pat Conroy; ★★☆

P'tang, Yang Kipperbang (1982); Director: Michael Apted; Writer: Jack Rosenthal; Actor: John Albasiny & Abigail Cruttenden; ★★★☆

Push (2009); Director: Paul McGuigan; Writer: David Bourla; Actor: Dakota Fanning; ★★

Que la Bête Meure (The Beast Must Die) (1969); Director: Claude Chabrol; Writer: Paul Gegauff & Claude Chabrol; Actor: Marc DiNapoli; ★★☆

Rabbit Proof Fence (2002); Director: Phillip Noyce; Writer: Christine Olsen; Story: Doris Pilkington Garimara; Actor: Everlyn Sampi, Laura Monaghan & Tianna Sansbury; ★★★☆

Race to Witch Mountain (2009); Director: Andy Fickman; Writer: Matt Lopez & Mark Bomback; Story: Alexander Kay; Actor: Alexander Ludwig & AnnaSophia Robb; ★★★

Rag Nymph (1997); Director: David Wheatley; Writer: T R Bowen; Story: Catherine Cookson; Actor: Perdita Weeks; ★★

Railway Children, the (1970); Director: Lionel Jeffries; Writer: Lionel Jeffries; Story: E Nesbit; Actor: Jenny Agutter, Sally Thomsett & Gary Warren; ★★★★★

Railway Children, the (2000); Director: Catherine Morshead; Writer: Simon Nye; Story: E Nesbit; Actor: Jamima Rooper, Claire Thomas & Jack Blumenau; ★★★☆

Ratcatcher, the (1999); Director: Lynne Ramsay; Writer: Lynne Ramsay; Actor: William Earle, Lynne Ramsay (Jr), Leanne Mullen & Michelle Stewart; ★★★☆

Reaping, the (2007); Director: Stephen Hopkins; Writer: Carey & Chad Hayes; Story: Brian Rousso; Actor: AnnaSophia Robb; ★★★

Rebel without a Cause (1955); Director: Nicholas Ray; Writer: Stewart Stern; Story: Robert M Lindner, Irving Shulman; Actor: James Dean & Natalie Wood; ★★★☆

Resident Evil: Apocalypse (2004); Director: Alexander Watt; Writer: Paul WS Anderson; Actor: Sophie Vavasseur; ★

Return to Oz (1985); Director: Wakter Murch; Writer: Walter Murch & Gill Dennis; Story: Frank Baum; Actor: Fairuza Balk & Emma Ridley; ★★★☆

Return to the Blue Lagoon (1991); Director: William A Graham; Writer: Leslie Stevens; Story: Henry de Vere Stacpoole; Actor: Garette Patrick Ratliff & Courtney Phillips; ★★

Ring of Endless Light, a (2002); Director: Greg Beeman; Writer: Marita Giovanni & Bruce Graham; Story: Madelaine D'Engle; Actor: Mischa Barton, Scarlett Pomers & James Whitmore; ★☆

Roxy Hunter & the Secret of the Shaman (2007); Director: Eleanore Lindo; Writer: Robin Dunne & James Kee; Actor: Aria Wallace; ★

Run the Wild Fields (1999); Director: Paul Kaufman; Writer: Rodney Vaccaro; Story: Rodney Vaccaro; Actor: Alexa Vega; ★☆

Russkies (1987); Director: Rick Rosenthal; Writer: Alan Jay Glueckman, Sheldon Lettich & Michael Ninkin; Actor: Leaf & Summer Phoenix, Peter Billingsley, Stefan DeSalle & Whip Hubley; ★★☆

RV: Runaway Vacation (2006); Director: Barry Sonnenfeld; Writer: Geoff Rodkey; Actor: Josh Hutcherson, Joanna 'Jojo' Levesque & Chloe Sonnenfeld; ★★

Sacrifices of the Heart (2005); Director: David Cass Sr; Writer: Patti Davis; Actor: Chase Wilmot; ★

Safety of Objects (2001); Director: Rose Trouch; Writer: Rose Trouch; Story: A M Homes; Actor: Alex House, Kristen Stewart & Charlotte Arnold; ★★

Samson & Delilah (2009); Director: Warwick Thornton; Writer: Warwick Thornton; Actor: Rowan McNamara & Narissa Gibson; ★★★

Sandlot Kids (1993); Director: David Mickey Evans; Writer: David Mickey Evans & Robert Gunter; Actor: Tom Guiry; ★

Schindler's List (1993); Director: Steven Spielberg; Writer: Steven Zaillian; Story: Thomas Keneally; Actor: Anna Mucha & Magdalena Dandaurian; ★★★☆

School of Rock (2003); Director: Richard Linklater; Writer: Mike White; Actor: Miranda Cosgrove, Kevin Clark, Aleisha Allen, Caitlin Hale, Jaclyn Neidenthal, Jordan-Claire Green, Maryam Hassan & Rebecca Brown; ★★★★☆

Scrooge (1951); Director: Brian Desmond-Hurst; Writer: Noel Langley; Story: Charles Dickens; Actor: Glynn Dearman; ★★☆

Searchers, the (1956); Director: John Ford; Writer: Frank S Nugent; Story: Alan LeMay; Actor: Natalie & Lana Wood; ★★★★

Secret Garden, the (1949); Director: Fred M Wilcox; Writer: Robert Ardrey; Story: Frances Hodgson Burnett; Actor: Margaret O'Brien, Dean Stockwell & Brian Roper; ★★★★

Secret Garden, the (1993); Director: Agnieszka Holland; Writer: Caroline Thompson; Story: Frances Hodgson Burnett; Actor: Kate Maberly, Heydon Prowse & Andrew Knott; ★★★★☆

Secret Life of Bees (2008); Director: Gina Prince-Blythewood; Writer: Gina Prince-Blythewood; Story: Sue Monk Kidd; Actor: Dakota Fanning & Nate Parker; ★★★☆

Sense and Sensibility (1995); Director: Ang Lee; Writer: Emma Thompson; Story: Jane Austin; Actor: Emilie François; ★★★★

Seven Years in Tibet (1997); Director: Jean-Jacques Annaud; Writer: Becky Johnston; Story: Heinrich Harrer; Actor: Jamyang Jamsho & Sonam Wangchuk; ★★★

Shadow of Doubt, a (1992); Director: Aline Issermann; Writer: Aline Issermann; Actor: Sandrine Blancke; ★★★★

Shadrach (1998); Director: Susana Styron; Writer: Susana Styron & Bridget Terry; Story: William Styron; Actor: Scott Terra & Monica Bugajski; ★★

Shane (1952); Director: George Stevens; Writer: AB Guthrie Jr & Jack Sher; Story: Jack Schaefer; Actor: Brandon de Wilde; ★★★★☆

Shattered Family (1993); Director: Sandy Smolan; Writer: Blair Ferguson; Actor: Tom Guiry & Colleen Ford; ★☆

Shattered Silence (2012); Director: John Stimpson; Writer: Marcy Holland & John Stimpson; Actor: Jenn Proske; ★☆

She's the Man (2005); Director: Andy Fickman; Writer: Ewan Leslie, Karen McCullah Lutz & Kirsten Smith; Story: Ewan Leslie; Actor: Amanda Bynes; ★★

Silent Hill (2006); Director: Christopher Gans; Writer: Roger Avary; Story: Christopher Gans & Nicolas Boukrief; Actor: Jodelle Ferland; ★★★

Single Santa Meets Mrs Claus (2004); Director: Harvey Frost; Writer: Pamela Wallace; Actor: Dominic Scott Kay, Mackenzie Fitzgerald & Katie Coe; ★★

Sixth Sense (1999); Director: M Night Shyamalan; Writer: M Night Shyamalan; Actor: Haley Joel Osment & Mischa Barton; ★★★★☆

Skin (2008); Director: Anthony Fabia; Writer: Helen Crawley, Jessie Keyt & Helena Kriel; Actor: Ella Ramangwane; ★★★

Slumdog Milllionaire (2008); Director: Danny Boyle; Writer: Simon Beaufoy; Actor: Ayush Makesh Khedekar, Azharuddin Mohamad Ismail, Rubina Ali & Tanvi Ganesh Lonkar; ★★★★

Snow Day (2000); Director: Kris Koch; Writer: Will McRobb & Chris Viscardi; Actor: Mark Webber & Zena Grey; ★★★

So dear to my heart (1948); Director: Harold Schuster; Writer: John Tucker Battle, Maurice Rapf & Ted Sears; Story: Sterling North; Actor: Bobby Driscoll & Luana Patten; ★★★

Son of Babylon (2009); Director: Mohamed Al-Daradji; Writer: Jennifer Norridge, Mohamed Al-Daradji & Mithan Ghaza; Actor: Yasser Talib; ★★★☆

Son of Ranbow (2007); Director: Garth Jennings; Writer: Garth Jennings; Actor: Bill Milner, Will Poulter & Jules Sitruk; ★★★☆

Song of the South (1946); Director: Wilfred Jackson & Harve Foster; Writer: Dalton Raymond, Morton Grant & Maurice Rapf; Story: Joel Chandler Harris; Actor: Bobby Driscoll & Luana Patten; ★★★

Sorcerer's Apprentice, the (2001); Director: David Lister; Writer: Brett Morris; Actor: Byron Taylor & Roxanne Burger; ★☆

Sound of Music (1965); Director: Robert Wise; Writer: Ernest Lehman; Story: Richard Rogers, Oscar Hammerstein, Howard Lindsay & Russel Crouse; Actor: Nicholas Hammond, Duane Chase, Angela Cartwright, Charmain Carr, Debbie Turner, Heather Menzies & Kym Karath; ★★★★★

Spirit of the Beehive (1973); Director: Victor Erice; Writer: Francisco J Querejeta; Actor: Ana Torrent & Isabel Telleria; ★★★★

St Trinian's (2007); Director: Oliver Parker & Barnaby Thomson; Writer: Piers Ashworth & Nick Moorcroft; Story: Ronald Searle; Actor: Talulah Riley, Mischa Barton, Chloe & Holly Mackie; ★★

Stand by Me (1986); Director: Rob Reiner; Writer: Reynold Gideon & Bruce A Evans; Story: Stephen King; Actor: Wil Weaton, River Phoenix, Corey Feldman & Jerry O'Connell; ★★★★☆

Station Agent, the (2003); Director: Tom McCarthy; Writer: Tom McCarthy; Actor: Raven Goodwin; ★★☆

Stepmom (1998);   Director: Christopher Columbus;   Writer: Gigi Levangie, Jessie Nelson,Steven Rogers,Karen Leigh Hopkins & Ron Bass; Story: Gigi Levangie; Actor: Jena Malone & Liam Aiken; ★★★☆

Stolen (2011); Director: Justin Chadwick; Writer: Stephen Butchard; Actor: Inokentijs Vitkevics, Gloria Oyewumi & Jessie Clayton; ★★★

Stolen Children (1992); Director: Gianni Amelio; Writer: Sandro Petraglia, Stefano Rulli & Gianni Amelio; Actor: Valentina Scalici & Guiseppe Ieracitano; ★★★☆

Stormbreaker (2006); Director: Geoffrey Sax; Writer: Anthony Horowitz; Story: Anthony Horowitz; Actor: Alex Pettyfer & Sarah Bolger; ★★☆

Story of an African Farm (2004); Director: David Lister; Writer: Thandi Brewer & Bonnie Rodini; Story: Olive Schreiner; Actor: Kasha Kropinski, Anneke Weidemann & Luke Gallant; ★★☆

StreetDance (2010); Director: Max & Dania; Writer: Jane English; Actor: George Sampson; ★★★☆

Sundays & Cybele (1962); Director: Serge Bourguignon; Writer: Antoine Tudal, Serge Bourguignon & Bernard Eschasseriaux; Story: Bernard Eschasseriaux; Actor: Patricia Gozzi; ★★★☆

Super 8 (2011); Director: J J Abrams; Writer: J J Abrams; Story: ; Actor: Joel Courtney & Elle Fanning; ★★★★

Susannah of the Mounties (1938); Director: William A Seiter; Writer: Robert Ellis & Helen Logan; Story: Muriel Denison, Fidel La Barba & Walter Feris; Actor: Shirley Temple & Martin Good Rider; ★☆

Swallow and Amazons (1974); Director: Claude Whatham; Writer: David Wood; Story: Arthur Ransome; Actor: Simon West, Zanna Hamilton & Sophie Neville; ★★★

Switching Goals (1999); Director: David Steinberg; Writer: David Kukoff & Matt Roshkow; Story: ; Actor: Ashley & Mary-Kate Olsen; ★★☆

Taxi Driver (1996); Director: Martin Scorsese; Writer: Paul Schrader; Actor: Jodie Foster; ★★★★

Tendre Cousines (Cousins in Love) (1980); Director: David Hamilton; Actor: Thierry Tevini & Valerie Dumas; ★

That Night (1992); Director: Craig Bolotin; Writer: Craig Bolotin & Alice McDermott; Story: Alice McDermott; Actor: Eliza Dushku, Katherine Heigl & Sarah Joy Stevenson; ★★★☆

There will be blood (2007); Director: Thomas Anderson; Writer: Thomas Anderson; Story: Upton Sinclair; Actor: Dillon Freasier & Sydney McCallister; ★★★

They Come back (2007); Director: John Bradshaw; Writer: Gary Boulton-Brown; Actor: Niamh Wilson; ★★☆

Thirteen (2003); Director: Catherine Hardwicke; Writer: Nikki Reed & Catherine Hardwicke; Actor: Evan Rachel Wood & Nikki Reed; ★★★

32A (2007); Director: Marian Quinn; Writer: Marian Quinn; Actor: Ailish McCarthy & Sophie Jo Wasson; ★★☆

This is England (2006); Director: Shane Meadows; Writer: Shane Meadows; Actor: Thomas Turgoose; ★★★☆

Tideland (2005); Director: Terry Gilliam; Writer: Terry Gilliam & Tony Grisoni; Story: Mitch Cullin; Actor: Jodelle Ferland; ★★★☆

Tiger Bay (1959); Director: J Lee Thompson; Writer: John Hawkesworth & Shelley Smith; Story: Noel Calef; Actor: Haley Mills; ★★★☆

Tightrope (1984); Director: Richard Tuggle; Writer: Richard Tuggle; Actor: Alison Eastwood & Jennifer Beck; ★★

Time Bandits (1981); Director: Terry Gilliam; Writer: Michael Palin & Terry Gilliam; Actor: Craig Warnock; ★★

Time to Kill, a (1996); Director: Joel Schumacher; Writer: Akiva Goldsman; Story: John Grisham; Actor: Raeven Larrymore Kelly & ; ★★☆

Time Traveller's Wife (2008); Director: Robert Schwentke; Writer: Bruce Joel Rubin; Story: Audrey Niffenegger; Actor: Brooklyn Proulx, Hailey & Tatum McCann; ★★

Times and Winds (Bes Vakit) (2007); Director: Reha Erdem; Writer: Reha Erdem; Actor: Özkan Özen, Elit Işcan & Ali Bey Kayali; ★★★

Timescape (1991); Director: David N Twohy; Writer: David N Twohy; Story: Lawrence O'Donnell & C L Moore; Actor: Ariana Richards; ★★

To Kill a Mockingbird (1962); Director: Robert Mulligan; Writer: Horton Foote; Story: Harper Lee; Actor: Mary Badham, Philip Alford & John Megna; ★★★★☆

Tomboy (2011); Director: Céline Sciamma; Writer: Céline Sciamma; Actor: Zoé Héran, Jeanne Disson & Malonn Lévana; ★★★★☆

Toto le Héros (1991); Director: Jaco Van Dormael; Writer: Jaco Van Dormael; Actor: Thomas Godet & Sandrine Blancke; ★★★★

Treasure Seekers, the (1996); Director: Juliet May; Story: Enid Nesbit; Actor: Felicity Jones & Keira Knightley; ★

Tremors (1989); Director: Ron Underwood; Writer: SS Wilson & Brent Maddock; Story: SS Wilson; Actor: Ariana Richards; ★★★

True Grit (2010); Director: Joel Coen & Ethan Coel; Writer: Joel Coen & Ethan Coel; Story: Charles Portis; Actor: Hailee Steinfeld; ★★★★

Turn of the Screw (1999); Director: Ben Bolt; Story: Henry James; Actor: Joe Sowerbutts & Grace Robinson; ★★☆

Turn of the Screw (2009); Director: Tim Fywell; Writer: Sandy Welch; Story: Henry James; Actor: Josef Lindsay & Eva Sayer; ★★★

Uncle Buck (1989); Director: John Hughes; Writer: John Hughes; Actor: Macaulay Culkin, Gaby Hoffman & Jean Louisa Kelly; ★★★

Under the Mud (2006); Director: Solon Papodopoulos; Actor: Jasmine Mubory; ★★

Unfinished Life (an) (2005); Director: Lasse Hallström; Writer: Mark & Virginia Korus Spragg; Story: Mark Spragg; Actor: Becca Garner; ★★

Untamed Love (1994); Director: Paul Aaron; Writer: Peter Nelson; Story: Torey Hayden; Actor: Ashlee Lauren; ★★☆

Urban Ghost Story (1998); Director: Genevieve Joliffe; Writer: Chris Jones; Story: Genevieve Joliffe; Actor: Heather Ann Foster; ★★★

Village of the Damned (1995); Director: J Carpenter; Writer: David Himmelstein; Story: John Wyndham; Actor: Lindsey Haun; ★

Wah-Wah (2005); Director: Richard E Grant; Writer: Richard E Grant; Actor: Zac Fox & Nicholas Hoult; ★★★☆

Walkabout (1971); Director: Nicolas Roeg; Writer: Edward Bond; Story: James Vance Marshall; Actor: Jenny Agutter & Lucien John; ★★★★★

War of the Worlds (2005); Director: Steven Spielberg; Writer: David Koepp; Story: HG Wells; Actor: Justin Chatwin & Dakota Fanning; ★★★★

Water (2005); Director: Deepa Mehta; Writer: Deepa Mehta; Actor: Sarala ; ★★★

Water Babies, the (1978); Director: Lionel Jeffries; Writer: Michael Robson; Story: Charles Kingsley; Actor: Tommy Pender & Samantha Gates; ★

Water Lilies (Naissance des Pieuvres) (2008); Director: Céline Sciamma; Writer: Céline Sciamma; Actor: Pauline Acquart, Adèle Haenel & Louise Bianchere; ★★★★

Waterworld (1995); Director: Kevin Reynolds; Writer: Peter Rader, David Twohy & Joss Whedon; Actor: Tina Majorino; ★★★☆

Well, the (1951); Director: Leo C Popkin & Russell Rouse; Writer: Russell Rouse & Clarence Green; Actor: Gwendoline Laster; ★★☆

Whale Rider (2002); Director: Niki Caro; Writer: Niki Caro; Story: Witi Ihimaera; Actor: Keisha Castle-Hughes; ★★★★

When Zachary Beaver came to town (2003); Director: John Schultz; Writer: John Schultz; Story: Kimberley Willis Holt; Actor: Jonathan Lipnicki, Sasha Neulinger, Amanda Alch & Joanna McCray; ★★

Whistle down the Wind (1961); Director: Bryan Forbes; Writer: Keith Waterhouse & Willis Hall; Story: Mary Bell; Actor: Haley Mills, Alan Barnes & Diane Holgate; ★★★★

Wicker Man, the (1973); Director: Robin Hardy; Writer: Anthony Shaffer; Actor: Geraldine Cowper & Jennifer Martin; ★★☆

Wild Child (2008); Director: Nick Moore; Writer: Lucy Dahl; Actor: Emma Roberts; ★★

Wizard of Oz, the (1939); Director: Victor Fleming; Writer: Noel Langley, Florence Ryerson & Edgar Allan Woolf; Story: Frank Baum; Actor: Judy Garland; ★★★★★

Woodsman, the (2005); Director: Nicole Kassell; Writer: Nicole Kassell & Steven Fechter; Story: Steven Fechter; Actor: Hannah Pilkes; ★★★

Wuthering Heights (1992); Director: Peter Kosminsky; Writer: Anne Devin; Story: Emile Brontë; Actor: Jessica Hennell; ★

Wuthering Heights (2003); Director: Coky Giedroyc; Writer: Peter Bowker; Story: Emile Brontë; Actor: Declan Wheeldon, Joseph Taylor & Alexandra Pearson; ★

XXY (2007); Director: Lucia Puenzo; Writer: Lucia Puenzo; Story: Sergio Bizzio; Actor: Inés Efron; ★★★☆

Yours, Mine & Ours (2005); Director: Raja Gosnell; Writer: Ron Burch & David Kidd; Actor: Drake Bell, Miranda Cosgrove & Haley Ramm; ★☆

Zombies: Wicked little things (2006); Director: J S Cardone; Writer: Ben Nedivi; Story: Boaz Davidson; Actor: Chloë Grace Moretz & Scout Taylor-Compton; ★☆

Index

10,000 Years BC...470, 538
2012...59, 68, 69, 128, 141, 173, 189, 210, 375, 486, 530, 538, 542, 555

A

About a Boy..113, 231, 496, 530, 538
Acquart, Pauline...174, 201, 359, 372, 429, 536, 557
Adamcova, Kristina...322, 325, 496, 549
Adamson, Andrew...237, 542
Addams Family Values..84, 266, 305, 331, 532, 534, 538
Adolescent Malice...54, 368, 373, 375, 534, 538
Adventures of Baron Munchausen...185, 331, 532, 538
Adventures of Huck Finn..195, 212, 286, 301, 360, 482, 532, 538
Adventures of Sharkboy and Lavagirl.........................29, 179, 183, 275, 343, 485, 488, 538
Agutter, Jenny....45, 56, 64, 81, 99, 185, 186, 216, 222, 336, 367, 370, 409, 535, 543, 553, 557
Aiken, Liam...411, 413, 548, 555
Akeelah and the Bee...................................65, 66, 113, 130, 164, 165, 178, 217, 534, 539
Akhtar, Qasim...217, 334, 550
Akinshina, Oksana...63, 137, 372, 466, 495, 517, 535, 549
Alas de Mariposa.......................33, 62, 96, 97, 149, 163, 302, 310, 431, 459, 465, 532, 539
Alaska...114, 174, 181, 237, 242, 259, 418, 531, 534, 539
Alch, Amanda...339, 342, 375, 536, 557
Alcott, Louisa May..79, 549
Alfredson, Tomas...548
Ali, Rubina...205, 365, 493, 555
Alice (1988)...272, 539
Alice in the Cities.....................................56, 101, 102, 104, 105, 226, 228, 229, 369, 528, 539
Alice Upside Down...160, 162, 339, 411, 415, 449, 531, 534
Alice's Adventures in Wonderland....65, 67, 134, 162, 222, 223, 258, 270, 271, 274, 315, 521, 537, 539
Aliens..153, 531, 532, 539
Aliens in the Attic..153, 531, 532, 539
All I want for Christmas.......................................107, 162, 175, 277, 335, 382, 530, 534
Allbright, Landry..545
Allen, Aleisha...65, 160, 162, 230, 266, 540, 554
Allen, Elizabeth..539
Almgreen-Doré, Isabelle..289
Along came a spider..539
Alvarado, Trini..386
Amazing Panda Adventure..28, 217, 218, 237, 248, 371, 539
Amedore, John Patrick...534
Amelio, Gianni..555
Amenábar, Alejandro...552

American Haunting, an...289, 296, 313, 501, 530
Amityville Horror..............60, 127, 289, 294, 297, 298, 311, 312, 313, 411, 426, 469, 530, 539
Anderson, Bobbie..347, 389, 547
Anderson, Melissa..448, 549
Anderson, Thomas...556
Andre.......................87, 88, 174, 238, 242, 255, 256, 338, 371, 532, 539
Andrews, Virginia...544
Angel of Pennsylvania Avenue................................87, 88, 154, 162, 227, 532, 539
Angela (1994) 252, 311, 312, 328, 331, 338, 340, 360, 365, 367, 370, 426, 509, 514, 519, 534, 539
Angus, Thongs and Perfect Snogging..50, 86, 127, 196, 199, 325, 329, 345, 347, 358, 534, 539
Anita & Me..217, 219, 322, 539
Annie (1982).........................26, 27, 101, 121, 153, 162, 176, 241, 242, 491, 492, 539
Annie (1999)...24, 121, 162, 176, 539
Annunciation.................50, 308, 343, 365, 370, 373, 406, 497, 533, 534, 539
Anson, Jay...539
Apted, Michael...553
Aquamarine...196, 199, 533, 539
Are We There Yet.............................65, 81, 127, 129, 160, 227, 230, 540
Argento, Dario...553
Armstrong, Gillian...543, 549
Arngrim, Alison...549
Arnold, Charlotte...327, 554
Asher, Jane..535, 545
Ashley, Lauren..551
Ashton, Emily...63, 310, 330, 402, 467, 552
Astin, Sean...343, 447, 535, 545
Atchison, Doug..539
Atonement.......................................39, 58, 163, 355, 356, 532, 540
Aubrey, James...304, 549
Audition................................60, 176, 302, 305, 315, 433, 469, 470, 533, 540
Audrey Rose....................................103, 307, 313, 314, 403, 532, 540
Austin, Lynn..546

B

Babel..............................30, 58, 242, 324, 389, 392, 474, 533, 540
Back to the Secret Garden..206, 532, 540
Background (1953)...383, 386, 387
Bad News Bears..................25, 57, 108, 151, 155, 159, 160, 168, 171, 172, 534, 540
Bad Seed.........27, 36, 39, 46, 50, 54, 58, 62, 94, 161, 168, 302, 303, 469, 540
Badham, Mary...............46, 56, 58, 130, 151, 153, 158, 159, 212, 483, 556
Baio, Scott..44, 342, 541
Baker, Henriette..553
Bale, Christian.....................43, 56, 57, 64, 100, 161, 433, 435, 544
Balk, Fairuza...270, 286, 554

Balkin, Karen..358, 542
Ball-Trap on the Côte Sauvage..252, 538, 540
Ballard, Carroll...57, 366, 367, 544
Balletshoes...83, 126, 176, 366, 371, 531, 540
Banerji, Subir..427
Baquero, Ivana...128, 271, 274, 320, 372, 442, 552
Barbie Dance Stars..177
Barrie J M...278, 344, 553
Barry, Ian..547
Barrymore, Drew.................23, 36, 82, 268, 278, 292, 313, 363, 407, 484, 535, 544
Barton, Mischa. 163, 164, 232, 255, 266, 268, 271, 274, 276, 286, 295, 322, 409, 548, 554, 555
Bartusiak, Skye McCole...447, 473, 543
Bastard out of Carolina 59, 64, 97, 324, 333, 373, 375, 459, 467, 495, 515, 521, 531, 534, 537, 540
Battle Royale...132, 138, 141, 468, 533, 540
Baudon, Clothilde..161, 547
Baum, Frank...109, 141, 186, 190, 554, 557
Baxter, Deborah...186, 477, 546
Beaches (1988).....................50, 118, 162, 176, 196, 197, 198, 229, 413, 414, 540
Beattie, Amber...352, 434, 438, 541
Beaudene, Raquel..205, 346, 535, 545
Because of Winn Dixie..241
Because of Winn-Dixie.......................155, 237, 242, 243, 311, 425, 449, 531
Beck, Jennifer...23, 63, 330, 556
Bedknobs and Broomsticks..270, 444, 532, 540
Bedtime Stories...530, 534, 540
Beeman, Greg...554
Beer, Sally..342, 369
Beer, Shannon...67, 349
Beethoven...240, 532, 533, 540
Before Women had Wings.....................219, 221, 424, 459, 466, 468, 530, 540
Beguiled, the...354, 355, 532, 534, 540
Bell, Jamie...........................23, 29, 42, 56, 58, 150, 151, 160, 175, 273, 335, 341, 411, 540
Bell, Martin...546
Bell, Mary...55, 250, 302, 308, 309, 315, 557
Bella, Rachael...206, 534, 543
Belle, Camilla...206, 292, 470, 538, 540, 549
Benjamin, Richard...550
Bennett, Eliza...81, 551
Bennett, Skye..126
Benson, Sally..550
Berger, Katya...367, 371, 373, 499, 501, 535, 549
Berri, Claude...547
Berrington, Stephanie..354, 544
Berthome, Timia...547

Besson, Luc...548
Bialik, Mayim..50, 162, 176, 197, 540
Big (1988)..42, 75, 138, 195, 224, 282, 323, 540
Big Momma's House 2...89, 177, 178
Billingsley, Peter...114, 554
Billy Elliot..23, 29, 42, 56, 58, 65, 115, 147, 148, 150, 164, 175, 273, 335, 341, 357, 360, 411, 502, 531, 534, 540
Birch, Thora 82, 91, 107, 127, 153, 162, 174, 175, 181, 190, 196, 198, 242, 277, 287, 327, 329, 332, 372, 534, 539, 546, 552
Birds, the..72, 290, 292, 298, 330, 531
Birkin, Andrew...55, 541, 550
Birkin, Ned...29, 55, 136, 362, 541
Bizzio, Sergio...558
Black Beauty..254, 533, 541
Blackwell, Nicola...23, 150, 335, 341
Blair, Linda...56, 62, 112, 313, 372, 544
Blame it on Fidel.................................40, 52, 61, 64, 326, 330, 369, 447, 450, 520, 532, 541
Blancke, Sandrine..57, 81, 328, 371, 506, 536, 554, 556
Blatty, William Peter..544
Bless the Child..314, 473, 541
Blom, Per..359, 547
Bloom, Jeffrey...544
Blue Butterfly (2003)..108, 396, 453, 530, 541
Blue Butterfly (2004)..335, 534
Blue Lagoon.28, 30, 41, 54, 65, 76, 82, 103, 132, 133, 134, 228, 322, 323, 326, 330, 348, 365, 366, 369, 429, 531, 534, 541
Blythe, Charlotte..331, 338, 367, 370, 519, 534
Blyton, Enid.............................78, 92, 97, 152, 155, 180, 242, 250, 387, 464, 532, 544
Body Snatcher, the...202, 391, 533, 541
Boettcher, Ashley..539
Boeuf, Dorothée...553
Bogdanovich, Peter...551, 552
Böhm, Kathi..258
Bolger, Emma..23, 249, 258, 417, 451, 546, 547
Bolger, Sarah..64, 78, 311, 412, 417, 451, 555
Bolotin, Craig...556
Bolt, Robert...543
Bomann, Brittney...109, 253, 281, 284, 544, 549
Boorem, Mika..474, 539, 547
Boorman, John..433, 442, 461, 544, 546
Booth, Freddie..289, 410, 551
Booze-Mooney, Katie..543
Boucant, Corinne...536, 553
Bould, Hannah...278, 419, 430, 553
Bourguignon, Serge...556

Boy Called Dad, a..407, 541
Boy in the Striped Pyjamas, the......................184, 352, 433, 434, 438, 449, 532, 541
Boyd, Jenna...177, 473, 543, 550
Boyle, Danny..41, 51, 62, 144, 365, 550, 555
Boynton, Lucy..83, 126, 164, 176, 226, 540, 550
Bradley, Portia..311, 355, 390, 551
Bradshaw, John...544, 556
Brady Bunch Movie.............................30, 50, 78, 86, 87, 89, 331, 358, 532, 541
Brain, Alexandra...93, 544
Breslin, Abigail 23, 27, 41, 49, 57, 58, 63, 82, 91, 108, 112, 121, 125, 130, 149, 165, 166, 171, 174, 186, 189, 241, 321, 332, 410, 412, 415, 426, 427, 463, 543, 549, 551, 552
Brewster, Anna...217
Bridarolli, Lia...547
Bridge to Terabithia.....65, 86, 87, 151, 152, 153, 160, 163, 168, 204, 334, 410, 422, 425, 532, 541
Brooke Ellison Story, the..........................61, 92, 371, 389, 390, 396, 398, 400, 519, 532, 541
Brookes, Rafiella...34, 304
Brooks, Richard...548
Brothers Grimm...273, 533, 541
Brown, Rebecca...160, 554
Brown, Thomas..88, 153, 535, 546
Browning, Emily...81, 548, 550
Bruce, Jane..82, 483, 552
Bruchon, Pascale..339, 341, 536, 553
Buddha Collapsed out of Shame...462, 541
Bugajski, Monica..212, 312, 367, 372, 430, 431, 554
Bugsy Malone................................44, 46, 52, 69, 162, 163, 187, 342, 533, 541
Bundy, Laura Bell..335, 489, 548
Burger, Roxanne...536, 555
Burke, Charlotte................................112, 164, 266, 337, 345, 370, 536, 552
Burnett, Angela...66, 548
Burnett, Charles...548
Burnett, Frances Hodgson..89, 540, 549, 554
Burnham, Terry...547
Burton, Tim...541
Butterfield, Asa..184, 433, 438, 449, 541
Butterfly Effect, the................................485, 506, 519, 530, 534, 541
Bynes, Amanda...169, 189, 555

C

Cain, Christopher...539
Calef, Noel...556
Camomile Lawn................................66, 121, 124, 141, 353, 372, 504, 541
Campion, Jane...553
Candleshoe..152, 153, 154, 532, 541

Capote, Truman..542
Caro, Niki..27, 36, 49, 149, 174, 557
Carpenter, J..557
Carpenter, John..545
Carr, Charmain..162, 325, 555
Carroll, Joan..550
Carroll, Lewis..................................186, 221, 222, 271, 272, 273, 495, 521, 537, 539
Carter, Angela..542
Carter, Ann..52, 202, 203, 270, 387, 440, 543, 552
Cartwright, Angela..162, 555
Cartwright, Veronica..290, 540, 542
Cascio, Salvatore..58, 111, 542
Case 39..112, 289, 303, 315, 470, 532, 541
Casper (1995)..297, 343, 448, 534, 541
Casper meets Wendy..................................286, 287, 288, 297, 531, 538, 541
Cass, David..554
Cassavetes, Nick..551
Castle-Hughes, Keisha...24, 27, 36, 49, 50, 57, 58, 67, 149, 150, 174, 255, 308, 372, 406, 551, 557
Casto, Marine..342, 372, 534, 545
Catch that Kid..151, 160, 170, 532, 541
Cattarinich, Domenico..549
Celia (1988)..................152, 153, 154, 237, 241, 244, 248, 251, 259, 271, 275, 304, 418, 467
Cement Garden 26, 29, 30, 76, 82, 130, 132, 136, 323, 346, 362, 367, 373, 413, 414, 415, 419, 420, 428, 431, 534, 541
Chabert, Lacey..182, 549
Chadha, Gurinder..539
Chapin, Billy..51, 82, 483, 552
Charlie and the Chocolate Factory..................................65, 78, 80, 258, 541
Charlotte's Web..56, 57, 65, 78, 110, 237, 241, 242, 250, 334
Chatwin, Justin..82, 102, 437, 557
Cheaper by the Dozen (1950)..447, 541
Cheaper by the Dozen 1..78, 79, 87, 243, 483
Cheaper by the Dozen 2..40, 80, 336, 531
Chester, Vanessa Lee..................................66, 154, 219, 266, 291, 549
Child of Divorce..382, 387
Child, the..259
Child, the (1977) (Harry Novak presents..)..23
Children of Theatre Street..175, 370, 533, 542
Children, the (2008)..23, 34, 267, 302, 304
Chitty Chitty Bang Bang..........................35, 36, 40, 68, 69, 107, 283, 284, 289, 315, 531, 542
Chlumsky, Anna 65, 81, 128, 155, 163, 164, 321, 335, 337, 339, 342, 358, 402, 415, 422, 423, 425, 536, 551
Chocolat..448, 483, 530, 542
Christmas Box..532, 542

Christmas Memory, A..29, 153, 362, 531, 542
Christopher, Dyllan...111, 384, 545
Chronicles of Narnia..
    Prince Caspian..179, 252, 309, 532, 542
    The Lion, the Witch and the Wardrobe. .25, 28, 82, 174, 189, 221, 237, 259, 270, 286, 309, 444, 478, 532, 542
Chucky...196, 289
Cider with Rosie...................................81, 111, 342, 369, 530, 534, 538, 542
Cinema Paradiso...58, 111, 334, 528, 530, 542
Claridge, Jessica..258, 395, 451, 544, 546
Clark, Barney...118, 484, 494, 552
Clark, Larry..51, 356, 357, 548
Clarke, Emmy...164, 551
Clarkson, Amelia...491
Clayton, Jack..547
Clayton, Jessie...481, 555
Cleaner (2007)..66, 173, 415, 417, 463, 542
Cohen, Jeff..224, 545
Cold Light of Day................................371, 372, 497, 511, 512, 519, 530
Cold Sweat...462, 473, 530, 542
Cole, Marcus..542
Cole, Rosalie..542
Coleman, Charlotte..95, 310, 359, 552
Coleman, Holliston...314, 473, 541
Collet-Serra, Jaume...23, 552
Colletti, Ian..148
Columbus, Christopher..545, 546, 551, 555
Company of Wolves.....................84, 238, 290, 300, 321, 325, 340, 371, 497, 532, 534, 542
Connelly, Jennifer..58, 268, 449, 553
Conner, Isabel...289, 294, 313, 539
Conroy, Pat...553
Contact (1997)..309, 417, 418, 531, 542
Cookson, Catherine...490, 510, 553
Coomes, Carol..161, 547
Cooper, Justin..108, 548
Corcoran, Donna...52, 390, 551
Corrina, Corrina..............................80, 117, 210, 211, 371, 410, 420, 421, 426, 428, 531, 542
Cosgrove, Miranda...554, 558
Côté, Michel..361, 519, 542
Coulthard, Alice..362, 414, 431, 541
Courage of Lassie.................................26, 238, 239, 240, 241, 244, 533, 542
Courtney, Joel...556
CRAZY (2005)...361, 519, 532, 542
Cría Cuervos............................48, 176, 237, 305, 331, 370, 374, 415, 416, 418, 528, 531, 542
Crichton, Michael...548, 549

Criman, Denis..351
Cristiano, Guiseppe..474, 547
Cross, Joseph..411, 415, 547
Crossing, the..488, 531
Cruttenden, Abigail..28, 30, 311, 340, 536, 553
Csupo, Gabor..541
Cuarón, Alfonso..545, 546, 549
Culkin, Kieran..231, 331
Cullam, Mitch..134, 225, 493
Cullinan, Thomas..540
Curious Case of Benjamin Button, the..58, 533, 542
Curly Sue..108, 371, 532, 543
Curse of the Cat People, the..52, 202, 203, 270, 532, 543
Cyberbully (2011)..486

D

Dahl, Roald..179, 286, 541, 542, 547, 550
Dance like the Flower Fairies..177, 282
Dandaurian, Magdalena..454, 554
Danes, Claire..350, 535, 547, 549
Danielle Steel's Daddy..387
Dann, Patty..550
Dante, Joe..544
Dark, the (2005)..23, 237, 292, 296, 530
Dart, Iris Rainer..540
Davies, Valentine..550
Davis, Andrew..540
Davis, Aree..266, 546
Day at the Beach, A..301, 390, 391, 393, 459, 464
Daykin, Jennifer Rae..551
Dayton, Jonathan & Valerie Faris..549
de Felitta, Frank..540
De Vere Stacpoole, Henry..541
de Wilde, Brandon..23, 55, 56, 87, 223, 231, 238, 554
Dean, James..95, 96, 554
Dear Frankie..113, 389, 394, 530, 543
Death Defying Acts..50, 58, 155, 266, 267
Definitely, Maybe..23, 63, 332, 531
del Toro, Guillermo..320, 442, 552
Denison, Muriel..556
Dennis (1993)..179, 329, 462, 532, 534, 543
Denton, Allegra..546
Dercourt, Denis..552
DeSalle, Stefan..179, 554
Descher, Sandy..35, 68, 147, 189, 535, 548

Devil's Child, the...206
Devito, Danny..550
Di Camillo, Kate..540
Diables, les..................................101, 102, 104, 132, 174, 224, 225, 347, 396, 532
Diary of Anne Frank, the...................81, 84, 95, 322, 339, 437, 441, 532, 534, 543
Diaz, Kristel..375, 535, 549
Dickens, Charles..118, 140, 545, 552, 554
Dicker, Karen..258, 547
Dickie Roberts, Former Child Star...43, 177, 543
Digging to China...224, 225, 352, 530, 535, 543
Dill, Drica...547
Ding, Yi..28, 218, 371, 539
Dirty Dancing...175
Disson, Jeanne...157, 202, 536, 556
Doctor Dolittle..30, 65, 238, 268, 532, 543
Doctor Zhivago...114, 132, 440, 538, 543
Dodgson, Charles...221, 222, 272, 273, 521
Donato, Marc...108, 335, 396, 534
Dooley, Taylor..183, 343, 538
Dotrice, Karen...464, 550
Douglas, Andrew..539
Down will come Baby.................50, 85, 320, 375, 422, 424, 462, 474, 476, 530, 532, 543
Dreamchild...162, 222, 223, 272, 532, 543
Dreamer...25, 57, 237, 242, 252, 253, 259, 532, 543
Driftwood..................................23, 52, 101, 108, 117, 120, 122, 366, 371, 532, 543
Driscoll, Bobby.................51, 81, 123, 219, 223, 249, 250, 251, 273, 484, 485, 555
Driss, Manelle..427, 544
Drum, the...28, 65, 533
Drummond, Clare...370, 434, 553
Du Chatinier, Samuel...365
Du Maurier, Daphne..540
Duff, Hilary...79, 287, 288, 297, 541
Dugger, Florrie...162, 541
Duigan, John..548
Duke, Patty...46, 58, 390, 394, 395, 396, 550
Dululle, Yannick..473, 542
Dumas, Valerie..350, 556
Dunst, Kirsten.............56, 109, 130, 161, 298, 299, 339, 350, 467, 489, 535, 547, 548, 549
Durbin, Deanna...32
Dürrenmatt, Friedrich...542
Dushku, Eliza..57, 87, 200, 328, 331, 405, 411, 556
Dust Factory......................49, 160, 168, 311, 345, 421, 429, 430, 535, 543
Dustbin Baby................40, 101, 103, 106, 109, 111, 121, 371, 384, 543
Dwan, Alan..543

E

Earl, Elizabeth...99, 199, 280, 370, 435, 544
East of Sudan..185, 532, 535, 543
Eastwood, Alison...241, 249, 330, 556
Edlington, Gemma..547
Edney, Beatie (Beatrice)......................................301, 390, 391, 453, 459, 464, 543
Edwards, Hugh...304, 315, 483, 549
Edwards, Sebastian Rice...23, 28, 331, 433, 442
Efron, Inés..62, 363, 367, 536, 558
Eleniak, Erika...343, 535
Elf (2003)..85, 276, 277, 532, 543
Ellison, Brooke & Jean...541
Eloise at the Plaza...76, 371, 532, 538, 543
Emerald Forest...28, 200, 370, 475, 532, 544
Empire of the Sun................56, 57, 64, 100, 132, 161, 433, 435, 441, 532, 544
Engström, Blanca...328
Enid (2009)......................................36, 92, 97, 387, 388, 462, 464, 538, 544
Erice, Victor..442, 555
Eschasseriaux, Bernard..556
ET the Extra-Terrestrial.............23, 82, 89, 278, 284, 296, 308, 309, 343, 363, 535, 544
Etel, Alex...311, 327, 416, 431, 448, 478, 550
Evans, David Mickey...540, 554
Evans, Nicholas..253, 398, 546
Evans, Richard...542
Exorcism of Emily Rose...307, 316
Exorcist, the...............23, 56, 60, 62, 112, 296, 312, 313, 372, 373, 403, 461, 530, 544
Explorers......................................28, 76, 109, 179, 343, 382, 530, 535, 544
Eyes of an Angel..25, 241

F

Fabia, Anthony...555
Fairy King of Ar...281, 532, 544
Fairy Tale..
    a true story (1997).............................99, 196, 199, 278, 280, 366, 370, 417, 429, 435
Fallen Angel.........................45, 61, 160, 168, 237, 257, 343, 459, 509, 512, 519, 530, 535, 544
Family Gathering, a...251, 533, 544
Fanning, Dakota.....26, 27, 34, 46, 49, 51, 55, 56, 58, 63, 65, 82, 101, 102, 117, 118, 128, 162,
    164, 167, 173, 196, 211, 235, 238, 239, 242, 250, 252, 253, 268, 292, 293, 301, 327, 334,
    372, 416, 417, 425, 431, 433, 437, 449, 452, 474, 495, 497, 535, 536, 541, 543, 546, 550,
    553, 554, 557
Fanning, Elle......30, 58, 148, 242, 271, 278, 310, 355, 375, 383, 392, 474, 490, 540, 542, 552,
    553, 556
Father Goose...354, 434, 435, 533, 544
Father of My Children...51, 55, 371, 427, 530, 544

Favreau, Jon..543
Fawsett, J..543
Fechter, Steven..557
Feig, Paul..545
Felsette, Laurelle & Nicole...544
Felton, Tom...38, 153, 490, 546
Ferdin, Pamlyn...47, 354, 355, 534, 540
Ferland, Jodelle....51, 56, 58, 110, 112, 134, 164, 224, 225, 269, 271, 289, 292, 295, 303, 331, 355, 373, 416, 420, 460, 470, 483, 484, 493, 536, 541, 550, 555, 556
Feuillet, Benjamin...40
Fickman, Andy...545, 553, 555
Fieder, Gary...543
Field of Dreams..78, 297, 532, 544
Fincher, David..542, 552
Fine, Anne...384, 551
Firestarter...23, 268, 292, 313, 484, 531, 535, 544
Fish Tank...53
Five Children and It...100, 281, 282, 444
Five on a Treasure Island...242, 544
Five Pennies, the..46, 110, 162, 532, 544
Flack, Karen...370, 546
Fleming, Erik..551
Fleming, Ian...542
Fleming, Victor..557
Flickan..328
Flightplan...113, 410, 419, 530, 544
Flint, Rebecca...37, 38, 44
Flowers in the Attic.......................................81, 409, 447, 449, 474, 544
Fly away Home...80
Fly Away Home......................45, 57, 115, 116, 117, 128, 237, 248, 329, 366, 372, 426
Forbes, Bryan..557
Forrest Gump...168, 390, 391, 495, 504, 530, 544
Forster, Allison..45, 82, 338, 350, 535, 545
Forsyth, Bill...545
Foster, Blake...343
Foster, Heather Ann..112, 298, 372, 557
Foster, Jodie...27, 30, 35, 41, 43, 44, 45, 52, 54, 56, 62, 63, 134, 136, 152, 153, 154, 162, 168, 186, 187, 256, 302, 305, 342, 346, 367, 370, 373, 419, 473, 513, 515, 519, 522, 541, 544, 549, 556
Fowler, Connie May..540
Fox and the Child..151, 237, 238, 246, 533, 544
Fox, Zac...311, 387, 426, 557
François, Emilie..46, 51, 81, 554
Franklin, Pamela...141, 315, 372, 547
Freaky Friday..30, 81, 111, 173, 320, 532, 544

Free Willy................................110, 112, 123, 237, 239, 255, 256, 533, 544
Free Willy 3...
   the rescue..256
Freundlich, Bart...541
Frid, Amelia..467
Friedkin, William..544
Friend, Jessie-Ann...27, 28, 182, 183, 344, 464, 535, 550
Fuhrmann, Isabelle..552
Fukasaku, Kenta...540
Fullerton, Fiona..162, 272, 539
Fulton, Grace...52, 86, 494, 551, 552
Furrh, Chris...138, 549
Fywell, Tim..557

G

Gainsbourg, Charlotte....26, 56, 82, 94, 117, 136, 148, 151, 346, 362, 366, 367, 370, 373, 414, 420, 431, 514, 535, 541, 547
Gale, Jean...347, 547
Gamble, Mason...179, 329, 543
Game Plan..116, 531, 545
Gans, Christopher..555
Garland, Judy.....................32, 39, 45, 50, 55, 110, 162, 176, 180, 304, 493, 557
Garner, Becca...557
Garner, Peggy Ann..42, 54, 94, 108, 382, 491, 547
Garris, Mick...546
Gates, Samantha...557
Gatins, John...543
Gautier, Alice...371, 427, 544
Gavras, Julia...541
Genova.........................50, 117, 370, 415, 416, 417, 418, 419, 425, 428, 449, 531, 545
Getty, Balthazar...138, 549
Ghost and Mrs Muir...27, 297, 530, 545
Gibbs, Holly...551
Gibson, Brian..553
Giedroyc, Coky..558
Gigi..26, 51, 555
Gilbert, Lewis...545
Gilbert, Melissa..81, 153, 154, 402, 448, 549
Gilliam, Terry...............51, 56, 134, 185, 270, 271, 273, 315, 331, 460, 493, 538, 541, 556
Glanzelius, Anton..111, 160, 168, 243, 409, 413, 551
Glatter, Lesli Linka..552
Glenn, Julie...176, 370, 547
Glove, Solomon...67, 349
Godden, Rumer..353, 545
Godet, Thomas...328, 371, 536, 556

Godfrey, Hannah..283, 418, 547
Goldbacher, Sandra...197, 366, 540, 550
Golden Compass, the...40, 42, 185, 309, 310, 532, 545
Golden, Arthur...550
Good Mother, the...327, 371, 387, 388, 530, 545
Good Year, a...342, 372, 533, 534
Good, Meagan...544
Goodell, Gregory..543
Goodnight Mr Tom...123, 411, 417, 444, 532, 545
Goodwin, Raven..66, 555
Goonies, the...89, 179, 224, 343, 447, 532, 535, 545
Gordon, Hannah Taylor..441, 547
Gordon, Hilary & Rebecca...184, 551
Gordon, Susan...46, 162, 544
Gorovaia, Irene...534
Gould, Aidan..475, 548
Gould, Jadin...108, 117, 483, 548
Gozzi, Patricia...47, 120, 224, 225, 352, 402, 556
Graham, William A..554
Grant, Miriam..278, 430, 553
Grant, Richard E...214, 387, 468, 496, 511, 557
Gray, Carsen...344, 536, 553
Great Balls of Fire..110, 353, 372, 508, 532, 535, 545
Great Expectations...163, 164, 205, 343, 345, 535, 545
Great Rock & Roll Swindle...373
Green, Jordan-Claire...554
Greenburg, Zack O'Malley..401
Greene, David..547
Greengage Summer...353, 535, 545
Gressner, Nicolas..549
Grey, Zena...555
Greystoke..
      the Legend of Tarzan..28, 133, 532, 545
Greyvenstein, Leigh..281, 544
Grezel, Sylvie...465, 553
Griffiths, Mark...540
Grimes, Karolyn...311, 547
Grinch, the...471, 532, 545
Grint, Rupert..35, 46, 169, 285, 335, 452, 545, 546
Grisham, John..211, 556
Grogan, Clare...345, 350, 545
Groome, Georgia..23, 41, 46, 50, 55, 62, 86, 118, 127, 199, 208, 325, 329, 345, 347, 358, 516,
      517, 534, 539, 549
Grounded...111, 187, 190, 342, 384, 531, 535, 545
Grow Your Own..217, 218, 421, 428, 545

Guiry, Tom..81, 124, 554, 555
Gupta, Uma Das..402, 552

H

Hack, Olivia...50, 541
Hadjimatheou, Katherina...540
Hadzihalilovic, Lucile..26, 51, 175, 547
Haibruge, Berangere...173, 324, 367, 370, 547
Hale, Caitlin..554
Haley Joel Osment...56, 265, 295, 403, 555
Hall, Adrian...68, 283, 542
Hall, Bug...29, 161, 204, 360, 535, 549
Hall, Peter..541
Hall, Rebecca..66, 121, 372, 541
Halloween (1978)...292, 293, 302, 306, 528, 545
Halloween 4..
    The Return of Michael Myers..130, 532, 545
Halloween 5..
    Revenge of Michael Myers..268
Hallstrõm, Lasse..542, 551, 557
Hamilton, David..350, 556
Hamilton, Zanna...556
Hampton, Christopher...540
Hand that Rocks the Cradle..545
Haney-Jardine, Perla..117, 415, 449, 545
Hanford, Cody...327, 535
Hann-Byrd, Adam...489, 548
Hansen-Løve, Mia..51, 544
Happening, the...292, 532
Hard Candy............................23, 56, 58, 60, 303, 406, 503, 513, 516, 519, 533, 545
Harding, Sarah...553
Hardwicke, Catherine...551, 556
Harlin, Renny...542
Harling, Laura..491, 547
Harris, Danielle..130, 268, 545
Harris, Joanne...542
Harry Potter..28, 35, 36, 38, 39, 42, 46, 48, 52, 69, 79, 121, 123, 124, 131, 153, 169, 195, 196,
    199, 202, 262, 265, 275, 284, 285, 286, 293, 300, 309, 334, 340, 410, 447, 452, 485, 489,
    490, 520, 532, 535, 545, 546
Harry Potter (2) and the Chamber of Secret...545
Harry Potter (3) and the Prisoner of Azkaban..546
Harry Potter (4) and the Goblet of Fire..546
Hassan, Maryam...554
Haun, Lindsey...557
Haunted Mansion, the...266, 532, 546

Hawes, James..544
Hawke, Ethan...28, 56, 109, 343, 535, 544
Heavenly Creatures.............................302, 358, 359, 532, 535, 546
Heidi...23, 96, 109, 121, 125, 130, 141, 189, 206, 207, 208, 226, 249, 258, 395, 449, 451, 462, 475, 531, 546
Heigl, Katherine..556
Hellman, Lilian...542
Henderson, Sarah...............................51, 347, 356, 357, 373, 403, 548
Henley, Georgie.................................55, 174, 237, 252, 309, 478, 542
Hennell, Jessica...349, 557
Henry, Justin...24, 61, 383, 386, 548
Hepburn, Dee..160, 350, 545
Héran, Zoé............................153, 156, 157, 169, 371, 449, 536, 556
Hewitt, Alexandra...371, 543
Hewitt, Love..281, 334, 551
Hicks, Scot..552
Hidden in America..60, 115, 141, 531, 546
Hidden Places...76, 105, 114, 221, 236, 546
Hide and Seek....................57, 117, 128, 239, 293, 415, 416, 417, 449, 546
Hideous Kinky.............................114, 187, 323, 370, 372, 468, 520, 530, 546
High Wind in Jamaica, a.................186, 247, 301, 304, 370, 419, 477, 503, 532, 546
Highmore, Freddie.....................42, 56, 58, 100, 281, 342, 541, 544, 545
Hill, Dana.............................45, 160, 168, 257, 343, 509, 535, 544
Hirokazu, Kore-eda..552
His Teeth...481, 521
Hitchcock, Alfred...290, 540
Hoath, Florence..............................99, 199, 280, 417, 540, 544
Hocus Pocus...82, 286, 287, 533, 546
Hodges, Eddi..42, 161
Hoffman, Gaby. .24, 81, 82, 83, 86, 90, 107, 109, 111, 127, 173, 190, 198, 199, 297, 320, 383, 544, 550, 552, 557
Hoffman, Michael...552
Hofrichter, Suzi..177, 202, 391, 546
Hogan, P J...553
Holgate, Diane...250, 308, 557
Holland, Agnieszka...339, 554
Holmes, Brittany Ashton.................................29, 204, 360, 535
Home (2008)..365, 450, 532, 546
Home Alone.......................................23, 29, 83, 130, 137, 546
Home Sweet Homicide..108
Honey, I Shrunk the Kids.................42, 78, 81, 88, 153, 184, 243, 532, 535, 546
Honey, the Kids Rule the World...343
Hooper, Tobe...553
Hoot...484, 485, 533, 546
Hope and Glory..............23, 25, 28, 327, 331, 352, 433, 442, 530, 546

Hope Floats...50, 127, 378, 385, 388, 448, 528, 530, 546

Hopkins, Billy...547

Hopkins, Stephen...549, 553

Horowitz, Anthony..555

Horse for Danny, a..124, 253, 531, 546

Horse Whisperer.................58, 78, 237, 242, 252, 253, 254, 255, 390, 397, 398, 519, 532, 546

Hoult, Nicholas..113, 231, 383, 538, 557

Hounddog (2008).....26, 34, 57, 63, 68, 118, 128, 162, 167, 238, 242, 301, 310, 315, 327, 372, 431, 459, 495, 497, 521, 531, 535, 546

House, Alex...327, 554

How to Kill your Neighbour's Dog.......................................177, 202, 237, 391

Howard, Ron..545, 550

Howes, William..304

Hughes, Allen...548

Hughes, John..543, 546, 550, 557

Hughes, Ken..542

Hughes, Richard...503, 546

Humphreys, Michael Conner..168, 391, 544

Hurd-Wood, Rachel.............................284, 289, 296, 313, 344, 501, 536, 539, 553

Hurst, Fannie...547

Hussein, Waris...550

Huston, John..539

Hutcherson, Josh......29, 65, 86, 87, 90, 153, 160, 163, 164, 168, 179, 195, 204, 333, 334, 339, 341, 422, 490, 535, 541, 548, 549, 554

Hutchinson, Lucy..543

Huton, Timothy...543

Hyde, Tracy..162, 175, 336, 337, 550

I

I am Slave...23, 60, 459, 462, 479, 480, 532, 546

I Know Where I'm Going...409

I Love You, I Love You Not...29, 218, 350, 535

Ice Palace, the (Is-slottet).............................106, 203, 327, 358, 365, 367, 370, 531, 537, 547

Ihimaera, Witi...557

Imagine That...85, 531, 547

Imitation of Life...114, 213, 218, 258, 547

Impudent Girl, an (L'effrontée). 56, 94, 117, 148, 151, 161, 176, 189, 365, 366, 370, 514, 531, 535, 547

In a Stranger's Hand...476, 547

In America...64, 78, 311, 412, 417, 451, 547

In Name Only..382

In Search of the Castaways..........................45, 102, 103, 153, 185, 335, 547

Iñárritu, Alejandro González..540

Ingalls Wilder, Laura...549

Ingenious..283, 309, 418, 531, 547

Inn of the 6th Happiness...547
Inn of the Sixth Happiness..434, 439
Innes, Michael..541
Innocence..258, 259
Innocence (2004)............26, 39, 51, 55, 111, 119, 173, 175, 202, 203, 324, 367, 370, 373, 547
Innocents, the...125, 141, 297, 372, 532, 547
Interview with the Vampire...................................161, 298, 299, 339, 532, 535, 547
Ionesco, Eva..54, 96, 538
Irvin, Britt..535, 547
Irvin, Sam...550
Iscan, Elit...332
Işcan, Elit...556
Izumi, Ayaka...176, 469, 540

J

Jack (2003)..361, 530, 535, 547
Jack Frost (1998)..113, 411, 415, 530, 547
Jackson, Sherry...54, 386, 390
Jacquet, Luc..544
Jager, Anna Franziska...173, 243, 367, 371, 551
Jakob the Liar...49, 370, 441, 547
Jakub, Lisa..384, 551
James and the Giant Peach...162, 179, 532, 547
James, Henry...126, 141, 267, 289, 297, 547, 557
James, Liam...128, 538
Jane Eyre..................38, 54, 83, 103, 119, 121, 123, 124, 126, 208, 462, 491, 531, 547
Jason, Sybil..44, 54, 390
Jean de Florette...418, 533, 538, 547
Jeffries, Lionel..553, 557
Jeffries, Marc John...266, 546
Jeles, Andras...539
Jig...175
Jimenez, Marianella...335, 396, 534, 541
Joey (1997)...26, 116, 237, 251, 547
Joffe, Mark..550
Johansson, Scarlett. 33, 36, 56, 58, 61, 68, 83, 253, 255, 366, 396, 397, 404, 537, 546, 550, 551
John, Lucien...64, 81, 186, 216, 370, 409, 557
Johnny Mad Dog..433, 440, 532, 547
Johnson, Joe..548
Joliffe, Genevieve...557
Jones, Ella...198, 372, 550
Jones, Kirk...551
Jones, Peter...82, 141, 348, 541
Jordan, Neil..542, 547
Josephson, Elva...141, 348, 369, 541

Journey of Natty Gann.......57, 102, 152, 153, 155, 226, 227, 242, 246, 247, 483, 531, 535, 548
Journey to the Centre of the Earth...179, 533, 548
Jovovich, Milla..141
Julia (2008)...475, 531, 548
Jumanji...109, 130, 283, 335, 485, 489, 531, 548
Jungle 2 Jungle...28, 345, 530, 548
Jungle Book...238, 532, 548
Junior Miss..94
Juno..58, 61, 65, 404, 406, 531, 548
Jurassic Park...66, 237, 291, 292, 352, 533, 548
Just you and me, kid...366

K

Kagan, Jeremy...548
Kamikaze Girls...197
Kampmeier, Deborah...................................26, 68, 162, 310, 315, 497, 521, 546
Kan, Hanae...49, 552
Karath, Kym...163, 555
Kartheiser, Vincent...114, 174, 181, 242, 539
Karwien, Eleanore...322, 325, 372, 553
Kassell, Nicole...62, 460, 496, 519, 521, 557
Kassovitz, Peter...547
Kaufman, Paul...554
Kay, Dominic Scott...277, 536, 555
Keerthana...370, 436, 552
Kelley, Ryan...345, 429, 535, 543
Kelly, Brian...547
Kelly, Raeven Larrymore...211, 473, 556
Kendrick, Ellie...322, 437
Kenny, Holly...112, 217, 334, 550
Kerrigan, Michael...544
Kervel, Nina...52, 64, 326, 369, 450, 541
Kes (1969)...28, 49, 156, 238, 365, 548
Keynes, Skandar...82, 309, 542
Kidron, Beebon...552
kids (1995).....................23, 33, 51, 65, 343, 347, 355, 356, 357, 373, 403, 433, 533, 535, 548
Killer of Sheep...28, 41, 55, 66, 468, 532
King, Stephen...268, 274, 544, 555
King, Vanessa...322, 372, 505, 548
Kingsley, Charles...557
Kinnaman, Melinda..111, 151, 160, 169, 171, 328, 370, 551
Kinski, Nastassia...33, 53, 520
Kisner, Jeremy James...205, 346, 535, 545
Kiss at Midnight, a...108, 117, 483, 531
Kitaura, Ayu...552

Klavan, Andrew..........543
Kleister, Randal..........541
Knight, Eric..........548
Knight, Maxim..........86, 552
Knights of the South Bronx..........49, 66, 164, 165, 530, 548
Knott, Andrew..........254, 554
Koch, Kris..........555
Koenig, Laird..........549
Kohoutová, Kristýna..........272, 539
Kosminsky, Peter..........557
Kraft, Sammi Kane..........108, 156, 534, 540
Kramer v Kramer..........24, 61, 76, 80, 90, 382, 383, 386, 387, 388, 548
Kramer, Lloyd..........540
Krieger, Samantha..........392, 550
Kropinski, Kasha..........124, 214, 279, 468, 555
Krueger, Lisa..........550
Kubrick, Stanley..........34
Kurys, Diane..........325, 553
Kyle, Alexandra..........211

L

Lambada..........177
Landis, Forrest..........87, 483
Landon, Michael..........549
Lang, Walter..........541, 542
Langrick, Margaret..........345, 536, 551
Langton, Sara..........327, 443, 546
Lanskaya, Yelena..........546
Lassie..........240, 242
Lassie (2005)..........25, 49, 237, 242, 246, 548
Lassie Come Home..........238, 240, 245, 247, 548
Last Mimzy, the..........265, 532, 548
Last time I saw Paris..........531, 535, 548
Laster, Gwendoline..........557
Laughton, Charles..........51, 552
Launder, Frank..........541, 545
Lauren, Ashlee..........372, 493, 557
Laurents, Kathren..........240, 551
Laurin..........304, 352, 371, 548
Lawn Dogs..........227, 231, 232, 234, 257, 271, 274, 275, 276, 286, 322, 370, 532, 548
Lawston, Marlene..........419, 544
Laxton, Richard..........545
Lean, David..........543, 552
Leandersson, Lina..........363, 487, 535, 548
Lee Thompson, J..........556

Lee, Harper..130, 556
Lee, Laurie..111, 342, 474, 542
Lee, Sophie..218, 421, 428, 545
Leeds, Marcie..162, 197
Lemony Snicket's A Series of Unfortunate Events................75, 81, 105, 123, 432, 548
Lena..
    My 100 children..548
Leon................27, 34, 56, 58, 221, 227, 231, 232, 234, 235, 352, 431, 531, 532, 548
Lerman, Logan..484, 506, 546
LeRoy, Mervyn..52, 540
Lester, Mark................23, 29, 118, 162, 175, 336, 494, 502, 544, 550, 552
Let Me In................63, 290, 300, 315, 363, 372, 488, 495, 530, 535
Let the Right One In................29, 60, 299, 363, 459, 485, 487, 489, 531, 535
Leung, Katie..334, 535, 546
Lévana, Malonn..371, 556
Levangie, Gigi..555
Levant, Brian..540
Levesque, Joanna 'Jojo'..199
Levin, Mark................49, 204, 333, 339, 341, 548, 549, 552
Levin, Mark & Jennifer Flackett..49, 552
Lewis, CS................270, 308, 309, 542
Lewis, Hilda..550
Lewis, Jenny..386
Lewis, Myra..545
Liar Liar (1997)..108, 531, 548
Liar, Liar................60, 61, 127, 322, 372, 459, 495, 504, 505, 506, 508, 509, 510, 519, 532, 548
Life with Mikey..42
Life-Size................46, 90, 117, 128, 129, 153, 160, 176, 178, 224, 282, 321, 415, 418, 531, 548
Lily, Morgan..128
Lilya 4-ever................23, 63, 132, 137, 207, 208, 366, 372, 463, 466, 495, 517, 532, 535, 549
Lindqvist, Ajvide................63, 299, 315, 363, 487, 548
Linklater, Richard..540, 554
Lipnicki, Jonathan..339, 342, 557
Lishman, Bill..544
Lister, David..555
Little Giants..168
Little Girl who lives down the Lane, the...27, 45, 132, 136, 168, 237, 256, 302, 305, 346, 367, 370, 373, 391, 509, 513, 515, 516, 549
Little House on the Prairie................75, 78, 81, 99, 153, 154, 166, 402, 411, 448, 452, 532, 549
Little Lips (Piccole Labbra)................367, 371, 373, 459, 495, 499, 535, 549
Little Manhattan................29, 65, 69, 90, 160, 195, 204, 333, 339, 341, 489, 490, 532, 535, 549
Little Miss Sunshine................58, 78, 82, 149, 164, 166, 321, 410, 415, 427, 533, 549
Little Otik (Otesánek)................275, 322, 325, 496, 533, 549
Little Princess................118, 192, 201, 219, 274, 275, 314, 432, 447, 451, 484, 491, 549
Little Rascals................29, 63, 161, 204, 331, 360, 533, 535, 549

Little Secrets..40, 43, 90, 161, 199, 383, 532, 535, 549

Little Unicorn...76, 109, 237, 242, 252, 253, 254, 284, 525, 549

Little Women...............................78, 79, 83, 91, 99, 148, 163, 350, 413, 467, 491, 549

Locke, Sharyl...544

Loew, Arthur..540

Lofting, Hugh...543

Lohan, Lindsay. .56, 100, 117, 128, 129, 153, 160, 176, 178, 224, 282, 321, 372, 418, 548, 552

Lolita 32, 33, 34, 37, 43, 47, 50, 55, 56, 62, 68, 69, 70, 114, 127, 141, 206, 258, 354, 373, 374, 375, 376, 495, 496, 498, 499, 500, 502, 503, 508, 519, 521, 531, 535, 537, 549

Loncraine, R..551

London to Brighton...23, 41, 46, 55, 62, 118, 207, 208, 516, 531, 549

Long Day Closes..531, 549

Lonkar, Tanvi Ganesh...62, 83, 175, 493, 555

Lord of the Flies....................28, 30, 50, 76, 132, 138, 187, 265, 304, 315, 468, 483, 533, 549

Lost in New York..49, 533, 549

Lost in Space...181, 447, 533, 549

Lost World..

    Jurassic Park...66, 154, 266, 291, 531, 549

Lovely Bones, the...58, 118, 429, 430, 512, 533, 535, 549

Lovers of the Arctic Circle...205, 348, 375, 531, 535, 549

Lowe, Maya...544

Lowry, Dick...546

Ludwig, Alexander..66, 553

Lynch, Evanna..546

Lyne, Adman...549

Lynskey, Melanie...302, 358, 535, 546

Lyon, Sue...32, 33, 34, 62, 326, 498, 501, 519

Lyonne, Natasha..534

M

Maberly, Kate...............................87, 89, 121, 207, 240, 339, 370, 395, 450, 536, 554

Mace, Alex..552

Mackendrick, Alexander...390, 546, 550

Mackhmalbaf, Hana...541

Madach, Imre..539

Magdalene Sisters...49, 310, 490, 491, 505, 516, 549

Magdelene Sisters...119

Magic Door, the...525, 531, 549

Magic Island..................................27, 28, 87, 179, 182, 183, 265, 273, 344, 464, 531, 535, 550

Majorino, Tina 117, 162, 174, 210, 219, 238, 242, 255, 256, 272, 371, 420, 421, 425, 459, 468, 474, 539, 540, 542, 557

Malèna..30, 323, 502, 533, 550

Malle, Louis..553

Malone, Jena....44, 59, 64, 69, 97, 129, 172, 309, 324, 333, 373, 385, 389, 417, 418, 467, 495, 515, 521, 534, 540, 542, 546, 555

Mamma Mia!...175
Man in the Moon...83, 337, 350, 366, 533, 550
Man on Fire.......................56, 65, 235, 259, 459, 462, 474, 533, 550
Man who sued God, the...307, 531, 550
Mandy (1952)..............................78, 389, 390, 392, 393, 394, 550
Mann, Alakina..............................293, 296, 310, 415, 463, 466, 552
Manny & Lo.............58, 61, 65, 132, 133, 134, 366, 372, 404, 406, 532, 550
Manõn de Source...418
Mantegna, Gina..545
Marano, Vanessa..371, 396, 398, 400, 541
March, William..540
Marcus, Paul...546
Marquez, Ramona...................36, 38, 39, 93, 127, 387, 488, 542, 544
Marsh, Isabella Nightingale...369
Marshall, Connie...108, 447, 551
Marshall, Garry...540
Marshall, Rob...479, 539, 550
Marshall, Sean...162
Martineza, Francesca..389, 390
Martinsen, Hilde Nyeggen..........................327, 358, 367, 370, 547
Mary Poppins...........85, 90, 118, 180, 224, 238, 384, 428, 464, 494, 533, 550
Matheson, Richard..542
Matilda...46, 52, 65, 269, 287, 533, 550
Matthews, Paul...544, 549
Mavity, Abigail...108, 117, 548
Mayfield, Les...550
Mayle, Peter..545
Mazurowna, Ernestine...418, 547
McBride, Jim...545
McCallister, Sydney..205, 467, 556
McCarthy, Ailish..199, 338, 536, 556
McCarthy, Tom..555
McCormack, Leigh..549
McCormack, Patty.........27, 36, 39, 46, 49, 54, 57, 58, 62, 161, 168, 540
McCormick, Haley...219, 487, 552
McCray, Joanna...557
McDermott, Alice..556
McElhone, Jack...113, 389, 394, 543
McEwan, Ian...136, 356, 540, 541
McGibbon, Lewis...327, 431, 478, 550
McGuigan, Paul...553
McIlvaine, Julia...153, 542
McKenna, Alex...26, 116, 251, 547
McMurray, Lilita..53, 520
McNamara, Sean..541

Me without You..25, 90, 196, 197, 198, 372, 531

Meadows, Shane...556

Medem, Peru..348, 375, 549

Meehan, Thomas...539

Meet me in St Louis. 23, 27, 39, 51, 54, 56, 58, 78, 79, 162, 176, 200, 370, 447, 450, 452, 533, 550

Mehta, Deepa..557

Melhuish, Amy...540

Melissa P (100 strokes of the brush before bed)........95, 354, 355, 357, 371, 462, 531, 535, 550

Melody.....................................29, 113, 162, 175, 187, 333, 335, 336, 337, 531, 550

Memoirs of a Geisha....................96, 109, 111, 119, 372, 431, 462, 479, 532, 550

Menzies, Heather..41, 162, 555

Mermaids....................................113, 127, 173, 318, 355, 531, 535, 550

Mero, Julia..539

Messengers, the...295, 533, 550

Metchik, Asher..81, 111

Meyers, Nancy..552

Mghoi, Natalie..480, 546

Michael, Sinead...93, 544

Miike, Takashi..540

Milestone, Lewis...552

Millar, Gavin..543

Miller, Claude...547

Miller, George..539, 549

Miller, Kristina...544

Miller, Mandy...387, 389, 390, 392, 393, 453, 550

Miller, Rebecca...311, 312, 338, 519, 539

Millions (2004).......................................311, 327, 416, 431, 448, 478, 531, 550

Mills, Haley...40, 100, 110, 151, 153

Mills, Hayley....25, 32, 34, 45, 55, 102, 103, 117, 121, 152, 153, 158, 159, 161, 185, 229, 250, 291, 302, 308, 335, 353, 397, 433

Mills, Zach...221, 551

Minnelli, Vincente...51, 55, 56, 550

Miracle on 34th Street.................52, 53, 76, 107, 270, 277, 307, 382, 392, 496, 531, 550

Miracle Worker, the.........................46, 58, 390, 392, 393, 394, 533, 550

Miracles Still Happen...185

Mischief Night..106, 112, 217, 334, 550

Misérables, les...121, 550

Miss Potter..148, 164, 176, 224, 226, 533, 550

Missing, the..112, 473, 531

Missing, the (2003)..112

Mixed Company (1974)...211, 471, 551

Miyazaki...237

Mockingbird Don't Sing........................324, 372, 395, 459, 466, 519

Moden, Julio...549

Moffett, Sharyn...54, 202, 382, 387, 391, 447, 541, 551
Mom at Sixteen..60, 61, 65, 84, 404, 406, 407, 531, 551
Mommy Market, the...81
Momsen, Taylor..471, 545
Monaghan, Laura...215, 553
Monahan, Brent...539
Monkey Business (1998)..163, 237, 240, 533, 551
Moodysson, Lukas...63, 517, 549
Moore, Ashleigh Aston...190, 198, 330, 552
Moore, Colleen..47, 332
Moore, Nick...557
Moore, Stephanie...548
Moretz, Chloë Grace..63, 89, 173, 177, 178, 289, 290, 298, 300, 338, 349, 363, 372, 494, 495,
    535, 538, 539, 540, 548, 558
Morris, Willie..242, 490, 551
Morshead, Catherine..553
Morton, Alicia..24, 121, 162, 539
Moscow, David..282, 540
Mosquito Coast...180, 184, 335, 533, 551
Mr Blandings builds his Dream House..447, 533
Mr Magorium's Wonder Emporium...221, 533
Mrs Doubtfire..................................52, 157, 252, 325, 382, 383, 384, 385, 388, 531, 551
Mubory, Jasmine...312, 557
Mucha, Anna...454, 554
Mullan, Carrie..370, 372, 546
Mullan, Peter...549
Mullen, Leanne...203, 514, 553
Mulligan, Robert..550, 556
Mummy Returns, the..289, 410, 533, 551
Munchie..29, 127, 128, 281, 334, 448, 462, 485, 488, 489, 531, 551
Muniz, Frankie...200, 334, 490, 551
Murakami, Ryu...540
Murphy, Gloria...543
My American Cousin...65, 95, 110, 345, 533, 536, 551
My Brother the Pig...58, 83, 242, 533
My Dog Skip..39, 52, 200, 211, 242, 334, 490, 533, 551
My Girl (1991)............64, 65, 128, 129, 155, 163, 321, 337, 339, 358, 402, 415, 422, 425, 536
My Girl 2..30, 335, 339, 342, 415, 536, 551
My House in Umbria......................................125, 164, 226, 234, 421, 426, 428, 551
My Life as a Dog (Mit Liv Som Hund). 111, 126, 151, 160, 168, 169, 171, 242, 243, 328, 365,
    370, 409, 413, 425
My Queen Karo...173, 243, 312, 365, 367, 371, 531, 551
My Sister's Keeper. .58, 61, 78, 82, 91, 112, 124, 349, 389, 396, 398, 409, 412, 413, 427, 462,
    519
My Year without Sex..311, 355, 360, 390, 533

My Year Without Sex...178
Mystery of Natalie Wood...44, 52, 53, 494, 520, 533, 551

N

Nabokov, Vladimir.....................24, 346, 354, 375, 496, 498, 499, 502, 508, 521, 537, 549
Nanny McPhee..................38, 81, 85, 90, 107, 118, 128, 224, 237, 274, 286, 384, 531, 551
Nativity Story, the..67, 307, 308, 406, 533, 551
Nativity!...20, 48, 307, 533, 536, 551
Naylor, Phyllis Reynolds...539
Neidenthal, Jaclyn..554
Nelson, Jessie..542, 555
Nelson, Ralph...544
Nelson, Tim...552
Nesbit, E..336, 444, 450, 553
Never Say Goodbye...382
Neville, Sophie...556
Newell, Harry...344
Newell, Mike...546
Newman, Mimi..550
Night of the Hunter...51, 82, 99, 129, 294, 483, 552
No more Baths! Kids stand up for a friend...........................213, 219, 221, 485, 486, 552
No Reservations...76, 108, 121, 125, 410, 426, 427, 552
Nobody Knows.........................49, 76, 102, 112, 113, 132, 135, 136, 414, 428, 552
Noël-Bruneau, Bertille...238, 246, 544
Noonan, Chris..550
North Star...25, 433, 440, 533, 552
North, Sterling...555
Now and Then......78, 86, 90, 109, 127, 152, 153, 180, 185, 196, 198, 199, 200, 231, 327, 328, 329, 330, 372, 383, 536, 552
Nowhere to Run...231, 330
Noyce, Phillip..553
Nutcracker, the (2010)...30, 58, 278, 355, 533, 552

O

O'Brien, Margaret23, 27, 39, 48, 51, 54, 56, 58, 70, 79, 89, 121, 162, 176, 200, 207, 287, 294, 370, 395, 450
O'Neal, Tatum. 25, 55, 57, 58, 104, 116, 129, 151, 155, 156, 160, 171, 172, 229, 238, 267, 372
O'Neil, Chris...265
O'Neill, Amy...81, 153, 184, 535
O'Rourke, Heather...................................33, 52, 69, 243, 266, 289, 293, 294, 295, 315, 372
Oberer, Amy...335, 534
Odgers, Hester..245, 548
Ohgo, Suzuka...111, 372, 431, 479, 550
Olga..440
Oliver Twist...76, 118, 484, 494, 532, 552

Oliver!..23, 118, 162, 336, 494, 502, 532, 552
Oliveri, Robert...81, 184, 546
Olsen, Mary-Kate..151, 160, 172, 556
Omen, the...23, 60, 265, 306, 312, 313, 314, 533
One fine day..552
One Fine Day...78, 531
Oranges are not the Only Fruit.....................................63, 95, 123, 310, 330, 359, 402, 467, 552
Orphan (2009)...................................23, 33, 121, 122, 301, 303, 355, 356, 392, 552
Orr, Wendy..552
Ortega, Kenny...546
Others, the (2001)..267, 293, 296, 310, 414, 421, 463, 466
Our First Christmas...86, 552
Oyewumi, Gloria...481, 555
Özen, Özkan..87, 556

P

Page Turner...161, 533, 552
Page, Ellen...56, 58, 61, 303, 406, 503, 513, 545, 548
Pagnol, Marcel...547
Paige, Yasmin...83, 126, 366, 371
Palmer, Keke.....................65, 66, 130, 164, 165, 173, 178, 217, 415, 463, 539, 542, 548
Panabaker, Danielle..407
Panettiere, Hayden...160, 168, 345, 429, 535, 543
Panic Room..473, 531, 552
Paper Moon.........................58, 104, 106, 129, 155, 156, 229, 267, 372, 532, 552
Paperhouse.........................112, 164, 266, 268, 337, 345, 370, 533, 536, 552
Papodopoulos, Solon...557
Paquin, Anna..45, 48, 57, 58, 116, 117, 128, 161, 247, 248, 323, 329, 337, 366, 372, 426, 491, 544, 553
Paradise (1991).....................42, 108, 127, 153, 196, 327, 332, 372, 485, 502, 520, 531, 552
Parent Trap...30, 76, 100, 372, 382, 552
Parker, Alan...52, 69, 541, 550
Parker, Lindsey..544
Pasquin, John..548
Pasternak, Boris...543
Patela, Laura...544
Paterson, Katherine...204, 410, 541
Pather Panchali...402, 427, 533, 552
Patten, Luana..219, 250, 251, 555
Patterson, James..539
Patterson, Sarah........................84, 300, 321, 325, 340, 371, 497, 534, 542
Pearson, Alexandra..558
Peck on the Cheek (Kannathil Mutthamittal)............60, 101, 102, 103, 109, 370, 436, 443, 552
Peguero, Yajira..356, 548
Pendleton, Aidan..87, 88, 338, 539

584

Penn, Arthur..550
Peppermint Soda (Diabolo Menthe)...............................322, 325, 372, 531, 553
Perez, Conchita...176, 370, 416, 542
Perfect Teacher...531, 553
Peter Pan...............78, 80, 81, 154, 188, 192, 221, 277, 278, 280, 284, 333, 344, 533, 536, 553
Peterson, Amanda...343, 535, 544
Pettis, Madison...116, 545
Phenomena...58, 268, 449, 531, 553
Phillips, Courtney...27, 141, 326, 370, 554
Phoebe in Wonderland......................82, 148, 271, 310, 383, 392, 490, 533, 553
Phoenix, Leaf...82, 109, 179
Phoenix, River............................27, 29, 109, 184, 335, 425, 544, 551, 555
Phoenix, Summer...82, 109, 554
Photographing Fairies..............................278, 280, 297, 409, 419, 429, 533, 553
Piano, the..48, 57, 161, 323, 337, 531
Piccoult, Judy..463, 551
Pied Piper...................................54, 370, 433, 434, 478, 532, 553
Pilkes, Hannah......................................62, 301, 508, 519, 557
Pilkington Garimara, Doris...215, 553
Pipoly, Danuel...50, 138, 315
Plimpton, Martha..335, 545, 551
Pocket Money (L'Argent de Poche)..........20, 55, 323, 339, 341, 460, 465, 533, 536, 553
Polanski, Roman...................................43, 53, 326, 391, 464, 543, 552
Polletin, Katia...258
Polley, Sarah..185, 331, 538
Pollyanna.............23, 30, 39, 40, 80, 121, 122, 123, 125, 130, 207, 240, 390, 397, 398, 531, 553
Polson, John...239, 546
Poltergeist (1982)..........................33, 49, 243, 289, 293, 294, 403, 553
Poltergeist II
   the other side...................................266, 294, 295, 372, 533, 553
Pomers, Scarlett...255, 554
Popkin, Leo C & Russell Rouse...557
Popplewell, Anna...............................90, 197, 252, 309, 372, 542, 550
Porter, Alisan..108, 371, 543
Portman, Natalie.............34, 56, 58, 234, 235, 352, 431, 548
Potter, Dennis...543
Pratt, Kyla...86, 268, 543
Pretend you have Big Buildings..447
Pretty Baby.......27, 34, 54, 62, 63, 112, 211, 348, 353, 365, 366, 371, 373, 459, 467, 477, 495, 500, 519, 536, 553
Prince of Tides...............................90, 91, 383, 459, 467, 518, 519, 533, 553
Proulx, Brooklyn...224, 556
Prowse, Heydon...................................339, 395, 536, 554
Ptang, Yang Kipperbang..........................65, 333, 340, 536
Puenzo, Lucia...558

Push (2009)..49, 56, 164, 268, 292, 531, 532, 553

Q

Quilligan, Veronica..154
Quinn, Aileen...162, 176, 491, 492, 539
Quinn, Marian...556
Quinnell, A J...259, 550

R

Raab,Ellie..241
Rabbit Proof Fence...........................44, 65, 214, 215, 258, 372, 462, 490, 531, 553
Race to Witch Mountain...66, 268, 532, 553
Racing Stripes..237
Radcliffe, Daniel 34, 35, 36, 38, 42, 43, 48, 68, 69, 169, 285, 293, 334, 452, 489, 535, 545, 546
Rag Nymph..27, 121, 462, 490, 510, 511, 519, 532, 553
Rahman, Mani...436, 552
Railway Children, the......28, 30, 45, 56, 60, 78, 81, 99, 101, 103, 222, 336, 447, 450, 533, 553
Ramangwane, Ella...213, 215, 372, 472, 555
Ramsay, Lynne..370, 452, 553
Ramsay, Lynne (Jr)...553
Randall, Ethan...107, 175, 335, 534, 539
Ransome, Arthur...190, 556
Ratcatcher, the..................28, 49, 203, 370, 422, 423, 430, 447, 452, 514, 533, 553
Raven-Simoné...65, 86, 543
Ray, Charlie...160, 204, 339, 341, 490, 535, 549
Ray, Satyajit...552
Reaping, the...23, 49, 268, 292, 313, 484, 532
Rebel without a Cause..94, 95, 96, 140, 554
Redford, Robert....................................152, 249, 253, 254, 358, 396, 397, 546
Reeve, Christopher...398, 541
Reitman, Jason...548
Rennison, Louise...539
Resident Evil..
    Apocalypse...290, 304, 554
Return to Oz...102, 141, 270, 531, 554
Return to the Blue Lagoon.........................27, 133, 326, 330, 348, 370, 531, 554
Ricci, Christina......103, 152, 153, 173, 185, 190, 198, 266, 297, 305, 327, 328, 329, 331, 343,
    355, 372, 448, 534, 536, 538, 541, 550, 552
Rich Kids...386
Richalet, Julie...161, 552
Richards, Ariana...66, 156, 291, 352, 548, 556, 557
Richards, Dakota Blue...40, 185, 310, 543, 545
Richards, Kyle...293, 545
Richter, Jason James...110, 112, 123, 255, 256, 544
Riding in Cars with Boys...407

Ring of Endless Light, a..163, 255, 256, 266, 268, 409, 533, 554
Ripley, Heather...35, 36, 40, 68, 107, 283, 290, 542
Ritchie, Michael...540
Rivera, Jodie (as Amanda Shepherd)...546
Riza, Bella...114, 187, 323, 372, 468, 546
Robb, AnnaSophia.....66, 87, 151, 152, 153, 160, 163, 204, 240, 242, 249, 268, 292, 311, 313, 334, 422, 425, 449, 484, 540, 541, 553
Roberts, Emma...168, 199, 346, 536, 539, 557
Robertson, Andrew...30, 136, 323, 346, 362, 414, 431, 541
Robinson, Grace...141, 315, 557
Robinson, Nick...123, 417, 444, 545
Robinson, Phil Alden..544
Robson, Mark...547
Rodriguez, Robert..538
Rollin, Jean...549
Ronan, Saoirse.....39, 50, 58, 118, 155, 163, 164, 266, 267, 356, 429, 430, 512, 535, 540, 543, 549
Rooper, Jemima...99, 152, 544
Rose, Bernard..552
Rose, Jack...544, 553
Rosenberg, Stuart..539
Rosman, Mark...548
Roth, Bobby...543
Rottiers, Vincent..101, 104, 347, 373, 396, 534, 543
Rottlander, Yella...539
Rousso, Brian..553
Rowling, JK...35, 262, 265, 545, 546
Roxy Hunter & the Secret of the Shaman..162, 531, 554
Ruggia, Christophe..543
Run the Wild Fields......................................29, 101, 152, 153, 155, 236, 445, 483, 554
Rundgren, Kiki..329, 551
Rushton, Jared...42, 88, 195, 540, 546
Russell, Chuck...541
Russell, Jay...39, 52, 551
Russkies..76, 82, 109, 114, 179, 531, 554
RV...
    Runaway Vacation...533, 554
Ryan, Natasha...289, 298, 313, 539
Ryder, Winona..................113, 163, 164, 350, 353, 355, 372, 413, 508, 535, 545, 549, 550
Ryne, Miranda Stuart...........................311, 328, 331, 338, 370, 426, 514, 519, 534, 539

S

Sabu...28, 65, 238, 543, 548
Sacrifices of the Heart..130, 554
Safety of Objects, the..327, 531, 554

Salenger, Meredith........................57, 70, 101, 102, 152, 153, 155, 227, 246, 247, 483, 535, 548
Salvatores, Gabrielle...547
Sampi, Everlyn...44, 65, 215, 553
Samson and Delilah...215, 471
Sanchez, Ashley...292, 545
Sanchez, Maite...374
Sandlot Kids...168, 187, 533, 554
Sangster, Thomas...128, 551
Sansbury, Tianna...215, 553
Sarala...479, 557
Sax, Geoffrey...555
Sayer, Eva...84, 141, 161, 267, 302, 304, 315, 542, 557
Scanlon, Jack...438, 541
School of Rock...160, 161, 163, 533, 554
Schreiner, Olive...555
Schultz, John...539, 557
Schumacher, Joel...556
Schuster, Harold...555
Schwentke, Robert...544, 556
Sciamma, Céline...144, 156, 157, 158, 174, 556, 557
Scorsese, Martin...515, 556
Scott Fitzgerald, F...542, 548
Scott, Ridley...545
Scott, Terry...550
Scrooge...79, 80, 140, 418, 533, 554
Searchers, the...103, 476, 532
Seaton, George...550
Secret Garden...30, 51, 56, 87, 89, 100, 121, 140, 207, 208, 240, 339, 366, 370, 395, 447, 450, 536, 554
Secret Life of Bees.................................46, 56, 65, 118, 196, 211, 258, 301, 425, 447, 452, 536, 554
Segat, Jonathan...178, 360, 390, 551
Seiter, William A...556
Sense and Sensibility...46, 51, 81, 409, 531, 554
Seuss, Dr...545
Seven Years in Tibet...223, 532, 554
Shadow of Doubt, a...57, 495, 506, 533, 554
Shadrach...212, 219, 312, 365, 367, 372, 430, 431, 533, 554
Shane (1952)...222, 223, 554
Shankland, Tom...34, 542
Shankley, Amelia...162, 222, 273, 543
Shankman, Adam...40, 337, 540, 542
Shattered Family...81, 124, 532, 555
Shattered Silence (2012)...459, 486, 489, 521, 531, 555
Shepherd, Amanda...287
Sheridan, Jim...417, 547

Sherin, Ed..548

Sheshadri, Leah...283, 547

Shields, Brooke 27, 28, 30, 34, 36, 41, 43, 47, 54, 62, 63, 65, 96, 112, 141, 211, 322, 323, 348, 353, 366, 369, 371, 373, 374, 467, 497, 500, 501, 515, 519, 534, 536, 541, 553

Shimizu, Momoko..552

Shoot the Moon...382

Shriner, Will..546

Shute, Nevil...434, 553

Shyamalan, M Night..545, 555

Siberling, Brad..541

Siegel, Donald...540

Silent Hill..80, 110, 164, 269, 292, 295, 416, 483, 532, 555

Sinclair, Gordon John...26, 45, 82, 341, 345, 350, 535, 545

Sinclair, Marianne (author Hollywood Lolita). .43, 47, 53, 68, 69, 70, 141, 230, 258, 352, 354, 375, 376, 493, 497, 521

Sinclair, Upton..556

Single Santa Seeks Mrs Claus...277

Sirk, Doug...547

Sixth Sense, the...56, 265, 295, 403, 519, 533, 555

Skin...213, 215, 372, 459, 472, 533, 555

Slade, D..545

Slater, Ryan...218, 371, 539

Slumdog Millionaire........41, 51, 62, 83, 119, 132, 144, 165, 175, 205, 365, 390, 492, 525, 532

Small, Eric..543

Smart, Rebecca...152, 153, 154, 241, 244, 271, 275, 304, 418, 467, 541

Smit-McPhee, Kodi..290, 300, 363, 535, 548

Smith, Robert..544

Smollett, Jurnee..65, 86, 87, 88, 266, 372, 544

Snow Day...45, 81, 110, 347, 533, 536, 555

So dear to my heart...555

So Dear to my Heart...123, 238, 249, 531

Sobieski, Leelee...124, 253, 345, 546, 548

Solomon, Courtney...539

Son of Babylon...226, 441, 443, 454, 531, 555

Son of Ranbow...531, 536, 555

Song of the South....................................81, 219, 223, 250, 273, 484, 485, 489, 533, 555

Sound of Music, the...27, 38, 41, 60, 69, 80, 107, 117, 162, 174, 251, 318, 325, 434, 435, 531, 555

Spellman, Cathy Cash...541

Spenser, Jeremy..383, 387, 453

Spielberg, Steven.....23, 52, 56, 66, 69, 100, 266, 291, 294, 308, 437, 438, 544, 545, 548, 549, 553, 554, 557

Spirit of the Beehive..........................48, 198, 230, 290, 292, 302, 306, 441, 442, 528, 533, 555

Spirited Away..237

Spragg, Mark...557

Spyri, Johanna..141, 207
Stahl, Nick...82, 130, 231, 550
Stand by Me........................27, 28, 64, 180, 196, 198, 199, 320, 365, 425, 533, 555
Stassner, Ingrid...239, 306, 540
Station Agent, the...66, 533, 555
Steele, Tarra...324, 372, 395, 466, 551
Steinberg, David...556
Steinfeld, Hailee.........................27, 52, 58, 64, 148, 185, 243, 252, 557
Stephens, Harvey..265, 313, 314, 552
Stephenson, John...544
Stepmom.........26, 86, 129, 172, 349, 385, 388, 411, 413, 414, 531, 536, 555
Sterling, William...539
Stevenson, Robert...540, 547, 550
Stevenson, Sarah Joy...556
Stewart, Kristen.........................160, 170, 171, 473, 541, 550, 552, 554
Stewart, Michelle..370, 553
Stockwell, Dean................55, 108, 132, 181, 220, 223, 366, 395, 554
Stolen (2011)..23, 60, 479, 480, 555
Stolen Children...................105, 112, 226, 227, 447, 452, 516, 555
Stone, Abigail..296, 371, 543
Stone, Carol..84
Stone, Norman..553
Stoner, Alyson...........79, 160, 162, 336, 339, 411, 415, 449, 534, 539, 542
Storesund, Line..327, 358, 367, 370, 547
Stormbreaker...28, 531, 555
Story of an African Farm..................123, 124, 214, 279, 468, 532, 555
Stranks, Susan...................................82, 141, 348, 369, 375, 541
Streatfeild, Noel...126, 176, 540
StreetDance.....................................42, 160, 175, 176, 533, 556
Streisand, Barbra..553
Stuckey, Sophie..296, 543
Sturridge, Charles..544, 548
Styron, William...554
Sulfaro, Guiseppe...30, 323, 550
Summer Magic..161
Sundays & Cybele...............120, 224, 225, 230, 352, 402, 492, 499, 532, 556
Super 8..40, 58, 531, 556
Susannah of the Mounties.................................186, 219, 532, 556
Švankmajer, Jan.............................272, 275, 276, 496, 539, 549
Swaine, Dominique..............47, 50, 56, 373, 498, 501, 519, 535, 549
Swallows and Amazons.............................81, 151, 174, 180, 181
Swanson, Kristy...81, 409, 449, 544
Swift, David...541, 552, 553
Swift, Susan...313, 540
Switching Goals..........................151, 160, 169, 172, 533, 556

Szilagyi, Steve..553
Szinetar, Dora..304, 352, 371, 548

T

Talib, Yasser...226, 443, 555
Tamahori, Lee..539
Taubman, Tiffany...331
Taxi Driver...35, 43, 54, 62, 63, 373, 515, 519, 532, 556
Tay, Daniel...85, 543
Taylor-Compton, Scout...111, 355, 536, 558
Taylor, Byron..282, 284, 485, 536, 549, 555
Taylor, Elizabeth..................26, 32, 38, 53, 238, 239, 240, 241, 244, 245, 249, 542, 547, 548
Telleria, Isabel..198, 290, 302, 306, 442, 555
Temple, Shirley................................32, 36, 44, 57, 162, 186, 219, 258, 339, 374, 484, 556
Tendres Cousines..350, 502
Terry, Georgina...23, 240, 396, 397, 553
Tevini, Thierry...350, 502, 556
That Night............57, 87, 200, 328, 331, 366, 372, 404, 405, 406, 411, 415, 419, 531, 536, 556
There will be Blood..205, 467, 531
Theroux, Paul...551
They Come Back...295
Thirteen (2003)..23, 25, 51, 94, 201, 219, 338, 358, 536, 556
Thirty-two A (32A).................25, 65, 101, 196, 199, 338, 360, 372, 497, 530, 536, 556
This is England..327, 525, 531, 536, 556
Thivisol, Victoire...448, 483, 542
Thomas, Betty...541, 543
Thomas, Claire...553
Thomas, Henry...23, 82, 343, 535, 544
Thompson, Lee..217
Thomsett, Sally...45, 336, 553
Thomson, Cassi...86, 552
Tideland. 25, 51, 56, 64, 134, 224, 225, 270, 271, 295, 331, 355, 373, 420, 460, 493, 531, 536, 556
Tiger Bay............25, 110, 121, 122, 151, 152, 153, 158, 159, 227, 229, 231, 232, 433, 532, 556
Tightrope...23, 63, 241, 330, 331, 531, 556
Time Bandits..179, 185, 533, 556
Time to Kill, a..211, 472, 533, 556
Time Traveller's Wife, the...151, 224, 372
Times & Winds..30, 64, 87, 97, 330, 332, 533
Timescape (1991)...156, 531, 556
To Kill a Mockingbird. 46, 56, 58, 117, 118, 130, 148, 151, 153, 154, 155, 159, 198, 211, 212, 231, 420, 483, 556
Tokar, Norman...541
Tomboy (2011)................................144, 151, 153, 156, 169, 369, 371, 449, 533
Tomlinson, Eleanor...199, 347

Tooth..311
Tornatoro, Guiseppe...323, 550
Toto le Héros...............................40, 57, 65, 82, 328, 346, 371, 389, 536, 556
Tovey, Roberta...546
Trachtenburg, Michelle...544
Trading Hearts..386
Treasure Seekers...189, 531, 556
Tremors...291, 292, 533, 557
Treu, Blair..40, 43, 161, 549
Trouble along the Way...386
True Grit.......................27, 52, 58, 64, 148, 185, 189, 243, 252, 531, 557
Truffaut, Eva..55, 536, 553
Truffaut, Francois..341, 553
Tuchner, Michael...540
Tuggle, Richard...556
Tung, Sandy...539
Turgoose, Thomas..327, 525, 536, 556
Turn of the Screw..............23, 30, 60, 84, 121, 125, 126, 141, 161, 267, 279, 297, 557
Turner, Ann...541
Turner, Debbie...162, 555

U

Ulloa, Juanma Bajo..539
Uncle Buck...24, 83, 94, 95, 230, 533, 557
Under the Mud...49, 90, 123, 312, 532, 533, 557
Underwood, Ron...557
Unfinished Life, an.....................127, 152, 237, 249, 358, 396, 467, 557
Untamed Love...372, 484, 493, 531, 557
Uppal, Chandeep...217, 322, 539
Urban Ghost Story.......................112, 290, 298, 325, 372, 404, 557

V

Vaccaro, Rodney..554
Vakit, Bes..556
Valiente, Sara..348, 375, 549
Valverde, Marie...550
Van Allsburg, Chris...548
van den Berg, Rudolf...542
Van Dormael, Jaco...57, 556
Vaneau, Yara...544
Vaquero, Laura.....................................33, 62, 163, 164, 302, 310, 431, 539
Vassilieva, Sofia....................................82, 349, 371, 412, 543, 551
Vavasseur, Sophie...290, 554
Vega, Alexa..............101, 152, 153, 155, 236, 445, 483, 484, 486, 554
Verne, Jules...547, 548

Vesaas, Tarjei.....547
Vidal, Christina.....42
Vieira, Asia.....327, 371, 387, 545
Village of the Damned.....269, 304, 557
Vincent, Alex.....196, 289, 314, 542
Virgin Spring.....110
Voskanian, Robert.....542

W

Wachs, Caitlin.....334, 490, 551
Wah-Wah.....311, 383, 386, 387, 426, 531, 557
Walkabout.....64, 81, 185, 186, 216, 239, 258, 367, 370, 409, 532, 557
Wallace, Aria.....554
Wang, Wayne.....540
War of the Worlds.....56, 82, 101, 102, 103, 113, 433, 434, 436, 557
Ward, Kylo.....407, 541
Wasson, Sophie Jo.....199, 338, 536, 556
Water (2005).....25, 111, 459, 463, 479, 480, 496, 557
Water Babies.....494, 533, 557
Water Lilies.....25, 105, 157, 173, 174, 201, 359, 372, 429, 533, 536, 557
Waterworld.....474, 532, 557
Watson, Emma.....35, 36, 83, 126, 169, 202, 285, 334, 335, 366, 371, 490, 520, 545, 546
Webb, Marc.....538
Wedekind, Frank.....547
Weeks, Perdita.....27, 121, 371, 510, 511, 515, 542, 553
Weidemann, Anneke.....124, 214, 468, 555
Weidler, Virginia.....53, 382
Weir, Peter.....551
Weisman, Sam.....543
Weld, Tuesday.....34, 96, 326, 484, 544
Well, the.....212, 533
Welles, Orson.....436
Welling, Nick.....553
Wells, HG.....436, 557
Wells, Stewart.....360
Wendel, Lara.....55, 538
Wenders, Wim.....104, 528, 539
Wesley, Mary.....66, 124, 141, 353, 504, 541
Westerman, Carlie.....114, 221, 546
Westmore, Lucy.....114, 543
Whale Rider.....24, 27, 36, 49, 50, 51, 58, 96, 97, 149, 150, 151, 174, 200, 237, 255, 256, 366, 372, 557
Wheatley, David.....553
Wheaton, Wil.....27, 29, 425
When Zachary Beaver came to Town.....339, 342

Whistle down the Wind...81, 110, 117, 151, 152, 159, 229, 237, 242, 249, 250, 291, 302, 308, 309, 352, 557

Whitaker, Forest...546

Whitesell, John...540

Whitman, Mae..50, 127, 385, 448, 546, 552

Wicker Man, the..313, 533, 557

Widdows, Sarah...506, 519, 541

Wilcox, Fred M..542, 548, 554

Wild Child...94, 95, 168, 346, 536, 557

Williams, Paul Andrew..542, 549

Wilmot, Chase...130, 554

Wilson, Anna...343

Wilson, Jacqueline...103, 106, 384, 543

Wilson, Mara..46, 52, 107, 252, 269, 277, 384, 550, 551

Wilson, Ruth...491

Wilson, Sandy...551

Winick, Gary..541

Winslet, Kate...30, 114, 246, 302, 323, 358, 535, 546

Winterson, Jeanette...552

Winterton, Michael...545

Wise, Robert...541, 543, 555

Witherspoon, Reese................................41, 58, 337, 350, 366, 371, 535, 550

Wizard of Oz....45, 60, 67, 75, 109, 110, 141, 176, 179, 186, 274, 283, 284, 286, 304, 532, 557

Wood, Elijah 42, 43, 108, 195, 196, 212, 301, 305, 327, 332, 360, 372, 482, 485, 502, 538, 552

Wood, Evan Rachel. 23, 40, 50, 85, 94, 112, 161, 199, 201, 224, 225, 352, 358, 375, 383, 424, 473, 476, 535, 536, 543, 550, 556

Wood, Lana...521, 554

Wood, Natalie......23, 44, 50, 52, 53, 94, 95, 103, 107, 108, 117, 122, 277, 297, 366, 371, 476, 521, 543, 545, 550, 554

Woodsman, the.....................................60, 61, 62, 301, 460, 496, 506, 509, 519, 521, 533, 557

Woolcock, Penny...550

Wright, Bonnie..334, 545, 546

Wright, John...540

Wryn, Rhiannon Leigh...265, 548

Wuthering Heights...67, 123, 349, 471, 531, 532, 557, 558

Wyler, William..358, 542

Wynorski, Jim...551

X

XXY...61, 62, 362, 363, 367, 533, 536, 558

Y

Yates, David...546

Yelchin, Anton..361, 535, 547

York, Susannah..353, 545

Young, Robert...547
Young, Terence...542
Yours, Mine & Ours...86, 531, 536, 558

Z

Zathura...
    a space adventure..179
Zeiff, Howard...551
Zima, Yvonne...84, 115, 421, 424, 426
Zombies...
    Wicked little things..........................23, 111, 267, 304, 355, 494, 531, 536, 558

CPSIA information can be obtained at www.ICGtesting.com
Printed in the USA
LVOW05s1153201214

419707LV00001B/1/P